PROCESSES AND PRODUCTION METHODS (PPMs) IN WTO LAW

Despite a decades-long debate, starting with the *Tuna-Dolphin* disputes of the 1990s, questions on the status of national regulatory measures linked to processes and production methods in WTO law have remained unsolved. Likewise, labelling requirements relating to unincorporated aspects of a product's life cycle remain strongly contested. Ongoing disputes at the WTO, as well as global social and environmental challenges relating to economic activities show how topical and important the search for adequate answers still is. *Processes and Production Methods (PPMs) in WTO Law* identifies and comprehensively analyses the key legal problems concerning such measures, setting them in the context of the current debate and its economic and regulatory background. Christiane R. Conrad develops a new approach to this debate which draws on the objectives and established economic rationales of the WTO Agreements.

CHRISTIANE R. CONRAD is an attorney at law and in-house lawyer with a telecommunications company in Germany. She was a member of the Collaborative Research Centre 'Transformations of the State' at the University of Bremen, and she has also been a Visiting Fellow at Georgetown University Law Center.

CAMBRIDGE INTERNATIONAL TRADE
AND ECONOMIC LAW

As the processes of regionalization and globalization have intensified, there have been accompanying increases in the regulations of international trade and economic law at the levels of international, regional and national laws.

The subject matter of this series is international economic law. Its core is the regulation of international trade, investment and cognate areas such as intellectual property and competition policy. The series publishes books on related regulatory areas, in particular human rights, labour, environment and culture, as well as sustainable development. These areas are vertically linked at the international, regional and national level, and the series extends to the implementation of these rules at these different levels. The series also includes works on governance, dealing with the structure and operation of related international organisations in the field of international economic law, and the way they interact with other subjects of international and national law.

Series Editors

Dr Lorand Bartels, *University of Cambridge*
Professor Thomas Cottier, *University of Berne*
Professor William Davey, *University of Illinois*

Books in the series:

Trade Policy Flexibility and Enforcement in the WTO: A Law and Economics Analysis
Simon A. B. Schropp

The Multilaterization of International Investment Law
Stephan W. Schill

The Law, Economics and Politics of Retaliation in WTO Dispute Settlement
Edited by Chad P. Bown and Joost Pauwelyn

Non-Discrimination in International Trade in Services: 'Likeness' in WTO/GATS
Nicolas Diebold

Processes and Production Methods (PPMs) in WTO Law: Interfacing Trade and Social Goals
Christiane R. Conrad

PROCESSES AND PRODUCTION METHODS (PPMs) IN WTO LAW

Interfacing trade and social goals

CHRISTIANE R. CONRAD

CAMBRIDGE UNIVERSITY PRESS
Cambridge, New York, Melbourne, Madrid, Cape Town,
Singapore, São Paulo, Delhi, Mexico City

Cambridge University Press
The Edinburgh Building, Cambridge CB2 8RU, UK

Published in the United States of America by Cambridge University Press, New York

www.cambridge.org
Information on this title: www.cambridge.org/9781107694156

© Christiane R. Conrad 2011

This publication is in copyright. Subject to statutory exception
and to the provisions of relevant collective licensing agreements,
no reproduction of any part may take place without the written
permission of Cambridge University Press.

First published 2011
First paperback edition 2013

A catalogue record for this publication is available from the British Library

Library of Congress Cataloguing in Publication Data
Conrad, Christiane R.
Processes and production methods (PPMs) in WTO law : interfacing trade
and social goals / Christiane R. Conrad.
p. cm. – (Cambridge international trade and economic law ; 5)
Includes bibliographical references and index.
ISBN 978-1-107-00812-0 (hardback)
1. Foreign trade regulation. 2. World Trade Organization. I. Title. II. Series.
K3943.C656 2011
382'.92–dc22
2011014116

ISBN 978-1-107-00812-0 Hardback
ISBN 978-1-107-69415-6 Paperback

Cambridge University Press has no responsibility for the persistence or
accuracy of URLs for external or third-party internet websites referred to in
this publication, and does not guarantee that any content on such websites is,
or will remain, accurate or appropriate.

The *Parties* to this Agreement,
Recognizing that their relations in the field of trade and economic endeavour should be conducted
with a view to raising standards of living,
ensuring full employment,
and a large and steadily growing volume of real income and effective demand,
and expanding the production of and trade in goods and services,
while allowing for the optimal use of the world's resources in accordance with the objective of sustainable development,
seeking both to protect and preserve the environment
and to enhance the means for doing so in a manner consistent with their respective needs and concerns at different levels of economic development

Marrakesh Agreement Establishing the
World Trade Organization
signed in Marrakesh, Morocco, on 15 April 1994

As of today, 153 countries and other WTO members as well as 29 candidate countries have committed themselves to the above objectives.

CONTENTS

List of figures and tables   *page* xv
Preface and acknowledgements   xvii
Table of GATT 1947 Reports   xix
Table of WTO Reports   xxi
List of abbreviations   xxvi

Introduction   1

I   Foundations: the relevance of NPA measures at the interface of domestic regulation, economic globalization and world trade law   7

1   Setting the stage for legal analysis   11
   1.1   Brief introduction to the topic   11
   1.2   The crucial cases   13
      1.2.1   *Tuna-Dolphin I* (1991)   13
      1.2.2   *Tuna-Dolphin II* (1994)   15
      1.2.3   *Shrimp Turtle* (1998)   16
         1.2.3.1   The Panel Report   17
         1.2.3.2   The Appellate Body Report   18
         1.2.3.3   *Shrimp Turtle – Article 21.5* (2001)   20
   1.3   Overview of the PPM debate   20
      1.3.1   Emergence of the PPM debate   21
      1.3.2   Developments in academia and practice   22
      1.3.3   Concepts and terms central to the 'PPM debate'   25
         1.3.3.1   The product–process distinction   25
         1.3.3.2   Processes and production methods   27
         1.3.3.3   'Product-related' and 'non-product-related' PPMs   28
      1.3.4   Unanswered questions and legal uncertainty   29
   1.4   Identification of key legal issues   31
      1.4.1   Customs tariffs   32
         1.4.1.1   Article II   32
         1.4.1.2   The relevance of international rules   33
         1.4.1.3   Obligation to most-favoured-nation treatment   35
      1.4.2   Import prohibitions or other quantitative restrictions   36

vii

         1.4.3   Non-tax internal regulation   38
         1.4.4   Internal taxes and other internal charges   39
                  1.4.4.1 Indirect taxation and NPAs   40
                  1.4.4.2 Direct taxes and NPAs   43
         1.4.5   Border tax adjustment   43
                  1.4.5.1 Imports   44
                  1.4.5.2 Exports   45
         1.4.6   Anti-dumping duties   46
         1.4.7   Subsidies   48
                  1.4.7.1 Subsidies linked to NPAs   48
                  1.4.7.2 Low standards as illegitimate subsidization   51
         1.4.8   General exceptions   52
                  1.4.8.1 The particular exceptions   53
                  1.4.8.2 The introductory provision of Article XX   54
         1.4.9   Technical barriers to trade and sanitary and
                  phytosanitary measures   55
         1.4.10   Summary   56
   1.5   Delineation and foundations of the legal analysis   57
   1.5.1 Scope of the analysis   57
          1.5.1.1 General object of research: trade in goods   57
          1.5.1.2 Scope of the legal analysis   60
   1.5.2 Terms and concepts   61
          1.5.2.1 NPA measures   61
          1.5.2.2 Processes and production methods or 'PPMs'   62

2 Putting the debate into perspective: analysis of the
   socio-economic context   64
   2.1 National regulation and NPAs   65
        2.1.1 Overview of regulation   66
               2.1.1.1 General domestic regulation   66
               2.1.1.2 The notion of social regulation   68
               2.1.1.3 Different modes of regulation   70
        2.1.2 Differences and similarities in regulatory cultures: the example of the
               United States and Europe   74
               2.1.2.1 Regulation in the United States   75
               2.1.2.2 Regulation in Western Europe   78
               2.1.2.3 Assessment of differences and similarities   81
        2.1.3 The economic case for state intervention   83
               2.1.3.1 Basic considerations on free markets and the economic
                        role of governments   84
               2.1.3.2 Categories of economic rationales for regulation   86
                        2.1.3.2.1 Regulation to safeguard competitive markets   87
                        2.1.3.2.2 Regulation addressing market failure   88
                        2.1.3.2.3 Regulation in pursuit of distributional or
                                   social objectives   90
               2.1.3.3 Preliminary conclusion   91

2.2 International trade and NPA measures   92
  2.2.1 Design parameters of the multilateral trading system   92
    2.2.1.1 Object and purpose of the WTO Agreements   92
      2.2.1.1.1 Identification   93
      2.2.1.1.2 Relevance   96
    2.2.1.2 Economic rationales of the multilateral trading system   98
  2.2.2 The interface of domestic regulation and international trade   100
    2.2.2.1 The general debate on domestic regulation   100
    2.2.2.2 NPA measures and international trade in goods   103
  2.2.3 Political arguments in the international debate   104
    2.2.3.1 Effective and efficient protection of national or foreign objects   104
    2.2.3.2 Sovereignty and extraterritoriality   106
    2.2.3.3 Unilateralism   108
    2.2.3.4 Competitiveness and effective regulation   110
    2.2.3.5 Summary   113

II Legal analysis: reviewing the status of NPA measures *de lege lata*   115

3 Preliminary considerations: applicability of WTO law and other international law to NPA measures   119
  3.1 Applicability of WTO law to NPA measures   120
  3.2 The relevance of conventional international law in WTO dispute settlement   121
    3.2.1 No closed self-contained regime   122
    3.2.2 General applicability of international law   124
    3.2.3 Conflicts with other international treaties and instruments   128
      3.2.3.1 Existence of a conflict of norms   128
      3.2.3.2 Applicable conflict rules   132
        3.2.3.2.1 Asymmetrical conflicts   133
        3.2.3.2.2 Symmetrical conflicts   134
      3.2.3.3 Conflicts of norms, NPAs and the example of CITES   138
  3.3 NPA measures and the law on state responsibility   140
  3.4 Conclusion   145

4 Consistency with GATT obligations   147
  4.1 The scope of the national treatment obligations   149
    4.1.1 The use of specific terms   150
      4.1.1.1 Narrow interpretation: products   151
      4.1.1.2 Broad interpretation: 'affecting'   152
      4.1.1.3 Preliminary conclusion   155
    4.1.2 Comparison of Article III:2 and 4   156
    4.1.3 Measures 'of the same nature'   158
    4.1.4 Summary and conclusion   161

CONTENTS

4.2 The principle of non-discrimination and the 'like products' concept 162
    4.2.1 Introduction to the principle of non-discrimination 162
        4.2.1.1 General problems inherent to the principle 163
        4.2.1.2 Clear prohibition of origin-based discrimination 165
        4.2.1.3 Non-discrimination and NPAs 167
    4.2.2 Interpreting the 'like products' concept with special consideration of NPAs 168
        4.2.2.1 The DSB approach: 'objective' determination 169
            4.2.2.1.1 Main features 170
                4.2.2.1.1.1 Relevant factors 172
                4.2.2.1.1.2 Varying importance of factors 174
                4.2.2.1.1.3 Degree of 'likeness' under different provisions 177
            4.2.2.1.2 Relevance of NPAs 179
                4.2.2.1.2.1 Processes and production methods 179
                4.2.2.1.2.2 Output and producer characteristics 183
                4.2.2.1.2.3 Price 189
                4.2.2.1.2.4 National policies and regulatory regimes 192
            4.2.2.1.3 Relevance of 'minor' physical differences 196
                4.2.2.1.3.1 Editorial content 197
                4.2.2.1.3.2 Environmental impacts 200
                4.2.2.1.3.3 Toxicity and risk 201
                4.2.2.1.3.4 Genetic modifications 203
            4.2.2.1.4 Summary 204
        4.2.2.2 The 'aim and effects' theory 206
            4.2.2.2.1 Rationales and main elements 207
                4.2.2.2.1.1 The criteria 208
                4.2.2.2.1.2 Scope and relevance 209
                4.2.2.2.1.3 Diversity of opinions 210
            4.2.2.2.2 Significance for NPA measures 211
            4.2.2.2.3 The 'aim and effects' theory in WTO adjudication 212
                4.2.2.2.3.1 *US – Malt Beverages* (1992) 213
                4.2.2.2.3.2 *US – Taxes on Automobiles* (1994) 214
                4.2.2.2.3.3 *Japan – Alcoholic Beverages* (1996) and *EC – Bananas* (1997) 215
                4.2.2.2.3.4 Subsequent jurisprudence 218
            4.2.2.2.4 Critique 220
        4.2.2.3 Market-based or economic approaches 222
            4.2.2.3.1 Rationales and main elements 223
            4.2.2.3.2 Significance for NPA measures 226
            4.2.2.3.3 Relevance in WTO adjudication 228
            4.2.2.3.4 Critique 232
    4.2.3 Summary 236
4.3 Detrimental treatment and NPA measures 240
4.4 Conclusions 244

5 Limits to the justification of NPA measures under the general exceptions 247

5.1 Particularities in interpreting Article XX 249
- 5.1.1 Relevance of international law for interpretation 249
  - 5.1.1.1 Basic framework of interpretation 250
  - 5.1.1.2 GATT and WTO case law 252
  - 5.1.1.3 Signatories-based approach 254
    - 5.1.1.3.1 Congruence within disputes 255
    - 5.1.1.3.2 Incongruence within disputes 257
  - 5.1.1.4 Objective approach 258
    - 5.1.1.4.1 The nature of interpretation 258
    - 5.1.1.4.2 Relevance of international instruments 260
    - 5.1.1.4.3 Summary 263
    - 5.1.1.4.4 Excursus: *inter se* understanding on interpretation 264
- 5.1.2 Other interpretative questions 265
  - 5.1.2.1 No restrictive interpretation 265
  - 5.1.2.2 Static or evolutionary interpretation? 267
- 5.1.3 Summary 269

5.2 General concerns regarding justifiability of NPA measures 269
- 5.2.1 Vagueness of basic objections 270
- 5.2.2 Review of arguments against justifiability 272
  - 5.2.2.1 Irreconcilability with WTO objectives and purpose 272
  - 5.2.2.2 *Per se* violation of the chapeau 274
  - 5.2.2.3 Violation of the sovereignty principle 275
- 5.2.3 Result 281

5.3 The scope of Article XX 281
- 5.3.1 The geographical scope and the problem of extraterritoriality 281
  - 5.3.1.1 Insufficient GATT and WTO case law 283
  - 5.3.1.2 The text of the particular exceptions 284
    - 5.3.1.2.1 Direct references to the geographical scope 285
    - 5.3.1.2.2 Indirect reference: the means–end relationship 286
      - 5.3.1.2.2.1 'necessary' 286
      - 5.3.1.2.2.2 'relating to' and 'imposed for' 288
      - 5.3.1.2.2.3 Implications for the geographical scope 291
    - 5.3.1.2.3 Indirect reference in exception (g): domestic restrictions 295
      - 5.3.1.2.3.1 History and relevant case law 295
      - 5.3.1.2.3.2 Distinction between foreign and shared resources 297
  - 5.3.1.3 Object and purpose 300
  - 5.3.1.4 Negotiating history 302
  - 5.3.1.5 Alternative approaches to extraterritoriality 305
  - 5.3.1.6 Conclusions on the geographical scope 308
- 5.3.2 Subject coverage of the particular exceptions 309
  - 5.3.2.1 Exclusivity of listed policies 310

CONTENTS

- 5.3.2.2 Coverage of other policies   311
  - 5.3.2.2.1 Protection of the environment   311
  - 5.3.2.2.2 Human rights and labour standards   313
- 5.3.2.3 Summary   316
- 5.3.3 Special consideration of the public morals exception   316
  - 5.3.3.1 Open subject coverage   317
  - 5.3.3.2 Standards of right and wrong   321
  - 5.3.3.3 The geographical scope   323
    - 5.3.3.3.1 Location of moral standards   323
    - 5.3.3.3.2 Location of the threat   324
    - 5.3.3.3.3 Preliminary conclusions   326
  - 5.3.3.4 Requirements relating to the means–end relationship   326
    - 5.3.3.4.1 Motivation for moral NPA trade measures   327
    - 5.3.3.4.2 Suitability   328
    - 5.3.3.4.3 Necessity   329
      - 5.3.3.4.3.1 'Relative' and 'absolute' necessity   330
      - 5.3.3.4.3.2 WTO jurisprudence on 'weighing and balancing'   331
      - 5.3.3.4.3.3 Other approaches   338
    - 5.3.3.4.4 Conclusions for an adequate 'necessity' test   339
      - 5.3.3.4.4.1 Step 1   340
      - 5.3.3.4.4.2 Step 2   341
      - 5.3.3.4.4.3 Step 3   342
- 5.3.4 Summary   343
- 5.4 The chapeau and other requirements regarding the application of measures   345
  - 5.4.1 A 'balancing process' under the chapeau?   347
  - 5.4.2 The requirements   349
    - 5.4.2.1 Introductory remarks   350
    - 5.4.2.2 General requirements and principles   352
      - 5.4.2.2.1 An 'unavoidable' standard of justifiability?   352
      - 5.4.2.2.2 Relevance of different conditions in countries   353
      - 5.4.2.2.3 Special and differential treatment   356
        - 5.4.2.2.3.1 The principle of SDT   356
        - 5.4.2.2.3.2 Relevance of SDT for the chapeau   359
      - 5.4.2.2.4 Due process and general principles   359
    - 5.4.2.3 Specific problem fields   361
      - 5.4.2.3.1 No prohibition of unilateral measures   361
      - 5.4.2.3.2 Are serious negotiations obligatory?   362
    - 5.4.2.4 Specific requirements for NPA measures   364
      - 5.4.2.4.1 Relevant characteristics of NPA measures   365
      - 5.4.2.4.2 Consultations and negotiations   366
      - 5.4.2.4.3 Implementation periods   367
      - 5.4.2.4.4 Transfer of technologies, administrative and financial support   369
- 5.5 Conclusions   372

CONTENTS

6 The status of PPM measures under the TBT Agreement and the SPS Agreement 374
  6.1 Introduction 374
  6.2 The TBT Agreement and PPMs 374
    6.2.1 Applicability of the TBT Agreement 375
      6.2.1.1 Categorization of relevant norms linked to unincorporated PPMs 376
      6.2.1.2 Technical regulations and standards 377
      6.2.1.3 Labelling requirements 381
        6.2.1.3.1 The EU regulatory framework on egg labelling 383
        6.2.1.3.2 Coverage with respect to labelling of PPMs and NPAs 385
          6.2.1.3.2.1 Labelling of unincorporated PPMs 385
          6.2.1.3.2.2 Other NPAs 388
    6.2.2 Substantive provisions 389
      6.2.2.1 No *per se* illegality 389
      6.2.2.2 Substantive requirements on technical regulations and standards 393
        6.2.2.2.1 Overview of substantive requirements 393
        6.2.2.2.2 The distinction between regulations and standards 395
      6.2.2.3 Legitimacy of the objective pursued: special consideration of consumer information 396
        6.2.2.3.1 Consumer information as an internationally recognized value 398
        6.2.2.3.2 Consumer information as precondition for the functioning of markets 405
        6.2.2.3.3 Preliminary conclusions 410
      6.2.2.4 Necessity 412
    6.2.3 The relationship of the TBT Agreement and the GATT 414
    6.2.4 Special and differential treatment 415
  6.3 The SPS Agreement 419
  6.4 Result 421

III Outlook: new perspectives on the legal status of NPA measures 423

7 The interface of international trade and public policies: an overview over existing proposals for reform 427
  7.1 Review 427
    7.1.1 Denial of competence? 428
    7.1.2 Changes at WTO level 432
      7.1.2.1 Substance 433
      7.1.2.2 Procedure 438
    7.1.3 Institutional changes and governance-related suggestions 440

xiv   CONTENTS

            7.1.3.1 Institutional changes   440
            7.1.3.2 Governance in a multi-level system   443
    7.2 Comment   448

8   A regulation-based perspective on NPA trade measures   451
    8.1 Regulatory problems linked to international trade   452
        8.1.1 Side-effects of international trade   453
        8.1.2 The regulatory dilemma   454
            8.1.2.1 Effectiveness of unimpaired national regulation   454
            8.1.2.2 Effectiveness of impaired national regulation   456
        8.1.3 Market failure and the lack of international institutions   461
        8.1.4 Regulatory failure is not in line with objectives and key rationales
              of the WTO   463
        8.1.5 Conclusions   466
    8.2 Applying the regulation-based perspective   467
        8.2.1 Deduction of the regulation-based approach   467
        8.2.2 Categorization of national regulation   469
            8.2.2.1 Category 1: Regulation reducing market imperfections   469
            8.2.2.2 Category 2: Regulation addressing market failure   473
            8.2.2.3 Category 3: Distributive regulation   478
        8.2.3 General conditions of consistency   481
            8.2.3.1 General requirements   481
            8.2.3.2 National regulation and SDT   482
        8.2.4 Conclusions   483

Summary and concluding remarks   485
Bibliography   494
Index   513

FIGURES AND TABLES

Figure

4.1 Determination of detrimental treatment under GATT Article III   240

Table

8.1 Regulation-based approach to WTO conformity of NPA measures   479

PREFACE AND ACKNOWLEDGEMENTS

This book is a revised and updated version of my Ph.D. dissertation, which was accepted by the Law Faculty of the University of Berne in 2008. The sub-title of my dissertation, 'A contribution to the debate on the impact of WTO law on national regulation pursuing social goals', shows the broader context of my doctoral research which led to this book. As a member of the project group 'Social regulation and world trade' at the Collaborative Research Centre 'Transformations of the State', I placed a strong focus on the interplay of national social regulation and international trade, and, in particular, on the status of national regulatory measures under the law of the WTO. I found that despite a decades-long debate, the status of such measures – both from a legal and a political perspective – still remains unresolved. Existing regulatory measures show, that despite legal uncertainty, states do not totally refrain from exercising their power to enact such measures. However, there can be no doubt that the existence of the WTO Agreements and the heated legal and political debates on the legality of certain measures of national social regulation, which have been taking place at an international and, above all, at a transnational level, may lead to a chilling effect on the exercise of national powers. These, however, are still necessary to solve certain problems in cases where no capable institutions at other governance levels are in place. This book analyses the problem and offers a new 'regulatory' perspective, which might help to realize the common goals of national regulators and members of the WTO.

Writing this book would not have been possible without the encouragement, advice, help and support of many people, only a few of whom can be mentioned here. First and foremost, I owe particular gratitude to my supervisor, Professor Thomas Cottier, who inspired me to write this thesis in the first place. His advice and encouragement have been much needed major driving forces throughout my work. I am grateful also to Professor Ernst-Ulrich Petersmann for his comments and for reviewing my dissertation in the proceedings at the Law Faculty of the University of Berne. This work benefited greatly from discussions with scholars and practitioners representing various academic disciplines and international backgrounds at the World Trade Institute (WTI) in Berne – thanks to the staff at the WTI for making this possible, and many thanks to my fellow Ph.D. students for candid comments and exciting discussions. I undertook important parts of my research at the Institute of International Economic Law (IIEL) at Georgetown University Law Center in Washington DC, which likewise offered ample opportunity to engage in academic and political exchange of thoughts in an atmosphere most beneficial for academic research. I enjoyed and gained a lot from discussions with Michelle Grando, Hong-Liu Gong and other fellows at the Institute, and especially with Professor John H. Jackson and Professor A. Jane Bradley, to both of whom I owe particular gratitude. Many thanks also to Professor Steve Charnovitz for thought-provoking comments on an earlier paper, and thanks to Tomer Broude and the Hebrew University of Jerusalem for granting me the opportunity to participate at a roundtable on the *EC – Biotech* case.

I particularly wish to remark on the support provided by the Collaborative Research Centre 'Transformations of the State' and by the University of Bremen, without which this book would not have been possible. I would like to express my appreciation to the project directors, Professor Josef Falke and Professor Christian Joerges and to my fellow researchers at the Centre, among them Matthias Leonhard Maier, Thorsten Hüller and Alexia Herwig, for their comments on earlier versions and for providing an inspiring and supportive research environment.

TABLE OF GATT 1947 REPORTS

Australia – Ammonium Sulphate: Working Party Report, the Australian Subsidy on Ammonium Sulphate, GATT/CP.4/39, adopted 3 April 1950, BISD II/188   172, 174, 175

Belgium – Family Allowances: Belgian Family Allowances, G/32, adopted 7 November 1952, BISD 1S/59   21, 166, 192, 193, 194

Border Tax Adjustments: Working Party Report on Border Tax Adjustments, adopted 2 December 1970, L/3464, BISD 18S/97   45

Canada – FIRA: Canada – Administration of the Foreign Investment Review Act, L/5504, adopted 7 February 1984, BISD 30S/140   155

Canada – Gold Coins: Canada – Measures Affecting the Sale of Gold Coins, L/5863, 17 September 1985, unadopted   190

Canada – Ice Cream: Canada – Import Restrictions on Ice Cream and Yoghurt, L/6568, 36S/68, adopted 4 December 1989   265

Canada – Herring: Canada – Measures Affecting Exports of Unprocessed Herring and Salmon, L/6268, 35S/98, adopted 22 March 1988   288, 289, 296

EEC – Animal Feed Proteins: EEC – Measures on Animal Feed Proteins, L/4599, adopted 14 March 1978, BISD 25S/49   172, 174, 175, 190

EEC – Minimum Import Prices: European Economic Community – Programme of Minimum Import Prices, Licences and Surety Deposits for Certain Processed Fruits and Vegetables, L/4687, adopted 18 October 1978, BISD 25S/68   170

EEC – Parts and Components: European Economic Community – Regulation on Imports of Parts and Components, L/6657, adopted 16 May 1990, BISD 37S/132   43

Germany – Sardines: Treatment by Germany of Imports of Sardines, G/26, adopted 31 October 1952, BISD 1S/53   33, 174

Italy – Agricultural Machinery: Italian Discrimination against Imported Agricultural Machinery, L/833, adopted 23 October 1958, BISD 7S/60   153, 155, 165, 166

Japan – Alcoholic Beverages I: Japan – Customs Duties, Taxes and Labelling Practices on Imported Wines and Alcoholic Beverages, L/6216, adopted 10 November 1987, BISD 34S/83   39, 40, 41, 50, 172, 173

Japan – SPF Dimension Lumber: Canada/Japan – Tariff on Imports of Spruce, Pine, Fir (SPF) Dimension Lumber, L/6470, adopted 19 July 1989, BISD 36S/167   34, 35, 175

Spain – Unroasted Coffee: Spain – Tariff Treatment of Unroasted Coffee, L/5135, adopted 11 June 1981, BISD 28S/102   32, 36, 175, 176, 196, 205

Spain – Soyabean Oil: Spain – Measures Concerning Domestic Sale of Soyabean Oil – Recourse to Article XXIII:2 by the United States, L/5142, 17 June 1981, unadopted   167

Thailand – Cigarettes: Thailand – Restrictions on Importation of and Internal Taxes on Cigarettes, DS10/R, adopted 7 November 1990, BISD 37S/200   287

Tuna-Dolphin I: United States – Restrictions on Imports of Tuna, DS21/R, 3 September 1991, unadopted, BISD 39S/155   14, 15, 16, 22, 37, 38, 151, 153, 155, 156, 158, 159, 179, 180, 184, 191, 195, 212, 276, 283, 284, 289, 291, 302, 303, 310, 311, 350

Tuna Dolphin II: United States – Restrictions on Imports of Tuna, DS29/R, 16 June 1994, unadopted   15, 16, 17, 22, 37, 38, 147, 151, 152, 153, 155, 157, 158, 181, 184, 195, 196, 252, 271, 283, 285, 305, 350

United States Customs User Fee, L/6264, 35S/245, adopted 2 February 1988   265

US – Malt Beverages: United States – Measures Affecting Alcoholic and Malt Beverages, DS23/R, adopted 19 June 1992, BISD 39S/206   41, 153, 184, 185, 189, 207, 208, 213, 214, 216

US – Pork from Canada: United States – Countervailing Duties on Fresh, Chilled and Frozen Pork from Canada, DS7/R, 38S/30, adopted 11 July 1991   265

US – Sugar: United States – Imports of Sugar from Nicaragua, L/560, 31S/67, adopted 13 March 1984   144

US – Section 337 Tariff Act: United States Section 337 of the Tariff Act of 1930, L/6439, adopted 7 November 1989, BISD 36S/345   153, 160, 161, 183, 184, 205, 287, 310

US – Spring Assemblies: United States – Imports of Certain Automotive Spring Assemblies, L/5333, adopted 26 May 1983, BISD 30S/107   54

US – Superfund: United States – Taxes on Petroleum and Certain Imported Substances, L/6175, adopted 17 June 1987, BISD 34S/136   151

US – Taxes on Automobiles: United States – Taxes on Automobiles, DS31/R, 11 October 1994, unadopted   23, 54, 155, 156, 157, 158, 166, 186, 187, 189, 190, 191, 200, 201, 205, 207, 208, 209, 212, 214, 215, 216

US – Tuna I: see *Tuna-Dolphin I*

US – Tuna II: see *Tuna-Dolphin II*

TABLE OF WTO REPORTS

Argentina – Hides and Leather: Argentina – Measures Affecting the Export of Bovine Hides and the Imports of Finished Leather, Panel Report, WT/DS155/R and Corr.1, 19 December 2000, adopted 16 February 2001, DSR 2001:V, 1779   152, 155, 218, 338, 339, 352, 353

Australia – Salmon: Australia – Measures Affecting Importation of Salmon, Panel Report, 12 June 1998, modified by Appellate Body Report, 12 June 1998, WT/DS18/AB/R, adopted 6 November 1998, DSR 1998:VIII, 3327   208

Brazil – Retreaded Tyres: Brazil – Measures Affecting Imports of Retreaded Tyres, Panel Report, 12 June 2007, modified by Appellate Body Report, 3 December 2007, WT/DS332/AB/R, adopted 17 December 2007, DSR 2007:IV, 1527   287, 288, 331

Canada – Autos: Canada – Certain Measures Affecting the Automotive Industry, Panel Report, 11 February 2000, modified by Appellate Body Report, 31 May 2000, WT/DS139/AB/R, WT/DS142/AB/R, adopted 19 June 2000, DSR 2000:VI, 2985   154, 155, 162, 163, 166, 167

Canada – Periodicals: Canada – Certain Measures Concerning Periodicals, Panel Report, 14 March 1997, modified by Appellate Body Report, 30 June 1997, WT/DS31/AB/R, adopted 30 July 1997, DSR 1997:I, 481   40, 43, 154, 156, 178, 197, 198, 199, 218, 274

Canada – Wheat Exports and Grain Imports: Canada – Measures Relating to Exports of Wheat and Treatment of Imported Grain, Panel Report, 6 April 2004, upheld by Appellate Body Report, 30 August 2004, WT/DS276/AB/R, adopted 27 September 2004, DSR 2004:VI, 2739   165

Chile – Alcoholic Beverages: Chile – Taxes on Alcoholic Beverages, Panel Report, 15 June 1999, modified by Appellate Body Report, 13 December 1999, WT/DS87/AB/R, WT/DS110/AB/R, adopted 12 January 2000, DSR 2000:I, 281   230, 240

China – Audiovisual Entertainment Products: China – Measures Affecting Trading Rights and Distribution Services for Certain Publications and Audiovisual Entertainment Products, 12 August 2009, modified by Appellate Body Report, WT/DS363/AB/R, 21 December 2009, adopted on 19 January 2010   318, 333, 335

Dominican Republic – Import and Sale of Cigarettes: Dominican Republic – Measures Affecting the Importation and Internal Sale of Cigarettes, Panel Report, 26 November 2004, modified by Appellate Body Report, 25 April 2005, WT/DS302/AB/R, adopted

19 May 2005, DSR 2005:XV, 7425   53, 102, 152, 154, 160, 169, 170, 171, 173, 174, 175, 176, 177, 178, 179, 201, 202, 204, 205, 206, 218, 219, 220, 221, 230, 231, 232, 236, 239, 246, 248, 288, 294, 332, 333, 336, 380

EC – Asbestos: European Communities – Measures Affecting Asbestos and Asbestos Containing Products, Panel Report, 18 September 2000, modified by Appellate Body Report, 12 March 2001, WT/DS135/AB/R, adopted 5 April 2001, DSR 2001:VII, 3243   53, 102, 159, 160, 161, 169, 170, 171, 173, 174, 176, 177, 178, 179, 201, 202, 204, 206, 210, 219, 220, 221, 230, 231, 232, 236, 237, 239, 288, 294, 332, 336, 380, 456

EC – Bananas III: European Communities – Regime for the Importation, Sale and Distribution of Bananas, Panel Report, Complaint by Ecuador, Mexico, United States, Guatemala and Honduras, 22 May 1997, modified by Appellate Body Report, 9 September 1997, WT/DS27/AB/R, adopted 25 September 1997, DSR 1997:II, 591   131, 174, 206, 218, 415

EC – Biotech: European Communities – Measures Affecting the Approval and Marketing of Biotech Products, Panel Report, WT/DS/291/R, WT/DS/292/R, WT/DS/293/R, 29 September 2006, adopted 21 November 2006, DSR 2006:III, 847   134, 203, 204, 206, 220, 253, 254, 255, 268, 420

EC – Certain Computer Equipment: European Communities – Customs Classification of Certain Computer Equipment, Panel Report, 5 February 1998, modified by Appellate Body Report, 5 June 1998, WT/DS62/AB/R, WT/DS67/AB/R, WT/DS68/AB/R, adopted 22 June 1998, DSR 1998:V, 1851   33, 35, 257, 302

EC – Chicken Cuts: European Communities – Customs Classification of Frozen Boneless Chicken Cuts, Panel Report, Complaint by Brazil and Thailand, 30 May 2005, modified by Appellate Body Report, 12 September 2005, WT/DS269/AB/R, WT/DS286/AB/R and Corr. 1, adopted 27 September 2005, DSR 2005:XIX, 9157   152, 252, 268

EC – Hormones: EC Measures Concerning Meat and Meat Products (Hormones), Panel Report, 18 August 1997, Complaint by Canada and the United States, modified by Appellate Body Report, 16 January 1998, WT/DS26/AB/R, WT/DS48/AB/R, adopted 13 February 1998, DSR 1998:I, 135   103, 208, 266, 293

EC – Poultry: European Communities – Measures Affecting the Importation of Certain Poultry Products, Panel Report, 12 March 1998, modified by Appellate Body Report, 13 July 1998, WT/DS/69/AB/R, adopted 23 July 1998, DSR 1998:V, 2031   131, 256

EC – Seal Products: European Communities – Measures Prohibiting the Importation and Marketing of Seal Products. Request for Consultations by Canada, 4 November 2009, WT/DS400/1. Request for Consultations by Norway, 5 November 2009, WT/DS401/1.   188

EC – Tariff Preferences: European Communities – Conditions for the Granting of Tariff Preferences to Developing Countries, Panel Report, 1 December 2003, modified by Appellate Body Report, 7 April 2004, WT/DS246/AB/R, adopted 20 April 2004, DSR 2004:III   50, 193, 355

Guatemala – Cement I: Guatemala – Anti-Dumping Investigation Regarding Portland Cement From Mexico, Panel Report, 19 June 1998, modified by Appellate Body

TABLE OF WTO REPORTS xxiii

Report, 2 November 1998, WT/DS60/AB/R, adopted 25 November 1998, DSR 1998:IX, 3767   129

India – Autos: India – Measures Affecting the Automotive Sector, Panel Report, 21 December 2001, modified by Appellate Body Report, 19 March 2002, WT/DS146/AB/R, WT/DS175/AB/R, adopted 5 April 2002, appeal withdrawn, DSR 2002:V, 1821   166, 167, 174

Indonesia – Automobiles: Indonesia – Certain Measures Affecting the Automobile Industry, Panel Report, WT/DS54/R, WT/DS55/R, WT/DS59/R, WT/DS64/R and Corr. 1, 2, 3 and 4, 2 July 1998, adopted 23 July 1998, DSR 1998:VI, 2201   42, 167, 175, 194, 229

Japan – Alcoholic Beverages II: Japan – Taxes on Alcoholic Beverages, Panel Report, 11 July 1996, modified by Appellate Body Report, 4 October 1996, WT/DS8/AB/R, WT/DS10/AB/R, WT/DS11/AB/R, adopted 1 November 1996, DSR 1996:I, 97   42, 125, 170, 172, 178, 199, 215, 216, 217, 218, 223, 228, 229, 251, 252, 390

Japan – Film: Japan – Measures Affecting Consumer Photographic Film and Paper, Panel Report, WT/DS44/R, 31 March 1998, adopted 22 April 1998, DSR 1998:IV, 1179   218, 221

Korea – Alcoholic Beverages: Korea – Taxes on Alcoholic Beverages, Panel Report, 17 September 1998, modified by Appellate Body Report, 18 January 1999, WT/DS75/AB/R, WT/DS84/AB/R, adopted 17 February 1999, DSR 1999:I, 3   40, 199, 224, 229, 233

Korea – Dairy: Korea – Definitive Safeguard Measure on Imports of Certain Dairy Products, Panel Report, 21 June 1999, modified by Appellate Body Report, 14 December 1999, WT/DS98/AB/R, adopted 12 January 2000, DSR 2000:I, 3   50

Korea – Various Measures on Beef: Korea – Measures Affecting Imports of Fresh, Chilled and Frozen Beef, Panel Report, 31 July 2000, modified by Appellate Body Report, 11 December 2000, WT/DS161/AB/R, WT/DS169/AB/R, adopted 10 January 2001, DSR 2001:I, 5   167, 192, 287, 288, 294, 331, 332, 333, 335

Mexico – Taxes on Soft Drinks: Mexico – Tax Measures on Soft Drinks and Other Beverages, Panel Report, 7 October 2005, modified by Appellate Body Report, 6 March 2006, WT/DS308/AB/R WT/DS308/R, adopted 24 March 2006, DSR 2006:I, 43   156, 169, 175, 178, 231

Shrimp Turtle: United States – Import Prohibition of Certain Shrimp and Shrimp Products, Panel Report, 15 May 1998, modified by Appellate Body Report, 12 October 1998, WT/DS58/AB/R, adopted 6 November 1998, DSR 1998:VII, 2821h   16, 17, 18, 19, 20, 24, 26, 52, 53, 54, 55, 97, 125, 131, 161, 182, 196, 249, 251, 252, 253, 254, 258, 260, 265, 266, 267, 268, 270, 271, 273, 274, 275, 283, 284, 290, 296, 297, 300, 304, 310, 311, 312, 319, 335, 346, 348, 351, 353, 354, 360, 361, 362, 363, 364, 368, 369, 370, 371

Shrimp Turtle – Article 21.5 Malaysia: United States – Import Prohibition of Certain Shrimp and Shrimp Products – Recourse to Article 21.5 of the DSU by Malaysia, Panel Report, 15 June 2001, upheld by Appellate Body Report, 22 October 2001, WT/DS58/AB/RW, adopted 21 November 2001, DSR 2001:XIII, 6481   20, 26, 94, 152, 248, 271, 272, 354, 361, 362, 363

Turkey – Importation of Rice: Turkey – Measures Affecting the Importation of Rice, Panel Report, Complaint by the United States, WT/DS334/R, 21 September 2007, adopted 22 October 2007, DSR 2007:VI, 2151   165

Tuna-Dolphin III: United States – Measures Concerning the Importation, Marketing and Sale of Tuna and Tuna Products, Request for Consultations by Mexico, 28 October 2008, WT/DS381/1, Panel report expected in February 2011   185, 414

US – 1916 Act: United States – Anti-Dumping Act of 1916, Panel Report, Complaint by the EC, 31 March 2000, and by Japan, 29 May 2000, upheld by Appellate Body Report, 28 August 2000, WT/DS136/AB/R, WT/DS162/AB/R, adopted 26 September 2000, DSR 2000:X, 4793   169

US – Offset Act ('Byrd Amendment'): United States – Continued Dumping and Subsidy Offset Act of 2000, Panel Report, 16 September 2002, modified by Appellate Body Report, 16 January 2003, WT/DS217/AB/R, WT/DS/234/AB/R, adopted 27 January 2003, DSR 2003:I, 375   360, 367

US – Cotton Yarn: United States – Transitional Safeguard Measure on Combed Cotton Yarn from Pakistan, Panel Report, 31 May 2001, modified by Appellate Body Report, 8 October 2001, WT/DS192/AB/R, adopted 5 November 2001, DSR 2001:XII, 6027   229

US – FSC: United States – Tax Treatment for 'Foreign Sales Corporations', Panel Report, 8 October 1999, modified by Appellate Body Report, 24 February 2000, WT/DS108/AB/R, adopted 20 March 2000, DSR 2000:III, 1619   167

US – FSC (Article 21.5 – EC): United States – Tax Treatment for 'Foreign Sales Corporations' – Recourse to Article 21.5 of the DSU by the European Communities, Panel Report, 20 August 2001, modified by Appellate Body Report, 14 January 2002, WT/DS108/AB/RW, adopted 29 January 2002, DSR 2002:I, 55   167

US – Gambling: United States – Measures Affecting the Cross-Border Supply of Gambling and Betting Services, Panel Report, 10 November 2004, modified by Appellate Body Report, 7 April 2005, WT/DS285/AB/R, adopted 20 April 2005, DSR 2005:XII, 5797   155, 317, 318, 319, 322, 323, 333, 334, 335, 336, 347, 348

US – Gambling (Article 21.5): United States – Measures Affecting the Cross-Border Supply of Gambling and Betting Services – Recourse to Article 21.5 of the DSU by Antigua and Barbuda, Panel Report, WT/DS285/RW, 30 March 2007, DSR 2007:VIII, 3105   351, 355, 364

US – Gasoline: United States – Standards for Reformulated and Conventional Gasoline, Panel Report, 29 January 1996, modified by Appellate Body Report, 29 April 1996, WT/DS2/AB/R, adopted 20 May 1996, DSR 1996:I, 3   50, 52, 124, 134, 166, 171, 186, 187, 188, 249, 285, 286, 289, 290, 291, 296, 300, 311, 339, 346, 347, 350, 351, 353

US – Hot Rolled Steel: United States – Anti-Dumping Measures on Certain Hot-Rolled Steel Products from Japan, Panel Report, 28 February 2001, modified by Appellate Body Report, 24 July 2001, WT/DS184/AB/R, adopted 23 August 2001, DSR 2001:X, 4697   415

US – Section 301 Trade Act: United States – Sections 301–310 of the Trade Act of 1974, Panel Report, 22 December 1999, WT/DS152/R, adopted 27 January 2000, DSR 2000:II, 815   41

US – Shrimp: see *Shrimp Turtle*

US – Softwood Lumber IV: United States – Countervailing Duty Determination with Respect to Certain Softwood Lumber from Canada, Panel Report, 29 August 2003, modified by Appellate Body Report, 19 January 2004, WT/DS257/AB/R, adopted 17 February 2004, DSR 2004:II, 571   49

US – Tuna and Tuna Products: see *Tuna-Dolphin III*

ABBREVIATIONS

AAA	Agricultural Adjustment Administration
AB	Appellate Body
AD Agreement	Agreement on Implementation of Article VI of the General Agreement on Tariffs and Trade 1994 (Anti-Dumping Agreement)
CAC	Codex Alimentarius Commission
CAFE	Corporate Average Fuel Economy law
CITES	Convention on International Trade in Endangered Species of Wild Fauna and Flora
CFC	Chlorofluorocarbon
DSB	Dispute Settlement Body
DSU	Understanding on Rules and Procedures Governing the Settlement of Disputes
EC	European Community/European Communities
ECOSOC	United Nations Social and Economic Council
EEC	European Economic Community
EU	European Union
FDA	Food and Drug Administration
FTC	Federal Trade Commission
GATS	General Agreement on Trade in Services
GATT 1947	General Agreement on Tariffs and Trade 1947
GATT 1994	General Agreement on Tariffs and Trade 1994
GMO	Genetically Modified Organism
GPA	Agreement on Government Procurement
GSP	Generalized System of Preferences
HS	Harmonized System: Harmonized Commodity Description and Coding System of the World Customs Organization
ICJ	International Court of Justice
ILO	International Labour Organization

IMF	International Monetary Fund
Marrakesh Agreement	Marrakesh Agreement Establishing the World Trade Organization
MEA	Multilateral Environmental Agreement
MFN	Most-Favoured-Nation treatment
MMPA	Marine Mammal Protection Act
NAFTA	North American Free Trade Area
NGO	non-governmental organization
NIOSH	National Institute for Occupational Safety and Health
NIRA	National Industrial Recovery Act
Note	GATT, Annex I Notes and Supplementary Provisions, Ad Article III
NPA	non-physical aspect
NPA measure	national measure linked to an NPA
NRA	National Recovery Administration
OECD	Organization for Economic Cooperation and Development
OJ	Official Journal
OSHA	Occupational Safety and Health Administration
PPM	processes and production methods
PPM measure	national measures linked to a PPM
RIAA	Reports of International Arbitral Awards
SCM Agreement	Agreement on Subsidies and Countervailing Measures
SDT	special and differential treatment of developing countries
SPS Agreement	Agreement on the Application of Sanitary and Phytosanitary Measures
TBT Agreement	Agreement on Technical Barriers to Trade
TED	turtle excluder device
TRIPS	Agreement on Trade-Related Aspects of Intellectual Property Rights
UN	United Nations
UNCLOS	United Nations Convention on the Law of the Sea
UNEP	United Nations Environment Programme
UNICEF	United Nations International Children's Emergency Fund
VCLT	Vienna Convention on the Law of Treaties

WCO	World Customs Organization
WEO	World Economic Organization (fictitious)
WHO	World Health Organization
WTO	World Trade Organization

Introduction

Freer international trade, fostered by the WTO Agreements, has led to strong economic integration, to growth and to an increase in aggregated global welfare. At the same time, however, political integration has lagged behind. Nation-states, as well as the global community, are facing intensifying social conflicts and pressing environmental problems, such as air and water pollution or climate change. Despite a high degree of international economic integration and an increase in global wealth, global society's problem-solving capacities are rather poor. Views on the extent to which international trade has contributed to these problems diverge considerably. It has been observed that the environmental and social costs of goods production and consumption are hardly ever completely reflected in market prices: thus, goods are traded internationally for prices that do not reflect their true costs, for instance, in terms of pollution, related health damage or other social hardship. While scientists and researchers from different disciplines have been investigating extensively the serious medium- and long-term effects of these neglected costs on the economy, the environment and on humankind, corresponding changes in the global economic systems are not yet conceivable. There are good reasons to believe that, together with technological progress, international trade has enormous potential as a tool to tackle these global problems successfully. However, political stakeholders and society still need to develop sufficient will and capabilities to tap the potential and utilize this tool effectively.

Against this backdrop, it is not surprising that the impact of WTO law on national social policies and regulation has been at the centre of political and scholarly attention in recent years. The broader problem encompasses the relationship of the multilateral trading system to social policies, such as protection of the environment, health, human rights, labour rights or culture and minority rights, and it occurs in all areas of trade, namely, trade in goods, services and intellectual property rights.

This book addresses but a small portion of this larger problem. It discusses the question, under which conditions states may link product measures to aspects other than physical characteristics of a product, or to put it differently, to non-physical aspects (NPAs), in order to pursue social policy objectives. Such NPA measures distinguish between physically identical products based on aspects not revealed in the product itself. Examples for NPA measures are national measures linked to a process or production method (PPM) without physical impacts on the end products, such as an import prohibition for products produced by small children, or tax or tariff reductions for products produced by ecological methods.

The production process, however, has traditionally been a core field of national regulation. In the – hypothetical – absence of international trade, the regulation of production, products, their sale, consumption and waste disposal and other socially important issues would take place within a single territory and would therefore fall into the jurisdiction of a single regulator. Since goods are actually traded internationally on an immense scale, production and consumption of goods in the contemporary world are decoupled: production and consumption, or use, take place in territories of different states and within different regulatory regimes and legal frameworks. Products produced according to the rules in force in the country of production are traded to countries and consumers which possibly regulate production within their own territories in an entirely different way.

There are different motivations that may lead legislators and regulators to link measures to NPAs such as production. First, they may intend to discourage or to encourage certain aspects of production, no matter where. Second, they may want to satisfy calls for measures by domestic populations in cases where the public feels strongly about certain aspects, for instance, where child labour is concerned. Third, if domestic regulations are stricter, regulators may aim at protecting their domestic production from competition with foreign products that have been produced in a cheaper way due to softer regulation abroad. Fourth, national regulators may find it necessary to supplement internal regulation with trade measures in order to maintain effectiveness of regulation, and last, but not least, regulators may actually pursue plainly protectionist goals. Of course, a mix of the above and other motives and rationales also need to be taken into consideration. Whatever the motivation, if applied to imports, NPA measures inherently relate to foreign facts. Border measures linked to NPAs often have an extraterritorial reach which are considered to be problematic: due to the tight net of transnational economic and business relations and great economic interdependencies, measures with an extraterritorial reach may cause considerable effects on the economy and social life within other states. For this reason, some feel that states must be prevented from imposing their domestic regulatory framework via NPA measures on other countries, and fear that the functioning of the multilateral trading system could otherwise be put at risk.

Since the debate has sometimes been tense and attitudes hardened, it has often been overlooked that there is broad international agreement on the need to address certain social problems, including those created or exacerbated by unsustainable production. Thus, the debate is characterized as a debate on the means to achieve certain goals, namely, through the use of measures affecting international trade, while the ultimate goals pursued will seldom be called into question. This work tries to identify basic rationales and common ground with the potential to do justice to the different dimensions of the problem. In a first step, it is necessary to untangle the complex issues involved. Thus, this work addresses the legal questions arising with respect to NPA measures, while taking into account their political and economic context and relevance. The analysis of the status of NPA measures *de lege lata* and *de lege ferenda* is based on three important considerations emerging from the socio-economic context of the problem. First, the absolutely prevailing view in economic theory holds that government intervention and regulation are necessary in certain situations. This implies that from an economic point of view, regulatory NPA measures should be considered adequate under certain circumstances. Second, the WTO Agreements, constituting the foundations of the multilateral trading system, must be interpreted in line with basic economic rationales of the system and its objectives. Third, it is believed that WTO law, forming part of the much larger realm of public international law, must be construed in a coherent way that does not impair the essential problem-solving capacities of global society.

The book is organized in three parts. Part I, 'Foundations', provides the background relevant to the legal questions at issue. This part pays tribute to the threefold nature of the object of the analysis: it starts with the legal dimension by identifying the legal key issues to be explored comprehensively in the main part. The object of the analysis, national NPA measures, also has a political and an economic dimension. The political dimension concerns the relevance of NPA measures for domestic regulation and touches upon questions of sovereignty, while the economic dimension encompasses, on the one hand, the economic rationales for government intervention in free markets, and economic effects of NPA measures, on the other hand. From an economic perspective, national regulation is needed in order to ensure the proper functioning of markets, to prevent or reduce market failure or to correct market outcomes if these do not conform to basic ideas of fairness and equity. The perspective of this work on the three dimensions, however, is the perspective of international trade law. By transferring the problem to the international stage, a fourth dimension is introduced into the analysis: due to international trade, NPA measures apply to foreign goods, and the congruence of the legal, political and economic dimension with national territorial borders is erased. Part I closes with a review and explanation of the legal, political and economic arguments relevant to the legal status of NPA measures in the international debate.

Part II, 'Legal analysis', is the main part of this work, and takes the perspective of international trade law as it stands and analyses the legal status of NPA measures. Accordingly, it starts with the preliminary question of whether multilateral trade agreements are the right standard for assessing NPA measures. Since NPA measures usually relate to public policies other than trade, other international law may also be applicable and possibly trump provisions of WTO Agreements in the case of conflicts. In most cases, however, the WTO Agreements will apply to NPA measures due to their inherent trade relevance. Since this analysis is limited to measures applying to products, the review is limited to the relevant multilateral agreements on trade in goods, in particular, the GATT 1994 and the TBT Agreement. The analysis focuses on the legal issues that have been identified as crucial in Part I of this work. It begins in Chapter 4 with an assessment of whether NPA measures violate GATT obligations, such as the obligation to provide national treatment, and explores the relevance of the non-discrimination principle and of the notion 'like products' to NPA measures in depth. Finding considerable legal uncertainty on these issues, this work assumes, in line with the prevailing view, that most NPA measures would automatically violate basic obligations under the non-discrimination principle. Chapter 5, therefore, explores justification under the general exceptions. Although the language of Article XX does not accord a special status to NPA measures, there are some particularities relevant for the justification of NPA measures, both with respect to provisional justification and to the chapeau. This chapter concludes that there is considerable flexibility in Article XX, which allows justification of some important NPA measures. However, the flexibility is limited: not all NPA measures that might be considered legitimate by global society or by different national societies are justifiable under the general exceptions as they stand. Of the set of NPA measures, some PPM measures fall into the scope of some of the particular agreements on trade in goods.

INTRODUCTION

Chapter 6 discusses primarily the importance of the TBT Agreement. It finds that the TBT Agreement is applicable to labelling requirements, and also where unincorporated PPMs are concerned. An important finding of this particular analysis is the consideration that consumer information as the predominant objective of most labelling laws concerning PPMs must be considered a legitimate objective under the TBT Agreement.

Part III provides a broader 'Outlook' on the topic. The legal assessment of NPA measures under the existing WTO Agreements in Part II shows that, despite a decades-long debate and a few relevant reports of the GATT and WTO adjudicatory bodies, the legal status of NPA measures under WTO law, including the scope for justification, is still characterized by considerable legal uncertainty. Taking into account that the legal status of NPA measures is actually the most important application of the even broader and more politically dominated debate on the interface of WTO law and non-economic public policies, the so-called 'linkage' or 'trade and ...' debate, the legal uncertainty, even on the meaning of specific words in the legal texts, can hardly be a surprise. The broader debate exceeds the borders of WTO law and ultimately aims at solving conflicts or trade-offs between different public policies at the global level. It has produced a large number of reform proposals that would be highly relevant to the WTO as an institution and likewise to the legal status of NPA measures. Part III begins in Chapter 7 with an outline of the broader debate and reviews some proposals of a substantial, procedural or institutional nature that are highly relevant for WTO law. Against the backdrop of these proposals, the final chapter develops a specific perspective that could be utilized in determining whether NPA measures should be consistent with WTO law. This perspective is founded on the assumption that NPA measures as part of national regulation are, under certain conditions, needed to maintain the functioning of markets or to correct market outcomes. Given that markets are no longer national, it seems that, depending on the economic rationales underlying the NPA measures at issue, there may be a greater or smaller overlap with the key economic rationales of the multilateral trading system on, the one hand, and with its fundamental objectives, on the other. Three important findings arising from an application of this perspective are particularly relevant for NPA measures: first, squaring aims and effects of national regulatory measures with objectives and economic rationales of the multilateral trading system gives a good indication of whether or not a particular measure should be consistent with WTO law. Second, information requirements must not be merely justifiable, but should be *prima facie* consistent with WTO law. Third, in order to bring NPA measures in line with the WTO objective of sustainable development and the principle of special and differential treatment for developing countries, regulators ought to be obliged to consider and mitigate the economic effects of national NPA measures on developing countries.

PART I

Foundations: the relevance of NPA measures at the interface of domestic regulation, economic globalization and world trade law

In spite of numerous legal problems related to measures linked to non-physical aspects (NPA measures), the debate on such measures cannot be reduced to a problem of law. The issue is highly complex, due to the relevance of facts central to other disciplines as well. Any attempt to solve the PPM debate based on only one of the relevant disciplines, namely, law, economics, international relations or political science, is bound to fail. A sustainable solution needs to take all aspects of the debate and their implications into consideration. Therefore, the legal status of NPA measures needs to be analysed, taking into account other dimensions. With respect to the agreements underlying the multilateral trading system, implications of economic theory need to be taken into account. Furthermore, since the economic interests of WTO members diverge, and since perceived restrictions on national sovereignty go beyond merely economic issues, the debate has huge political implications. Any solution should address those diverging national and political perspectives and reconcile them. The two chapters forming Part I provide the background relevant to the legal analysis *de lege lata*, as well as to newer perspectives on the issue as offered in Part III.

1

Setting the stage for legal analysis

Legal uncertainty relating to measures linked to non-physical aspects under the law of the WTO is not a new phenomenon. Albeit with a focus on measures linked to processes and production methods (PPMs), it has been debated intensely in legal, economic and political circles since the early 1970s. Nevertheless, most legal questions underlying the debate have remained unsettled. The fact that this analysis builds on a decades-old debate facilitates the analysis in some respects, but also raises difficulties. The debate has given structure to the large problem-field, and it has developed concepts, some of which are used in this analysis. However, other concepts and terms developed and used in the debate have remained blurred, and their usefulness is doubtful. The intention of this chapter is to illustrate the topic and to identify the concepts and terms used in the subsequent parts of this analysis. It begins with a brief illustration of the topic detached from the legal debate, followed by a description of the landmark cases of GATT and WTO dispute settlement. The next section focuses on the debate that emerged around these disputes, the so-called 'PPM debate'. It describes the basic concepts and terms developed for and used in this debate. Section 1.2 briefly reviews the legal status of the most important types of measures relevant to the debate in order to identify the legal core issues. Based on the key legal issues so identified, the final section rethinks the concepts and the terms central to the so-called PPM debate and defines those used in the remainder of this work.

1.1 Brief introduction to the topic

Product regulation usually refers to the physical properties of products. In this way, all risks or dangers to consumers' health from use or consumption of a product can be addressed, since such dangers must logically arise from ingredients, materials or other physical properties of a product. There are, however, also measures that distinguish between products because of an aspect that is not physically incorporated into it.

The latter type of measure is the object of this analysis. Such measures are characterized by a link to an aspect other than physical product characteristics, or in other words, to a non-physical aspect or NPA. This NPA is reflected in the objective or factual elements of a measure. The legal consequences of an NPA measure, just like other measures, apply to products. For instance, exemptions from VAT could be granted to products which have been traded in a 'fair' way, or an import ban might stop the importation of certain timber originating in countries which do not pursue general reforestation policies. In both examples, legal consequences are applied to products because of certain NPAs linked to those products in some way. The range of facts, aspects and actual events to which NPA measures can be linked is almost unlimited.

Perhaps the most important group of NPAs comprises aspects of production, or more precisely, a process or production method, or PPM.[1] A common example for a measure linked to a PPM, or a PPM measure, is an import ban on fish caught with driftnets without so-called turtle excluder devices.[2] This ban distinguishes between tuna products based on a PPM, namely, the way in which the tuna have been caught. Another well-known example of a PPM measure is a labelling requirement for eggs, which requires producers and importers to print a code on each egg disclosing the respective farming method for chickens before placing these eggs on the market.[3]

Although PPMs arguably represent the most common subset of NPAs, it is important to note that the set of potential NPAs is much larger. As shown above, there are numerous other NPAs to which measures can be linked. A more recent example for a producer, rather than a process-related NPA measure, is European legislation prohibiting the placing on the market of seal products if these do not result from hunts traditionally conducted by Inuit and other indigenous communities and contribute to their subsistence.[4] A hypothetical and producer-related example from the field of environmental and health policies would be the requirement on the importation of oil that certain security standards for drilling rigs and

---

[1] PPMs are a subset of NPAs only if the respective aspect of production does not shape or otherwise physically affect the end-product itself. The distinction between product-related and non-product-related PPMs is addressed in more detail below.
[2] The example is based on the famous *Tuna-Dolphin* cases outlined in more detail in the next section.
[3] Example is discussed in more detail in Chapter 6, below.
[4] Article 3:1, Regulation (EC) 1007/2009 of 16 September 2009, OJ of the European Union, L 286/36 of 31 October 2009.

refineries are observed by the exploiting company. Since the concept of NPA measures is so broad, even measures linked to aspects completely unrelated to the product to which they apply would constitute NPA measures. For instance, the general observance of basic human rights or labour standards in the country of origin would be such an aspect. Hence, the set of possible NPAs is vast, since it covers aspects close to the product at issue as well as aspects completely unrelated to a product or its production, and NPAs can in principle relate to any subject matter in any area of life. From this perspective, economic sanctions would be another subset of NPA measures, which is not, as will be detailed below, the focus of this analysis. In sum, NPA measures could be understood as a generic term delimiting a large set of measures, with PPM measures forming the most common and relevant subset.

There is a widely held belief that the WTO Agreements, and particularly the GATT, do not permit national measures linked to aspects other than physical product characteristics. Since all measures linked to NPAs by definition accord different treatment to physically identical products, they are suspected of violating the GATT and other WTO Agreements in as far as they apply to imports. This work analyses the legal status of NPA measures and tests the presumptions underlying the conventionally held understanding that such measures are illegal. The following section outlines some disputes arising under GATT and the WTO which can be considered the landmark cases for this subject.

1.2 The crucial cases

The legal debate gained momentum with several disputes arising in dispute settlement. Most of them dealt with classical production-based trade measures, allegedly supplementing national policies, and so became landmark cases in the debate. Since they are well-suited to illustrate the problem and its wider implications, this section briefly sketches these disputes to show the crucial legal developments in GATT and WTO dispute settlement over the previous two decades.[5]

1.2.1 Tuna-Dolphin I (1991)

The provision central to the dispute between Mexico and the United States was section 101(a)(2) of the US Marine Mammal Protection Act (MMPA)

---

[5] For a general overview and interpretation of these disputes see Hudec (2000).

of 1972. It stated that 'the secretary of state shall ban the importation of commercial fish or products from fish *which have been caught with commercial fishing technology which results in the incidental kill or incidental serious injury of ocean mammals in excess of United States standards*'.[6] In the dispute, Mexico mainly challenged the following measures of the United States and their respective legal foundations: (1) a ban on the importation of fish which had been caught with certain commercial fishing technology; (2) a ban on importation from intermediary countries which have not themselves acted to prohibit importation from countries using such technology; (3) the possible extension of both import prohibitions to all fish products from these countries; and finally (4) the application of labelling provisions for tuna from Mexico. Interestingly, at the time both parties seemed to be of the view that measures linked to PPMs were permissible under the GATT. For this reason, the United States insisted that the provisions regulated production, while this was vehemently opposed by Mexico.[7] Mexico denied that the measures were PPMs because they aimed at protecting dolphins rather than at the production of tuna.[8] Apparently, both parties to the dispute felt that regulation of production is a legitimate activity in line with the GATT.

The Panel Report, although never adopted by the contracting parties, is known for its remarkable findings and reasons why GATT Article III[9] did not apply to the import prohibition. The panel gave a main reason and supported it with an auxiliary one. It stated, first, that the Note Ad Article III, deferring import restrictions from Article XI to the scope of Article III, could not apply since it covered only measures that were applied to the product 'as such'. The above measure directly regulated only the sale of tuna and could not possibly affect tuna as a product.[10] The panel then sought further safeguards and concluded, secondly, that even if Article III did apply, the measure would not meet its requirements. However, by using the term 'requirements' the panel seemingly did not mean to conclude that the measure actually violated Article III:4, but rather that it did not even fall into its scope: in its view, Article III:4

---

[6] Panel report in *Tuna-Dolphin I* (1991), No. 2.5 (added italics indicate relevant NPAs contained in the objective elements of the challenged regulation).
[7] *Tuna-Dolphin I* (1991), No. 3.18.
[8] *Tuna-Dolphin I* (1991), No. 3.17.
[9] If not indicated otherwise, all articles cited in this work refer to the General Agreement on Tariffs and Trade (GATT 1947, as stipulated in No. 1(a) of the GATT 1994, Marrakesh Agreement, Annex 1A).
[10] *Tuna-Dolphin I* (1991), No. 5.14.

called for a comparison of the treatment of products, and the regulation could not possibly affect tuna as a product.[11] In consequence, the panel established a violation of Article XI and proceeded to examine justification under Article XX. The panel considered two of the specific exceptions, namely, Article XX(b) and (g), and placed emphasis on the aspect of extraterritoriality. It found both exceptions to be limited to measures within the jurisdiction of the importing country,[12] and supported its conclusion by denying other requirements for justification.[13] In consequence, the panel concluded that the import bans[14] imposed by the United States were in violation of the GATT.

1.2.2 Tuna-Dolphin II (1994)

The *Tuna-Dolphin II* dispute was essentially based on the same facts and concerned the same provision of the US MMPA. This time, the European Economic Community (EEC) and the Netherlands complained about the measures. The panel in *Tuna-Dolphin II* was aligned with the decision of the *Tuna-Dolphin I* panel in 1991 regarding the application of Article III. Albeit not explicitly, the panel asserted the product–process distinction by pointing to less favourable treatment of like products not produced in conformity with certain policies.[15] It reached the same conclusion as the first panel, namely, that the Note Ad Article III was not applicable and that the measure was inconsistent with Article XI.[16]

The discussion on extraterritoriality under Article XX(b) and (g) is once again of particular relevance to the PPM debate. One of the merits of this report, and an important difference compared with the 1991 *Tuna-Dolphin* report, is the distinction between territorial jurisdiction and jurisdiction based on nationality. The panel reached a different conclusion on this point, finding that policies within a country's jurisdiction regarding its nationals and vessels fell within the range of policies covered by Article XX(g).[17] Ultimately, however, the panel reached the conclusion that the measures were not 'primarily aimed at' the conservation of an exhaustible natural resource, nor 'necessary' in the sense of Article XX(b). The reasons for this decision are most remarkable: while examining specific

---

[11] *Tuna-Dolphin I* (1991), No. 5.15.   [12] *Tuna-Dolphin I* (1991), Nos. 5.26, 5.27 and 5.32.
[13] *Tuna-Dolphin I* (1991), No. 5.33.
[14] Above measures (1) and (2); the panel did not consider measures (3) and (4) inconsistent with the GATT.
[15] *Tuna-Dolphin II* (1994), No. 5.8.   [16] *Tuna-Dolphin II* (1994), Nos. 5.9 and 5.10.
[17] *Tuna-Dolphin II* (1994), Nos. 5.20 and 5.33.

elements of Article XX, the panel essentially relied on the basic objectives and principles of the GATT to support its findings. It argued that Article XX could not be interpreted so as to permit contracting parties to adopt trade measures as a means to force other contracting parties to change policies within their jurisdiction. The balance of rights and obligations among the parties and, in particular, the right of access to markets would be seriously impaired.[18] Although differing in its reasoning, like the panel in *Tuna-Dolphin I*, this panel also found the measures in question to be illegal under the GATT. Nevertheless, the *Tuna-Dolphin II* panel went one step further. While the *Tuna-Dolphin I* panel had mostly focused on the extraterritorial effects of the measure at issue, which would not be acceptable under Article XX, the *Tuna-Dolphin II* panel rejected the measures based on the more general reason that such measures would undermine the multilateral trading system, thus reinforcing the prevailing view at the time that this type of measure was unjustifiable *per se*.[19] The contracting parties were mostly very appreciative of the outcome of the *Tuna-Dolphin* disputes.[20]

1.2.3 Shrimp Turtle (1998)

While both *Tuna-Dolphin* reports remained unadopted, the *Shrimp Turtle* panel was established under the WTO, and consequently, following an appeal, the reports were adopted by the DSB. Subject to this dispute were, for instance, section 609(a) and (b) of Public Law 101–102[21] which requested ('shall') the Secretary of State to initiate negotiations for agreements with all foreign governments which have persons or companies engaged in commercial fishing operations which might adversely affect certain species of sea turtles. Section 609(b) also prescribed a ban on importation of shrimp harvested with a certain method, stating 'the importation of shrimp or products from shrimp *which have been harvested with commercial fishing technology which may affect adversely such species of sea turtles* shall be prohibited not

---

[18] *Tuna-Dolphin II* (1994), Nos. 5.26 and 5.38.
[19] See, e.g., Jackson (1994); Reiterer (1994); Schlagenhof (1995), p. 127.
[20] Note by the Secretariat, 23 March 1995, Item 4: The Provisions of the Multilateral Trading System with respect to the Transparency of Trade Measures ... WT/CTE/W/5 (95-0633), IIICh(i). The fact that both reports remained unadopted must be ascribed to the ongoing NAFTA negotiations between Mexico and the United States at the time.
[21] As codified at 16 United States Code (USC) § 1537. Annex I, *Shrimp Turtle*, Appellate Body Report (1998).

later than May 1, 1991'.[22] According to paragraph 2 of this section, the importation of shrimp was banned unless the President had certified to Congress that the harvesting nation had a regulatory programme and an incidental catch rate comparable with that of the United States', or that the particular fishing environment of the harvesting nation did not pose a threat to sea turtles. Section 609 was seen together with guidelines for assessing the comparability of foreign regulatory programmes, and for certifying other harvesting nations. After several earlier revisions, the 1996 Guidelines also provided that other measures the harvesting nation had been undertaking to protect sea turtles were to be taken into account in determining the comparability of national programmes.[23]

The complainants felt that the embargo on shrimp and shrimp products enacted by section 609 constituted quantitative restrictions contrary to Articles XI:1 and XIII:1, was not justified by Article XX and resulted in an impairment of their benefits.[24]

1.2.3.1   The Panel Report

In response to the arguments brought forward by the parties, the panel did not address whether the measure constituted a violation of Article III, but started out by determining a violation of Article XI. It briefly considered a violation of Article I, then exercised judicial economy and did not further review the respective allegations.[25]

The panel proceeded to examine the measure under Article XX, limiting its review to the chapeau of this provision.[26] Unlike the panel in the *Tuna-Dolphin* reports, this panel went straight to the object and purpose of GATT and the WTO Agreements, locating its considerations with the reasoning on 'unjustifiable discrimination'. The panel warned that such types of measure would affect the security and predictability of the multilateral trading system as a whole. It argued that if the measures were justified, market access for goods could become subject to an increasing number of conflicting policy requirements for the same product, and that this would rapidly lead to the end of the WTO multilateral trading system.[27]

While the tenor is similar to the Panel Report in *Tuna-Dolphin II*, arguing with general considerations with respect to intention and functioning

---

[22] Emphasis added.   [23] *Shrimp Turtle* (1998), Panel Report, No. 2.14.
[24] *Shrimp Turtle* (1998), No. 3.1.   [25] *Shrimp Turtle* (1998), Nos. 7.17 and 7.23.
[26] *Shrimp Turtle* (1998), No. 7.62.   [27] *Shrimp Turtle* (1998), Nos. 7.44 and 7.45.

of the world trading system, the panel makes an interesting about-turn on the issue of extraterritoriality. It states explicitly that it does not base its findings on an extra-jurisdictional application of US law, alluding to its view that many governmental measures can have an effect outside the jurisdiction of the respective government, and thus implying that this aspect was irrelevant to its decision. In contrast, the panel considered of paramount importance whether a domestic law seeking justification under Article XX operates 'so as to affect other governments' policies in a way that threatens the multilateral trading system'.[28] Nevertheless, the report lacks determination regarding its findings. It concludes: 'However, our findings regarding Article XX do not imply that recourse to unilateral measures is always excluded, particularly after serious attempts have been made to negotiate; nor do they imply that, in any given case, they would be permitted.'[29]

For the purpose of outlining the development of the PPM debate, one other aspect of the Panel Report deserves attention. The decision of the defending party not to raise as a defence the issue of whether the measure was permissible from the perspective of national treatment under Article III:4 can be interpreted as implicit acceptance of the product–process doctrine.[30]

1.2.3.2 The Appellate Body Report

Apart from procedural matters, the appeal by the United States was limited to the panel's finding that the measure constituted unjustifiable discrimination and thus was not within the scope of measures permitted under Article XX.[31] In consequence of this limitation, the Appellate Body did not address the question of which GATT obligations had been violated in the first place, but discussed the relevance of the General Exceptions in Article XX.

The Appellate Body explicitly rejected the panel's approach to look into object and purpose of GATT and WTO. It found that the multilateral trading system was not an interpretive rule which could be employed in the appraisal of a given measure under the chapeau of Article XX,[32] but that the intention of the chapeau was to prevent

---

[28] *Shrimp Turtle* (1998), No. 7.51.   [29] *Shrimp Turtle* (1998), No. 7.61.
[30] Hudec (2000), p. 217.
[31] *Shrimp Turtle* (1998), Appellate Body Report, No. 98.
[32] *Shrimp Turtle* (1998), Appellate Body Report, No. 116, with reference to *US – Gasoline* (1996), p. 22.

abuse or misuse of a specific exemption provided for in Article XX.[33] The Appellate Body regarded the measures as being provisionally justified by Article XX(g). With respect to extraterritoriality of the protected value, the Appellate Body simply pointed out that the sea turtles at stake were all known to occur in waters over which the United States exercises jurisdiction,[34] and that the vast majority of the nations of the world shared the policy of protecting sea turtles.[35] The Appellate Body even stated that 'conditioning market access on whether exporting Members comply with, or adopt, a policy or policies unilaterally prescribed by the importing Member may, to some degree, be a common aspect of measures falling within the scope of one or another of the exceptions (a)–(j) of Article XX'.[36]

The Appellate Body then proceeded to examine the chapeau of Article XX, and found that the measure was applied in a manner that constituted unjustifiable and arbitrary discrimination between countries where the same conditions prevail. In the reasoning for unjustifiable discrimination, the Appellate Body stressed that it is not acceptable for one WTO member to require other members to adopt essentially the same comprehensive regulatory programme to achieve a certain policy goal without taking into consideration different conditions in territories of other members.[37] It argued that the United States had also failed to engage all member states exporting shrimp to its territory in serious across-the-board negotiations with the objective of concluding bilateral or multilateral agreements before enforcing the import prohibition. The Appellate Body considered this to be a serious flaw,[38] with other flaws amounting to arbitrary discrimination. In this respect, it cited the rigidity and inflexibility with which officials made the determination for certification, a prerequisite for importation, without considering which measures might be appropriate to conditions prevailing in different exporting countries, and a denial of basic fairness and due process to member states applying for certification.[39]

In sum, the Appellate Body reached essentially the same finding as the panel, namely, that the measure was not entitled to justification under

[33] *Shrimp Turtle* (1998), Appellate Body Report, Nos. 158–60.
[34] *Shrimp Turtle* (1998), Appellate Body Report, No. 133.
[35] *Shrimp Turtle* (1998), Appellate Body Report, No. 134.
[36] *Shrimp Turtle* (1998), Appellate Body Report, No. 121.
[37] *Shrimp Turtle* (1998), Appellate Body Report, No. 164.
[38] *Shrimp Turtle* (1998), Appellate Body Report, Nos. 166–72.
[39] *Shrimp Turtle* (1998), Appellate Body Report, Nos. 177 and 181.

the chapeau of Article XX because it discriminated unjustifiably and even arbitrarily between countries where the same conditions prevailed.[40] In addition to its application of the chapeau and important dicta, it overruled the panel's finding of *per se* inadmissibility of a certain type of unilateral trade measure, namely, a PPM measure. This is what made the Appellate Body Report in *Shrimp Turtle* so important.[41]

1.2.3.3 Shrimp Turtle – Article 21.5 (2001)

The *Shrimp Turtle* dispute did not end with the Appellate Body Report in the original dispute, but continued as a compliance case. Approximately two years after the DSB had adopted the panel and the Appellate Body Report, one of the appellants in the *Shrimp Turtle* dispute, Malaysia, again requested establishment of a panel. Malaysia complained that the United States had failed to comply with the DSB's recommendations, and that its measures were inconsistent with Article XI and remained unjustified.[42] Eventually, the Appellate Body rejected all arguments brought forward by the appellant. The decision basically supported the findings of the Appellate Body in the original dispute, but added some details with respect to justification of the measures under Article XX.

1.3 Overview of the PPM debate

This section recounts the emergence of the legal debate, its milestones and the present state of play, without, however, delving into the legal arguments brought forward. The purpose of this section is to describe the traditional debate as such, with the concepts and terms prevailing in that debate. For instance, the distinction between products, on the one hand, and production processes, on the other, are central to the debate. This section exceptionally ignores differences between PPM measures and other measures linked to NPAs and sticks to the terms and concepts used in the debate. The subsequent sections will then review the crucial terms and concepts and define their use for the remainder of this book.

---

[40] *Shrimp Turtle* (1998), Appellate Body Report, No. 184.
[41] E.g., H. Chang (2000) calls the report the most important ruling to date, for Jackson (2000a) it is one of the two most profound cases that have come through the appellate process, and Berger (1999) characterizes it as a positive milestone and environmental breakthrough.
[42] *Shrimp Turtle – Article 21.5* (2001), Panel Report, No. 3.1.

1.3.1 Emergence of the PPM debate

The *Belgium – Family Allowances* Panel Report of 1952 constitutes early evidence for the then prevailing view that the GATT did not allow the contracting parties to apply to imports measures linked to the existence or not of certain policies in the country of origin.

The focus of the PPM debate, however, has been on measures linked to PPMs. A document important for the emergence of a distinction between measures linked to products and measures linked to production, particularly with respect to environmental measures, is a note of the GATT Secretariat from 1971. The note had been drafted in preparation for the UN Conference on the Human Environment in order to survey issues that national anti-pollution measures might raise for international trade. The study explores the rationales for national import restrictions in cases where the production process causes pollution, and finds that the interest usually stems from a desire to compensate domestic producers for extra costs assumed in pollution control. It then explicitly rejects the relevance of pollution control by explaining that:

> protection because of higher costs than those prevailing ... elsewhere is precisely what GATT seeks to limit, in the interests of ensuring the most efficient use of resources on a worldwide basis.[43]

The note then went on to generalize this argument with respect to a whole range of national policies:

> The fact that the new pollution control differences would result directly from governmental regulation would not make them unique: national standards concerning labour, social security, taxation and safety already have a varying impact on costs from one country to another which GATT does not recognize as grounds for protection.[44]

This view was confirmed two decades later in the 1992 study on 'Trade and the Environment'. The GATT Secretariat stated that in principle, it was:

> not possible under GATT's rules to make access to one's own market dependent on the domestic environmental policies or practices of the exporting country.[45]

In sum, the early debate was overall clear as to the inconsistency with GATT obligations of measures linked to production or other policies.

---

[43] GATT (1971), p. 13.   [44] GATT (1971), p. 13.   [45] GATT (1992), p. 10.

Arguments invoked to support the finding that PPM measures violate GATT obligations were of a most fundamental nature and a possible justification of such measures was not even discussed explicitly.

1.3.2 Developments in academia and practice

At the time of the *Tuna-Dolphin* disputes in the early 1990s, the view that production-based trade measures should be considered illegal prevailed also among trade officials and scholars.[46] There was a general fear that the acceptance of trade measures conditioning market access to the adherence to domestic standards would result in 'chaos and anarchy'.[47] The *Tuna-Dolphin* cases were interpreted to state very clearly that process-based regulations were incompatible with the GATT.[48] The arguments, especially in the early debate, were mostly politically motivated,[49] which is to some extent also reflected in the *Tuna-Dolphin* reports. Some even wondered whether the panel had their own political motivation to reject the US measures despite allegedly noble intentions underlying them. It was contemplated that:

> the Panel served to further the argument that process-based regulations are necessary for environmental sustainability. By leaving no way in which the current GATT system can be used or manipulated to permit such regulations, the Panel urged and challenged the Contracting Parties to resolve these issues on a multilateral basis.[50]

---

[46] See, e.g., Schoenbaum (1992); Reiterer (1994), p. 113, who states that restrictions based on non-product-related PPMs are generally considered discrimination and violate basic principles of the GATT; OECD (1994), p. 7, Commission of the European Communities, Communication from the Commission to the Council and the European Parliament on Trade and Environment, COM(96)54 final of 28 February 1996, p. 14. Jackson (1992) understands 'both the Article III (including some Article XI questions) and the Article XX exceptions to apply to the product standards and to life and health within the importing country, but not to extend these concepts and exceptions to "processes" outside the territorial limits of jurisdiction.' He therefore sees the need that the 'GATT system must give specific and significant attention to this trade-off in order to provide for exceptions for environmental purposes'.

[47] Schoenbaum (1992), p. 703.

[48] Zreczny (1994), p. 81 (focusing on the *Tuna-Dolphin I* Panel Report).

[49] Puth (2003), p. 66. Also, Geradin (2000), p. 97 attested a general hostility of WTO members for process-related restrictions (for 1998). The third-party submissions in *Tuna-Dolphin I* (1991) show a general rejection of the US measures without always linking the arguments to GATT provisions, while the arguments of the same third parties were of a much more legal nature in *Tuna-Dolphin II* (1994).

[50] Zreczny (1994), p. 83, with respect to the *Tuna-Dolphin I* decision.

1.3 OVERVIEW OF THE PPM DEBATE

However, with environmental problems moving to the centre of attention in politics in the early 1990s, the distinction between trade measures aiming at products and those aiming at production processes faced increasing criticism. The GATT and, a few years later, the WTO were often accused of preventing national policies which preserved the environment or supplied other public goods of high quality,[51] and the illegality of production-based trade measures was one important aspect of the alleged shortcomings. The general idea and reasoning behind this criticism was increasingly met with approval,[52] without, however, leading to the multilateral solution that some had hoped for.

Another effect of the *Tuna-Dolphin* cases was that the debate increasingly took on a legal character. The panels' findings that the production-based measures at issue violated GATT obligations also mostly met with approval among scholars. The legal distinction between measures linked to products and measures linked to production gained ground and led some to consider its status as legal doctrine.[53] Both panel reports also sparked a whole series of scholarly publications commenting on and discussing the legal status of measures linked to processes and production methods,[54] mostly referred to as 'PPMs'.[55] Although the distinction was increasingly met with criticism, the concept of the product–process distinction was further refined. Trade measures distinguishing between

---

[51] See, e.g., Ralph Nader, 16 March 1994: 'The Uruguay Round is crafted to enable corporations to play this game at the global level, to pit country against country in a race to see who can set the lowest wage levels, the lowest environmental standards, the lowest consumer safety standards', quoted in Roessler (1998).

[52] For instance, as early as 1992 Arthur Dunkel, then Director General of GATT, stated at a Conference on Business and the Environment in Bangkok on 23 January 1992: 'And the Uruguay Round has brought new elements into the picture, such as … sanitary and phytosanitary measures, and agreement that processes and production methods may be used to distinguish one product from another' (GATT/1527). In 1998, the European Parliament, referring to the Panel Report in *US – Taxes on Automobiles* of 11 October 1994 with respect to the 'gas guzzler tax', urged the Commission to advocate at the WTO Ministerial Conference in Geneva that the WTO should draw up a Statement of Understanding to enable otherwise identical products to be differentiated where the production or processing of such products have different impacts on the environment (Sitting of the European Parliament of 30 April 1998, *Official Journal of the European Commission*, C 152/80).

[53] See, e.g., Hudec (1998), p. 624; Hudec (2000).

[54] On the product–process distinction in general see, e.g., Zreczny (1994); Hudec (1998); Appleton (1999); Hudec (2000); Howse and Regan (2000); Jackson (2000a); Charnovitz (2001a); Puth (2003); Kysar (2004).

[55] The abbreviation 'PPMs' is not used in a uniform way, but is nevertheless central to the legal debate. See section 1.3.3, below.

products because of PPMs were believed to be inadmissible *per se*, but only provided that the respective production process would not have a physical impact altering the end product. The reason that trade measures based on the product itself were considered legal was that physical differences were traditionally seen as relevant. Those production methods which affect products physically needed to be considered permissible as well. Hence, in addition to the product–process distinction, a further distinction between so-called product-related and non-product-related PPMs emerged.[56]

The view of a *per se* illegality of trade measures based on processes was finally challenged by the Appellate Body Report in the *Shrimp Turtle* dispute in 1998. To reiterate, although the product–process doctrine and related questions regarding whether or not production-based measures violate national treatment provisions was not even addressed in the respective report,[57] the Appellate Body confirmed that such measures were in principle justifiable. However, the United States, which defended several PPM-based trade measures, lost its case, and the report gave sufficient leeway for interpretation; in particular, the precise conditions that would need to be fulfilled for justification have since remained unclear.

By the turn of the twenty-first century, arguably most legal scholars writing on this problem had repudiated the idea of *per se* illegality of PPM-based trade measures.[58] Some even went beyond the reasoning offered by the Appellate Body Report and challenged the primary assumption that PPM-based trade measures violate GATT obligations, based on the product–process distinction, in the first place. Since the *Shrimp Turtle* dispute, no panel has yet been established to settle a dispute relating to a NPA or PPM measure.

In recent years, however, the focus of the debate has shifted. With the increasing importance of non-tariff barriers to trade, and the conclusion of several other multilateral agreements on trade in goods in the Uruguay Round, the importance of the GATT declined. Questions

---

[56] Hudec (2000), p. 191.
[57] The Appellate Body in its *Shrimp Turtle* Report did not address the PPM problem, although India, Pakistan and Thailand as Joint Appellees had brought this argument forward (Appellate Body Report on *Shrimp Turtle* (1998), No. 42).
[58] See, e.g., van den Bossche, Schrijver and Faber (2007), Puth (2003), Charnovitz (2001a), Hudec (2000), Bronckers and McNelis (2002), Howse and Regan (2000) and Thaggert (1994) criticizing the product–process distinction with different arguments, but see, e.g., Jackson (1997, 2000a) p. 236 and Berrisch (2003), p. 88, who state that the distinction remains useful but should not be applied too rigidly.

relating to product labelling or to requirements regarding traceability of products, potentially falling into the scope of other WTO Agreements, attracted considerable attention. Especially in the Western developed world, labelling schemes including provisions relating to PPMs or other NPAs have been adopted. The discussion on PPM labelling schemes addresses numerous questions relating to the scope of the TBT Agreement, the permissibility of such schemes under its provisions and the relationship of the TBT Agreement and the GATT. No dispute dealing with such questions has yet been decided before the adjudicatory bodies.

1.3.3 Concepts and terms central to the 'PPM debate'

The debate on PPMs has been based on some concepts and terms widely accepted today. Despite their broad acceptance, the use of these concepts and terms has not been consistent. Disagreement continues to prevail over their precise legal meaning and relevance. This section briefly outlines the key features and basic rationales of these concepts and gives an overview over key terms of the debate and over the different meanings they are given.

1.3.3.1 The product–process distinction

Underlying the PPM debate is the presumption that trade measures can be sub-divided into measures that are linked to products and measures that are linked to production, and that both groups of measures have a different legal status under the GATT. The term 'product–process doctrine' to depict this distinction was coined by Hudec in 1998.[59] Hudec explained that it had long been assumed among governments that only national measures distinguishing between products based on their physical qualities could be in line with the GATT obligation to accord national treatment. He observed that:

> under this so-called 'product–process doctrine', product distinctions based on characteristics of the production process, or of the producer, that are not determinants of product characteristics are simply viewed as *a priori* illegitimate.[60]

---

[59] The relevance of a distinction between production process and product was recognized much earlier, and is known in political science as well as in law. See, e.g., Zrecny (1994), pp. 81–133.
[60] Hudec (1998), p. 624.

The merits of the product–process distinction are seen in drawing a bright line, as a rule to prevent abuses through trade measures.[61] It was warned that in abandoning the distinction, other 'handholds' to deal with the vast possibilities of such abuses would be needed.[62] These arguments express concerns about the legal situation that would be created if the product–process doctrine were abandoned. Proponents of the product–process doctrine point to the possible creation of a vast loophole in the GATT,[63] since countries might then be allowed to link trade measures to all aspects subject to national regulation, such as the protection of labour or minority rights, religious requirements or cultural traditions.[64] These concerns are often expressed by comparing the rejection of a distinction with a slippery slope or the opening of Pandora's Box. The distinction, however, has also been criticized by a number of scholars. Hudec, for instance, declared the product–process doctrine a potentially lethal threat to process-based regulation. Well aware of the Appellate Body's more favourable stance towards possible justifications of environmental measures under Article XX, Hudec still remained worried about the uncertain scope of Article XX, both with respect to the kinds of measure that might possibly be justified, as well as with respect to coverage of related issues such as human rights or labour rights.[65]

Since the distinction between products and production has considerable logical appeal, it is often overlooked that the legal content of the concept is vague. The concept is mostly invoked as evidence in support of a particular legal finding, namely, that PPM measures must be considered *prima facie* illegal under the GATT. The underlying reasoning, in contrast, remains obscure: for instance, it is not apparent which GATT obligations are violated, whether justification of production-based measures under Article XX is possible or not, and, if so, under which conditions.[66] In his

---

[61] Jackson (2000a), pp. 303, 304, Zrecny (1994), p. 93.
[62] Jackson (2000a), pp. 303, 304.
[63] Opinion stated by Venezuela, in *Tuna-Dolphin I* (1991) Panel Report, No. 4.27.
[64] Cf. Jackson (1992), pp. 1243, 1244, who gives further examples.
[65] Hudec (2000), p. 188.
[66] Hudec (2000), p. 187, for instance, interprets the doctrine to mean that PPM measures, depending on the law in question, would violate either GATT Article III or Article XI. He interprets the doctrine as permitting justification under Article XX. Jackson (1997), p. 236, in contrast, implies that Article XX cannot justify measures that accord different treatment to identical products because of aspects of production. Earlier, however, it was advocated that justification could not be considered at all (cf. Panel Report in *Tuna-Dolphin I* (1991), No. 4.1 (Submission of Australia) and No. 3.31 (Mexico), Panel Report in *Tuna-Dolphin II* (1994), No. 4.38 (Submission of New Zealand).

authoritative article on the subject, Hudec gave a very specific meaning to the product–process doctrine. In his view, the distinction is actually related to the Ad Note to Article III. He considered that measures relating to production, which are merely part of a larger national regulatory framework, were in line with the obligation to accord national treatment in Article III, if they treated foreign products no less favourably than domestic products. However, in order to be referred to Article III, measures applied to imports at the border must fall into the scope of the Ad Note to Article III. Hudec interpreted the product–process distinction to limit the Ad Note to internal regulations based on the physical characteristics of the product.[67] Hence, such measures would quasi-automatically violate Article XI.

The reason for the obscurity of the product–process distinction is that it is attached to the legal text of the GATT only loosely. Although the distinction is mostly based on the Panel Reports outlined in the previous section, the distinction has never been explicitly accepted by the adjudicatory bodies. Whether or not the product–process distinction has legal value depends on the relevant provisions of the agreements, which will be analysed comprehensively in Part II.

1.3.3.2 Processes and production methods

The concept of processes and production methods (PPMs), serves to flank the product–process distinction. Under the product–process distinction, measures relating to the production process are assumed to have a special legal status. The objective elements which lead to this legal status, accordingly, are the processes and production methods to which such measures are linked.

Though the concept is used mostly with respect to the GATT, it is likewise linked only loosely to GATT language. The first exhaustive discussion of the relevance of PPMs in international trade law was provided by the Organization for Economic Cooperation and Development (OECD) in its 1994 report. The OECD stated that the abbreviation PPMs refers to 'processes and production methods',[68] and advocated a definition that slightly exceeded the literal meaning of the words as: 'the way in which products are manufactured or processed and natural resources extracted or harvested'.[69] Presumably, due to the absence of a legal definition or reference in the agreements, the abbreviation PPMs and the term processes

---

[67] Hudec (1998), p. 191.   [68] OECD (1994), p. 7, OECD (1997), p. 7.
[69] OECD (1997) p. 7.

and production methods have subsequently been used in a very inconsistent way. In recent years, the term has been understood much more broadly, for instance, as the 'sum of all activities necessary to place the product on the market'.[70] These differences might be one reason why the option to completely avoid this term has sometimes been preferred, citing the 'process–product problem'[71] or simply the 'PPM debate'[72] instead.[73] Eventually, it was recognized that the term simply seems to have a number of different meanings.[74]

1.3.3.3 'Product-related' and 'non-product-related' PPMs

In the course of the debate on the product–process doctrine, the additional distinction between 'product-related' and 'non-product-related' PPMs'[75] was developed and has become an analytical concept that is widely accepted.[76] It is geared towards the physical differences between end-products produced with different PPMs. While production will usually change the properties of the end-product and are so revealed in it or related to it, some aspects of production are 'non-product-related' in the sense that they do not alter any physical characteristics of the merchandise. In other words, some PPMs are incorporated in the end-product by means of the physical impact they exert on it, and other PPMs are unincorporated in the sense that they do not leave any physical traces on or in the merchandise.

---

[70] Puth (2003), p. 44.   [71] Jackson (2000a), p. 429.
[72] See Quick and Lau (2003).
[73] As Hudec points out, there is a divide between different meanings of the term PPM, on the one hand, and the boundaries of the GATT legal doctrine, on the other (Hudec (2000), p. 187, fn. 1).
[74] Hudec (2000), pp. 187–217.
[75] Sometimes, the terms incorporated and unincorporated PPMs are used as a more precise alternative (cf., e.g., WTO, Trade and Environment: Background Document, April 2004, p. 17). Also Charnovitz (2001a), p. 13, speaks of a misnomer and calls the distinction popular but flawed. His concerns, however, do not target the substantive and factual difference between incorporated and unincorporated PPMs, but consequential conclusions drawn from the distinction thus do not refer to the categorization as such.
[76] Charnovitz (2001a), p. 11. However widely accepted the distinction is, it has also been suggested that it would be preferable to forbear from using the rather complicated construction of two categories of PPMs and instead divide between product-based and production-based trade measures (see Winter (2003), p. 129; Howse and Regan (2000), p. 250; Bartels (2002), p. 384, who distinguishes with boycott measures a further category). Other concepts exist as well, e.g., Geradin (2000), p. 92, who distinguishes between direct restrictions on trade, product standards and process standards, thus ignoring considerable overlaps between these categories.

1.3 OVERVIEW OF THE PPM DEBATE

The additional distinction gives an indication that it is the existence of physical differences between end-products rather than the fact that a measure relates to production that is crucial for its legal status under the GATT. Some scholars therefore suggested a different perspective and terminology, shifting the focus away from the rather narrow term 'production'. Hudec, for instance, stated that:

> product distinctions based on characteristics of the production process, or of the producer ... cannot be used as a justification for different treatment of foreign and domestic goods. When dealing with a product distinction based on *such non-product criteria*, WTO panels are instructed to ignore the *non-product criteria* and to determine whether any difference of treatment between foreign and domestic products can be justified under the other test of legitimacy provided in Article III – the 'like product' test and its allied doctrines.[77]

While Hudec chooses the term 'non-product criteria', others have suggested approaching the discussion from a different angle. PPM-based measures were defined as 'any trade measure or domestic regulation or tax that distinguishes products by looking beyond perceptible characteristics',[78] by referring to 'non-product-related trade measures'.[79] Again, which term is best suited for the legal discussion depends on the provisions of the GATT.[80] The cursory legal analysis in section 1.4 clarifies which legal problems under the GATT are crucial for trade measures linked to NPAs, and whether or not PPM measures do have a legal status that is distinct from other measures.

1.3.4 Unanswered questions and legal uncertainty

The difficulty in describing the current state of play in the debate on PPM measures is threefold. First, the debate does not focus on a delimited question, but touches upon numerous legal questions, the answers to which are interlinked. Second, as apparent from the description above, there is great diversity of opinion in the literature on each of these questions. Third, for

---

[77] Hudec (1998), p. 624 (emphasis added). [78] Charnovitz (2001a), p. 11.
[79] Puth (2003), p. 29, distinguishes between product-related and non-product-related trade measures (author's translation from German).
[80] The adjectives 'product-related' and 'non-product-related' PPMs are confusing: by definition, production methods 'relate' to products, even if they do not have an impact on the physical characteristics of the end-product. This work therefore prefers the adjectives 'incorporated' and 'unincorporated'. For the relevance of the distinction see Chapter 6 below on the special status of PPM measures under the TBT and the SPS Agreements.

different reasons, such as the special facts of the cases and claims raised by the parties, the existing dispute settlement reports are not only very few, but these few even fail to address the legal problems comprehensively. Likewise, the WTO Secretariat still detects disagreement between members over consistency of PPM measures with the WTO Agreements.[81]

Nevertheless, it seems to be widely believed that the basic lines along which PPM measures are assessed under WTO law have been established. For instance, with respect to a violation of GATT obligations, some take for granted that there is a prevailing view which holds that Article XI prohibits trade restrictions that target the production process instead of the product 'as such'.[82] This view seems to be in line with the *Tuna-Dolphin* reports and with the *Shrimp Turtle* reports, the latter completely disregarding Article III. However, the *Tuna-Dolphin* reasoning for non-applicability of Article III has been strongly criticized.[83] The possibility of an 'Article III defence' of trade measures being a corollary to national policies has been vigorously vindicated,[84] and Article III has also been the starting point for other approaches to finding a solution to the PPM problem.[85]

Assuming that PPM measures violate GATT obligations, it could be argued that as a consequence of the *Shrimp Turtle* dispute it is widely accepted that production-based trade measures are in principle justifiable under Article XX.[86] However, due to the specificities of that case, the general consensus seems to be limited to PPM measures applied with a jurisdictional link, such as the territorial link underlying the measures in the *Shrimp Turtle* dispute due to the nature of the turtles at issue as a migratory species. From this perspective, the reasoning in the *Shrimp Turtle* dispute seems to be unsuited as a basis for generalizations. Furthermore, there is no doctrine of *stare decisis* under WTO law, and even though the *Shrimp Turtle* dispute as *quasi de facto* precedent is a strong case for future acceptance of unilateral trade measures, it is possible that the Appellate Body might change or adjust its rulings. Even assuming that PPM measures are in principle justifiable, the conditions for justification

---

[81] WTO (2004), p. 17, fn. 75.   [82] E.g., Puth (2003), pp. 29, 30.
[83] E.g., Puth (2005), p. 589, fn. 27; Quick and Lau (2001), p. 108, call the argumentation 'questionable', an early critique of the approach to Article III by the *Tuna-Dolphin* panels by Thaggert (1994).
[84] Howse and Regan (2000), pp. 249–89.
[85] See also the 'aims and effects' theory, discussed in more detail in Chapter 4, section 4.2.2.2, below.
[86] Cf. the summary of the product–process distinction by Porges and Trachtman (2003), at p. 798; recently, e.g., Ferrell (2005), p. 376; Showalter (2005), at p. 869; van Calster (2000), at p. 12; Petersmann (1994), at p. 156.

under Article XX, including those contained in the chapeau, have hardly been further refined.

In sum, whether there is such a prevailing view holding on to the product–process distinction or not remains unclear. The different views discussed in the literature and among practitioners are instead evidence of an astonishing legal uncertainty relating to some of the most fundamental provisions of the GATT.

1.4 Identification of key legal issues

This section synoptically analyses fictitious PPM and NPA measures in order to identify the crucial provisions and key terms determining their legal status. The synoptical analysis addresses such measures merely in a cursory and very general way, since the key legal questions so identified are analysed in depth in Part II of this work. To date, most analyses have approached the PPM debate from the point of view of a particular policy field, such as the environment or labour and human rights.[87] Such approaches have the advantage that the consequences of any favoured solution are also limited to a particular policy field. This book nevertheless uses a different and more abstract approach in order to address legal problems common to different policy fields. By de-coupling the object of research from particular policy fields the legal 'common denominators' of these trade measures can be identified. The intention is to link the fundamental and far-reaching problems dominating the broader debate to the more specific legal questions of the relevant provisions in the WTO Agreements.

Despite their extensive political as well as factual implications, the theoretical legal problems are approached from a strictly legal perspective in this section, using the relevant sources of law and interpretation at hand. It is only the examination of problems under the existing agreements and WTO adjudication that will allow for a judgement as to how far the current legal situation is appropriate to the far-reaching problems, and, if not, which changes would be necessary for a better solution. The wider implications are therefore considered in the subsequent evaluation of the existing legal status of these measures in Part III of this work.

[87] For an environmental perspective see, e.g., Schlagenhof (1995); Wiers (2001); Charnovitz (2002); Gaines (2002); Cottier, Tuerk and Panizzon (2003); Puth (2003); Winter (2003); for the human rights and labour standards perspective, e.g., Howse and Trebilcock (2005), at pp. 288, 289; Macklem (2002), at p. 627; and, e.g., Nielsen (2007) for a focus on animal welfare and biodiversity.

The following summarized legal analysis of the most important types of trade measures serves to identify those interpretative questions which are crucial to the PPM debate. The analysis draws on case law, widely accepted results of scholarly debates and conventional views among scholars. Once a relevant legal issue is found to be of particular importance for the legal status of measures linked to NPAs, it is identified as a crucial legal problem to be addressed in Part II. Also, the identified questions allow for inferences regarding the common features of all those measures which trigger these particular legal problems, and, as a corollary, on the true scope of the debate. The object of the analyses are different fictitious policy measures linked to PPMs, such as bans on importation, tariff measures, national regulation, taxation, charges and so forth.

1.4.1 Customs tariffs

Although a main purpose of GATT and WTO is the substantial reduction of all tariffs, in general customs duties in the form of tariffs are explicitly legal under the GATT.[88] Once members have bound certain tariff rates in their Schedules of Concession under Article II, they have committed themselves not to levy more than the codified tariff, the ceiling, on a particular item.[89] This prohibition, however, does leave room for a number of tariff measures that states may take, for example, in the, now rare, case of unbound items, or in the case of bound items the raising of customs duties which remain below the ceiling. It is, however, questionable if states could take any of these tariff measures if they were linked to NPAs.

1.4.1.1 Article II

While it is arguably unusual in practice, NPAs can, and do, serve as a basis for tariffs. The legal status of tariffs based on NPAs is one of the subjects that is not explicitly regulated by the GATT. It is closely related to the issue of product classification, which is problematic due to the lack of a comprehensive and internationally harmonized classification system. The GATT itself does not determine whether tariffs may be based on NPAs, nor does it regulate questions of tariff qualification or reclassification in the nomenclature.[90] Article II merely obliges members to accord a certain treatment to products as described in a Schedule, subject to the

---

[88] See, e.g., GATT Article II:1(b). [89] Jackson (1969), p. 201.
[90] Panel Report, *Spain – Unroasted Coffee* (1981); Jackson (1969), at p. 212.

terms, conditions or qualifications set forth therein.[91] There are no further requirements that members have to observe in the description of the items and, correspondingly, in the classification of goods according to their trade policy. Articles II:3 and II:5 contain only vague injunctions that reclassification may not impair the value of any of the concessions provided for in the appropriate Schedule. Therefore, reclassification may be subject to a non-violation complaint.[92]

In the absence of further regulation in Article II, it can be concluded that countries are authorized to introduce sub-positions in their tariff nomenclatures and to freely draft descriptions of the items.[93] In principle, therefore, WTO members could be free in their product classification for tariff purposes, and in binding tariffs according to product-related and non-product-related criteria, such as unincorporated PPMs or other NPAs, as long as the country does not violate obligations under its Schedule.

1.4.1.2 The relevance of international rules

The legal status of tariff measures linked to NPAs might, however, also depend on other international agreements bearing on GATT law.[94] Tariff negotiations in the Uruguay Round were held on the basis of the Harmonized System (HS), and concessions were made in terms of its nomenclature.[95] International endeavours to harmonize tariff classification must therefore be taken into account. The International Convention on the Harmonized Commodity Description and Coding System of the World Customs Organization (WCO) entered into force on 1 January 1988. Meanwhile, almost all WTO members have adopted or apply the HS,[96] a product nomenclature developed by the WCO in order to achieve

---

[91] GATT Article II:1(b).
[92] Matsushita, Schoenbaum and Mavroidis (2004), p. 116; cf. Panel Report, *Germany – Sardines* (1952), No. IV. The non-violation complaint is regulated in Article XXIII:1(b).
[93] van Calster (2000), p. 38.
[94] It is generally held that the WTO legal system is largely, but not entirely, self-contained (Matsushita, Schoenbaum and Mavroidis (2004), p. 76). This is also true with respect to tariffs, as the Agreement on Customs Valuation (Agreement on Implementation of Article VII of the General Agreement on Tariffs and Trade, Annex 1A of the WTO Agreement) refers explicitly to the Customs Cooperation Council (CCC), which is based on an international convention of 1950 and has developed the Harmonized System. The HS therefore bears on WTO law with respect to customs and classification, cf. DSB report in fn. 95, below.
[95] Appellate Body Report, *EC – Certain Computer Equipment* (1998), No. 89.
[96] As of 30 June 2010, the number of contracting parties to the HS Convention was 138 (WCO, General Secretariat, NG0169E1a, 29 July 2010), with the HS being used by more than 200 countries and economies as the basis for their tariff classification, see

uniform tariff classification. Countries use the HS as a basis for their customs tariffs. Under the nomenclature, tariff treatment distinguishing between products on grounds of NPAs is not prohibited. However, in most cases the tariffs are classified according to a short description, mostly based on product names,[97] and thus refer to the end-product as such and not to NPAs.[98] Pursuant to the General Rules for the Interpretation of the Harmonized System, classification shall be determined according to the terms of the nomenclature's headings.[99] Also, materials and substances shall be taken into account in classification.[100]

However, it is not indicated whether these descriptions may refer to physical characteristics only, or to other aspects also. While most of the headings refer to physical product characteristics, it is wrong to conclude that this practice, however well-established, is the only one permissible. It has to be noted that a minority of headings in the HS refer explicitly to aspects other than physical characteristics of the finished product. For instance, the HS refers to 'paintings … executed entirely by hand',[101] and thus to a product which has been produced with a certain production method. Another note refers to different ways of printing,[102] and is thus also linked to production.

It also cannot be assumed that members that adhere to the HS have to stick to physical characteristics under those headings that refer to physical characteristics only. This is because tariff classification below subheading level remains in the hands of the state imposing tariff rates.[103] In this respect, the Panel Report in *Japan – SPF Dimension Lumber* stated that the HS:

---

www.wcoomd.org/files/1.%20Public%20files/PDFandDocuments/Conventions/Hsconve21.pdf, accessed 30 July 2010.

[97] A crucial rule is contained in No. 3(a), which is applicable if *prima facie* a good is classifiable under several headings. In this case, the heading which provides the most specific description shall be preferred to others. This rule implies that the references in headings are to be understood as short descriptions of the goods to be classified.

[98] Therefore, the misleading assumption that tariff classification of like or identical products will necessarily be the same, e.g. Quick and Lau (2003), at p. 431.

[99] International Convention on the Harmonized Commodity Description and Coding System (HS Convention), Annex, The General Rules for the Interpretation of the Harmonized System, amended as of 26 June 2004, No. 1

[100] HS Convention, No. 2(b).

[101] HS Convention, section XXI, Chapter 97, Heading 01.

[102] HS Convention, section X, Chapter 49, Note 2.

[103] Article 3 of the HS Convention requires that members 'shall use all the headings and subheadings of the Harmonized System without addition or modification, together with their related numerical codes', while not prohibiting further sub-categorization.

1.4 IDENTIFICATION OF KEY LEGAL ISSUES

did not entail any obligation as to the ultimate detail in the respective tariff classifications. Indeed, this nomenclature has been on purpose structured in such a way that it leaves room for further specifications.[104]

Finally, the HS is not the only criterion for interpreting concessions under the GATT. The respective states' classification practice during negotiations has to be taken into account as a supplementary means of interpretation.[105] This means, that while a practice distinguishing between products for the purpose of tariff classification prior to negotiations may be maintained, a subsequent modification in tariff classification is problematic. From this point of view, a distinction within the boundaries set by earlier concessions according to the sub-headings of the HS would be legal because it would not violate the prohibition of raising a tariff rate beyond the ceiling. Hence, if a country respects the bound rates in its Schedule, it might, for example, be permissible for a country to leave untouched the tariff for a certain product, while reducing the tariff for identical products which were produced in a different way, for instance, in order to provide an incentive for ecological production.

1.4.1.3 Obligation to most-favoured-nation treatment

A differentiation in tariff rates based on NPAs is nevertheless questionable under the WTO core principle of non-discrimination, namely the obligation to provide most-favoured-nation (MFN) treatment according to Article I. The MFN principle has a twofold impact on Article II. The imposition of tariffs is permitted subject to MFN treatment according to Article II:1(a),[106] which requires that treatment provided for in the appropriate Schedule is binding for the commerce of the other contracting parties, thus not allowing any differences in treatment because of the product's origin. As tariffs linked to NPAs do not distinguish between products based on their origin, this dimension of MFN treatment would not be violated by a sub-categorization – at least not on the surface.

This may be different in the case of the second dimension of MFN treatment under Article II, which is a direct consequence of Article I:1 and the obligation not to discriminate among trading partners with respect to customs duties. In this case, the general obligation to accord MFN treatment prohibits discrimination between 'like' products and

---

[104] Panel Report, *Japan – SPF Dimension Lumber* (1989), p. 31.
[105] Appellate Body Report, *EC – Certain Computer Equipment* (1998), No. 92.
[106] Bhala and Kennedy (1998), p. 78.

applies to scheduled products as well as to others.[107] Whether there is a discrimination or not depends primarily on the choice of objects to which advantages have been granted. The standard applicable in order to determine a case of discrimination is the 'likeness' or not of the products in question. A differentiation in tariff rates is permissible only if the products concerned are not considered 'like'.[108] On the one hand, if all products within one sub-heading of the HS were looked upon as 'like' in the sense of Article I:1, and if further sub-positions allowed for different tariff treatment, then the finding of discrimination would be inevitable, with the consequence that further differentiation under sub-headings was impermissible *per se*. On the other hand, assuming that tariff classification alone, including the sub-heading level, was an indication of likeness or unlikeness would lead to the circular reasoning that the issue of discrimination could never be relevant regarding customs duties. Therefore, some degree of sufficient reason for a distinction between products below sub-heading level is required.[109] The view that tariff classification alone is an indication for 'likeness' in Article I:1 has been objected by members and scholars alike.[110]

Despite the apparent freedom of members to classify their tariffs under Article II,[111] and despite the fact that the HS classification is partly based on NPAs, whether a tariff linked to NPAs will be *prima facie* legal or not ultimately depends on the definition of the term 'like' in Article I:1.

1.4.2 Import prohibitions or other quantitative restrictions

Article XI lays down a general prohibition of certain trade measures that become effective at the border, namely, all import restrictions other than duties, taxes or other charges. This prohibition applies to any import restriction, regardless of whether the measure is based on products, production processes or any other circumstance not revealed in the product. However, even for border measures such as quantitative restrictions there

---

[107] Panel Report, *Spain – Unroasted Coffee* (1981), IV, No. 4.3; Jackson (1969), p. 204.
[108] Panel Report, *Spain – Unroasted Coffee* (1981), IV, No. 4.4.
[109] In *Spain – Unroasted Coffee* (1981), IV, No. 4.6, the Panel stated that there need to be sufficient reasons to allow for a different tariff treatment by establishing new positions or sub-positions.
[110] van Calster (2000), p. 39; Jackson (1969), p. 215.
[111] It is therefore misleading that Puth (2003), p. 285, points out that members are free to differentiate in their tariff nomenclature between products based on production methods, mentioning the example of a country introducing separate sub-positions for non-chlorine bleached paper and other paper.

1.4 IDENTIFICATION OF KEY LEGAL ISSUES

is an exit option for the otherwise inescapable outcome of *prima facie* illegality.[112] This option is based on the conflict rule[113] contained in the Note Ad Article III (henceforth: the Note), and it is of particular importance for import restrictions linked to NPAs. It stipulates:

> Any ... law, regulation or requirement of the kind referred to in paragraph 1 which applies to an imported product and to the like domestic product and is collected or enforced in the case of the imported product at the time or point of importation, is nevertheless to be regarded as an internal ... law, regulation or requirement ... and is accordingly subject to the provisions of Article III.

The Note is directed at cases where an internal regulation applies to both the imported and the 'like' domestic product. Specifically, it aims at a situation where an internal regulation is applied at the border to an imported product with trade-restrictive effects. While normally the prohibition of quantitative restrictions in Article XI would be applicable, the Note refers this situation to the scope of Article III, the national treatment provision. As will be detailed in the next section, this could mean that the measure would be permissible if it treated the imported product at least as favourably as the 'like' product of national origin.[114]

However, to reiterate, it is controversial whether or not the Note can possibly apply to import restrictions linked to PPMs or NPAs. The proponents of the product–process distinction base their argumentation on the language of the Note, which explicitly refers to regulations applying to 'products' and allegedly implies that the Note is not applicable to PPM measures.[115] Article III would then not be applicable, with the consequence that the measure would be prohibited as a quantitative restriction. A similar line of argumentation was used by both *Tuna-Dolphin* panels in the early 1990s. Both panels argued that the relevant measures did not refer to the product 'as such', as was required by the Note and by Article III. Therefore, the panels held that neither the Note nor Article III

---

[112] The relationship between Article XI and Article III is under discussion. In the *Tuna-Dolphin* disputes, the panel first analysed applicability of Article III, and when it found it to be inapplicable, it concluded on violation of Article XI.

[113] For the qualification of the Note as a conflict norm see Cottier, Tuerk and Panizzon (2003), p. 158.

[114] In this sense also, the GATT secretariat has stated that the basic intention of GATT rules is that a country can do anything to imports or exports that it does to its own products. Consequently, non-discriminatory environmental policies would ordinarily not be subject to any GATT restraints (GATT (1992), p. 8).

[115] Panel Reports, *Tuna-Dolphin I* (1991), No. 5.14, *Tuna-Dolphin II* (1994), Nos. 5.9 and 5.10.

were applicable. This line of argument was first established in the *Tuna-Dolphin I* dispute,[116] and with a slightly different rationale it was repeated in *Tuna-Dolphin II*.[117] As a consequence, internal PPM regulation which constitutes a quantitative restriction under Article XI would be prohibited *per se*. As mentioned above, however, these disputes cannot be regarded as constituting a line of well-established case law, and there is also considerable criticism of the product–process distinction in the literature. According to the contrary opinion that the Note is applicable, the legality of PPM-based quantitative restrictions depends on the national treatment standards of Article III.[118] Whether the legal status of import restrictions linked to NPAs is reviewed under Article XI or Article III thus depends on interpretation of the scope of the Note Ad, particularly on the interpretation of the term 'products'.

1.4.3 Non-tax internal regulation

Internal regulation, including social regulation, does not directly affect international trade and is at first glance not subject to WTO law, the primary objective of which is the regulation of trade and the prevention of discrimination.[119] However, national regulation can have a considerable impact on international trade, for example, if it has a bearing on imports. Therefore, almost all domestic regulation, in particular regarding health, the environment and labour markets, can be regarded as potential non-tariff barriers to trade.

Article III is the crucial norm in determining how the WTO regime polices the regulatory activities of its members.[120] At its core, Article III imposes on the contracting states the prohibition to discriminate between 'like' domestic and imported products. First of all, this means that internal regulation is subjected to GATT scrutiny only in the event that such regulation has an impact on imported products. To reiterate, depending on the interpretation of the Note Ad, Article III could also be relevant in cases where internal regulation is applied to imported products when crossing the border.

Under Article III, whether a measure according different treatment to products is discriminatory or not depends first of all on the consideration

---

[116] *Tuna-Dolphin I* (1991), Nos. 5.14 and 5.15.
[117] *Tuna-Dolphin II* (1994), No. 5.9.
[118] Cottier, Tuerk and Panizzon (2003), p. 158.   [119] GATT (1992), p. 7.
[120] Hudec (1998), p. 620.

1.4 IDENTIFICATION OF KEY LEGAL ISSUES

that the products in question are 'like products'. The word 'like', however, is not defined in the GATT.[121] Since it is inherently a term of comparison, it cannot be defined in an absolute way. Which products are to be considered 'like', depends on the characteristics relevant for the comparison. The opponents of the legality of NPA measures limit the relevant characteristics to physical ones and conclude that identical products produced with different unincorporated PPMs must always be 'like' each other. Therefore, a treatment distinguishing between products because of NPAs or unincorporated PPMs would be discriminatory. If, in contrast, a wider definition of likeness, including, for instance, NPAs, were applied the comparison might lead to the finding that even physically identical products might not necessarily be 'like' each other in the sense of Article III. As a consequence, trade measures differentiating between products because of NPAs would thus be allowed under WTO law, even without recourse to justification. Some scholars also argue that there is an additional condition for finding that a measure is discriminatory. They hold that only measures with underlying protectionist aims or effects could be considered discriminatory in the sense of the GATT. From this point of view, the determination of whether a measure pursues protectionist aims and effects is crucial. Since this theory was developed and applied mostly with respect to the assessment of tax measures under Article III, this issue is discussed in the next section.

To summarize, whether or not internal regulation that applies to imports and is linked to NPAs is illegal depends again on the meaning of the term 'like products'.

1.4.4 Internal taxes and other internal charges

Taxes are not bound in the member states' schedules of concession, and their introduction remains in the jurisdiction of member states.[122] The idea of using internal taxes and charges linked to NPAs as policy instruments to pursue various policy objectives is based on their potentially high efficiency and transparency.[123] Internal taxes and charges linked to NPAs can be categorized into indirect taxation applying to products,

---

[121] See also, Panel Report, *Japan – Alcoholic Beverages I* (1987), p. 24.
[122] van Calster (2000), p. 417.
[123] See, e.g., Commission of the European Communities, Communication from the Commission to the Council and the European Parliament on Trade and Environment, COM(96)54 final of 28 February 1996, p. 16; OECD, C/MIN(99)14, of 12 May 1999, No. 67, regarding general possible options for dealing with measures underlying PPMs.

40   SETTING THE STAGE FOR LEGAL ANALYSIS

business taxation linked to NPAs relating to the taxed corporation (direct taxation) and direct charges linked to NPAs (e.g., emission trading).[124] Imported products can be subject to both internal indirect taxation and border tax adjustment, which will be discussed subsequently.

1.4.4.1 Indirect taxation and NPAs

Taxes are a traditional instrument for internalizing externalities,[125] such as environmental damage caused by production.[126] The use of taxes as market instruments in order to promote certain methods of production, for example, through imposing a lower VAT on products which have been produced with less emissions and gradually increasing the tax rate for deteriorating emission output, is rather common.[127]

Indirect taxation is subject to Article III:2. Article III:2 consists of two interrelated sentences, the relationship of which is explained by the Note Ad Article III, paragraph 2. The Note can be read so as to indicate that the proper order for examination of a measure is first to check consistency with the first sentence of Article III:2, and only if the measure is not found to violate this sentence, to put it under the scrutiny of the second sentence.[128]

The first sentence of Article III:2 establishes two conditions that cumulatively lead to impermissibility of tax measures. The imported product would, first, need to be 'like' the domestic product the treatment of which

---

[124] This categorization disregards the type of externality states address with these measures. Since externalities are related to targets and intentions of measures and, as such, relevant for justification, not for WTO violations in the first place. In the literature, however, some scholars distinguish between domestic, transboundary or global, and extraterritorial production externalities. Van Calster (2000), p. 423, in contrast, speaks of a type characterized by local consumption or production externalities in the exporting or importing state which is not the state imposing the taxes.

[125] Hunter, Salzman and Zaelke (2002), p. 135.

[126] See, e.g., an initiative of the European Commission in the Green Paper on Integrated Product Policy (COM(2001)68, 7 February 2001) to apply a reduced VAT rate on products with a certain eco-label. In its resulting Communication (COM(2003)302, 18 June 2003) the European Commission declared that it would not pursue this particular initiative any further in reaction to comments received from Member States and other stakeholders.

[127] See for an overview on suggestions for market-based instruments, Commission of the European Communities, Green Paper on Market-based Instruments for Environment and Related Policy Purposes, COM(2007)140 final, 28 March 2007.

[128] See, e.g., Appellate Body Report, *Canada – Periodicals* (1997), pp. 22–3; Appellate Body Report in: *Japan – Alcoholic Beverages I* (1987), pp. 18–31; likewise van Calster (2000), p. 47; a different approach being followed by the panel in *Korea – Alcoholic Beverages* (1998).

1.4 IDENTIFICATION OF KEY LEGAL ISSUES

is the standard relevant for the comparison. Second, the tax or other internal charge imposed on the imported product would need to be in excess of the one applied to like domestic products. The latter condition, namely, different tax treatment, does not feature any particularities when it comes to NPA measures – even the smallest amount of an excess in taxation is considered too much.[129] In contrast, the first condition – 'likeness' of the products in question – is again crucial for the permissibility of measures linked to NPAs.

As mentioned in the previous section, the shortcomings of the term 'like products' have inspired a theory that despite its broader implications was first developed with respect to tax measures. This theory is often referred to as the 'aims and effects test'.[130] It postulates that a measure can possibly violate Article III:2 only if its nature is contrary to the object and purpose[131] of Article III as a whole.[132] In order to identify this object and purpose, the language of Article III:1 – 'internal taxes and other internal charges ... should not be applied to imported or domestic products so as to afford protection to domestic production' – was interpreted so as to limit the purpose of Article III to a prohibition of those regulatory distinctions between products which intend to, and which actually do, protect domestic production. As a consequence, regulatory distinctions applied so as to achieve policy purposes unrelated to protection would be allowed by Article III:1.[133] For the limited purpose here to identify the crucial GATT provisions and legal theories for assessing NPA measures, it is not necessary to delve into the complex debate.[134] It has been pointed out earlier that NPA measures are often imposed as a tool for environmental or social policies, and that therefore it could be argued that they should be presumed to pursue legitimate aims. As regards protective effects, it is not possible to make a general statement regarding measures linked

---

[129] Appellate Body Report, *Japan – Alcoholic Beverages I* (1987), p. 23.
[130] Cf. Chapter 4, section 4.2.2.2, for a more detailed analysis of the 'aims and effects' theory.
[131] For the importance of object and purpose for interpretation see Panel Report in *US – Section 301 Trade Act* (1999), para. 7.22.
[132] The 'aims and effects test' was originally applied with respect to the interpretation of the notion of likeness in Article III in general. Later, it was seen to be relevant under Article III:2 only, and finally its has been seen to originate from the language 'so as to afford protection' in Article III:1 (cf. Hudec (1998)). However, the point of the test is beyond the scope of the notion of likeness (cf. Hudec (2002)).
[133] Panel Report, *US – Malt Beverages* (1992), para. 5.25.
[134] Cf. Chapter 4, section 4.2.2.2, for a more detailed analysis of the 'aims and effects' theory.

to NPAs: just as other measures, also measures linked to NPAs may or may not have protective effects, depending on the product market and the NPAs prevailing in different countries. Protective aims and effects depend on the circumstances in a real case and cannot be addressed in a general way. Nevertheless, considering the particularity that NPA measures usually serve to implement legitimate non-trade policies, the aims and effects test is certainly relevant for the legal status of NPAs.

If the respective products are not found to be 'like', a tax measure has yet to comply with the conditions laid down in the second sentence of Article III:2 together with the related Note. Hence, a violation of the second sentence requires that imported and domestic products are 'directly competitive or substitutable' and in competition with each other and that the directly competitive or substitutable imported and domestic products are 'not similarly taxed'. The reference in Article III:2 to the first paragraph is interpreted as requiring additionally that the dissimilar taxation of the directly competitive or substitutable imported domestic products is 'applied ... so as to afford protection to domestic production'.[135]

The first requirement, the existence of a directly competitive relationship between the imported and the domestic product, is to be decided on a case-by-case basis, taking the relevant market into account.[136] There is broad agreement that the set of directly competitive and substitutable products is the broader category as compared with the set of 'like products' relevant to the first sentence of Article III:2.[137] In analysing whether products produced with different NPAs are directly competitive and substitutable this last consideration is crucial. If physically identical products are considered 'like products', regardless of the circumstances of production, then such products must *a fortiori* be directly competitive or substitutable. Even if it is assumed that the presumption of likeness of identical products can be rebutted, arguing that such products are not even directly competitive or substitutable would place an even higher burden on the party denying competitiveness and substitutability of products. The second requirement, the existence of dissimilar taxation, does not provide any particularities when it comes to NPAs. The final requirement for a violation of the second sentence of Article III:2, namely, the application of the dissimilar tax 'so as to afford

---

[135] Appellate Body Report, *Japan – Alcoholic Beverages II* (1996), p. 24.
[136] Appellate Body Report, *Japan – Alcoholic Beverages II* (1996), p. 25.
[137] Appellate Body Report, *Japan – Alcoholic Beverages II* (1996), p. 19; Panel Report, *Korea – Alcoholic Beverages* (1998), para. 10.38.

1.4 IDENTIFICATION OF KEY LEGAL ISSUES

protection to domestic production', is assumed to be relevant for tax measures based on NPAs.[138]

In sum, the key issues bearing on the legal status of NPA-based indirect taxation are again the meaning of the term 'like products', now in Article III:2, and the related notion of 'directly competitive and substitutable'. Since measures linked to NPAs often pursue non-trade policies, and these could be presumed legitimate, the 'aims and effects test' is also highly relevant for measures linked to NPAs.

1.4.4.2 Direct taxes and NPAs

States could also distinguish in the direct taxation of producers based on the production methods they use. For instance, producers maintaining production facilities that do not meet safety standards could be subject to higher income taxation than producers using safer technologies. States could also use tax credits as incentives to producers to favour certain production methods. However, according to the prevailing opinion direct taxes have to be regarded as outside the scope of this provision,[139] even if this is questionable from an economic point of view.[140] Direct taxation, referring to NPAs or to other possible characteristics, therefore, cannot violate Article III:2.[141]

1.4.5 Border tax adjustment

Products described in the schedules of concession are not only exempt from ordinary customs duties in excess of those set forth therein, but they are in principle also exempt from all other duties or charges of any kind in connection with their importation.[142] Nevertheless, charges which correspond to the domestic tax burden may be collected on importation of a product under GATT law, but they must be applied on a non-

---

[138] See Howse and Regan (2000), p. 249.
[139] Jackson (1969), § 12.7, p. 285, who recognized this language as one of the major loopholes of the GATT Working Party on Border Tax Adjustment, Report, adopted on 2 December 1970, BISD 18S/97, at para. 14; Matsushita, Schoenbaum and Mavroidis (2004), p. 168; van Calster (2000), p. 421, Puth (2003), p. 257; Panel Report, *Argentina – Hides and Leather* (2000), para. 11.159, referring to Appellate Body report, *Canada – Periodicals* (1997), para. p. 20, cf. Christian and Hufbauer (2004).
[140] Matsushita, Schoenbaum and Mavroidis (2004), p. 168; van Calster (2000), p. 421; Jackson (1989), p. 215.
[141] However, differentiation of direct taxation may amount to subsidization and could therefore be problematic under WTO law, as is discussed below at section 1.4.7.
[142] Panel Report, *EEC – Parts and Components* (1990), para. 5.4.

discriminatory basis, both with regard to like domestic products and to those originating from the territory of other members of the WTO.[143] Such border tax adjustment can also occur on exportation. In this case, taxes to which products were subjected before exportation are rebated.

1.4.5.1 Imports

There are two provisions in the GATT applying to the import levy side of border tax adjustment, namely Article II:2(a) and the general Note Ad Article III.[144] Article II:2(a) permits the imposition of a charge equivalent to an internal tax on the like domestic product on importation of a product, provided the tax is consistent with the provisions of Article III:2 and national treatment requirements. The general part of the Note Ad clarifies that a tax measure is subject to the provisions of Article III if it applies to both the imported and the like domestic product, even if it is enforced in the case of the imported product at the time or point of importation.

The exception contained in Article II:2(a) as described above refers to charges equivalent to internal taxes 'in respect of the like domestic product'. According to the prevailing opinion, indirect taxes levied on products, such as the European VAT, are eligible for border tax adjustment.[145] The general rule, therefore, is that in the case of indirect taxation, the legal position of products is the same for both those bound and those unbound in the country's schedules of concessions, and that border tax adjustments are permissible if consistent with Article III:2.

If indirect taxes are linked to NPAs, however, this rule is problematic. Since the exception in Article II:2(a) contains the term 'like domestic product', the permissibility of border tax adjustment based on NPAs is subject to interpretation of 'likeness', even before the national treatment standard under Article III:2 is applied. The permissibility of border adjustment of indirect taxes linked to NPAs thus depends on an interpretation of the notion of likeness under three provisions: namely, the Note Ad; Article II:2(a); and Article III:2 as detailed above, but only if this interpretation permits a distinction based on NPAs.

---

[143] Article II:2(a) together with Article III:2; Matsushita, Schoenbaum and Mavroidis (2004), p. 167, referring to Panel Report *Indonesia – Automobiles* (1998).

[144] Jackson (1969), § 12.7, p. 295.

[145] This opinion has prevailed since the adoption of the Report of the Working Party on Border Tax Adjustment, above fn. 140, at para. 14. However, the distinction between direct and indirect taxes is too simplistic from an economic point of view and rests today merely on tradition and practicality, Matsushita, Schoenbaum and Mavroidis (2004), p. 480.

In principle, it should also be possible to adjust direct taxation.[146] However, since border tax adjustment for bound items is allowed only thanks to the Article II:2(a) exception, adjustment of direct taxes is generally perceived as being prohibited by the GATT.[147] This means that if NPAs are used as a basis for domestic direct taxes, states are not allowed to level the playing field for imported products through border tax adjustment. The general prohibition on additional duties and charges contained in Article II is inapplicable only in the insignificant case of unbound items.[148] According to the Note Ad, border tax adjustment would in this case be subject to the national treatment requirements in Article III.

1.4.5.2 Exports

The export side of border tax adjustment is mainly regulated by the GATT and the SCM Agreement. Due to the traditional economic beliefs underlying the distinction between direct and indirect taxes, border tax adjustment for direct taxes on the export side is illicit in general.[149]

In contrast, border adjustment of indirect taxes is allowed under certain conditions. First, Article VI:4 ensures that products must not face the imposition of anti-dumping or countervailing duties because they were exempt from taxes borne by 'like products' destined for domestic consumption in the country of origin. This is also true for the refund of such duties or taxes. The Note Ad Article XVI confirms this intention by clarifying that the exemption or remission of direct taxes in the case of products destined for exportation shall not be regarded as a subsidy.

Also, different indirect taxation, if linked to NPAs, leads to some particularities. The notion of the 'like domestic product' leads to a vice-versa scenario compared with the problems occurring in cases of border tax adjustment on importation. The state of origin can refund a producer of products which have been manufactured in an environmentally sound manner and which, because of the country's taxation rules, are subject to less tax than products produced in a more damaging manner. This measure could be justified by the same reasoning that underlies the imposition

---

[146] Cf. Christian and Hufbauer (2004).
[147] Matsushita, Schoenbaum and Mavroidis (2004), p. 479.
[148] In developed countries, an average of 1 per cent of product lines still remain unbound, while the percentage of unbound product lines in developing countries and countries in transition is estimated between 2 and 27 per cent (WTO (2010) p. 25).
[149] Tax adjustment is qualified as prohibited export subsidies under SCM Article 3.1(a) read together with Annex I(e). However, there are convincing arguments against the prohibition of adjustment of direct taxation, cf. van Calster (2000), p. 426.

of lower indirect taxes for products that have been produced in an environmentally friendly way, namely, the higher costs of production. The state could argue that the producer when exporting its products is unable to reap the fruits of his environmentally friendly production, because the lower tax rate applies in the country of origin only. In order to level the playing field, the higher rebate should offset the competitive disadvantage resulting from the higher standard and thus higher costs of production. Again, the notion of likeness, this time in Article VI:4 and in the Note Ad Article XVI, would be crucial for the permissibility of such a refund.

1.4.6 Anti-dumping duties

Anti-dumping duties could come into consideration as a tool to prevent imports of products that have been produced using certain production methods. Importing states might be particularly prone to using this tool in cases where the domestic industry complains about imported products that are cheaper than domestically produced products due to lower standards in the country of exportation. This situation is mostly discussed with respect to environmental standards: producing in low-standards countries is often branded as 'eco-dumping', while 'social dumping' refers to production with lower labour standards. Since anti-dumping duties are usually based on a comparison of prices, it would seem at first glance to be impermissible to link anti-dumping duties to NPAs. This problem has not yet become relevant at the WTO, and therefore this analysis is limited to some basic considerations.

According to Article VI:1, anti-dumping duties are permitted basically to offset dumping if products are introduced into the commerce of the importing country at less than their normal value, and if there is a threat of, or an actual material injury to, the domestic industry of the importing country. The definition of dumping in GATT Article VI and in Article 2 of the AD Agreement provide for different ways to determine dumping.

The first method is a comparison of the export price of the product and the comparable price 'for the like product' when destined for consumption within the country of production. This method only allows anti-dumping duties targeting NPAs if industries in the exporting countries produce part of the total product output in a cheaper manner by ignoring certain standards, and part of total output of a particular product in a more expensive manner, presumably observing such standards. In this case, the importing country could cite the fact that the cheaper products exported into third countries were 'like' the more expensive products

1.4 IDENTIFICATION OF KEY LEGAL ISSUES

produced under the observation of higher standards. The export price might then be compared with the price of like products produced with higher standards in the exporting country, and consequently found to be priced too low. Since physically identical products would be considered to be 'like', the comparison between products produced with cheap production methods for exportation and 'like' products produced with safer/cleaner or simply more expensive production methods in the exporting country result in the assertion of dumping. Hence, the importing country would be allowed to impose anti-dumping duties, provided all other requirements were fulfilled. On the other hand, should NPAs be recognized as a determinant of 'likeness', then these products would not be 'like' each other, and consequently no case of dumping could be established. The legal definition of the term 'like product' in Article 2.6 of the AD Agreement does not solve this uncertainty explicitly. The definition stresses 'identity' of products, or products being 'alike in all respects', and thus arguably requires a very high degree of likeness. But although the definition does mention product characteristics and 'all respects' as determinants of likeness, it does not clarify whether or not the term 'characteristics' and the relevant 'respects' refer to physical aspects only, or if non-physical aspects should also be taken into account. However, the very idea of a comparison of prices in different countries shows that the AD Agreement aims at the prevention of predatory price competition only – but not at the prevention of low prices in general.

Another way of determining dumping could be suitable to support anti-dumping tariffs linked to NPAs. To simplify, the basic definition of dumping is the introduction of a product into the commerce of another country at less than that product's normal value (Article 2:1 AD Agreement). Article 2:4 AD Agreement states that the comparison between export price and normal value must be governed by 'fairness'. One could argue that it is inherently unfair to exploit competitive advantages which arise from non-observance of minimum standards and thereby from highly polluting or risky production in countries where such standards do not exist or are not being enforced. It might be argued that applying 'fairness' in the comparison requires levelling the playing field retroactively by considering costs arising from adhering to certain minimum standards, even if such 'costs' did not arise in monetary terms, since standards were ignored. This argumentation might be used particularly in cases where international agreements establishing minimum standards exist, but are ignored by producers and authorities alike. The crucial issue with respect to anti-dumping duties is, therefore, the meaning of the term 'fairness'.

However, here it also seems to be crucial that the intention of the anti-dumping agreement, as apparent, for instance, from GATT Article VI, is limited to the protection of industries from injury due to unfair competition. The term 'fairness' alone cannot be considered sufficient to establish that beyond that there is an intention to protect the environment or social rights by supporting the observance of certain minimum standards. Therefore, NPA duties justified with protection against so-called eco-dumping or social dumping cannot be considered as consistent with the AD Agreement.[150]

1.4.7 Subsidies

Two different situations relating to subsidies linked to NPAs need to be distinguished. On the one hand, there are ordinary domestic subsidies that promote certain NPAs, such as environmentally friendly production methods. This situation will usually occur in industrialized countries that can afford financial incentives as instruments to pursue certain social policies. On the other hand, there is the argument that countries that maintain low environmental or other social requirements, which allow enterprises to shift considerable external costs to the environment and society, 'subsidize' their industries in an illicit way. It is often assumed that many developing countries or countries in transition refrain from adopting higher standards and allow enterprises to pollute for free.

1.4.7.1 Subsidies linked to NPAs

NPA measures that constitute subsidies are subject to the SCM Agreement.[151] According to Article 1, subsidies require some form of income or price support in the sense of GATT Article XVI or a financial contribution by a public body (Article 1.1(a)(1) and 1.1(a)(2)), a corresponding benefit which was conferred (Article 1.1(b)), and specificity as detailed in Article 2. Tax incentives or credits normally imply a financial contribution in the form of government revenue foregone and therefore constitute indirect subsidies.[152] The following considerations are therefore equally valid for tax measures as well as for direct contributions.

---

[150] Against the permissibility of anti-dumping duties because of NPAs also Puth (2003), p. 221. Given this finding of inconsistency, the legal analysis in Part II does not take up this discussion.

[151] All provisions mentioned in this chapter refer to the SCM Agreement, if not otherwise indicated.

[152] Lopez-Mata (2001), p. 578; but see also Ruge (2002), according to whom tax privileges to producers belong to the group of direct subsidies.

1.4 IDENTIFICATION OF KEY LEGAL ISSUES

The objective elements of financial contribution from a public body and the existence of a benefit are not contingent upon whether the subsidy in fact supports a certain production method rather than a producer or a product. Thus, incentives targeting the use of certain PPMs or other NPAs must be considered a financial contribution, and almost always the very idea of an incentive will be to confer a benefit. Hence, the targets of subsidization could be relevant on the first level of the finding of a subsidy only if this fact was connected to the element of specificity (Article 1.2, Article 2).

The third element, specificity, was introduced as a tool to separate acceptable subsidies from unacceptable ones and to limit the use of countervailing duties.[153] Only subsidies which are not specific to certain industries, which means to an enterprise or industry or group of enterprises or industries, are permitted and not countervailable.[154] The question arises as to whether the criterion of specificity excludes from the scope of prohibited subsidies those measures that promote NPAs in order to achieve legitimate policy goals.

An example of a subsidy pursuing a legitimate policy goal is a financial incentive to use certain filters in production plants in order to reduce air pollution. Yet even if the use of a certain filter is an objective element not limited to certain enterprises, the tax incentive could nevertheless be considered specific under Article 2.1(b) because it would be doubtful whether the objective element is 'economic'[155] in nature. Furthermore, subsidies or incentives may often be inherently limited to certain industries, since only the production of certain goods leads to a specific type of pollution that needs to be avoided by specific filters. Therefore, subsidies linked to NPAs might still be considered specific to a particular industry – even if the limitation to a certain industry was by nature of the objective of the measure.[156] Subsidies linked to NPAs will therefore usually fall into the scope of the SCM Agreement.

This broad definition of specificity is arguably a result of the original 'traffic light' structure of the SCM Agreement. The SCM Agreement is

---

[153] Wilcox (1998), pp. 153, 154.
[154] SCM Agreement Article 8.1(a) (expired in 1999), also Article 1.2 read with SCM Agreement Parts III and IV (*argumentum e contrario*), see also Matsushita, Schoenbaum and Mavroidis (2004), p. 264; Kube (2001), p. 24; Horlick and Clarke (1994) p. 42.
[155] The so-called 'SME-footnote' No. 2 to the SCM Agreement requires 'criteria or conditions which are neutral, which do not favour certain enterprises over others, and which are economic in nature and horizontal in application, such as number of employees or size of enterprise.'
[156] Cf. the reasoning of the Panel rejecting Canada's arguments in *US – Softwood Lumber* (2003), No. 7.116 (which was not appealed before the Appellate Body).

not based on a concept of violations and justification comparable with the structure of the GATT. Instead of providing possibilities for justifying a subsidy, the SCM Agreement explicitly provided a category of non-actionable ('green light') subsidies. Articles 8 and 9 stipulated objective facts qualifying a subsidy as permitted and non-actionable. Among these in Article 8.2(c) there used to be a category of subsidies relating to compliance with environmental requirements, which would under certain conditions be relevant to tax measures supporting the use of environmentally friendly production processes. The provisions on quasi-permitted subsidies in SCM Agreement Part III were originally introduced for a five-year period. They expired in 1999, and have not been replaced since. Therefore, it must be concluded that a non-protectionist intention alone is not sufficient to qualify a subsidy as unspecific, because that would make the provisions on 'green light' subsidies redundant and would thus violate the rule of effective treaty interpretation.[157] Furthermore, the fact that members did not extend application of these provisions by consensus according to SCM Agreement Article 31 must not be ignored. Arguably, members were not convinced of the legitimacy of the quasi-permitted subsidies.[158] Interpreting the term 'specificity' in a way that qualifies production-based tax incentives as non-actionable would, therefore, mean floating out the vote of WTO members not to extend the experimental period of five years for 'green light' subsidies.

Most subsidies targeting NPAs would thus belong to the category of actionable subsidies, which under certain conditions can result in the imposition of countervailing duties. In determining whether the subsidy has resulted in adverse effects to the interests of other members according to Article 5, the term 'like products' is again crucial. According to Article 6.3(a), an adverse effect exists, for example, if serious prejudice to the interests of other members arises, such as in cases where the effect of the subsidy is to displace or impede the imports of a 'like product' of another member. This seems to imply that whether or not a subsidy is actionable may depend on the products that are considered 'like'. It could

[157] The principle of effective treaty interpretation (as defined by the Appellate Body in *US – Gasoline* (1996), p. 23) states that 'interpretation must give meaning and effect to all the terms of a treaty. An interpreter is not free to adopt a reading that would result in reducing whole clauses or paragraphs of a treaty to redundancy or inutility'. This principle has been observed by the Appellate Body in numerous other disputes, e.g., *Japan – Alcoholic Beverages I* (1987), p. 11; *Korea – Dairy* (2000), pp. 23, 24, Nos. 80–2; *EC – Tariff Preferences* (2004), p. 69, No. 172.

[158] See Sykes (2003), pp. 22–3, arguing 'green light subsidies' are questionable from an economic point of view.

be assumed that a narrow or broad interpretation of the term 'like', taking into account or ignoring aspects of production, may predetermine the finding or not of serious prejudice to the interests of other members. However, it seems that for the determination of adverse effects, the definition would in practice hardly be relevant: Article 6.4 explicitly confirms that a change in 'relative shares of the market to the disadvantage of the non-subsidized like product' is sufficient for a finding of serious prejudice. Therefore, it seems that a subsidy linked to NPAs would usually be found to cause serious prejudice to the interests of other members and thus be actionable under the SCM Agreement. Although this finding may often not be satisfactory, it seems that the problem here is that Part IV on non-actionable subsidies has lapsed.

To conclude, the assessment of subsidies linked to NPAs does not differ from the assessment of other subsidies under the SCM Agreement. Due to the broad definition of serious prejudice, it will in practice be irrelevant for the assessment of whether or not the subsidies are actionable.[159]

1.4.7.2 Low standards as illegitimate subsidization

The argument that low environmental or social standards constitute illegitimate subsidies is based on considerations similar to those prevalent in the debate on eco-dumping detailed above. While the allegation of eco-dumping focuses on the competitive advantages of producers, the allegation of a regulatory subsidy focuses on the role of the state or government in conferring an advantage on enterprises producing within the regulating state.

From a legal point of view, the existence of a subsidy in the sense of the GATT and the SCM Agreement is assessed on the basis of the relevant provisions. Thus, a regulatory subsidy constituted by the adoption of low standards falls into the scope of the SCM Agreement if it meets the requirements for a subsidy as laid down in Article 1. To reiterate, in order to meet the definition, a subsidy needs to consist of a financial

---

[159] It is, however, interesting that Ruge (2002) suggests justifying subsidies established for environmental policies under GATT Article XX. If one subscribes to this view, then the specificities of NPA measures under Article XX, as outlined in Part II, would also become relevant to subsidies linked to NPAs. However, it seems questionable whether Article XX could be applicable to subsidies falling into the scope of the SCM Agreement, since the SCM Agreement may constitute *lex specialis*. Ruge does not explore this more fundamental question and the consequences of this construction. While this approach bears considerable problems that go beyond the scope of this work, it seems that this approach would be worth being considered, given the lack of provisions on non-actionable subsidies.

contribution that confers a benefit and that is specific in accordance with the provisions of Article 2.

It is, however, doubtful whether the first requirement, namely, a financial contribution, is met. The contribution could consist of either government revenue foregone, the provision of goods and services other than general infrastructure, or any other form of income or price support.[160] The normal case of government revenue foregone, as explained in footnote 1 of the SCM Agreement, is an exemption from duties or taxes, not the complete absence of such duties. It is also questionable as to whether low standards that result in external costs can be considered a good or service. Against the finding of income or price support provided by low standards, the fact that there is no direct impact on the national budget has been invoked.[161]

The existence of a financial contribution need not be gone into, however, since the third requirement, namely, specificity, is not met in the case of low environmental and social requirements. Since these will usually be generally applicable, and neither conditioned by any criteria nor limited to certain enterprises in the sense of Article 2, regulatory subsidization does not fall into the scope of the SCM Agreement, nor does it violate GATT Article VI or Article XVI.[162]

1.4.8 General exceptions

For the purpose of this analysis it is here assumed that trade measures linked to NPAs violate the obligations of the member state imposing the measure. In this case, the legal status of the measure depends on justification under the general exceptions in Article XX.[163] Article XX is a general provision and does not distinguish between strictly product-based measures, on the one hand, and NPA measures, on the other. Even before applying Article XX, the question arises as to whether, as an expression of domestic policy requirements, NPA measures pose *per se* a threat to the multilateral trading system and are in general excluded from

---

[160] See Article 1.1(a)(1)(ii), (iii) and (a)(2)

[161] Puth (2003), pp. 223–5. Puth rejects the finding of a financial contribution under any of the alternatives in Article 1 altogether.

[162] Against the consideration of low standards as illegitimate subsidization also Puth (2003), p. 226. Given the rejection of a special relevance of NPAs for subsidies, the legal analysis in Part II does not need to address this issue in more detail.

[163] Article XX is seen as exception 'justifying' otherwise illegal measures, e.g., Appellate Body Report, *US – Gasoline* (1996), IV, p. 22; Appellate Body Report, *Shrimp Turtle* (1998), No. 123; in scholarship, e.g., Lowenfeld (2002), p. 35.

1.4 IDENTIFICATION OF KEY LEGAL ISSUES

justification.[164] It has been argued that GATT Article XX allows for exceptions from GATT obligations, which in turn imply a focus on products, not on the production process, and that, consequently, also Article XX could not help to render process-based measures permissible under the GATT.[165] From this perspective, the product–process distinction would extend beyond the GATT violation side and bear on justification under the general exceptions.

1.4.8.1 The particular exceptions

Only measures which fall into the scope of any of the listed particular exceptions can be provisionally justified. All measures linked to NPAs have either a direct effect via regulation or an indirect effect via economic incentive on an NPA, such as a production method. This impact leads to several problems relevant to the listed policies.

The first problem field relates to the scope of the particular exceptions. Since the list of measures which can potentially be justified under Article XX is exclusive, many NPA measures might fall outside the scope of Article XX. Such aspects targeted by measures linked to NPAs which do not appear in the list of measures are, for instance, workers' rights or conditions of employment, culture, religion or the natural environs of production sites. As a consequence of the traditionally restrictive interpretation of the general exceptions[166] many measures linked to NPAs would not be justifiable.

The second problem, often referred to under the key term 'extraterritoriality', relates to the location of production and the values protected by the listed policies.[167] There is consensus that states may take measures to protect those values that are located within their borders. However, where international trade is concerned, production takes place within and without the territory of the state imposing the measure. While direct regulation is limited to the national territory, the effects of measures linked to NPAs applying to products may well exceed these borders. For reasons outlined in Chapter 2, measures linked to NPAs are usually designed in a general way so that they apply to both domestic and foreign products. The extreme instance of this problem is a measure designed to protect certain

---

[164] Panel Report, *Shrimp Turtle* (1998), Nos. 7.44 and 745.
[165] Jackson (1997), p. 236.
[166] E.g., Panel Report, *EC – Asbestos* (2000), fn. 221, No. 8.272 with further references. This analysis concludes, however, that this interpretative rule is not valid, see Chapter 5, section 5.1.2.1, below.
[167] Cf. Bartels (2002), p. 355.

values that are located exclusively outside national borders. An example could be a European country imposing a law according to which lumber originating in rain forests requires a certificate on forestation in order to be sold in its market. A different aspect of the extraterritoriality problem is the question of measures linked to NPAs designed to promote values outside national borders by imposing measures that are not based on the production process in a narrow sense, but on the existence and enforcement of certain policies in the country of origin.[168] Article XX, however, is silent regarding the location of protected values.

Therefore, in addition to those subject matters covered by Article XX, the relevance of extraterritorial effects is a crucial question to be analysed in Part II.

1.4.8.2 The introductory provision of Article XX

The so-called chapeau stipulates that trade measures capable of justification must not be applied in a manner that would constitute (1) a means of arbitrary discrimination between countries where the same conditions prevail, or (2) a means of unjustifiable discrimination between countries where the same conditions prevail, or (3) a disguised restriction on international trade.[169] All these requirements mostly relate to the manner in which the measure is applied,[170] and serve to find out, both from a substantive and procedural point of view, whether the measure constitutes an abuse or misuse of the provisional justification made available in any of the particular exceptions.[171]

Trade measures linked to NPAs feature some common characteristics that could be relevant to these requirements. To reiterate, by conditioning market access or other advantages to the production methods or other NPAs favoured under national law, these measures promote national production standards outside the importing state's territory. It seems that the prohibition on discrimination between countries where the same conditions prevail must be interpreted comprehensively. A one-size-fits-all approach could then constitute unjustifiable discrimination in the sense of the chapeau, as this approach does not take into consideration

---

[168] Measures of this category were challenged in both *Tuna-Dolphin* cases.
[169] Appellate Body Report, *Shrimp Turtle* (1998), No.150.
[170] Appellate Body Report, *Shrimp Turtle – Article 21.5* (2001), No. 118, Appellate Body Report in *US – Gasoline* (1996), V, p. 22, quoting Panel Report, *US – Spring Assemblies* (1983), para. 56.
[171] Appellate Body Report, *Shrimp Turtle* (1998), No. 160.

the different conditions that occur in different member states.[172] Since NPAs, if applied to imports, relate to aspects outside the territory of the state imposing the measure, differences between countries of origin must arguably be more important than in the case of exclusively product-based measures. The principle of special and differential treatment of developing countries could in this respect be highly relevant. Therefore, the question of how far differences between countries need to be taken into account in order for NPA measures not to constitute discrimination needs to be explored in more detail.

Another aspect relevant to NPA measures under the chapeau is unilateralism. In the *Shrimp Turtle* dispute, it was argued that in the case of a trade measure with the general policy objective of protecting certain values beyond the imposing state's borders, concerted and cooperative efforts beforehand were necessary. The lack of such efforts would indicate unjustifiable discrimination.[173] The question of what precisely these efforts to negotiate solutions before imposing a unilateral measure must consist of, as regards, for instance, phase-in periods, transfer of technologies or general assistance remains as yet unresolved and is also subject to the analysis in Part II. Similar concerns with respect to arbitrary discrimination arise when it comes to certification schemes linked to NPAs. Arbitrary discrimination could be assumed because of the characteristics of the requirements imposed. In addition, the lack of transparency in the administration of a trade measure may contribute to the finding of arbitrary discrimination.[174]

Due to the broad and general requirements in Article XX, especially in the chapeau, interpretation of Article XX with a view to its particularities is also highly relevant for the legal status of NPA measures.

1.4.9 Technical barriers to trade and sanitary and phytosanitary measures

NPA measures that constitute technical barriers to trade, namely, technical regulations and standards, fall under the scope of the TBT Agreement. The TBT Agreement is based on the principle of non-discrimination. Article 2.1 establishes in a GATT-like fashion both the obligations to accord national treatment and MFN treatment. Hence, the

---

[172] Appellate Body Report, *Shrimp Turtle* (1998), Nos. 164 and 165.
[173] Appellate Body Report, *Shrimp Turtle* (1998), No. 172.
[174] Appellate Body Report, *Shrimp Turtle* (1998), Nos. 183 and 184.

concept of 'like products' is crucial for the legal status of technical barriers to trade that are linked to NPAs. In contrast to most other multilateral trade agreements, the TBT Agreement refers explicitly to 'processes and production methods' in the definitions for technical regulations and standards in Annex 1. The explicit mention of PPMs suggests that these do have a special status under the TBT Agreement. Crucial to the legal status of technical regulations and standards linked to NPAs is therefore the 'like products' concept. Also, the relevance of measures linked to PPMs is explored in Part II.

The SPS Agreement, in contrast, aims for the protection of certain values. Therefore, the agreement does not include non-discrimination provisions comparable with those of the GATT or the TBT Agreement. Nevertheless, the SPS Agreement does mention 'processes and production methods' explicitly. Therefore, while the 'like product' concept is irrelevant under the SPS Agreement, the legal status of PPM measures deserves special consideration in Part II.

1.4.10 Summary

This section has given the legal status of different types of NPA measures a cursory analysis, with a view to determining the crucial legal provisions and terms that lead to particularities in their legal status. The following issues have been identified as crucial:

- the concept of 'like products' as, for example, in GATT Article I:1, Article III:2, including a comparison with 'directly competitive and substitutable', Article III:4, Article VI:4 and the Note Ad Article III and Article XVI, the TBT Agreement;
- the term 'products' with respect to the scope of the GATT Article III and the related Note;
- the relevance of numerous specificities inherent in NPA measures, such as extraterritorial effects or unilateralism, for their justifiability under GATT Article XX; and
- the relevance of measures linked to PPMs under the TBT and the SPS Agreements.

These legal issues are constitutive for the debate on PPMs and are analysed and discussed in detail in Part II. The cursory analysis allows for some preliminary conclusions that influence the structure of this work as well as the concepts and terms used therein, as described in the following section.

1.5 Delineation and foundations of the legal analysis

The preliminary conclusions in the previous section provide the material basis which allows the main analysis to be focused on the crucial key questions. This section sets the stage for the analysis in more formal terms. The following sections delineate the scope of the analysis and define crucial terms and concepts used throughout the rest of this work.

1.5.1 Scope of the analysis

The topics and questions discussed in this book are not only cross-cutting within the field of trade in goods. More than that, they are in principle relevant to all fields of international trade, and therefore problems addressed in this volume in a broader sense become relevant under a large number of multilateral and plurilateral trade agreements. Since all these agreements differ in important respects due to sectoral or topical particularities, a one-size-fits-all solution will not be possible. Legal problems relating to non-physical aspects of internationally traded goods occurred as early as the beginning of the twentieth century. These problems have led to several disputes under the GATT 1947 and to numerous publications on the topic. Nevertheless, it has not so far been possible to arrive at a generally accepted conclusion on the topic. A basic idea of this analysis is to offer a comprehensive analysis of the problems relating to trade in goods in order to review the legal discussion and to come up with insights that may allow for solutions to address the problem in a more general way.

The following sections show that in-depth research in these specific fields is needed in order to structure the problem and to find solutions adequate to their relevant particularities.

1.5.1.1 General object of research: trade in goods

This work focuses on non-physical aspects of goods and related legal problems when such goods are traded internationally. NPAs may likewise create problems when it comes to trade in services and they may well also become relevant for other major areas of international trade, such as international public procurement.

NPAs relating to products play a rather one-dimensional role when it comes to international trade in goods: a product is produced somewhere in a certain manner including NPAs, it is subsequently shipped elsewhere, and thus leaves the manner in which it was produced behind.

Obviously, NPAs can become relevant as well when it comes to trade in services.[175] Also services can be provided in different ways, under different circumstances, by different persons and, ultimately, by use of different methods which do not affect the actual services or their quality; hence, non-physical aspects will lead to problems similar to those connected to trade in goods.

Since under the GATS services can be supplied in four different modes, NPAs have the potential to become relevant in ways that differ from those relevant to trade in goods. An example of a constellation of similarities with trade in goods could be financial or call services that are supplied in a cross-border way, which means in the sense of GATS Article I:2(a) that only the service itself crosses the border. In this case, all NPAs of the service and the service supplier would remain in the country of supply. Non-physical aspects that might find their way onto the political agenda of the country of service consumption and thus lead to a request for adequate trade measures could be the working conditions in call centres abroad, such as minimum age of the call centre agents, maximum working time, agents' right to breaks and so forth. This situation of service supply, as well as the non-physical aspects related to it, are comparable with the situation where products produced in one country are then exported into another country for consumption abroad. Acknowledging these apparent similarities, this work in some instances refers to GATS provisions and related case law which sheds light on issues originally emerging from the sphere of trade in goods.[176]

If, on the other hand, services are, for instance, supplied by foreign individuals within the country of consumption, which means in the fourth mode of supply under GATS Article I:2(d), then the NPAs become relevant within the country importing the service. This situation differs in important ways from that of the import of goods. Likewise, service supply by commercial presence in the country of consumption and consumption abroad, the other modes of service supply addressed by the GATS, differ in important aspects from trade in goods. Problems in connection with the allocation of regulatory jurisdiction, that are necessarily

---

[175] As Diebold correctly points out, one cannot speak of 'processes and production methods' with respect to services due to their intangible nature (Diebold (2008), p. 70). The concept of non-physical aspects, as explained in the following section, which is given preference in this analysis, is of a more abstract nature than the concept of PPMs and would thus be adequate to illustrate similar problems related to services.

[176] Comparable are, e.g., the general exceptions in GATT and GATS, as discussed in the US – Gambling reports, see below, Chapter 5, section 5.3.3.

1.5 DELINEATION AND FOUNDATIONS OF THE LEGAL ANALYSIS 59

relevant to NPAs and international trade, are multidimensional under the GATS. Hence, a legal concept such as the product–process distinction is less natural when applied to services, since international trade in services has a bearing in multiple ways on territoriality and the allocation of territorial jurisdiction.[177] Furthermore, the basic legal disciplines on domestic regulation relating to market access obligations differ in important ways from those set forth in the GATT. The GATT is characterized primarily by obligations to national and most-favoured-nation (MFN) treatment. Under the GATS, in contrast, WTO members are obliged to adhere to rules on domestic regulation (GATS Article VI) and to the arguably more intrusive rules relating to market access (GATS Article XVI), with positive obligations for each member depending on their specific commitments in various sectors inscribed in their Schedules, on the one hand, and on possible conditions or qualifications, on the other.

While some findings and ideas that result from the present analysis in the field of trade in goods may be transferable to related problems in trade in services, this book does not focus on trade in services. Given the important and crucial differences between goods and services and related problems in international trade, together with the crucial differences between both fields of law, the relevance of non-physical aspects of services in international trade law poses numerous new questions and is a separate topic for in-depth research.[178]

Another example of the extremely broad significance of the problem is the importance of NPAs for both national and international public procurement. Public procurement laws are highly relevant for international trade of both goods and services. Many national procurement laws allow for, or even require, the consideration of social or other implications of tenders. Therefore, the question arises as to how far non-physical aspects, PPMs and social policy objectives may legally be considered in the award of contracts by national governments that are party to the plurilateral WTO Agreement on Government Procurement (GPA). Indeed, the GPA, similarly to GATT and GATS, imposes MFN and national treatment obligations on its parties without clarifying whether non-physical aspects may be of relevance to the tenderer or not. Interestingly, the GPA in its

---

[177] Trachtman (2003), p. 76
[178] See Vranes (2009b), pp. 963–87, for an analysis of national regulatory measures with impacts on trade in services. He concludes that in contrast to the GATT, the impact of the GATS on regulatory freedom depends on the actual country-specific commitments and on limitations contained in a member's schedules, on the one hand, and on the interplay of GATS Articles VI, XVI and XVII, on the other.

Article XXIII establishes specific exceptions for measures relating to a few non-physical aspects, namely, 'to the products or services of handicapped persons, of philanthropic institutions or of prison labour'. Due to the explicit reference to some non-physical aspects, these exceptions may be invoked to show the sensitivity of the GPA to such aspects, as well as an exclusion *a contrario* of non-physical aspects in general. However, a distinction between products and processes similar to the distinction under the GATT could also be rejected due to the explicit wording of the GPA with respect to processes and methods of production in specifications. The general status of non-physical aspects under international public procurement law can still be characterized as open.[179] While this work does not delve into the specific field of public procurement, in as far as tenders relating to goods are concerned the basic ideas presented in this work may to some extent also be applicable to this field of law.

1.5.1.2 Scope of the legal analysis

Trade in goods is regulated not only by the GATT, but by all multilateral agreements as listed in Annex 1A of the Marrakesh Agreement. Non-physical aspects and related trade measures may also pose legal problems where trade in agricultural products is concerned. Furthermore, non-physical aspects may play a role when it comes to subsidies or anti-dumping measures, to cite but two examples.

The focus of the legal analysis in this work, however, is on the GATT as the most general and fundamental agreement on international trade in goods. Given the abstract nature of the legal questions relevant to this topic, it is nevertheless possible to transfer concepts and findings of this analysis to problems linked to non-physical aspects under the provisions of the specific multilateral agreements on trade in goods. Therefore, this work occasionally refers to other multilateral agreements, without however delving into the broader relevance of non-physical aspects for those agreements as a whole. The exceptions in this respect are the TBT and the SPS Agreements, for in contrast to the GATT both address the relevance of processes and production methods explicitly. This particularity cannot be ignored in basic research, since it is only the wording of these agreements that may allow the drawing of conclusions as to the drafter's view on PPMs and related problems.

---

[179] For more on the relevance of non-economic concerns, in particular human rights concerns, in national and international public procurement rules see McCrudden (1999), p. 37.

1.5 DELINEATION AND FOUNDATIONS OF THE LEGAL ANALYSIS 61

Therefore, Chapter 6 is dedicated to the legal status of non-physical aspects under both agreements.

The approach of this work is to address legal problems related to non-physical aspects in a more abstract way, which allows one structure the problems and to draw conclusions that are broadly applicable. These are developed based on the text of the GATT. Their applicability to specific provisions within and without the GATT, however, needs to be assessed on a case-by-case basis by considering the concepts and principles developed in this work.

1.5.2 Terms and concepts

Addressing the legal problems in detail requires this work to distinguish between different groups of trade measures, the legal status of which differs to some extent under WTO law. The concepts underlying these groups and the terms used to signify them are described and defined in this section. A difficulty this analysis has met is the fact that some terms and concepts used have been central to the so-called PPM debate. Due to their long-lasting use in this debate they have become well-established, although their use has remained inconsistent and as a corollary their precise meanings have remained blurred. This section not only delineates certain groups of trade measures subject to this analysis, but also explains and defines the terms used to identify them in this book.

1.5.2.1 NPA measures

The cursory analysis has confirmed that the term 'like products' in particular is crucial for the special legal status of PPM measures. It is used in various applications of the principle of non-discrimination in multilateral trade agreements, and there is disagreement as to which factors determine whether or not products are 'like'. While physical differences between products are generally held to be relevant for the determination of 'like products', aspects which do not lead to physical differences are mostly considered to be irrelevant. This means, that it is particularly the fact that a measure links legal consequences to an aspect not physically incorporated in a product which predetermines the particular and contested legal status of such measures. Therefore, the crucial question with respect to the term 'like products' relevant to this work is whether aspects that are not physically incorporated in the product, such as certain production methods which leave the product unchanged, can be of any relevance for the determination of 'likeness'.

For the legal problems discussed in this work, it will therefore be irrelevant whether or not the aspect imposing legal consequences on an internationally traded good relates to production or to any other aspect, such as transportation, origin, certain characteristics of producers or workers involved in production. The term 'PPM measure', or more precisely non-product-related (npr-PPMs), which have been well established in the PPM debate, are therefore not quite accurate in their description of the core legal problem. Arguably for this reason, Hudec coined another term, namely, 'non-product aspect',[180] which, however, could not establish itself in the debate. 'Non-product aspect', just as the term 'non-product-related' PPM, seems peculiar or even contradictory, since it is the contested measure itself which, beyond doubt, creates a link between the particular aspect at issue and the traded product.

To reiterate, the fact which leads to the presumed special legal status is the fact that a measure links legal consequences to something other than physical aspects of a product, or, to put it differently, to non-physical aspects. Thus, the term 'non-physical aspect', or 'NPA', seems to depict the element that is at the core of the legal discussion most clearly. Also, since the term 'processes and production methods' is explicitly included in some of the WTO Agreements, the term NPA makes it possible to distinguish between the more general legal problems, particularly under the GATT, and specific problems linked to PPMs, as described in the following section. For this reason, preference is here given to the term NPA, which is used throughout the legal analysis.

As a corollary, measures linked to NPAs, or NPA measures, in this work signify the group of all measures which have the fact that they refer to a non-physical aspect in their objective elements in common, and thus make certain legal consequences contingent upon NPAs.

1.5.2.2 Processes and production methods or 'PPMs'

Processes and production methods as legal terms are explicitly included in both the TBT and SPS Agreements. The meaning of this term as legal wording must be distinguished from the inconsistent use of the term in the PPM debate.[181]

---

[180] Hudec (1998), see above at fn.77.
[181] See above, section 1.3.3.2. To reiterate, the term PPMs is not used in a uniform way. Very often, the term PPMs is equalized with unincorporated PPMs. This is not correct, given the fact that only incorporated PPMs are relevant under the SPS Agreement, as detailed below. Also, the abbreviation PPMs is often used to indicate PPM measures rather than aspects of production. E.g., Charnovitz (2001a) summarizes all of these aspects and

1.5 DELINEATION AND FOUNDATIONS OF THE LEGAL ANALYSIS 63

The literal meaning of the term production, however, is a stage in a product's life cycle. The life cycle of a product can be described as starting with research and development and then continues with planning. Then the actual production process begins. Depending on the nature of the product, production consists of various stages, such as input of raw materials, manufacture and assembly, possibly at different locations. After the product has been produced, other stages in the product life cycle follow, such as packaging and transportation to destination. Following distribution, the product is sold, consumed and finally disposed of. Taking a closer look at the production stage itself, in economic terms simply defined as the conversion of inputs into outputs, shows that this limited stage also consists of various elements. Production comprises different input aspects, such as facilities or human labour, while the throughput stage of production comprises the actual production methods and processes used. A production method is, thus, but one element in the throughput stage of production. From this point of view processes and production methods are the factual aspects which merely constitute the throughput stage of production, and thus just one aspect among many others occurring in the product life cycle. The literal meaning of production, or production methods, is therefore very limited. PPMs are therefore a specific objective fact, and the explicit mention in the TBT and the SPS Agreements suggests that measures linked to PPMs have a specific legal status as opposed to other measures, including other NPA measures. While there may be good reasons not to limit the meaning to the throughput stage of production, there is no apparent reason to stretch the meaning of the term beyond the production stage of the product life cycle, given that the term is part of the legal wording of the TBT and the SPS Agreements.

It should be noted, however, that only unincorporated PPMs are a subset of the larger set of NPAs. The distinction between PPMs, unincorporated PPMs and NPAs and respective measures therefore remains important. In order to allow for precise distinctions, this work uses the abbreviation to refer to PPMs only as objective facts and as far as the TBT and SPS Agreements are concerned, and to PPM measures if the measures themselves are concerned.

> trade measures relating to them in a broader category of 'PPMs'. The meaning he gives to the term PPMs is consequently very broad and would possibly equal the concept of NPA measures used here.

2

Putting the debate into perspective: analysis of the socio-economic context

NPA measures pose a multidimensional problem. At first glance, NPAs are a subject of domestic regulation, and as such part of the internal affairs of any given state. But if NPA measures apply to goods, then in the case of imported goods they automatically refer to activities and conditions located within another country, namely, the country of production. Due to international trade, NPA measures are inherently linked to subjects usually considered to fall into the internal affairs of other states. This means that beyond WTO law, NPA measures touch upon the concept of national sovereignty, which is a key concept of international relations and public international law. More than that, NPA measures have effects upon trade and businesses. Such effects are economic by nature, and they may constitute the very purpose of the measure or merely a side-effect. The WTO Agreements are based on economic rationales, and hence the economic effects of NPA measures cannot be ignored in assessing their permissibility under WTO law.

Domestic regulation, for example, regulation of production, can take many forms. First, regulation of production may be direct regulation through prohibitions, obligations or requirements. Direct regulation of production, however, is limited to production inside the regulator's jurisdiction. Second, production can be influenced through regulation which applies to a product, but is linked to the way in which it has been produced. Regulators might use incentives or disincentives, for example, in terms of taxes or other charges, to encourage or discourage the use of certain production methods without, however, prescribing the preferred production methods in an absolute way. In this latter case of indirect regulation, regulators may apply measures either to products of national origin only, or to all products including imports. While in the first mode of regulation, the direct regulation of production, there will be effects on international trade through modifications of the competitive conditions, the second mode of regulation has a direct effect on international trade since it is directly applied to imports. The effects on the competitive conditions of products are even more visible in the latter case. This book addresses only the second mode of regulation, here termed 'indirect regulation'.

This chapter explores the multiple dimensions of the topic as background relevant to the legal analysis in Part II, and crucial for the regulation-based approach presented in Part III. Section 2.1, focuses on the domestic side of NPAs. It describes domestic regulation in general, respective national and regional differences, as well as the economic case for regulation with a special focus on NPA regulation. Section 2.2 then turns towards the international dimension. It outlines the economic rationales that motivated states to conclude the GATT and later the WTO Agreements, and reviews the most important economic and political arguments for and against NPA measures with effects on international trade.

2.1 National regulation and NPAs

This work explores domestic measures that apply to goods, but ultimately intend to influence other facts or situations, such as the production process. This chapter gives an overview of regulation in general and regulation of production in particular. Although regulation has been a prominent subject for scholarly analysis in different disciplines, among them law, political science and economics, there is no universally accepted definition of the term 'regulation'. Also, different political and administrative traditions and considerable differences in the understanding of regulation in different countries are described, using the example of the United States and Europe. This chapter also places emphasis on the economic case for regulation. While the choice of modes, extent and intensity of regulation are subject to political discussion, it seems that the basic economic rationales for regulation are widely accepted. It is an evident fact that to a greater or lesser extent, all states do regulate, whether they are free market economies, planned or mixed economies.

Different regulatory traditions and attitudes among WTO members make the debate on NPA measures more difficult. Different views on the need to regulate NPAs also prevail within countries, and foreign NPA measures can appear even more suspicious. Even the major Western trading nations, as, for instance, the United States, on the one hand, and European countries or the EC, on the other, have different regulatory traditions and different views on the proper role of the state, its government and regulatory bodies. In consequence, they may assess the need for regulation in general, and the need for regulation of production in particular, as differently as they assess the need to link measures to NPAs in the first place. An examination of the different regulatory traditions and the different underlying views shows that despite some differences, domestic NPA regulation within different WTO members has a great deal in common. These similarities, together with the economic rationales of the WTO, constitute the common ground on which the adequate legal status of NPA measures should be built.

2.1.1 Overview of regulation

Domestic regulation by its very nature differs from one country to another, and there are different connotations or meanings given to the term in different scholarly disciplines. Meaning and use of the term 'regulation' differ, for instance, with respect to the mode of regulatory activity, as well as with respect to controlled activities or situations.

2.1.1.1 General domestic regulation

Regulation is certainly not a new phenomenon. In 483 AD, the Roman emperor Zeno proclaimed a prohibition of all monopolies, combinations and price agreements. This edict is often cited as one of the earliest instances of anti-monopoly regulation.[1]

The term 'regulation' is used in jurisprudence as well as other social sciences. It is, therefore, important to note that the term is used in a number of different senses and different contexts.[2] In its very core, regulation refers to some form of intervention and control. For instance, economists discovered regulation as object of research with the emergence of public choice theory in the late 1940s, and have been exploring regulation by focusing on the behaviour of voters, regulators and other political agents and institutions in different political systems. Political scientists, in contrast, discuss regulation from the more organizational perspective of policy implementation and rule-making. Even within the legal discipline, regulation is used in two different senses. On the one hand, the term denotes a specific type of legal act, namely, a piece of secondary legislation issued to implement statutes which have been adopted by the constitutionally competent legislator. In the EU, for example, regulations are rules characterized by general and direct applicability.[3] Regulations as delegated legislation can be adopted by any regulator to which authority

---

[1] See, e.g., Majone (1996a), p. 9. [2] Baldwin and Cave (1999), p. 2.
[3] Article 249 EC Treaty.

has been delegated. From this perspective, the nature of the issuing body is not decisive for the legal character of a norm as regulation. On the other hand, regulation is used in a more general sense to denote the totality of official rules accounting for state control and supervision. The different perspectives on regulation, adopted by different scientific disciplines, account for some of the differences in meaning and connotation.

Regulation in its *broadest sense* denotes a process 'consisting of the intentional restriction of a subject's choice of activity by an entity not party to, or involved in, that activity'.[4] This definition includes all forms of social control or influence that affect behaviour. It is accordingly irrelevant whether this behaviour-affecting influence is exerted by the state or by any other institution or organization. It seems that especially in Europe, scholars seem to use regulation in a broad sense, referring to the whole realm of legislation, governance and social control.[5] Since the object of this analysis is state regulation, this definition is too broad and not suitable for this work.

A different and *narrower definition* of regulation places emphasis on the form of influence and defines regulation as a specific set of commands. This definition requires the existence of a binding set of rules applied by an agency or other specific body assigned with the task of supervising the regulated field. Health and safety at work or anti-trust legislation as applied by the relevant agencies might serve as examples for regulation in this narrow sense. This definition is commonly used in the United States and gives a specific meaning to the term which fits the specific domestic regulatory culture. Majone stresses the necessity of detailed knowledge of regulators and marks this as an important difference between regulation in a narrow sense and simple legislative activity, such as passing laws.[6] Also, Selznick's famous definition of regulation as sustained and focused control exercised by a public agency over activities that are generally valued by society[7] stresses the importance of a specialized regulatory agency and is, therefore, close to the narrow definition. According to this definition, EC regulations, which are mostly enacted by the European institutions including the parliament, would not qualify as 'regulation', since the parliament does not satisfy the requirements for a specialized regulatory agency. However, depending on the substance of rules enacted by European institutions, these rules could be as problematic under WTO law just as are comparable

---

[4] Mitnick (1980). [5] Majone (1996d), p. 49.
[6] See Majone (1996b), p. 9. [7] Selznick (1985), pp. 363, 364.

rules issued by independent US agencies. Hence, the narrow definition is also not suitable for this analysis.

An *intermediate view* describes regulation as deliberate state influence, thus stressing the role of the state as regulator, while the coverage of activities of this definition is open. In this sense, regulation encompasses all state actions designed to influence industrial and social behaviour.[8] The intermediate view incorporates all activities constituting regulation under the narrow definition, but additionally includes influence from other public actors or institutions. However, non-state regulation by other social institutions as covered by the broad definition is excluded. The merit of this definition is that it does not distinguish between regulations on grounds of the regulating body, whether this is a special agency, a ministry or even parliament itself. Also, the intermediate view covers other modes of influence besides influence through commands, such as influence through incentive-based regimes. Regulation is more than a concept prohibiting undesired behaviour. Since regulation may also facilitate certain behaviour, or even make certain behaviour possible in the first place, it includes a 'green light' approach as well.

In this book the term 'regulation' is used in the sense of the intermediate view. The focus of this analysis is to a large extent on national rules that regulate social behaviour and situations and have an effect on international trade. Due to the huge differences in legislation and rule-making in WTO members, the substance of regulation is crucial for the debate, while the nature of the regulating body adopting the respective norms is irrelevant. The term regulation is therefore used as a generic term that comprises all national measures, whether laid down in constitutions, statutory law, secondary law, recommendations or other measures.

2.1.1.2 The notion of social regulation

Regulation is often understood in the sense of intervention in the free play of market forces. Hence, commonly cited examples for regulation are regulation of fair competition, mergers, entry of undertakings and their activities in naturally monopolistic markets such as network industries, or the regulation of production and product safety regulation. In recent years, however, the term 'social regulation' has emerged in literature. This section explores the meaning of social regulation and its relationship to measures linked to NPAs.

---

[8] Baldwin and Cave (1999), p. 3

Social regulation is used as a generic term, and it is usually illustrated by examples such as regulation to implement health, safety, anti-discrimination or environmental policies.[9] Majone, for instance, adds that 'social regulation' refers to all regulation aimed at the supply of public goods, such as environmental protection, nuclear safety, product safety or consumer protection and information.[10] There have also been attempts to define social regulation in an abstract way, for example, as 'those forms of regulatory control that are not directly concerned with the control of markets or other specific aspects of economic life, but instead aim to protect people or the environment from the damaging consequences of industrialization'.[11] This definition approaches the term by placing emphasis on the primary regulatory goals, namely, protection of the public interest, rather than by describing the regulated objects or sectors.

It seems, however, that a precise distinction between regulation that regulates markets and regulation that has the objective of protecting people or the environment is neither feasible nor desirable. Most regulation aimed at the protection of people or the environment does so precisely by restricting or guiding market activities. For instance, rules on product safety are intended to protect the public interest, namely, consumers' health, but usually achieve these objectives by establishing requirements directed at producers. In fact, a large proportion of regulated activities have an obvious and intended impact on economic activities, although they primarily pursue social objectives. For instance, regulation of opening hours for retail stores, conditions for the use of public facilities or requirements for the transportation of live cattle all bear directly on economic activities while primarily pursuing social goals. The same is true for the regulation of network industries, in as far as regulation aims at providing basic infrastructure even in sparsely populated areas. On the other hand, there are, indeed, also rules that protect people without simultaneously having a direct effect on economic activities. For example, rules in the field of education, such as rules on the minimum number of breaks between lessons for school children, are rules without a direct effect on markets. Although these rules do not protect children from the damaging consequences of industrialization, it seems that the term 'social regulation' should encompass precisely this type of regulation. However, the economy is not merely linked, but ultimately forms an important part

---

[9] E.g., Vogel (1997), p. 98; Joerges (2006), p. 500.
[10] Majone (1996d), p. 52.   [11] Hawkins (1989), p. 663.

of social life. Hence, there must be an overlap between economic and social regulation.

In the context of WTO law, the term 'social regulation' is often used in a vague sense to illustrate the perceived conflict between free trade and state regulation in general.[12] This means that social regulation in the context of WTO law ought to be understood to refer to all national social regulation with an actual or potential impact on international trade. Hence, social regulation in this sense is regulation that is close to the market or economic activities, and therefore capable of affecting international trade, while ultimately aiming at protecting social values. As in the national sphere, in WTO law also a precise distinction between social and economic regulation would fall short of reflecting both fields and the fact that they are inextricably linked.

Since social regulation is characterized by its social objectives,[13] it comprises regulation linked to products as well as regulation linked to NPAs. Although most regulation linked to NPAs allegedly pursues social objectives, NPA measures must not be regarded as a sub-set of social regulation. Whether or not NPA measures do actually pursue legitimate social objectives or not must be assessed on a case-by-case basis, as is apparent from the legal analysis in Part II. Since NPA measures that pursue such legitimate objectives actually constitute social regulation, the legal status of national NPA measures under the law of the WTO is highly relevant for the more general debate on the impact of WTO law on social regulation.

2.1.1.3 Different modes of regulation

A large part of domestic regulation aims at physical product characteristics. Requirements relating to shape or size of products, as well as to materials or ingredients are designed to increase compatibility of products or consumer safety. The focus of this investigation, in contrast, is regulation of non-physical aspects, such as unincorporated production methods. As with other subjects of regulation, NPAs can also be regulated in two different modes, namely, directly or indirectly.[14] Direct regulation of NPAs means regulation through prohibitions, requirements and obligations. Indirect regulation aims at the same regulatory objective, namely, an NPA, but is applied to products. It is a regulatory tool that uses incentives to encourage or discourage certain behaviour or certain results by

---

[12] E.g., Cho (2003) repeatedly refers to 'non-trade (social) concerns' without giving a more precise definition.
[13] Also Nadakavukaren Schefer (2010), p. 1.
[14] On the distinction see Majone (1997), p. 265.

distinguishing between products based on NPAs. Even the provision of information by public bodies could be considered a 'soft' tool of indirect regulation. Information alone can, indeed, be effective in changing behaviour and expectations, although the mere provision of information implies neither legal consequences nor coercive powers.[15]

There is, however, scope for overlap between product regulation, on the one hand, and direct or indirect regulation of production, on the other. Product characteristics are clearly always a result of production, for instance, through the use of certain ingredients or a particular method or condition of production. Also, regulation of products combined with regulation of production is rather common. Often, states rely on direct regulation only. However, indirect regulation can be used as an alternative or as a supplement to prevent loopholes. In sum, states use several methods of regulation, and often these methods are combined.

Regulation of production as the most common set of NPAs is here used to illustrate differences between the various modes of regulation. At least in most industrialized countries, production is highly regulated in a direct way. Direct regulation of production may refer to use, treatment or storage of certain materials or substances, to the use of specific technical equipment or to waste management, to name but a few examples. In addition, the workplace is highly regulated in order to ensure reasonably safe conditions for workers at their workplace, and such regulation may have a bearing on production.

Often, direct regulation is drafted in terms of certain results instead of prescribing certain activities or actions that need to be taken. A classical example is the regulation of industrial production with national regulations relating to industrial air pollution. National regulations will often establish certain ceilings for specific air pollutants, such as sulphur dioxide or nitrogen oxide, often with respect to specific types of installations. Although such regulations might suggest certain methods, they will usually leave the choice of the best method to reach the required results up to the producer or operator of installations. In order to obtain an authorization for operation, the operator will need to show that the installation conforms to the requirements established by the state. During operation,

---

[15] Majone (1997). It seems, however, important to distinguish between information issued by public bodies, which may be considered soft indirect regulation, on the one hand, and legal requirements to publish information, on the other. The latter requirements are often linked to legal consequences and as such constitute direct regulation of information. For the relevance of information as a precondition for the functioning of markets see below Chapter 4, section 4.2.2.3.2.

authorities are usually entitled to check whether or not the operation still meets the requirements and to take appropriate action if this is not the case.[16] In this way, the state hosting production facilities or installations can exercise control over production on its territory. Naturally, the requirements for the operation of certain installations vary considerably from one state to another.

Requirements with respect to certain production methods or the use of certain equipment are comparatively rare. Often, even if certain equipment is required in principle, regulations will leave other ways to reach, for example, an equivalent reduction of pollution up to the operator's discretion.[17] However, when it comes to regulation of consumption regulators will often offer incentives or disincentives to influence behaviour. For instance, consumers using catalysers in their cars may be rewarded with tax reductions or other advantages. This difference between regulation of consumption and regulation of production can be explained with the additional margin in knowledge and producers' power to innovate, which consumers lack. A change in consumer behaviour might be easier to reach than results in terms of output values.

In other instances, regulators choose to regulate production directly, even though the regulatory objective could also be expressed in terms of product characteristics. This will often be the case if physical differences are difficult to detect. For instance, in order to prevent the spread of bovine spongiform encephalopathy (BSE) many states prohibit the use of animal proteins in ruminant feed since those proteins are suspected of causing BSE in food-producing ruminants. In addition to these strictly product-related requirements, some states have set up certain requirements for production. Especially in cases where small physical differences in product characteristics imply dangers or risks for consumers, a prohibition of substances in end-products may not be sufficient to reach the level of protection envisaged by the regulator, because it is difficult to oversee compliance. For instance, in addition to product regulation in the form of prohibition of certain feed, Swiss regulators added direct and indirect regulation of production to achieve their desired level of protection. They

---

[16] See, e.g., the German Technical Instructions on Clean Air Control ('TA Luft') which detail obligatory emission values and respective ceilings for specific industries and requirements for operating various installations. Technische Anleitung zur Reinhaltung der Luft, 24 July 1998, Gem. Ministerialblatt vom 30. Juli 2002 (GMBl. 2002), Heft 25–29, pp. 511–605.

[17] See, e.g., the requirement to use soot filters in the German Clean Air Technical Instruction, 5.4.10.15.1 (above fn. 16).

required that loose feed must not be transported in vehicles or containers that are also used for the transportation of dangerous animal waste or carcasses.[18] This regulation concerns feed both as a product and as a raw material used in meat production. A similar example for the regulation of meat production processes is Regulation (EC) 183/2005 of the European Community laying down requirements for feed hygiene. The main objective of this regulation is consumer protection by ensuring feed safety throughout the food chain, including feed for food-producing animals. The rules and conditions laid down with this regulation relate to hygiene requirements to be observed by feed operators as well as farmers when feeding food-producing animals. Since this regulation is not content with the establishment of requirements regarding end-products, namely, feed or food derived from animals, these requirements constitute direct regulation of production. However, the regulation is also supplemented with indirect regulation of production that is applied to imports. Article 23 of the regulation states:

> Feed business operators importing feed from third countries shall ensure that importation takes place only in accordance with the following conditions:
>
> (a) the third country of dispatch appears on a list ... of third countries from which imports of feed are permitted;
> ... and
> (d) the feed satisfies: (i) the requirements laid down in this Regulation, and in any other Community legislation laying down rules for feed.[19]

Ultimately, the regulation requires European feed business operators to import only feed that meets two basic requirements: first, the feed has to be dispatched in certain enlisted countries; and, second, it has to live up to the requirements laid down in the regulation. Those requirements, as explained above, go beyond physical product characteristics. They relate to hygiene during feed production and placing on the market, and to conditions ensuring traceability, registration and approval.[20] Although

---

[18] Article 28, Verordnung des EVD vom 10. Juni 1999 über die Produktion und das Inverkehrbringen von Futtermitteln, Zusatzstoffen für die Tierernährung, Silierungszusätzen und Diätfuttermitteln (FMBV), SR: 916.307.1-V (as of 1 September 2006).

[19] Regulation (EC) 183/2005 of the European Parliament and of the Council of 12 January 2005 laying down requirements for feed hygiene, published 8 February 2005, OJ, L 35/1.

[20] Regulation (EC) 183/2005, Articles 1 and 2.

import of feed not satisfying these requirements is not directly prohibited, the obligation of feed business operators to ensure that imports live up to the requirements can be regarded as equalling a prohibition. The example shows that product regulation can be supplemented with both direct and indirect regulation of production, and with corresponding trade measures, if imports are concerned.

Finally, it is noteworthy that the common distinction between products, on the one hand, and production, on the other, suggests that all regulation is either product regulation or regulation of production. This distinction is misleading. As mentioned above, there is a whole realm of economic activities and behaviour which is highly regulated and does not fit into any of these categories. For instance, regulation of the conditions for transportation is neither product regulation nor regulation of the production process. The same is true for measures with respect to the location of production facilities, requirements for licences or approvals or general regulation with respect to a 'fair' treatment of workers, for instance, with respect to minimum wages or maximum working hours. All these aspects can be regulated directly or indirectly with measures applying to products.

To summarize, regulation often consists of a conglomerate of measures that, in part, constitute product regulation and, in part, both direct and indirect regulation of production. These instruments will often be designed to supplement each other and are concurrently capable of reaching the desired level of regulation. It seems that none of the above modes of regulation are *per se* suspicious of constituting illicit protection.

2.1.2 Differences and similarities in regulatory cultures: the example of the United States and Europe

Differences in NPA regulation between different states create barriers to international trade. To a great extent, these differences are due to different regulatory traditions. While this work cannot provide a comprehensive historical overview of the different traditions of some of the major players in international trade, it seems important to show some basic lines of differences and to explore the underlying reasons. To this end, this section describes regulatory developments in the United States, on the one hand, and different European states, on the other. These states have been chosen for this work by way of example only, due to the fact that considerable research exists which facilitates understanding of regulatory traditions and developments. Of course, regulatory cultures in other

WTO members may differ to a great extent from these examples. Such differences may relate to history, experience and practice of regulation and, as a corollary, are apparent in related scholarship.[21] Despite obvious differences in regulatory traditions and practices, it is here presumed that regulatory cultures in WTO members also have a great deal in common. Differences prevail as regards the question of how and to what extent to regulate. In contrast, the different regulatory cultures seem to converge when it comes to the more fundamental question as to whether regulation is necessary at all in a given situation.

2.1.2.1 Regulation in the United States

The regulatory history of the United States was influenced by a general belief in the markets as the best tool for an efficient allocation of resources. Nevertheless, the first federal regulatory commission with the purpose of intervening in the free market, the Interstate Commerce Commission, was created as early as 1887. Many other regulatory agencies followed. For instance, one of the most important regulatory agencies in the United States today, the Federal Trade Commission (FTC), was established in 1914 with the purpose of preventing unfair methods of competition in commerce.[22] Regulation in the United States gained further momentum after the stock market crash of 1929. During the Great Depression, the US Congress under the Franklin D. Roosevelt Administration passed a number of statutes that contained regulatory programmes and established new regulatory agencies in order to improve general public welfare and standards of living. The 1933 National Industrial Recovery Act (NIRA),[23] for instance, was intended to promote cooperation between industries, induce united action between labour and management and authorized the president to establish agencies to effect these policies. A few days later, the National Recovery Administration (NRA) was formed. With the NIRA as its basic tool, the NRA was able to negotiate deals with the major industries to promote public welfare through minimum wages and a limit on working hours in exchange for an exemption from anti-

---

[21] Regulation in the Anglo-American sense as used in this work is distinct from the object of research of 'régulation theory' which originates in France. Régulation theory analyses capitalism and its transformations, and posits that the variable structures of each economy are determinants of its own economic cycles. See, e.g., Boyer and Saillard (2002), pp. 36–44.

[22] For more details on the developments that led to the establishment of the FTC see Winerman (2003).

[23] Public Law National Industrial Recovery Act, 16 June 1933, ch. 90, 48 Stat. 195.

trust laws.[24] Also in 1933, Congress passed the Agricultural Adjustment Act[25] which created the Agricultural Adjustment Administration (AAA), aimed at reducing crop surplus. Both the AAA and the NRA worked for about two years until they were found to be unconstitutional by the US Supreme Court. However, the New Deal gave birth to other agencies that still exist today. The Securities Act of 1933 was designed to provide full disclosure of the character of securities being offered for sale and to prevent fraud. The Securities and Exchange Commission, with the power to enforce the Securities Act of 1933 as well as several other statutes, was created in 1934. To this day, it registers, regulates and oversees basically all aspects of securities trading and is among the most important government agencies in the United States. The regulation wave of the 1930s was in response to an existential crisis of the country. However, the increased regulation brought about conflicts as well. It appeared that efficient regulation required isolation from the influences of day-to-day politics, and at the same time it needed to be reconciled with democratic principles and a public demand for accountability. This situation led to the emergence of the US-style independent regulatory agencies, which are established by statute and operate and decide in a transparent and open manner.[26]

After the Second World War, government regulation became extremely common in the United States. Regulation of prices and of conditions for market entry into industries such as transportation, communications and utilities was well established by the 1960s. Various official bodies regulated airlines, communication services, media, electricity and gas. The scope of regulation, as well as the number of regulatory bodies, expanded even further during the following decade. Between 1969 and 1974 what has been called 'the regulation binge' occurred, with thirty-five regulatory programmes enacted by Congress and signed by the government which led to a number of new regulatory agencies.[27] Among those programmes were several that began to cover issues such as oil prices, environmental pollution, safety of the workplace or on the highway and protection of investors.[28] Both the National Institute for Occupational Safety and Health (NIOSH) and the Occupational Safety and Health Administration (OSHA) were established in 1970 by the Occupational Safety and Health Act. Also in 1970, President Nixon and Congress created the Environmental Protection Agency (EPA). The EPA develops

---

[24] For more details on the NRA see Schlesinger (1958), pp. 87–176.
[25] 7 USCS § 624, Act of 12 May 1933.   [26] Woolcock (1998), p. 260.
[27] Lowi (1986), p. 2.   [28] For more detailed information see Breyer (1990), pp. 7–58.

and enforces regulations that implement environmental laws enacted by Congress, such as the Clean Air Act and its amendments, the Clean Water Act and the Resource Conservation and Recovery Act.

In examining the origins of this 'new regulation', Lowi observed with a view to the US experience that the history of regulatory policy developed in line with phases of general ethical development regarding the allocation of responsibility, or a shift of the crucial question 'who is to blame' toward questions of cost.[29] Shared responsibility in a state resulted quickly in responsibility of state and government, and costs were finally spread over society as a whole. Lowi interprets these developments as a larger consensus moving towards a welfare state public philosophy, even before there was an actual welfare state. He sees striking parallels between this development and the development of regulatory policy. The dawn of national regulatory policy was around 1890, when concrete, specific, traditional objects, namely, railways, via oil, sugar and other trusts were regulated. From 1906 to 1914, more abstract objects such as the quality of goods and of commerce in general were subject to regulation. This period was followed by the regulation of the environment as regulation of conduct after 1946, and extended to what is seen as the peak of regulation in the 1970s.

The expansion of regulation was then stopped by several major reforms starting from the mid-1970s. With the expanding scope and intensity of regulation, the economic burdens it created became apparent, and public dissatisfaction began to grow.[30] It was argued that just as markets could fail, so could regulation. Market failure no longer seemed to be as persuasive an argument for regulation, since regulatory failure in the case of government intervention might result in even more serious consequences.[31] In his 1971 analysis, Stigler posits that by its very nature the regulatory process in some respects always benefits the regulated industry,[32] and he later points to the problem that because of this specialization and constant association, the regulator develops a compliant attitude towards the regulated industry,[33] a problem now often referred to as 'regulatory capture'. Technological innovation, together with ideological and economic forces, induced some major reforms which were enacted in order to reform or dismantle traditional regulatory structures. By the end of the 1970s, both the gas and the airline industries

---

[29] Lowi (1986), pp. 7–9, n. 209.   [30] Breyer (1990), p. 15.
[31] Majone (1996b), p. 17.   [32] Most fundamental on public choice theory Olson (1965).
[33] See Stigler (1975b), p. 145.

had been reformed. In the 1980s the motor carriers industries and the railways followed, and in the 1990s, most prominently, the telecommunications sector. These reforms restructured whole industries, and they amounted in part to a revision of earlier regulation, or 'deregulation'. Objects of such deregulation were industries that were structurally competitive, such as airlines, trucking, railways, natural gas and telecommunications. However, deregulation did not stop there. Several classical fields of regulation, such as health, safety and the environment, were subjected to reform pressure. While reforms in these areas did not amount to deregulation, other tools were used in order to achieve the regulatory goals. Strict regulation was in part replaced by disclosure of information, tax schemes, marketable rights and bargaining.[34] In sum, a long history of regulation with its peak around 1970 was followed by regulatory reforms, which restructured some key industries in order to provide for less rigid regulation.

The US regulatory culture is characterized by the existence of specialized agencies established with the task of regulation. In his early analysis with respect to regulation in the United States, Stigler emphasizes the role of the regulatory agency with a specialized knowledge of the regulated activity, and calls the agency an 'inevitable instrument' of public control.[35] The role of the regulatory agency is also stressed in Selznick's definition of regulation as sustained and focused control exercised by a public agency over activities that are generally valued by society,[36] and also Majone states that sustained and focused control by a public agency with detailed knowledge of the regulated activity constitutes a distinguishing feature of US-style regulation.[37] He concludes that regulatory policy-making in this sense requires 'not bureaucratic generalists, but specialized agencies or commissions capable of fact-finding, rule-making, and enforcement'.[38]

2.1.2.2 Regulation in Western Europe

According to Majone, regulation as understood in the United States has to be distinguished from simple law-passing. European scholars, in contrast, often tend to understand regulation as referring to the whole realm of legislation, governance and social control.[39] These differences in meaning are due to the historical differences in the modes of regulation in Europe and the United States.

---

[34] For more detailed information see Breyer (1990), pp. 7–58.
[35] See Stigler (1975b), p. 145. [36] Selznick (1985), pp. 363, 364.
[37] Majone (1996a), p. 2. [38] Majone (1996a), p. 2. [39] Majone (1996d), p. 49.

Although the history of regulation varies between the different countries in Europe, the main mode of economic regulation in Europe was public ownership rather than regulation.[40] Public ownership became widespread in the nineteenth century with the development of industries such as gas, electricity, water, railways and telephone services.[41] In addition, control of economic activities was reached by softer regulatory instruments, such as through price control or licensing. In fact, this mode of regulation has a long history in Europe. For example, in Britain, the Tudor and Stuart periods from the end of the fifteenth century to the beginning of the eighteenth century saw regulation on a hitherto unprecedented scale as described by Ogus.[42] The amount of regulation can be explained by a constant striving to prevent threats to the power of the monarch, including external threats as well as internal threats from popular uprisings due to bad harvests or high unemployment.[43] In addition, the influence of some strong interest groups, such as landowners and later the merchant class, contributed to regulation. Key areas of regulation in these periods were trade, employment, agriculture and land use.[44] Over time, the motivation for regulation has changed.

In contrast to US-style regulation, however, regulation in Europe has traditionally been exercised directly by the government through delegation to ministries, inter-ministerial committees or other semi-public corporatist bodies.[45] The first US-style regulatory agencies, namely, independent agencies which enacted statutory regulation, were established only after the Second World War. The first such agency in Europe, although significantly weaker than comparable agencies in the United States, was the British Monopolies and Merger Commission created in 1948,[46] another followed in 1954 with the British Independent Television Agency.[47] In general, independent anti-cartel or competition authorities were among the first to be established in Europe. After the creation of the British Monopolies and Merger Commission in 1948, the French Commission technique des ententes et des positions dominantes was established in 1953, followed by the German Bundeskartellamt in 1958.

---

[40] Majone (1996b), p. 11.
[41] For a detailed description of nationalization and privatization in Britain see McEldowney (1995), pp. 408–23.
[42] Ogus (1992).   [43] Ogus (1992), p. 3.   [44] Ogus (1992), p. 5.
[45] Majone (1996b), p. 10. See also Majone (1997) on the lack of competences of the new agencies of the European Community as compared with US-style regulatory agencies.
[46] The British Monopolies and Merger Commission was replaced by the Competition Commission in 1999.
[47] Baldwin and Cave (1999), p. 2.

An important example that illustrates the move from the European preference for public ownership to regulation and regulatory agencies was the Treaty of Paris, which established the European Coal and Steel Community. The choice of the option of a common market in steel over the internationalization of this sector has been at least partly ascribed to US influence in Europe after the Second World War.[48] Another related development was the enactment of anti-cartel clauses and competition laws in different European countries. In Germany, supporters of an anti-cartel law faced opposition from German industries. Also due to American insistence, an anti-cartel law, albeit a weak one, was approved by the German Parliament.[49] The introduction of an anti-cartel law in Germany in 1957 coincided with the Treaty of Rome establishing the European Economic Community, which includes a number of competition and anti-trust provisions. In most European countries, the enactment of competition laws after the Second World War brought about the existence of independent regulatory bodies enforcing these laws. Only shortly after the 'regulation binge' in the United States from the end of the 1960s to the mid-1970s, Western Europe also witnessed an increase in regulatory agencies or 'autorité administrative indépendante'.[50]

European scholarship started paying attention to regulation as a specific form of public control mostly in the late 1980s and 1990s, curiously with the beginning of the deregulation wave. As a result of the different modes of regulation that co-existed, the keyword 'deregulation' in Europe has been used to describe all kinds of measures which were intended to open markets and to free economic activities from unnecessary regulatory burdens.[51] Accordingly, deregulation is understood to refer to denationalization and liberalization of former publicly owned industries, as well as to restructuring and regulatory reform in general. Deregulation in Europe was triggered by increasing dissatisfaction with the economic performance of nationalized companies. Also the European Community has been playing an active role in boosting the process of deregulation in Europe. In fact, European legislation has often forced member states to deregulate, in whole or in part, certain industries, most prominently transportation industries.

A good example, for differences in deregulation between Europe and the United States also, is deregulation of rail transportation. For instance,

---

[48] Majone (1996d), p. 50.   [49] Majone (1996d), p. 52.
[50] For examples of such agencies in Britain and France see Majone (1996d), p. 48.
[51] E.g., Boss, Laaser, Schatz *et al.* (1996), p. 1.

in Germany deregulation of the rail system started in 1994 with a reform which eradicated debts and combined the national Deutsche Bundesbahn and the former East German Deutsche Reichsbahn, and transferred both into the legal form of a stock corporation. The Deutsche Bahn AG remained in public ownership, but has since been preparing to debut on the stock exchange at some future date. Besides privatization, the reform also included the establishment of a new public agency, the federal rail authority, Eisenbahnbundesamt, to take over the public functions of the incumbent. In 1988, railways in Sweden became subject to a major reform which opened the market for transportation services to some extent, although the reform did not include privatization. In Britain, the railways were privatized in 1993. While the US rail system has also been subject to deregulation, it is the only rail system in the world that had been totally privately owned from its inception.

While deregulation is most commonly used to describe the recent reform processes with respect to air, land and water transportation, telecommunications, postal services, financial services, reforms in other trades and industries have also been referred to as deregulation. In Germany, other reforms with respect to entry and practising of certain trades and services were intended to deregulate and foster competition in craft industries, the liberal professions, such as lawyers, notaries, accountants and auditors, retail and biotech industries.[52]

2.1.2.3 Assessment of differences and similarities

A traditional difference between US-style and European-style regulation lies in the form of regulation, namely, the imposition of rules on private agents, on the one hand, and public ownership, on the other. Another difference is with regard to the regulator, namely the US-style independent regulatory agency versus regulation by governments and ministries. US-style regulatory agencies seem to operate in a more transparent, open and, in general, more rules-based way, while in Europe political control seems to preponderate. There, regulators, although directly politically accountable, are provided with considerable discretionary powers.[53]

It has been posited that since the establishment of the United States, the country and its regulatory practice have been guided by two important presumptions. First, it was assumed that the market should be the general institution to form developments, and that the state should intervene only if necessary. Second, there was a general presumption of private

---

[52] E.g., Boss, Laaser, Schatz et al. (1996), p. 1.   [53] Woolcock (1998), p. 261.

ownership; hence, the preference of regulation over nationalization in the case of market failure.[54] Since American society appreciated market activities in general, the answer to such market failure has been control as well as protection through regulation. It has been argued, that, in contrast, political opinion in Europe since the end of the nineteenth century has been rather hostile to the market ideology. Majone invokes this attitude as the deeper reason why in perceived cases of market failure the political answer was nationalization and planning rather than regulation.[55] According to him, the differences between the US style and European style of regulation reflect significant ideological and institutional differences with respect to political control of market processes.[56]

Interestingly, recent developments suggest that the borders between the different styles of regulation are increasingly blurred. First of all, with deepening European integration and an increasing importance of European institutions, as shown, for example, through the widespread acceptance of a number of important decisions by the European Court of Justice, European countries are on the way to a more rules-based approach.[57] Second, the deregulation wave starting in the late 1970s in the United States was soon followed by the beginning of major regulatory reforms with respect to privatization of formerly national industries. As a result of deregulation, new regulatory structures had to be erected in place of what was there before, and, consequently, it has been suggested that the term deregulation should be replaced or combined with the term re-regulation.[58]

For this work, however, the similarities between the different regulatory cultures are most important. From the description above, it seems that despite differences in the form of regulation and in the regulating bodies, there is considerable convergence as regards the more basic question of whether or not to regulate at all. To a large extent, the objects of regulation are identical. For instance, general market activities have been subject to regulation both in the United States and Europe, albeit several decades later. The idea of regulation in both cultures has been to prevent monopolies and unfair competition. Although timing differed considerably, basic infrastructure and network industries were subject to regulation and deregulation both in the United States and Europe, and the same is true for environmental regulation. Calls for government regulation aimed at the prevention of climate change from within the

---

[54] Woolcock (1998), p. 259.   [55] Majone (1990b), p. 2.   [56] Majone (1990b), p. 2.
[57] Woolcock (1998), p. 264.   [58] Kay and Vickers (1990), p. 223.

economy[59] may well contribute to convergence in the long run. Since both regulatory cultures chosen here are market economies, the reason for the fundamental similarities may lie in the economic rationales for state intervention, which are detailed in the next section.

2.1.3 The economic case for state intervention

Despite fundamental differences in economic schools of thought, there is comparatively little disagreement among economists about microeconomic foundations and the basic rationales for free markets and trade. Samuelson and Nordhaus, for instance, regard a market economy as:

> an elaborate mechanism for coordinating people, activities, and businesses through a system of prices and markets. It is a communication device for pooling the knowledge and actions of billions of diverse individuals. Without central intelligences of computation, it solves problems of production and distribution involving billions of unknown variables and relations, problems that are far beyond the reach of even today's fastest supercomputer. Nobody designed the market, yet it functions remarkably well.[60]

According to the prevailing neo-classical micro-economic theory, markets function in this sense because they follow an internal logic. Free markets lead to redistribution activities and a re-allocation of resources that lingers on until an equilibrium state is reached. Under free market conditions, this equilibrium is characterized by the fact that no further exchange is possible which would result in a benefit for one individual without at the same time placing at a disadvantage any other agent. This equilibrium result of a free market is referred to as Pareto efficiency.[61] Given that markets have the potential to allocate resources most efficiently, the question about the economic role of government arises.

---

[59] 'Beim Klimaschutz ist viel Staat erwünscht', Wirtschaftswoche, 27 November 2007. The article refers to a poll among businesses, co-authored by David Elshorst of Clifford Chance, according to which 80 per cent opined that more regulation was necessary in order to force businesses to address climate change.
[60] Samuelson and Nordhaus (2005), p. 26.
[61] While the Pareto optimal equilibrium is superior to all alternative outcomes, it is based on individual demand curves which depend on the income level of agents. Thus, a Pareto optimal market outcome does not imply that the final reallocation of resources is fair or just (Sen (1999), pp. 24–6). As detailed in the following sections, this insight is important for the rationales of regulation as an alternative or a supplementary tool to free markets.

2.1.3.1 Basic considerations on free markets and the economic role of governments

The idea, that free market activities pursued by individuals in their pure self-interest lead to benefits for society as a whole goes back to Adam Smith. One of the major developers of classical economics, he expressed doubts about the success of actions specifically designed to promote public welfare in his book, *The Wealth of Nations*:

> Every individual naturally inclines to employ his capital in the manner in which it is likely to afford the greatest support to domestic industry, and to give revenue and employment to the greatest number of people of his own country ... By pursuing his own interest he frequently promotes that of the society more effectually than when he really intends to promote it. I have never known much good done by those who affected to trade for the public good.[62]

Any regulation implies an intervention in the market and thereby endangers the optimal result theoretically achieved by market forces and free competition. Presuming the superiority of markets to achieve an optimal allocation of resources, choosing regulation as a tool over free markets makes sense only if two conditions are fulfilled: first, in the specific situation, the market must have failed to achieve the desired output; and, second, state intervention must be suitable to achieve the objective instead.[63]

A minority of economists, however, might challenge this justification and support a strict *laissez-faire* approach instead.[64] Their argument could be based on two grounds. First, they could challenge the assumption of market failure and plead for leaving the solution of almost all problems up to the market. The number of problems which are admitted for solution through the political process would therefore be strictly limited. Second, even in situations where markets fail, resorting to state intervention is not necessarily advisable. In the case of regulatory failure, paternalistic government intervention leads to inefficient results or to an undesirable distribution of income. Some hold that market failure is usually the lesser of two evils.[65]

---

[62] Smith (1776), vol. 4, ch. 2 ('Of restraints upon the importation from foreign countries').
[63] Breyer (1979), pp. 549 et seq.
[64] For instance, the traditional Austrian and Chicago schools of economic thought ascribed a very constrained economic role to the government, which in its extreme could even be limited to enforcing private property rights.
[65] For an interpretation of the liberal tradition as represented by Milton Friedman see Nowotny (1999), pp. 13–17.

However, the large majority of economists agree on several instances in which markets fail to achieve either an efficient allocation of resources or in which the market outcome does not match a specific public policy objective. This is hardly surprising, since according to the traditional neo-classical model, markets function in the sense that they achieve an optimal allocation of resources only provided the preconditions assumed by the model are in place.[66] Since the real world does not live up to any of these preconditions, it is unavoidable that markets fail. Nevertheless, economists may disagree when it comes to the precise circumstances which cause markets to fail, and in addition there is also disagreement about form, design and intensity of state intervention. According to the nature of different situations of market failure, different tools of state intervention, such as public supply of utilities and services of general interest, public ownership, public control, direct regulation and taxes, come into consideration. Corresponding to the diverging views of economists, state practice with respect to regulation also differs considerably. Some states prefer to leave the supply of certain services entirely up to private companies, while others choose public supply or strict regulation of the respective industry. Indeed, it is here presumed that questions of the choice of the adequate regulatory instrument and the intensity of regulation are of a political nature.

Nevertheless, it is widely recognized that markets can, and do, fail. In these situations, market forces cannot lead to an optimal allocation of resources. In such cases, the state is assigned the task of intervening effectively, and, indeed, market failure has been recognized by scholars of different disciplines as a normative justification of regulation.[67] Regulation or public ownership, respectively, was supposed to remedy inefficiencies engendered by different types of market failure.[68] Another case for regulation, even where strictly speaking the market does not fail, is the divergence of results of market distribution from the distributional preferences of a society. Since from an economic point of view, cases of market failure and distributional matters are valid reasons for regulatory activities, these are grouped accordingly into three categories as detailed in the next section.

---

[66] For more details on the particular preconditions see section 2.1.3.2.2 below.
[67] E.g., Majone (1996b), p. 9; Samuelson and Nordhaus (2005), p. 322; Jackson (2002), p. 123.
[68] See Majone (1996c), p. 28.

2.1.3.2 Categories of economic rationales for regulation

Before discussing several categories of economic objectives of state intervention, a few remarks will be made in order to clarify the objective and limits of the following categories. This chapter purposely ignores the findings of public choice theory. Public choice theory is concerned with the way in which decisions are reached in the political process. A well-known argument based on this theory is that regulation is often a result of the political market and of political influence of well-organized groups representing special interests rather than the public welfare. Other concerns analysed by this branch of economics are, for example, regulatory capture or the short-term orientation of politicians seeking re-election. To some extent, these concerns are certainly justified. However, this work is concerned with normative issues, and it assumes that regulation is employed by a 'good' government or 'good' agencies which act in the public interest according to well-established economic rationales for regulation.[69] Also, government functions in general are not the object of this research. Even in the impossible event that markets were perfectly competitive, governments would still be needed in order to ensure the functioning of societies in general and of the market in particular by ensuring public safety, a judicial system or by offering public services such as education and health care.[70]

The focus of this chapter is on rationales for regulating the economy, albeit in a broad sense, which includes social regulation linked to economic activities. Reasons for regulation can be grouped into three categories as detailed below.[71] The first are market deficiencies due to the real-life conditions of the markets, which differ from the theoretical model. This type of regulation tries to approximate real-life market conditions to the idealized preconditions of the theoretical model. The second category is market failure. In cases of market failure, market mechanisms are not suitable for reaching an efficient allocation of resources, due to the characteristics of the specific market or the properties of the traded product. Regulation in this case replaces the market or creates a market artificially, rather than merely supporting the functioning of a free market. The third category contains reasons of distributional justice or other normative

---

[69] See also Baldwin and Cave (1999), pp. 9 *et seq.*
[70] Samuelson and Nordhaus (2005), p. 318.
[71] These categories have been established for the approach suggested in Part III. Although economists agree on the basic types of market failure, there are different views on how to group them. The different views on each particular category will briefly be discussed in the following sections.

considerations. In certain situations, the market is suitable for reaching an 'efficient' allocation of resources, but the 'efficient' distributional result achieved by the market will hardly ever be in accordance with the result desired by society. In this case, regulation intends to correct or adjust distribution by a market. These categories should not be understood as exclusive, but are suitable to categorize different instances of state intervention according to their rationales.[72]

2.1.3.2.1 Regulation to safeguard competitive markets

The hypothesis that markets are capable of achieving Pareto efficient results according to the neo-classical model is based on certain presumptions on the conditions of the market. The entire set of necessary preconditions is here referred to as 'perfect competition'. Often, the preconditions are limited to price-taking, or the absence of market power, product homogeneity and free entry and exit of market participants.[73] In a broader sense, a perfectly competitive market, or a 'complete market',[74] is in addition also characterized by perfect mobility and perfect and complete information of firms and consumers.[75] No instance of any concentration of market power which leads to an influence on other agents or transactions is allowed. Technology is presumed to produce diminishing returns, and in consequence firms stay comparatively small and numerous.[76] There are no transaction costs, and the use of purchased goods needs to be exclusive and rights need to be transferable. For the purposes of this work, a broad definition of perfect competition that includes all preconditions for the functioning of markets according to the traditional model is preferable.[77]

---

[72] The categories are similar, but not identical, to the ones listed by Deardorff (2000), pp. 71–84. Deardorff discusses both imperfect markets and market failure as one category, while he distinguishes between regulation for distributive and regulation for non-economic reasons. From a global point of view also, social regulation implies a distribution of resources, e.g., in case of safety requirements for workers or environmental regulation. Since social as well as distributive regulation depends upon the preferences of the society supporting the regulation, this work deals with these issues in a single category.

[73] E.g., Pindyck and Rubinfeld (2004), p. 252. Samuelson and Nordhaus even equal the term 'perfect competition' with price-taking (2005, p. 148).

[74] E.g., Sen (1999), p. 68.

[75] E.g., Frank (2005), pp. 350–3. Also Samuelson and Nordhaus view perfect information as a precondition for the functioning of markets (2005, p. 162).

[76] Goodwin, Nelson and Ackerman (2004), p. 438.

[77] Whenever any of the preconditions for the functioning of markets is not in place, markets fail. Since perfect competition is a precondition for the functioning of markets, it is here regarded as the first category of economic rationales for regulation. This does

In the real world, perfect competition obviously does not exist and is unachievable. However, according to the neo-classical model, imperfectly competitive markets are not capable of achieving optimal results. Furthermore, since these imperfections are preconditions for the functioning of markets, markets themselves are unable to generate such conditions. Hence, there is a need to supply perfect competition or, rather, the need to reduce market imperfections as much as possible. In modern economies, increasing efficiency by promoting competition is therefore the primary economic function of the government.[78]

Indeed, a large amount of state regulation serves to ensure the proper functioning of a free market by trying to improve satisfaction with respect to the listed conditions. For instance, distortions of the free play of market forces can result from the anti-competitive behaviour of market participants, such as agreements or concerted practices of competitors, or predatory pricing of a single firm or undertaking. Anti-trust or competition laws serve to counter such behaviour and to ensure competitive conditions. Similarly, markets are bound to fail if monopolistic structures prevail and, accordingly, many market-based economies prohibit at least hard-core cartels. Monopolies lead to problems such as reduced supply and higher prices. An important shortcoming of real-life markets as compared with the model is the existence of considerable information asymmetries. In part, this shortcoming is also addressed by regulation prescribing the disclosure of certain information to producers.[79] Even the provision of basic infrastructure could be seen as falling into this category, since it reduces transaction costs and increases mobility.

2.1.3.2.2 Regulation addressing market failure

Market failure, including market failure due to imperfect competition, is an important objective of government intervention[80] and, therefore, a classical case for regulation.[81] Under certain conditions, even otherwise perfectly competitive markets are not a suitable tool to reach an efficient allocation of resources, because the characteristics of the specific market

---

not contradict the view that the absence of perfect competition, namely, a situation of imperfect markets, constitutes a case of market failure (e.g., Sen (1999), p. 307). However, in order to avoid duplication, imperfect competition is not mentioned in the second category, market failure.

[78] Samuelson and Nordhaus (2005), p. 35.
[79] For the legal status of respective regulation see Chapter 6, section 6.2.2.3 and Chapter 8, section 8.2.2.1, below.
[80] Cottier and Khorana (2005), p. 260.   [81] Majone (1996c), p. 28.

prevent the functioning of markets. Such situations are referred to as market failure, and in such cases public policies can potentially remedy the sub-optimal outcomes achieved by markets.[82]

An important instance of market failure occurs in the case of goods without market prices.[83] In such cases, the properties of the good do not allow markets to function. Problems arise if goods are not excludable, not rival, or neither. For instance, goods are not rival if their consumption does not limit supply. This may be the case if the fixed costs of production are extremely high, while the average costs decline with increasing production, as is the case in most network or infrastructure industries such as railways, electricity or water services. In this case, a natural monopoly arises since the market conditions are such that a good can be offered at minimal cost by a single firm or seller. The negative effects of monopolies, however, will occur regardless of whether the monopolistic position has been obtained by illegitimate market activities or because of natural conditions. Other examples are purely public goods that are neither excludable nor rival. In this case, the market does not function because the good is available to everyone, whether or not a consumer is willing to pay for consumption. Thus, the supply of the good is discouraged. An example is a police force, which society chooses to afford for itself in order to maintain law and order. In this case, even those who are not willing to pay for such services profit from additional safety in their lives.

Also externalities lead to market failure.[84] Externalities occur if the supply of a good leads to costs that are not reflected by the market price, since the costs are borne by third parties which for some reason cannot interfere in the bargaining process. An example of negative externalities, which is particularly important to the debate on NPAs, is environmental pollution, caused by production as a production externality, or waste disposal, as a consumption externality. There is no doubt that environmental pollution places a burden on society and on people living in the polluted environment, yet the market prices of goods, even if produced with heavy side-effects in terms of pollution, will hardly reflect damage to, and costs borne by, others. Today, the environment is mostly treated as a public good and does not have a market value adequately represented in the bargaining process. This instance of market failure is mostly countered with

---

[82] Mankiw (2006) at pp. 204, 212 regarding externalities, at p. 224 regarding common resources and public goods.

[83] For more on non-private goods see e.g. Mankiw (2006), pp. 223–37; Sen (1999), pp. 316–24.

[84] Mankiw (2006), at pp. 203–19; Sen (1999), pp. 306–7.

direct regulation of potentially polluting activities, but also with incentive regimes, or with systems that assign property rights so as to internalize costs.

In sum, in cases of market failure markets are not a suitable means to achieve an efficient allocation of resources. Regulation can then constitute an alternative tool, either to overcome the conditions which lead the market to fail or to correct the allocation of resources achieved by the market.

2.1.3.2.3 Regulation in pursuit of distributional or social objectives

In other instances, market mechanisms do not fail in the sense described above, but fail to bring about an allocation of resources preferred by a given society. More often than not, Pareto efficient market outcomes do not correspond to ideas of fairness or equity. Preferences of societies, as reflected in moral or ethical norms and general ideas of fairness, will mostly not be satisfied by the allocation of resources achieved by free and efficient markets.[85] Whether or not there is a need to remedy an 'unfair' allocation of resources is ultimately a political question that depends on the level of 'fairness' demanded by a specific society and needs to be answered in the political process. Arguably all countries in the world have adopted some income-distributing policies that try to correct market outcomes and to achieve the desired allocation of resources by other means. For instance, regulation is often used to provide for continuity and availability of services to all members of society – a result, which often could not be reached by market forces. For instance, the market price of public transportation, especially to remote areas with low population density, would be unaffordable for potential consumers, and as a corollary this service would not be supplied. However, for society as a whole it may be desirable to have basic infrastructure and to maintain settlements even in remote areas of a country, for example, in order to maintain an agricultural industry or simply to preserve more traditional lifestyles in regions used as recreational areas for the urban population.

Also, regulation may be chosen to influence market outcomes so that they better reflect a society's attitudes in terms of distributional justice and social welfare. Many societies choose to transfer resources to individuals who are unable to participate in the market or otherwise disadvantaged. However, the mode and extent of resource transfer may differ

---

[85] Mankiw (2006), p. 430.

considerably from one society to another. For that reason, certain services like health or education are often strictly regulated or even provided by the state. Another instance of regulation guided by moral or normative objectives is regulation relating to the workplace. If a sufficient workforce is available, safety in the workplace would not normally be provided by market mechanisms due to the usually weaker bargaining power of those employed.[86] Hence, in some societies, the workplace is highly regulated and safety ensured by mandatory requirements imposed on industry. Also, as detailed above, the market would fail to protect the environment. To reiterate, this is partly due to the character of the environment as a public good. Despite environmental pollution being the result of market failure, regulation to protect and preserve the environment also has a distributional dimension. Free markets will not usually bring about the specific level of a healthy environment demanded by society. Instead, it is feared that they could lead to pollution havens, inhabited by the poor, while only the wealthy population could afford to live in less polluted areas.[87] Hence, nationally applicable environmental regulation ensures a minimum level healthy environment that corresponds to this society's preferences and that allows all members of society to benefit.

2.1.3.3 Preliminary conclusion

All economic rationales for regulation are relevant to regulation of NPAs, and of production in particular. The regulation of production is as diverse as the production process itself. If, for instance, publication of information on certain details of the production process is prescribed, then the rationale for such regulation might be to improve knowledge of market agents in order to ensure the proper functioning of the market. Production regulation that requires producers to reduce pollution might address environmental concerns and falls into the category of regulation to deal with market failure. Much of production regulation, however, can be attributed to societal preferences, and thus to the third category, as the example of safety at the workplace illustrates.

Although these categories centre around apparently distinct aspects of the market, namely, preconditions for market functioning, cases of market failure and distributional correction of Pareto optimal results, there is considerable overlap between these categories. For instance, both the

---

[86] Breyer categorizes this and other motivations for regulation as paternalistic. See Breyer (1984), p. 238.
[87] See, e.g., Boyce (2004), who observes a correlation between the location of polluting industries and poverty of the local population, both among and within states.

first and the second category are concerned if markets fail because of the absence of perfect competition in a broader sense. Externalities can be considered a case of market failure as well as a case of market imperfection, if the absence of externalities is seen as a characteristic of perfect markets. Both the second and the third category are concerned, for example, if markets fail, and if the impacts of failure are more severe for one part of the population than for another. The categorization should therefore be understood as a rough approximation illustrating the interrelation of regulation and markets as different and interrelated tools serving the objective of improving welfare.

2.2 International trade and NPA measures

The review of disputes on NPA measures in Chapter 1 has shown that NPA measures have the potential to restrict international trade. This section explores the relationship between international trade and NPA measures more comprehensively. The next section provides an overview over the economic foundations underlying the multilateral trading system, as well as its principal objectives. Both are necessary for the interpretation of the agreements in Part II. Furthermore, economic rationales and objectives will be referred to in developing an approach to the legal status of NPA measures in Part III. Section 2.2.2 discusses the interface of domestic regulation and international trade in general, and the relevance of NPA measures in particular, and the focus of section 2.3.2 is on the political and economic arguments invoked for and against such measures.

2.2.1 *Design parameters of the multilateral trading system*

This section gives an overview of some fundamental issues of the multilateral trading system, which are here referred to as its design parameters. These include the principal objectives and purpose of the multilateral trading system established by the WTO Agreements, and the basic economic rationales underlying the system. The overview begins with an identification of the main objectives of the GATT and the WTO Agreements and discusses their relevance. Section 2.2.1.2 then identifies and explains the economic theory on which the system is built.

2.2.1.1   Object and purpose of the WTO Agreements

Objectives and purpose are derived from the text of the WTO Agreements, primarily from the preambles. Since the objectives and purpose of

2.2 INTERNATIONAL TRADE AND NPA MEASURES

agreements are not usually justiciable rights and obligations, their relevance from a legal perspective is discussed subsequently.

2.2.1.1.1 Identification

The objectives of the GATT 1947 are stated primarily in the first recital of the preamble:

> Recognizing that their relations in the field of trade and economic endeavour should be conducted with a view to raising standards of living, ensuring full employment and a large and steadily growing volume of real income and effective demand, developing the full use of the resources of the world and expanding the production and exchange of goods.

The parties agree to conduct their economic relations 'with a view to' achieving a whole list of economic and non-economic objectives relating to issues such as living standards, employment and the resources of the world. The first and primary objective explicitly stated is 'raising standards of living'. Interestingly, this objective refers to the well-being of individuals rather than to the benefits for each party's economy. All other objectives concern in different ways the ideal of a healthy and sustainable economy. The GATT and the failed ITO, respectively, were negotiated in the post-war situation after the Second World War, and the text only partly reflects the concerns at that time. The primary idea guiding the establishment of these institutions was the prevention of another world war, and related to this objective was the intention to 'increase the pie' for all rather than to struggle over it.[88] It was understood that free trade would benefit all nations and that, consequently, free trade represented a common goal. This is apparent especially in the last part of first recital, expressing the intention to make 'full use of the resources of the world'. Hence, the objectives of the GATT 1947 were of an economic nature and referred to the socio-economic well-being of individuals, as well as to the well-being of the economy as a whole.

When the WTO was established, none of the above socio-economic objectives was abandoned. Apart from a few minor changes, the text of the GATT 1947 preamble was fully included in the preamble to the Marrakesh Agreement.[89] While preserving the traditional goals, however, new objectives were added. The former reference to the resources of the world was reframed into 'while allowing for the optimal use of the

---

[88] Cf. Jackson (2002), p. 122.
[89] See Marrakesh Agreement, Preamble, 1st recital, as reproduced at the beginning of this book.

world's resources in accordance with the objective of sustainable development, seeking both to protect and preserve the environment'. In addition to the reference to sustainable development and the environment, the last phrase of the first recital points to the needs and concerns of the parties 'at different levels of economic development'. Also, the second recital, although drafted in a complicated manner, points to the needs of developing countries and especially the least developed among them, and recognizes 'the need for positive efforts' to ensure that these countries 'secure a share in the growth in international trade commensurate with the needs of their economic development'.

Jackson, who considers the traditional GATT and WTO objectives together with concerns and developments relating to the reduction of poverty and financial crisis, identifies at least five prominent objectives of the WTO system as to:

> keep the peace, promote world economic development and welfare, work towards sustainable development and environmental protection, reduce the poverty of the poorest part of the world, and manage economic crises that might erupt partly due to the circumstances of globalization and interdependence.[90]

Indeed, the text of the Marrakesh Agreement is unambiguous about the objectives of the multilateral trading system in as far as sustainable development, economic development of developing and least developing countries and environmental preservation and protection are concerned.[91] However, there are some other social policies, such as the preservation of traditions, culture or the protection of minorities, which arguably would not fall into the broad range of objectives of the WTO Agreements. This depends, however, on the interpretation of the term 'sustainable development'. Despite the absence of a precise definition of the term in the WTO Agreements themselves, it seems obvious that the use of the term reflects its definition in the famous Brundtland report.[92]

---

[90] Jackson (2006), p. 86.
[91] For the objective of sustainable development, this has been explicitly recognized by the panel in *Shrimp Turtle – Article 21.5 Malaysia* (para. 5.54: 'In that framework, assessing first the *object and purpose* of the WTO Agreement, we note that the WTO preamble refers to the notion of "sustainable development". This means that in interpreting the terms of the chapeau, we must keep in mind that sustainable development is one of the objectives of the WTO Agreement' – original emphasis).
[92] See Brundtland Report (1987). The report defines sustainable development as 'development that meets the needs of the present without compromising the ability of future generations to meet their own needs'.

2.2 INTERNATIONAL TRADE AND NPA MEASURES

Accordingly, the term aims at economic development that is sustainable in the sense that the present use of the world's resources is limited by the rights of future generations. Meanwhile, the term is understood to aim at the integration of economic, social and environmental concerns.[93] Although its legal relevance is not yet entirely clear, it is uncontested that the concept is of some relevance whenever WTO law is interpreted or applied.[94] While the text of the Marrakesh Agreement was drafted in the early 1990s, WTO members reaffirmed their commitment to the objective of sustainable development in the Doha Ministerial Declaration in 2001, by stating:

> We strongly reaffirm our commitment to the objective of sustainable development, as stated in the Preamble to the Marrakesh Agreement. We are convinced that the aims of upholding and safeguarding an open and non-discriminatory multilateral trading system, and acting for the protection of the environment and the promotion of sustainable development can and must be mutually supportive.[95]

In sum, the various objectives of the multilateral trading system comprise both economic and non-economic objectives. The economic objectives relate to the economic well-being of individuals and of economies as a whole, and to economic optimality in the reallocation and use of globally available resources. The non-economic objectives comprise objectives such as sustainable development, protection and preservation of the environment and economic development of developing countries, and last but not least, lasting peace. It is important to note that given the breadth of the objectives, conventional claims of a clash of objectives between the multilateral trading system and particular social policies, such as environmental policies, must be considered wrong. In contrast, the objectives of the multilateral trading system are perfectly in line with the objectives of environmental policies and a broad range of other social policies. The perceived clash of objectives is actually an inconsistency in the means chosen to pursue these goals.[96]

---

[93] Bürgi Bonanomi (2007), p. 13; see also Appellate Body Report, *Shrimp Turtle* (1998), No. 129, fn. 107, with further references.
[94] Bürgi Bonanomi (2007), p. 21. See also pp. 20–1 for an overview of relevant reports of the WTO adjudicatory bodies.
[95] Doha Ministerial Declaration, adopted on 14 November 2001, WT/MIN(01)/DEC/1, No. 6.
[96] See below, section 2.2.1.2.

2.2.1.1.2 Relevance

One could doubt the legal relevance of the objectives of the WTO Agreements, given that these are primarily contained in the preambles. Preambular statements do play an important role in treaty interpretation, particularly in identification of the treaty's object and purpose, although such statements are not formally legally binding in the same way that operational provisions can be.[97] This proposition of the relevance of objectives and purpose of the treaty is based first of all on general principles of international law, namely, on the sovereignty of states, which gives states the freedom to accede or not to accede to international treaties, and on the principle *pacta sunt servanda*, which requires WTO members to act in good faith.[98] The object and purpose of a treaty is not in itself an obligation, but the consent of states to be bound by a treaty also extends to its object and purpose, in as far as these are reflected in the text of the treaty. This can be concluded from the Vienna Convention on the Law of Treaties (VCLT), which ascribes great importance to the object and purpose of treaties and to the requirement to act in 'good faith'. For instance, according to VCLT Article 18, a state is generally obliged to refrain from defeating the object and purpose of a treaty after it has signed the treaty or otherwise expressed its consent, even before the treaty has entered into force. This rule must *a fortiori* be applicable to a state that has signed a treaty for the period of its operation. The extension of consent to object and purpose of a treaty is also apparent in the exclusion of reservations to treaties if the reservation is incompatible with object and purpose of the treaty.[99] Finally, object and purpose are a guiding consideration in the interpretation of the entire text of a treaty.[100] While the WTO Agreements consist of a several treaties, the WTO is also an international organization, with a large membership and organized into several bodies, including decision-making and adjudicatory bodies. Therefore, it could even be argued that object and purpose of the WTO Agreements are even more crucial for WTO members, since they are members, and therefore constitutive elements of an international organization rather than merely signatories to an international treaty. In this sense, the parties to the Marrakesh Agreement and WTO members declared explicitly that they

---

[97] Cordonier Segger (2009), before fn. 47.
[98] The VCLT preamble, 3rd recital, states: '*Noting* that the principles of free consent and of good faith and the *pacta sunt servanda* rule are universally recognized'.
[99] VCLT, Article 19(c).
[100] VCLT, Article 31:1.

are *'Determined* to preserve the basic principles and to further the objectives underlying this multilateral trading system.'[101]

However, reference to object and purpose of the WTO Agreements has been viewed rather critically in WTO case law. Its relevance for an interpretation of specific obligations was rejected by the Appellate Body in *Shrimp Turtle*. In this dispute, the panel had invoked the object and purpose of the WTO Agreements as an argument for its finding that the US import prohibition for shrimps violated WTO obligations. The Appellate Body reprimanded the panel for not having looked 'into the object and purpose of the *chapeau of Article XX*', but rather into 'the object and purpose of the *whole of the GATT 1994 and the WTO Agreement*, which object and purpose it described in an overly broad manner' (original emphasis). It then criticized the panel for having arrived at the very broad formulation that measures that 'undermine the WTO multilateral trading system' must be regarded as 'not within the scope of measures permitted under the chapeau of Article XX'. The Appellate Body stated:

> Maintaining, rather than undermining, the multilateral trading system is necessarily a fundamental and pervasive premise underlying the *WTO Agreement*; but it is not a right or an obligation, nor is it an interpretative rule which can be employed in the appraisal of a given measure under the chapeau of Article XX.[102]

The Appellate Body's statement, however, relates to a situation where a panel invoked objective and purpose of the agreements as a basic argument for its conclusion that a WTO member had violated its obligations. Indeed, inconsistency of a measure with the object and purpose of a treaty alone cannot provide a stable basis for a finding of a violation.

It is, therefore, noteworthy that in the same report the Appellate Body explicitly acknowledged the legal relevance of the preamble by stating that it 'informs not only the GATT, but also the other covered agreements'.[103] It could, therefore, be argued that object and purpose of the agreements may still be referred to as an argument for showing that a measure is consistent with WTO law. This could be especially relevant for an interpretation of the particular exceptions listed in Article XX. Certainly, an interpretation oblivious of object and purpose of a treaty would not be consistent with the VCLT canon of interpretation. While the Appellate Body's view on the importance of object and purpose of the

---

[101] Marrakesh Agreement, Preamble, 5th recital.
[102] Appellate Body Report, *Shrimp Turtle* (1998), No. 116 (original emphasis).
[103] Appellate Body Report, *Shrimp Turtle* (1998), No. 129.

WTO Agreements might be clarified in future reports, the frequent reference to preambular language by the adjudicatory bodies and government officials indicates that the objectives as reflected in the preamble are, indeed, legally relevant.[104]

Against this legal reasoning could be invoked the argument that despite the formal consent to be bound by the WTO Agreements expressed through signature or accession, many WTO members actually acceded for pragmatic reasons rather than because of their belief in object and purpose of the WTO. Given the fact that WTO membership comprises the large majority of the countries in the world, including all major trading nations, participation of states in international trade is more and more contingent on WTO membership. Hence, the economic pressure on states to accede to the WTO is enormous. Although a secret disagreement would be legally irrelevant, especially with regard to future amendments or additional agreements, the economic constraints cannot be ignored, and persistent identification with object and purpose of the WTO Agreements cannot be assumed too easily.

However, the assumption that WTO objectives constitute the biggest common denominator is not based on legal arguments only. As has been shown above, it is the convincing substance of the objectives of the WTO Agreements that renders the assumption that states would subscribe to them as plausible, regardless of the arguably diverse motivations for accession.

2.2.1.2 Economic rationales of the multilateral trading system

The motivation of countries to become parties to the GATT and later members of the WTO is based on neo-classical economic theory and on the claim that free trade is economically beneficial to all countries. Also, the economic rationales underlying the multilateral trading system can be derived from the preambles. There the parties determined not only the objectives, but also the means to achieve them, namely, by fostering free trade among the parties. Both preambles of the GATT and the Marrakesh Agreement use nearly identical language to express the commitment of the parties to contribute to the stated objectives 'by entering into reciprocal and mutually advantageous arrangements directed to the substantial reduction of tariffs and other barriers to trade and to the elimination

---

[104] Cf. also Charnovitz (2007a), pp. 687–8.

2.2 INTERNATIONAL TRADE AND NPA MEASURES 99

of discriminatory treatment in international trade relations'.[105] Thus, the parties intended to remove the most important obstacles to trade and to eliminate discrimination.

The multilateral trading system established with the WTO Agreements is based on two interlinked presumptions derived from classical and neo-classical theory: the first principle is the efficiency of competitive markets, and the second principle is the theory of comparative advantage.[106] The latter theory of comparative advantage, developed by David Ricardo at the beginning of the nineteenth century, holds that even a country that is less efficient in the production of any good will profit from free trade, if it specializes in the production of the good which it can produce at relatively low costs and if it exports them.[107] This will enable the country to import more of the goods it needs compared with autonomy. Thus, respective specialization in combination with international trade will improve the country's income or endowment with goods in absolute terms. Interestingly, according to the theory, smaller economies will profit more than bigger economies, since they affect world market prices least, but ultimately all countries win.[108] Ricardo's theory has also met criticism, since it is based on a number of assumptions to which reality does not live up. Among these assumptions is that there is full employment, that prices reflect marginal costs of production and that there are no externalities.[109] Nevertheless, its basic validity is widely recognized and it has been termed 'one of the deepest truths in all of economics'.[110]

Nevertheless, even the critics of the theory of comparative advantage will usually subscribe to the first key principle of the WTO Agreements, namely, the efficiency of free and competitive markets. The economic forces behind international trade are diversity of natural resources, differences in tastes and in production costs. An agreement to remove trade barriers means opening domestic markets to foreign competition in exchange for market access to foreign markets for domestic producers. Trade is trade, whether it involves people within a nation or people in different countries. By opening national markets, trading opportunities

---

[105] Except for replacing the word 'commerce' with 'international trade relations', see 2nd recital of the GATT and 3rd recital of the Marrakesh Agreement.
[106] Jackson (2000c), p. 372.   [107] See Samuelson and Nordhaus (2005), p. 296.
[108] Samuelson and Nordhaus (2005), p. 298.
[109] See, e.g., Lammenett (1964), pp. 163–4 for an overview over the assumptions of the free trade theorem.
[110] Cf. Samuelson and Nordhaus (2005), p. 302.

are expanded[111] with all related advantages, namely, additional consumption and production opportunities, economies of scale and the benefits of increased competition in terms of quality and price. From a global perspective, free trade in competitive markets allows the world to move to the frontier of its production–possibility curve.[112] While these theories do not address the precise distribution of the additional income among the trading nations, they are unambiguous in their finding that the 'economic pie', namely, total production, is increased in absolute terms.

The multilateral trading system established with the WTO Agreements is based on the understanding that freer international trade is a suitable means to promote the objectives listed in the preambles of the various WTO Agreements. Although the primary goal of the WTO Agreements is to foster free trade, the Agreements are clear in their determination of freer trade as the suitable tool to achieve other ultimate economic and non-economic objectives.

2.2.2 *The interface of domestic regulation and international trade*

Domestic regulation bears on international trade and vice versa. Recognizing this fact, the GATT negotiators in 1947 inserted several provisions addressing this interface. Most importantly, they inserted an obligation for all contracting parties to accord national treatment in Article III. The text of this provision was drafted in an extremely broad way, and in consequence the obligation to refrain from discrimination encompasses the entire field of national regulation, provided that it has some effect on imported products. In response to possible impacts of increased international trade on domestic regulations, the negotiators stipulated in Article XX that 'nothing in [the GATT] shall be construed to prevent the adoption or enforcement by any contracting party of measures' necessary to pursue any of several listed policies that were considered legitimate. This section outlines the continuing debate on the general interface of international trade and domestic regulation and explains why NPA measures are particularly relevant in this respect.

2.2.2.1 The general debate on domestic regulation

In recent years, WTO members have increasingly focused attention on domestic regulation, both with a view to lower non-tariff barriers

---

[111] Samuelson and Nordhaus (2005), pp. 293–5.
[112] Samuelson and Nordhaus (2005), p. 300.

2.2 INTERNATIONAL TRADE AND NPA MEASURES

to trade and to maintaining the ability of WTO members to regulate their internal affairs effectively. WTO members explicitly recognize the importance of domestic regulation in pursuing national policy objectives, especially with respect to trade in services.[113] Evidence of WTO members' awareness of problems arising from the impact of domestic regulation on international trade and vice versa can be found in the existence of the Working Party on Domestic Regulation, which was established by the Council for Trade in Services in 1999.[114] The Working Party was established to continue the work of the previous Working Party on Professional Services, but its mandate also encompassed new tasks as laid down in Article VI:4 of the GATS. Accordingly, among the new tasks was the development of generally applicable and sector-specific disciplines to ensure that measures relating to licensing requirements, technical standards and qualification requirements do not constitute unnecessary barriers to trade in services.[115] The Working Party on Domestic Regulation was very active, holding numerous formal and informal meetings, and discussing a large number of communications and proposals by WTO members. However, members and public alike have remained suspicious with regard to the disciplines to be developed. Many WTO members felt it was important to state explicitly their view that they nevertheless retained the right to adopt and implement domestic regulations which they deemed to be necessary to pursue legitimate policy objectives,[116] and that 'domestic regulations should be formulated and developed in response to changing legal, social and economic environments and differing circumstances in the territory of each Member'.[117] Others, however, expressed concerns about the interpretation of what constitutes such legitimate policy objectives and wondered if there could possibly be such a thing as 'illegitimate

---

[113] See also the Doha Ministerial Declaration, adopted on 14 November 2001, WT/MIN(01)/DEC/1, No. 7: 'We reaffirm the right of members under the General Agreement on Trade in Services to regulate, and to introduce new regulations on, the supply of services.'

[114] Decision on domestic regulation, adopted by the Council for Trade in Services on 26 April 1999, S/L/70 (28 April 1999), Preamble.

[115] E.g., Decision on domestic regulation, adopted by the Council for Trade in Services on 26 April 1999, S/L/70 (28 April 1999), Nos. 2 and 3.

[116] Cf., e.g., Switzerland, Communication from Switzerland, Proposal for Disciplines on Technical Standards in Services, 1 February 2005, S/WPDR/W/32, No. 1. This point was explicitly approved, e.g., by Singapore (No. 13) and Thailand (No. 28) (see Report on the Meeting held on 7 and 18 February 2005, Note by the Secretariat, S/WPDR/M/29, 11 July 2005).

[117] See Report on the Meeting held on 7 and 18 February 2005, above fn. 116, No. 2.

national policy objectives'.[118] With respect to domestic regulation, the services negotiations have been engaging and fruitful, resulting in a draft text of disciplines by the chairperson of the Working Party,[119] despite the deadlock of negotiations on market access. Nevertheless, views of WTO members diverge substantially on the nature of possible rules and disciplines. While the United States stresses the importance of enhanced transparency without being interested in additional horizontally applicable disciplines, the EU's focus is on licensing requirements and procedures. There is no common position among developing countries, which are split according to their different economic interests. Some developing countries are most interested in disciplines on qualification requirements with respect to mode 4, the presence of natural persons in the territory of the receiving country, while others are in favour of strong disciplines on domestic regulation in order to minimize trade-restrictive effects, while a third group emphasizes the right to regulate and introduce new regulatory measures.[120]

Due to the earlier conclusion of the GATT, the debate on the interface of domestic regulation and international trade in goods has a much longer history. With the lowering of tariffs, non-tariff barriers, often in the form of domestic regulation, moved to the centre of attention. Some of the trade-restrictive effects of non-tariff barriers were addressed with the conclusion of the TBT and the SPS Agreements during the Uruguay Round, which cover some of the most important instances of non-tariff barriers. Also, a number of disputes at the WTO contributed to the clarification of some of the tensions between domestic regulation and the objective of freer international trade. Noteworthy in this respect is the *EC – Asbestos* case, which resulted in the confirmation that France had not violated any obligations by prohibiting imports of products containing asbestos.[121] The findings of the Appellate Body on this dispute seem to express respect for the regulatory autonomy of WTO members. Other

---

[118] See Report on the Meeting held on 7 and 18 February 2005, above fn. 116, the Philippines (No. 29), more general concerns were expressed by Australia (No. 33), Chile (No. 19) and Hong Kong, China (No. 18).

[119] The consolidated draft text by the chair was issued on 10 July 2006 (10 (26) *Bridges Weekly Trade News Digest*, Services: Domestic Regulation Leaps Forward, Market Access Stands Still, 19 July 2006).

[120] See 10 (26) *Bridges Weekly Trade News Digest*, Services: Domestic Regulation Leaps Forward, Market Access Stands Still, 19 July 2006; Report of the Meeting held 22 June 2005, Note by the Secretariat, S/WPDR/M/30, 6 September 2005.

[121] Appellate Body Report in: *EC – Asbestos* (2001), Nos. 155–75, 192–3.

disputes, such as the *EC – Hormones* disputes, however, constitute proof of continuing tensions.

Another strand of the debate emerged in the late 1960s to early 1970s, when environmental problems moved to the forefront of public attention. Until recently, the broader impacts of international trade on the environment and on other subjects usually protected by national regulation, such as health and safety, social rights or culture and minorities, have been subject to the so-called 'trade and' debate.[122] Finally, NPA measures also form part of the interface of domestic regulation and international trade.[123] However, a body comparable to the Working Party on Domestic Regulation under the Council of Trade in Services is missing.

2.2.2.2 NPA measures and international trade in goods

This section explains the distinguishing features of NPA measures and why these are problematic when applied to imports. As shown above, domestic regulation is mostly linked to NPAs in order to replace or to supplement direct regulation. NPA measures are characterized by two aspects: first, they apply to products, and, second, they refer to an NPA in their objective elements. An example of an NPA measure is a measure that distinguishes between meat products because of aspects that are not incorporated in the meat itself, such as farming methods, or conditions in which live cattle are transported to the slaughter house, or any other aspect that is not physically present in the meat itself.

It is the combination of both features that renders NPA measures suspicious under WTO law. Since NPA measures apply to products, the existence of freer international trade due to the multilateral trading system implies that NPA measures are applied not only to domestic products, but also to imports. Hence, NPA measures inherently have an effect on international trade – although this effect is not *per se* more (or less) trade-restrictive than effects of measures linked to physical product characteristics.

Therefore, it is the other feature that renders NPA measures particularly suspicious if applied to imports. The fact that NPAs are by definition not incorporated into the physical product characteristics is relevant in a twofold way. First, as opposed to other product measures, NPA measures applied to imports cannot be justified by dangers or risks for the territory

---

[122] For more on this debate see below Part III, Chapter 7.
[123] See the crucial disputes and overview over the debate on PPMs above, Chapter 1, section 1.2 and section 1.3.

of the regulating state arising from the product. This is because they cannot be more or less dangerous than identical products unrelated to the respective NPA. This aspect relates to justification of the measure. Second, the NPAs that lead to the distinction between products are located outside the territory of the regulating state. This means that the regulating state links a measure to an aspect beyond its jurisdiction. Hence, there are doubts about the competence of the regulating state to issue NPA measures applying to imports.

The relevance of this feature is linked to several political arguments for and against permissibility of NPA measures, which are reviewed in the next section.

2.2.3 Political arguments in the international debate

The debate on NPA measures is predominantly political. Because of the economic and political implications of NPA measures, the positions among WTO members and other stakeholders diverge considerably. This section summarizes the most important arguments brought forward in the debate. The distinctive features of NPA measures and their implications are invoked both to reject and to support them, thus the arguments are presented according to themes.

2.2.3.1 Effective and efficient protection of national or foreign objects

The single most important argument for adopting NPA measures, just as any other type of regulation, is the need to regulate effectively. Typically, the objective of NPA measures relates to the NPA in question. For example, if a measure refers in its objective elements to the use of certain pesticides in agricultural production, then the objective pursued with the legal consequences of the measures is to discourage or even encourage the use of those pesticides.[124] The ultimate objective of the measure in this case could be to protect the environment, in particular, the soil and ground water, from the use of a harmful substance present in certain pesticides or from an excessive amount of pesticides. As detailed above, the state imposing this NPA measure might intend to complement direct domestic regulation of the use of pesticides or it might rely on discouraging or encouraging the use of pesticides without regulating the use directly.

---

[124] See also Howse and Regan (2000), at pp. 272–3, who illustrate how economic incentives inherent to NPA measures render them effective regulatory instruments.

In the case of the protection of national objects, direct regulation and NPA measures will often be combined: if a production method is prohibited, then it makes sense to prohibit the sale of the products generated in violation of the rule. Otherwise, if profits could be generated legally with products that have been produced in violation of rules, producers would be encouraged to cheat and to reap profits while ignoring the rules. Setting economic disincentives for the use of prohibited production methods may also be cheaper for the state imposing the production rule: the enforcement of direct regulation requires costly control mechanisms. Economic disincentives may suffice to keep producers from using prohibited NPAs, since the economic implications in the case of discovery would mean that the costs of production cannot be covered by the sale of the products produced. In competitive markets, producers would most likely report to authorities should they fear that their competitors save costs by making use of illegal NPAs. This means that if the protected object is located within the regulating state, both direct and indirect regulation are suitable, or even necessary, for reaching regulatory goals in an efficient way. However, these arguments are limited to the domestic sphere: NPA measures make sense only if they apply to products produced domestically. Since production abroad usually cannot possibly affect the object of protection, for instance, the quality of soil in the regulating state, the application of NPA measure to imports cannot be justified by these arguments.

However, should the goal of regulation be the protection of certain objects no matter where they are located, the regulatory argument for NPA measures is even stronger: if enforcement of direct regulation is difficult or even impossible, for example, because the regulating state does not have jurisdiction on the territory of the object of protection, NPA measures may be the only effective tool for the regulating state in order to achieve its regulatory goals. In this situation, however, the legitimacy of this regulatory argument is contested by obvious counter-arguments relating to the sovereignty of the state affected by the NPA measure, which will be explored in the following section. In the case of multilateral environmental agreements aimed at the protection of objects located within the territories of all or several signatories, in contrast, sovereignty will usually not be a counter-argument, provided that all members have agreed on the terms of the agreement. Since in this situation direct regulation is impossible for all but one member, one of the remaining tools to influence NPAs in the exporting state is to make treatment of imported products dependent on the respective NPA. Sales prohibitions in other countries may be desired by all states, or even only by the state, in which the object of protection is located: as explained above, indirect regulation leading to economic disincentives for producers may be more effective and less costly for the affected state. Charnovitz cites a number of historical and current examples for NPA measures in multilateral environmental agreements to show the broad acceptance of NPA measures even in the international sphere.[125] Among his examples are prohibitions on the landing of fish taken in violation of certain rules as agreed upon between Mexico and the United States, or a prohibition on the sale of certain seabirds caught in nets as laid down in an early agreement between Denmark and Sweden. Unilateral measures taken in order to enforce the objectives of certain international agreements, however, may be contested if NPA measures are not laid down in the treaty at issue.

In sum, the validity of the regulatory argument depends on the location of the object of protection. It is, however, questionable if the protection of objects beyond the territory of the regulating state is legitimate at all, and if so, under which conditions. If the measure is applied to both domestic and imported products, it might be valid if the protected object is located abroad or constitutes shared resources or a global common. This extraterritorial reach of NPA measures leads to sovereignty concerns on the part of the country of production as detailed in the next section.

2.2.3.2 Sovereignty and extraterritoriality

NPA regulation has an impact on production via incentives or disincentives. Because of the economic advantages or disadvantages accorded with the measures, any producer trading in the respective product will calculate costs and benefits of a change in production in order to satisfy the requirements of the measure. Should the benefits outweigh the costs, producers will change the way in which they produce even if their production facility is not located in the regulator's jurisdiction. If the costs outweigh the benefits, producers will accept the economic disadvantages or direct their products towards different markets.[126]

Opponents of production-based trade measures argue that by linking trade measures to aspects of production, the state imposing the measure would exceed its jurisdiction. They argue that the competence to regulate production activities rests with the state on whose territory production takes place. By applying measures to products based on aspects of

---

[125] Charnovitz (2002), p. 70.
[126] See on the relevance of extraterritoriality and related arguments, e.g., Howse and Regan (2000), pp. 274–9.

production, the imposing state would interfere with the direct regulation of the country of production. Ultimately, production-based measures would be used as tools to illicitly impose the internal regulatory framework of one state on other states. It is feared that unilateral measures restricting trade, for example, based on different environmental conditions in other countries, would invite chaos and retaliation.[127] It would be irrelevant that there were no legal effect on the producing state, since the economic effects would be strong enough that the conditions, although not legally binding, would be *de facto* compulsory for foreign producers. This strong factual effect is a consequence of free international trade, and for many countries good economic and trade relations are essential. For this reason, linking measures to activities within another state's territory would violate, or at least undermine, this state's sovereignty, and therefore production-based trade measures would be impermissible. Sovereignty concerns are of paramount importance in the political debate, where NPA measures are often perceived as a means of cultural or environmental imperialism.

Interestingly, the proponents of production-based trade measures also invoke sovereignty, albeit the sovereignty of the importing state. The claim is that the importing state has jurisdiction to regulate under which conditions products may be traded, consumed or used on its territory. Therefore, its sovereignty would allow the application to products of measures linked to any aspect it deemed important, whether or not the aspect would be physically incorporated into the product. Accordingly, the freedom to design measures applying to products in its territory and respective regulation were just an expression of the importing state's internal sovereignty. As regards the concerns about violating other states' sovereignty, proponents of production-based measures argue that trade measures by their very nature are not capable of interfering with other states' sovereignty. Production-based measures apply to products in the territory or on the way to the territory of the importing and regulating state. They could not lead to a physical or legal effect in the exporting country's jurisdiction. Even if production-based measures imply economic incentives or disincentives, any change in production abroad would be a consequence of autonomous and voluntary decisions made by producers abroad. Furthermore, proponents argue that factual economic side-effects of internal regulation, whether merely product-related or

---

[127] Schoenbaum (1992), p. 723.

production-related, are common in international relations and that such side-effects are inevitable. As Howse and Regan put it:

> If 'sovereignty' is the issue, one could as well say that to deny the importing country the right to exclude shrimp caught by a method it abhors would be an invasion of *its* sovereignty.[128]

The arguments referring to sovereignty and extraterritoriality are based on different understandings of sovereignty. According to the meaning of sovereignty underlying the opponents' argument, internal sovereignty implies an active right to regulate internal activities, as well as a passive right to non-interference. Thus, any measure having an impact on internal activities is a violation of a state's sovereignty – whether or not the impact would be economic pressure rather than legal obligation. The proponents of NPA measures, in contrast, understand sovereignty as a legal concept implying full autonomy in any state action and behaviour, which is not limited by possible side-effects on other states. Accordingly, a state may choose the conditions under which it allows importation of products. Factual effects of internal rules on conditions in other countries are thus nothing but an inevitable and common side-effect of sovereign internal regulation.

While the above opposing views on extraterritorial effects of regulation are still prominent in the political debate, recent scholarship has explored reconciling approaches. The adequacy and usefulness of the traditional concept of sovereignty in today's world and the allocation of power in a system of multi-level governance move to the centre of the debate.[129]

2.2.3.3 Unilateralism

Unilateralism arguments should not be confused with the related complexities of an extraterritorial reach. While aspects of extraterritoriality are usually invoked to challenge legitimacy of NPA trade measures in principle, unilateralism is mostly perceived as crucial when it comes to the question of justification. Even the Rio Declaration on Environment and Development of 1992, a symbol of a new international awareness of a common responsibility for the world's resources, states in Principle 12 that: 'Unilateral actions to deal with environmental challenges outside the jurisdiction of the importing country should be avoided.' Unilateralism can relate to two interlinked situations. First, unilateralism relates to the standards adopted with a particular measure. Production-based measures

---

[128] Howse and Regan (2000), p. 274 (original emphasis).   [129] Cf. below Chapter 8.

are usually drafted based on the domestic regulatory framework, which so functions as a reference standard. Alternatively, production-based trade measures can also be based on international standards as laid down in international treaties or in documents issued by specialized international organizations. While in the former situation, the state would, indeed, assess foreign activities applying national standards, in the latter case a state would assess foreign activities applying benchmarks that have been agreed upon by a larger number of countries. For the latter situation, the contested legal relevance of other international agreements under WTO law is crucial.[130]

The second meaning of unilateralism relates to the number of countries adopting the measure. Only a production-based measure imposed by a single country might then be referred to as unilateral action, while the same measure taken by several countries together, possibly authorized by an international agreement, might have to be assessed differently. These situations also occur in combination. For instance, if the domestic standard of a country is based on an international standard, and this country imposes a production-based measure enforcing this standard, then the country acts unilaterally in the sense of taking this measure deliberately, albeit that the standard is shared internationally.

In contrast to the previous aspects which both proponents and opponents interpret to imply exactly the opposite of what the other side suggests, there is no consistent line of argument for opponents and proponents when it comes to unilateralism. While only a few voices condemn any unilateral action *per se*, the relevance of unilateralism is mostly discussed with respect to justification of NPA measures. In sum, rather than characterizing any unilateral activity as illegitimate, most scholars deem it appropriate to differentiate. Bodansky, for example, admits, on the one hand, that unilateral action is mostly available to powerful states and that at times only a thin line may divide leadership from coercion. On the other hand, he points out that, although questionable from a process standpoint, a threat of, or actual, unilateral action may play a critical role in the development of international standards and may often be the only means of promoting and enforcing shared values. He concludes that any particular unilateral action should be evaluated to determine whether or not it advances desired ends.[131] Thus, situations might be assessed differently depending on dialogue and cooperation before a unilateral action

---

[130] See below Chapter 3, section 3.2. [131] Bogdansky (2000), pp. 346, 347.

is taken, depending on the number of states referring to the same measure, or depending on the level of international acceptance of the applied standard.

2.2.3.4 Competitiveness and effective regulation

The impacts of NPA regulation on the competitiveness of domestic firms are invoked both in support of and against NPA measures. The argument is based on the reciprocal effects of regulation and international trade. Internal NPA regulation, such as high environmental standards, lead to compliance costs for the domestic industry. In the absence of international trade, the regulatory goals would be reached at the cost of a rise in prices of the respective products borne by domestic consumers. International trade, however, leads to a different situation. Compliance costs then place domestic industries at a disadvantage vis-à-vis their foreign competitors. Hence, domestic industries would lose market share or even be driven out of the market altogether. Interestingly, the regulatory goals, in as far as they are limited to the environment of the regulating state, would still be achieved – albeit at the cost of a loss of an industry.

The competitiveness side of the argument relates to costs which are usually caused by direct regulation and affect the industries that are legally obliged to observe the regulations. For instance, if industrial emissions must not exceed certain maximum levels for various pollutants, companies will have to take measures in order to reach these requirements. Depending on how high or low the thresholds are, companies will resort to specific filters or limit the use of certain materials. The additional costs created by these measures would need to be considered in calculating the price of the end-product. Competitors producing in foreign countries with less restrictive environmental regulation, in contrast, would not need to take any of these measures and would, consequently, be able to sell their products at a lower price. Hence, the competitive disadvantage for companies producing in the state imposing the stricter regulation.

Proponents of NPA measures argue, therefore, that such measures, for example, a prohibition of all paper products processed with chlorine, must be applied to both domestic and foreign products in order to level the playing field. Since only companies adhering to the conditions can profit from selling paper products at all, the additional costs borne by complying companies in contrast to companies producing elsewhere under conventional and cheaper conditions can be offset. By offering better indirect tax rates for products produced using methods conforming to domestic regulations, or by imposing tariffs on those imported goods which do not conform to these standards, the regulating state would provide indirect compensation to all companies which conformed to the requirements. This indirect compensation would offset the competitive advantages for foreign producers arising from lower regulatory requirements in other countries. A low level of requirements and obligations with respect to environmental protection and other objects of protection could even be seen as an illegitimate subsidization in order to attract industries from other countries, or as a form of dumping.[132]

Opponents of NPA trade measures, however, point out that there is nothing about any state's regulatory framework that could justify any compensation.[133] They argue that compensation for costs relating to production would be in contradiction with the very idea of free trade and comparative advantages. According to this view, lower requirements or a less cost-intensive regulatory framework with respect to production forms the comparative advantage of the country of production, and, consequently, NPA trade measures would jeopardize the realization of the benefits of international trade, namely, the most efficient allocation of resources, between different countries and ultimately the improvement of living standards around the world. Advantages in the treatment of products based on conformity with domestic production requirements are therefore viewed as an illegitimate subsidization.

These different views seem to result from different understandings of the objectives of the WTO Agreements and the economic rationales of markets and free trade as outlined above. The proponents of NPA measures argue that it has to be permissible to regulate effectively in cases of market failure, for instance, in cases of negative externalities. If because of global markets direct regulation is not sustainable, it must be legitimate to design suitable supplements to domestic regulation, if the regulatory goals are legitimate. NPA measures would then be the suitable supplement to ensure effectiveness of national regulation.

The opponents of NPA trade measures build their arguments on the very idea of markets and comparative advantage. They perceive the occurrence and handling of externalities as an internal matter of the state. According to this view, the state competent to regulate has to bear the consequences of its internal regulatory framework. If the regulator decides to raise levels of protection by introducing a more restrictive regulatory

---

[132] See above Chapter 1, sections 1.4.6 and 1.4.7; also Howse and Trebilcock (2005), at pp. 265–71; or Schneuwly (2003), p. 122, who considers the argument that bad working conditions constitute a form of dumping 'rational' from an economic perspective.

[133] See, e.g., Griffin (2000).

framework instead of otherwise dealing with externalities, then this state has also to accept the costs of such regulation, namely, that its industries will operate with a competitive disadvantage vis-à-vis companies producing in countries with a less restrictive regulatory framework. From this point of view, regulatory differences result in desirable regulatory competition, which enables producers to choose among different settings the set that suits them best. While some countries are disadvantaged when it comes to natural resources, they may find that they have a comparative advantage in production of goods due to a regulatory framework attractive to companies. According to this view, NPA measures which neutralize this advantage, by 'levelling the playing field', are contrary to the very idea of comparative advantage and division of labour, since of all countries those poor in natural resources would be deprived of the benefits of free trade to which they are entitled under the WTO Agreements. They see each country's specific design and degree of regulation as part of a country's factor endowment, in the same way as natural resources or labour. Since it would be contrary to the idea of international trade to compensate companies for additional costs due to a lack of natural resources in the country of production, it would be illegitimate to compensate companies for additional costs due to a restrictive legal framework in the country of production. Invoking the competitive disadvantages of producers producing in a regulatory framework with a high level of social protection is therefore often dismissed as an illicit 'economic' argument.[134]

Apparently, both views diverge when it comes to the proper functioning of markets. The proponents plead for regulation as an alternative tool in cases of market failure, arguing that in global markets lacking direct regulation NPA trade measures are the second-best solution. The opponents agree in as far as the right of any country to regulate production activities on its territory is concerned. However, they disagree on the conclusion that the proponents draw for global markets, namely, the right to link trade measures to NPAs. Ultimately, proponents of NPA measures and opponents at this point disagree about the preconditions for markets. Proponents of NPA measures hold that social or environmental costs must be reflected in product prices, so that the regulating function of markets promotes products with the best relationship between quality and social, environmental as well as economic costs of production. Opponents of NPA measures are of the view that social and environmental costs should not necessarily be reflected in market prices.

[134] E.g., Charnovitz (2002), p. 106.

2.2.3.5 Summary

The arguments described above relate to economic and other political concerns in a globalized world. They show that the issue of NPA measures is indeed multidimensional, since it relates to legal, political and economic aspects as well as national and international consequences that need to be taken into account. The aspects of sovereignty and extraterritoriality have a legal as well as a political character, with unilateralism being a possible tool for differentiation. The arguments relating to comparative advantage, on the one hand, and effectiveness of regulation, on the other, however, are primarily of a political and economic nature. All arguments brought forward, however, touch upon fundamental questions relating to the problem-solving capacities within the multi-layered system of governance, with special consideration of the role of the nation-state and of the system of international law in general. Beyond that, the arguments show differences in the understanding of 'fairness' concepts, which may, however, be rooted in the differences between countries rather than in actual normative disagreement. The validity of the respective arguments both from a legal and economic perspective is explored in more detail below.[135]

---

[135] See, e.g., below Chapter 5, section 5.2 and section 5.3.1.

PART II

Legal analysis: reviewing the status
of NPA measures *de lege lata*

This part explores the legal key issues identified in Part I based on the WTO Agreements as they stand. Before entering the narrow field of WTO law, Chapter 3 discusses the applicability of WTO law and other international law to NPA measures. Since NPA measures will often relate to non-trade public policies covered by international agreements, conflicts of norms are inevitable. Under certain circumstances, it is conceivable that other international agreements will prevail over the WTO Agreements – in this case, the legal status of NPA measures under WTO law would be irrelevant. Usually, however, the WTO Agreements, and most importantly the GATT, will determine the legal relations among WTO members.

Chapter 4 begins with the analysis under WTO law. Consistency of national measures with GATT obligations is examined in two steps. The first step in the examination regards a possible violation of GATT obligations and asks whether a measure falls into the scope of the obligation. If so, the question whether or not the measure violates the obligation stated in the provision is addressed. Measures not falling into the scope of obligations cannot possibly violate the agreement. The second step follows only in cases where the measure was found cumulatively to fall into the scope of an obligation and to violate it. It examines whether the measure is justified by any one of the exemptions contained in the GATT, most importantly in Article XX. Accordingly, Chapter 4 analyses the inconsistency of NPA measures with obligations stated in the GATT. The analysis focuses on the underlying concepts and questions identified in Chapter 1 as crucial for the legal status of NPA measures. Based on the findings of this analysis, this work adopts the view that most trade-restrictive NPA measures would violate GATT obligations. Chapter 5, therefore, examines the precise conditions of justification with special consideration of the relevant particularities of NPA measures. The last chapter of the legal analysis, Chapter 6, addresses the special legal status of PPM measures under the other multilateral agreements beyond the GATT, namely, the TBT and the SPS Agreements which explicitly address PPMs.

3

Preliminary considerations: applicability of WTO law and other international law to NPA measures

The perception that NPA measures with restrictive effects on international trade violate GATT obligations is based on the presumption that the respective provisions of the GATT are applicable to NPA measures. This chapter briefly reviews this basic presumption, taking into account that the WTO forms part of the highly fragmented system of international law. While the applicability of WTO law will usually not be under dispute, the applicability of other international law may in some cases be controversial. This situation is particularly relevant to NPA measures.

The national or – in the case of the EC – supra-national, NPA to which a measure is linked inherently relates to a matter other than the tradable good. Depending on its objectives, an NPA measure will usually relate to a subject matter or policy other than trade, for instance, to an aspect of environmental or social policy. Even if the particular aspect at issue is of a strictly national nature, as a corollary of the more and more dense system of international law, the aspect at issue or related aspect may likewise be subject to other public international law, for example, under an international or bilateral treaty. This is particularly true for NPA measures of an environmental nature, but likewise, for example, for national NPA measures touching upon matters of human rights. In these situations, the question arises whether WTO law is exclusively applicable among WTO members, whether it may be excluded by another relevant legal regime, or whether both legal regimes apply concurrently.[1] In the latter case, the consequences of a concurrent application of different legal regimes may prove to be crucial.

For the purposes of this analysis, it is important to note that NPA measures do not necessarily – and arguably not even usually – serve to fulfil the imposing state's obligations under an international treaty. To

---

[1] The direct applicability of international law as a legal question is unrelated to the issue of the relevance of international law for interpretation of GATT provisions. The latter question is discussed below in Chapter 5, section 5.1.1.

date, disputes at the WTO have concerned NPAs adopted in a national or supra-national political process, without the implementing WTO member being obliged to adopt the NPA under an international treaty. While the highly controversial questions discussed in this chapter may in some cases play an important role for the legal assessment of an NPA, they may be entirely irrelevant in others. Likewise, the relevance of this question is not limited to NPA measures. However, given that NPA measures usually serve to implement non-trade public policies, the question may be of particular importance to the legal status of an NPA measure.

The following sections hold that WTO law is part of international law. Section 3.1 briefly addresses the general applicability of WTO law. Section 3.2 focuses on applicability of other conventional international law and on possible conflicts of norms. Finally, section 3.3 discusses specifically whether the international law on state responsibility is applicable and whether it could lead to a justification of NPA measures outside the GATT general exceptions.

3.1 Applicability of WTO law to NPA measures

NPA measures are adopted by nation-states or – in the case of the EC – by a supra-national organization. Just as other regulatory measures, NPA measures are also drafted in order to tackle issues on the political agenda of a given state, whether or not similar issues are subject to other international agreements. However, the legislative or executive body adopting a specific NPA measure will often pursue environmental or other social objectives.[2] Given their specific primary objectives, NPA measures will usually not be designed to focus on international trade, but on other policies. Trade issues may even not be addressed directly. For these reasons, applicability of WTO law to NPA measures in some cases may be doubted.

Since there is no universal applicability of WTO law, applicability of WTO law requires first of all that the state adopting a specific NPA measure is bound by the WTO Agreements. Provided that this is the case, the NPA measure must fall within the scope of application of any of the WTO Agreements. In the case of trade in goods, for an NPA measure to fall within the scope of a GATT provision some actual or potential effect on goods imported into the territory of a WTO member is required. In the

---

[2] See above Chapter 1, section 1.5.2.1 and Chapter 2, section 2.1.1.2 on characteristics and nature of NPA measures.

case of NPA measures applying to goods, it will hardly be possible to completely avoid such effects, and in consequence GATT provisions will usually be applicable. Whether or not the NPA measure in question actually violates an obligation, however, is not a question of the applicability of the WTO Agreements. Possible violations must be assessed by consideration of the facts of the case and of the specific elements of relevant provisions, as will be detailed in the following chapters.

Thus, provided the above preconditions are met, WTO law will normally be applicable to NPA measures. For the question of applicability of WTO law it is irrelevant whether or not the NPA measure in question has been adopted in pursuit of purely national interests or objectives, which will often be the case, or if the measure has been adopted in order to comply with bilateral or multilateral international treaties.

Applicability of WTO law does not necessarily preclude applicability of other international regimes to the same facts. Of interest for the status of NPA measures under WTO law, however, is predominantly the question of whether or not other international law is relevant in WTO dispute settlement.

3.2 The relevance of conventional international law in WTO dispute settlement

Several issues pertaining to the relevance of international law for WTO law need to be distinguished, namely, questions regarding jurisdiction, applicability of international law and its relevance for interpretation.[3]

Among these issues, the question of jurisdiction or competence of the adjudicatory bodies is the least problematic, since there is agreement that jurisdiction is limited to claims under the agreements covered by the WTO.[4] This is apparent from DSU Article 3.2, which stipulates that the system serves to preserve WTO members' rights and obligations contained in the covered agreements. Also the panel's Standard Terms of Reference in DSU Article 7.1 clarify that matters referred to the DSB are to be examined 'in the light of the relevant provisions in (name of the covered agreement(s) cited by the parties to the dispute', and that the findings shall assist the DSB with recommendations or rulings 'provided for in that/those agreement(s)'. Legal rights and obligations outside the WTO

---

[3] Marceau (2001), p. 1082, distinguishes between jurisdiction and applicable law; Pauwelyn (2003), p. 456, creates an extra category for international law used as an interpretative tool. This article draws on Pauwelyn's three-category approach.

[4] E.g., Matsushita, Schoenbaum and Mavroidis (2004), p. 23; Pauwelyn (2003), p. 443.

system are not to be preserved by the dispute settlement system, and are not an object of this analysis.

This section addresses the question of whether the law applicable in WTO dispute settlement exceeds the realm of the WTO Agreements. It asserts the general applicability of international law, and therefore proceeds to ask which norms prevail in cases of conflict. The third, and similarly controversial, question, namely, the relevance of international law as an interpretative tool, is of greatest relevance to the status of NPA measures under WTO law. This topic is discussed in Chapter 6 below with respect to a GATT provision, for which this question of interpretation is of paramount importance, namely, Article XX.[5]

3.2.1   No closed self-contained regime

Against the general applicability of other international law and treaties it could be argued that the WTO is a self-contained regime.[6] The term 'self-contained regime' was explicitly used in a judgment by the International Court of Justice in the *Tehran Hostages* case of 1980 to characterize the rules of diplomatic law. The Court, focusing on secondary rules, explained this concept as a regime 'which, on the one hand, lays down the receiving State's obligations regarding the facilities, privileges and immunities to be accorded to diplomatic missions and, on the other, foresees their possible abuse by members of the mission and specifies the means at the disposal of the receiving States to counter any such abuse'.[7] In this sense, a self-contained regime is a sub-category of the *lex specialis* principle, namely, a special set of rules which also provides a specialized system for reacting to breaches, with the consequence that the general law of state responsibility does not apply.[8] The term is also used in the broader sense to denote a union of rules laying down particular rights, duties and powers, and

---

[5] See below Chapter 5, section 5.1.1
[6] The international law concept of a self-contained regime dates back to the *SS Wimbledon* case of 1923 before the Permanent Court of International Justice, where the court found that the Treaty of Versailles contained special provisions for the Kiel Canal in Germany. It concluded that the underlying idea of this regime was not to be sought via analogy to other rules on other waterways but by arguing *a contrario*, and thus excluded these other general rules (case of the *SS Wimbledon*, PCIJ Series A. No. 1 (1923), pp. 23–4).
[7] Case concerning the *United States Diplomatic and Consular Staff in Tehran*, ICJ Reports (1980), p. 40, para 86.
[8] Fragmentation of International Law: Difficulties Arising from the Diversification and Expansion of International Law, Report of the Study Group of the International Law Commission, A/CN.4/L.682, 13 April 2006, Nos. 124, 125.

3.2 RELEVANCE OF CONVENTIONAL INTERNATIONAL LAW

respective administrative rules, which seek precedence in regard to general international law.[9]

With respect to the WTO, the term self-contained regime is mostly[10] used in that broader sense to express general concerns that the organization operates, at least to some extent, in isolation from public international law, that it seeks to maintain a monopoly over interpretation and application of its law and that it purports to exclude recourse to other fora.[11] This would be especially relevant to the interpretation of the general exceptions in Article XX, since these concern policies outside the WTO's core competency of international trade. If the WTO were considered to be a closed self-contained regime, recourse to either general international law or to other specific fields of international law would not be allowed when dealing with non-trade policies and interests.

However, none of the special treaty regimes existing today can be characterized as a closed 'self-contained regime' in the sense of a treaty regime that operates in total isolation of general international law.[12] While it has been observed that due to its narrow focus on tariffs, the GATT 1947 operated largely as a self-contained regime, this conclusion cannot be reached for the WTO with its much wider subject coverage and its quasi-judiciary which touches frequently upon other regulatory areas.[13] Although views on the status of the GATT differ, it is nevertheless widely recognized that the WTO cannot be considered a self-contained regime.[14] The WTO covered agreements contain institutionalized links to international law, for example, in DSU Article 3.2, which establishes that the dispute settlement

[9] Koskenniemi and Mosley (2004), p. 127.
[10] See, however, Bartels (2002), who endorses the position that WTO law supersedes general international law with respect to the limitation of secondary rules to countermeasures as authorized by dispute settlement, at pp. 391–401. This finding may be justified for the dispute settlement system, but should not be extended to the set of rules forming the organization as a whole (cf. Fragmentation of International Law Report, above fn. 8, No. 134, also Pauwelyn (2003), p. 39).
[11] Report of the International Law Commission (ILC) on the work of its fifty-sixth session (2004), A/CN.4/549, of 31 January 2005, paras. 123–4.
[12] ILC, (2004), A/CN.4/549, of 31 January 2005, para. 122.
[13] Cottier and Oesch (2005), p. 513.
[14] See, e.g., against the GATT as a self-contained regime: Kuijper (1994), p. 228; Hahn (1996), p. 161; for the GATT as a self-contained regime Charnovitz (2001a), p. 793; against the WTO as a closed self-contained regime, e.g., Pauwelyn (2003), p. 37; Koskenniemi and Leino (2002), p. 571; Marceau (1999), pp. 107, 108 and (2002), pp. 766, 767; Charnovitz (2001a), p. 793; Mavroidis (2000b), p. 765; Palmeter and Mavroidis (1998), p. 413. Also the Consultative Board on the Future of the WTO (2004) did not consider the WTO as a self-contained regime. It stated: 'The WTO legal system is part of the international legal system, but it is a *lex specialis*.' (*The Future of the WTO*, p. 39, No. 168).

system serves 'to clarify the existing provisions of those agreements in accordance with customary rules of interpretation of public international law'. Based on this provision, the Appellate Body stated in even more general terms that this 'direction reflects a measure of recognition that the *General Agreement* is not to be read in clinical isolation from public international law'.[15]

As opposed to the norms at issue in the *Kiel Canal* case, the multilateral trading system established by the WTO Agreements is almost globally applicable and indirectly affects most areas of social life. Therefore, it seems clear that the agreements covered by the GATT and the WTO are integral parts of the larger system of public international law,[16] and that the proposition that the WTO constitutes a closed self-contained regime must be dismissed. Beyond that, however, uncertainty remains about the relationship between public international law and WTO law.

3.2.2 General applicability of international law

While in scholarly literature, there is near consensus in dismissing the proposition of the WTO as a self-contained regime, the actual consequences of this finding are highly controversial. It seems that the majority of scholars express doubts as to a general exclusion of international law from the scope of applicable law. Van Damme, for instance, holds that it 'is not a question of whether general international law applies, but when and how much general international law applies, and whether secondary and/or primary rules apply'.[17] Indeed, declining application of general international law, including general principles such as due process and good faith, would contradict the nature of the WTO Agreements as international treaties.[18] There is much more hesitance on the part of scholars, as well as the dispute settlement bodies, in applying treaties from different sub-systems of international law; for instance, multilateral environmental agreements.[19] The applicability of general principles of international law, however, does not help in the increasing number of cases under WTO

---

[15] Appellate Body report, *US – Gasoline* (1996), p. 17, after fn. 34.
[16] Matsushita, Schoenbaum and Mavroidis (2004), p. 76.
[17] Van Damme (2009), p. 21.
[18] Van Damme (2009), p. 19; in this sense also Marceau (2001), p. 1081; Pauwelyn (2003), p. 27.
[19] Tietje (2006), at pp. 194, 195, holds that MEAs are not directly applicable, but is in favour of taking MEAs into account when interpreting WTO law.

3.2 RELEVANCE OF CONVENTIONAL INTERNATIONAL LAW

dispute settlement, where parties claim that a particular international treaty is applicable.

WTO law itself lacks a general clarification of the applicable sources of law.[20] Only in rare cases do the WTO covered agreements contain explicit rules. Obviously, other conventional international law is applicable in the rare event that the WTO covered agreements so provide, as, for example, in the case of protection of intellectual property in TRIPS Article 1.[21] There is also an instance of explicit reference to certain rules of customary international law in DSU Article 3.2, which stipulates that the existing provisions of the covered agreements are to be clarified 'in accordance with customary rules of interpretation of public international law'. The rules of interpretation laid down in VCLT Article 31 and 32, which are regarded as having attained the status of rules of customary or general international law, are therefore considered to be applicable.[22] Another customary rule, namely, the principle of effective treaty interpretation, has been accepted by the adjudicatory bodies as a corollary of the general rules of interpretation contained in the VCLT.[23] Jurisprudence under both the GATT and WTO has also confirmed the applicability of a few general principles of law, such as the principle of *abus de droit*.[24] The status of the remaining body of general international law, including conflict rules, however, is unclear under the terms of the agreement. For this reason, the prevailing view holds that there is no direct applicability of multilateral agreements in WTO dispute settlement procedures.

A supporter of the broader applicability of general international law is Pauwelyn, who pleads for application of 'the entire universe of legal norms' relevant to a case to assess the validity of a WTO claim.[25] His motive is twofold: on the one hand, he seeks to preserve the unity of international law through a process of horizontal and vertical integration and through the prevention of contradictory decisions on the same subject by different international tribunals,[26] while on the other hand, he acknowledges the diversity of WTO members, which implies that WTO law must yield

---

[20] In this respect, the DSU differs from statutes of other international judicial bodies, such as the International Court of Justice or the International Criminal Court (cf. Van Damme (2009), p. 13).
[21] Matsushita, Schoenbaum and Mavroidis (2004), pp. 67–9; Ohlhoff (2003), Recital 40.
[22] For Article 31: prevailing view since Appellate Body Report, *US – Gasoline* (1996), p.17; for Article 32: prevailing view since Appellate Body Report, *Japan – Alcoholic Beverages II* (1996), p. 10.
[23] Appellate Body Report, *US – Gasoline* (1996), p. 23, with fn. 45.
[24] Appellate Body Report, *Shrimp Turtle* (1998), para. 158.
[25] Pauwelyn (2003), pp. 117–18, 461.   [26] Pauwelyn (2003), pp. 117–18.

to more specific law.²⁷ Pauwelyn argues that a different approach would necessarily violate the principle of *pacta sunt servanda*, since otherwise states could escape the obligations to which they had agreed outside the realm of the WTO, as these would not be applicable inside the safe haven of WTO dispute settlement.²⁸ Additionally, since the DSU had been created and existed within the system of international law, no confirmation that general international law applies to the WTO treaty would be needed.²⁹ Pauwelyn finds that references to some rules of international law, for example, in DSU Article 3.2, do not imply an exclusion of others. Therefore, unless the WTO treaty has contracted out of international law, the latter continues to apply.³⁰ Pauwelyn emphasizes that WTO rules 'apply differently to different WTO members depending on whether or not they have accepted other non-WTO rules', and that there is a complicated matrix of rights and obligations between WTO members.³¹ Given the high number of multilateral treaties and the high number of WTO members, it seems natural that the legal relations among different WTO members diverge. According to Pauwelyn, this approach should be adopted not only by the WTO adjudicatory bodies, but by all international tribunals. He grants that with his approach decisions of different tribunals might conflict if different interpretations of the same norms were applied by different tribunals. However, in order to avoid this situation, Pauwelyn suggests that international tribunals should take into account each other's decisions and judgments.³²

Pauwelyn puts forward more arguments to support his view. Not entirely convincing, however, is the argument that the terms of Article 38:1 of the Statute of the International Court of Justice have effectively been brought into WTO dispute settlement by Articles 3:2 and 7 of the DSU.³³ Article 38(1) is neither a rule of interpretation, nor is the ICJ Statute a set of rules applicable between the parties. Others, however, have argued that DSU Article 3.2 relates to VCLT Article 31:3(c),³⁴ and so creates a link between any relevant rule of international law applicable between the parties and WTO law. Also, the adjudicatory bodies should be able to

---

[27] Pauwelyn (2003), pp. 487–92.   [28] Pauwelyn (2003), pp. 117, 118.
[29] Marceau (2001), p. 1081, Pauwelyn (2003), pp. 465–7.
[30] Pauwelyn (2003), p. 465.   [31] Pauwelyn (2003), p. 476.
[32] Pauwelyn (2003), p. 118.
[33] Palmeter and Mavroidis (1998), p. 399. As a dogmatic argument this is not convincing, since Article 38 of the Statute of the ICJ is not a rule 'applicable in the relations between the parties', as requested by VCLT Article 31:3(c), to which DSU Article 3:2 refers. Article 38 of the Statute merely regulates procedures before the ICJ.
[34] Prevailing view since Appellate Body Report, *US – Gasoline* (1996), p. 17.

3.2 RELEVANCE OF CONVENTIONAL INTERNATIONAL LAW

apply all rules applicable between the parties, since DSU Article 11 grants panels authority to 'make such other findings as will assist the DSB in making the recommendations'.[35]

Not surprisingly, Pauwelyn's view has also prompted criticism. Trachtman[36] rejects applicability of international treaties, as this would imply that human rights or environmental treaties could modify WTO obligations. Trachtman points out that even if other international law is applicable between WTO member states, this does not imply that the law is also applicable in WTO dispute settlement. He holds that international legal tribunals are courts of limited jurisdiction that may apply law only to the extent authorized in their mandates, and that in the case of the DSU the affirmative mandate is defined as the covered agreements. He concedes that there is an 'interfunctional choice-of-law problem, between law that arises in different sectors of the international legal system', but criticizes Pauwelyn of trying to impose a particular order where none exists. Trachtman does not dispute, however, that general international law may be used to interpret WTO law.

Nevertheless, while the applicability of international treaties as yet remains controversial, the view that adjudicatory bodies should in principle be able to apply all rules of international law to the extent necessary to solve a dispute is preferred by this author.[37] Sir Hersch Lauterpacht made the important finding that treaties rank first in the hierarchical order of the sources of international law.[38] Given the importance of international treaties and considering that the WTO does not stand in clinical isolation from international law, the conclusion that international treaties must also be taken into consideration by the WTO dispute settlement bodies seems necessary. Even though doctrinal reservations as to the mandate of the dispute settlement bodies may remain, the reality of an ever larger body of international treaties cannot be ignored. In private law, it is well accepted that courts apply foreign law if national law or the will of the

---

[35] Matsushita, Schoenbaum and Mavroidis (2004), p. 24; Pauwelyn (2003), p. 469.
[36] Trachtman (2004), pp. 855–61.
[37] Marceau (1999) opines that not all sources of law may be applied under the DSU (p. 110). Marceau's view is based on the presumption that this would imply allowing WTO panels and the Appellate Body the 'enforcement of outside obligations', and therefore she concludes that this would overload the multilateral trading system. This, however, is rather a question of jurisdiction (see above), not of the law applicable, since only claims under the WTO covered agreements can be subject to dispute settlement. Marceau limits the role of other international law consequently to a tool of interpretation for WTO law, on this subject see below at Chapter 5, section 5.1.1.
[38] Lauterpacht (1970), p. 87.

parties so requires. It would be curious if the Appellate Body, in order to fulfil its explicit task of deciding on questions of law, were required to ignore law applicable between the parties to a dispute, even in cases where applicability of certain treaties would be demanded by both parties.

In sum, it is generally acknowledged that some general principles of international law are directly applicable in WTO law, and there are strong arguments for likewise applying conventional international law.[39] For the purposes of this analysis, it is important to note that affirming the general applicability of the huge body of conventional international law neither predetermines the applicability of specific international treaties for a certain dispute, nor does it imply which norm ultimately prevails in the case of conflict.

3.2.3 Conflicts with other international treaties and instruments

Applicability of non-WTO international law implies a potential for conflicts. From the huge body of international law all rules that are relevant according to their *ratione materiae* and *ratione personae* may be applicable. If different norms apply, conflicts may arise.

A precise determination of scope and legal consequences of the norms in question is needed in order to decide on the existence or not of a conflict of norms. In the case of a finding of conflict, the question of whether a treaty norm indeed prevails over the conflicting WTO provision then needs to be answered by conflict rules, which could be spelled out in the WTO covered agreements, in the treaty from which the conflicting norm derives or in general international law.[40] Section 3.2.3.1 focuses on the definition of a conflict of norms, with section 3.2.3.2 summing up applicable conflict rules.[41]

3.2.3.1 Existence of a conflict of norms

According to a narrow definition, a conflict of norms arises if various norms apply to the same facts (*ratione materiae*) and contain contradictory

---

[39] An entirely different question is the relevance of international treaties for interpretation of the WTO covered agreements, which will be discussed below in the context of Article XX, see below at Chapter 5, section 5.1.1.

[40] Pauwelyn (2003), pp. 473, 436–9.

[41] The rules on interpretation, which may in many cases lead to a negation of conflict in the first place, are discussed in Chapter 5 below with respect to a GATT provision, for which interpretation is of paramount relevance, namely, Article XX (at Chapter 5, section 5.1.1).

3.2 RELEVANCE OF CONVENTIONAL INTERNATIONAL LAW

obligations to the same body or person (*ratione personae*). Merely different or diverging provisions are not sufficient for the finding of a conflict.[42] The WTO adjudicatory bodies have confirmed a narrow definition of conflict, under which only mutually exclusive provisions can be regarded as conflicting.[43] The role which international treaties have actually played in WTO dispute settlement is indeed small. So far, not one measure based on a multilateral environmental agreement (MEA) has actually been challenged before GATT/WTO dispute settlement. The reason may be that the vast majority of international conventions do not contain any trade measures. Even if they do, conflict potential with respect to WTO law can be regarded as limited, since many provisions fall to some extent within the scope of the general exceptions in Article XX(b) and (g).[44]

With respect to the *ratione materiae*, some authors consider the potential for conflicts, particularly between MEAs and the WTO Agreements, extremely low. Puth, for instance, argues that due to the principle of sustainable development as adopted in the 1992 Rio Declaration on Environment and Development[45] (Rio Declaration) and the accompanying Agenda 21, the potential for conflicts has declined. Since the principle of sustainable development is reflected in the preamble of the Marrakesh Agreement, and since the concept of sustainable development comprises both systems, namely, international trade law and international environmental law, it would in Puth's view be alien to the system to assume irresolvable conflicts between both sets of norms. Following the Rio Declaration, the concept ought to be taken into account in the drafting process of international conventions, so that conflicts of norms would be excluded from the outset. Prior conventions, on the other hand, ought to be interpreted in a harmonizing way according to the postulate of

---

[42] The narrow definition of a conflict of norms is not uncontested, see, e.g., Vranes (2009a), pp. 19–21. Some authors advocate a wider definition, according to which, e.g., permissions that are incompatible with obligations under other treaties would also be solved by conflict rules (e.g., Vranes (2009a) pp. 30–7; Pauwelyn (2003)). This section shows that the existence or not of a conflict of norms and the applicability of conflict rules needs to be determined on a case-by-case basis, taking into account the parties involved and the treaties and provisions that may lead to such conflict.

[43] Appellate Body Report, *Guatemala – Cement I* (1998), para. 65; Panel Report, *Indonesia – Automobiles* (1998), No. 14.99.

[44] Neumayer (2002) considers it far from clear that the measures provided for in the Montreal Protocol, CITES, the Basel Convention and the CBD might conflict with WTO norms, while he sees sufficient potential for conflicts between the Cartagena Protocol on Biosafety and the SPS Agreement (at pp. 147–50).

[45] United Nations General Assembly, Report of the United Nations Conference on Environment and Development, A/CONF.151/26 (Vol. I), of 12 August 1992.

integration, which is inherent to the principle of sustainable development. Agreements covered by MEAs and the WTO therefore co-exist on equal footing and without conflict.[46] Puth concludes that the concept of sustainable development not only allows, but actually requires, the rejection of conflicts between MEAs and the WTO covered agreements, making the application of conflict rules superfluous.[47]

Puth's view is closely related to the concept of harmonizing interpretation of general international law. This concept has been developed based on the assumption of good faith, which implies that states have taken their other obligations under international law into account when negotiating international treaties, so that their obligations are to be regarded as cumulative rather than exclusive.[48] Moreover, VCLT Article 31.3(c) requires that 'any relevant rules of international law' should be taken into account, and so promotes coherence in international law. However, the presumption against conflict in international law must not be overstated. It merely serves to place the burden of proof for relying on a provision of a new law on the party claiming that the new law prevails over the old law.[49] While in many cases interpretation may be sufficient to avoid a finding of conflict between MEAs and the WTO covered agreements,[50] it would not be reasonable to assume the absence of conflict in general. Given the increasing body of bilateral, regional and multilateral treaties, a considerable overlap in subject matter and the asymmetry of parties to the respective agreements the potential for conflict cannot be ignored.

Also, by ascribing this meaning to sustainable development as reflected in the Rio Declaration, this principle is elevated to a rule of interpretation of general international law comparable to the rules on interpretation contained in the VCLT. This, however, is not in line with the legal quality of the Rio Declaration, regardless of the large number (178) of governments that adopted the declaration. Rather than constituting evidence of a certain legal quality, the large number may well be a consequence of the character of the declaration as an advisory statement of purpose, thus constituting 'soft law' that is not binding on the signatories.[51] While

---

[46] Puth (2003), pp. 160, 161. [47] Puth (2003), p. 167.
[48] Marceau (2001), p. 1089, referring to Wilfried Jenks, The Conflict of Law-Making Treaties, *British Yearbook of International Law* (1953), 425 *et seq.*
[49] Pauwelyn (2003), p. 244.
[50] This view is supported by Marceau (2001), pp. 1089–90, and firmly rejected by Vranes (2009a), p. 21, who stresses that coherence cannot be achieved by defining away evident problems.
[51] Wirth (1995), p. 602.

3.2 RELEVANCE OF CONVENTIONAL INTERNATIONAL LAW 131

the Rio Declaration has been most influential at the political stage, the principle of sustainable development has not yet been codified in an agreement. Although the principle is mentioned in the preamble of the Marrakesh Agreement establishing the WTO, and therefore may indeed be invoked to 'add colour, texture and shading' to the adjudicatory bodies' interpretation of the agreements,[52] applying the principle of sustainable development to generally negate conflicts with MEAs over-emphasizes this principle vis-à-vis the texts of MEAs and the WTO Agreements as 'hard' international law. Respect for the sovereign drafters of international agreements means giving importance to the text of conflicting provisions and to the text of the treaties.

For the finding of a conflict, the *ratione personae* of two norms also needs to overlap. The question arises if relevant international treaties, the contracting parties of which are not identical to WTO members, can possibly be relevant under WTO law. Since WTO membership is large and potentially relevant international conventions are numerous, an incongruent situation will occur frequently. To reiterate, conventional law mentioned in the WTO covered agreements is applicable to the extent to which it is referred. With similar reasoning, panels have applied some other international instruments in a few cases. For instance, the *EC – Bananas III* panel found that the meaning of the Lomé Convention to the extent referred to in the respective waiver had become a GATT/WTO issue.[53] The Appellate Body confirmed this view. Since the GATT contracting parties had granted a waiver for certain GATT provisions to the EU, limited to the extent necessary for what was required by the Lomé Convention, the adjudicatory bodies found that they had no alternative but to determine what the relevant provisions of the Lomé Convention actually required.[54] In a few other instances, panels also decided to apply bilateral agreements, because of a close connection between the agreement in question and the GATT, because the agreement was consistent with GATT objectives, and because both parties had requested recourse to GATT arbitration or did not object application of the agreement in question, respectively.[55]

In sum, the relevance of conventional law not referred to in the agreements covered by the WTO remains problematic, both with respect to the *ratione materiae* and the *ratione personae*. Since it is almost impossible

[52] Appellate Body Report, *Shrimp Turtle* (1998), paras. 153, 155.
[53] Panel Report, *EC – Bananas* (1997), No. 7.98.
[54] Appellate Body Report, *EC – Bananas* (1997), paras. 164–7.
[55] Arbitration award in *Canada/European Communities* (1990), pp. 4, 5; Panel Report, *EC – Poultry* (1998), paras. 196–201.

that parties to a specific international treaty are identical to WTO membership, most conflict situations would involve at least one WTO member also bound by a multilateral treaty. Therefore, it is necessary to distinguish between conflict situations based on the extent of congruence or not of WTO members and signatories of the respective treaty.

3.2.3.2 Applicable conflict rules

In contrast to the NAFTA, which in Article 104 lays down explicit rules for cases of inconsistencies between its provisions and certain environmental and conservation agreements, the agreements covered by the WTO do not contain any explicit rules for dealing with conflicts between prior or later conventional law. Since the norms of general international law are applicable in WTO law, the prevailing conflict rules apply.[56] Accordingly, it is clear that peremptory norms of international law prevail over trade rules.[57] While the relevance of this rule seems small, it implies that at least those human rights that constitute *ius cogens* would prevail if in conflict with WTO law.[58] Likewise, obligations *erga omnes* are applicable in the relations of all WTO members.[59]

The most relevant conflict rules are contained in the VCLT, for example, in Article 30. In order to be applicable, the rules reflected in the VCLT would need to have attained the status of general international law, since not all WTO members have signed the VCLT, and since the conflict rules are not part of the rules on interpretation mentioned in DSU Article 3.2. While prevailing case law in GATT/WTO jurisprudence holds that VCLT Articles 31 and 32 merely reflect customary international law, the adjudicatory bodies have not so far determined the status of other articles of the VCLT. The VCLT contains conflict provisions based on widely recognized traditional legal rules, such as *lex posterior derogat legi priori*. The prevailing view holds that the VCLT in general essentially codifies customary international law,[60] and that it is therefore applicable in relations among WTO members.[61] Vranes, for instance, argues that the above

---

[56] Pauwelyn (2003), p. 356.   [57] See also VCLT Article 53.
[58] Cottier (2002), p. 114. Cleveland (2002) points out that none of the major human rights treaties allows for unilateral sanctions, p. 153.
[59] With respect to human rights, Cottier, Pauwelyn and Bürgi recommend that WTO panels ought to disapply trade law if and when under international law human rights law prevails, Cottier, Pauwelyn and Bürgi (2005b), p. 24.
[60] E.g., Wallace (2002), p. 230.
[61] McRae (2000), p. 38; Pauwelyn (2001), p. 545, Marceau (2001), p. 1095, fn. 33 (for the *lex posterior* and *lex specialis* rules); Pauwelyn (2003), p. 148, cites the law of treaties as a prominent example for general customary international law, see also p. 315.

conflict rules, whether codified or not, simply derive from the structure of any legal order and are ultimately inherent in the necessary task of determining the sense of a legislator's – or a sovereign state's – enactments.[62] Even the United States, as the most important trading nation which has not yet ratified the VCLT, has apparently recognized that the convention is a 'primary source of international law concerning treaties, even for non-parties',[63] albeit pointing out that not all provisions of the VCLT are a mere codification of customary international law. Although not mentioned in the VCLT, the rule *lex specialis derogat legi generali* is also widely supported in doctrine[64] and thus applicable in WTO law.[65]

3.2.3.2.1 Asymmetrical conflicts

The asymmetrical conflict situation occurs in the case of a dispute between one WTO member that has ratified a relevant treaty, including norms in conflict with GATT rules, and another WTO member that is not bound by the same treaty. Here, the conflict rule in VCLT Article 30:4(b) comes into consideration, which stipulates that in the case of 'a State party to both treaties and a State party to only one of several treaties, the treaty to which both States are parties governs their mutual rights and obligations'. In this case it is irrelevant which of the treaties precedes the other one. Article 30:4(b) is simply a confirmation of the *pacta tertiis* rule in VCLT Article 34.[66] It could therefore additionally be regarded as a conflict-avoiding rather than a conflict-solving rule, since the relationship between both parties is governed by the earlier treaty only and no conflict between the parties of the specific dispute can possibly arise.[67] This,

---

[62] Vranes (2009a), pp. 45–50.
[63] Congressional Research Service, Treaties and Other International Agreements; The Role of the United States Senate, A Study Prepared for the Committee on Foreign Relations, 106th Congress, 2nd Session, S. Pt. 106–71, pp. 43, 44.
[64] Sinclair (1984), p. 96; Fragmentation of International Law: Difficulties Arising from the Diversification and Expansion of International Law, Report of the Study Group of the International Law Commission, Draft conclusions of the work of the Study Group, A/CN.4/L.682/Add. 1, 2 May 2006, p. 5, No. 5.
[65] The General interpretative note to Annex 1A reflects an application of the *lex specialis* rule in WTO law, albeit limited to conflicts within the WTO Agreements. For application of the rule to conflicts between WT law see Marceau (2001), p. 1092 (and fn. 27 with further references), p. 1095; Verdross and Simma (1984), Article 640.
[66] VCLT Article 34: 'A treaty does not create either obligations or rights for a third State without its consent.'
[67] Pauwelyn (2003), pp. 383–4, 427–9. In consequence of this rule, however, the state bound by both treaties will be unable to fulfil its obligations under one treaty without breaching the other one. The consequences for this state are subject to the rules on state responsibility and not subject of this analysis.

however, does not preclude the situation where a party that is a signatory to an international treaty containing conflicting provisions finds itself in a position where it is necessary to act in breach of one international contract in order to comply with another one. As a corollary of such action, conflicts with other contracting parties to that treaty may arise which, however, would then possibly be governed by the violated treaty. In sum, the agreement to which both states are parties is applicable in their relations, while the other agreement is not.

3.2.3.2.2 Symmetrical conflicts

In contrast, the symmetrical conflict situation is characterized by the fact that all parties to a dispute are signatories to the same successive treaties which nevertheless contain conflicting provisions. This situation of conflicting norms arises if an NPA measure that is prescribed by, or under, a broader conflict definition, based on a successive multilateral treaty norm violates GATT obligations. Given the huge number of WTO members and, as a corollary, the difficulties in amending the covered agreements it seems preferable that the legal relationships among WTO members differ to some degree. Otherwise, the agreements could easily become 'a collection of rules "written in stone"'.[68] WTO members would actually be prevented from moving forward in other areas of international law by way of international treaties, in as far as the potential for conflict with WTO norms might arise. VCLT Article 30:4(a), read together with Article 30:3, prescribes for that particular situation of a symmetrical conflict, that the provisions of the earlier treaty are applicable only to the extent they are compatible with the later treaty. Although there are good arguments against application of that provision, the basic idea expressed and codified by the VCLT is that obligations under an international treaty with more than two members are not necessarily the same in the legal relationships among all members.[69] For determining these relationships, however, it is necessary to determine the appropriate conflict rule governing a particular conflict.

---

[68] Pauwelyn (2003), p. 475.
[69] For a unity of WTO law in this sense, however, Marceau (2001), p. 1105. The consequence of this view would be that WTO law would indeed be applied in isolation of other international law, a result that the Appellate Body has explicitly rejected in *US – Gasoline* (1996), p. 17, after fn. 34. The *EC – Biotech* (2006) Panel's argumentation against a treaty's relevance as an interpretative tool must be read in the context of an asymmetrical situation (see below Chapter 5, section 5.1.1).

3.2 RELEVANCE OF CONVENTIONAL INTERNATIONAL LAW

In the case of a symmetrical conflict, the *lex posterior* rule would come into consideration. In some cases, for example, if in the above instance both WTO members have also ratified the CITES, applying this rule would lead to a number of difficulties. The problem is not that the rule does not apply because the treaties in their entirety do not regulate the same subject matter, and that therefore Article 30 of the VCLT would not be applicable.[70] Even if the WTO covered agreements regulate trade, other international instruments deal with the same subject matter in as far as they contain trade-related provisions. It is the specific provisions at issue, rather than the treaties in their entirety which are capable of creating a genuine conflict.[71] Even when it is considered that the subject matter is identical and the provisions are in conflict, it is the timeline for the conclusion of the treaties that would provide problems for the application of the *lex posterior* rule. For instance, it could be argued that the CITES prevails over possibly conflicting rules of the GATT 1947. However, it could easily be argued that the WTO covered agreements, including the GATT 1994 and reinforcing the GATT 1947, prevail over the CITES. Additionally, one would need to take into account the day of accession, which differs considerably for most WTO members and CITES contracting parties, and both the WTO as an organization, and the CITES as an international agreement constitute larger legal frameworks which have evolved over time. The rules of both systems are constantly being confirmed, implemented, adapted and expanded by means of decisions, interpretations and, last but not least, by the accession of new states.[72] According to Pauwelyn, treaties with these features fall into the category of 'continuing' or 'living treaties', which are impossible to deem as preceding or subsequent in any sequential order.[73] Indeed, the *lex posterior* rules contained in Article 30 do not go well with the complexities arising from international treaties with memberships of a hundred or more, for instance, establishing an organization with bodies authorized to make decisions, as opposed to the relatively simple relationships created in bilateral treaties. Pauwelyn is, therefore, right in concluding that it would arguably be against the will of the contracting parties or members and would lead to arbitrary solutions to 'freeze' these rules by artificially allotting a certain point of time to a treaty as an instrument.[74] Hence, the *lex posterior* rule must be rejected

---

[70] This formalistic argument is made by Puth (2003), p. 164, who rejects applying VCLT Article 30 for this reason.
[71] Pauwelyn (2003), p. 367.   [72] Pauwelyn (2003), p. 379.
[73] Pauwelyn (2003), pp. 378, 379.   [74] Pauwelyn (2003), p. 380.

in the case of the CITES and for other treaties succeeding the agreements covered by the WTO.[75]

From a different perspective, an MEA that has been concluded after the WTO Agreements, contains trade-related provisions, and has been ratified by nearly all WTO members, such as the CITES, could constitute a modification of the WTO Agreements in the sense of VCLT Article 41.[76] The legality of such an *inter se* agreement, which (as opposed to an amendment) modifies the legal rights and obligations under the WTO covered agreements for the states participating in that agreement, would need to be assessed under this provision.[77] A crucial condition for the legality of a modification under Article 41 is that the MEA does not affect 'the enjoyment by other parties of their rights' under the WTO Agreements.[78] MEA provisions which allow for justification of measures beyond GATT Article XX for signatory states could well be able to affect actual trade flows, but would certainly not affect the rights of other WTO members.[79] Consequently, a modification could be allowed and the legal relations between the WTO members party to the *inter se* agreement would be modified accordingly.[80] Since the rights and obligations would then be modified, there would be no need to apply the conflict rules contained in Article 30.[81] However, there are two important arguments against applying the rules on modifications as contained in VCLT Article 41. First, the provisions in the VCLT regarding amendments and modifications of international treaties indicate that they regard intentional and express amendments and modifications. This would, for example, explain why both VCLT Articles 40 and 41 provide for notification requirements regarding all other contracting states. MEAs or other multilateral treaties containing trade-related provisions are not, however, negotiated in order

---

[75] Against an application of these rules also Hilf (2000), pp. 483, 484.
[76] Pauwelyn (2003), pp. 315–18.
[77] The reason is that according to VCLT Article 30:5, Article 41 prevails over Article 30:4. See also Pauwelyn (2003), p. 382.
[78] VCLT Article 41:1(b)(ii). [79] Pauwelyn (2003), pp. 318, 319.
[80] In favour of the applicability of MEAs as *inter se* agreements modifying the legal relations among the signatories is, e.g., Mavroidis (2000b), p. 77.
[81] Pauwelyn, in contrast, sees a persisting conflict of norms between the *inter se* agreement and the earlier treaty. Pauwelyn (2003), pp. 382–3. His view, however, means ignoring the nature of a modification. With the modification, the legal relations between the parties are transformed, so that there is no room for conflict between them. However, the same effect would be reached by applying the conflict rules in Article 30:4(a) together with Article 30:3, namely, that the later agreement (the *inter se* agreement) would prevail.

3.2 RELEVANCE OF CONVENTIONAL INTERNATIONAL LAW

to amend or modify other treaties.[82] It seems that this situation is better referred to the conflict rules on successive treaties as laid down in Article 30. Second, and perhaps more important, there are difficulties in determining a chronological order of different multilateral treaty regimes as described above. Additionally, since the WTO must be considered a continuing or living treaty regime, just as the *lex posterior* rule, Article 41 on treaty modifications with its specific requirements cannot in general apply to the relationship between the agreements covered by the WTO and other conventional international law.

Since neither the *lex posterior* rule nor rules on modifications apply with respect to the WTO Agreements, the principle *lex specialis derogat legi generali* comes into consideration. The first precondition for applying the *lex specialis* rule is that both norms address the same subject matter in a general sense, and that one of them addresses a certain aspect of that matter in a more special or concrete way. It has been argued that the WTO covered agreements and other international instruments often do not deal with the same subject matter, in as far as the latter instruments contain environmental or other social policies.[83] Crucial, however, is the content of the norm in question. Moreover, if international instruments include trade-related provisions, such as authorizations for restrictions of trade in certain products, then these specific norms concern the same subject matter as the GATT, namely, trade in goods, but in a more specific way. Whether or not a conflicting provision in an international treaty constitutes *lex specialis* vis-à-vis the GATT, must be determined on a case-by-case basis. However, since the basic principles and provisions of the GATT apply to trade in general and with respect to all groups of products, and the conflicting treaty's trade effects may be limited to specific products and possibly even be combined with special circumstances or NPAs, the *lex specialis* rule will in many instances lead to the non-WTO provision prevailing over the WTO provision.[84] This line of thinking is, for example, confirmed in NAFTA which gives priority to trade obligations contained in certain environmental and conservation agreements.[85]

---

[82] In this sense also Puth (2003), pp. 166, 167.
[83] Schlagenhof (1995), p. 150, with respect to the Montreal Protocol on Substances that Deplete the Ozone Layer, Winter (2003), p. 137, with respect to the CITES.
[84] Pauwelyn (2003), p. 389.
[85] NAFTA Article 104:1 reads: 'In the event of any inconsistency between this Agreement and the specific trade obligations set out in: (a) the Convention on International Trade in Endangered Species of Wild Fauna and Flora ... (b) the Montreal Protocol on Substances that Deplete the Ozone Layer ... (c) the Basel Convention on the Control of Transboundary Movements of Hazardous Wastes and Their Disposal ... or (d) the

138   PRELIMINARY CONSIDERATIONS

To summarize, provisions in international agreements allowing for trade-restricting measures, with the trade restrictions limited to certain products and to specific circumstances, will often constitute *lex specialis* as compared with general GATT obligations. This conclusion applies to all trade-related provisions in international agreements whether or not they are linked to NPAs. This finding does not imply a modification of the WTO Agreements, since only the legal relations amongst WTO members also party to the respective international agreement are affected.

3.2.3.3   Conflicts of norms, NPAs and the example of CITES

While the discussion on conflicts of international norms is highly interesting and most relevant against the backdrop of an increasing fragmentation of international law, it may be less relevant to the legal status of NPA measures under WTO law than one might assume. An example for an international treaty with potentially conflicting provisions is the Convention on International Trade in Endangered Species of Wild Flora and Fauna (CITES). A WTO member having ratified CITES may, for example, provide for the confiscation or return to the state of export of certain specimens, if specimens are traded in violation of the convention (CITES Article VIII:1). The CITES mainly restricts trade in certain endangered species, and therefore whole groups of products according to their physical characteristics. However, some trade restrictions contained in the CITES relate specifically to NPAs.

For instance, since the CITES regards trade in *wild* flora and fauna, the domesticated forms of some prohibited species are excluded from the convention.[86] Other restrictions apply to specimens from populations stemming from certain regions, but not to specimens of the same species from other regions – also in these cases, the distinction does not refer to physical differences between the restricted products and unrestricted like products. Some specimens are exempt from restrictions subject to PPMs: for example, some restrictions do not apply to specimens of certain fauna species that have been artificially propagated.[87] Measures implementing these rules must therefore distinguish between identical

---

agreements set out in Annex 104.1, such obligations shall prevail to the extent of the inconsistency, provided that where a Party has a choice among equally effective and reasonably available means of complying with such obligations, the Party chooses the alternative that is the least inconsistent with the other provisions of this Agreement.'

[86] E.g., CITES Appendix I, *Bos Gaurus* and *Bos Mutus*.
[87] E.g., CITES Appendix II, *Euphorbia* spp.

3.2 RELEVANCE OF CONVENTIONAL INTERNATIONAL LAW   139

products based on their geographical origin and on the way in which they have been propagated.

A CITES member's requirement to present permits and certificates as provided for in CITES on importation of *Euphorbia trigona* shall serve as an example for a possible conflict of norms with the GATT. According to CITES Article IV, states having ratified the CITES shall require the prior presentation of either an export permit or a re-export certificate on the importation of any specimen of a species listed in Appendix II, including the specimen *Euphorbia trigona*. This obligation, however, does not apply to artificially propagated specimens of *Euphorbia trigona*.

For the purposes of the example, it is assumed that both the importing country A and the exporting country B are WTO members and CITES signatories. Given that the CITES entered into force in 1975 and had almost universal membership of 175 states as at 31 December 2009, and that as of 14 March 2007, 138 CITES members were concurrently WTO members, at which date the WTO had a membership of 150 in total,[88] this setting is most likely. In the example, the first precondition for a conflict of norms, namely, a total or partial overlap in the *ratione personae*, is met. The CITES regulates international trade in endangered species, thus trade in specific goods. Therefore, an overlap with the *ratione materiae* regulated by the GATT is also apparent.

According to the narrow definition, however, an overlap does not necessarily imply a conflict. In order for the above considerations on conflicts to apply, it is necessary to further assess whether the CITES requires its members to implement the above measures in a way that actually contradicts that member's obligations under the GATT. This assessment requires a precise analysis on scope of application and legal consequences of the norms in question. In order for a conflict to arise, there needs to be a violation of the GATT.

For example, an exporter situated in country B and trying to export wild *Euphorbia trigona* specimen into the territory of country A might fail to present export permits. Country A, aware of its obligations under CITES, could decide to return the products to country B. Country B could now claim that the import restriction introduced by country A constitutes a violation of A's obligations under the GATT, namely, a quantitative restriction prohibited by Article XI, and a violation of the GATT obligation to provide MFN treatment under Article 1, since artificially propagated

---

[88] For an overview of membership in some of the most important MEAs and the WTO see the matrix on trade measures in: WTO (2007b), pp. 130–8.

specimens of *Euphorbia trigona* imported from other countries are not subject to the import restrictions introduced by A. In the assessment, whether or not B's claim is sound or not, several highly controversial legal issues of WTO law need to be decided, in particular the meaning of 'like products', the scope of Articles III and XI, and, ultimately, the scope of the general exceptions in Article XX. The scope of the general exceptions, which reflect policies often underlying NPAs, is of utmost relevance to the finding of a conflict or not.[89] Should the protection of endangered species fall within the scope of any of the general exceptions and should the measure at issue conform to the requirements stipulated in the chapeau, the finding of a conflict and application of conflict rules would be barred at the outset. In this case, it would be entirely irrelevant whether or not the state restricting imports of endangered species were a CITES signatory or whether the measure was adopted unilaterally, based on the internal political process.

The analysis of the crucial legal issues mentioned above are detailed in the following chapters. The example shows, however, that in many cases of NPA measures – even those adopted in order to comply with international agreements – not so much the rules on conflicts of norms will be decisive, but the analysis of scope and subject matter of the GATT itself.

3.3 NPA measures and the law on state responsibility

Under customary international law on state responsibility, countermeasures come into consideration if a state has committed an illegal act and refuses to negotiate an amicable solution. Countermeasures can then be used as a legitimate tool of persuasion to take up such negotiations[90] and to discontinue with the illicit behaviour by inducing compliance.[91] Countermeasures in this sense are measures to counter violations of rules of international law by other states, and are therefore the exercise of secondary rights, as opposed to measures taken by way of primary right established under an international agreement.[92] Since international instruments often create obligations, but rarely contain enforcement mechanisms, economic sanctions could well be a tool to promote

---

[89] In case a measure would indeed be justified under Article XX, the possibility of also raising a non-violation complaint under the GATT would not lead to a conflict of norms between the GATT and the CITES, since in this case the measure authorized by the CITES would by definition not be in violation of GATT obligations.
[90] Mavroidis (2000b), p. 772.   [91] Pauwelyn (2003), p. 229.
[92] Bartels (2002), p. 392.

3.3 NPA MEASURES AND THE LAW ON STATE RESPONSIBILITY 141

observance of such obligations. This topic is therefore most relevant to NPA trade measures. The question arises as to whether NPA trade bans or other restrictions could be justified as countermeasures under customary international law. This would first of all require that customary international law on state responsibility be applicable in the relations between WTO members.

Against applicability of these rules, it has been suggested that with respect to countermeasures the GATT is a self-contained regime in the sense that both unauthorized countermeasures and countermeasures external to the GATT are prohibited. Bartels argues that since WTO members are not allowed to enforce their WTO rights with countermeasures unless they are authorized to do so, it seems obvious that they should be prohibited from doing so in order to enforce their other rights.[93] Consequently, he suggests not discussing measures in terms of their unilateral or multilateral character, but rather considering whether the measures are exercises of secondary rights in response to a violation of an obligation.[94] Only countermeasures that have been authorized by the WTO would then remain an option for WTO members.[95] This prohibition would apply even if countermeasures were lawful under the rules on state responsibility, and the right to apply countermeasures would be restored only in the case of a breakdown of the WTO system.[96] In support of his claim, Bartels invokes the negotiating history and official documents, as, for instance, a 1982 GATT Ministerial Declaration. In this declaration, the GATT contracting parties undertook 'to abstain from taking restrictive trade measures, for reasons of a non-economic character, not consistent with the General Agreement'.[97] This declaration can be regarded as evidence against the permissibility of trade measures as sanctions or political pressure. Bartels concludes that countermeasures as exercises of merely secondary rights ought not to be permissible under GATT Article XX, even if they would not be prohibited by general rules of state responsibility.[98]

To reiterate, from the point of view of conflict, the claim of a (limited) self-contained regime can be translated into an application of the *lex specialis* rule. The conflict in this case would be between treaty norms and norms of customary international law. Since the rules on state

---

[93] Bartels (2002), pp. 394–6.   [94] Bartels (2002), p. 392.
[95] Bartels (2002), pp. 391–402.   [96] Bartels (2002), p. 395.
[97] Ministerial Declaration on Dispute Settlement, adopted on 29 November 1982, L/5424, BISD 29S/9.
[98] Bartels (2002), p. 402.

responsibility cannot be regarded as *jus cogens*, contracting out must be considered permissible. Treaty law, namely, WTO law, would therefore prevail, provided that the norms at issue contract out of general international law. In other words, there is a presumption of applicability of general international law, which may be rebutted by means of treaty interpretation.[99] Pauwelyn sees this rebuttal as successful in as far as it regards the use of countermeasures for violations of WTO obligations. Not only is the remedy, namely, the suspension of concessions, equated with countermeasures under the WTO Agreements, the objective of the system since the GATT 1947 has also shifted from rebalancing to compliance and, hence, resembles more the structure of the law on state responsibility.[100]

It is necessary, however, to distinguish between countermeasures for breaches of WTO law as authorized by the DSU, on the one hand, and countermeasures to remedy violations of other international law, on the other.[101] The finding that the WTO Agreements contracted out of international law as regards countermeasures for breaches of WTO law does not, however, answer the crucial question for the purposes of this analysis; namely, the question of whether general international law remains applicable regarding breaches of other international law, such as convention obligations with respect to the protection of human rights or the environment, or *ius cogens*. Bartels argues that the establishment of a system of countermeasures for WTO violations and the prohibition on WTO members applying other countermeasures to enforce their WTO rights implies that the prohibition applies to countermeasures with respect to their other rights.[102] However, this conclusion is not compelling. Charnovitz, for instance, points out that of all international organizations it is the WTO where the use of trade sanctions is most self-contradictory and calls into question whether WTO rules were actually meant to superintend instruments that other treaties use to achieve compliance.[103] Also Pauwelyn's observation that the 'DSU does not say anything on countermeasures taken in response to *non-WTO breaches*', such as breaches under a human

---

[99] Pauwelyn (2003), p. 236.   [100] Pauwelyn (2003), p. 230.
[101] On the former case see Charnovitz (2001b). Of course, the same set of facts may be relevant from the perspective of countermeasures and/or sanctions in different ways: a country might impose economic sanctions on a state for a breach of core human rights. If that state is a WTO member, it might challenge the measure under WTO law, and the adjudicatory could authorize the complainant to adopt countermeasures as long as the sanction is in place. This situation would combine a trade sanction with countermeasures authorized by the DSB.
[102] Bartels (2002), p. 396.   [103] Charnovitz (2001a), p. 817–18.

3.3 NPA MEASURES AND THE LAW ON STATE RESPONSIBILITY

rights treaty, is not entirely correct. From the perspective of the WTO agreements any trade-restrictive measure constitutes a breach of basic WTO obligations. Its permissibility is then a question of justification, for example, under the provisions of the respective agreement. Both GATT[104] and GATS[105] contain general and security exceptions which allow states to take trade-restrictive measures in order to protect essential interests outside the realm of trade. Hence, since certain legitimate non-economic reasons for justification are reflected in the treaties, the WTO treaty is not completely 'silent' on this issue, although there is no distinction between simple unilateral non-economic measures and those that constitute countermeasures. Therefore, countermeasures for non-WTO breaches, just like other unilateral measures, may be justified under Articles XX and XXI. Therefore, the existence of exceptions for measures pursuing certain non-economic policies is strong evidence for the view that the GATT has indeed contracted out of international law on state responsibility. If these exceptions do not cover countermeasures for the specific subject matter at issue, then this is a consequence of the scope of these exceptions, which must, given the principle of effective treaty interpretation, be considered as a deliberate expression of the will of the WTO members. Also from the perspective of international law on treaties, the deliberate waiving of rights under international law, in this case the right to reprisals, by sovereign states is lawful: there is no *ius cogens* requiring states to take reprisals in certain situations which Article XXI would violate. Rather than excluding international law, Article XXI seems to mirror in a legitimate way public international law on state responsibility.[106] Therefore, even the finding that the scope of Articles XX and XXI limits the use of countermeasures more than the law on state responsibility would not prevent the conclusion that the GATT has contracted out of international law.

Against this finding has been argued that the law on countermeasures under the DSU would aim at compensation rather than at ending the illegal behaviour, and that given the lack of effectiveness it could not be assumed that a complete contracting out was intended.[107] However,

---

[104] GATT Articles XX and XXI.   [105] GATS Articles XIV and XIV bis.
[106] Hahn (1996), pp. 363–8. In 1996, Hahn observed a growing uneasiness among WTO stakeholders and academics with the finding that reprisals or sanctions beyond the scope of Article XXI violate the GATT. WTO law would not sufficiently allow for appropriate answers in case of breaches of international law on the environment and social issues (pp. 368–73).
[107] Zeitler (2000), p. 191. Murase made the more general point that as 'a fact of life in international law [that] its procedural law is not always perfect, in which case an aggrieved state must be permitted to seek remedies unilaterally', Murase (1995), p. 369.

countermeasures as authorized by the DSB must not be confused with countermeasures under general international law, which may be justified under the general exceptions; certainly, the adjudicatory bodies cannot authorize NPA measures as legitimate countermeasures against violations of non-WTO law. From a more normative than dogmatic perspective, Frowein has argued that the existence of general exceptions in the GATT cannot lead to an exclusion of the right of reprisals. Since armed reprisals are prohibited in international law, peaceful economic reprisals ought to remain applicable since they remain the most important avenue for sanctioning unlawful behaviour.[108] Frowein's concerns that it might be too strong a restriction on a state's ability to take effective non-violent action are certainly legitimate: it would not be satisfactory to conclude even in cases of severe violations of international law that WTO law would prevent WTO members from resorting to the more peaceful means of influence, namely, economic sanctions.

Whether or not there is an actual need to fall back on customary international law for countermeasures can be decided upon only after having determined that the scope of the general and security exceptions does not allow an adequate political response in all cases. It should be noted, that the *United States – Imports of Sugar from Nicaragua* panel report cannot be invoked as an argument in this direction, since the opportunity to clarify the ability of the GATT exceptions to deal with such cases was missed.[109] However, certain preconditions for justification under Article XXI security exceptions suggest that at least in some cases of severe breaches of *ius cogens* a fallback on the law on state responsibility ought to be possible. Here, particularly the exception in Article XXI(c) for the maintenance of international peace and security is noteworthy. Since only action in pursuance of 'obligations' under the UN Charter is permitted, WTO members are not allowed to take action if the UN merely recommends such action.[110] Thus, at least in situations of severe human rights or other *ius cogens* violations by a WTO member in which inaction or deadlock at the UN prevails, a fallback on the law on state responsibility ought to be justified. However, the scope of Article XX, including the public morals

---

[108] Frowein (1994), pp. 374–6.
[109] Panel Report, *United States – Imports of Sugar from Nicaragua* (1984). The Panel did not examine whether the measure was justified, since the United States refused to acknowledge that the dispute involving highly political matters was within the ambit of the GATT, at 3.11 and 4.4.
[110] Only decisions under Article 41 UN Charter are covered by Article XXI(c) (Berrisch (2003), p. 158).

exceptions, must not be underestimated and needs to be assessed carefully before recourse to the general law on state responsibility is taken.

In sum, in the relations between WTO members, GATT Articles XX and XXI constitute *leges speciales* vis-à-vis general customary international law on countermeasures. Resorting to the law on state responsibility must therefore be limited to exceptional circumstances. A justification of NPA measures under general international law is therefore excluded, with the rare exception of severe violations of *ius cogens* in the event of political deadlock at the UN.

3.4 Conclusion

The applicability of WTO law to NPA measures with trade effects will not usually present any particular problems. However, since NPAs may often also be subject to non-WTO international law, the applicability of other rules of international law may prove crucial for their legal status. It is widely recognized that the WTO is in general not a closed self-contained regime, but part of the system of international law. Thus, it is here argued that non-WTO international law is in principle applicable among WTO members with the consequence that the legal relationships between WTO members differ.

According to the *pacta tertiis* rule, only treaties to which the respective states are parties can govern the legal relations between them. Therefore, conflicts of norms contained in different international agreements can arise only in the legal relations between states that are parties to the respective agreements. A convention cannot apply if one party to the legal relationship under WTO law is not a party to the convention. In this situation, a conflict of norms cannot arise. If a conflict arises, the *lex posterior* conflict rule cannot apply, since the WTO covered agreements are 'continuing' or 'living' treaties. Multilateral treaties also cannot be regarded as *inter se* agreements which modify the relations among the parties according to VCLT Article 41. In contrast, the *lex specialis* rule is applicable as a conflict rule of customary international law. Accordingly, provisions regulating trade in certain products only or trade in certain products if these are related to certain NPAs, must be considered *lex specialis* compared with the provisions of the agreements covered by the WTO. Whether or not the *lex specialis* rule applies, however, has to be determined on a case-by-case basis.

In consequence of the *lex specialis* rule, WTO members have contracted out of international law to a certain extent and therefore must refrain from relying on the law on state responsibility for justifying measures in violation of the WTO covered agreements. The exceptions provided for in the agreements, such as GATT Articles XX and XXI as far as trade in goods is concerned, would be applicable instead.

This means that in assessing the legitimacy of NPA measures all relevant international law needs to be taken into account and that conflict rules determine which of several conflicting provisions prevails. If an international norm applies in the legal relations among certain WTO members, provisions allowing for NPA trade measures may thus prevail over conflicting GATT obligations if they constitute *lex specialis*. A convention that contains such special provisions and that has been ratified by only one of the disputing WTO members, however, is not applicable. In contrast, the exceptions contained in the WTO agreements indicate that WTO members have almost completely contracted out of the general international law on state responsibility. NPA measures that serve to induce compliance of a WTO member with its obligations under non-WTO law are usually allowed only to the extent that they are covered by these exceptions. In possibly rare cases of severe violations of *ius cogens* that are not covered by the exceptions, however, resorting to the law on countermeasures could possibly come into consideration.

4

Consistency with GATT obligations

When GATT violations through NPA measures are at issue, recent discussions have tended to focus mainly on justification of those measures under Article XX, while questions on the violation of the GATT are often neglected. One reason for this shift might be the assumption that NPA measures are *per se* illegal under the GATT,[1] or that the WTO adjudicatory bodies would at least rule to this end.[2] Also, since a view promoted in the earlier debate, namely, that NPA measures are excluded from justification, has lost ground, the attention is now mostly on the precise conditions of justification. Another reason could be the almost general perception that production-based measures are typically used as tools to pursue legitimate national policies, such as protection of the environment, and therefore in principle are justifiable under Article XX. The respondent in one of the classical PPM disputes, *Tuna-Dolphin II*, shrugged off the pressure to rebut the claims that its measures violated the GATT, and called the whole discussion about violation of the GATT an almost 'academic exercise', claiming that the measures were clearly within the scope of the general exceptions and consequently justified.[3] Despite these explanations, it seems that there is a general hesitance when it comes to addressing the issue of a GATT violation. Indeed, related questions eventually touch upon the very core of the GATT, and apparently there is little trust in its 'load-bearing capacity'. Indeed, an assessment of GATT violations through NPA measures is a legally and normatively difficult and highly complex issue.

Others have warned, with good reason, that the determination of a GATT violation should not be neglected. Indeed, a focus on the

---

[1] See, e.g., Swinbank (2006), who invokes the embeddedness of non-physical 'credence characteristics' in consumer goods, but simply assumes that GATT rules, particularly non-discrimination provisions, prohibit NPA measures.
[2] Charnovitz (2002), p. 92, states that 'any optimism that future WTO panels will tolerate origin-neutral PPMs in the context of Article III would be unfounded'.
[3] Panel Report (unadopted), *Tuna-Dolphin II* (1994), No. 3.6.

justification side has its obvious drawbacks. A premature shift of attention to justification might rely too heavily on the general exceptions, which have traditionally been interpreted narrowly and might offer a thin safety net rather than a comfortable way out by escaping the claim of a GATT violation in the first place.[4] Only specific policies are listed as possible justifications for GATT violations. Furthermore, it is often postulated that as an exception to the rule, Article XX would need to be interpreted narrowly. Therefore, it is feared that many measures which ought to be considered legitimate would fail before a WTO tribunal. If measures are already considered to be consistent with GATT obligations, however, they do not come under the scrutiny of the general exceptions. In consequence, a careful assessment of whether or not measures actually violate GATT obligations is imperative.

The above concerns ultimately concern the scope of GATT obligations vis-à-vis WTO members' sovereign right to freely take the measures which they deem to be appropriate in order to achieve specific policy objectives. The more broadly the GATT obligations are interpreted, the more pressure is put on national legislators and governments, which need to resort to justifying their measures under the limited exceptions in Article XX. In contrast, a too narrow interpretation of GATT obligations would result in loopholes which would allow national governments to veil protectionist and trade-restrictive measures as legitimate sovereign decisions which would be *per se* in line with GATT obligations. In interpreting the agreements, it is therefore important to consider the scope of GATT obligations for the determination of the GATT exceptions and vice versa.

The core question that underlies the discussions below, therefore, is where to draw the dividing line between illegitimate GATT violation and *per se* permissible national measures. The most crucial of the questions that need to be answered in order to draw that line adequately are the scope of obligation to provide MFN treatment under Article I, the relationship between Article XI and Article III, and the scope of the obligation to national treatment under Article III. These legal problems are closely interrelated, first, because of a partial identity in language in different provisions, and, second, because the legal concepts used are similar. There is, for instance, the notion of 'like products' which occurs about fifteen times in various GATT provisions and which is crucial for both MFN as well as national treatment.

---

[4] See, e.g., Howse and Regan (2000), p. 253.

This chapter starts with the scope of national treatment obligations and the question as to whether NPA measures fall within or without the scope of Article III. Section 4.2 discusses, arguably, the most crucial issue, relevant for MFN treatment as well as for national treatment, namely, the concept of 'like products'. It begins with a brief introduction to the legal principle of non-discrimination. This core principle underlying the GATT is of particular importance to the PPM debate, because the way it is interpreted is decisive for the legal status of production-based measures. Section 4.3 then analyses the concept of 'like products', and considers different approaches and their relevance for NPA measures. The chapter concludes with a summary of the results.

4.1 The scope of the national treatment obligations

Just as with any regulation, NPA measures can also take different forms. Therefore, whether or not the national treatment obligation in Article III is applicable to NPA measures depends on the type of respective measure. For example, direct NPA regulation could be subject to Article III:4, NPA tax measures as a particular sub-set of this group could be covered by Article III:2, and NPA border measures could fall under the national treatment standards if referred to Article III through application of the Note Ad Article III.

Arguably the most far-reaching argument relevant to the legal status of NPA measures is with regard to the range of measures which fall under the GATT, and more precisely, under the national treatment obligation. The gist of the arguments discussed in this section is the consideration that both Article III and its interpretative Note cover only measures directed at products 'directly' or at products 'as such', while measures directed at other aspects are excluded from their scope. Following the logic of the argument, NPA measures would be excluded, since they were not directed at the product itself.

It is important to note, however, that the legal consequences of this argument depend on the type and design of the measure in question. The claim that internal NPA measures fall outside the scope of the GATT and in consequence violate Article III would simply be inconsistent and is therefore not discussed in the following analysis. The claim that NPA measures fall within the scope of Article III and are *per se* legal, on the other hand, presumes applicability of Article III, a topic explored in the following sections. In contrast, excluding NPA border measures from the scope of application of Article III and of the respective Note could in some instances lead to a quasi-automatic violation of GATT obligations, but it could also lead to a finding of legality in other cases. For instance, internal NPA measures which would not be covered by Article III would remain entirely outside of the scope of the GATT. It could be argued that in consequence such measures would defy any scrutiny under GATT provisions, and would be *per se* legal. In contrast, if NPA border measures were regarded as falling outside the scope of the Note Ad Article III and as a corollary also outside the scope of Article III, they would indeed quasi-automatically be in violation of the prohibition of quantitative restrictions in Article XI.

The following sections disentangle the main claim, namely, that NPA measures do not fall into the scope of Article III and the Note Ad. Three single arguments supporting it are identified. First, there is the use of certain terms, such as the term 'product', in Article III and the Note Ad, which could imply that only measures applying to products 'as such' fall into the scope of these provisions. The second argument focuses on the scope of the Note Ad Article III, drawing on differences between Article III:2 and Article III:4. The third argument draws on the relationship between Article III and the Note Ad in general. These arguments are closely interrelated in as far as they are linked to the same concept or even word used in a provision.

Each section gives a general description of the argument and then discusses the relevant statements of the GATT and WTO adjudicatory bodies. Since very few reports address this claim directly, the analysis is supplemented with the consideration of reports that bear on related questions and allow for conclusions relevant to this analysis.

4.1.1 *The use of specific terms*

Some argue that the use of the word 'products' leads to a limitation of the scope of both Article III and the related interpretative Note. The word 'products' appears in Article III:1, 2 and 4. Paragraphs 1 and 2 deal with taxes and other regulation 'applied to ... products' and paragraph 4 deals with treatment that is 'accorded to ... products'. Also the Note Ad Article III includes the word 'product'. It deals with the precarious distinction between prohibited quantitative restrictions under Article XI, on the one hand, and internal measures, on the other, and is therefore also relevant for the determination of the scope of Article III. The Note states that:

> Any ... regulation ... which applies to an imported product and to the like domestic product and is collected or enforced in the case of the imported

4.1 SCOPE OF THE NATIONAL TREATMENT OBLIGATIONS 151

product at ... importation, is nevertheless to be regarded as an internal ... regulation ... and is accordingly subject to the provisions of Article III.[5]

4.1.1.1 Narrow interpretation: products

The narrow interpretation refers to the repeated use of the word 'product', which it regards as evidence of a limitation of the scope of these provisions to measures that refer to 'products as such', in the sense that measures directed at other aspects would be excluded from the scope. It was adopted by both *Tuna-Dolphin* panels, which held that the interpretative note and Article III were not applicable to the measures in question. Its reasoning, however, was very brief. Both panels clearly drew their conclusions from the language of Article III read together with the Note.[6]

The *Tuna-Dolphin I* panel discussed the applicability of Article III and the respective Note to an import ban. To this end, it quoted several passages of the text of Article III:1 and III:4, and found that Article III covered only measures affecting 'products as such'.[7] The panel then continued its reasoning and eventually concluded that the Note Ad Article III also covered only measures that are applied to the 'product as such'.[8] In examining the measure at issue, the panel found that the regulation on domestic harvesting of tuna to reduce the incidental taking of dolphins did not directly regulate the sale of tuna, and in consequence could not affect tuna 'as a product'. Therefore, the import prohibition on certain tuna products could not possibly constitute internal regulations covered by the Note Ad Article III.[9] It then proceeded to claim *arguendo* that even if the measure were covered by the Note, the measure would not meet the requirements of Article III, because it 'could not possibly affect tuna as a product'.[10] The

---

[5] GATT, Annex I Notes and Supplementary Provisions, Ad Article III, before paragraph 1.
[6] Panel Report, *Tuna-Dolphin I* (1991), para. 5.11; Panel report, *Tuna-Dolphin II* (1994), No. 5.8.
[7] Panel Report, *Tuna-Dolphin I* (1991), No.5.11.
[8] Panel Report, *Tuna-Dolphin I* (1991), Nos. 5.11 and 5.14. The Panel based its reasoning explicitly on the Working Party Report on Border Tax Adjustments, which had been adopted by the contracting parties in 1970. Although the report related to tax measures, the Panel saw it as a need of consistency to adopt the same reasoning also for 'regulations not applied to the product as such' (at 5.13). Possibly, the Panel intended to follow a line of case law, albeit relating to taxes, as reflected for instance in the Panel Report in *US – Superfund* (1987), at para. 5.2.4.
[9] Panel Report, *Tuna-Dolphin I* (1991), No. 5.14.
[10] Panel Report, *Tuna-Dolphin I* (1991), No. 5.15. Also, the *Tuna-Dolphin II* (1994) Panel discussed both the scope of application of the Note Ad Article III and Article III itself, even if it mingled both questions into the discussion on the application of the Note Ad Article III, cf. *Tuna-Dolphin II* (1994), at No. 5.8.

Tuna-Dolphin II panel in this respect basically confirmed the findings of the earlier panel, stressing the importance of the word 'products' in both Article III and the Note.[11]

After the *Tuna-Dolphin* disputes, no other panel or the Appellate Body required that measures should apply to 'products as such' or placed comparable emphasis on the words 'product' or 'products'. In the *Argentina – Hides and Leather* dispute of 2000, the respondent invoked this language to support its claim that the measure at issue was not covered by Article III,[12] but the panel did not take up this argument. As will be shown in the next sub-section, other panels seem to have preferred a broader interpretation instead.

4.1.1.2 Broad interpretation: 'affecting'

A different approach to the scope of national treatment obligations, adopting a broader interpretation, has also been based on language. In contrast to the narrow interpretation, this approach places emphasis on the verb 'to affect'.[13]

Article III:1 and III:4 refer to measures '*affecting* the internal sale, offering for sale, purchase, transportation, distribution or use'.[14] Not only the verb 'to affect',[15] but the remainder of the sentence is an indication for an indirect rather than direct relationship between the aspect affected by the measure and the product. Measures embraced by both paragraphs may affect any of several listed stages of the product life cycle rather than the product in terms of physical properties. Also, Article III:1 mentions explicitly quantitative requirements regarding 'mixture, *processing* or *use* of products'.[16] Since any measure referring to ingredients or parts of a product would fall under 'mixture', the rule of effective treaty interpretation[17] could be invoked to argue that the other aspects listed explicitly, namely, 'processing', need to be given specific meaning. Since measures affecting the physical properties of products will usually be covered by the aspect 'mixture', one could argue that the word 'processing' refers to

---

[11] Panel Report, *Tuna-Dolphin II* (1994), No. 5.8.
[12] Panel Report, *Argentina – Hides and Leather* (2000), at No. 11.157.
[13] See also Howse and Regan (2000), p. 255 ('broad reading of "affecting the sale"').
[14] Emphasis added.
[15] For the broadness of the verb 'to affect' see also, Panel Report, *Dominican Republic – Import and Sale of Cigarettes* (2004), at No. 7.280.
[16] Emphasis added.
[17] For its validity under WTO law, cf. Appellate Body Report, *EC – Chicken Cuts* (2005), No. 214, with further references in fn. 413.

4.1 SCOPE OF THE NATIONAL TREATMENT OBLIGATIONS 153

those aspects of production that do not affect the physical properties of a product.

These latter arguments apply also when it comes to the Note Ad Article III. Nevertheless, there is an important difference in language between the Note and some paragraphs of Article III.[18] While the language of Article III contains the preposition 'of', the Note refers to regulation of the kind referred to in paragraph 1 which *applies to* an imported product and *to* the like domestic product'. The choice of the words 'applies to', as opposed to 'affecting', might suggest a narrower interpretation. It seems more difficult to subsume a regulation prohibiting certain fishing techniques under a law which 'applies to' a product, than under a regulation which 'accords' some kind of treatment to a product or 'affects' the sale of a product.

In both GATT and WTO dispute settlement, the broader interpretation has so far been used or discussed exclusively with respect to Article III. A famous example for this approach is the report of the early and frequently cited GATT panel in the *Italian Agricultural Machinery* dispute.[19] This panel had argued that by the selection of the word 'affecting' in relation to products the drafters of Article III:4 had intended to cover not only the laws and regulations which directly governed the conditions of sale or purchase, but also any laws or regulations which might adversely modify the conditions of competition between products.[20] Later GATT panels also followed this approach, both before[21] and after[22] *Tuna-Dolphin I*. The 1994 panel in *US – Taxes on Automobiles*, published shortly after the *Tuna-Dolphin II* report, finally stated explicitly that measures do not need to regulate a product directly to fall

---

[18] The Panel cited a difference in the language of the Note Ad Article III compared with Article III:1 and III:4 several times, but nevertheless did not probe into this point, cf., e.g., Panel Report, *Tuna Dolphin I* (1991), No. 5.14.
[19] Panel Report, *Italy – Agricultural Machinery* (1958), No. 64 at para. 12.
[20] Panel Report, *Italy – Agricultural Machinery* (1958), No. 64 at para. 12.
[21] See, e.g., Panel Reports in *Canada – FIRA* (1984), Nos. 5.8, 5.9, and in *US – Section 337 Tariff Act* (1989), No. 5.10. In 1984, the Panel in *Canada – FIRA* applied Article III:4 to undertakings by foreign investors to purchase goods of Canadian origin, submitted in order to have their investment proposals approved, and found they constituted violations, without discussing the coverage of Article III at all. The 1989 *US – Section 337 Tariff Act* Panel basically ignored the importance of the word 'products' and instead found that measures applying to persons rather than to products, such as patent laws, and even the respective enforcement measures at issue also affected the sale of products as set out in Article III.
[22] E.g., the *US – Malt Beverages* (1992) Panel examined tax credits for smaller breweries under Article III:2 without discussing its applicability, thus implying that Article III covers measures which do not relate to the product directly (at Nos. 5.18, 5.19).

within the scope of Article III.[23] It stated that instead it was sufficient that a measure affected the conditions of competition, and that therefore internal measures based on factors unrelated to the product as such, as for instance a measure applied to a producer, could indeed fall into the scope of Article III:4.[24]

Since the establishment of the WTO, no panel has addressed this question directly, but other panels have followed the approach to apply a broader interpretation, whether dealing with product-based measures or others.[25] For instance, in the 1997 *Canada – Periodicals* dispute, the panel examined a tax measure on periodicals under Article III:2. The excise tax at issue was applied to split-run editions of periodicals and therefore obviously not linked to the physical product, but to its content. The excise tax, however, did not depend on the content of periodical in absolute terms, but only on the content in comparison with the content of other editions which were distributed outside Canada.[26] The respondent claimed that the measure was, in fact, a regulation of advertisement services rather than one that would be covered by the GATT provisions on trade in goods. The panel reasoned that there were overlaps in the subject matter, and did not further discuss whether the measure truly applied to 'products as such'. The panel continued its examination, focusing on the question of 'likeness' of the products at issue, and found that the measure was in violation of Article III:2.[27] This decision is of some interest, because in contrast to earlier cases it used the broader interpretation even for a measure under Article III:2 – a provisions which uses the words 'apply … to … products' instead of the apparently broader term 'affecting' used in paragraph 4. Finally, the panel in the 2000 *Canada – Autos* dispute dealt again with Article III:4, examining a measure which required a certain Canadian value added to obtain the benefit of duty-free importation of motor vehicles. The measure was based on a factor other than physical

---

[23] Panel Report, *United States – Taxes on Automobiles* (1994), at No. 5.45.

[24] Panel Report, *United States – Taxes on Automobiles* (1994), at No. 5.45. The Panel bolstered this view also by referring to the findings of the early *Italy – Agricultural Machinery* (1958) case.

[25] In several more recent disputes the Panels stated explicitly that the term 'affecting' in Article III:4 of the GATT 1994 had 'a broad scope'. See Panel Report *Mexico – Taxes on Soft Drinks* (2005), which found that a measure conditioning exemptions from tax measures and bookkeeping requirements for manufacturers on the use of cane sugar had an effect on the use of beet sugar (at No. 8.108), and Panel Report, *Dominican Republic – Import and Sale of Cigarettes* (2004), at No. 7.280.

[26] Panel Report, *Canada – Periodicals* (1997), No. 2.7.

[27] Panel Report, *Canada – Periodicals* (1997), No. 5.30.

4.1 SCOPE OF THE NATIONAL TREATMENT OBLIGATIONS 155

characteristics, namely, an origin requirement in the specific form of a minimum requirement of Canadian value added in production, and in this respect resembles the *Italy – Agricultural Machinery* dispute. The *Canada – Autos* panel found that the requirement, which clearly was not based on physical product properties, affected conditions of competition and violated Article III:4,[28] and so implicitly applied the broader interpretation.[29]

4.1.1.3 Preliminary conclusion

Although both *Tuna-Dolphin* panel reports remained unadopted, the narrow interpretation must not be dismissed too easily. Since the adoption of both reports, several other panels have emphasized their value in providing useful guidance,[30] including the 'product as such' argument,[31] which, however, has not specifically been used to exclude NPA measures from the scope of Article III. Furthermore, in scholarship the frequent use of the word 'product', which could be seen as an antipode to the production of goods, has also been cited as a possible textual basis for the product–process distinction.[32]

Nevertheless, the broad interpretation seems preferable.[33] Scholars have argued that the reference to 'products' conveys nothing about a distinction between products as opposed to production, but simply indicates that the GATT is about trade in goods.[34] This view also finds support in a number of panel reports both before and after the *Tuna-Dolphin* disputes, as detailed above. These panels applied a much broader interpretation of the scope of Article III, which also comprised regulations not exclusively directed at products.[35]

---

[28] Panel Report, *Canada – Autos* (2000), at Nos. 10.80, 10.90.
[29] Not only have both *Tuna-Dolphin* reports remained unadopted, more importantly, a number of Panel Reports before and after the *Tuna-Dolphin* reports indicate that the interpretation focusing on the word 'products' were too narrow. Although focusing on Article III instead of the Note, these Panels applied a much broader interpretation, which comprised regulation and laws not based on products alone.
[30] See, e.g., the more recent panel report in *US – Gambling* (2004), at No. 6.526 and fn. 980.
[31] See, e.g., Panel Report, *Argentina – Hides and Leather* (2000), there fn. 539.
[32] See, e.g., Jackson (2000b), pp. 303–4.
[33] For the broader interpretation see, e.g., also Howse and Regan (2000), p. 254; Hudec (2000), p. 194. Hudec even argued that the Panel's statement, which emphasized the broader term 'affecting' as well as the word 'products', could also be read as a reference to Article III's very broad coverage.
[34] Howse and Regan (2000), p. 254.
[35] E.g., Panel Reports in *Italy – Agricultural Machinery* (1958), at para. 12; *Canada – FIRA* (1984), Nos. 5.8, 5.9; *United States – Section 337 Tariff Act* (1989), No. 5.10; *US – Taxes on*

The same reasoning must then also apply to the Note in order to prevent an unjustified inconsistency in the scopes of the Note and Article III itself. Interestingly, the reasoning of the *Tuna-Dolphin I* panel for the narrow interpretation of the Note supports this conclusion. The panel invoked the text of Article III for its interpretation of the scope of the Note. It first discussed the scope of Article III and then transferred the result to its discussion on the scope of the Note. As shown above, the narrow interpretation adopted by the *Tuna-Dolphin* panels with respect to Article III must be considered overruled. Since these panels arrived at their narrow interpretation of the Note only via their narrow interpretation of Article III, their findings on the Note cannot be sustained. Consequently, the use of the term 'products' in the text of Article III and the Note cannot be invoked to exclude NPA measures from their respective scopes.

4.1.2 Comparison of Article III:2 and 4

The panel in *Tuna-Dolphin I* in 1991 also compared Article III:2 and Article III:4 in order to determine the scope of the Note Ad Article III, and concluded from this comparison that measures which do not refer to the 'product as such' do not fall into the scope of the Note Ad.[36] To reiterate, in consequence, the measure at issue in this dispute was found to violate Article XI.

The panel stated that Article III applied the national treatment standard to both regulations and taxes, and thus the interpretation and considerations of Article III:2 on tax measures should be taken into account when interpreting the provisions of Article III:4.[37] It then looked into the interpretation of Article III:2, referred to the Report of the Working Party on Border Tax Adjustment and found that paragraph 2 did not allow for border tax adjustment for taxes not directly levied on products.[38] It concluded that as a consequence of this limitation, the Note also covered only taxes borne by the product. The panel then went one step further by finding that it would be inconsistent to limit the Note to taxes borne by products with respect to Article III:2, and to open at the same time the scope of the Note for regulation not applied to the product 'as such'.[39] Instead,

---

Automobiles (1994), at No. 5.45; *Canada – Periodicals* (1997), No. 2.7, *Mexico – Taxes on Soft Drinks* (2005), No. 8.108.
[36] Hudec (2000), p. 195.   [37] Panel Report, *Tuna-Dolphin I* (1991), No. 5.13.
[38] Panel Report, *Tuna-Dolphin I* (1991), No. 5.13.
[39] Panel Report, *Tuna-Dolphin I* (1991), No. 5.13.

4.1 SCOPE OF THE NATIONAL TREATMENT OBLIGATIONS 157

the panel found that the scope of the Note should be interpreted consistently for both types of measures, namely, more narrowly, so as to exclude internal regulation not applied to the product 'as such'. The panel did not add any substantive reasons for this conclusion to this rather formalistic argument.

The same argumentation was made by the complainants in *Tuna-Dolphin II*. The EEC and the Netherlands claimed that the import prohibition was a kind of border adjustment of the national harvesting regulations, which was impermissible since harvesting regulations did not apply to the product as such.[40] To support this conclusion, the complainants invoked the Panel Report in *US – Superfund*, in which the panel had stated that only taxes directly levied on products were eligible for border tax adjustment, with the policy purpose of the tax being irrelevant.[41] The panel in *Tuna-Dolphin II* did not refer to this particular claim in its findings.

However, the argument was also brought forward by the *US – Taxes on Automobiles* panel, albeit with respect to internal measures. Curiously, the conclusions drawn from the comparison differed considerably from those of the *Tuna-Dolphin I* panel.[42] Anticipating objections regarding the curious legal consequences of a limitation of the scope of Article III:4, the panel in *US – Taxes on Automobiles* made it clear that measures do not need to regulate a product directly to fall into the scope of Article III:4. According to the panel, such measures would be covered by Article III:4, but be considered violations of the national treatment obligation, because the comparison with Article III:2 showed that a differentiation between products must not be based on aspects unrelated to the product as such.[43] The motivation of the *US – Taxes on Automobiles* panel was to ensure the benefits of tariff commitments. It argued that the limitation of Article III:2 to taxes based on factors directly related to the product as detailed above showed one of the central purposes of Article III, namely, to ensure the security of tariff bindings.[44] The panel considered that the negotiated commitments must not be frustrated through measures which were based on factors unrelated to the product as such.[45] The outcome of negotiations could otherwise easily be jeopardized. The panel stated:

[40] Panel Report, *Tuna-Dolphin II* (1994), at No. 3.93.
[41] Panel Report, *US – Superfund* (1987), at No. 5.2.4.
[42] Panel Report, *US – Taxes on Automobiles* (1994), No. 5.52.
[43] Panel Report, *US – Taxes on Automobiles* (1994), No. 5.54.
[44] Panel Report, *US – Taxes on Automobiles* (1994), No. 5.53.
[45] Panel Report, *US – Taxes on Automobiles* (1994), No. 5.53.

> If it were permissible to justify under Article III less favourable treatment to an imported product *on the basis of factors not related to the product as such*, Article III would not serve its intended purpose.[46]

Thus, while the *Tuna-Dolphin* panels interpreted the scope of both Article III and the Note narrowly, the *US – Taxes on Automobiles* panel interpreted the scope broadly. Curiously, the narrow and the broad interpretations of Article III and the Note by the above panels did not lead to contradictory findings, but determined the same outcome: a measure based on aspects other than product characteristics was ultimately found to violate the GATT. This seeming contradiction is due to the nature of the Note as a conflict norm, and it shows that even a broad interpretation of the scope does not render NPA measures *per se* legal.[47]

The argument is not convincing. Although frequently cited, it is noteworthy that the Report of the Working Party on Border Tax Adjustments is wanting as regards substantive arguments for the distinction between taxes directly levied on products and other taxes. The Report predominantly referred to practice and invoked the convergence of views in considering indirect taxes not eligible for tax adjustment. More than that, it is questionable whether the considerations applying to border tax adjustments likewise apply to other regulations. And finally, the comparison between indirect taxes and measures directed at NPAs is lopsided. This becomes apparent at the example of direct taxes linked to NPAs. The Working Party Report does not offer any answers to the legality of adjustments of direct taxes on the basis of NPAs, if, for example, a country applies different VAT rates to products based on its environmental qualities.

4.1.3 Measures 'of the same nature'

A different strand of argumentation discussed by panels relates exclusively to the Note Ad Article III and is thus irrelevant for strictly internal measures. According to this view, the Note, which refers a measure from Article XI to the more advantageous standards of Article III:4, covers only those measures on imported products which are 'of the same nature' as

---

[46] Panel Report, *US – Taxes on Automobiles* (1994), No. 5.3. Emphasis added by this author.

[47] In consequence of the *Tuna-Dolphin* Panels' narrow interpretation, the border measures violated quasi-automatically the prohibition of quantitative restrictions. In consequence of the *US – Taxes on Automobiles* (1994) Panel's broader interpretation, the measure violated national treatment obligations.

4.1 SCOPE OF THE NATIONAL TREATMENT OBLIGATIONS

those applied to domestic products. In consequence, internal NPA regulation supplemented with corresponding border measures would not fall into the scope of the Note, because NPA regulation would *per se* be considered as having a nature different from border measures, which inherently imply some form of import restriction. Several panels have addressed this particular question on the scope of the Note regarding the relationship of the measure applying to the imported product and the measure applying to the domestic product.

The *Tuna-Dolphin I* panel discussed the scope of the Note extensively while reviewing a classical PPM measure, and it found that the measure covered by the Note needed to be 'of the same nature' as the measure applied to domestic products.[48] It then proceeded to cite as an example of measures 'of the same nature' an import prohibition which enforces an internal sale prohibition at the border and applies to both imported and domestic products.

However, the panel's finding lacks clarity. It is unclear what the panel means by referring to the 'nature' of a measure. The example for a measure 'of the same nature' does not suffice to add clarity. For instance, is it self-evident that an import prohibition is of the same 'nature' as a prohibition on selling a product domestically? It seems that these measures rather than having the same nature pursue the same goal, namely, the prevention of the distribution of a product. The difference between the nature and the goal of a measure could be crucial – many measures pursuing the same goal might be very different by nature, and many measures of the same nature might pursue entirely different goals.

Interestingly, the text of the Note does not explicitly require that the domestic measure and the measure applied to imports be 'of the same nature'. In fact, rather than referring to two different measures at all, the Note refers to a single law or measure, which applies to both the imported and the domestic product. Literally, the Note seems to require identity rather than similarity or being 'of the same nature'.

This literal interpretation, which would in turn considerably limit the scope of the Note, was brought forward by Canada in *EC – Asbestos*, but instantly rejected by the panel.[49] It was argued that the use of the word 'comme' in the French version of the GATT was an indication for the identity of measures applied to imported and domestic products. The panel disagreed. It stressed the difference in this respect between the

---

[48] Panel Report, *Tuna-Dolphin I* (1991), No. 5.11.
[49] Panel Report, *EC – Asbestos* (2000), No. 8.93.

French word 'comme' and the English 'and', and was of the view that among the different meanings of the word 'comme' was 'in the same way as'. It argued that a crucial aspect was that the measure led to the 'same result' for both imported and domestic products, and concluded that the French text excluded the interpretation that an identical measure was required.[50]

It also invoked the earlier Panel Report in *US – Section 337 Tariff Act*.[51] In this dispute, the panel had examined different measures under the Note, regardless of the fact that the measure applying to imported products was very different from the national laws which applied to domestic products. The measure at issue in the dispute, laid down in section 337 of the Tariff Act, was considered by the parties as an enforcement measure for national US patent laws.[52] The panel stated that in order to preserve the function of the obligation to provide national treatment, enforcement procedures could not be separated from the substantive provisions they serve to enforce.[53] On this basis, the panel in its interpretation slightly reformulated the Note to the end that:

> any law, regulation or requirement *affecting the internal sale of products* that is enforced in the case of the imported product at the time or point of importation is nevertheless subject to the provisions of Article III.[54]

The measures actually constituted treatment of persons rather than products. Since they were linked to the origin of the challenged products they were found suitable to affect the internal sale of foreign products.[55] Also the *EC – Asbestos* panel implicitly rejected the literal interpretation. It briefly touched upon this issue when it stated that the complete absence of domestic products would not suffice to exclude applicability of Article III, at least if the cessation of production is the consequence of the measure and not the reverse.[56]

---

[50] Panel Report, *EC – Asbestos* (2000), Nos. 8.92–8.924. The Dominican Republic took up this argument in the *Dominican Republic – Import and Sale of Cigarettes* (2004) dispute (see Panel Report, at No. 7.245). This Panel, however, did not consider the measure at issue a restriction to imports, and therefore did not address this point.
[51] Panel Report, *EC – Asbestos* (2000), at No. 8.95.
[52] Panel Report, *US – Section 337 Tariff Act* (1989), No. 3.6.
[53] Panel Report, *US – Section 337 Tariff Act* (1989), No. 5.10. The Panel speaks of enforcement measures otherwise 'escaping' the national treatment standard of Article III to address the alleged difference between enforcement measures and substantive provisions.
[54] Panel Report, *US – Section 337 Tariff Act* (1989), No. 5.10, emphasis added by this author.
[55] Panel Report, *US – Section 337 Tariff Act* (1989), No. 5.10.
[56] Panel Report, *EC – Asbestos* (2000), No. 8.91. This particular finding was not appealed.

4.1 SCOPE OF THE NATIONAL TREATMENT OBLIGATIONS 161

In sum, the question on the relationship between or identity of the measure examined under the Note, on the one hand, and corresponding internal regulation, on the other hand, has been addressed only rarely in dispute settlement. Most important for this argument are the Panel Report *Tuna-Dolphin I* in 1991 and the earlier Panel Report *US – Section 337 Tariff Act*. There seems to be consensus mainly in the rejection of a strictly literal interpretation of the Note, which would have required a single measure applying to both imported and domestic products for the Note to apply. While the unadopted *Tuna-Dolphin I* panel established the rather obscure requirement that measures should be 'of the same nature' to fall within the scope of the Note, the *US – Section 337 Tariff Act* panel, and without much discussion, applied the Note although the measures in question were very different. Also the dismissal of concerns about the absence of domestic products by the *EC – Asbestos* panel constitutes another hint that the 'of the same nature' requirement cannot be considered prevailing case law. Whether or not there is sufficient correlation between a measure to be considered under the Note and corresponding internal measures seems to depend on the relevant facts of the case at issue. It seems, however, that the mere fact that a measure applying to imported products at the border provides for different features than the national measure regulating the matter within a state's territory is not in itself sufficient to exclude the border measure from the scope of both the Note and Article III itself.

4.1.4 Summary and conclusion

The above analysis regards both the scope of Article III and the scope of the respective Note as a conflict norm. The claim that their scope would exclude NPA measures is based on the three interlinked arguments discussed above. The first one focuses on language, particularly on the term 'product', which some interpret to imply a distinction between measures directed at products, on the one hand, and measures directed at NPAs, on the other. This analysis rejects this argument and favours a broad interpretation. The second argument is based on a comparison between the scope of the national treatment obligations pertaining to tax measures and those pertaining to other regulation. It was used by two panels. and in both cases led ultimately to the illegality of the measures at stake. The analysis presented here concludes that the argument is merely formalistic and bare of substantive reasoning. Therefore, it is here rejected. Finally, the third argument focuses on the relationship between the border measure examined under the Note Ad and the corresponding national measure under Article III. Although it is not clear from existing case law how exactly the correlation between measures ought to be in order to render the conflict norm applicable, there is no apparent reason why the fact that a measure is based on an NPA should constitute an obstacle to its application.

In sum, this analysis favours a broad interpretation of the scope of both Article III and the Note. This implies that NPA measures fall into the scope of Article III and therefore are subject to scrutiny under the GATT national treatment rules. Likewise, NPA border measures are not barred from the scope of the Note, and may thus be assessed under the standards of Article III, provided the other conditions of the Note are met. Hence, as compared with other measures, NPA measures do not provide for any particularities as regards the scope of the national treatment obligations, or to put it differently: the fact that a measure is linked to an NPA, including a PPM, is irrelevant as regards the scope of Article III and the respective Note.

4.2 The principle of non-discrimination and the 'like products' concept

One of the crucial legal problems pertaining to NPA measures is inextricably linked to one of the most fundamental legal principles of GATT law, namely, the principle of non-discrimination. This chapter first gives a more general introduction to non-discrimination as a core principle of the WTO and then analyses the key terms that are constitutive for this principle under WTO law, most importantly the notion of 'like products'. Section 4.2.2 analyses the prevailing approach and relevant case law of the adjudicatory bodies and compares it with two alternative approaches and their relevance for NPA measures. Section 4.2.3 sums up the discussion and draws conclusions.

4.2.1 Introduction to the principle of non-discrimination

Non-discrimination is a widely used legal concept which is also of paramount importance to GATT and WTO law.[57] Its more concrete

---

[57] The GATT itself refers to 'the general principles of non-discriminatory treatment' in Article XVII. The Appellate Body, albeit with respect to MFN treatment, mentions the pervasive character of the principle of non-discrimination (Panel Report, *Canada – Autos*

applications in the GATT are two major obligations, namely, most-favoured nation (MFN) and national treatment. Both sub-principles are indispensable cornerstones of an open international trading system.[58] The principle of non-discrimination appears in a number of GATT provisions as well as in the text of other multilateral agreements on trade in goods.[59]

4.2.1.1 General problems inherent to the principle

The basic idea of non-discrimination in the GATT is that like products shall be treated in a like way, no matter where they originate. The first sub-principle, namely, MFN treatment, obliges WTO members to treat imports originating in different nations equally, while the obligation to national treatment requires that imported goods be treated no worse than domestically produced goods, once they have cleared customs and border procedures.[60] According to the language of non-discrimination provisions, violations are determined in two steps. First, it has to be established that the set of products at issue are 'like products'. In a second step, it is analysed whether the treatment accorded to the foreign product at issue is 'less favourable' than the treatment accorded to the 'like' domestic product, or the 'like product' originating in a third country, respectively. In contrast to non-discrimination provisions in other regulatory systems, the non-discrimination concept in WTO law does not consider whether there is a legitimate rationale or regulatory intent for the difference in treatment.[61] The language of the non-discrimination provisions implies instead that any difference in treatment with the less favourable treatment accorded to foreign products is discriminatory.[62] While the second step of the analysis does not usually pose any particular problems, it is the first step which bears a major difficulty: the objects between which discrimination is forbidden are not stated clearly.

(2000), No. 82), also Hilf (2001), at 117, Cottier and Mavroidis (2002a). Goettsche calls it a principle of structure central to the WTO (2005, p. 117). Also in other contexts the principle of non-discrimination has often been cited as one of the WTO core principles, e.g., Jenny (2003), with respect to the integration of competition policies in the WTO.

[58] Cottier and Mavroidis (2002b), p. 389.
[59] Under the GATT, the 'like products' concept is incorporated in Articles I, II, III, VI, VII, IX, XI, XIII, XVI and XIX, and in the Notes Ad Articles I, III, V, VII ('like merchandise') and XVI.
[60] Jackson (1997), p. 213.   [61] Hudec (1998), p. 626.
[62] Nevertheless, some argue that the real question determining discrimination in WTO law is the regulatory purpose of the challenged measures. This argumentation is addressed in more detail below, section 4.2.1.2.

The non-discrimination principle in the GATT prohibits only discrimination between 'like products'. Hence, interpretation of this concept is at the centre of the debate. 'Likeness' is not legally defined in the GATT, and the GATT contracting parties and later WTO members failed to develop a general definition or interpretation of this term. By its very nature as a term of comparison, the term 'like' cannot be defined in an abstract way. Since there is no such thing as two identical products, it is a truism that all products are inherently different. 'Likeness' in the sense of the non-discrimination principle is, therefore, a question of degree rather than a question of yes or no. In order to be functional, the term thus needs to be given meaning. Since the concept 'like products' is constitutive for GATT core obligations, a broader definition implies that more measures violate GATT obligations. If, on the other hand, the definition is narrower, fewer products are considered 'like', and as a corollary, more measures would conform to the respective GATT provisions,[63] since distinctions between products that are not 'like' are *per se* permissible. Hence, the crucial question is which criteria determine whether or not products are 'like'.

In extreme cases, where measures distinguish between products that are different in most respects, such as apples and cars, the concept does not lead to difficulties. Distinctions between such obviously different products cannot violate the non-discrimination provision. This means that great physical differences obviously play a role. In contrast, the language of the non-discrimination provisions implies that product origin is not a valid criterion. Due to the reference to 'imported' and 'domestic products' in the agreements, there is consensus among scholars and in GATT and WTO jurisprudence that distinguishing between products based on their origin amounts to a *de jure* discrimination which violates the GATT *a priori*.[64] However, while the use of measures which discriminate *de jure* has declined over time, governments have become more sophisticated in developing measures that provide an advantage to domestic products, without however plainly distinguishing between products based on their origin. It is widely recognized that such apparently origin-neutral measures can be prohibited as illegal *de facto*

---

[63] Mattoo and Subramanian (1998), p. 304.
[64] Cf., e.g., the language of Articles I:1 and III:1, 2 and 4. See also Cottier and Oesch (2005), p. 383; Prieß and Berrisch (2003), p. 80, recital 14 (on the principle of non-discrimination in general); Davey and Pauwelyn (2002), p. 25 (on the MFN principle in Article I:1); Hudec (1998), pp. 620–3. For relevant case law on this issue see the section below.

discriminations.⁶⁵ What exactly constitutes *de facto* discrimination, however, is highly controversial.

Therefore, it is not entirely clear whether measures that apply to relatively similar products and link different legal consequences to aspects other than origin violate the principle of non-discrimination or not. To give an example, it is not self-evident whether or not different alcoholic beverages are 'like products'. Thus, a measure linking a tax rate to the alcohol content of a beverage, thus singling out some alcoholic beverages from the broader category of alcoholic beverages in general, is problematic. Some have therefore argued that a decision on likeness cannot be objective, and that the decision always presupposes some normative judgement.⁶⁶ Therefore, it has been suggested that in the determination of likeness a consideration of the regulatory purpose underlying the measure should be included.⁶⁷

The principle of non-discrimination, however, is based on a comparison of products, combined with a comparison of treatment. Only treatment that is less favourable for one product than for another 'like' product can possibly violate any non-discrimination obligation. Therefore, the problem of determining *de facto* discriminations could, at least in part, be solved with a focus on the latter comparison. It could be argued that a discriminatory measure must to some extent have a discriminatory effect on foreign products. Hence, in the absence of a discriminatory effect, there would be no finding of discrimination. Different approaches to determine a discriminatory effect have been considered. While the two components of the non-discrimination principle, comparison of products and comparison of treatment, appear to be separate issues, they are in fact interrelated: the result of a comparison of treatment will always depend on the groups of products the treatment of which is compared.

4.2.1.2 Clear prohibition of origin-based discrimination

The clear prohibition of product discriminations based on origin has been translated into numerous reports by panels and the Appellate Body. These are unanimous in their rejection of origin as a legitimate determinant of likeness.⁶⁸ The *Italian Agricultural Machinery* dispute of 1958 is

---

[65] Cf., e.g., Van den Bossche, Schrijver and Faber (2007), p. 20; Cottier and Oesch (2005), p. 383; Cottier and Mavroidis (2002a), p. 4; Cottier and Mavroidis (2002b), pp. 390–1; Ehring (2002), p. 922; Mattoo and Subramanian (1998); Jackson (1997), p. 217.
[66] Davey and Pauwelyn (2002), p. 38.   [67] See below in this, section 4.2.1.2.
[68] See, e.g., Panel Reports *Turkey – Importation of Rice* (2007), No. 7.214, *Canada – Wheat Exports and Grain Imports* (2004), No. 6.164, with further references in fn. 246, Nos.

one of the earlier disputes which rejected origin as a legitimate aspect for distinctions.[69] Ever since, panels and the Appellate Body have repeated the irrelevance of product origin as a basis for distinctions. A distinction based on the origin of a product is a *de jure* discrimination and *a priori* in violation of the GATT non-discrimination principle.

Although it is a commonplace that *de jure* discriminations violate the GATT, there are still disputes dealing with measures which rather bluntly discriminate based on product origin. To give a more recent example, the *India – Autos* dispute of 2002 rejected the auto components licensing policy adopted by the Indian Government under the Foreign Trade Act of 1992. This policy was applied in combination with certain Memoranda of Understanding, which were to be signed by Indian car manufacturers wishing to import certain automotive kits and by the Indian Director General of Foreign Trade. According to the law as laid down in a Public Notice, the Memoranda required manufacturers to use certain minimum amounts of local parts and components, and obliged them to broadly balance the value of imports with equivalent exports. In cases where a manufacturer did not sign a Memorandum, import licences could be denied.

The dispute resembles that in *Belgium – Family Allowances*, in that a national measure makes imports subject to an exemption or licence, respectively. While the Belgian measures subject to the dispute constituted an obvious discrimination on its face, since exemptions were granted according to countries of product origin, the Indian requirement for import licences obliging manufacturers to indigenization provides for a general discrimination of products of foreign origin vis-à-vis products of domestic origin. The panel in *India – Autos* left no doubt about the relevance of this aspect for the determination of likeness – this time, however, with respect to the obligation to national treatment under Article III:4. First, with respect to the indigenization requirement, the panel stated that in cases where origin was the sole criterion distinguishing the products, it would be correct to treat such products as like products within the meaning of Article III:4.[70] With respect to the trade balancing requirement, the

---

6.262–6.264; *Canada – Autos* (2000), No. 10.29; *US – Malt Beverages* (1992), No. 5.5, for a different origin-based measure see also No. 5.20; *US – Taxes on Automobiles* (1994), Nos. 5.46–5.49, with respect to origin in terms of location of the production site inside or outside of the customs territory of the United States, at No. 2.15; Panel Report *US – Gasoline* (1996), No. 6.9.

[69] Panel Report, *Italian Agricultural Machinery* (1958), No. 15.6.

[70] Panel Report, *India – Autos* (2001), No. 7.174. None of these issues were decided on by the Appellate Body, since India withdrew its appeal.

4.2 THE PRINCIPLE OF NON-DISCRIMINATION

panel stated the relevance of origin for likeness quite clearly: 'Such differences in origin would not alone be such as to make products unlike.'[71] This quote is the most recent in a series of disputes that expressed the same conclusion, namely, the irrelevance of origin for the determination of likeness under Article III:4.[72] Measures using origin as basis for a distinction can, for example, consist of local content requirements[73] or in other advantages granted in connection with the use of domestic products only.[74] All these measures violate GATT obligations *a priori*.

4.2.1.3 Non-discrimination and NPAs

As shown above, the 'like products' concept is of paramount importance for the question whether or not NPA measures violate GATT obligations. Of crucial interest is the question of whether NPAs may be taken into account when determining if products are 'like' or not. On the one hand, one could argue that NPA measures by definition distinguish between 'like' products. This conclusion, however, would be based on the controversial presumption that only physical aspects are permissible factors for the determination of likeness. As shown above, the criteria relevant to the determination of likeness are subject to an ongoing debate.

The criteria relevant for the determination of likeness depend on the purpose of the comparison. To give an example, if asked whether two monozygotic twins bear a resemblance or not, people might come up with different answers. While friends might find them extremely different, strangers might find a striking degree of similarity, and none of the

---

[71] Panel Report, *India – Autos* (2001), No. 7.302.
[72] E.g., Panel Report *US – FSC (Article 21.5 – EC)* (2001), No. 8.133 with respect to tax exemptions. In the 2000 *Korea – Beef* dispute, the panel rejected the consideration of origin for distinguishing between products with respect to treatment of imported products on the national market through a dual retail system (at No. 618). Its findings with respect to likeness of imported and domestic beef were not appealed. See also, e.g., Panel Report *Spain – Soyabean Oil* (1981), No. 4.7, with respect to Article III:4.
[73] See, e.g., the *Canada – Autos* (2000) dispute on the requirement of certain Canadian Value Added (CVA) (Panel Report, at Nos. 10.65–10.131). Canada had granted duty free imports to certain manufacturers included in a list. Only manufacturers which had produced in Canada were eligible for the respective import duty exemption. The Panel found the measures to violate both MFN and national treatment, implying that the tariff exemption had not been granted to other producers of 'like' cars. Hence, the distinction based on the identity of the manufacturer and location of production was found to be in violation of the GATT.
[74] This is now explicitly stipulated in the TRIMS Agreement, Article 2 together with the Illustrative List contained in the Annex to the agreement. Cf. for a local content requirement also the panel report *Indonesia – Autos* (1998). This Panel only assumed a violation of Article III:4, but exercised judicial economy (at No. 14.93).

answers would be wrong. The different assessments would obviously be due to the different standards applied by both groups: while friends might intuitively consider character and internal values crucial, strangers who do not have a personal relationship would rely on the only information available, namely, outer appearance. Similarly, whether or not products are considered 'like' depends entirely on the relevant standards. Hence, the crucial question is which aspects are relevant in the determination of likeness for the purposes of the various GATT provisions at issue. Once this question has been answered and products have been determined as 'like', the assessment of a possibly discriminatory measure will proceed to the second step: only the additional finding of less favourable treatment to imported products renders a measure discriminatory.

4.2.2 Interpreting the 'like products' concept with special consideration of NPAs

The above questions are particularly sensitive, since answering them ultimately determines the scope and content of the most fundamental GATT obligations. On the one hand, there are concerns that too broad an interpretation of the non-discrimination principle would imply disciplines on national legislation, which might unduly restrict policy space for rational and legitimate political decisions of national governments and legislators, and which could lead to excessive scrutiny of internal legislation by the WTO adjudicatory bodies.[75] On the other hand, since today the importance of *de jure* discrimination has become small and since *de facto* discrimination in various forms with all their negative impacts on conditions of competition for imported products prevail, it seems self-evident that WTO obligations must not be construed too narrowly.

The following sections discuss three exemplary approaches to the 'like products' concept. All approaches explore ways to balance both concerns in determining the correct extent to which national measures should be subjected to WTO scrutiny, and are thus highly relevant to the legal status of NPA measures. Although these approaches are presented in different sections of this chapter, they do not stand in isolation, but rather differ in the degree of importance which they ascribe to certain aspects. It should also be noted, that the 'like products' concept is used in a number of different provisions and contexts. The following sections focus on its use in Articles I, III and the Note Ad Article III. While the meaning of the term

---

[75] See Ehring (2002), pp. 921 *et seq.*

varies according to the differences in language and purpose, as will be shown below, the basic considerations in the following discussion apply – to a greater or lesser extent – to all provisions using the 'like products' concept.

4.2.2.1 The DSB approach: 'objective' determination

The analysis of the 'like products' concept naturally begins with the approach taken by the *quasi*-judicial organs of the WTO, namely, the panels and the Appellate Body, as revealed in a number of reports pertaining to this question. The notion of 'like products' has been a prominent subject in disputes since the earliest times of the GATT, and there is a large number of DSB reports on this matter.[76] In addition to WTO reports, there is also a substantial volume of secondary literature discussing these reports.

Despite the absence of the doctrine of *stare decisis* in WTO law, reports adopted in GATT and WTO dispute settlement are of paramount importance in WTO law. The WTO adjudicatory bodies treat their previous reports themselves often just as precedents by meticulously citing relevant prior decisions.[77] The great importance of reports under the GATT 1947 forms part of the GATT 1947 acquis as defined under Article XVI of the Marrakesh Agreement, and has been recognized as providing guidance to the WTO.[78] But it is not only WTO bodies who pay considerable attention to decisions of the Appellate Body, but also the private sector.[79] The approach of the adjudicating bodies can be regarded as prevailing opinion and is therefore presented as a starting point for considering possible alternative approaches.

Panels and the Appellate Body are widely believed to have ruled consistently that trade measures based on NPAs and PPMs are illegal. Taking a closer look, however, this simple interpretation of the various reports is wrong. Instead, panels and the Appellate Body do not seem to have developed a coherent approach to the legal issues pertaining to such measures. The following sections examine the relevant case law and identify the basic lines of the approach so far adopted by the WTO adjudicatory bodies.

---

[76] For a good summary of prevailing case law see panel report *Mexico – Taxes on Soft Drinks* (2005), No. 8.28. For earlier case law on 'like products' see fn. 58 in the Appellate Body report *EC – Asbestos* (2001), No. 88, with numerous references.
[77] Iwasawa (2002), p. 290.
[78] E.g., Appellate Body Report, *US – 1916 Act* (2000), No. 61. See for the contradictory approach of the Appellate Body to this question Iwasawa (2002), pp. 289, 290, fn. 3.
[79] Jackson (2005), at p. 664.

4.2.2.1.1 Main features

Particularly in the earlier days of the GATT's existence, panels often chose rather 'pragmatic' solutions and simply side-stepped a determination of 'like products'. For example, panels would adapt the sequence of examination of cumulative conditions to the effect that in consequence of a requirement which had not been satisfied, the panel was spared the difficulties of tackling the issue of likeness.[80] Nevertheless, over the years two key insights in the interpretation of the 'like products' concepts emerged as a result of a consistent development in GATT and later WTO case law. First, it was determined that whether two products are 'like' is to be made on a case-by-case basis, in order to allow a fair assessment in each case of the elements which constitute a similar product.[81] Second, there was the recognition that the notion of likeness does not have to be interpreted in a uniform way for all provisions which make use of it.[82] This idea was later also expressed by the Appellate Body in *EC – Asbestos*, which stated that the notion of likeness must be interpreted in the light of the context, the object and purpose of the provision at issue, and of the object and purpose of the covered agreement in which the provision appears.[83]

Until today, both rules have consistently been followed. In its probably best known quote, the Appellate Body in *Japan – Alcoholic Beverages II* illustrated both assumptions by invoking the image of a stretched or squeezed accordion to stress the inherent flexibility of the concept of likeness. Both aspects were mingled when the Appellate Body stated that:

> the width of the accordion in any one of those places must be determined by the particular provision in which the term 'like' is encountered as well as by the context and the circumstances that prevail in any given case to which that provision may apply.[84]

A more recent attempt of a definition via the dictionary in the *EC – Asbestos* dispute proved that the crucial issues of interpretation could not be resolved with the textual method only: the Appellate Body found that the dictionary meaning left many interpretative questions open.[85] Nevertheless, its dicta and findings on the 'like products' concept must

---

[80] E.g., Panel Report, *EEC – Minimum Import Prices* (1978), at para. 4.12.
[81] This prevailing case law is based on the Report of the Working Party on Border Tax Adjustment, adopted on 2 December 1970, BISD 18S/97, at para. 18.
[82] E.g., Panel Report, *Japan – Alcoholic Beverages II* (1996), para. 6.20.
[83] Appellate Body Report, *EC – Asbestos* (2001), No. 88.
[84] Appellate Body Report, *Japan – Alcoholic Beverages II* (1996), H 1(a), p. 21.
[85] Appellate Body Report, *EC – Asbestos* (2001), Nos. 90–92.

4.2 THE PRINCIPLE OF NON-DISCRIMINATION

be considered authoritative. Most importantly, the Appellate Body drew conclusions on the function of the concept. Although its considerations regarded Article III:4, they are also insightful for other instances of references to the concept. The Appellate Body stated:

> Thus, a determination of 'likeness' under Article III:4 is, fundamentally, a determination about the nature and extent of a competitive relationship between and among products.[86]

In addition, the Appellate Body identified three different interpretive questions which should be addressed in order to give proper meaning to the concept.[87] These questions are in line with the main features developed in earlier reports, but they provide a more detailed structure for interpretation, and with the third issue even adds a new dimension to the concept of likeness.

The Appellate Body first mentions the question of the *characteristics or qualities* which are important in assessing 'likeness'.[88] The Appellate Body refers here to the aspects that have to be taken into account in any given real-life case when determining likeness, and which are not specified in the legal texts.[89] These aspects can also be referred to as the 'determinants' of likeness. The second interpretive question regards the *degree of similarity* which is required under each provision.[90] The term 'like' can be attributed a wider or narrower meaning and so decides the scope of the respective obligation. The Appellate Body then identified a third, and arguably crucial, question, namely, *whose perspective* was relevant to judge likeness in the first place, and suggested as alternatives perspectives of consumers, producers or inventors of products.[91] Unfortunately, it did not exhaust the discussion on this question.

The above interrelated aspects of the concept and nature of likeness as identified by the Appellate Body do not yet provide a functional interpretation of 'likeness', but they do provide guidance in approaching the issue. The following sections briefly discuss each of the interpretive questions, with a special consideration of their relevance to NPA measures.

---

[86] Appellate Body Report, *EC – Asbestos* (2001), No. 99. In this respect, it is important to note the concurring statement of one member of the Appellate Body, who expressed substantial doubts about 'a "fundamentally" economic interpretation of "likeness" of products' (No. 154).
[87] E.g., Appellate Body Report, *EC – Asbestos* (2001), No. 101.
[88] Appellate Body Report, *EC – Asbestos* (2001), Nos. 92, 101 *et seq.*
[89] Cf., e.g., Panel Report, *US – Gasoline* (1996), No. 6.7.
[90] Appellate Body Report, *EC – Asbestos* (2001), No. 92 *et seq.*
[91] Appellate Body Report, *EC – Asbestos* (2001), No. 92.

4.2.2.1.1.1 Relevant factors

GATT and WTO case law on the question of which factors determine the 'likeness' of products has been very consistent. The jurisprudence traces back to the report of the Working Party on Border Tax Adjustment,[92] but it should be noted that the Working Party in turn drew from the previous experience of contracting parties within and without the GATT. The Working Party deliberated the issue in the late 1960s. It addressed the issue of the criteria for determining 'like' or 'similar products' with respect to various provisions in the GATT, although the report mostly focused on border tax adjustments. The relevant criteria it identified in its 1970 report were: (1) the product's end-uses in a given market; (2) consumers' tastes and habits; and (3) the product's properties, nature and quality.[93] The report implied, on the one hand, that the criteria determining likeness of products would be the same, regardless of which GATT provision was at issue. On the other hand, it advised that these criteria were mere suggestions and that problems arising from interpretation of the term should be solved on a case-by-case basis.[94]

Of the above criteria, particularly the criteria of physical characteristics and end-uses, gained great importance. The 1987 *Japan – Alcoholic Beverages I* panel emphasized that the criteria introduced by the Working Party were not exclusive (*'inter alia'*),[95] and that earlier GATT panels had also used the criterion of tariff classification.[96] The suitability of the latter criterion for the determination of 'likeness' was examined more thoroughly by the Appellate Body in *Japan – Alcoholic Beverages II* nine years later. The Appellate Body qualified the use of this criterion by noting that tariff bindings, as opposed to tariff classification under the Harmonized System, are often a result of state practice, and that least-developing country members in particular had submitted schedules with bindings which included very broad ranges of products, and which were obviously not suitable for the determination of 'likeness'. Other tariff bindings could, on the other hand, provide significant guidance. The Appellate Body thus confirmed the use of the criterion with the *proviso* that determinations be made on a case-by-case basis.[97] Other panel and Appellate Body reports

---

[92] Working Party on Border Tax Adjustment.
[93] Working Party on Border Tax Adjustment, para. 18.
[94] Working Party on Border Tax Adjustment, para. 18.
[95] Panel Report, *Japan – Alcoholic Beverages I* (1987), No. 5.6.
[96] Working Party Report, Panel Reports *Australia – Ammonium Sulphate* (1950), No. 8, and *EEC – Animal Feed Proteins* (1978), para. 4.2.
[97] Appellate Body Report, *Japan – Alcoholic Beverages II* (1996), p. 22 (H.1.a).

4.2 THE PRINCIPLE OF NON-DISCRIMINATION 173

followed, and the DSB approach to likeness has since been based on the criteria set up by the working party, supplemented with the criterion tariff classification.[98]

Consumers' tastes and habits, on the other hand, were treated as a weak criterion, especially in earlier case law. Most reports mentioned the criterion briefly in order to confirm an outcome that had already been established based on other criteria. The low importance of the consumers' tastes and habits criterion is illustrated, for example, by the Panel Report in the 1987 *Japan – Alcoholic Beverages I* dispute. The panel opined that products 'do not become "unlike" merely because of differences in local consumer traditions within a country'.[99] This case law, however, must be considered overruled. The Appellate Body in *EC – Asbestos* emphasized the importance of consumers' tastes and habits as a relevant criterion.[100]

The consumers' tastes and preferences criterion is particularly relevant for NPA measures: since consumer tastes and preferences are not qualified, these may often relate to aspects other than physical product characteristics. As advertising and marketing show, non-physical aspects often play an important role in consumer decisions. Therefore, some scholars argue that not only physical aspects, but also NPAs are relevant and might even be decisive for the determination of likeness.[101] Despite a large amount of case law on the definition of 'likeness', neither panels nor the Appellate Body have ever addressed this issue explicitly with respect to NPA measures.

The Appellate Body in *EC – Asbestos* authoritatively outlined the proper approach of panels to the determination of likeness as follows:

> the Panel should have examined the evidence relating to each of those four criteria and, then, weighed *all* of that evidence, along with any other relevant evidence, in making an *overall* determination of whether the products at issue could be characterized as 'like' (original emphasis).[102]

In sum, under the DSB approach the so-called Working Party criteria, tariff classification under the HS and any other relevant evidence are

---

[98] E.g., Appellate Body Report, *EC – Asbestos* (2001), No. 101. See also the analyses of likeness under Article III:2 and III:4 in the Panel Report *Mexico – Taxes on Soft Drinks* (2005), Nos. 8.27–8.36, 8.106.
[99] Panel Report, *Japan – Alcoholic Beverages I* (1987), at 5.9(b).
[100] Appellate Body Report, *EC – Asbestos* (2001), No. 130.
[101] E.g., Kysar (2004); Howse (2002), p. 515; Bronckers and McNelis (2000), p. 376, who recommend ascribing greater importance to consumer preferences (see also below at section 4.2.2.3).
[102] Appellate Body Report, *EC – Asbestos* (2001), No. 109.

relevant determinants of likeness. These must be assessed together in an overall determination of likeness. An open question under the DSB approach, however, remains whether highly important differences in one respect may be sufficient to outweigh similarities which are suitable to create a competitive relationship between the products in question.[103]

4.2.2.1.1.2 Varying importance of factors

The 'like products' concept is part of several provisions in the WTO Agreements, and, as stated above, the prevailing view holds that the meaning of the term 'likeness' is not the same under all of these provisions.[104] Corresponding to the different meanings of the concepts, the relevance of the different factors determining likeness might also differ from one provision to another. Therefore, for this analysis of the legal status of NPA measures, the question arises as to whether any of the criteria, such as physical product characteristics, is of paramount importance under all or some of the provisions, or if the various criteria in general are equally important.

Particularly in the earlier history of the GATT, examination of likeness of products was often superficial. Elaborations on this issue were sometimes limited to a single paragraph, even if with respect to several different provisions. In other cases, for the purpose of likeness under one provision a panel would also refer to its respective findings under another.[105] These practices would imply that the criteria determining likeness are identical under different provisions. Indeed, if the examination of likeness under one provision is comprehensive and leads to the same result from the perspective of each of the criteria, there would be no value added by repeating the examination for each provision. So far, neither in GATT nor in WTO dispute settlement has a clear stance been taken towards the question of whether one or several traditional criteria are of greater importance than others, or if the traditional criteria are of equal value.[106] However, there is evidence that the adjudicatory bodies, at least in some instances, considered certain criteria more important than others.

---

[103] See the concurring statement in Appellate Body Report, *EC – Asbestos* (2001), Nos. 152-3.

[104] Appellate Body Report, *EC – Asbestos* (2001), No. 88.

[105] E.g., for Articles I and III, Panel Report, *Indonesia – Autos* (1998), para. 14.141; *EEC – Animal Feed Proteins* (1978), Panel Report, Nos. 4.1, 4.2; Working Party Report on: *Australia – Ammonium Sulphate* (1950), No. 9 (referring to the argumentation in No. 8); for Articles I, III, X and XIII, e.g., Panel Report, *EC – Bananas III (ECU)* (1997), paras. 7.62–7.63; for Articles I and XIII GATT Panel Report, *Germany – Sardines* (1952), No. 11–12.

[106] Mavroidis (2005), p. 152.

4.2 THE PRINCIPLE OF NON-DISCRIMINATION

Likewise, in the early years of the GATT, panels found the criterion of tariff classification important for Article 1 and determined likeness of products in part, and even exclusively, by examining tariff classification.[107] A turn in this adjudication was indicated in 1981 by the decision in the *Spain – Unroasted Coffee* dispute. The panel in this dispute was not satisfied with the plain fact of tariff classification, but examined whether actual physical differences justified a distinct treatment.[108] In contrast, in *Indonesia – Automobiles*, the panel completely ignored the criterion of tariff classification for the determination of likeness, first for an examination under Article III:2,[109] but subsequently also for its examination of a violation of MFN treatment with respect to tariffs under Article I.[110] Instead, the panel based its findings mainly on the same end-uses and same basic properties, nature and quality.[111] Existing case law seems inconsistent on this point. Even for the objectives of Article I, the criterion of tariff classification is not *per se* of particular importance. In response to possible abuses of the nation's right to establish sub-headings in their tariff classification, other criteria have been considered as being of greater importance even when it came to the examination of tariff measures.[112]

It could be assumed that under Article III the criterion of tariff classification would be inferior to other criteria, namely, physical product characteristics. While panels still consider tariff classification under the HS as relevant for the determination of likeness under Article III,[113] there is no

---

[107] Working Party Report, *Australia – Ammonium Sulphate* (1950), No. 8; also Panel Report, *EEC – Animal Feed Proteins* (1978), No. 4.2.

[108] Panel Report, *Spain – Unroasted Coffee* (1981), No. 4.6. Note, however, that the Panel Report, *Japan – SPF Dimension Lumber* (1989) could be interpreted to a different end. In this dispute the Panel stressed, with some reservations, the importance of tariff classification and found that tariff differentiations were basically a legitimate means of trade policy (at para 5.10). The Panel found that a claim of 'likeness' had to be based on the tariff classification of the importing country, and that Canada with its reference to the North American concept of dimension lumber had not satisfied this requirement (at para. 5.13–5.14). Since the Panel considered itself unable to examine the claim in a broader context, because of the limitation of the claim to the issue of dimension lumber, the importance of this report with respect to the importance of tariff classification must not be overstated.

[109] Panel Report, *Indonesia – Autos* (1998), Nos. 14.109–14.110.

[110] Panel Report, *Indonesia – Autos* (1998), No. 14.141.

[111] Panel Report, *Indonesia – Autos* (1998), No. 14.110.

[112] As shown by *Spain – Unroasted Coffee* (1981), see also above Chapter 1, section 1.4.1.

[113] See for more recent Panel Reports *Mexico – Taxes on Soft Drinks* (2005), Nos. 8.28, 8.29, and *Dominican Republic – Import and Sale of Cigarettes* (2004), No. 7.165.

doubt about the greater weight of the other traditional criteria, namely, physical properties, end-uses and consumers' tastes and habits.[114]

It would, however, be wrong to assume that any physical differences were of paramount importance in the determination of likeness under the DSB approach. Although there is consistent case law holding that physical properties need to be taken into account in the determination of like products, as, for example, ingredients in feed products, where their different vegetable, animal and synthetic origins led to the conclusion that the products are different,[115] it is also recognized that every physical difference is sufficient for the negation of likeness. In *Spain – Unroasted Coffee* the panel considered the organoleptic differences between different types of coffee resulting from geographical factors, cultivation methods, the processing of the beans and genetic factors. While the panel identified a number of smaller physical differences, it found that these could not justify different treatment.[116]

Particularly instructive on the weight of physical differences is the Appellate Body report in *EC – Asbestos*, which offers an interesting contrast to the *Spain – Unroasted Coffee* Panel Report. Here, great importance was given to a seemingly small physical difference in fibres of construction material. The panel in this dispute had found that certain materials containing asbestos fibre were 'like' similar materials not containing asbestos on the basis of physical similarities.[117] This finding was reversed by the Appellate Body.[118] The Appellate Body highlighted the relevance of the health risk that it considered to be relevant as physical properties.[119] Thus, a comparably small physical difference between materials was attributed great importance, because it implied carcinogenicity of the product. Nevertheless, the Appellate Body refrained from an ultimate decision on whether or not the products at issue were like. Despite its clear finding of carcinogenicity and other indications of likeness, the

---

[114] Appellate Body Report, *Japan – Alcoholic Beverages II* (1996), H 1(a).
[115] Panel Report, *EEC – Animal Feed Proteins* (1978), para. 4.2.
[116] Panel Report, *Spain – Unroasted Coffee* (1981), para. 4.6.
[117] Panel Report, *EC – Asbestos* (2000), No. 8.149.
[118] Appellate Body Report, *EC – Asbestos* (2001), No. 192(c) and (d).
[119] Appellate Body Report, *EC – Asbestos* (2001), Nos. 116, 128. See also the concurring statement of one member of the division who considered the difference to be of paramount importance: 'It is difficult for me to imagine what evidence relating to economic competitive relationships as reflected in end-uses and consumers' tastes and habits could outweigh and set at naught the undisputed deadly nature of chrysotile asbestos fibres, compared with PCG fibres, when inhaled by humans, and thereby compel a characterization of "likeness" of chrysotile asbestos and PCG fibres.' (No. 152).

4.2 THE PRINCIPLE OF NON-DISCRIMINATION

Appellate Body considered the lack of consideration of consumers' tastes and habits as one out of the four traditional criteria of likeness even more important. As a corollary, it dismissed Canada's claim of a violation of Article III:4, not because of the differences among the products in question, but because Canada had failed to supply evidence concerning consumers' tastes and habits and thus had not satisfied its burden of proof.[120] While one member expressed its view that in this case, the importance of physical differences were such that they would trump any evidence concerning other criteria, the majority of members held the view that even in this case a consideration of all criteria would have been necessary to come to a conclusion.

In sum, the existing case law suggests that the same criteria are relevant for assessing the likeness of products under all provisions using the concept.[121] Within the overall assessment to date, it then seems that the DSB approach holds that all traditional criteria need to be considered, although it would arguably be possible to attribute greater importance and weight to some evidence than to other evidence, depending on the particular characteristics of a case. For the purposes of this work it is important to note that, contrary to a popular belief, the DSB approach does not imply that any physical difference is sufficient to justify 'unlikeness' of products and differences in their treatment. Rather, the relevance of physical differences needs to be assessed on a case-by-case basis. While there is no doubt that physical differences are of great weight in the overall determination of likeness, it is also clear that none of the criteria which provide space for the consideration of NPAs, such as consumer tastes and habits, is excluded from the assessment under any provision using the 'like products' concept.

4.2.2.1.1.3 Degree of 'likeness' under different provisions

As stated above, 'likeness' of products is a question of degree rather than of a clear 'yes' or 'no'. Therefore, the question on the threshold for a finding of 'likeness' under different provisions including this concept arises. This threshold can be higher, so that a higher degree of similarity would be needed, or lower, so that little similarity might be sufficient to qualify

---

[120] Appellate Body Report, *EC – Asbestos* (2001), Nos. 141, 147.
[121] There is little case law regarding the term 'like products' under other GATT provisions. However, in many cases the object and purpose of the provision might provide guidance. For instance, the term 'like products' as used in Article II:2(b) obviously relates to the term in Article III:2, and similarly the use in Article XIII provides similarities to the concept as part of MFN treatment in Article I.

two products as 'like' under a given provision. On top of the scale of likeness would be 'identity' of two products – a concept, however, of merely theoretical value in the real world.

Since the famous accordion analogy in *Japan – Alcoholic Beverages II*, it is prevailing case law that the degree of similarity which is required by the 'like products' concept varies from one provision to another, and sometimes even within the paragraphs of a single provision. The Appellate Body used the image of a stretched or squeezed accordion in order to illustrate different degrees of product similarity,[122] or in other words, different degrees of 'likeness'. It also confirmed the conclusion of the panel that because of the second sentence of Article III:2, which provides for a different category of products other than 'like products',[123] the first sentence including the concept of 'like products' must be construed more narrowly.[124]

With respect to Article III:4, the Appellate Body in *EC – Asbestos* stated later that the product scope, 'although broader than the *first* sentence of Article III:2, [was] certainly *not* broader than the *combined* product scope of the *two* sentences of Article III:2 of the GATT 1994'.[125] This finding of the Appellate Body has since been repeated in other reports.[126]

This brief outline of relevant case law on the different degrees of likeness under various GATT provisions is sufficient for the present purposes. Compared with the relevance of NPAs as a factor for the determination of likeness, the importance of the question on the specific degree of likeness is limited for this analysis. Only to the extent they are considered relevant for likeness, could NPAs possibly contribute to a higher or lower degree of likeness among two products. In cases involving NPAs, there would by definition be an extremely high degree of physical similarity between the products at issue. Even presuming the relevance of NPAs, it would therefore seem that outweighing these physical similarities would be more likely under provisions requiring a high degree of 'likeness'. In contrast, under

---

[122] Appellate Body Report, *Japan – Alcoholic Beverages II* (1996), p. 21, fn. 47.
[123] Namely, the category of 'directly competitive or substitutable products' (GATT Article III:2 together with the Note Ad Article III, para. 2).
[124] Appellate Body Report, *Japan – Alcoholic Beverages II* (1996), p. 19/20, H 1(a). This finding on the degree of likeness required for Article III:2, first sentence, has been confirmed numerous times (e.g., Appellate Body report in *Canada – Periodicals* (1997), V. A, p. 21).
[125] Appellate Body Report, *EC – Asbestos* (2001), No. 99 (original emphasis).
[126] See, e.g., Panel Report, *Mexico – Taxes on Soft Drinks* (2005), at para. 8.105. This finding was not appealed.

provisions requiring a lower degree of likeness, it would seem even more difficult – although not impossible – to argue that a difference in NPAs outweighs physical similarities almost amounting to physical identity.

In contrast to NPAs, however, incorporated PPMs by definition cause at least minor physical differences. Since the *EC – Asbestos* report, it is acknowledged that also a comparably minor physical difference which is not even detectable from the outer appearance of a product can prevent a finding of likeness in WTO law – and this even under Article III:4 which requires a lower degree of likeness. However, this would depend on the facts of the case and on the weight attributed to the specific physical differences in question.[127]

4.2.2.1.2 Relevance of NPAs

This section reviews GATT and WTO disputes on measures linked to NPAs, or minor physical differences. It analyses the relevant discussions of the parties, panels and the Appellate Body and considers especially the importance ascribed to the NPAs or minor physical differences by the adjudicatory bodies. The review is structured according to the different aspects featuring in the discussion on 'likeness'.

4.2.2.1.2.1 Processes and production methods

A few disputes dealt with measures linked to PPMs in the narrow sense, namely, the *Tuna-Dolphin I* and *II* and the *Shrimp Turtle* disputes. In these cases, the panels found that Article III was not applicable, and accordingly they did not directly address the issue of 'likeness'.[128]

(i) *Tuna-Dolphin I* (1991): Mexico, the complainant in *Tuna-Dolphin I*, based its argumentation in part on its interpretation of the term 'like products' in Article III. Mexico assumed that domestic and imported tuna were 'like products' and observed that the respondent, the United States, applied measures to a hybrid 'tuna/dolphin' category.[129] It stated that 'a

---

[127] The problems of interpretation are caused by the nature of the concept: the term 'likeness' is a term of comparison, and therefore it is relative. For that reason, it is impossible to determine the degree of likeness of two products without having set the applicable standards previously. The Appellate Body in *EC – Asbestos* (2001), e.g., stated with respect to the same fibres that in some instances these were physically *very* different (at Nos. 121, 136, 139) and in another that they were *quite* different (No. 125), without, however, making transparent the standards for determining when products were *very* or *quite* different.

[128] See above, Chapter 1, section 1.2.

[129] Panel Report, *Tuna-Dolphin I* (1991), No. 3.16.

measure regulating a product could not legally discriminate between domestic and imported products based solely on the production process; to do so would violate Article III'.[130]

The United States replied with a different interpretation of the concept of 'likeness'. It argued that the 'like products' categories to be compared were tuna harvested using purse-seine nets by US vessels, on the one hand, and tuna harvested using purse-seine nets by vessels from other nations, on the other hand. The United States interpreted Article III:4 as not distinguishing between laws that have an impact on physical characteristics and laws that otherwise affect the sale etc. of products, but that it merely required that treatment accorded to imported products be no less favourable than that accorded to products of national origin.[131]

The parties thus based their argumentation on different interpretations of the same provision and wording. Mexico claimed that 'likeness' of products could not possibly be determined by a production process which leaves physical characteristics of a product untouched. The United States responded that the crucial aspect of Article III:4 is the non-protective treatment of domestic products. Implied in this argumentation is the assumption that the term 'likeness' is not to be determined on the basis of physical product characteristics alone. Instead, it assumes that national authorities might establish product categories autonomously, and that they are merely obliged to apply them in a non-discriminatory way.

To reiterate, the panel did not address the question directly. Instead, it considered whether the harvesting regulations applied to products at all and decided that this was not the case, since regulations governing the taking of dolphins could not possibly affect tuna as a product.[132] This consideration has nevertheless been interpreted as a rejection of process-based distinctions between otherwise like products and as a confirmation of the product–process distinction.[133] Since the panel's reasoning is very brief and its structure unclear this interpretation would, however, seem far-reaching. In fact, the panel merely concluded that the measure was neither covered by the Note nor by Article III,[134] and so declined to

---

[130] Panel Report, *Tuna Dolphin I* (1991), No. 3.16. Also Venezuela endorsed this finding, although the argumentation was only alternative to the finding that Article III should be applicable at all (at 4.27, 4.28). It should be noted that Mexico based its claim of a violation on different arguments, one being that PPM-based measures violated Article III, another being that the measures in the MMPA did not actually even constitute PPMs.
[131] Panel Report, *Tuna-Dolphin I* (1991), No. 3.20.
[132] Panel Report, *Tuna-Dolphin I* (1991), No. 5.15.   [133] Hudec (2000), p. 197.
[134] Panel Report, *Tuna-Dolphin I* (1991), Nos. 5.14, 5.15.

4.2 THE PRINCIPLE OF NON-DISCRIMINATION

make a finding on the relevance of production for the determination of likeness.[135]

(ii) *Tuna-Dolphin II* (1994): The parties to the *Tuna-Dolphin II* report focused in their argumentation on justification under Article XX. The complainants for the most part repeated the arguments against applicability of the Note, and alternatively invoked a violation of the national treatment standard of Article III for both the primary and the intermediary nation embargo.[136] In contrast to the first *Tuna-Dolphin* dispute, the respondent this time concentrated on justification of the measures under Article XX, and did not raise the so-called Article III defence.[137]

Also in this dispute, the panel was content to find the Note Ad Article III not applicable.[138] Interestingly, the panel pointed out that harvesting 'practices, policies or methods could not have any impact on the inherent character of tuna as a product',[139] and thus suggested that such aspects could not make products unlike. But the panel seems to simply have put the readers off the scent, since its conclusion was not violation of Article III, which would be the logical consequence of a distinction between like products, but instead the non-applicability of the Note Ad Article III. Still, this statement has been seen as a somewhat clearer statement of the product–process doctrine, even if primarily by assertion.[140]

(iii) *Tuna-Dolphin III* (2009): In 2008, Mexico requested consultations with the United States in relation to certain measures taken by the latter concerning the importation, marketing and sale of tuna and tuna products. Mexico's complaints concern certain measures and acts suspected of effectively prevent the labelling of Mexican tuna products as 'dolphin-safe', even if the harvesting means complied with the standards established by the Inter-American Tropical Tuna Commission. Mexico holds that its products are accorded treatment less favourable than like products of US origin, and that the contested rules violate Article III:4 of the GATT 1994. After consultations had failed in 2009, the dispute settlement body established a panel.[141] A report is expected for February 2011.

---

[135] In this direction also Howse and Regan (2000), p. 254, also Bronckers and McNelis (2002), pp. 366, 370.
[136] Panel Report, *Tuna-Dolphin II* (1994), Nos. 3.4, 3.5 and 3.93.
[137] The respondent did not argue that the measures were consistent with Article III in the first place. Panel Report, *Tuna-Dolphin II* (1994), No. 3.6.
[138] Panel Report, *Tuna-Dolphin II* (1994), No. 5.9.
[139] Panel Report, *Tuna-Dolphin II* (1994), No. 5.9.   [140] Hudec (2000), p. 201.
[141] *Tuna-Dolphin III*. Note by the Secretariat, 15 December 2009, WT/DS381/5.

(iv) *Shrimp Turtle*: The panel in the *Shrimp Turtle* dispute also failed to take a stand on the question of 'likeness'. The United States as respondent had again chosen not to argue that the measure was covered by the Note and that shrimp harvested with different methods were 'unlike' under Article III. Nevertheless, some of the complainants had provided an opportunity to address this issue. They argued with respect to MFN treatment that 'the method of harvest did not affect the nature of the product',[142] and with respect to Article XIII that 'all foreign shrimp and shrimp products had the same physical characteristics, end-uses, and tariff classifications and were perfectly substitutable'.[143]

An interesting statement was made by Japan in a third party submission. It submitted that the measures applied to 'like products', but nevertheless stated that 'in view of the increased awareness of the importance of policy objectives of environmental protection and resource conservation, it should be noted that certain cases required differential treatment according to process and production methods (PPMs) to tackle global and transboundary environmental problems'.[144] Japan did not clarify, however, whether it suggested that this differentiation should play a role in GATT violations or in justification.

The panel, having found a violation of Article XI, left the question unanswered.[145] The appeal by the United States did not address this matter, and consequently the Appellate Body was silent on this matter.[146] Also in the compliance dispute *Shrimp Turtle – Article 21.5*, the United States did not contest that its implementation measure violated Article XI. The panel thus relied mainly on the findings in the original dispute and on the US position for its finding of a violation of Article XI, and thus did not address the question of likeness.[147]

(v) Summary: Although the question on the relevance of PPMs for the determination of likeness arose in several disputes, up to the present time none of the adjudicatory bodies has addressed this question directly. Therefore, while PPMs have not been considered relevant as 'other evidence' or as a separate criterion in the determination of 'likeness', it would be wrong to conclude that the DSB approach clearly rejects the relevance

---

[142] India, Pakistan and Thailand, Panel Report, *Shrimp Turtle* (1998), No. 7.18
[143] India, Pakistan and Thailand, Panel Report, *Shrimp Turtle* (1998), No. 7.20.
[144] Panel Report, *Shrimp Turtle* (1998), No. 4.50.
[145] Panel Report, *Shrimp Turtle* (1998), Nos. 7.22, 7.23.
[146] Appellate Body report, *Shrimp Turtle* (1998).
[147] Panel Report, *Shrimp Turtle – Article 21.5 Malaysia* (2001), Nos. 5.22, 5.23.

of PPMs. The panels declined applicability of the Note Ad Article III and therefore did not arrive at a point where a finding on this issue would have been necessary. Also, taking into account that one of the main objectives of the dispute settlement system is to achieve a satisfactory settlement of the matter,[148] this gap in case law might to a large extent be due to the fact that the respondent in the above cases decided not to bring this argument forward. While there is hesitance towards the consideration of PPMs for the determination of 'likeness', the adjudicatory bodies have not so far negated their relevance either.

4.2.2.1.2.2 Output and producer characteristics

Some disputes dealt with measures that distinguished between products based on characteristics of the producer or on other producer-related aspects. While these aspects are not PPMs in the narrow sense, they are closely related.

(i) *United States – Section 337* (1989):[149] This dispute concerned allegedly discriminatory patent infringement proceedings initiated by the US International Trade Commission (ITC) under section 337 of the United States Tariff Act of 1930. This section is applicable to acts of unfair competition, such as the infringement of valid US patents. The proceedings originally subject to the complaint were based on section 337a, which applied section 337 specifically to the importation or sale of products produced abroad by a process covered by a US patent.[150] The EEC complained that the procedures of section 337 subjected imported goods to a treatment less favourable than the treatment accorded to goods of national origin.

This Panel Report for the determination of likeness seems of little importance at first glance. Indeed, despite applying Article III:4, the panel did not even mention the word 'likeness', because the facts of the case required assessing whether or not section 337 was discriminatory to imported products only in a most general way. However, the panel clearly assumed some products to be 'like', since it found a violation of

---

[148] DSU Article III:4.
[149] It has been argued that this dispute concerned a measure based on a PPM (Bronckers and McNelis (2002), p. 369). However, it seems more appropriate to categorize the challenged measure as producer-related, since it is not linked to a specific PPM, but to a condition relating to the producer, namely, the fact that a producer either holds a valid licence or otherwise infringes a US patent.
[150] Panel Report, *United States – Section 337 Tariff Act* (1989), No. 2.2.

Article III:4.[151] The products to be compared were foreign and US products allegedly or actually infringing US patents.[152] The panel's findings therefore merely seem to indicate that origin is irrelevant for the determination of likeness.

But the panel's findings can be interpreted to have a crucial meaning beyond that. The panel compared 'likeness' of two categories of products, namely, domestic products that had allegedly been produced under infringement of a US patent, on the one hand, and foreign products that likewise had allegedly been produced under infringement of a US patent, on the other hand. The choice of these categories for the comparison of treatment accorded to both categories is arguably based on valid reasons. Neither the parties nor the panel claimed that the categories should distinguish between foreign products that had allegedly been produced illegally and domestic product that had been produced with a valid licence. In this respect, this report differs from both *Tuna-Dolphin* cases in a most crucial respect. How would the panel have decided if the EEC had complained about the fact that its allegedly illegal products had been treated less favourably than legal US products? Panel and parties seem to accept naturally the legislatory rationales for a distinction between 'legal' and 'illegal', yet physically identical products. By this logic, it must be assumed that the panel might have considered an NPA, namely, the existence or not of a valid licence, crucial for finding physically identical products 'unlike'.

(ii) *United States – Malt Beverages* (1992):[153] The measures subject to the 1992 *US – Malt Beverages* dispute were a set of regulations of the respective product market through various US federal and state laws. While some of the measures were tax measures, and others imposed distribution, transportation, licensing and price affirmation requirements, all measures had in common that they affected trade in certain beverages. The challenged measures differentiated between beverages partly on the basis of their physical properties, as, for example, alcohol content,[154] partly on aspects which may or may not affect physical characteristics of a product, as, for example, the use of local ingredients,[155] partly on product

---

[151] Panel Report, *United States – Section 337 Tariff Act* (1989), No. 5.20.
[152] Panel Report, *United States – Section 337 Tariff Act* (1989), No. 5.10.
[153] Panel Report, *US – Malt Beverages* (1992).
[154] Panel Report, *US – Malt Beverages* (1992), No, 2.32, cf. also table IV on Beer Alcohol Content Requirements.
[155] Panel Report, *US – Malt Beverages* (1992), No. 2.13, excise tax rates based on the use of local ingredients in Michigan, Ohio and Rhode Island.

4.2 THE PRINCIPLE OF NON-DISCRIMINATION 185

origin, and partly on other aspects not constituting physical product properties. Here, the dispute is of interest mainly for the two latter types of measure.

One of those measures was the federal excise tax for beer, which was considerably lower for the first 60,000 barrels of beer produced by breweries not exceeding a certain annual production. This lower rate was not available for imported beers. In some states, tax exemptions had been available for qualifying smaller domestic breweries but were not granted to foreign brewers. These measures were thus based on a combination of origin and an NPA, namely, the size of the brewery, its production and location. The panel examined the measures under Article III:2 and stated without any further discussion that tax exemptions limited to domestic breweries meant less favourable treatment to the imported product inconsistent with the obligation to accord national treatment.[156] Having examined a measure which discriminated against foreign products *de jure*, the panel did not at this point address the question of whether the size of the brewery could be a suitable determinant for likeness or rather 'unlikeness' of products.

However, with respect to another measure the panel had to decide on a distinction in treatment based on an NPA regardless of the origin of the product. In Minnesota, an excise tax credit based on annual production was available for certain quantities of beer sold by brewers whose annual production did not exceed an indicated level. Whether the credit was available to foreign as well as to in-state breweries, remained contentious.[157] Accordingly, there was the possibility that beneficiaries of credits could have been smaller breweries of any nationality, and thus origin did not play a role. The panel, in examining a violation of national treatment under Article III:2 stated that in this respect 'beer produced by large breweries is not unlike beer produced by smaller breweries',[158] implying that the size of a brewery would not matter in the determination of likeness of the products. This statement seems to amount to a negation of the relevance of NPAs for the determination of 'likeness'.[159]

---

[156] Panel Report, *US – Malt Beverages* (1992), No. 5.5, for a different origin-based measure also at 5.20.
[157] Panel Report, *US – Malt Beverages* (1992), Nos. 2.11, 2.14.
[158] Panel Report, *US – Malt Beverages* (1992), No. 5.19.
[159] Interpreted to this end e.g. by Fauchald (2003), p. 455, in fn. 43, also Howse and Regan (2000), p. 263, while being uncertain about the precise meaning, suggest that this is what the quote appears to mean.

On closer examination, however, the statement is less persuasive. The double negation 'is not unlike' suggests that the panel hesitated or did not actually intend to decide whether or not beers brewed in breweries of different sizes are 'like' each other. The statement, therefore, can hardly be understood as a confirmation that only physical differences can be significant. Furthermore, the panel then made a strategic withdrawal by referring to the submission of the respondent, the United States, which had neither asserted that the nature of the beer was affected, nor that the size of the breweries had 'otherwise affected beer as a product'.[160] The panel seems to have based its decision on the parties' submissions and their shortcomings.

Interestingly, the fact that the panel did, indeed, mention the option that beer as a product could not only be affected in its nature, but also 'otherwise', has been interpreted to be, if not a direct statement, at least as a hint indicating that aspects other than the physical constitution of beer could in fact be relevant to the definition of a product.[161] The reason for this interpretation is based on the assumption that the 'nature' of a product refers to its physical characteristics and that 'otherwise' therefore can refer only to aspects other than physical aspects. This logic is, however, not compelling. Although the report in the *US – Malt Beverages* dispute is only vague in its implications, its most evident interpretation suggests that aspects relating to the producer and to the circumstances of production in general are irrelevant for the determination of likeness.[162]

(iii) *United States – Taxes on Automobiles* (1994): One of the measures subject to the unadopted *US – Taxes on Automobiles* dispute, namely, the Corporate Average Fuel Economy law (CAFE), dealt with producer or rather importer-based measures.[163] The CAFE law declared unlawful the failure of manufacturers and importers of automobiles to reach certain fuel economy values for their fleet and it allowed for civil penalties. The fuel economy values were calculated according to a formula set up by the US Environmental Protection Agency. For purposes of the calculation, automobiles were classified under different categories, referred to

---

[160] Panel Report, *US – Malt Beverages* (1992), No. 5.19.
[161] Howse and Regan (2000), p. 263.
[162] To this end interpreted by the Panel in *US – Gasoline* (1996), at No. 6.11, Charnovitz (2001a), who also classifies the measure as a producer characteristics PPM, at p. 37.
[163] Other measures subject to this dispute are discussed further below.

as model types, based on characteristics that were likely to significantly affect fuel consumption.[164] From this point of view the measure was based on physical properties of products. However, the CAFE was based on a calculation of the average fuel economy, taking into account all products manufactured or imported by persons who control, were controlled by, or were under common control with the manufacturer.[165] Furthermore, the CAFE measure allowed for an exception for manufacturers whose worldwide production was fewer than 10,000 cars,[166] and so referred to another producer-related NPA.

The panel found that the measure actually regulated the conduct of manufacturers and importers,[167] and that the treatment of automobiles under the CAFE law depended on factors such as the source of the cars and the control and ownership relationships of the producer or importer.[168] The panel followed the 'aims and effects' theory[169] and assumed with the regulation at issue 'likeness' of the products to which it applied. The panel's focus was on the above factors determining the different legal consequences accorded to particular products. It proceeded to examine whether the treatment accorded was actually less favourable for imports. With respect to fleet averaging as an NPA, the panel stated that 'Article III:4 does not permit treatment of an imported product less favourable than that accorded to a like domestic product, based on factors not directly relating to the product as such'.[170] Hence, the panel here rejected the relevance of an NPA for the determination of 'likeness'.

(iv) *United States – Gasoline* (1996): The measures subject to the *US – Gasoline* dispute resemble those subject to the above *US – Taxes on Automobiles* dispute in that they were based on a combination of absolute and relative elements. The measures were a complex system of composition and performance requirements for gasoline, the aim of which was to reduce pollution, particularly in certain highly polluted areas within the United States. The requirements were in part absolute, such as the prohibition of certain heavy metals, and in part relative by consisting

---

[164] Panel Report, *United States – Taxes on Automobiles* (1994), Nos. 2.21 and 2.5–2.13.
[165] Panel Report, *United States – Taxes on Automobiles* (1994), No. 2.16.
[166] Panel Report, *United States – Taxes on Automobiles* (1994), No. 5.39.
[167] Panel Report, *United States – Taxes on Automobiles* (1994), No. 5.45.
[168] Panel Report, *United States – Taxes on Automobiles* (1994), No. 5.46.
[169] This theory is discussed more comprehensively below section 4.2.2.2.
[170] Panel Report, *US – Taxes on Automobiles* (1994), No. 5.54.

of a minimum percentage reduction of certain emissions in relation to the actual levels of emissions of a previous year. For instance, refiners or importers of gasoline were prohibited from selling gasoline that emitted certain substances in greater amounts than were emitted in 1990. The individual baselines for the comparison were calculated on certain data provided by the refiner or importer on their 1990 gasoline, and in the absence of reliable data a statutory baseline was applied.[171] The requirements for establishing an individual and advantageous baseline were partly different for importers, refiners and blenders. The statutory baseline, for example, was applied to importers who failed to establish their individual baseline under a certain method.[172]

Pointing out the chemical identity of foreign and domestic gasoline, the panel, in line with the submissions of the parties, quickly reached its conclusion that the imported and domestic gasoline in question were like products under Article III:4,[173] and then ostensibly proceeded to establish whether the treatment accorded to imported gasoline was less advantageous. In fact, however, the panel returned to its examination of likeness by stating that the distinction which affected the treatment accorded to imported and domestic gasoline related to certain differences in the characteristics of refiners, blenders and importers, and the nature of the data held by them.[174] With this statement, the panel acknowledged that the measure in question in fact distinguished based on producer characteristics. In consequence, the panel concluded:

> However, Article III:4 of the General Agreement deals with the treatment to be accorded to like products; its wording does not allow less favourable treatment dependent on the characteristics of the producer and the nature of the data held by it.[175]

(v) *European Communities – Seal Products* (2009): Both Canada and Norway have requested consultations with the European Communities concerning an EC measure regarding the importation and marketing of seal products.[176] Subject of the contested regulation is a prohibition on the

---

[171] Panel Report, *US – Gasoline* (1996), Nos. 2.1–2.4.
[172] Panel Report, *US – Gasoline* (1996), No. 2.8.
[173] Panel Report, *US – Gasoline* (1996), No. 6.9.
[174] Panel Report, *US – Gasoline* (1996), No. 6.11.
[175] Panel Report, *US – Gasoline* (1996), No. 6.11. The United States did not appeal this finding (Appellate Body Report, *US – Gasoline* (1996), at II.A).
[176] *EC – Seal Products*. Request for Consultations by Canada, 4 November 2009, and Request for Consultations by Norway, 10 November 2009.

4.2 THE PRINCIPLE OF NON-DISCRIMINATION

importation of various seal products, such as meat and fur skins, derived from all species of pinnipeds. The regulation allows importation and placing on the market if seal products result from traditional hunts conducted by Inuit and other indigenous communities and where the products contribute to their subsistence. While the motivation for the regulation is the cruel harvesting methods usually applied, the wording of the regulation clearly aims at producer, or in this case hunter, characteristics. At the time of writing, the parties have not yet issued their legal arguments on the matter.

(vi) Summary: In an almost subliminal way, the early *Section 337* Report seemed to suggest that producer-related aspects can be relevant for the determination of like product categories. However, the panel was far from taking a clear stance in this question. A more direct statement, but of opposite nature, has been issued in the panel's reasoning in the 1992 *US – Malt Beverages* case, which rejected the relevance of overall output by a producer for the question of 'likeness'. However, the form in which it has been drafted suggests that the panel did actually not intend to address this question. In 2006, the European Communities complained about rules closely resembling the rules contested in the *Malt Beverages* dispute: an exemption from excise duties on wine produced in Canada and on a reduction of excise duties for the first 75,000 hl of beer and malt liquor produced and packaged in Canada per year by a licensed brewer.[177] The dispute settlement bodies did not get the chance to decide once more on producer-related regulations, since the parties reached a mutually agreed solution on the matter in 2008. The *US – Taxes on Automobiles* Panel Report approached this question from an entirely different angle, but also rejected the relevance of producer-related aspects. A manifest and far-reaching decision against the relevance of certain producer characteristics was, however, taken by the panel in the WTO *US – Gasoline* dispute. Although the more recent reports suggest irrelevance of producer-related aspects for the determination of likeness, the record of reports is not yet entirely consistent.

4.2.2.1.2.3 Price

In several earlier GATT disputes the parties considered whether prices could play a role in determining likeness. The argument, however, was

---

[177] *Canada – Tax Exemptions and Reductions for Wine and Beer*, Request for Consultations by the European Communities, 4 December 2006, WT/DS354/1.

never explicitly addressed by the respective panels.[178] For instance, in the GATT dispute on *EEC – Animal Feed Proteins* of 1978, the representative of the respondent argued that:

> price could be a fundamental criterion for the evaluation of what constituted a like product in the case of the EEC measures. Price considerations, for example, justified the exclusion of fish meal and meat meal because their higher prices did not make them competitive and substitutable with vegetable proteins.[179]

Here, the panel did not need to address the argument, since it arrived at the conclusion that the products in question were not like for several other reasons.

The same question was discussed more extensively in the 1994 *US – Taxes on Automobiles* dispute mentioned above. One of the challenged measures, the so-called luxury tax, was based on the retail price of any four-wheel vehicle in the United States. An additional 10 per cent tax was added on the amount of the retail price exceeding US$30,000, and the tax applied to domestic and imported cars alike.[180] There was disagreement among the parties on the question of whether or not cars selling above and below this retail price were like products for the purpose of Article III:2.[181] The complainant, the EC, based its submission on two main strands of argumentation. First, it argued that despite minor differences in design and parts all passenger vehicles were 'like' products.[182] Second, the EC claimed a disparate impact of the distinction on imported cars, demonstrated by data which showed that the price threshold had been chosen at a level which disadvantageously affected European cars vis-à-vis domestically produced cars.[183] However, the EC also addressed the obvious argument that the measure distinguished between cars above and below the threshold of US$30,000 on the basis of its retail price, and therefore on an aspect not inherent in the cars' physical properties. The EC called the US$30,000 threshold artificial and not corresponding to objective product differences,[184] and so implied that cars above and below that threshold were like products. With respect to the latter argument,

---

[178] Cf., e.g., Panel Report, *Canada – Gold Coins* (1985).
[179] Panel Report, *EEC – Animal Feed Proteins* (1978), No. 3.4.
[180] Panel Report, *US – Taxes on Automobiles* (1994), Nos. 2.1, 2.2.
[181] Panel Report, *US – Taxes on Automobiles* (1994), No. 5.4.
[182] Panel Report, *US – Taxes on Automobiles* (1994), No. 3.55.
[183] Panel Report, *US – Taxes on Automobiles* (1994), No. 3.64.
[184] Panel Report, *US – Taxes on Automobiles* (1994), No. 3.97.

4.2 THE PRINCIPLE OF NON-DISCRIMINATION

the respondent, the United States, first insisted that the measure was clearly based on objective criteria, namely, the price, which was a suitable tax base, as the pure existence of most tariffs which were assessed on the basis of price clearly indicated.[185] The United States then construed its main argument in a similar way to its argumentation in *Tuna-Dolphin I* by alleging that the criteria underlying the created categories were not intrinsically discriminatory and instead based on neutral fiscal and social policies.[186] With this argumentation the United States did not assert that the products were unlike, but rather aimed at the fact that the measure itself was not discriminatory.

The panel began its reasoning by stating that since two individual products could never be the same in all respects, the crucial question was which differences may form the basis of regulatory distinctions between products.[187] It first reviewed the classical determinants of likeness, which it found were often the basis for regulatory distinctions in the implementation of non-protectionist policies. Then the panel concluded:

> Non-protectionist government policies might, however, require regulatory distinctions that were not based on the product's end-use, its physical characteristics, or the other factors mentioned. Noting that a primary purpose of the General Agreement was to lower barriers to trade between markets, and not to harmonize the regulatory treatment of products within them, the Panel considered that Article III could not be interpreted as prohibiting government policy options, based on products, that were not taken so as to afford protection to domestic production.[188]

With this statement, the panel confirmed that in addition to the classical criteria for likeness other aspects should also be accepted as a basis for distinctions in the implementation of non-protectionist policies, and implied that a product's price might well constitute such an aspect.[189] Indeed, the panel found that cars above and below the luxury tax threshold were neither 'like' nor 'directly competitive or substitutable' in the sense of Article III, because it could not state protectionist goals of the regulation.[190] The report, however, was not adopted.

---

[185] Panel Report, *US – Taxes on Automobiles* (1994), No. 3.93.
[186] Panel Report, *US – Taxes on Automobiles* (1994), No. 3.67.
[187] Panel Report, *US – Taxes on Automobiles* (1994), No. 5.6.
[188] Panel Report, *US – Taxes on Automobiles* (1994), No. 5.8.
[189] Since the Panel followed 'the aim and effects' theory (see below, section 4.2.2.2), it continued its examination of likeness by considering whether the aims and effects of the measure were so as to afford protection.
[190] Panel Report, *US – Taxes on Automobiles* (1994), Nos. 5.15, 5.16.

The panel in the 2000 *Korea – Various Measures on Beef* dispute also briefly considered the relevance of a considerable price differential between domestic and imported products for the determination of likeness,[191] and this even though the respondent had not contested the 'likeness' of the products at issue. The panel reiterated Korea's explanation for the price differential, namely, the relative cost of production, quality differences, consumer preferences and the existence of a legal quota, and then came to the conclusion that the products in question were 'like'.[192] It is not clear why the panel considered prices under the discussion of likeness at all, since the crucial question was less favourable treatment. Nevertheless, the mere fact that the panel discussed the price differential indicates that it suspected prices might indeed be relevant for 'likeness'.

To summarize, price as an aspect relevant for the determination of likeness has been brought up in several GATT and WTO disputes. However, only one panel seriously considered prices in the determination of likeness, and its report was not adopted.

4.2.2.1.2.4 National policies and regulatory regimes

This section reviews disputes regarding measures that were in some way linked to policies or regulatory regimes in the country of production or the country of destination.

(i) *Belgium – Family Allowances* (1952): The relevance of the early GATT case *Belgium – Family Allowances* to NPA measures is controversial. In this dispute, the panel decided on a Belgian law which imposed a charge on imported products under certain circumstances and provided for exemptions from this charge for countries whose system of family allowances was equivalent to that of Belgium. An exemption had been granted to some contracting parties, while it had been refused to others. Without, however, giving precise legal reasoning, the panel stated that:

> The consistency or otherwise of the system of family allowances in force in the territory of a given contracting party with the requirements of the Belgian law would be irrelevant in this respect, and the Belgian legislation would have to be amended insofar as it introduced a discrimination between countries having a given system of family allowances and those which had a different system or no system at all, and made the granting of the exemption dependent on certain conditions.[193]

---

[191] Panel Report, *Korea – Various Measures on Beef* (2000), No. 618.
[192] Panel Report, *Korea – Various Measures on Beef* (2000), No. 618.
[193] Panel Report, *Belgium – Family Allowances* (1952), para. 3.

4.2 THE PRINCIPLE OF NON-DISCRIMINATION

The panel's very hesitant recommendations implied its finding that the Belgian measures were discriminatory and violated Article I and possibly Article III:2.[194]

The brief and rather obscure reasoning of the panel allows for different interpretations. Some understand the report as indicating that only aspects inherent in the product, not differences in the characteristics of exporting countries may lead to different treatment under Article I.[195] This conclusion has even been broadened up so as to imply that only physical product characteristics could possibly be taken into account in determining likeness of products.[196]

In fact, the issue of likeness had not been discussed by the panel directly. Not even the defendant invoked the position that the products at issue were not 'like', and this seems to reflect the prevailing view among the contracting parties. It is noteworthy that in the frequent discussions of the complaint at the Sixth and Seventh Session, involving many statements by different countries not being parties to the dispute, the issue of 'likeness' was simply not mentioned. Others, however, expressly reject a possible relevance of the *Belgian Family Allowances* case to the NPA issue. One of the arguments is that the Belgian measure treated products differently based upon the country of origin,[197] thus categorizing the measure as being discriminatory on its face.

The case does, however, go beyond mere discrimination because of the products' origin. The Belgian measures linked the treatment of imported products to a particularly shaped domestic non-trade policy of another contracting party. While the system of exemptions was clearly country-based, the conditions for being granted an exemption were not intrinsic to a country.[198] They were not expressed in terms of geography, but in terms of a certain domestic policy.

It has been suggested that the parties and the panel particularly criticized the fact that the Belgian authorities had granted exemptions in cases where the exporting country had a system that did not fully comply with that of Belgium. The decision could therefore also be interpreted as merely criticizing the inconsistency of the Belgian authorities in implementing

---

[194] Panel Report, *Belgium – Family Allowances* (1952), para 8.
[195] Jackson (1997), p. 218, fn. 19. Also Charnovitz (2001a), who categorizes the measure as a non-product-related PPM tax.
[196] E.g., Statement by the EC in *EC – Tariff Preferences* (2003), Panel Report, No. 4.55; also Schoenbaum (1997), p. 271, who extended the meaning of the *Belgium – Family Allowances* (1952) case to production methods in general.
[197] Howse and Regan (2000), p. 263.   [198] Charnovitz (2005), p. 12.

their law equally with respect to different GATT contracting parties, instead of a rejection of the entire system of additional charges. The facts of the case were such that the practice of granting exemptions was inconsistent even with the spirit of the Belgian law itself and clearly led to discrimination based on origin. Thus, under the less far-reaching interpretation the dispute shows merely that the origin of products cannot be a legitimate determinant of 'likeness'.

It is this latter aspect which does indeed imply that there is hardly any relevance in this case to the question of likeness. Under Article I, MFN treatment has to be granted 'unconditionally' to like products. The requirement of a certain system of family allowances in a country could be seen as a condition for the treatment accorded to imported products. The meaning of the report would then be limited to the question of whether the country granted a certain preference unconditionally, while the question of 'likeness' would be irrelevant.[199] This view finds support in the circumstances of the dispute itself. None of the parties invoked 'unlikeness', and the panel focused in its examination on the question of unconditional granting of exceptions.[200] The Panel Report has also been interpreted to this end by a later Panel.[201]

While it is granted that the panel did not address the question of 'likeness', one has to consider the indirect relevance of its interpretation of the term 'unconditionally' for the term 'like products' in Article I:1. The existence of the term 'unconditionally' might even be seen as an indication that aspects not incorporated in product characteristics must not be considered in the determination of whether products are 'like' or not. Clearly, this discussion is limited to Article I, since only in this article does the 'like products' concept meet with the requirement of unconditionality. The dispute could thus be invoked to the end that policy requirements with respect to the exporting country are not suitable to determine 'likeness' under the MFN principle in Article I:1. If the policy requirements are seen as a condition, then this would render their relevance for the question of 'likeness' naught.

---

[199] Charnovitz (2005), fn. 51, also Hudec (1990) who does not mention the question of likeness in his exhaustive analysis of the case. Also the GATT *Analytical Index* of 1989 discusses the case as relevant to the question of unconditionality, not to the issue of 'likeness', at Article I-4 (so does the *Analytical Index, Guide to WTO Law and Practice*, of 1994).

[200] Panel Report, *Belgium – Family Allowances* (1952), Nos. 3, 4.

[201] Panel Report, *Indonesia – Autos* (1998), Nos. 14.143–14.144.

4.2 THE PRINCIPLE OF NON-DISCRIMINATION 195

Nevertheless, the significance of this dispute must be considered to be low. The main reason is that the report, obviously wanting in legal reasoning, is also obscure in its findings. Neither reasoning nor recommendations clarify in which way exactly the Belgian measures violated GATT obligations.[202] Furthermore, since the complaint was supported by several other nations, such as Austria and Finland, Belgium was under considerable political pressure and had based its line of argumentation on difficulties due to domestic requirements of a parliamentary decision and had already agreed to settle the matter rather than denying a violation.[203] Finally, the chairman of the Working Party stated that the legal issues of the dispute were so involved that the panel had considered that it was for the contracting parties to arrive at a conclusion,[204] and so practically devaluated the report's legal significance.

(ii) *Tuna-Dolphin I and II:* One strand of Mexico's arguments to support the impermissibility of the US MMPA was the fact that the MMPA was not 'even' a PPM, because it was not aimed at producers, but instead aimed at governments in terms of programmes and policy results.[205] This argumentation implies that even if a PPM could be considered relevant to the notion of 'like product' under Article III, this would be irrelevant to the *Tuna-Dolphin I* dispute. Since the MMPA was based on government programmes and results rather than on PPMs, it was linked to an aspect irrelevant for the determination of likeness. This argumentation, which regarded the primary nations embargo, was not taken up by any other party. Many third parties argued instead that the measure was not covered by Article III because of its extraterritorial effect. The panel, as detailed above, made its findings with a different argumentation and did not address the point made by Mexico.

To reiterate, in the *Tuna-Dolphin II* dispute the parties also focused on Article XX and did not address the question of likeness. However, one of the third parties, Australia, took up Mexico's argument of the *Tuna-Dolphin I* dispute. It first reasoned that all tuna products were like, and then argued that the fact that an intermediary nation had imported tuna

---

[202] Hudec (1990), p. 149.
[203] Statements of the Belgian, Austrian and Finish Representatives, Summary Record of the Sixth Session, Twenty-first Meeting on 23 October 1951, document GATT/CP.6/SR.21, of 26 October 1951, at p. 2.
[204] Statement of Chairman Isbister, Summary Record of the Seventh Session, Fourteenth Meeting on 7 November 1952, document SR7/14 of 10 November 1952, at p. 10.
[205] Panel Report, *Tuna-Dolphin I* (1991), No. 3.17.

from other countries could not transform its own tuna products into 'unlike' products.[206] It explicitly stated that 'even if processing methods were held to be relevant to like product concepts, the standards for the products subject to the intermediary nation embargo did not involve any consideration of the method of processing of that product'.[207] Similarly, Venezuela argued that the GATT did not permit the restriction of imports of products only because the exporting country had environmental policies different from the country imposing the restriction.[208] Most other third parties implied that imported and domestic tuna products were like products, implicitly denying the relevance of national policies for the determination of likeness. Due to its different argumentation and findings under Article XI, this panel also did not address this discussion in its findings.[209]

(iii) Summary: To date, national policies or regulatory regimes have never been considered as permissible determinants of likeness. While the Panel Report most crucial in this respect, namely, *Belgium – Family Allowances*, found that the Belgian measures violated GATT obligations, the report is not suited to drawing broader conclusions on this question. Likewise, the issue was not addressed in either the *Tuna-Dolphin* or the *Shrimp Turtle* disputes. However, the opinions of third parties, expressly or implicitly voiced in their submissions, show a clear rejection of the idea that different regimes could render products 'unlike'.

4.2.2.1.3 Relevance of 'minor' physical differences

To reiterate, with the *Spain Unroasted Coffee* Panel Report it became apparent that not just any physical difference is sufficient to render products 'unlike'.[210] On the other hand, there are a number of disputes involving measures that distinguished between products based on

---

[206] Panel Report, *Tuna-Dolphin II* (1994), No. 4.6.
[207] Panel Report, *Tuna-Dolphin II* (1994), No. 4.6.
[208] Panel Report, *Tuna-Dolphin II* (1994), No. 4.43.
[209] For similar reasons, the adjudicatory bodies in *Shrimp Turtle* also address this question. While the parties focused on Articles XI and XX, Japan as a third party explicitly stated its opinion with respect to 'likeness' that neither differences in practices nor in policies could have any impact on the inherent character of shrimp as products. Without always pointing it out explicitly, most third-party countries assumed likeness of imported and domestic shrimp products as self-evident. Panel Report: *Shrimp Turtle* (1998), e.g., Australia at 4.5, or Nigeria at 4.56.
[210] See above, section 4.2.2.1.1.2.

4.2 THE PRINCIPLE OF NON-DISCRIMINATION

physical differences, which must be considered extremely small in absolute terms. This section analyses the adjudicatory bodies' rationales in ascribing greater or lesser importance to minor physical differences.

4.2.2.1.3.1 Editorial content

In *Canada – Periodicals*, a panel had to decide whether imported split-run editions of a magazine are 'like' other domestic editions of magazines under Article III:2.[211] Split-run editions were defined as 'periodicals with the same or similar editorial content as those published in foreign countries, which contain an advertisement directed to the Canadian market'.[212] The United States complained that Canada prohibited the import of split-run editions, and in addition had enacted a regulation, which, although due to the import prohibition it was not applied in practice, imposed an 80 per cent excise tax on the value of advertisements contained in split-run periodicals.[213]

The aspect decisive for a differentiation between products under the Canadian measure was contentious among the parties. Canada claimed that the measure was based on the difference in editorial contents of imported split-run editions and domestic magazines, and based its argumentation on the assumption that differences in editorial content should be considered as differences in characteristics of the products themselves.[214] Canada argued that periodicals with editorial content developed for the Canadian market and split-runs substantially reproducing foreign editorial content were not 'like products',[215] since there was a significant objective difference between a split-run and a magazine with original content for the Canadian market.[216] The complainant denied that the measure differentiated based on editorial content, and argued instead that the tax measure was based on the mere existence of a product sold in a country other than Canada, and the extent of that product's similarities to, and differences from, the product sold in Canada. This would amount to an extraneous factor, which was not to be considered for 'likeness' under the national treatment obligation.[217]

---

[211] Panel Report, *Canada – Periodicals* (1997), No. 5.22.
[212] Panel Report, *Canada – Periodicals* (1997), No. 5.1.
[213] Panel Report, *Canada – Periodicals* (1997), No. 2.6.
[214] Panel Report, *Canada – Periodicals* (1997), No. 3.66.
[215] Panel Report, *Canada – Periodicals* (1997), No. 3.61.
[216] Panel Report, *Canada – Periodicals* (1997), No. 3.71.
[217] Panel Report, *Canada – Periodicals* (1997), Nos. 3.64, 3.65.

In this respect, the panel followed the argumentation of the complainant and stated that the objective requirements the Canadian tax measure was based on were extraneous factors. The panel stated:

> Putting these external factors aside, imported 'split-run' periodicals and domestic non 'split-run' periodicals can be extremely similar.[218]

It then continued its examination of 'likeness' under Article III:2 by construing a hypothetical case of a periodical with a Canadian and a US edition, where the publication of the latter was discontinued. The panel found:

> These two editions would have common end-uses, very similar physical properties, nature and qualities. It is most likely that the two volumes would have been designed for the same readership with the same tastes and habits. In all respects, these two volumes are 'like'.[219]

Two aspects of the panel's examination are of particular interest. First, the panel decided to 'put aside' for its examination the 'external factors' on which the Canadian measure was based. This could indeed amount to a negation of any relevance such external factors could have for the 'likeness' of products. The panel seems to use the word external in a spatial sense, since it refers to the definition of split-run magazines which relies on factors external to the Canadian market.[220] Second, the panel proceeded in the further examination considering the conventional determinants of likeness, namely, end-uses, physical properties and consumers' tastes and habits, without, however, mentioning editorial content as a separate criterion for likeness. This omission, however, does not mean that the panel ignored the relevance of editorial content for the determination of likeness in general. On the contrary, the panel seems to have acknowledged that different editorial content might lead to (minor) differences in the physical properties, since it stated that the physical properties would be only 'very similar' instead of 'identical'. In addition, the panel refers to the readership and their tastes and habits. Since it is the editorial content that is decisive for the readership of periodicals, the panel implied that it took the editorial content into account when finding that the periodicals were 'like'. It can therefore be concluded that the panel considered editorial content to be relevant for the determination of likeness, mostly under the criterion consumer tastes and habits.

---

[218] Panel Report, *Canada – Periodicals* (1997), No. 5.25.
[219] Panel Report, *Canada – Periodicals* (1997), No. 5.25.
[220] Panel Report, *Canada – Periodicals* (1997), No. 5.24.

4.2 THE PRINCIPLE OF NON-DISCRIMINATION

The Panel Report, including its findings on the likeness of split-run and non-split-run periodicals, was appealed by the respondent.[221] Reviewing the panel's examination of this question, the Appellate Body strongly criticized the panel's legal reasoning as illogical, and found that this reasoning was based on an inadequate factual analysis. Due to these insufficient facts, and mindful of its own limited mandate to review and decide only questions of law, the Appellate Body reversed the panel's findings without completing the analysis on the question of likeness.[222] Nevertheless, and despite Canada's protests, the Appellate Body proceeded to examine whether split-run and non-split-run periodicals, if not like, might instead be directly competitive and substitutable under the terms of Article III:2, second sentence. It reviewed the facts provided in the Panel Report and reached the conclusion that they did indeed meet these requirements.[223]

The Appellate Body then addressed the relevance of the contents of periodicals under Article III:2. It stressed the relevance of contents for the direct competitiveness and substitutability by stating:

> Our conclusion that imported split-run periodicals and domestic non-split-run periodicals are 'directly competitive or substitutable' does not mean that all periodicals belong to the same relevant market, whatever their editorial content. A periodical containing mainly current news is not directly competitive or substitutable with a periodical dedicated to gardening, chess, sports, music or cuisine.[224]

Although this statement does not relate to the question of 'likeness' under the first sentence of Article III:2 directly, the last sentence allows for some important conclusions. It is indeed settled that the concept of direct competitiveness and substitutability under the second sentence of Article III:2 is broader than, and thus comprises, the like product concept under the first sentence.[225] Therefore, while all products that are 'like' under the first sentence are also directly competitive and substitutable, the reverse conclusion is not permissible. For the determinants of likeness vis-à-vis the determinants of direct competitiveness and substitutability this means

---

[221] Appellate Body Report, *Canada – Periodicals* (1997), III(b), p. 16.
[222] Appellate Body Report, *Canada – Periodicals* (1997), V.A., after fn. 42, pp. 22–3.
[223] Appellate Body Report, *Canada – Periodicals* (1997), VI.B.1, p. 29.
[224] Appellate Body Report, *Canada – Periodicals* (1997), VI.B.1, p. 28, after fn. 51.
[225] Appellate Body Report, *Canada – Periodicals* (1997), VI.B.1, p. 28, after fn. 51 (calling the second sentence the 'broader prohibition'). See for more explicit statements, Panel Report in *Korea – Alcoholic Beverages* (1998), No. 10.36, with reference to Panel Report *Japan – Alcoholic Beverages II* (1996), No. 6.22 (findings were implicitly confirmed by the Appellate Body on appeal, through formulation 'in all other respects', Appellate Body Report, *Japan – Alcoholic Beverages II* (1996), after fn. 50, p. 23); Jackson (1969), p. 282.

that if an aspect prevents the assumption of direct competitiveness and substitutability, this aspect *a minore ad maius* also prevents the assumption of likeness under the first sentence. This would be the case for 'editorial content' of periodicals. The Appellate Body stated that although split-run and non-split-run magazines may be directly competitive and substitutable, the actual editorial content, such as current news, technology or cuisine, is suitable to prevent competition among periodicals. Since the Appellate Body found that editorial content is suitable to prevent competitiveness, it implied that this aspect would necessarily also be suitable to exclude 'likeness' under the first sentence of Article III:2.

In sum, from the above reports it is not clear whether editorial contents would be used as a separate criterion, or rather constitute a sub-aspect of the classical criteria product properties, or consumer tastes and habits, as suggested by the panel. Nevertheless, there is no doubt that editorial content played an important role for the determination of 'likeness'. Although it is granted that different editorial content leads to physical differences between split-run magazines, there is no reason to believe that these physical differences are any 'larger' than physical differences between split-run or non-split-run magazines, or between two different magazines of the same category. It is not the actually small physical difference between different magazines, but the intellectual importance ascribed to the difference, for instance, by consumers.

4.2.2.1.3.2 Environmental impacts

Differences in environmental impacts are a result of physical differences among products. Nevertheless, the environmental impact through use or consumption is not in itself a physical product property, but merely a consequence of physical differences. Respective measures are therefore linked to data expressing the environmental impact, rather than to the actual physical differences.

The *US – Taxes on Automobiles* panel reviewed a tax imposed on manufacturers and importers of automobiles for the sale of each automobile according to its fuel economy. The graduated excise tax was aimed at the environmental impact of exhaust fumes and referred to the sale of automobiles. This so-called 'gas guzzler tax' was based on calculated, not on actual, fuel economy. The calculation was based on model types which shared major design characteristics influencing fuel efficiency.[226] The tax was triggered by a failure to meet these fuel-economy requirements. With

---

[226] Panel Report, *US – Taxes on Automobiles* (1994), No. 5.18.

respect to 'likeness' of automobiles the EC argued that a difference in fuel economy was not sufficient to make one automobile 'unlike' another,[227] while the United States argued that the regulatory distinctions were made on permissible objective criteria in terms of fuel economy.[228]

The panel, following the aims and effects theory, recalled the importance of the question of whether or not the measure had been applied 'so as to afford protection'.[229] It analysed protective aims and effects with respect to each of the pairs of products to be compared, and found that the measure was not applied so as to afford protection. As a corollary, it did also not distinguish between 'like' products.[230] The panel stated that for the purpose of Article III:2, imported automobiles above the threshold were not 'like' domestic products below the threshold,[231] even if the difference in fuel economy was not an actual one but the result of a calculation based on average consumption of certain model types. The panel so legitimized the regulatory distinction and granted considerable leeway to legislators for the design of national policies.

However, since the Panel Report was not adopted, and since no other dispute discussed distinctions between products based on their economic impact through consumption, a prevailing case law on the relevance of environmental impacts cannot be stated.

4.2.2.1.3.3 Toxicity and risk

The *EC – Asbestos* dispute concerned measures distinguishing between different construction materials, namely, cement-based products containing chrysotile asbestos fibres, on the one hand, and cement-based products containing other fibres, on the other. The panel in the *Asbestos* case had discussed whether a risk linked to a product should be taken into account for the determination of 'likeness' of products, and decided against, arguing that otherwise the effect of Article XX(b) would be nullified.[232] Consequently, it considered both categories of cement products 'like' under Article III:4. This decision was strongly criticized in scholarly literature,[233] and it was reversed on appeal. The Appellate Body found that toxicity or health risks could be considered as a separate criterion or

---

[227] Panel Report, *US – Taxes on Automobiles* (1994), No. 5.19.
[228] Panel Report, *US – Taxes on Automobiles* (1994), No. 5.20.
[229] Panel Report, *US – Taxes on Automobiles* (1994), No. 5.23.
[230] Panel Report, *US – Taxes on Automobiles* (1994), No. 5.36.
[231] Panel Report, *US – Taxes on Automobiles* (1994), Nos. 5.26, 5.32, 5.37.
[232] Panel Report, *EC – Asbestos* (2000), No. 8.130.
[233] E.g., Charnovitz (2001a), at p. 40.

among the existing criteria of product properties and consumers' tastes and habits. However, whether as separate criterion, defining aspect, or sub-category of physical properties or consumers' tastes and habits,[234] the Appellate Body found that the physical difference was highly significant and its consideration for the determination of likeness under Article III:4 was indispensable.[235] One member of the Appellate Body even made a concurring statement, stressing that the importance of this particular physical difference between chrysotile asbestos and PCG fibres was paramount, thus excluding the possibility that any other evidence could possibly outweigh it and render such products 'like'.[236] With its findings, the Appellate Body elevated carcinogenicity or toxicity as relevant evidence in the determination of 'like products'.

The measure was correctly not seen as constituting an NPA measure in scholarly literature, since it was based on dangers inherent in the product.[237] Nevertheless, it seems that the difference in physical product characteristics is comparably smaller than the difference between other products which have been considered 'like' in previous disputes. What makes the decision important for NPA measures is the fact that the Appellate Body ascribed great importance to a relatively small physical difference by considering another value, namely, human health, for the determination of 'likeness' under Article III.[238]

The fact that the Appellate Body explicitly reversed a finding of a panel is sufficient to classify toxicity and respective health risks relevant for the determination of 'like products' under Article III:4, albeit not necessarily as a separate criterion. However, the broader meaning of this report is unclear: throughout the report, the Appellate Body maintained a tight bond between its considerations and the specific facts of the case. Therefore, whether or not other characteristics of equal importance for other public policy objectives could be considered relevant in

---

[234] Appellate Body Report, *EC – Asbestos* (2001), Nos. 114, 125, 126, and the 'concurring statement' of one member of the Appellate Body at Nos. 149–54.
[235] Appellate Body Report, *EC – Asbestos* (2001), Nos. 114, 115.
[236] Appellate Body Report, *EC – Asbestos* (2001), No. 152.
[237] Cottier, Tuerk and Panizzon (2003), at p. 158, Charnovitz (2001a), at p. 40.
[238] More than that, the report also pointed out that members may also draw distinctions between products which have been found to be 'like', provided that it does not accord less favourable treatment to 'the group of "like" *imported* products ... than that accorded to the group of "like" domestic products'. Appellate Body report in: *EC – Asbestos* (2001), No. 100. This statement suggests that there may be considerable leeway and flexibility for legitimate activities of national regulatory bodies, e.g., with respect to environmental policies. Cottier, Tuerk and Panizzon (2003), pp. 157, 158.

the 'like product' determination in the same way as toxicity remains to be seen.[239]

4.2.2.1.3.4 Genetic modifications

Genetic modification as such can be regarded as being part of the production process of certain products, and as such would constitute a so-called PPM.[240] From this point of view, genetic modification and products derived by it, such as seeds, feed and food, are sometimes regarded as an application of the so-called PPM debate. The opposing view, however, stresses that genetic modification is used only to modify the seeds of plants, while the cultivation of the actual plants and their seeds and fruits is nothing but conventional agricultural production.[241] From this point of view, not only the end-products but also the production process would be the same, genetic modifications would fail to justify any difference in treatment.

The crucial question is not so much whether genetic modification constitutes a PPM, but rather whether or not products derived from such modification differ physically from non-modified products. The panel in *EC – Biotech* touched upon this question only briefly, since the focus of the disputing parties' claims was on obligations under the SPS Agreement. Nevertheless, with respect to the challenged product-specific measures, the panel briefly discussed possible differences in treatment between the groups of imported and domestic biotech products, that is, genetically-modified products, and imported and domestic non-biotech, that is, conventional products. The panel refrained from taking a clear stance towards the question of 'likeness', since it could not establish actual differences in treatment.[242] However, the panel apparently also deemed less important the question of likeness than possible reasons for differences in treatment. It stated:

> In other words, Argentina is not alleging that the treatment of products has differed depending on their origin. In these circumstances, it is not self-evident that the alleged less favourable treatment of imported biotech products is explained by the foreign origin of these products rather than, for instance, a perceived difference between biotech products and non-biotech products in terms of their safety, etc.[243]

---

[239] See also Oesch (2003a), pp. 459, 460.   [240] Petersmann (2000), p. 254.
[241] Isaac and Kerr (2003), p. 36.
[242] Panel Report, *EC – Biotech* (2006), No. 7.2516.
[243] Panel Report, *EC – Biotech* (2006), No. 7.2514.

The panel's brief statement is to some extent evocative of the Appellate Body's findings in *EC – Asbestos*: here also a physical difference between products, albeit small, was viewed as having the potential to justify differences in treatment for the purposes of Article III:4. However, it seems that the panel in *EC – Biotech* takes this one step further: it seems to consider as paramount the question of whether or not origin has been the guiding reason for a regulatory distinction. Summarizing its considerations, the panel found:

> In our view, Argentina has not adduced argument and evidence sufficient to raise a presumption that the alleged less favourable treatment is explained by the foreign origin of the relevant biotech products.[244]

This statement implies that, with the exception of regulatory distinctions made for reasons of product origin, reasonable regulatory distinctions would be acceptable for the obligation established by Article III:4.

However, given that the panel merely briefly touched upon this question, and given the fact that due to the lack of an appeal of the decision the Appellate Body did not have the chance to possibly correct these findings, the panel's statements must not be overstated. However, as a matter of fact the panel's statements also show that minor physical differences created by genetic modifications may be crucial in the determination of likeness and of possible violations of Article III:4.

4.2.2.1.4 Summary

Under the DSB approach, 'likeness' is assessed on a case-by-case basis, considering the criteria established by the Working Party, namely: (1) the product's end-uses in a given market; (2) consumers' tastes and habits; and (3) the product's properties, nature and quality, supplemented by panels with the additional criterion (4) international tariff classification.[245] Among these criteria, criterion (3), physical properties of products, is of paramount importance. Not only have panels and the Appellate Body directly attributed greatest weight to this criterion, but by their nature the other criteria are also strongly influenced by the product's physical characteristics.[246] Not only the end-uses depend on physical characteristics, but also classification in international tariff systems is predominantly based on physical descriptions. Likewise, consumer preferences

---

[244] Panel Report, *EC – Biotech* (2006), No. 7.2514.
[245] See above at section 4.2.2.1.1.
[246] Appellate Body Report, *EC – Asbestos* (2001), No. 111.

4.2 THE PRINCIPLE OF NON-DISCRIMINATION

and tastes are influenced by physical factors. In some cases, however, the assessment might differ according to different criteria. Some tariff lines include product descriptions which refer to production methods, and more importantly, consumers' tastes and preferences can develop irrespectively of physical characteristics of a product. However, with the notable exception of the *Asbestos* decision, the latter criterion has never played a decisive role. In consequence of this ostensibly consistent case law, it is conventionally believed that there is not much room for the consideration of aspects other than physical product properties in determining which products are alike. The advantage of ascribing importance to physical differences has been seen to lie in the 'bright-line rule'[247] that this criterion establishes. Indeed, product distinctions based on physical differences are easy to administer, and as a corollary enforcement activities are also more transparent and easier to review.

However, the review of cases concerning NPA measures and measures that distinguish based on small physical differences shows that GATT and WTO case law is not as consistent as often assumed. NPAs were in most cases found to be irrelevant for the determination of likeness. While the adjudicatory bodies did not actually discuss this question with respect to PPMs, so far the record of cases relating to measures linked to national policies and programmes clearly reject their relevance. There are, however, some disputes which suggest that under certain circumstances NPAs may constitute a legitimate basis for distinctions. Although the *US – Section 337 Tariff Act* panel did not directly address this question, the report seems to suggest that the fact that whether or not a producer holds a valid licence for production might constitute an aspect which renders a product distinction legitimate. More explicit was the panel in the unadopted *US – Taxes on Automobiles* case, which found that prices may be a legitimate basis for distinctions for purposes of a luxury tax.

As regards the reverse case, it is recognized since the *Spain – Unroasted Coffee* dispute that not all physical differences, no matter how small, may justify product distinctions under Article III. Other disputes held that measures based on minor physical differences, namely, editorial content, differences affecting fuel consumption of cars, differences leading to health risks and genetic modifications may well be suitable for regulatory distinctions. In all reviewed cases, however, it was clear that the assessment of whether or not the physical difference rendered products 'unlike' did not focus on the physical difference as such, but on the importance

---

[247] Jackson (2000a), p. 303 (referring to the product–process distinction).

ascribed to the particular difference for normative reasons. While in the case of different editorial content, the minor physical differences were relevant from the viewpoint of consumers and the question of competitiveness, the physical differences leading to pollution or health risks were assessed under normative standards. The *EC – Asbestos* Appellate Body Report particularly ascribed great importance to health risks, although it refrained from a clear finding that the products at issue were 'unlike'.[248] Similarly, the panel in *EC – Biotech* considered that, for example, safety may well be an acceptable reason for a regulatory difference between products, whether like or not, if small physical differences prevail.

In sum, the traditional criteria for the determination of likeness remain well established for the determination of likeness. Nevertheless, a more recent development shows that the DSB does not refrain from reviewing evidence relating to these traditional criteria from a normative perspective and to weigh such evidence accordingly, thus ascribing greater weight even to smaller physical differences.

4.2.2.2 The 'aim and effects' theory

Given the importance of the 'like products' concept and given the fact that its interpretation has led to concerns about legal certainty and predictability in an ever more 'judicialized' WTO, practitioners and scholars have been contemplating alternatives or changes to the DSB's objective approach. Among these is the so-called 'aim and effects' test or theory.[249] The proponents of this theory basically hold that the aim and effects of a regulatory measure are crucial for the determination of whether or not affected products are 'like'. Underlying the theory is a specific view about what exactly the intention and function of the national treatment

---

[248] Instead, the Appellate Body merely reversed the Panel's respective finding, but nevertheless proceeded to assess the measure under the general exceptions. See also the concurring statement in the Appellate Body Report, *EC – Asbestos* (2001), Nos. 149–54.

[249] The 'aim and effects test' is highly controversial. Some interpreted the Panel Report in *Japan – Alcoholic Beverages II* (1996) (basically upheld by the Appellate Body) to explicitly reject the 'aim and effects' theory; this confirmed in *EC – Bananas III* (1997), Panel Report, as modified by the Appellate Body report, *EC – Bananas III* (1997), p. 91 (cf. WTO *Analytical Index, Guide to WTO Law and Practice*, 1st edition, Article III, No. 100, also Charnovitz (2002), p. 89; Hudec (2002), p. 117). However, as shown above, in *EC – Asbestos* (2001) the Appellate Body placed great importance on the regulatory intention of the measure, namely the prevention of health risks, in determining 'likeness'. This shows that, although the Appellate Body obviously has not considered the theory explicitly, its views on the underlying arguments are not yet settled. The test found support in scholarship, cf., e.g., Hudec (1998), p. 34; Matsushita, Schoenbaum and Mavroidis (2004) p. 176; Roessler (1996), pp. 29–31.

obligation in the GATT is. Hence, the theory is mostly relevant to the 'like products' concept in Article III.

The 'aim and effects' theory is not an entirely homogeneous approach. Some proponents stress the importance of possible protective effects, while others place more emphasis on the relevance of aims and regulatory intentions. Furthermore, in as far as the effects of measures are concerned, some focus on the determination of less favourable treatment, the second condition for discrimination, rather than on the 'like products' definition.

4.2.2.2.1 Rationales and main elements

The traditional DSB approach and the paramount importance it ascribed to the border tax adjustment criteria also met with criticism. Some critics feel that this approach leads to a scrutiny of national regulation that is far too rigid, confining national policy space excessively. Thus, underlying the theory of 'aim and effects' was the idea of bringing in line a review of national regulation with the basic objective of the GATT, namely, a ban on protectionism, with a view to leaving governments the necessary policy space to address legitimate non-trade concerns.[250] The legal starting point of the 'aim and effects' approach is Article III:1, which stipulates as a policy objective that the contracting parties should not apply internal taxes and other internal measures to imported or domestic products 'so as to afford protection'. The GATT panel in *US – Malt Beverages* was the first to take up these considerations. It interpreted Article III:1 as an expression of the basic purpose of the national treatment obligation in Article III.[251] Later, another panel argued that a primary purpose of the GATT was the lowering of barriers to trade between markets, and not the harmonization of product regulation within them. It therefore concluded that GATT Article III would not prohibit government policy options based on products, which were not taken so as to afford protection to domestic production.[252] Since the policy objective stated in GATT Article III:1 was interpreted to have a subjective or purpose element, which is indicated by the words 'so as to', and an objective element,[253] which consists in the measure's protective effects, the new approach to balance free trade objectives and legitimate domestic policies was termed the 'aim and effects' approach.

---

[250] Cottier and Oesch (2005), p. 403
[251] Panel Report, *US – Malt Beverages* (1992), No. 5.25.
[252] Panel Report, *US – Taxes on Automobiles* (1994), No. 5.8.
[253] Panel Report, *US – Taxes on Automobiles* (1994), No. 5.10.

4.2.2.2.1.1 The criteria

The first criterion of the 'aim and effects' test is the identification of regulatory purpose. It has been pointed out that regulatory purpose is not to be confused with the personal motivation of individual legislators. Instead, it would be crucial to ascertain the political forces which produce the measure or law at issue. These would come into play, however, only in case objective evidence, such as text, structure and foreseeable effects of a measure, and subjective evidence, such as ministerial statements or reports, would not lead to a clear finding.[254] Interestingly, the Appellate Body has already engaged in purpose review, albeit in disputes that were reviewed under the SPS Agreement, and it has been acknowledged that it came to plausible conclusions, and thus has proven its competence for such purpose inquiry.[255] There are, however, also other understandings of the 'aim and effects' approach. It has been argued that the review of the aim of a measure was not meant to include subjective elements, but that instead it was limited to an objective analysis of purpose, similar to the one that the Appellate Body, without, however, admitting it, applied in the *US – Malt Beverages* report.[256]

The effects part of the 'aim and effects' test refers to the protective effect which a measure can have on competitive conditions between products of different origins, and it can be assessed with statistical data and other relevant evidence. The first panel considering the GATT policy objective in assessing the legality of a trade measure, the *US – Malt Beverages* panel, was ambiguous regarding the relevance it attached to the actual effects of the measure. In one instance, it pointed out that the prohibition of a discriminatory measure is neither 'conditional on a trade effects test' nor 'qualified by a *de minimis* standard'.[257] However, when it came to various tax measures which linked different tax rates to beer depending on its alcohol content, the panel probed into the regulatory purpose of the measure. It then declared that there was no evidence submitted to the panel that the choice of the particular level of low and high alcohol content 'has the purpose or effect of affording protection to domestic production'.[258] In contrast, the *US – Taxes on Automobiles* panel placed great emphasis

---

[254] Regan (2002), pp. 458–60.
[255] Regan (2002), pp. 460, 461, invoking the Appellate Body report in *EC – Hormones* (1998), and the Panel Report in *Australia – Salmon* (1998).
[256] Hudec (1998), pp. 631, 632, referring to the arguments of the United States in this dispute.
[257] Panel Report, *US – Malt Beverages* (1992), No. 5.6.
[258] Panel Report, *US – Malt Beverages* (1992), No. 5.74.

on the effects of the measures at issue. In a review under both the first and second sentence of GATT Article III:2, the panel asked whether the measure at issue had 'the *effect*, in terms of conditions of competition', of affording protection to domestic products or production.[259] Accordingly, the panel's analysis focused on the conditions of competition of domestic and foreign products, and it was based on sales and trade-flow data, and on other available evidence such as manufacturing technology.[260]

4.2.2.2.1.2 Scope and relevance

Although only the second sentence of Article III:2 explicitly refers to Article III:1 and the policy objective it states, the 'aim and effects' test was considered an interpretive tool of wider application. Many scholars approved of the new approach, albeit for different reasons. The gist of the arguments is that since the legality of measures distinguishing between products should be assessed in the light of the very purpose of the GATT to prevent protectionism, protectionist aims or effects should be taken into account for the determination of an impermissible differentiation between 'like products'.[261] Also the language of both Articles III and I has been interpreted not to include anything that suggests that any regulatory policies other than favouritism between nations or protectionism should be inadmissible. Therefore, the aims and effects of a measure would need to be considered sensibly by the WTO adjudicatory bodies.[262]

A different argument for the relevance of regulatory purpose is the nature of the phrase 'like products' as a concept including a comparison. It has been argued that there would simply be no way to give content to this phrase without referring to the purpose of making the comparison.[263] Indeed, the fact that equality – and the phrase 'like products' refers to an undetermined degree of equality – is in itself an empty concept which derives meaning only from normative standards which need to be defined has been called an 'analytical truth'.[264] Identifying the purpose of the comparison would therefore be indispensable in order to find out which properties matter for the determination of likeness.[265]

Finally, it has been observed that the 'aim and effects' theory added nothing to what panels had been doing anyway. Robert E. Hudec stated

---

[259] Panel Report, *US – Taxes on Automobiles* (1994), Nos. 5.13, 5.25, 5.30, 5.34.
[260] Panel Report, *US – Taxes on Automobiles* (1994), Nos. 5.13, 5.14.
[261] Cottier (1998), p. 59; Regan (2002), p. 444.
[262] Howse and Regan (2000), pp. 262, 268.
[263] Regan (2002), pp. 446, 447.   [264] Westen (1983).
[265] Regan (2002), pp. 446, 447.

that in his view, GATT and WTO tribunals had been deciding all along based on an application of the 'aim and effects' criteria, whether consciously or unconsciously. He suspected that any panellist asked to decide on a particular regulatory measure would instinctively want to know whether the measure has a *bona fide* purpose, and to what extent its market effects were protective.[266] Therefore, he welcomed the 'aim and effects' test as an opportunity for panels to address these criteria of decision openly.[267]

4.2.2.2.1.3 Diversity of opinions

It should be noted that not all advocates of the 'aim and effects' test suggest the same kind of test or the same kind of analysis. While the classical 'aim and effects' test as applied by the above panels considered both elements equally important, some scholars stress the importance of regulatory purpose to an extent that renders the measure's actual protective effects almost irrelevant.[268] Other scholars, however, consider only a measure's protective effects and argue that this would make consideration of a measure's regulatory aims unnecessary, at least in cases where both the domestic and the foreign groups of 'like' products are impacted in the same way,[269] and even others supplement the theory with a necessity test under Article III.[270] This line of thinking was triggered by the observation that WTO jurisprudence to date offers no consistent guidance on the question, whether origin-neutral national rules violate national treatment only if they impose a greater disadvantage on imports than on domestic products, or whether it is sufficient that some imports are put at a disadvantage.[271] In sum, the relevance of trade effects is unclear. It has been argued that the phrase 'like products' needs to be given meaning on the basis of the WTO members' rights, namely, the right that products originating in their territory should not be discriminated against on grounds of their origin. This would mean that a 'discriminatory effects' test could be considered for both non-discrimination provisions, Article I and Article III alike.[272] The test should be located in the second step of the review of a discriminatory measure, namely, in determining whether the treatment which had been

---

[266] Hudec (1998), pp. 634, 635.
[267] Hudec (1998), p. 635; also Regan (2002), p. 205, referring to the Appellate Body Report in *EC - Asbestos* (2001).
[268] Regan (2002).   [269] Ehring (2002), p. 925.
[270] Mattoo and Subramanian (1998), pp. 313–21, Verhoosel (2002).
[271] Ehring (2002), pp. 921, 922.   [272] Davey and Pauwelyn (2002), p. 39.

accorded to some of the like products was less favourable than the treatment of other like products, rather than in the first step determination of 'likeness'.[273] Basically, this way of determining illegal *de facto* discriminations requires first a determination of 'like products' along the lines of the national measure in question. In a second step, a comparison is then made of whether the group of products which is accorded disadvantageous treatment is relatively greater among imports than among domestic products. If this is not the case, then this approach would decline existence of a de facto discrimination, regardless of the rationality of the measure in question.

4.2.2.2.2 Significance for NPA measures

The 'aim and effect' theory is as important for NPA measures as it is for any other ordinary trade measure: if a measure is neither adopted with protective intentions nor has a protective effect, then it should be considered to be in line with the GATT non-discrimination provisions. Measures linked to NPAs do not differ from other trade measures in a way which would make it more or less likely that they have protective aim or effects. Just as measures linked to products, also measures linked to NPAs can be tools of protectionism and discriminate *de facto*, or they can be entirely legitimate.

Nevertheless, the approach is especially relevant to measures linked to NPAs. The reason is that under the traditional DSB approach, domestic measures based on physical product characteristics are often *a priori* in line with obligations under Article III, because physical differences are recognized as a valid criterion for distinction. This rule applies whether or not there are any legitimate reasons for a different treatment. For example, there is no obvious need to accord different treatment to rice as opposed to wheat. However, since traditionally the treatment of both grains has differed, rice and wheat would not be considered as 'like products' under the GATT, and different treatment would be consistent with GATT obligations, regardless of actual protective effects of this distinction. Therefore, NPA measures are placed at a legal disadvantage. The aim and effects approach could to some extent correct this legal disadvantage. The approach would provide the opportunity to withdraw at least those NPA measures from GATT scrutiny which by their nature cannot impair basic GATT objectives.

---

[273] Ehring (2002); Davey and Pauwelyn (2002), pp. 39, 40.

However, the panel in *US – Taxes on Automobiles* seemed to deny the relevance of the aim and effect theory for NPA measures altogether. It rejected the relevance of the aim and effects of one of the challenged measures, the Corporate Average Fuel Economy (CAFE) regulation. The panel was of the view that:

> Article III:4 does not permit treatment of an imported product less favourable than that accorded to a like domestic product, based on factors not directly relating to the product as such. The Panel found therefore that, to the extent that treatment under the CAFE measure was based on factors relating to the control or ownership of producers/importers, it could not in accordance with Article III:4 be applied in a manner that also accorded less favourable treatment to products of foreign origin. It was therefore not necessary to examine whether treatment based on these factors was also applied so as to afford protection to domestic production.[274]

This finding, which takes up the *Tuna-Dolphin* line of argumentation, was apparently guided by the reasoning that the exclusion of a consideration of aim and effects was necessary in order to ensure the security of tariff bindings. The panel explained that the achievement of serious tariff negotiations would be jeopardized if tariff commitments could be frustrated by the application of measures which were 'triggered by factors unrelated to the product as such'.[275] Against the exclusion of NPA measures has been argued that it would be unjustified to view them as a class of particularly dangerous measures. Tariff commitments could be frustrated through product-related measures just as well as they can through NPA measures.[276] According to this view, there is no reason to exclude application of the 'aim and effects' approach to NPA measures.

4.2.2.2.3 The 'aim and effects' theory in WTO adjudication

The views which the GATT and WTO panels and the Appellate Body took on a consideration of aims and effects for the interpretation of non-discrimination provisions are ambiguous and will be reviewed briefly. In some earlier cases, panels considered aim and effects of challenged measures in order to determine likeness of products under Article III:2. This consideration had the potential to change the traditional DSB approach by introducing an additional criterion for the determination of like products.

---

[274] Panel Report, *US – Taxes on Automobiles* (1994), No. 5.54.
[275] Panel Report, *US – Taxes on Automobiles* (1994), No. 5.53.
[276] Howse and Regan (2000), pp. 263, 264.

4.2.2.2.3.1 US – Malt Beverages (1992)

The debate on an 'aim and effects' test was sparked by the *US – Malt Beverages* panel, which incidentally at least in part concerned NPA measures.[277] The panel's crucial remarks regarding the test were, however, made with respect to a measure which distinguished between products on grounds of their physical properties, namely, wines in which a specified variety of grapes was used. The panel began its reasoning by stating that the intention of Article III was not to prevent contracting parties from using their fiscal and regulatory powers for purposes other than to afford protection to domestic production. This limited purpose of Article III would have to be taken into account in interpreting the term 'like products' in Article III.[278] The panel then proceeded to apply this standard to the measure at issue and found that given the limited growing range of the specific variety of grape, the tax treatment implied a geographical distinction which afforded protection to local production of wine to the disadvantage of wine produced where this type of grape cannot be grown. The panel briefly stated that the United States did not claim any public policy purpose for this Mississippi tax provision other than to subsidize small local producers and concluded that the wines at issue were therefore 'like products', and that the measure had to be presumed to afford protection to Mississippi vintners in violation of Article III:2, first and second sentence.[279]

With respect to other measures distinguishing between beer on the ground of alcohol content, the panel observed that:

> once products are designated as like products, a regulatory product differentiation, e.g., for standardization or environmental purposes, becomes inconsistent with Article III even if the regulation is not 'applied ... so as to afford protection to domestic production'. In the view of the Panel, therefore, it is imperative that the like product determination in the context of Article III be made in such a way that it does not unnecessarily infringe upon the regulatory authority and domestic policy options of contracting parties.[280]

The panel applied these standards and found that 'there was no evidence submitted to the Panel that the choice of the particular level has

---

[277] For more facts of the case see above, section 4.2.2.1.2.2(ii). For the conditions for in-state rates see, Panel Report, *US – Malt Beverages* (1992), table 1, at p. 7.
[278] Panel Report, *US – Malt Beverages* (1992), No. 5.25.
[279] Panel Report, *US – Malt Beverages* (1992), No. 5.26.
[280] Panel Report, *US – Malt Beverages* (1992), No. 5.72.

the purpose or effect of affording protection to domestic production', and drew the conclusion that low and high alcohol content beer therefore need not be considered 'like products' under Article III:4.[281]

The Panel Report was adopted and welcomed as a first step towards a more flexible view of the concept of like products.[282]

4.2.2.2.3.2 US – Taxes on Automobiles (1994)

The *US – Taxes on Automobiles* dispute concerned three measures. One was based on price, and the others on calculated fuel efficiency of certain automotive model types.[283] In its examination of a violation of GATT obligations through these measures the panel addressed the object and purpose of Article III:2 and III:4, and stated that according to its first paragraph, Article III serves only to prohibit regulatory distinctions between products applied 'so as to afford protection to domestic production'.[284] It concluded that the determination of likeness under Article III:2 would in all but the most straightforward cases have to include an examination of the aim and effect of the particular tax measure.[285] The panel then stressed explicitly that:

> issues of likeness under Article III should be analysed primarily in terms of whether less favourable treatment was based on a regulatory distinction taken so as to afford protection to domestic production.[286]

On examination of the aims and effects of the luxury tax the panel found that there was no discriminatory effect on products of foreign origin, and concluded that the products could not be regarded as 'like products' under Article III:2.[287] The same finding was reached for the 'gas guzzler tax'.[288] The panel then proceeded to examine the third measure, the CAFE, under Article III:4. It did not get to examine whether the measure was applied so as to afford protection in the sense of the 'aim and effects' test, because it first found that the CAFE accorded treatment less favourable to imported products. The panel considered that as this treatment was based on origin and on factors not directly relating to the product as such, it was impossible to justify the measure under Article III, because

---

[281] Panel Report, *US – Malt Beverages* (1992), No. 5.73.
[282] Demaret and Stewardson (1994), p. 39.
[283] These measures are described above, section 4.2.2.1.2.2(iii).
[284] Panel Report, *US – Taxes on Automobiles* (1994), No. 5.7.
[285] Panel Report, *US – Taxes on Automobiles* (1994), No. 5.9.
[286] Panel Report, *US – Taxes on Automobiles* (1994), No. 5.9.
[287] Panel Report, *US – Taxes on Automobiles* (1994), No. 5.15.
[288] Panel Report, *US – Taxes on Automobiles* (1994), No. 5.37.

4.2 THE PRINCIPLE OF NON-DISCRIMINATION

this would not only frustrate tariff negotiations, but would also violate the obligation to unconditional MFN treatment under Article III:4 as referred to in Article I:1.[289]

With respect to the question of likeness, the report used the 'aims and effects' test to clear measures which would otherwise infringe the national treatment obligation in Article III. The panel framed two questions which express the dilemma in not unnecessarily restricting legitimate national policies and protecting WTO obligations sufficiently at the same time. It asked:

> which differences between products may form the basis of regulatory distinctions by governments that accord less favourable treatment to imported products? Or, conversely, which similarities between products prevent regulatory distinctions by governments that accord less favourable treatment to imported products?[290]

The panel saw the solution in taking the regulatory purpose and protective effects into account for determining whether the products at issue were 'like' under Article III:2. The adoption of the Panel Report in *US – Taxes on Automobiles* was blocked by the EC, but it has had a strong influence on the debate regarding the actual meaning of national treatment obligations in relation to legitimate national policies.[291]

4.2.2.2.3.3 *Japan – Alcoholic Beverages* (1996) and *EC – Bananas* (1997)

The *Japan – Alcoholic Beverages* dispute under the then newly established WTO concerned the Japanese Liquor Tax Law which provided for tax measures exclusively based on physical properties of the product, namely, on the alcohol content of beverages. The 'aim and effects' test was discussed by the parties, the panel and to some extent also by the Appellate Body. The parties had different opinions on the 'aim and effects' test. While the European Community and Canada rejected the test altogether, both Japan and the United States agreed on its application, but reached opposite conclusions with it.[292]

---

[289] Panel Report, *US – Taxes on Automobiles* (1994), Nos. 5.49, 5.54.
[290] Panel Report, *US – Taxes on Automobiles* (1994), No. 5.6.
[291] For a more comprehensive analysis of the application of the 'aim and effects test' in this dispute see Mattoo and Subramanian (1998), and Verhoosel (2002), pp. 52–4, who argues that the panel set the standard for *de facto* discrimination too high and was overly permissive of regulatory barriers.
[292] Panel Report, *Japan – Alcoholic Beverages II* (1996), see Nos. 4.12–4.14 for the EC's position, No. 4.23 for Canada's position, Nos. 4.17–4.18 for the US position and No. 4.19 for Japan's position.

The panel started its appraisal by stating that the test had no textual basis in Article III:2, first sentence, as there was no reference to paragraph 1. It then recalled a number of further arguments against the test, mostly concerning practicability. First, the panel mentioned the repercussions for the burden of proof of the complainant and invoked difficulties linked to the determination of both aim and effects of national measures. It referred to the multiplicity of aims, and to the problems of obtaining the legislative history of a measure.[293] The panel then moved on to another set of counter-arguments, invoking the principle of effective treaty interpretation with respect to the problem that many of the exceptions enlisted in Article XX would become redundant as a corollary to the test.[294] Finally, the panel addressed the two panel reports which had confirmed the test previously. It stressed that the Panel Report in *US – Taxes on Automobiles* had not been adopted, and it stated with respect to the *US – Malt Beverages* Panel Report, which had been adopted under the GATT, that it was inconsistent with the wording of the Article III:2 condition 'likeness' of products on the regulatory purpose of the measure.[295]

The Appellate Body did not address the panel's statements on the theory directly, but it stressed the difference in the first and second sentence of Article III:2 to support a different meaning of paragraph 1 for the rest of Article III. The Appellate Body stated with respect to the first sentence of Article III:2:

> There is no specific invocation in this first sentence of the general principle in Article III:1 that admonishes Members of the WTO not to apply measures 'so as to afford protection'. This omission must have some meaning. We believe the meaning is simply that the presence of a protective application need not be established separately ... in order to show that a tax measure is inconsistent with the general principle set out in the first sentence.[296]

Implying that the omission of the invocation of Article III:1 renders unnecessary a separate examination of a requirement that the measure is applied so as to afford protection, the Appellate Body Report in its subsequent elaborations on the interpretation of 'likeness' did not test the aims and effects of a measure as established by the two panels in 1992 and 1994. The Appellate Body, overall affirming the decision of the panel, did

---

[293] Panel Report, *Japan – Alcoholic Beverages II* (1996), No. 6.16.
[294] Panel Report, *Japan – Alcoholic Beverages II* (1996), No. 6.17.
[295] Panel Report, *Japan – Alcoholic Beverages II* (1996), No. 6.18.
[296] Appellate Body Report, *Japan – Alcoholic Beverages II* (1996), p. 18, H 1.

4.2 THE PRINCIPLE OF NON-DISCRIMINATION

not even address the key complaint of both appellants, and instead established a new 'doctrine'[297] regarding the function of Article III:1 as 'a general principle which informs the rest of Article III'.[298] For these reasons, the Appellate Body Report has sometimes been interpreted as rejecting the 'aim and effect' test,[299] while other voices in literature call this interpretation of the report at least much overstated.[300]

On the one hand, the Appellate Body clearly rejected the application of an 'aim and effect' test under Article III:2, first sentence, by pointing out that the first sentence was in fact an application of the general principle of Article III:1.[301] Also, under Article III:2, second sentence, the Appellate Body went as far as finding that whether or not a measure is applied so as to afford protection was not an issue of intent, and that it was not necessary for a panel to establish legislative or regulatory intent,[302] and so rejected an 'aim and effect' test even for this provision. However, the Appellate Body is not straightforward in its findings on what exactly panels have to examine in order to determine whether a measure is applied 'so as to afford protection'. It stated:

> Although it is true that the aim of a measure may not be easily ascertained, nevertheless its protective application can most often be discerned from the design, the architecture, and the revealing structure of a measure. The very magnitude of the dissimilar taxation in a particular case may be evidence of such a protective application, as the Panel rightly concluded in this case. Most often, there will be other factors to be considered as well. In conducting this inquiry, panels should give full consideration to all the relevant facts and all the relevant circumstances in any given case.[303]

This statement is confusing in two ways. First, it is unclear how the application of the measure can be discerned from the measure itself. If something can be revealed from the structure of a measure, this cannot be the application, since that is a question of practice. It has been suggested that what could be revealed instead is the aim or purpose of a measure.[304] It is

---

[297] Charnovitz (1997), p. 200.
[298] Appellate Body Report, *Japan – Alcoholic Beverages II* (1996), p. 18, G, after fn. 40.
[299] E.g., Charnovitz (1997), p. 200   [300] Howse and Regan (2000), p. 264.
[301] Appellate Body Report, *Japan – Alcoholic Beverages II* (1996), p. 18, H 1.
[302] Appellate Body Report, *Japan – Alcoholic Beverages II* (1996), p. 27, H 2 c, first paragraph.
[303] Appellate Body Report, *Japan – Alcoholic Beverages II* (1996), p. 29, second paragraph before fn. 62.
[304] This interpretation has been suggested with slightly different arguments by Regan (2002), pp. 476, 477.

also not entirely clear whether the Appellate Body considers the aim of a measure simply too difficult to ascertain or beyond that utterly unsuitable as evidence for protective application. Also, the statement regarding the 'other factors' which most often will have to be considered is obscure.

In *Japan – Alcoholic Beverages*, the Appellate Body relied to a great extent on the particular wording of Article III:2 and on the differences between this paragraph's first and second sentence. Its findings did not therefore prejudice the possible consideration of 'aim and effects' under Article III:4. In *EC – Bananas* (1997), however, the Appellate Body explicitly rejected a separate consideration of whether a measure also affords protection to domestic production according to paragraph 4.[305]

4.2.2.2.3.4 Subsequent jurisprudence

Due to the above quoted Appellate Body reports it seems that the traditional 'aim and effects' theory will most probably not be applied. Nevertheless, the requirement that a measure is not applied so as to afford protection according to paragraph 1 is not completely ignored by the adjudicatory bodies either. The *Japan – Film* panel, for example, explicitly rejected a consideration of whether the measure was applied so as to afford protection under Article III:4. Nevertheless, it declared that it would use the general principle contained in paragraph 1 'as a guide to interpreting Article III:4'.[306]

Since then, numerous reports have been adopted in disputes where the test might actually have been relevant, but where it has been rejected.[307] In other instances, the test was simply not applied, as, for example, in the 1997 reports in the *Canada – Periodicals* dispute. The panel applied the traditional approach in determining likeness, without taking into account aim and effects of the measure.[308] While the Appellate Body found that the panel had used an inadequate factual basis for the determination of likeness, it clearly confirmed that the panel had in theory used the proper test.[309]

---

[305] Appellate Body Report, *EC – Bananas* (1997), No. 216.
[306] Panel Report, *Japan – Film* (1998), No. 10.371.
[307] See with respect to Article III:2, first sentence, e.g., Panel Report in: *Argentina – Hides and Leather* (2001), Nos. 11.137–11.138, with respect to Article III:4, e.g., the Panel in *Dominican Republic – Import and Sale of Cigarettes* (2004), No. 7.202, which rejected the consideration whether the measure was applied so as to afford protection, quoting the above statement of *EC – Bananas III* (1997) Appellate Body Report in reviewing the tax stamp requirement.
[308] Panel Report, *Canada – Periodicals* (1997), No. 5.25.
[309] Appellate Body Report, *Canada – Periodicals* (1997), pp. 20–1, V.A.

4.2 THE PRINCIPLE OF NON-DISCRIMINATION

In more recent reports, however, the aims, and more importantly, the effects of measures have been attributed greater importance, albeit under the aspect of 'less favourable treatment'. This development started with the Appellate Body in *EC – Asbestos* which stated that the:

> term 'less favourable treatment' expresses the general principle, in Article III:1, that internal regulations 'should not be applied ... so as to afford protection to domestic production' ... a Member may draw distinctions between products which have been found to be 'like', without, for this reason alone, according to the group of 'like' *imported* products 'less favourable treatment' than that accorded to the group of 'like' *domestic* products.[310]

Furthermore, it implicitly acknowledged the relevance of public health risks, and thereby also the public policy aims underlying the French measure for the determination of 'likeness'. The Appellate Body formally qualified carcinogenicity of one set of fibres as nothing but a physical property.[311] However, the choice of words, such as 'undeniable public health risks',[312] is strongly evocative of public policies and shows that the Appellate Body did not merely detect a certain degree of physical difference. Although it did not explicitly discuss the 'aims' of the challenged measure it is apparent that its reasoning was guided by the fact that the physical difference between the products was such that reasonable public policies, in particular health policies, ought to be linked to it. Therefore, there is no doubt that the Appellate Body qualified the relevance of that particular physical difference by applying normative standards, which, however, it failed to specify.[313]

The Appellate Body in *Dominican Republic – Import and Sale of Cigarettes*, in contrast, focused on less favourable treatment. It considered that no detrimental effect of a measure on imports is sufficient to prove less favourable treatment, if 'the detrimental effect is explained by factors

---

[310] Appellate Body Report, *EC – Asbestos* (2001), No. 100 (original emphasis). The Panel in *EC – Biotech* (2006), No. 7.2514, applied a similar line of reasoning.
[311] Appellate Body Report, *EC – Asbestos* (2001), Nos. 115–18, 142.
[312] Appellate Body Report, *EC – Asbestos* (2001), Nos. 128, 142. The Appellate Body in this respect agrees with the Panel's factual findings; however, it disagrees with the relevance which the Panel ascribed to them. The Appellate Body finds that the carcinogenicity is 'one principle and significant difference between these products' (at No. 142).
[313] Instead, the Appellate Body apparently invokes obviousness, or common sense, for the legitimacy of the normative standards it applies by stating: 'We do not see how this highly significant physical difference *cannot* be a consideration in examining the physical properties of a product as part of a determination of "likeness" under Article III:4 of the GATT 1994' (Appellate Body Report, *EC – Asbestos* (2001), No. 114).

or circumstances unrelated to the foreign origin of the product, such as the market share of the importer in this case'.[314] An approach along similar lines, albeit with a stronger focus on public policy considerations, was applied by the *EC – Biotech* panel.[315] In spite of the as yet incoherent jurisprudence on this issue, there is strong evidence that the basic objective of preventing protectionism as guidance in the interpretation of the non-discrimination provisions in WTO law, particularly with respect to national treatment, is becoming more and more accepted.[316]

While the adjudicatory bodies currently do not apply the 'aim and effects' theory for the determination of like products under Article III, the related substantive problems, particularly the precise scope of the national treatment obligation and the relevance of non-economic public policy goals under Article III, are far from being settled.

4.2.2.2.4 Critique

The 'aim and effects' theory reflects concerns relating to the sheer unlimited scope of the national treatment obligations in Article III and a potentially excessive scrutiny of measures implementing legitimate public policies. Therefore, it might be justified to label the theory a public policy approach to Article III. The approach, however, has met strong reservations. The main points of critique claim, on the one hand, inconsistency with the GATT language and impracticability, on the other. Other concerns point to some difficulties, without, however, rejecting the approach altogether. For instance, it has also been pointed out that there are different variations of purpose and market effects, and there may be cases where evidence relating to these criteria points to different directions.[317]

The first point of critique concerning GATT language, however, is not convincing. Since the GATT simply does not offer any guidance as to the precise meaning of 'like products', a teleological interpretation bringing in line language and broader policy objectives of special GATT articles or the agreement as a whole cannot be rejected outright. Article III:2, second sentence, clarifies that Article III:1 contains 'principles' as opposed to a specific obligations. However, there is no further guidance on the relevance of these principles – but certainly, the principle of effective treaty

---

[314] Appellate Body Report, *Dominican Republic – Import and Sale of Cigarettes* (2005), No. 96.
[315] Above at section 4.2.2.1.3.4.
[316] See also Cottier and Oesch (2005), p. 407, who invoke the *EC – Asbestos* report as evidence for the relevance of non-protective motives and effects under Article III:4.
[317] Hudec (1998), p. 627.

interpretation requires that there needs to be legal relevance. A too strong focus on language always runs the risk of leading to an artificial interpretation of the text, missing the primary objectives of the treaty.[318] Also, the other interpretative argument relating to GATT Article XX is invalid. It has been argued that contrary to effective treaty interpretation the exploration of regulatory aims and effects would render the function of Article XX entirely redundant. However, Article XX would still be applicable in cases of violations of other GATT provisions, and in cases of *de jure* discriminations.[310] A more substantive point of critique concerns the interpretation of the non-discrimination provision in general, which some are afraid could jeopardize the goal of free trade. In this view, it is necessary to put all discriminatory measures, whether protectionist or not, under scrutiny of the national treatment provision.[320]

Reservations generally relating to impracticability concern implementation difficulties, subjectivity and a related lack in terms of security and predictability.[321] Critics of the approach point out that the determination of whether products are 'like' should not be based on an allegedly subjective criterion. Rather, the determination would need to be based on objective criteria, since otherwise panels would be able to decide for themselves which regulatory purposes would be acceptable for differentiations.[322] However, it is not correct to equalize the 'aim and effects' test with a predominantly subjective approach. As shown above, the approach consists of an arguably subjective element in combination with an objective one, namely, effects. Even the subjectivity of the former element has been contested. Regan has argued that in spite of the term 'aim', the review in order to assess this element can be undertaken in a fairly objective way.[323]

This author's main objection regards the relevance of regulatory aims. It would seem awkward if one WTO member were allowed to take a particular measure because its aims were considered authentic, and another WTO member were not allowed to take it because of considerable doubts about the real motivation. If one imagined a measure taken to protect the environment, as, for example, a sales and import prohibition on products

---

[318] An example for the confusion that has been created in this respect could be the Panel's statement in *Japan – Film* (1998), above at section 4.2.2.2.3.4.
[310] Howse and Regan (2000), p.266.
[320] Cho (2003), pp. 25–7 (commenting on *EC – Asbestos*); Cho (2005), p. 654 (commenting on the relevance of the 'aim and effects' theory on PPMs).
[321] Gaines (2002), pp. 419, 426.   [322] Davey and Pauwelyn (2002), p. 38.
[323] Regan (2002), pp. 458–64.

containing CFCs which seriously harm the ozone layer, it seems obvious that not the motivation, but its suitability for a legitimate public policy purpose at issue should decide about its legality. Furthermore, it seems that a consideration of regulatory aims would require normative standards. In the absence of normative standards, the WTO adjudicatory bodies would lack the necessary tools to distinguish between impermissible *de facto* discrimination and genuine public policies.[324]

As regards protectionist effects, it seems that there are good arguments for the view that the GATT does not intend to discipline national regulation which does not have actual protectionist economic effects, albeit the language of the national treatment provision is not clear on this point.[325] However, it seems difficult to assess protective effects considering that markets are not static but dynamic. A measure having been found not to have any protective effects today may well have such effects tomorrow, because business and conditions of competition underlie permanent changes.

In any case, the potential of the 'aim and effects' test for shifting a number of national measures away from scrutiny under the GATT should not be overstated. Due to globalization, even the most genuine and rational internal measure will often have some protective effects. Since domestic producers usually also produce for the domestic market and thus operate in the national legal system under permanent adaptation to changes in this legal environment, it seems natural that foreign producers are at a disadvantage in this respect. The benefits of leaving the particular geographical market in the case of changing requirements will usually be greater for foreign producers than for domestic ones. This consideration is likely to be important when it comes to production methods, and even more so when it comes to other NPAs, on which producers might not have much influence.

4.2.2.3 Market-based or economic approaches

A set of different approaches to the 'like products' concept undertakes the determination of 'likeness' based on existence and degree of competitive

---

[324] See, e.g., Mattoo and Subramanian (1998), p 321, who recognize this problem, but argue that at least the most egregious cases of abuse could be identified easily.

[325] It is noteworthy that the crucial factual element required by the provision corresponding to GATT Article III:4 in the EC Treaty are the restrictive effects. The 'like products' concept does not appear in that Article (Article 28 EC Treaty reads: 'Quantitative restrictions on imports and *all measures having equivalent effect* shall be prohibited between Member States.' (emphasis added).

relationships. These approaches have in common that they focus on the position of the products in the marketplace, but they differ in the importance they ascribe to the competitive relationship vis-à-vis other criteria. This section first describes the basic features of economic approaches and then reviews GATT and WTO reports which to some extent reflect these basic features.

4.2.2.3.1 Rationales and main elements

The focus on markets for the interpretation of 'like products' is based on the insight that the 'GATT 1994 is a commercial agreement' and that 'the WTO is concerned, after all, with markets'.[326] The crucial question for the determination of likeness of different products from a market perspective is whether or not the products at issue are in competition.[327] Thus, even the traditional DSB approach is implicitly concerned with competitiveness and substitutability of products.[328] With respect to Article III, Vranes cites the telos of avoiding protectionism as basis for this approach. He claims that in order for a regulatory intervention to achieve protectionist goals, a competitive relationship between the domestic products protected and the disfavoured foreign products is required.[329]

Proponents of a market-based approach emphasize the perspective of actual market agents and plead for the use of economic analysis of substitutability based on economic data as a tool. According to the proponents of a market-based approach, the benefits of resorting to an economic analysis of the question of likeness would result in a resolution of disputes in a predictable and consistent manner through the use of transparent tools.[330] It would so reduce the range of possible outcomes of disputes, increase predictability and ultimately set limits to the undue discretion of the respective tribunals.[331]

As regards the details of the analysis, market-based approaches use as a point of departure the specific product market in question. In the main, proponents of market-based approaches suggest that the delineation of the relevant markets should be undertaken based on the meanwhile rather sophisticated competition law rules. Consumers would not consider products to be in competition for competition law purposes,

---

[326] Appellate Body Report, *Japan – Alcoholic Beverages II* (1996), at 25.
[327] Bronckers and McNelis (2002), p. 345.
[328] For recent developments see the analysis of WTO adjudication in the following section 4.2.2.3.3.
[329] Vranes (2009a), pp. 191–3.   [330] Choi (2003), p. 7.   [331] Choi (2003), p. 8.

and not to be in competition for other purposes,[332] and so market-based delineations offer clear answers. An analysis of 'likeness', applying a market-based approach, proceeds in several steps. A common feature of all market-based approaches is that as a first step they take physical characteristics into account, without, however, giving this criterion primary importance. Instead, they place great importance on consumers as agents in the market and on their decisions, and therefore attribute considerable weight to demand substitutability as the second step in an analysis.[333] Choi, an important advocate of market-based approaches, goes one step further and suggests a concept which, in addition to demand substitutability, also includes data on supply substitutability. He argues that, at least in the long run, high supply substitutability could mitigate the negative effects of discriminatory measures on foreign producers.[334] Hence, importance needed to be given to a producer perspective as well. However, Choi is also of the view that the consumer perspective provides the most immediate and conspicuous factor concerning competitive relationships. He acknowledges that demand-side substitutability deserves a major role in the determination of likeness, but insists that data on supply-side substitutability should be used to complement the overall assessment.[335] Choi also interprets the GATT as aiming at the protection of certain categories of potential competition. Even potentially protectionist measures, for example, in the case of taxation, can influence consumer behaviour. Thus, his approach takes into account latent demand and potential competition and substitutability in addition to the actual competitive relationship.[336]

Naturally, market-based approaches are concerned with questions about which economic methodologies are suitable to assess supply and demand substitutability, and which threshold or which degree of substitutability is sufficient to consider products 'directly competitive and substitutable', on the one hand, or 'like', on the other. For the analysis of demand substitutability, Choi suggests relying on direct view data on market segmentation, which can often be provided by the respective industry, and to refer to consumer surveys in cases where direct view data are not available. In order to include potential competition in the assessment,

---

[332] Bronckers and McNelis (2002), p. 359; Choi (2003), p. 33, see also there fnn. 142 and 143.
[333] Bronckers and McNelis (2002), also Choi (2003), chapter II.3.
[334] Choi (2003), p. 40.   [335] Choi (2003), p. 43.
[336] Appellate Body Report, *Korea – Alcoholic Beverages* (1999), Nos. 121–7. Choi considers future and potential substitution for both demand and supply substitutability (2003), chapter II, 3.2.4, pp. 71–81.

expanded questionnaires need to be drafted in order to include as many choices as possible.[337] For the assessment itself, Choi suggests a combination of methods which he refers to as 'Contingent Valuation Analysis on Proportional Cross-Price-Demand Substitutability'.[338] As regards the analysis of supply substitutability, Choi adapts the analysis developed for demand substitutability to the special situation of producers on the supply-side. Naturally, consumer surveys do not come into consideration as relevant data, instead, the analysis has to be based on a strict producer's view concerning production factors, market entry and demand substitutability.[339] According to Choi, the main benefit of both demand- and supply-side analyses would be an increase in consistency and predictability of the decisions of WTO tribunals in disputes involving determinations of 'like' or 'directly competitive or substitutable' products.[340]

While the market-based approach has been discussed mostly with respect to GATT Article III:2, disregarding most other provisions referring to the 'like products' concept, proponents of this approach are in

---

[337] Choi (2003), pp. 60–1.
[338] Choi (2003), chapter II, 3.2.2. The 'Contingent Valuation Analysis on Proportional Cross-Price-Demand Substitutability' (CVA-PCPDS) basically draws from an analysis of cross-price elasticity of demand, with methods that have been developed in competition law. There, cross-price elasticity is used as a criterion to define the scope of the relevant product market. Since this criterion also reveals the extent of a substitutive relationship between products (Choi (2003), pp. 54–6, invoking the *Indonesia – Autos* (1998) Panel, para. 14.177), Choi suggests borrowing this method with a few adaptations for purposes of the GATT. As appropriate minimum substitution rate for two products to be regarded as 'directly competitive or substitutable' the point at which price change rates equalize with substitution rates come into consideration. This point is called 'price-substitution equivalence standard' (PSE Standard) (Choi (2003), pp. 56, 57). The PSE Standard is supposed to serve as a basic standard, which may have to be adjusted in some situations. The PSE Standard is the lowest standard in a competitive relationship, and accordingly a specific threshold going beyond the PSE Standard could be defined with respect to the specific level of likeness in various provisions of the GATT (Choi (2003), p. 63). Choi is of the view that the benefits of the CVA-PCPDS outweigh some methodological problems, as resulting from the difficulty of drafting and interpreting questionnaires in a way that takes into account the numerous consumer choices in real life. Furthermore, a CVA-PCPDS can be complemented with other types of analysis, such as dynamic economic analyses.
[339] Choi (2003), p. 68.
[340] Choi (2003), pp. 62, 70. Also, there is no PSE standard on the supply side. Instead, the analysis refers to the average cross-price supply substitutability rate of the concerned industry (IASR standard) (Choi (2003), p. 68). With respect to the IASR standard, criteria on high or low substitutability should be based on the given situation and on the character of each industry (Choi (2003), p. 70). Nevertheless, the basic approach, the CVA-PCPDS used for the demand side, can be adapted into a 'Contingent Valuation Analysis on Proportional Cross-Price *Supply* Substitutability'.

support of a broader application under other provisions and agreements. They argue that the advantage of a market-based approach is that it brings together the different elements of the like product determination, and that it allows these elements to be given their proper weight in a coherent analysis.[341] Another benefit of the market-based approach is that the determination needs to be made with a view to the purpose of GATT rules, namely, to ensure fair competitive conditions between imported and domestic products. Some scholars tested the application of a market-based approach on anti-dumping provisions and on Article III:4 with respect to internal regulation, and reached the conclusions that the approach is suitable for both.[342] While all proponents of market-based approaches advocate broader application of the concept, opinions on the question of which provisions the approach is particularly suitable seem to differ. Choi advocates the application of his market-based analytical framework especially to the GATT non-discrimination provisions, for example, MFN and national treatment provisions, but holds that his approach is still workable as a basic framework.[343] Others highlight that the purpose of provisions which are suitable objects for a market-based approach has to be to establish or improve competitive conditions, without, however, indicating which provisions fulfil this requirement.[344] It has been recognized that today the application of market-based approaches might lead to considerable practical difficulties, while constant progress in information technologies might soon dispel these concerns.[345]

4.2.2.3.2 Significance for NPA measures

Just as the 'aim and effects' theory, the market-based approach to the determination of likeness also emphasizes criteria other than physical properties of products. For this reason, they are considered a possible way to avoid *a priori* illegality of many measures pursuing legitimate political purposes under WTO law. By giving considerable weight to consumer preferences via their decisions and behaviour as market participants, all aspects, which consumers deem important, can become crucial for the determination of likeness – whether these aspects are physically linked

---

[341] Bronckers and McNelis (2002), p. 347.
[342] Bronckers and McNelis (2002), pp. 357 *et seq.*
[343] Choi (2003), pp. 90, 91 *et seq.*   [344] Bronckers and McNelis (2002), p. 346.
[345] Choi (2003), pp. 84 *et seq.*

4.2 THE PRINCIPLE OF NON-DISCRIMINATION

to the product or not. Likewise, producer preferences could play a crucial role as well. If market participants would treat products differently because of PPMs or other NPAs, demand and/or supply substitutability between physically 'like' products could be lowered.[346] Cross-price elasticity between these products would then fall below a specific minimum threshold indicating likeness. As a consequence, even physically identical products could be found not to be in a competitive relationship with each other, depending on the impact certain NPAs may have on consumer preferences and tastes.[347] This means that in as far as consumers care to a sufficient degree for certain non-economic aspects, market-based approaches might render physically identical products 'unlike' for purposes of WTO law, and hence a difference in treatment accorded by WTO members would not be considered discriminatory or otherwise violate WTO law.

In its purest form, a market-based approach would consider the competitive relationship, as indicated by determinants such as cross-price elasticity of paramount importance. Nevertheless, at this point views diverge. Some scholars who in principle adhere to basic ideas of market-based approaches concede that a mere economic analysis cannot suffice to determine whether products are 'like', and stress that the determination of likeness also requires judgement on a qualitative basis.[348]

The suitability of the market-based approach to defend measures which pursue legitimate goals depends on the decision of consumers in a *quasi*-democratic way: consumers need to attribute sufficient weight to the aspect which decides on the distinction. Only if consumers are willing to pay higher prices for a product than for a competing product which has been produced in a different way, the competitive relationship between identical products can be ruled out. Because of this last qualification, it has been recognized that the market-based approach might lead to solutions for some, but not for all environmental regulation.[349] Thus, a market-based approach to determining 'likeness' could lead to legality of certain NPA measures and to illegality of others, depending on their relevance in the market.

---

[346] E.g., Vranes (2009a), p. 324, explains that if consumers perceive certain non-physical aspects as relevant and related to a product, this may indicate that otherwise similar products may be 'unlike' nonetheless.
[347] Van den Bossche, Schrijver and Faber (2007), p. 63, citing carpets made by children and non-battery cage hens as examples (at p. 64).
[348] Van den Bossche, Schrijver and Faber (2007), p. 57; Howse and Tuerk (2006), p. 91.
[349] Bronckers and McNelis (2002), p. 376.

4.2.2.3.3 Relevance in WTO adjudication

Economic approaches do not *per se* contradict the DSB approach to the question of 'likeness'. Rather, it seems that certain developments in WTO adjudication have influenced the approach and vice versa. The most apparent point of connection is the traditional DSB approach criterion of consumers' tastes and habits, due to which some elements of a competitive relationship have anyway been part of the traditional approach. Also, market elements have featured prominently in more recent case law. For instance, in several disputes regarding complaints about discriminatory taxes under Article III:2, both adjudicatory bodies stressed the significance of the market place for the determination of both 'directly competitive or substitutable' and 'like products'. The panel in *Japan – Alcoholic Beverages II* reiterated that Article III:2 together with the Note distinguished between 'like products', on the one hand, and 'directly competitive or substitutable products', on the other, and went on to elaborate that the wording made it clear that the appropriate test to define whether two products are 'like' or 'directly competitive or substitutable' is the marketplace.[350] It found that the decisive criterion for the determination of 'whether two products are directly competitive or substitutable is whether they have common end-uses, *inter alia*, as shown by elasticity of substitution'.[351] Even more important for all market-based approaches was the following statement of the panel:

> that independently of similarities with respect to physical characteristics or classification in tariff nomenclatures, greater emphasis should be placed on elasticity of substitution. In this context, factors like marketing strategies could also prove to be relevant criteria, since what is at issue is the responsiveness of consumers to the various products offered in the market.[352]

The Appellate Body explicitly approved of the panel's views on elasticity of substitution, and it fully confirmed the panel's reasoning that looking beyond the usual Working Party criteria at the 'marketplace' is appropriate.[353]

---

[350] Panel Report, *Japan – Alcoholic Beverages II* (1996), No. 6.22.
[351] Panel Report, *Japan – Alcoholic Beverages II* (1996), No. 6.22. The Appellate Body later fully approved of this view and quoted this statement in full length, Appellate Body Report, *Japan – Alcoholic Beverages II* (1996), at p. 25.
[352] Panel Report, *Japan – Alcoholic Beverages II* (1996), No. 6.28.
[353] Appellate Body Report, *Japan – Alcoholic Beverages II* (1996), p. 25.

4.2 THE PRINCIPLE OF NON-DISCRIMINATION   229

The statements of the adjudicatory bodies are of equal importance to the determination of both 'directly competitive or substitutable' and 'like' products. Since the group of 'like products' has been found to be a sub-set of the latter group of products, elasticity of substitution is relevant to the determination of 'like products' as well.[354] In the later *Korea – Alcoholic Beverages* dispute that dealt with similar facts, the panel applied the revised DSB approach as designed by panel and Appellate Body in *Japan – Alcoholic Beverages II* with respect to elasticity.[355] The panel, however, was careful in pointing out that it treated cross-price elasticity as only one of several evidential factors.[356] It stated that 'quantitative studies of cross-price elasticity are relevant, but not exclusive or even decisive in nature'. The problem which the panel saw in considering quantitative data is that consumers tend to buy what is familiar to them, thus placing imported goods in a naturally disadvantageous competitive position, especially if the analysis relates to experience-based consumer items.[357] Therefore, the panel assessed both an actual competitive relationship between the products at issue as well as a potential competitive relationship. For the latter, it considered the element of end-uses of great importance.[358] The Appellate Body supported the findings of the panel, and pointed out that 'latent demand' can be relevant in cases of experience goods, such as food and beverages, and that the panel did not err in buttressing its findings on a competitive relationship by referring to a 'strong potentially direct competitive relationship'.[359]

The panel's doubts about a possibly increased importance of cross-price elasticity vis-à-vis other factors were confirmed by the *Chile – Alcoholic Beverages* panel.[360] The panel expressed considerable doubts about measuring

---

[354] See, e.g., Appellate Body Report, *Korea – Alcoholic Beverages* (1999), No. 118, and Panel Report, *US – Cotton Yarn* (2001), rejecting the contrary view of the United States, No. 97.

[355] However, an assessment of whether there is a direct competitive relationship between two products or groups of products requires evidence that consumers consider or could consider the two products or groups of products as alternative ways of satisfying a particular need or taste (Panel Report, *Korea – Alcoholic Beverages* (1998), para. 10.40).

[356] Panel Report, *Korea – Alcoholic Beverages* (1998), para. 10.44.

[357] Panel Report, *Korea – Alcoholic Beverages* (1998), para. 10.50.

[358] Panel Report, *Korea – Alcoholic Beverages* (1998), para 10.78.

[359] Appellate Body Report, *Korea – Alcoholic Beverages* (1999), No. 124.

[360] Also other panels referred to substitutability, without however placing paramount importance on this criterion. For instance, the Panel in *Indonesia – Autos* (1998) referred to substitutability with respect to the determination of 'like products' in the SCM Agreement. Arguably, the importance of this finding cannot be generalized as indicative for a trend in WTO adjudication. The SCM Agreement provides a special and

the degree of substitutability econometrically, since such data would not always adequately reflect the extent of substitution.[361] It stated that studies measuring 'the relationship between dependent and independent variables are only part of the totality of factors a panel should take into account in determining the question of direct competitiveness or substitutability'.[362]

Finally, it should be noted that also the Appellate Body in *EC – Asbestos* dispute referred to the competitive relationship in the marketplace. It advised panels to consider especially those physical characteristics which are likely to influence the competitive relationship between products in the marketplace,[363] and then concluded that carcinogenicity and health risks are relevant because they bear on this relationship.[364] The Appellate Body found that the criteria 'end-uses' and 'consumers' tastes and habits' involve key elements relating to the competitive relationship between products: first, the extent to which products are capable of performing the same or similar functions, and, second, the extent to which consumers are willing to use the products to perform these functions.[365] With respect to the latter criterion, the Appellate Body found that evidence about the extent to which consumers are – or would be – willing to choose one product instead of another to perform certain end-uses is highly relevant in assessing the 'likeness' of those products under Article III:4 of the GATT 1994.[366] Interestingly, the Appellate Body considered the fibres in question as 'physically very different',[367] and invoked the high likeliness that consumers' tastes and habits would be influenced by health risks associated with products to support this finding. The approach taken can indeed be characterized as a *reasonable consumer* test,[368] since the Appellate Body conjectures on consumer choices in the case of full information rather than referring to actual market data or surveys.

In *EC – Asbestos*, the Appellate Body had identified as one out of three crucial questions pertaining to the issue of 'like products' the question

---

rather restrictive legal definition for the concept of 'like product'. The Panel's decision to transfer its negative findings on likeness under this analysis to the concept of 'like products' used in other provisions of the GATT (Panel Report, *Indonesia – Autos* (1998), at para. 14.175) is therefore questionable.

[361] Panel Report, *Chile – Alcoholic Beverages* (1999), para 7.69.
[362] Panel Report, *Chile – Alcoholic Beverages* (1999), para. 7.73.
[363] Appellate Body Report, *EC – Asbestos* (2001), No. 114.
[364] Appellate Body Report, *EC – Asbestos* (2001), Nos. 114–15.
[365] Appellate Body Report, *EC – Asbestos* (2001), No. 117.
[366] Appellate Body Report, *EC – Asbestos* (2001), No. 117.
[367] Appellate Body Report, *EC – Asbestos* (2001), No. 121.
[368] Mavroidis (2007), p. 242; Mavroidis (2005), p. 168

4.2 THE PRINCIPLE OF NON-DISCRIMINATION

'*whose perspective* is crucial for the determination'.[369] It seems that market-based approaches, which consider consumer as well as producer perspectives, ultimately offer an answer to this question, which the Appellate Body did not address any further in the report.

However, in the same report, the Appellate Body watered down the importance of consumer preferences. It incidentally pointed out that evidence on consumers' willingness to choose one product over another was especially relevant if products were physically quite different. The Appellate Body stated that a higher burden would be placed on complainants to establish existence of a competitive relationship for overcoming the indication that physically very different products are 'unlike'.[370] This statement can be interpreted to confirm the paramount importance of the first criterion, physical properties, while consumer preferences are useful to correct findings based on physical properties in unusual circumstances.

In the meantime, panels and the Appellate Body have used economic approaches in a number of cases. However, considerations of the competitive relationship between products, and the reference to economic data on cross-price elasticity, have not yet become standard tools in determining the likeness of products.[371] A considerable amount of reservation towards economic approaches underlies the concurring statement in *EC – Asbestos*. The concurring member of the Appellate Body suggested that in the face of clear scientific evidence showing that the asbestos fibres at issue were carcinogenic, the Appellate Body should have completed the analysis with respect to the finding that the fibres were not 'like', particularly given the lack of evidence relating to the other traditional criteria, such as end-uses and consumer tastes and habits. The reluctance of the other members to follow this suggestion, he presumed, was a result of their conception of the 'fundamental' role of economic competitive relationships in the determination of the 'likeness'. He apparently felt that the importance ascribed to, in this case even unknown, economic evidence would constitute a shift in WTO jurisprudence and stated that:

> the necessity or appropriateness of adopting a 'fundamentally' economic interpretation of the 'likeness' of products under Article III:4 of the GATT 1994 does not appear to me to be free from substantial doubt ... It

---

[369] Appellate Body Report, *EC – Asbestos* (2001), No. 92.
[370] Appellate Body Report, *EC – Asbestos* (2001), No. 118.
[371] Several disputes, in which the determination of likeness has played a crucial role, have been decided based on the traditional DSB approach. See, e.g., Panel Report, *Mexico – Taxes on Soft Drinks* (2005), paras. 8.27–8.36.

seems to me the better part of valour to reserve one's opinion on such an important, indeed philosophical matter, which may have unforeseeable implications.[372]

4.2.2.3.4 Critique

The idea of the market-based approach is to determine the meaning of 'likeness' in a way that is consistent with the main purpose of the GATT and the WTO, namely, to seize the advantages of free trade and functioning markets. The first advantage is that by introducing criteria which can be confirmed or confuted by hard evidence, market-based approaches reduce panels' and the Appellate Body's discretion in determining likeness or substitutability. Economic studies, based on statistical data obtained with polls or other sources, provide absolute numbers, and the determination of likeness is therefore checkable, in contrast to the traditional DSB approach which may sometimes be reminiscent of a 'rule of thumb'. By determining minimum thresholds of substitutability as criterion for likeness in different provisions and by relying on mathematical formulas, the determination of likeness seems to become a basically economic task put to the uses of the law.[373] Therefore, market-based approaches seem to increase predictability and transparency of WTO dispute resolution.[374] Practical problems in collecting data, which might impair reliability and validity of the results, seemingly do not militate against the approach in principle. The second advantage is that market-based approaches are apparently in conformity with one of the main GATT objectives, namely' to ensure fair competitive conditions. Since competitive conditions need to be ensured where competition exists, or could exist, a market-based assessment of the competitive relationship in question makes great sense. Third, it is claimed that the market-based approach has a democratic component. The approach relies heavily on consumer decisions and opinions and leaves it up to the people or to consumers, respectively, what is 'like' and what is not. The approach has even been seen as an expression of the self-determination rule of democracy, which provides for a better justificatory source than, for example, judicialization.[375] This latter aspect is important for NPA measures: consumers, via their purchasing decisions, could render distinctions between physically like products legitimate or illegitimate.

---

[372] Appellate Body Report, *EC – Asbestos* (2001), No. 154.
[373] Choi (2003), p. 155. [374] Choi (2003), p. 7. [375] Choi (2003), p. 155.

While these advantages seem plausible at first, it is questionable whether they can stand up on closer examination. Even if one agrees with the theoretical basis of the approach, namely, the determination of a precise competitive relationship, it is questionable whether market data are actually a better basis for the determination of a competitive relationship than objective assessments of products by experts, panellists and members of the Appellate Body. As has been pointed out by the DSB in *Korea – Alcoholic Beverages*,[376] it is not so much the actual, but the potential competitive relationship which ought to be decisive. Relying on actual market data, for the reasons explained in the report, are not useful as a basis for this determination, since this would mean cementing the *status quo* at an arbitrary point in time – a result impossible to bring in line with the benefits of dynamic markets. It is the very idea of opening up national markets to allow consumers to change preferences and markets to change with respect to available products. The question of whether or not a potential competitive relationship exists depends in the first instance on the end-uses of a given product, which most often is inextricably linked to its physical characteristics. This means that a careful determination of end-uses, whether by panellists or experts, may well be better suited as a basis for the determination of 'likeness' than an economic determination of actual or potential cross-price elasticity.

Also the alleged advantages relating to increased transparency and democratic value of market-based approaches to the determination of likeness are overstated. The fact that cross-price elasticity is computable does not necessarily mean that the determination is more objective. Computations would be based on numbers, which must be generated based on polls and comparisons. It is most likely that the opposing parties would base their argument on different polls and numbers, and that they would challenge the correctness of each other's data. Indeed, given the dynamic nature of markets, it may be impossible to collect data that remain valid for the term of the dispute. Counter-arguments relating to democratic value are self-evident. Since consumer decisions would be attributed greater value than the policies adopted by elected governments, national democratic procedures could be undermined. Indeed, with their purchasing power, consumers would hold a quasi-vote on possible distinctions. This vote, however, would be a consumer vote rather than a vote of the total electorate. Furthermore, 'voting' by purchase and consumption requires affluence. Since casting a vote

---

[376] See above at section 4.2.2.3.3.

includes a choice between a more and a less expensive product, only consumers with the necessary assets could actually choose according to their general preferences, while poor consumers need to give consideration to the price and thus favour the cheaper product – provided poor consumers can afford a certain product at all. This means that in affluent countries with a high number of wealthy consumers, consumer decisions are less influenced by prices, and hence consumers might be able to distinguish between greater numbers of products. With market-based approaches, the same measures might be considered legal in wealthy countries that would be found illegal in poor countries. Another disadvantage of the market-based approach is that consumer decisions or producer decisions are not always rational. Even the most irrational consumer decisions would then indirectly determine the policy space that is left to national governments. Considering the dimensions of the poverty gap in between and within WTO members, construing a link between purchasing power and democracy will usually be out of the question.

Furthermore, it remains questionable whether the theoretical basis of the approach itself is suitable. The approach is based on the premise that consumer preferences and demand substitutability are a crucial criterion for the determination of what constitutes 'like products' in WTO law. It is argued, that GATT law closely resembles competition law in that both ultimately deal with markets and try to foster competition. Since the determination of markets in competition law is based on studies of demand substitutability, it seems plausible then that the question of what constitutes 'like products' in GATT law could also be assessed based on substitutability criteria. There is no doubt about a close relationship between both fields of law, since both ultimately aim at upholding market functions. Nevertheless, it seems questionable whether the similarities allow the transfer of legal concepts in this particular respect, since both fields of law also differ in important respects. Competition law tries to protect market functions and competition by regulating the behaviour of market participants. The idea of the GATT Agreement, in contrast, is to open up national markets by reducing national barriers to international trade. Competition law addresses private companies, while the GATT places disciplines on the behaviour of states and public entities – including national regulation of markets. The GATT applies to a wide range of measures taken by states in general, whether in the form of quantitative restrictions, tariffs, anti-dumping duties or subsidies or domestic regulation in general.

4.2 THE PRINCIPLE OF NON-DISCRIMINATION

It is therefore important to determine the objective of any specific GATT provision before deciding whether or not concepts of competition law may be suitable to fulfil the specific purpose of the provision in question. Those GATT provisions, which, although addressing states, ultimately deal with the establishment of fair competitive conditions for private companies, seem most suitable for the application of market-based approaches, since here similarities with competition law are strong. Examples would be GATT disciplines on national anti-dumping duties, subsidies or CVDs, which interfere directly with the competitive conditions created by private companies. In contrast, the usefulness of competition law concepts for assessing the permissibility of internal measures from the perspective of the national treatment obligation is questionable. Internal regulation is not primarily concerned with enhancing competitive conditions, but in contrast to pursuing public policy objectives not in line with, but in spite of the market.

At this point, answering the question of whether a merely market-based approach is suitable for the determination of 'likeness' in Article III:4 of the GATT becomes an almost ideological task. Depending on one's view on the scope and purpose of the national treatment obligation, one can argue that a market-based approach could not possibly be a suitable basis for the determination of 'like products' where internal regulation is concerned. Market-based approaches rely to a great extent on consumers, and so would subject national measures, adopted by national legislators of governments, to a quasi-approval of consumers – since the market determines what is 'like' and what not. The problems of this approach become apparent when reasons for internal regulation are considered. States use internal regulation to correct and restrain market forces in order to achieve specific policy goals.[377] Determining 'likeness' based on results achieved by the markets would mean to subject regulation, that is, market-correcting measures, to the market. However, it is the very purpose of internal regulation to steer market results in order to achieve policy goals which cannot be achieved by the market. Hence, relying on market data for the determination of which national measures are permissible under GATT rules would merely reinforce market outcomes: only national measures distinguishing between products that would anyway be considered 'unlike' by market participants would then be permissible. Proponents of market-based approaches like to cite examples where consumers distinguish between environmentally friendly products and conventionally

[377] See above Chapter 2, section 2.1.

produced harmful products and so determine that such products are not 'like'. However, consumers may likewise distinguish between products for unacceptable reasons: it would be curious if regulatory distinctions, for example, between products produced by ethnic minorities, were allowed merely because a popular campaign would have led consumers in the regulating country to boycott these products, thus rendering them 'unlike' physically identical products.

Therefore, while the market-based approach might be very useful for the determination of likeness under some provisions of the WTO covered agreements, its usefulness for the national treatment obligation is here rejected.

4.2.3 Summary

The above approaches to the determination of 'likeness' have much in common. All stress the importance of physical characteristics and basically agree on the relevant criteria that have emerged in GATT and WTO adjudication. Indeed, while four groups of characteristics have been developed and accepted by the dispute settlement system, these can apparently be reduced to basically two different groups of criteria, namely, physical characteristics, on the one hand, and consumer preferences, on the other.[378] The remaining criteria reflect particular aspects which are, however, variations of the two basic sets and as such included in them. Product end-use, for example, is predominantly determined by a product's physical characteristics. Usually, there needs to be a certain degree in physical difference to make a product suitable or unsuitable for a particular end-use. The few cases where the end-use is determined by something else would be reflected by the criterion 'consumer tastes'. Tariff classification, on the other hand, is predominantly organized according to physical product characteristics, and with its sub-headings might be useful to determine which degree of difference between products is sufficient to consider products 'unlike'. Interestingly, this criterion disregards the aspect of consumer preferences, unless they are not already reflected in the classification as is the case in a few instances.

The criterion 'consumer tastes', in contrast, is rather unlimited, and gives a counterweight to physical characteristics. It can be used to broaden up as well as to narrow down sets of products which have been found to be

---

[378] The Appellate Body recognized certain interrelations between the criteria, but did not discuss these interrelations in-depths (Appellate Body report, *EC – Asbestos*, No. 102).

'like' under the criterion of physical differences. NPAs, as well as aspects leading to minor physical differences, which would mostly be irrelevant to the determination of 'likeness' under the criterion of physical characteristics, may be highly relevant to consumers. Therefore, it is the second set of criteria that has most potential to render products linked to NPAs 'unlike' under Article III.

The legal relevance of the 'like products' concept is enormous, since it features under many provisions in the GATT and in other agreements on trade in goods. Here, the 'like products' concept is decisive for the validity of national legislation and regulation, whenever there is an effect on trade in goods. Thus, it is not surprising that serious concerns about the precise meaning of the 'like products' concept remain. These concerns gave rise to the development of alternatives or supplements to the traditional DSB approach. While the 'aim and effects' theory ascribes greater importance to the existence of potential protectionist aims and effects, on the one hand, and to genuine public policy concerns, on the other, market-based approaches basically leave the determination of likeness up to the market and its actors.

NPA measures are well-suited to illustrate the differences to which the different approaches may lead. The objective approach, which has dominated GATT and most of WTO adjudication, ascribes little importance to the criterion of consumer preferences and basically considers physical differences and tariff classification as crucial. Thus, this approach would usually reach the conclusion that physically identical products are 'like'. Although the adjudicatory bodies in recent years have not applied a purely objective approach, as is apparent, for example, in the *EC – Asbestos* Report, measures distinguishing between products because of NPAs, such as production methods, would most likely be considered 'like' and therefore fall foul of national treatment obligations.

From the perspective of the public policy approaches, in contrast, the importance of physical differences is more limited, while legitimate public policies are at the centre of the determination. The strand of the 'aim and effects' theory which places emphasis on the nature of the public policies underlying the challenged measures would consider products 'unlike' each other if the reasons for the distinction are genuine and rational. This means that NPA measures – just like other measures – would be permissible depending on the genuineness of the underlying policy purposes. The strand that focuses on the measure's effects, on the other hand, would find measures *a priori* consistent with WTO law as long as imports are not disproportionately strongly affected by a restrictive measure, thus elegantly shifting the focus to the next step of the legal assessment: the requirement of less favourable treatment. Again, NPA measures might therefore be considered permissible as long as they would not put foreign products at an actual disadvantage.[379] Finally, market-based approaches leave the determination of 'likeness' up to the market, meaning that the relevance of NPAs would be up to market agents. As marketing practices show, consumers often do consider unincorporated PPMs and other NPAs highly relevant for their purchasing decisions, and it seems that the percentage of these consumers is rising, predominantly in states with a comparably high average income. Evidence for this is increasing in product advertising relating, for example, to 'sustainable farming', 'fair trade' or the famous, albeit not undisputed, 'dolphin-safe' labels on tuna tins. Even NPAs in their broadest sense, such as the offer of healthcare benefits to employees by the producer, are considered to be relevant to consumers.[380] For the purposes of certain WTO Agreements and provisions, market-based concepts will indeed be suitable to determine which products are like.[381] Some NPA measures might then be considered in line with WTO law. However, with respect to the GATT national treatment obligation, the 'like products' concept implicitly determines which national measures are *a priori* legitimate and which need justification under WTO law. Given that the competitive relationship between products can depend on an indefinite range of factors which are or are not relevant for the majority of consumers at a certain point in time, it is not plausible why this criterion should be decisive for 'likeness'. Even most irrational consumer choices would then be sufficient to justify national action affecting other producers or other economies. The determination of 'like products' based on substitutability for the purpose of Article III could then be used to contradict the very idea of the non-discrimination obligation.

Differences between the three approaches presented here are not only controversial, but quite fundamental. While the idea of substitutability is only to a small extent incorporated in the criteria applied by the DSB, the

---

[379] See the following section for an analysis of 'less favourable treatment' requirement for NPA measures.

[380] E.g., the company Starbucks advertises with its 'great workplace' and the benefits it offers to employees. E.g. Starbucks: 'Striking a balance', Corporate Social Responsibility, Fiscal 2004 Annual Report, p. 66, published at http://assets.starbucks.com/assets/csr-fy04-ar.pdf (last visited on 5 August 2010).

[381] E.g., under the AD Agreement, see above at section 4.2.2.3.

4.2 THE PRINCIPLE OF NON-DISCRIMINATION

aims and effects doctrine exclusively considers the nature of underlying national policies. The approaches illustrate well the different views on the scope of the GATT national treatment provision, which is fundamental to WTO law as well as to the relationship between the organization and its members. Given its importance, the lack of consensus on an adequate answer is disturbing, and it is appropriate that this situation has been called the 'deepest intuitive divide in WTO law'.[382]

Apparently, some basic ideas of the alternative approaches to the determination of likeness are reflected in more recent WTO adjudication. In discussing the relevance of health risks in the *Asbestos* case, the Appellate Body made clear that no evidence should be excluded *a priori* from the examination of likeness. It stated:

> We are very much of the view that evidence relating to the health risks associated with a product may be pertinent in an examination of 'likeness' under Article III:4 of the GATT 1994.[383]

The Appellate Body refuted the panel's argument that considering this aspect under Article III would largely nullify the relevance of Article XX(b). It seems that the Appellate Body at this point makes concessions to the aim and effects doctrine, which considers the genuineness of the underlying policies, such as health policies, as crucial in the determination of likeness. Likewise, there is no doubt that market-based approaches would also reach the same conclusion, since severe health risks will certainly bear on substitutability of affected products. However, given that the stated carcinogenicity of the products at issue are a consequence of their physical characteristics, a merely objective approach would at this point also arrive at the same conclusion. For this reason, the *EC – Asbestos* dispute is not well suited to drawing conclusions for tendencies in WTO jurisprudence relating to the legal status of NPA measures.

The alternative approaches have had considerable influence on the DSB approach in recent years. While some decisions show that the WTO adjudicatory bodies were inspired by ideas and contemplations considered crucial in the alternative approaches, the objective approach in the determinations of likeness clearly prevails. As a corollary, there are no indications that physically identical products would in future be considered 'unlike' each other in WTO dispute settlement because of different NPAs.

---

[382] Howse and Regan (2000), p. 257.   [383] *EC – Asbestos*, Appellate Body Report, No. 113

240   CONSISTENCY WITH GATT OBLIGATIONS

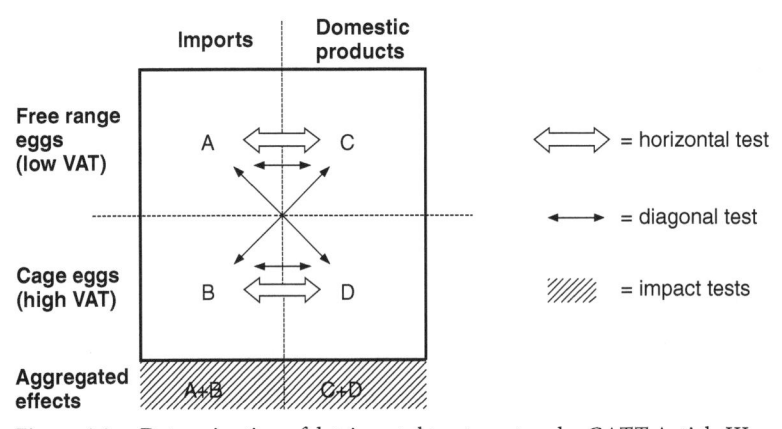

Figure 4.1: Determination of detrimental treatment under GATT Article III

4.3 Detrimental treatment and NPA measures

Once a measure has been found to be 'like', a second step in the legal assessment is needed to qualify the measures as violating the obligation to provide national treatment under Article III. While Article III:2 requires taxes or other internal charges 'in excess of those applied, directly or indirectly, to like domestic products', Article III:4 speaks of 'treatment no less favourable than that accorded to like products of national origin'. The basic idea underlying both norms is the proposition that treatment accorded to imported products ought to be at least as favourable as treatment accorded to like domestic products.

A comparison of treatment will in itself usually not pose any particular problems. More crucial is again the first step, namely, the determination of products or groups of products, the treatment of which is to be compared. A determination of 'like products' as detailed in the previous section does not answer, however, whether treatment of individual products is to be compared, or whether the comparison ought to focus on treatment of different groups of products as illustrated in the Figure 4.1 above. First of all, a 'horizontal test' comparing treatment to individual products could be applied,[384] comparing treatment along the dividing lines of the contested regulatory measure. As illustrated in Figure 4.1, it would thus compare treatment of product group A with that of C, and treatment of product group B with that of D. However, since this test accepts the

---

[384] Cf. Vranes (2009a), pp. 232–3 for a discussion on Chile's appeal in *Chile – Alcoholic Beverages*.

4.3 DETRIMENTAL TREATMENT AND NPA MEASURES

distinction established by the regulator and since it is ignorant as to product origin, it would not be suitable to detect any *de facto* discrimination.

Therefore, the WTO adjudicatory bodies so far have relied predominantly on a so-called diagonal test, albeit in some cases supplemented with a consideration of disparate impacts.[385] Also, the diagonal test focuses on the treatment of individual products by comparing the treatment of any imported product of the group of like products with the treatment of any domestic 'like product'. Thus, unlike under the horizontal test, the regulatory distinction among like products established with the contested measure is not accepted, but tested. The diagonal test compares treatments accorded to both imported product groups to both domestic product groups. In the diagram, each product group A and B would be compared with the treatment of each product group C and D. Comparing B with C will lead to the finding of taxes to imports in excess of those applied to domestic products.

As detailed in the previous section, the WTO adjudicatory bodies will usually not ascribe to NPAs the potential to render products 'unlike'. In consequence, for NPA measures, the diagonal test implies a finding of a violation of the non-discrimination standard, provided any disfavoured products are imported.

Suitability of the diagonal test, however, is not uncontested. Ehring and others plead for an asymmetric impact test, which compares domestic and foreign sub-groups according to the differentiation established in the contested national measure.[386] Under this approach, if as a whole and in proportion, the entire group of imports bears a burden equivalent to that of domestic products, a *de facto* discrimination cannot be established.[387] Objects of the comparison therefore are effects of treatments accorded to product groups rather than the treatment itself. Comparing the aggregated effects on the imported products groups A + B to the domestically produced product groups C + D leads to a finding of a violation of the national treatment requirement only, if the total of the detrimental effects on A + B are stronger than the total of the detrimental effects on C + D. Building in part on the lines of thinking established by the aim and effects doctrine discussed above, the asymmetrical test also aims at identifying only those protective effects which Article III:1 arguably seeks to prevent.

---

[385] See Ehring (2002), pp. 931–9 for an overview of relevant jurisprudence.
[386] Cf. Ehring (2002), pp. 921–47 and Vranes (2009a), pp. 235–51, 406, with similar graphs on the issue in both publications.
[387] Ehring (2002), p. 925.

Its basic idea is to release those national measures from scrutiny that are free from inadequately detrimental effects on imports and that are considered unsuitable to protect domestic producers.

Both methods of comparison, the diagonal and the asymmetric impact test, differ, first, in defining the sets of products and, second, in the consideration or not of certain variables to be compared such as volumes. Applying both methods may lead to contrary findings: while the diagonal test may result in a finding of discrimination, the asymmetrical impact test might lead to the conclusion that a measure is in line with the national treatment provisions. The determination of protective effects, however, is more complex than the above diagram suggests: results of the asymmetric impact test differ depending on the variables being compared and become even more complicated if specific product origin is taken into account.

Some of these difficulties are demonstrated by a short example: country A adopts an internal measure which ascribes lower VAT rates on the sale of free-range eggs than on cage eggs. It is assumed, that imported free-range eggs benefit from the lower VAT rates just as domestic free-range eggs, and that the same is true for national and imported cage eggs. At a given point in time, country A produces 100 cage eggs and 100 free-range eggs, thus a total domestic production of 200. For this example, it is assumed that country A imports 50 cage eggs and 900 free-range eggs from country B, and 450 cage eggs and no free-range eggs from country C.

The percentage of imported eggs that benefit from the lower VAT in this example amounts to more than 90 per cent – at first glance an indication that the measure is not protective. Focusing on the total number of products to which the higher VAT rate is applied, however, shows that 500 out of 600 and thus more than 80 per cent are imports. Both rates are accorded to the fact that the volume of imported products is seven times the volume of domestic production. Comparing the ratio of effects on both product groups according to their origin, thus ignoring the absolute volumes of imports and domestic production shows that 50 per cent of domestic products, but more than 70 per cent of all imports receive the beneficial treatment. Again, this seems to underline that the measure adopted by country A does not accord less favourable tax treatment to imports. However, the picture changes if imports from country C are considered: 100 per cent of imports from country C are subject to the higher VAT. Country C might therefore invoke the fact that the asymmetrical impact test shows that the contested measure clearly protects domestic producers from competition with products originating in country C, and that in addition country C's producers are placed at a disadvantage as compared with producers in country B.

The example shows that determining whether or not imported products are treated less favourably than domestic products is not a simple task. Nevertheless, the wording 'so as to afford protection' in Article III:1 provides a legal basis for exploring whether or not a contested measure actually has any protective effects. The relevance of this requirement with respect to taxes and other charges is reflected in the wording of Article III:2. The wording of Article III:4, in contrast, aims at a comparison of the treatment of products rather than on effects, which seems to speak in favour of the diagonal test. However, it is questionable whether the telos of Article III:4, focusing on national regulation in general, requires GATT signatories to abstain from distinguishing between 'like products' in their internal regulation, even in cases where those measures do not have any protective effects. Vranes, for instance, argues that the assessment of disparate impacts lies at the core of the concept of *de facto* discrimination.[388]

Furthermore, the above example shows that even the calculation of total trade effects will not always lead to clear findings. Relying on a pure calculation of aggregated effects in total would allow for collusion between different WTO members whose internal industries would be positively affected by such measures. Depending on volumes of trade between the colluding states, the disparate effects of such measures on other, possibly smaller, economies would have to be borne by national producers in these third economies, while the measure would overall be considered in line with the national treatment requirement. In this respect, the question arises as to how far the obligation to provide MFN treatment might be invoked by negatively affected WTO members, even if the asymmetrical test negates the existence of protective effects. Finally, it is important to bear in mind that a calculation of trade effects may do nothing more than reflect the situation at a certain point in time, that is, in the past, since even the latest numbers available will usually date back some time. Progressive changes in production volumes and trade flows, which are most likely in consequence of changing legislature in different WTO members, are therefore ignored.

Ehring suggests that the asymmetric impact test is applied in conjunction with the diagonal test, thus constituting a contributive factor

---

[388] Vranes (2009a), p. 240.

in the assessment of the compatibility of national measures with the WTO Agreements rather than replacing the diagonal test. He concedes that even if a measure does not have asymmetrical impacts, other factors might still lead to a finding of a violation.[389] The asymmetric impact test seems well suited as a corrective element, given that the diagonal test may lead to unnecessarily rigid and intrusive findings in cases where protective effects can be excluded. Given the strong interdependencies between national economies today, a total negation of protective effects and of disparate effects on other WTO members might be a rare exception. Therefore, even if the asymmetrical impact test were applied, NPA measures are most likely to fall foul of the national treatment obligation.

4.4 Conclusions

Internal regulation linked to NPAs, including regulation applied to imported goods at the border, falls into the scope of Article III and is assessed based on the standards established there. The language of Article III and its interpretative Note, in particular the frequent use of the term 'products', cannot be interpreted to exclude its application to NPA measures, as long as these affect trade in goods. The legitimacy of internal regulation linked to NPAs therefore depends on the interpretation of the national treatment obligation, especially on interpretation of the 'like products' concept. While it is well established that the concept can have different meanings under different provisions, many legal questions concerning its interpretation remain unsettled.

In particular, the prevailing objective approach to interpretation of the concept attaches great importance to the criterion of physical characteristics of products. It is this aspect of interpretation which is responsible for the conventional belief that measures distinguishing between products based on physical differences are legal, while measures based on NPAs are not. However, in this rigidity this belief is a misinterpretation of the objective approach. As shown above, GATT and WTO jurisprudence have attached importance to the smallest physical differences as well as to NPAs in some cases, and they also have ignored physical differences, albeit small ones, in other cases. The often quoted product–process distinction is therefore an over-simplification that does not characterize the approach correctly. The objective approach is based on a set of criteria, including consumer preferences; it therefore offers an, albeit limited,

[389] Ehring (2002). p. 928

4.4 CONCLUSIONS

flexibility for the consideration of NPAs. Nevertheless, it is conceivable that products would be considered 'like' despite differences in NPAs by the WTO adjudicatory bodies, even if the policy objectives they pursue are legitimate. While the advantage of the objective approach lies in high legal security and predictability, the disadvantage is that even apparently legitimate NPA measures would need to be justified under the arguably too restrictive general exceptions in Article XX.

There are several alternative interpretations of the concept of 'likeness'. These have above been summarized into two groups: the 'aim and effects' approaches, on the one hand, and market-based approaches, on the other. Both of these approaches have the potential to ascribe importance to NPAs and are therefore highly relevant to the legal status of NPA measures. If applied to NPAs, both approaches would lead to practical problems. While these are not of such importance that would disqualify these approaches altogether, both groups of alternative approaches are viewed critically by this author.

Since regulatory intentions are difficult to identify, the 'aim and effect' test would require normative standards for assessing regulations, if not *de facto* discrimination is to be permitted. Such normative standards, however, are not included in Article III. In the absence of any guidance from the text on such standards it remains unclear, how the adjudicatory bodies should apply this approach. The consideration of disparate economic effects, in contrast, which would render a measure protectionist, seems useful and could be applied more objectively and easily. Measures which apparently do not lead to any disparate economic effects cannot be viewed as protectionist and should thus not be considered as a violation of WTO law. However, given the high level of worldwide economic integration, the absence of any protectionist effects will be a rare exception in trade disputes.

Market-based approaches, applying criteria and tests well established in competition law, seem suitable for determining like products under some provisions of the WTO Agreements. However, given that the function of the national treatment obligation in Article III is indeed the function of a 'gatekeeper'[390] between the WTO legal system and domestic regulatory autonomy, these approaches are not suitable for determining likeness in any provision determining national treatment obligations. Given that market guidance and correction is the very idea of national regulatory measures, applying market-based approaches would imply

---

[390] Verhoosel (2002), pp. 4, 7.

a circular argument. In consequence, national regulation confirming 'assessments' of likeness by the market, that is, market participants, would be considered legal under WTO provisions. Since regulatory measures will usually be used to correct market outcomes, such measures would quasi-automatically fall foul of the national treatment obligation. Criteria set by markets are obviously not suitable for judging regulatory measures correcting market outcomes.

In sum, under the prevailing objective approach to the 'like products' concept, there is a high probability that NPA measures would be found to discriminate like foreign products and to violate GATT obligations, in particular, the national treatment obligation. Although both the normative and the economic justification of this approach are not free from doubts, its clear advantage is to draw a 'bright line' between permissible and impermissible measures and thus contribute to legal security and to the stability of the system. Likewise, also applying an asymmetrical impact test for the determination of less favourable treatment will not usually prevent NPA measures from falling foul of the obligation to accord national treatment under Article III. In consequence, the relevance of normative considerations underlying these measures is shifted to the general exceptions alone. This seems convincing, since as opposed to Article III, Article XX is explicitly concerned with normative issues and thus is the right place to assess the rationale and genuineness of regulatory measures affecting international trade.

It is important to note, however, that the interpretation of the 'like products' concept in GATT obligations is inseparably linked to the interpretation of the general exceptions. The development of the alternative approaches, as well as the consideration of health risks by the Appellate Body in the *Asbestos* case are, after all, nothing but regrettable evidence of a strong reluctance to apply the general exceptions as laid down in Article XX. Therefore, whether or not one or several aspects of the alternative approaches prevail, however, also depends on the parallel developments of adjudication with respect to the general exceptions. The adequate scope of the national treatment obligation with respect to NPA measures can be determined only together with the scope of the general exceptions. The following chapter shows, that distrust in Article XX is not justified – provided, however, that the potential offered by Article XX is actually seized by the adjudicatory bodies.

5

Limits to the justification of NPA measures under the general exceptions

Article XX contains a list of general exceptions to GATT obligations for measures relating to certain public policies. The list of privileged public policies contains general governmental 'police' and 'welfare powers',[1] such as the protection of life and health, national treasures, public morals, and other policies such as customs enforcement and trade with gold and silver. Measures pursuing any of the listed policies can be justified under Article XX if they conform to the requirements set out in the opening paragraph or chapeau. As is apparent from the title 'general exceptions' and strong language used in this provision[2] the exceptions apply to all material GATT obligations. Since the listed public policies in this sense override obligations, Article XX recognizes that the ability of any sovereign nation to act and promote the listed policy purposes is more important, even if such action is in conflict with various GATT obligations.[3] Thus, the general exceptions are an expression and application of the sovereignty principle.[4] They have the same status as other principles and norms and are indispensable for a well-balanced multilateral trading system.[5]

Since NPA measures that violate GATT obligations will often be linked to public policies, Article XX is of utmost importance to their legal status.[6]

---

[1] Jackson (1997), p. 233.
[2] 'nothing in this Agreement shall be construed to prevent the adoption ... by any contracting party of measures' (GATT Article XX).
[3] Jackson (1997), p. 233. Cho, in contrast, argues that the fact that the listed public policies are exceptions to the rule alone is in itself proof of a pro-trade bias. Cho (2003), p. 34.
[4] Tietje (1998), p. 311, Prieß and Berrisch (2003), p. 138.
[5] Cottier and Oesch (2005), p. 428
[6] Cho (2003), p. 34. Since different reasonable views on content and coverage of Articles III and XI with respect to measures linked to NPAs exist, which result in different conclusions on the question of whether such measures are in breach of WTO law in the first place, this chapter presumes in line with the arguments presented in Chapter 3 that a certain NPA measure violates GATT obligations. The analysis offered in this chapter is therefore relevant only in case that one subscribes to the view that NPA measures violate GATT obligations in general or because of the specific facts of the case. Also, as detailed

The list of public policies drafted by GATT negotiators in 1947, however, reflects the concerns of that time and thus appears in part anachronistic.[7] It is therefore questionable whether the particular exceptions are adequate and sufficient to enable states to meet contemporary challenges. So far, there have been relatively few disputes discussing justification of measures by Article XX, and most have focused on the health exception in Article XX(b), on exception (d) regarding measures securing compliance with GATT consistent laws or regulations, and on exception (g) regarding exhaustible natural resources. Only twice have WTO adjudicatory bodies held the contested measures to be justified.[8] In one dispute the measure related to product characteristics, namely, to whether or not a product contained asbestos, while the other dispute, *Shrimp Turtle – Article 21.5*, dealt with an NPA.

Due to the list of various public policies, Article XX constitutes the arguably most important gate in WTO law to other areas of public international law. The description of policies included in Article XX is very concise and contains a number of terms, the meaning of which is not further defined in Article XX. The interpretation of Article XX is therefore of utmost importance. Just as the applicability of public international law in WTO discussed in Chapter 3, so also the precise role of customary and conventional international law for the interpretation of WTO law is still highly controversial. Related questions are discussed at the outset of this chapter in section 5.1. Section 5.2 addresses another more general question, namely, whether NPA measures are capable of justification under the general exceptions at all, which it answers in the affirmative.

Sections C and D analyse application of Article XX to NPA measures in more detail. In WTO dispute settlement, justification by Article XX is assessed with a two-tiered analysis. First, the measure needs to be justified provisionally by determining whether it is covered by any of the particular exceptions. An important aspect in this respect is the question of whether there is a sufficient causal link between the measure at issue and

---

above, GATT obligations will not be violated, for example, if the international law applicable between the parties is *lex specialis vis-à-vis* the GATT and establishes a right to adopt the measures. In this case, problem fields linked to justification would be irrelevant.

[7] Cho (2003), p. 34.

[8] *EC – Asbestos* (2001), and *Shrimp Turtle – Article 21.5* (2001). The latter case, however, regarded measures not conforming to the requirements for justification in the original dispute (*Shrimp Turtle* (1998)), and that had subsequently been brought into conformity with the requirements in complying with the DSB recommendations in the original dispute. Under the GATT, there was not a single case of successful justification.

any of the listed policies. In a second step,[9] it is assessed whether the general requirements laid down in the chapeau are fulfilled.[10] Accordingly, section 5.3 focuses on coverage of the particular exceptions in Article XX(a)–(j), while section D analyses the requirements contained in the chapeau. Section 5.5 concludes that while Article XX provides considerable flexibility to justify certain NPA measures, this flexibility is not sufficient to justify all NPA measures that ought to be considered legitimate in the light of national and global contemporary concerns.

5.1 Particularities in interpreting Article XX

This section addresses several preliminary questions pertaining to the interpretation of Article XX. It focuses mainly on one particular aspect of the broader issue of treaty interpretation, namely, the relevance of other rules of international law for interpretation of the WTO Agreements. While in Chapter 3, the conditions for direct application of relevant international law have been identified, this section argues that international conventions, even if not directly applicable, may indeed be referred to for purposes of interpretation. The high importance of the question for NPA measures is again a consequence of the inherent link of such measures to non-trade public policies, and of the fact that often a large number of WTO members, but rarely all, will be parties to treaties or even instruments of 'soft law' regulating the subject matter.

5.1.1 Relevance of international law for interpretation

Given the succinct language of the particular exceptions in Article XX, which refer to various non-trade policies without further describing or explaining them, international agreements pertaining to the specific subject matter could offer useful guidance for interpretation. Interpretation is not only necessary for determining objective elements and scope of the particular exceptions, but also has the potential to serve as a tool for bringing in line seemingly conflicting norms, and is therefore crucial for the justification of NPA measures.

---

[9] This work adopts a two-step approach since the means–end relationship is understood as forming part of the first step of the analysis, namely, scope of the particular exceptions. Therefore, the approach adopted here does not differ substantively from the three-step examination as described in parts of literature (e.g., Cottier and Oesch (2005), p. 429).

[10] Appellate Body Report, *US – Gasoline* (1996), p. 22; confirmed in Appellate Body Report in *Shrimp Turtle* (1998), Nos. 118, 199.

VCLT Article 31(3)(c) states that treaties, customary international law and general principles of law are to be taken into account when interpreting provisions of international agreements in as far as they are applicable.[11] To reiterate, WTO members that are not parties to a certain convention are not bound by its provisions. The question of whether the same convention could nevertheless be relevant for interpretation in a dispute between WTO members is therefore highly controversial. There are basically three different views. Some scholars reject outright the use of conventional law for the interpretation of the WTO covered agreements, unless all WTO members are also parties to the referenced treaty. However, given the large number of WTO members, this situation will hardly ever occur. Others are in favour of reference to international treaties, provided that all members to a dispute have adopted the referenced treaty. A third view would refer to international treaties relevant to the subject matter, even if not all parties to a dispute are also parties to the referenced treaty. Before exploring these views, the following section summarizes the general rules for interpreting the WTO Agreements.[12]

5.1.1.1 Basic framework of interpretation

Interpretation of the WTO covered agreements conforms to the customary rules of interpretation of public international law.[13] Traditionally, there are five different schools of thought or approaches to interpretation,[14] and to a greater or lesser extent all of these are reflected in the Vienna Convention. VCLT Article 31(1) states the fundamental rule of treaty interpretation:

> A treaty shall be interpreted in good faith in accordance with the ordinary meaning to be given to the terms of the treaty in their context and in the light of its object and purpose.

The context to be taken into account for interpretation is set out in Article 31(2) and (3). More subjective elements, such as the preparatory works, in contrast, may be referred to as supplementary means only under certain circumstances, such as to confirm the meaning resulting from application of the general rule of interpretation, or if interpretation has left the

---

[11] Pauwelyn (2003), pp. 254, 255.
[12] Specific questions on the interpretation of the general exceptions is discussed below in section 5.1.2.
[13] DSU Article 3.2.
[14] For a brief overview on five different schools of thought on interpretation, namely, the subjective (historical), textual, contextual (systematic), teleological (functional) and logical (techniques of reasoning) methods, see Villiger (1985), pp. 327–8; for more details on the most important schools, see also McRae (2002).

meaning ambiguous.[15] Articles 31 and 32 adopt an integrated approach to interpretation,[16] albeit with a strong emphasis on the 'ordinary meaning' of terms.[17] State practice and decisions of courts and tribunals have shown that VCLT Articles 31 and 32 have usually been understood to state a predominance of textualism, with a consideration of context closely related to the actual text.[18]

The prevailing view, expressed in a number of judgments of international tribunals and by legal scholars, is that the rules of treaty interpretation incorporated in the VCLT Articles 31 and 32 are declaratory of customary international law.[19] Thus, these rules apply to interpretation of the WTO Agreements at the DSB even if members that are not signatories to the Vienna Convention are involved. Hence, the WTO's adjudicatory bodies have adopted a predominantly objective or textual approach to interpretation, as opposed to a subjective approach that would place emphasis on the intentions of the drafters.[20] This approach can be characterized as a textual approach which contains important teleological elements. In this sense, the Appellate Body stressed the inseparability of the words and purpose of a treaty:

> A treaty interpreter must begin with, and focus upon, the text of the particular provision to be interpreted. It is in the words constituting that provision, read in their context, that the object and purpose of the states parties to the treaty must first be sought. Where the meaning imparted by the text itself is equivocal or inconclusive, or where confirmation of the correctness of the reading of the text itself is desired, light from the object and purpose of the treaty as a whole may usefully be sought.[21]

Of special interest here is the third paragraph of VCLT Article 31, which relates to subsequent agreements, practice and to other relevant rules to be taken into account together with the context. VCLT Article 31(3)(c) states that 'any relevant rules of international law applicable in the relations between the parties' shall be taken into account. In particular, the meaning of 'between the parties' is controversial, as will be discussed below in more detail. VCLT Article 31(3)(c) has been considered a constitutional

---

[15] VCLT Article 32.   [16] Villiger (1985), pp. 343–5.   [17] Wallace (2002), p. 240.
[18] McRae (2002), before IV.A.
[19] *Libya* v. *Chad* (1994), ICJ 6, 8–9, at 41. See also Sinclair (1984), p. 19 with further references. Villiger (1985), in contrast, stated that in his view there were merely just emerging customary rules on the basis of the 1966 draft articles (p. 342, at no. 508).
[20] Established case law since Appellate Body Report, *Japan – Alcoholic Beverages* (1996), p. 11.
[21] Appellate Body Report, *Shrimp Turtle* (1998), para. 114.

norm in international law, allowing a view 'outside the four corners of a particular treaty to its place in the broader framework', and so reducing fragmentation and increasing coherence in international law.[22] Although the applicability of VCLT Article 31(3)(c) in WTO law is established,[23] the question of which conventional international law may be referred to for purposes of interpretation, under which precise conditions and to which end remains unanswered.[24]

5.1.1.2 GATT and WTO case law

In 1994, the GATT *Tuna-Dolphin II* panel took the position that only treaties which have been signed by all parties to the GATT could constitute primary means of interpretation under VCLT Article 31.[25] It therefore refused to take into account the bilateral and multilateral treaties cited by the parties. In contrast, the Appellate Body in *Shrimp Turtle* referred to several international instruments, although neither all WTO members nor all parties to the dispute had signed and ratified them. A crucial issue in this dispute was the interpretation of 'exhaustible natural resources' in GATT Article XX(g) and the question of whether it included living as well as non-living resources. The Appellate Body found it pertinent that 'modern international conventions' used the term in a specific way, comprising both living as well as non-living resources. It mentioned the UNCLOS, the Convention on Biological Diversity, Agenda 21 and the Resolution on Assistance to Developing Countries,[26] despite the fact that not all parties and third parties to the dispute had signed and ratified these instruments. The Appellate Body avoided disclosing under which category of tool for interpretation listed in VCLT Article 31 it considered these international instruments.[27] However, the language of the report suggests that it had referred to them in determining the ordinary meaning of the terms of the treaty in the light of its object and purpose according to the general rule of treaty interpretation in VCLT Article 31(1). This is indicated by

---

[22] McLachlan (2005), p. 281.
[23] It has explicitly been confirmed by the Appellate Body that also the second and third paragraph of Article 31 are declaratory of customary international law. (Appellate Body Report, *EC – Chicken Cuts* (2005), No. 192. See also Appellate Body report, *Japan – Alcohol* (1996), p. 10).
[24] The Appellate Body in *EC – Chicken Cuts* (2005) confirmed applicability of VCLT Article 31:3(c) without, however, applying it to the international law at issue.
[25] Panel Report, *Tuna Dolphin II* (1994), No. 5.19.
[26] Appellate Body Report, *Shrimp Turtle* (1998), para. 130.
[27] Charnovitz (2007a) even considers unclear whether the Appellate Body had invoked these treaties as sources of law or as facts (at p. 700).

the statement that against the backdrop of the 'recent acknowledgment by the international community' of the importance of the protection of species it would be 'too late in the day' to suppose that exception (g) 'may be read as' referring only to non-living natural resources. Furthermore, the Appellate Body considered the objective of the treaty via reference to the principle of effective treaty interpretation, which indicates the teleological component of VCLT Article 31(1).[28] This shows that the Appellate Body in referring to these instruments had explored the 'ordinary meaning' of terms as reflected in Article 31(1), rather than considering them as 'context' in the sense of Article 31(2) or as another interpretative tool provided for in Article 31(3). Nevertheless, the Appellate Body attributed great importance to these instruments, without further discussing the fact that several parties had not signed or ratified the conventions.[29]

The more recent *EC – Biotech* panel also discussed the importance of non-WTO treaties as interpretative tools in the sense of the Vienna Convention, but it reached an entirely different conclusion. The panel distinguished between taking into account international law as an interpretative element as 'context' under VCLT Article 31(3)(c), on the one hand, and considering such law as evidence of the ordinary meaning of the terms, on the other. The panel found that 'parties' in the VCLT meant the parties bound by the treaty that is interpreted, not merely the parties of a dispute. It concluded:

> This understanding of the term 'the parties' leads logically to the view that *the rules of international law* to be taken into account in interpreting the WTO agreements at issue in this dispute *are those which are applicable in the relations between the WTO Members.*[30]

The panel rejected taking into account both multilateral treaties invoked by the defendant, since the complainant was not party to these treaties.[31] Although it stressed that this was not a situation where all parties to a

---

[28] Charnovitz (2007a). Also Pauwelyn seems to interpret the Appellate Body's statement in this direction, although he does not distinguish between considering the ordinary meaning of terms and the common intentions of all WTO members ('and/or'). Pauwelyn (2003), p. 260.

[29] It should be noted, however, that the relevant international instruments considered by the Appellate Body in *Shrimp Turtle* (1998) worked in favour of the United States as respondent. Therefore, the fact that the United States had not ratified or even signed some of these instruments was less problematic in this case than it could have been if they would have been disadvantageous to one of the parties that has not signed or ratified them.

[30] Panel Report, *EC – Biotech* (2006), para. 7.68 (added emphasis).

[31] Panel Report, *EC – Biotech* (2006), paras. 7.73–7.75.

dispute were at the same time also parties to a particular international agreement, the above quote shows that the panel's arguments and conclusions were of a more general nature. It is thus suggested that even if the parties to the dispute were also parties to relevant international agreements, this would not have prompted the panel to reach a different conclusion, as long as not all WTO members were parties to that agreement.[32] With respect to the role of international treaties as evidence for the ordinary meaning of terms, on the other hand, the panel's considerations remain obscure. It referred to the Appellate Body in *Shrimp Turtle* and recognized that international treaties may indeed be relevant as evidence for the interpretation of certain terms, regardless of number and identity of the signatories. Nevertheless, the panel did not consider it necessary or appropriate to rely on the treaties invoked by the defendant.[33]

In sum, WTO jurisprudence on the relevance of international treaties is still in flux. While it has been established that international treaties *may* be considered as evidence for the ordinary meanings of terms in the WTO agreements, panels have not yet made use of this option. The relevance under VCLT Article 31(3)(c) of international agreements that have not been ratified by all WTO members is likewise not yet settled. Different approaches to the latter question in scholarship are discussed in the following section.

5.1.1.3 Signatories-based approach

Most legal scholars approach the issue of the relevance of international law for interpretative purposes based on the identity and congruence of WTO members and states that are signatories to the international agreement in question. They distinguish between situations of perfect congruence of membership, on the one hand, and congruence or incongruence within disputes, on the other. In the latter case, relevance would depend on whether either all parties, or at least one party, to the dispute is simultaneously a party to an international convention pertaining to the subject matter. The basis for this approach is Article 31(3)(c). If this paragraph is interpreted to include all parties, an international treaty would be relevant for interpretation of WTO law only in cases where all WTO members are also parties to the other agreement. For a situation of perfect congruence, there is agreement in scholarship and GATT/WTO jurisprudence that conventional international law accepted by all WTO members shall

---

[32] Panel Report, *EC – Biotech* (2006), para. 7.72.
[33] Panel Report, *EC – Biotech* (2006), paras. 7.95–7.96.

5.1 PARTICULARITIES IN INTERPRETING ARTICLE XX   255

be considered for interpretation of the covered agreements.[34] This view is consistent with the VCLT Article 31(3)(c), which stipulates that international instruments applicable between 'the parties' shall be taken into account. Views on the case of a situation of congruence or even incongruence within disputes, however, diverge considerably.

5.1.1.3.1   Congruence within disputes

The relevance of international law for the legal relationship between several WTO members, all of whom have signed or ratified an international agreement, is controversial. Some scholars are of the view that international treaties may also be referred to for interpreting terms of the WTO Agreements if at least the disputing WTO members have accepted the respective treaty.[35] Marceau, for example, invokes the principle of good faith to support this view. She argues that based on this principle, it can be assumed that states have negotiated their treaty obligations taking into account all their other obligations under international law.[36] Marceau therefore finds that states' obligations are cumulative and should be read together, and that this requires taking into account all relevant rules in international law that are applicable between the same parties.[37]

Other scholars oppose this view.[38] The main objection is the idea that, particularly with respect to interpretation, it is important that the unity of WTO law be preserved. Lennard stresses the importance of arriving at the same interpretation for all WTO members. He contemplates that interpretation of a treaty takes place regardless of the actual occurrence of a dispute, and that even if there is no dispute provisions need to be given

---

[34] Puth (2003), p. 196; Pauwelyn (2003), p. 257–263; Lennard (2002), p. 36; Marceau (2002), pp. 780–2; Panel Report, *Tuna-Dolphin II* (1994), para. 5.19; Panel Report, *EC – Biotech* (2006), para. 7.68.

[35] For instance, French (2005), pp. 306–7; Marceau (2001), p. 1087; Palmeter and Mavroidis (1998), p. 411. Palmeter and Mavroidis are in favour of considering international agreements between the parties to a dispute under both Article 31:3(c) and 31:3(b).

[36] Marceau (2001), p. 1089.

[37] Marceau (2001), p. 1089. This view apparently underlies Switzerland's submission with respect to the relationship between MEAs and the WTO Agreements. Switzerland argues: 'In that sense WTO rules should, according to international law, always be interpreted in a manner that they do not constitute a conflict with MEA rules. And vice versa, MEAs rules must be interpreted in a way that they to not create a conflict with WTO rules. This is a reflection of the general principle *pacta sunt servanda*, that requires that states should try to fulfil their obligations resulting from one treaty without violating their other obligations' (WTO, Submission by Switzerland, TN/TE/W/61, 10 October 2005).

[38] E.g., McLachlan (2005); Lennard (2002); Pauwelyn (2003).

meaning and effectiveness. According to Lennard, this can be done only by treating the parties to a particular treaty as a single body, whether or not the parties are disputants on a particular issue at a particular point in time.[39] He is afraid that it would create great uncertainty and that the informal precedent-setting value of Appellate Body reports would be greatly diminished if the same WTO rights and obligations had different meanings in the context of different WTO members.[40] Pauwelyn, who favours application of conventional law provided it is binding upon both disputing parties, also rejects a different interpretation of the WTO covered agreements depending on which WTO members are involved in a dispute, fearing a threat to the 'uniformity of WTO law'.[41] His reasoning is based on the principle of *pacta tertiis*, which means not only that a state cannot be held by a treaty it did not sign, but also that a treaty it did not sign must not affect interpretation of treaty provisions which are binding to it.[42] Pauwelyn opines that the language of VCLT Article 31(3)(c), which mentions rules applicable 'between the parties', also indicates that only rules which reflect the common intentions of all parties to the treaty, as opposed to the parties in a particular dispute, may be referred to for interpretation.[43] He finds that the existence of Article IX:2 of the Marrakesh Agreement, which provides the possibility of an authoritative interpretation by WTO membership and requires a three-quarters majority of the members supports his view. He suggests that the rules on an authoritative interpretation imply that bilateral treaties, signed by merely two WTO members, must not be referred to as an interpretative resource.[44] However, he concedes that conventional law not signed by all WTO members may also play a role for interpretation of WTO norms – either as historical background or if it otherwise reflects the 'common intentions' of WTO members.[45]

As Oesch observes, in several disputes, the WTO dispute settlement bodies did refer to international agreements other than the covered agreements according to DSU Articles 1 and 2 for interpreting WTO law.[46] In *EC – Poultry*, for example, the panel interpreted the Oilseeds Agreement, a bilateral agreement between the EC and Brazil, since it considered it part

---

[39] Lennard (2002), p. 37.   [40] Lennard (2002), p. 38.
[41] Pauwelyn (2003), p. 476. Nevertheless, Pauwelyn, as detailed above in Chapter 4, is in favour of applying multilateral agreements if all parties of a dispute are at the same time party to that agreement.
[42] Pauwelyn (2003), p. 257.   [43] Pauwelyn (2003), p. 258.
[44] Pauwelyn (2003), p. 259.   [45] Pauwelyn (2003), p. 260.
[46] Oesch (2003b), pp. 218–21.

of the historical background of the EC concessions at issue. Interpretation of the Oilseeds Agreement was necessary in order to interpret and determine the EC's obligations under the WTO agreements vis-à-vis Brazil. In *EC – Certain Computer Equipment*, the panel did not consider the Harmonized Commodity and Coding System and its Explanatory Notes in its interpretation of the schedules at issue. This fact was later strongly criticized by the Appellate Body. However, these disputes do not allow the drawing of conclusions on a general tendency: the dispute settlement bodies in both cases had good reasons for considering international agreements in interpretation. The bilateral Oilseeds Agreement was considered part of the historical background of the EC concessions at issue, furthermore, it was used to interpret concessions with a limited scope of application in terms of subject matter with relevance only to the parties of the dispute – thus, the importance of the WTO dispute settlement bodies' interpretation of the concessions would not exceed the realm of that particular dispute between the EC and Brazil. The HS, the international agreement discussed in *EC – Certain Computer Equipment*, in contrast, was of much great relevance, since a large number of WTO members were also parties to it. However, since the Uruguay Round negotiations were in part based on the HS, the latter must again be considered as historical background and is, furthermore, so closely related to the GATT and the WTO Agreements that without doubt it falls into the core competency of the WTO and dispute settlement bodies alike. The above disputes thus cannot serve as an indication for WTO jurisprudence adhering to either of these views.

In sum, even if the use of the term 'parties' is inconsistent within VCLT Article 31, the language seems to suggest a reading of the term 'parties' in section (3)(c) as meaning the parties to the treaty whose provisions require interpretation, in this case the WTO members. In consequence, Article 31(3)(c) would not allow referring to conventional law for interpretation, even in cases where both parties to a particular dispute were bound by that treaty. However, this reading of Article 31(3)(c) is not compelling, and even those who reject relevance for interpretation concede that there are certain exceptions to this strict interpretation.

5.1.1.3.2 Incongruence within disputes

For those who subscribe to the view that international law is relevant for interpretation if all parties to a dispute are signatories to the other treaty, the question remains whether or not conventional international law can also be relevant if only one or even none of the parties in a dispute are signatories of the treaty to be referred to.[47] The prevailing view in scholarship seems to reject the relevance of conventions in this situation. WTO jurisprudence is not clear on this issue. To reiterate, the Appellate Body in *Shrimp Turtle* based its interpretation of certain terms in international instruments not ratified by all parties to the dispute, while the panel in *EC – Biotech* denied any reference to other conventional law.

5.1.1.4 Objective approach

The approach to the relevance of other international law preferred by this author is based on the objective nature of interpretation as opposed to rule-making. It suggests that all international instruments have the potential to be relevant for interpretative purposes regardless of number and identity of their signatories.[48] The next sections explain why this approach is especially suitable for interpretation of Article XX, which deals in succinct language with subject matters that do not constitute a WTO core competence.

5.1.1.4.1 The nature of interpretation

By their very nature, treaties and other legal rules are drafted using general language in order to allow the application of these rules to a whole range of foreseeable and unforeseeable facts. The goal of interpretation is thus to identify the appropriate meaning of a rule from the whole range of possible meanings. Interpretation is necessary to determine which real-life situations are covered by the objective elements laid down in a provision providing for certain legal consequences. It follows certain rules depending on the context in which interpretation takes place and results in a description of the rules with other words which allows the determination of the meaning with respect to a specific real-life situation. The nature of interpretation is passive in the sense that it explores the meaning of an existing treaty instead of creating new rules. A mere clarification of terms is not to be equated with gap-filling or law-making, but is simply necessary for the task of interpretation, which results in a description of obligations that already exist.[49]

---

[47] Marceau (2001), p. 1107, is of the view that even then the MEA in question should be taken into account, for instance when assessing the importance of the value or interest at issue.

[48] Puth (2003), p. 201. Puth bases this view in part on the maxim of integration underlying the concept of sustainable development. The following elaborations state, however, that the nature of interpretation as opposed to rule-making itself requires taking into account international instruments, regardless of the concept of sustainable development.

[49] Bacchus (2005), pp. 16, 17.

As opposed to interpretation, the process of rule-making leads to the creation of new rights and obligations. Rule-making, as opposed to treaty interpretation, therefore requires agreement among the parties of a treaty. The distinction between legitimate interpretation and illicit rule-making is thus of great importance. If the adjudicatory bodies make a finding beyond the permissible interpretation, they start engaging in illicit rule-making. Indeed, the line between interpretation and illicit rule-making is fine, and only in the grey area between both processes is reference to the principle *in dubio mitius* permissible. The difficulties in distinguishing between interpretation and rule-making are inherent to any system of law with a division of powers, but they leave untouched the importance of the distinction.

It could, however, be argued that the distinction between interpretation and rule-making is important to sophisticated legal systems, such as national legal systems, while its importance in the legal framework created by the WTO covered agreements is low. National legal systems are based on a division of powers, and on a system of checks and balances, which does not exist sufficiently within the WTO. The distinction between interpretation and rule-making is a corollary of a system of checks and balances. In a system of checks and balances, expansive interpretation of laws by the judiciary can be corrected by other bodies. The WTO, however, is not a system with checks and balances, and expansive interpretation cannot be expected to be corrected internally. The WTO legislature, namely, WTO membership, is basically incapable of such action. This situation could be viewed from two perspectives: on the one hand, it could be argued that given the impossibility of correction, the WTO 'judiciary' would be required to restrict itself and to refrain from expansive interpretation; on the other hand, one might argue that the 'judiciary' needs to take over part of the legislative role in order to provide an alternative in times of political impasse. However, both views are unacceptable: the task of the adjudicatory bodies has been laid down in the WTO Agreements by the legislature, namely, WTO membership. The dispute settlement system serves to clarify the existing provisions,[50] and, as explained above, clarification requires interpretation. A hesitant approach to interpretation by the adjudicatory bodies would mean a failure to perform. Neither is extensive judicial activism permitted: the DSB cannot add to or diminish the rights and obligations contained in the agreements.[51]

[50] DSU Article 3:2, second sentence.   [51] DSU Article 3:2, third sentence.

5.1.1.4.2 Relevance of international instruments

The previous section described the nature of treaty interpretation as an objective and reviewable process, which, as opposed to rule-making, does not add to or distract from the rights and obligations created with the WTO covered agreements. It is therefore here suggested that international instruments may constitute evidence of the ordinary meaning of terms and as such are suitable and even necessary tools of interpretation. As a consequence of the objective and passive nature of interpretation the identity of the parties to the instrument at issue is therefore not decisive, although it is relevant for the weight ascribed to it as evidence.[52] The 'ordinary' meaning of a term means the normal, regular and common use of a term, which can by necessity only be determined in the realm of international law outside of the provisions and treaty at issue. This means that the higher the number of signatories or the greater the acceptance of a treaty or even an instrument of soft law character, the greater the importance that can be ascribed to an international instrument as evidence for the 'ordinary' meaning of certain terms. Weighing the importance of documents as evidence also means that the adjudicatory bodies would not be free in referring to any document relevant in terms of subject matter, since wide acceptance of that document would be a precondition.

Since language is in a constant process of change, reference to modern international conventions as interpretative tools is insightful. This has been demonstrated by the Appellate Body in *Shrimp Turtle*: without clarifying why it considered several international conventions that specifically dealt with the subject matter at issue and how these were relevant to the dispute, there is no doubt that the Appellate Body actually ascribed

---

[52] This suggestion is not to be confused with Pauwelyn's and Marceau's suggestion of considering international instruments as evidence for certain factual or factual-legal circumstances, such as environmental harmfulness of certain products or the 'necessity' of a measure to protect human health (Pauwelyn (2003), pp. 463–5, Marceau (2001), p. 1126). Both suggestions must be rejected since legal arrangements between states cannot constitute evidence of factual questions. International instruments are nothing more than agreements among states reached by means of diplomacy on certain questions. Such agreements, even if concerning facts, are *per se* unsuitable to replace the process of fact finding. International treaties can be invoked as evidence for agreement or consensus among the parties. An entirely different issue is factual evidence that has been considered elsewhere, e.g., during the negotiations of an international convention or before another tribunal, that is then reconsidered before a WTO tribunal. In this case, the normal rules on fact finding would apply. The approach suggested here, in contrast, suggests the consideration of the use of terms in international instruments as evidence for their ordinary meaning.

great importance to these conventions for interpretation of the language of exception (g).[53] Apparently, not only explicit agreement among the parties can be legitimate as an interpretative tool: although its legitimacy may be great, such agreements will rarely be at hand. Legitimacy, however, can also be derived from wide participation by states or other international organizations in a convention or document, if that document uses the term in a different and neutral context, and so demonstrates what the ordinary meaning of the term is, or can be. Even if legitimacy derived from international instruments is not perfect – unless the instrument has been accepted at a global level – it will nevertheless often be preferable compared with the practice of relying on arbitrarily chosen dictionaries, however good their reputation.[54]

Against this view could be invoked the sovereign right of any state to freely shape their international relations, including their international obligations. States may naturally refrain from adopting certain international obligations by refusing to sign or ratify international treaties, and according to the *pacta tertiis* rule these treaties cannot be invoked to their disadvantage. However, sovereignty is actually not a concern here, since these instruments may be referred to as evidence for the ordinary meaning of terms, but not as a tool to modify rights and obligations contained in the agreements.[55] As explained above, reference to international agreements cannot shape the rights and obligations of parties, since these exist already. Language and the ordinary meaning of terms are beyond sovereignty, since it emerges out of usage and practice. States have no say on the meaning of terms, unless, of course, they conclude explicit understandings on the meaning of certain terms together with the other parties, or unless they subject their concerns in a reservation where possible.[56]

---

[53] See below section 5.1.2.2.
[54] Bacchus (2005) seems to prefer the use of dictionaries because he sees only two alternatives, namely, a subjective interpretation based on the view of every WTO member, or a subjective interpretation based on the view of the members of the adjudicatory bodies (at p. 13). At the same time, he is reluctant to take a broader view of the context that is to be taken into account (at p. 16), because he fears that a too broad context could result in adding to or subtracting from the obligations contained in the agreement. It seems, however, that Bacchus ignores the fact that the 'ordinary' meaning of a term can by definition only be found outside the treaty and dispute at issue. Only the use of the term outside the treaty at issue can constitute evidence on the ordinary, i.e., the normal, regular and common, use of the term. For a general critique of a narrow textualism, demonstrated with GATS schedules of concessions, see Ortino (2006).
[55] Also Puth (2003), pp. 199–201.
[56] Against considering such instruments, e.g., Pauwelyn (2003), pp. 257–63. For Pauwelyn, the common intentions of all WTO members are crucial. This implies that only a situation

Another argument against the consideration of other international rules is the language of the Vienna Convention. In Article 31:2 and 3 it provides explicitly for several ways in which international instruments can be considered for interpretation. It could be argued that these paragraphs must be interpreted using the principle *expressio unius est exclusio alterius*[57] to mean that international instruments can be considered only under the conditions set out in these paragraphs and in the way established therein. In consequence, international instruments that have neither been signed nor otherwise accepted by all parties would be excluded as a means of interpretation. However, this argument seems to overstate the importance of the 'context' over the 'ordinary meaning to be given to the terms of the treaty'. The single most important maxim of interpretation according to Article 31 is that it has to be undertaken 'in good faith', and primary importance must be given to the ordinary meaning of terms. The Vienna Convention gives primacy to a textual interpretation,[58] and it is inconceivable that it would exclude any tools for exploring the 'ordinary meaning' of a term.

Last, but not least, it seems that any other interpretation would render Article 31 unsuitable for treaties with a large number of parties, and this even more if such treaties constitute 'living treaties'.[59] An interpretation of Article 31, especially paragraph 3(c), as underlying the congruence-based approach, would mean that reference to the ever larger and richer body of international rules and instruments relating to specific subject matters would practically be excluded. The absurdity of such interpretation becomes apparent if one considers that the GATT was drafted in 1947, and that the language contained therein to an ever larger extent no longer reflects the factual situation in the contemporary world. Therefore, it has been suggested that the strict interpretation of paragraph 3(c) should be qualified and to allow taking into account of treaties that are not binding on all parties to the principal treaty, or even not binding at all.[60] While this approach addresses concerns similar to

---

of perfect congruence as outlined above, and multilateral treaties which otherwise reflect these common intentions can be considered for interpretation of the WTO agreements.

[57] Lord McNair expresses the principle thus: 'If I agree that my brother may play with my railway engine and my motor car, it is obvious that I have not given him permission to play with my model aeroplane.' McNair (1986), pp. 399–400.

[58] Lennard (2002), pp. 21–2.

[59] See above section 3.2.3.2.

[60] In this direction also McLachlan (2005), pp. 308–9, albeit with respect to the ICJ *Case concerning Oil Platforms (Iran v. United States)*.

the objective approach to interpretation suggested here, it would result in incoherent interpretation of the WTO Agreements and is therefore here rejected.

In sum, determining the ordinary meaning of terms as required by VCLT Article 31 requires using all interpretative tools available. In the absence of related understandings of all parties, international documents and instruments, regardless of their signatories, may be considered as evidence for the ordinary meaning of terms under Article 31:1, provided they are relevant in terms of subject matter and of sufficient importance in terms of general acceptance.

5.1.1.4.3 Summary

In general, interpretation is independent from acceptance or rejection by the drafters or signatories of a text. The prevailing congruence-based approach ignores the basic nature of interpretation as opposed to rule-making. Thus, the distinction between situations of congruence or incongruence of WTO members and signatories of other international instruments misses the point.[61] Furthermore, the practical exclusion of other international law pertinent to a specific question would increase inconsistency between different sub-systems of international law.[62] Thus, an objective approach to interpretation is preferable. An objective approach implies that, regardless of whether any of the parties to a dispute is signatory of a certain international instrument, the instrument can constitute evidence for the ordinary meaning of terms, and this is so even if the interpretation supported by the respective document would be disadvantageous for party that has not signed or ratified it. The value of the document as evidence would be diminished only marginally. The same line of argument applies to a situation where both parties to a dispute have signed an international instrument relevant for interpretation. In all cases, the suitability of an instrument as evidence depends on its level of acceptance, which needs to be ascertained on an objective basis.

---

[61] Pauwelyn bases his view on the congruence-based approach, but also favours reference to instruments, if these reflect the 'common intentions' of all WTO members (Pauwelyn (2003), pp. 257–63). Although he affirms that WTO members' acceptance or not is relevant for the consideration of a legal instrument, this view is consistent with the approach suggested here since the common intentions may well reflect the crucial 'ordinary meaning' of a term.

[62] Marceau (2002), pp. 780–1.

5.1.1.4.4 Excursus: *inter se* understanding on interpretation

The question could arise as to whether a sub-group of WTO members could agree on a specific interpretation of a term or provisions in the WTO covered agreements, with effects limited to the relations between themselves. According to the objective nature of interpretation it is, however, a logical necessity that the interpretation of WTO law is the same for all WTO members.[63] An *intérpretation partagée* effecting only the relations between certain parties is therefore impossible.[64] An understanding between a sub-group of WTO members that is not consistent with the ordinary meaning of terms would necessarily be irrelevant for interpretation, if not it could itself be considered evidence for a change of the ordinary meaning. The formal conclusion that WTO members can modify the legal relations among themselves, but are unable to change the meaning of terms of the WTO Agreements with effects limited to the relations among themselves, however, seems unconvincing at first glance: the logical principle *a maiore ad minus* comes into mind, which would suggest that changing the meaning of terms is 'less' compared with a change of legal obligations. However, this seeming contradiction is resolved if one considers the legal nature of an understanding signed by a sub-group of WTO members that ascribes a meaning to a term or provision which exceeds the ordinary meaning of that term. In this case, the fine line between interpretation and rule-making has been crossed. Yet this does not render the understanding impermissible. Since the WTO members are in principle entitled to freely design their legal relationships, the understanding on interpretation would in fact constitute an agreement that modifies the rights and obligations in the relations between the parties to the understanding. In this way, the understanding becomes applicable law and conflict rules decide on whether the understanding or the covered agreements prevail. This understanding explicitly ascribes meaning to the terms of the WTO covered agreements, intentionally changing the meaning of this agreement, and it is open to WTO members only. It can, therefore, as opposed to other multilateral treaties, be considered an *inter se* agreement between WTO members, and its permissibility would then depend on the conditions established by VCLT Article 41. In consequence, the sub-group of WTO members would have achieved what they intended, albeit not by changing the interpretation of terms of the WTO agreements but by changing their legal relations with

---

[63] Puth (2003), p. 201. [64] Puth (2003), p. 201.

an *inter se* agreement. So far, however, no such understanding has ever been concluded.

5.1.2 Other interpretative questions

Since Article XX is a provision containing general exceptions and dealing with policies outside the core competencies of GATT and WTO it could prompt the application of special rules of interpretation. Before exploring the scope and meaning of the particular exceptions and the chapeau in more detail, this section discusses whether there are any special rules for interpreting the general exceptions.

5.1.2.1 No restrictive interpretation

GATT panels have traditionally held that provisions which constitute exceptions needed to be interpreted narrowly.[65] They regarded Article XX as a limited and conditional exception to GATT obligations and concluded that the principle of narrow interpretation applied.[66] Also, some legal scholars approve of this principle.[67]

This principle or legal method also referred to as *exceptiones sunt strictissimae interpretationis* holds that exceptions to rules by their very nature ought to be interpreted narrowly.[68] It refers to a situation where a set of rules has been created to provide a general and widely applicable regulation, while the set also provides for exceptions to the general rule in the case of circumstances that are explicitly specified. The basic argument is that an overly generous interpretation of exceptions contradicts and undermines the purpose of the general rule. However, this view ignores

---

[65] The practice of interpreting provisions which were considered exceptions narrowly used to be well established. Provisions which had been interpreted in this way were, e.g., GATT Article II:2 lit c (Panel Report, *United States Customs User Fee* (1987), para. 84) and GATT Article VI:3 (Panel Report, *United States – Pork from Canada* (1990), para. 4.4). However, this practice was not without exception. In *Canada – Ice Cream* the Panel mentioned the principle that exceptions be interpreted narrowly, but implied that the requirements in Article XI:2(c)(i) anyway were extremely difficult to comply with (para. 59).

[66] Panel Report, *Tuna-Dolphin I* (1991), No. 5.22.

[67] Berrisch (2003), p. 139, Tietje (1998), p. 311, van Calster (2000) p. 71. According to Heintschel von Heinegg (2004), p. 145, rec. 19), the principle is at least in some cases covered by the VCLT canon of interpretation if object and purpose of the treaty so require.

[68] This principle has been applied for instance by the ICJ in the *North Sea Continental Shelf* case, judgment of 20 February 1969, p. 186. This principle needs to be distinguished from the rule that *singularia non sunt extendenda*, which prohibits construing analogies in case of lists or enumerations, and which will be discussed below.

the fact that exceptions also contain special rules that are generally applicable if the special facts provided for are existent.[69] The Appellate Body in *EC – Hormones* explicitly rejected the validity of this principle. It stated:

> merely characterizing a treaty provision as an 'exception' does not by itself justify a 'stricter' or 'narrower' interpretation of that provision than would be warranted by examination of the ordinary meaning of the actual treaty words, viewed in context and in the light of the treaty's object and purpose, or, in other words, by applying the normal rules of treaty interpretation.[70]

Indeed, the principle is based on incorrect assumptions. For example, it is argued that an exception is characterized by the fact that analogies are not permitted.[71] However, it is not possible to characterize a norm as an exception, and to conclude from this characterization that it needs to be interpreted narrowly. Whether or not a norm should be interpreted narrowly is a question that can be answered only by interpretation.[72] Applying the principle therefore involves the danger of disregarding the very text of the provision to be interpreted.[73] This would be contrary to the approach of textual interpretation, which has the highest priority in the canon of treaty interpretation. The specific balance of rights and obligations laid down in the WTO Agreements as a result of multilateral negotiations must be derived from the text of the provisions. The right of a WTO member to invoke one of the particular exceptions, as explicitly provided for by the agreement, must not be rendered illusory, while at the same time the substantive rights of other WTO members granted in the GATT must not be eroded.[74] In sum, the right to invoke an exception and the rights of WTO members under the other provisions of the GATT are of equal importance. The prevailing view therefore holds that the principle of narrow interpretation of exceptions is unacceptable.[75] One scholar, in contrast, suggests that the principle *in dubio mitius* could

---

[69] Germann (1967), p. 62. [70] Appellate Body Report, *EC – Hormones* (1998), No. 104.
[71] Schneider and Schapp (2006), p. 155.
[72] Germann (1967), p. 323, Schneider and Schapp (2006), p. 155, Federal Court of Justice (civil law cases) of Germany, BGHZ 17 (1955), 266, 277.
[73] See also Feddersen (2002), p. 137.
[74] Appellate Body Report, *Shrimp Turtle* (1998), No. 156. Although the Appellate Body made these statements with respect to the chapeau of Article XX, these statements have a general meaning that is valid inasmuch for the particular exceptions.
[75] Matsushita, Schoenbaum and Mavroidis (2003), p. 66; Feddersen (2002), p. 139; Puth (2003), p. 297; Epiney (2000), p. 81, Manzini (1999), pp. 825–8; Germann (1967), p. 62; Bydlinski (1991), p. 440.

be of use in the interpretation of the general exceptions. Since Article XX contains exceptions to GATT obligations and thus determines the parties' space for unlimited policy choices, it could indeed be assumed that the negotiators intended the preconditions for invoking the exceptions to be strictly limited to those that are specifically mentioned in this Article.[76]

However, given that the function of Article XX is to strike a balance between GATT obligations vis-à-vis other WTO members and the right to autonomously pursue certain important interests, both principles, *in dubio mitius* and the principle of narrow interpretation, seem equally unsuitable to guide interpretation of Article XX. In line with the prevailing view, it is here assumed that the interpretation of the general exceptions follows the normal rules of treaty interpretation.

5.1.2.2 Static or evolutionary interpretation?

Since the public policies and interests listed in Article XX were drafted in the 1940s, the question arises whether interpretation aims at exploring the meaning of the respective terms at that time or their contemporary meaning. This question is closely related to the relevance of the subjective or historical method of interpretation. To reiterate, under the express terms of the VCLT, the preparatory work of the treaty is merely a supplementary means of interpretation that may be resorted to only in a few specific situations. Against the backdrop of more than half a century of practice since the GATT entered into force, the value of the GATT negotiating history has been questioned in general.[77]

With respect to the general exceptions, the WTO adjudicatory bodies seem to have ascribed little importance to the negotiating history, while adopting a more flexible and modern interpretation. With respect to exception (g) and the meaning and scope of the term 'exhaustible natural resources', the Appellate Body in *Shrimp Turtle* stressed that the words were crafted more than 50 years ago, and that they must be read 'in the light of contemporary concerns of the community of nations about the protection and conservation of the environment'.[78] In order to explore the contemporary meaning, the Appellate Body drew on other rules of international law because it considered that they were informative and

---

[76] Charnovitz (2007a), p. 701, invoked this argument with respect to geographical limitations of the general exceptions.
[77] Jackson (1992), pp. 1241, 1242.
[78] Appellate Body Report, *Shrimp Turtle* (1998), No. 129.

pertinent to the subject matter. It gave two arguments to support its approach. First, it stated that the WTO members in 1994 were fully aware of the importance of environmental protection. Second, it invoked the generic character of the term 'natural resources', which rendered it evolutionary, together with the fact that the International Court of Justice had stated that the interpretation of such terms cannot remain unaffected by subsequent developments of law.[79]

The Appellate Body's new 'evolutionary interpretation' of certain terms in Article XX has been adopted by other panels.[80] Although the Appellate Body's concerns about the evolutionary rather the static character of certain terms were specifically aimed at the language of exception (g), the logic of ascribing greater importance to contemporary international developments than to negotiating history applies to other exceptions as well. The new approach of evolutionary interpretation has mostly been well received in the literature.[81] Indeed, giving greater weight to contemporary concerns seems imperative given the intention and function of the general exceptions. These allow states to deviate from GATT obligations if certain important state interests are at stake, and such interests naturally change over time. Since Article XX is drafted in a succinct language, many terms used therein are vague and can be considered generic. Therefore, the evolutionary approach is crucial for the scope of the general exceptions in terms of subject matter. Since NPA measures are often linked to public policies and state interests, the approach may prove to be highly relevant for NPA measures. The relevance for the scope of one or another of the particular exceptions is discussed in the respective sections below.[82]

---

[79] Appellate Body Report, *Shrimp Turtle* (1998), No. 130, fn. 109, referring to the ICJ's *Namibia Advisory Opinion* (1971), ICJ Reports, p. 31.

[80] Panel Report, *EC – Biotech* (2006), No. 7.94. Also the Panel in *EC – Chicken Cuts* (2005) took account of the evolutionary approach, although it did not apply this approach to its interpretation of the schedules of concessions (at No. 7.99, fn. 144).

[81] E.g., Graber (2006), p. 571, favouring the inclusion of cultural policies; Abbott (2005), p. 84, Pauwelyn (2004), pp. 924–7, Marceau (1999), p. 121; more critically Raustiala (2000), pp. 405–10, Charnovitz (2002), p. 108, favouring negotiation of new rules as first best tool. Against the evolutionary approach, e.g., Kelly (2005), who argues that this approach is contrary to the role of the Appellate Body in the WTO's consensus-based system of governance.

[82] The question of evolutionary interpretation of terms included in paragraphs (a)–(j) does not prejudice in any way the question of exclusivity of the particular exceptions as listed in Article XX. For the latter discussion see below under section 5.3.2.1.

5.1.3 Summary

The interpretation of the general exceptions, just as any other provision in WTO law, follows the customary rules of interpretation, including those laid down in the Vienna Convention. Thus, the prevailing approach is an integrated approach that, however, places great emphasis on textual interpretation. In as far as generic or vague terms are concerned, an evolutionary interpretation is indicated. Finally, there is no rule of narrow interpretation of the general exceptions.

With respect to NPAs, especially the relevance of other international agreements as an interpretative tool is highly controversial. There is consensus that in as far as international instruments have been accepted by all WTO members these may be taken into account together with the context under VCLT Article 31:3(c). Whether or not this is possible if not all WTO members, or even not all parties to a particular dispute, have signed and ratified the treaty in question, is contested. While there are different views in legal scholarship, adjudicatory bodies in some cases have adopted a more flexible approach without, however, always clearly identifying the category of means of interpretation under which international instruments have been considered. It is here suggested that in principle all international instruments pertaining to the respective subject matter can be relevant for interpretation. International instruments and other documents often constitute evidence for the contemporary ordinary meaning of terms, and as such ought to be referred to regardless of whether or not they have been accepted by all WTO members or parties to a dispute. However, the importance as evidence of such instruments depends on the relevance of the document in terms of subject matter, on its nature or bindingness, as well as on its international acceptance. Low acceptance, especially related to the meaning of the term at issue, would exclude the usefulness of a document as evidence, even if the document were highly relevant to the subject matter.

5.2 General concerns regarding justifiability of NPA measures

As shown above in Chapter 4, the product–process distinction claims that measures linked to production violate basic GATT obligations. A similar distinction has also been applied to the general exceptions in Article XX: in several disputes, NPA measures relating to production were considered to be unjustifiable. This section reviews the different arguments and finds no basis for assuming *per se* unjustifiability of measures linked to production or other NPAs.

5.2.1 Vagueness of basic objections

There are various general objections to the justifiability of NPA measures, which are closely interrelated and often not adequately distinguished in the debate. For instance, in a comment on the *Shrimp Turtle* Appellate Body Report, Alan Oxley, the former Ambassador of Australia to the GATT, stated:

> First, the AB has placed the WTO in the business of determining environment policy for the members of the WTO ... Second, if countries can restrict trade on the basis of how a product is made, it sets at risk the basis of all international trade, the capacity of WTO members to exploit their comparative advantages in the global economy. Third, the ruling ignores WTO member preferences that unilateral trade restrictions with extraterritorial reach should be avoided, and that respect for national sovereignty should be the guiding principle in international endeavours to improve the environment.[83]

His concerns relate, on the one hand, to a perceived loss of national sovereignty and to an impairment of the objectives of the multilateral trading system, on the other. He is of the view that the sovereignty principle is violated by involving the WTO in determining environmental policies against the will of WTO membership, and by allowing for unilateral trade measures with an inherent extraterritorial link. His statement also expresses a fear that NPA trade measures could jeopardize the achievement of WTO objectives. Linking trade measures to the differences prevailing between WTO members would mean linking trade measures to the very basis of any comparative advantage, thus undermining the core concept underlying the objectives and functions of the multilateral trading system. Beyond the concerns relating to sovereignty and the functioning of the system, the perceived impairment of WTO members' ability to seize their comparative advantages is considered to be unfair.

Among the various objections, as expressed in the quote above, impairment of national sovereignty is often the primary concern. References to an 'imposition of policies upon other countries' or to the 'subordination of a country's jurisdiction' suggest that the concerns about the extraterritorial reach of measures linked to NPAs are related to traditional ideas

---

[83] Oxley (2002), pp. 18, 19.

5.2 JUSTIFIABILITY OF NPA MEASURES

on national sovereignty.[84] The basic reasoning is that since regulation of production or other activities, as well as the respective objects of protection, are in the exclusive jurisdiction of the country on whose territory the regulated activities take place, linking trade measures to extraterritorial NPAs disrespects, and possibly undermines, internal policies adopted by the country of production.

Also the arguments invoked in GATT and WTO case law are characterized by vagueness. Both the *Tuna-Dolphin II* panel and the *Shrimp Turtle* panel came to the conclusion that the general exceptions would not permit measures conditioning market access for imports upon the adoption of certain policies in the country of origin similar to those which prevail in the country of importation. While the *Tuna-Dolphin I* panel rejected the general consistency of such measures invoking the scope of any one of the relevant particular exceptions,[85] the *Shrimp Turtle* panel reached the same conclusion based on an interpretation of the chapeau in the light of the objective and purpose of the WTO Agreement.[86] Although the panel chose as the proper location for these considerations the chapeau, its main argument was not strictly related to its language, but was of a teleological nature.[87]

Parts of academia, especially in the mid-1990s, approved of the gist of the panels' arguments and supported this specific consequence of the product–process distinction. The main concern related to the consequence of interpreting Article XX as also covering production processes outside territorial limits of jurisdiction, since this would create a loophole or slippery slope with the potential to undermine the policy objectives of trade liberalization.[88] Hence, GATT principles would generally exclude justification of trade measures with extra-jurisdictional application to impose environmental policies on other states.[89] There were also claims that since GATT Article XX allows for exceptions from GATT obligations, which in turn imply a focus on products as opposed to production,

---

[84] E.g., Mexico, the complainant in the first *Tuna-Dolphin* dispute, stressed that GATT Article XX did not allow any country to 'impose measures in the implementation of which the jurisdiction of one contracting party would be subordinated to the legislation of another contracting party' (Panel Report, *Tuna-Dolphin I* (1991), No. 3.31). Also, Ecuador as a third party in *Shrimp Turtle* (1998) found it unacceptable that a state could be allowed 'to impose its domestic policy objectives upon other states' (Ecuador, Appellate Body Report in *Shrimp Turtle* (1998), No. 63).
[85] Panel Report, *Tuna-Dolphin II* (1994), Nos. 5.26, 5.39.
[86] Panel Report, *Shrimp Turtle* (1998), Nos. 7.45–7.47.
[87] See the quote below at p. 273, fn. 94.   [88] Jackson (2000a), p. 306.
[89] Jackson (1992), pp. 1243–4, Kelly (2005), pp. 480–1, Schoenbaum (1992), p. 713.

it could not help but render process-based measures permissible under the GATT. Exceptions for human health etc. would be limited to health in the importing country.[90]

On appeal, however, the Appellate Body in *Shrimp Turtle* explicitly rejected the panel's view that process-based measures are not justifiable under Article XX. The Appellate Body's findings and reasoning were mostly well received,[91] and it seems that in the course of time both environmentalists and the trade community approved of them.[92] However, because of the specific facts of the *Shrimp Turtle* case, it is controversial whether the Appellate Body's findings on justifiability of a PPM measure in this report imply a more general acceptance of NPA measures.[93] Therefore, the next section analyses the opponents' arguments in more detail.

5.2.2 Review of arguments against justifiability

The question of whether WTO members can possibly justify NPA measures depends, on the one hand, on the provisions of the GATT, and, since the WTO is not a self-contained regime, on provisions of general international law, on the other. Justification of such measures could be impermissible: (1) because of an irreconcilability with GATT and WTO objectives and purpose; (2) because they quasi-automatically violate the chapeau of Article XX; or (3) because they violate a peremptory norm (*ius cogens*) of international law.

5.2.2.1 Irreconcilability with WTO objectives and purpose

One of the main arguments for *per se* unjustifiability of NPA measures is that such measures are irreconcilable with the objectives and the basic purpose of the multilateral trading system. The *Shrimp Turtle* panel, for instance, argued that the PPM measure at issue would impair the functioning of the multilateral trading system. It stated that:

> if an interpretation of the chapeau of Article XX were to be followed which would allow a Member to adopt measures conditioning access to its market for a given product upon the adoption by the exporting Members of

---

[90] Jackson (1997), p. 236.   [91] Cf. Appleton (1999), p. 478.
[92] E.g., CIEL, Mann and Porter (2003) find that the *Shrimp Turtle* case would significantly 'expand the scope for considering nontrade international law in matters of WTO law' (at p. viii), Jackson (2000b), pp. 303–7; Sands (2000), p. 299.
[93] Feddersen, e.g., interprets the respective statements indeed to reject an exclusion of such measures from the scope of Article XX (Feddersen, 2002, p. 205). See also below at section 5.3.1.1.

certain policies, including conservation policies, GATT 1994 and the WTO Agreement could no longer serve as a multilateral framework for trade among Members as security and predictability of trade relations under those agreements would be threatened. This follows because, if one WTO Member were allowed to adopt such measures, then other Members would also have the right to adopt similar measures on the same subject but with differing, or even conflicting, requirements. If that happened, it would be impossible for exporting Members to comply at the same time with multiple conflicting policy requirements.[94]

The Appellate Body, however, reproached the panel for not having looked into object and purpose of the chapeau, but at object and purpose of the whole of the GATT and the WTO Agreement, and this in an 'overly broad manner'.[95] It pointed out that the multilateral trading system is a fundamental and pervasive premise underlying the WTO Agreement, but that it is neither a right nor an obligation of its own. Thus, it could not serve as an interpretive rule to be used for interpretation of the chapeau.[96]

The Appellate Body approached this question from a different angle. It remarked that the domestic policies embodied in measures comprised by Article XX have been recognized as important and legitimate in character, and then stated:

> It is not necessary to assume that requiring from exporting countries compliance with, or adoption of, certain policies (although covered in principle by one or another of the exceptions) prescribed by the importing country, renders a measure *a priori* incapable of justification under Article XX. Such an interpretation renders most, if not all, of the specific exceptions of Article XX inutile, a result abhorrent to the principles of interpretation we are bound to apply.

Its arguments are convincing. The strong language of the chapeau ('nothing in this agreement shall be construed to prevent the adoption') does not limit the range of policy tools for members to pursue any of the listed policy objectives. Therefore, a *per se* exclusion of a particular group of measures would be contrary to the function and importance which the contracting parties to the GATT ascribed to the policies mentioned in Article XX (a)–(j). In this sense, the existence of the particular exceptions and implied recognition of paramount policy objectives shows that even measures that are irreconcilable with basic economic rationales of international trade can be consistent with WTO law.

---

[94] Panel Report, *Shrimp Turtle* (1998), No. 7.45.
[95] Appellate Body Report, *Shrimp Turtle* (1998), No. 116.
[96] Appellate Body Report, *Shrimp Turtle* (1998), No. 116.

5.2.2.2 *Per se* violation of the chapeau

In contrast to the particular exceptions, which reflect certain national policies, the introductory clause of Article XX addresses the manner in which a measure is applied, rather than its actual contents. Its purpose and object is generally the prevention of abuse of the exceptions listed in Article XX.[97] In order to be justifiable, a measure which falls within any of the particular exceptions needs to be applied reasonably.

The panel in *Shrimp Turtle* found that the process-based measures in question would quasi-automatically violate the chapeau of Article XX. To reiterate, the panel argued that the challenged measure, or other similar measures which might be adopted, might threaten the security and predictability of that system.[98] In the panel's view this implied that this particular type of measure constitutes abuse, more precisely unjustifiable discrimination, and that they could not be within the scope of measures permitted under the chapeau.[99] The Appellate Body rejected the panel's view. It found that:

> conditioning access to a Member's domestic market on whether exporting Members comply with, or adopt, a policy or policies unilaterally prescribed by the importing Member may, to some degree, be a common aspect of measures falling within the scope of one or another of the exceptions (a) to (j) of Article XX.[100]

In consequence, the Appellate Body reversed the panel's finding that the measures were outside the scope of the general exceptions.[101] Although in the end the challenged measures were not found to be justified, the Appellate Body clarified that they were not in principle unjustifiable. Also with respect to the chapeau, it would not seem adequate to exclude a group of measures from the possibility of justification. Also from the point of view of application of NPA measures as opposed to the application of other measures there is no common feature that would render application of the former *per se* abusive of the general exceptions.[102]

---

[97] Appellate Body Report, *Canada – Periodicals* (1997), p. 22, context of fn. 43.
[98] Panel Report, *Shrimp Turtle* (1998), para. 7.44.
[99] Panel Report, *Shrimp Turtle* (1998), paras. 7.49, 7.62.
[100] Appellate Body Report, *Shrimp Turtle* (1998), No. 121.
[101] Appellate Body Report, *Shrimp Turtle* (1998), Nos. 122–3.
[102] In this direction also Quick (2000), p. 245. For a more comprehensive survey on WTO case law, which concludes that PPM measures are not considered to fall outside the scope of Article XX, see Charnovitz (2002), pp. 92–101.

5.2.2.3 Violation of the sovereignty principle

NPA measures could be *per se* illegal if they were in violation of peremptory norms of public international law, that is, *ius cogens*. To reiterate, the general objections against these measures relate to their alleged extraterritorial reach and corresponding violations of other WTO members' national sovereignty. Therefore, the question arises as to whether such measures fall foul of the international law principle of equal sovereignty of states, and whether this rule constitutes *ius cogens*.[103] The general concept of *ius cogens*, as well as the question of which norms qualify as such, however, is controversial under international law. Since some opponents of measures with an alleged extraterritorial reach have actually considered the 'sovereignty principle' as *ius cogens*,[104] this section discusses whether or not NPA measures violate this principle. However, an in-depth analysis of the much debated and complex concept of state sovereignty is beyond this work. This section gives, first, a general introduction to the concept with respect to trade measures, and then discusses the question specifically with respect to alleged extraterritorial effects of NPA measures.

State sovereignty is not legally defined. It is traditionally understood, however, that sovereignty has an internal and an external side. Internal territorial sovereignty in this sense has been interpreted to mean 'the right to exercise therein, to the exclusion of any other state, the functions of a state'.[105] The external side of sovereignty regards the relationship of a state towards other states. It has been suggested that external sovereignty simply means independence, and that the latter term should therefore replace the too emotive term 'sovereignty'.[106] Part of the external sovereignty of a state is the principle of non-intervention, which prohibits intervention in the internal affairs of another state, or its *domaine réservé*, by other

---

[103] For the purposes of the VCLT 'a peremptory norm of general international law is a norm accepted and recognized by the international community of States as a whole as a norm from which no derogation is permitted and which can be modified only by a subsequent norm of general international law having the same character' (VCLT Article 53).

[104] E.g., Malaysia as one of the complainants in *Shrimp Turtle* (1998) claimed that the contested measures had violated the sovereignty principle, which it considered *ius cogens* (No. 3.275). Against the qualification of sovereignty and independence as *ius cogens*, e.g., Mosler (1980), pp. 69 *et seq.*, Ipsen (2004), p. 193, at No. 60, Dahm, Delbrück and Wolfrum (2002), p. 716; in favour of the qualification as *ius cogens* not of the sovereignty principle, but of the related right to self-determination: Cassese (1995), p. 140.

[105] *Island of Palmas Case* (1928), RIAA II, at 838.

[106] Malanczuk (1987), pp. 17, 18; James (1986), p. 5.

states.[107] A crucial feature is the freedom of governments from direct orders and control by other governments.[108] Equal sovereignty of states is a concept included in the UN Charter, which in Article 2:1 stipulates 'the principle of the sovereign equality of all its Members'. Despite considerable critique, it is still prevailing and important in international relations. Sovereignty is a principle with inherent borders. As a corollary to every state's 'equal' sovereignty, a state's sovereignty is delimited by the sovereignty of its fellow states.[109]

Sovereignty concerns with respect to NPA measures are twofold.[110] On the one hand, sovereignty allows for legislative jurisdiction and the authority to independently regulate all internal affairs, including production, and all other activities or situations taking place within the territory of the state. Also, since the goods that enter the state as a result of international trade circulate freely within its territory, and since they are bought, used and consumed within its territory, a sovereign state is entitled to take measures to determine which products may be imported into its territory and under which conditions.[111] In this sense, in the absence of treaty-based rights, it is the prerogative of any state to freely regulate conditions of importation as well as internal affairs, even if such regulations have restrictive effects on international trade.[112] On the other hand, it could be argued that internal sovereignty, which implies the independence of government and as a corollary the absence of orders and control exercised by other governments, requires the absence of any influence, whether of a legal or factual nature, which undermines a country's internal regulation.[113]

Opponents of NPA measures have invoked the principle of non-intervention as an important aspect of sovereignty.[114] This principle is, for example, reflected in the Charter of Economic Rights and Duties of States, which stipulates that:

---

[107] Cf., e.g., the UN General Assembly's Declaration on the Inadmissibility of Intervention in the Domestic Affairs of States and the Protection of Their Independence and Sovereignty, 21 December 1965.
[108] Malanczuk (1987), p. 78.   [109] Meng (1994), pp. 39, 48.
[110] See also Thaggert (1994), p. 82.
[111] Cf. United States in Panel Reports, *Tuna Dolphin I* (1991), No. 3.65 and *Shrimp Turtle* (1998), No. 3.167.
[112] Wiers (2001), p. 103.
[113] Cf. Australia in Panel Report, *Tuna-Dolphin I* (1991), Nos. 4.2–4.3.
[114] New Zealand as third party in *Tuna-Dolphin I* (1991) invoked this principle to support its view that the contested measures were not justifiable under GATT Article XX. Panel Report, *Tuna-Dolphin I* (1991), No. 4.38.

> Every State has the sovereign and inalienable right to choose its economic system as well as it political, social and cultural systems in accordance with the will of its people, without outside interference, coercion or threat in any form whatsoever.[115]

Thus, under the Charter, NPA measures with extraterritorial links may be considered illicit interference in the economic, social or political system of sovereign trading partners. In sum, both proponents, as well as opponents, of NPA measures invoke their 'sovereignty' to support their directly opposed views on the legal status of NPA measures.

There is little hard law defining the contents of the complex and blurred sovereignty principle. From an international law perspective, however, the above concerns can be translated into questions of jurisdiction. Jurisdiction, or legal authority, is a central feature of state sovereignty and concerns a state's power to affect people, behaviour, legal relationships and circumstances, by means of legislative, executive or judicial action.[116] In order to perform its tasks and functions, every state has jurisdiction over certain activities, objects and relationships. While enforcement jurisdiction is nearly exclusively territorial, legislative jurisdiction can also be based on other grounds, such as nationality; for example, in criminal matters. In the field of anti-trust law, states have assumed jurisdiction on the grounds of effects within their territory, even if the behaviour that caused the effects had taken place in another state. This line of thought, which is most controversial, has been termed the 'effects doctrine'. Since there is a general presumption against the extraterritorial application of legislation, extraterritorial jurisdiction often leads to legal problems under international law. By applying a regulation to the territory of a different state, or to activities or objects otherwise under the authority of a different state, a state can exceed its jurisdiction, and the regulation can collide with the jurisdiction of the other state.[117] There are three different cases of exercises of jurisdiction with extraterritorial aspects. First, is the exercise of authoritative acts, including law enforcement, relating to activities outside its territory, or within the territory of a different state. Such prescriptive acts of states concerning foreign objects or activities without consent of the respective state are illegal under international law.[118] Second, is the case of extraterritorial jurisdiction with an

---

[115] Article 1 of the Charter of Economic Rights and Duties of States, adopted by the UN General Assembly in 1974.
[116] Shaw (1997), p. 572, Meng (1994), p. 13.   [117] Meng (1994), p. 87.
[118] Meng (1994), p. 116.

extraterritorial aspect is characterized by the fact that the legal consequences of the authoritative act of a state require action or omission of an action outside the regulating country's borders. This type of extraterritorial jurisdiction is called extraterritorial regulation: although the regulation can be enforced only within the regulating country, the prescribed action or omission ought to take place abroad. Third, an extraterritorial aspect can be part of the objective elements describing the preconditions of the legal consequences of an act of state. In this case, the legal consequences apply within the regulating country, while they are linked to certain circumstances abroad without, however, requiring certain activities. This type of extraterritorial jurisdiction is here referred to as 'extraterritorial nexus'. Excluded from the concept of extraterritorial jurisdiction, in contrast, are measures the objective elements of which, as well as their legal consequences, are confined to the regulating country's territory, although they may nevertheless bear on other countries because of economic or other factual side-effects. Examples of measures with merely factual extraterritorial impact are the rise of interest rates by a national bank, which may affect the economic situation in other countries, or a prohibition of weapon exports, which may affect the ability of other countries to lead wars.[119] According to Meng, only the latter type of measure does not create any problems of extraterritorial jurisdiction, since states are entitled to define their own legal order and situation, even if their activities have factual effects on other states.[120] In contrast, extraterritorial regulations, as well as measures with an extraterritorial nexus, are problematic under international law.

NPA trade measures are linked to objects, activities and other aspects, which if applied to imports do not belong to the territorial jurisdiction of the state utilizing the measure or which even belong to the jurisdiction of another state. An example of such extraterritorial aspects in a measure's objective elements is the adherence to certain production standards in other countries. The legal effect of such measures could consist in the prohibition of imports, or in other consequences linked to the observation or not of certain requirements to which the import or internal sale is subjected. Consequently, the legal effects concern the territory of the country imposing the measure. Since there is no prescriptive extraterritorial

---

[119] Meng (1994), p. 77.
[120] Meng (1994), p. 77, Bartels (2002), in contrast, criticizes Meng's view as too narrow, since a lack of enforceability in itself is not sufficient to qualify such measures as inoffensive, given the possibility of considerable factual effects.

5.2 JUSTIFIABILITY OF NPA MEASURES

regulation, NPA measures are here considered to fall into the category of measures with an extraterritorial nexus. This means, that despite the absence of an extraterritorial effect of a legal nature, this type of extraterritorial measure can lead to conflicts. For example, one has to ask whether the interests of concerned individuals or states need to be taken into account because of principles of economic rationality.[121] Due to their link to extraterritorial circumstances NPA measures may well have considerable factual extraterritorial effects. Since the effects are not of a strictly legal quality, they have been termed 'persuasion'. Persuasion is an effect not *qua* legal authority, but *qua* psychological or economic pressure, either because the concerned individual is striving to comply, or because a cost–benefit assessment leads to the decision that compliance is preferable to non-compliance.[122] Instead of regulating extraterritorial affairs, countries link measures to NPAs, such as protection of human rights in the country of production, rather in their own interest in order to promote values such as respect for human rights in other countries.[123]

The above categorization shows a crucial difference between measures linked to NPAs and measures which are exclusively linked to product characteristics that is often neglected. Both types of measures have in common that they might bring foreign producers to comply with the requirements established by the importing country, mostly for economic reasons. However, NPA measures differ from exclusively product-based measures in that they link legal consequences to extraterritorial facts. Product-based measures, on the other hand, link legal consequences to the physical characteristics of a product which is circulating or about to circulate within the territory of the regulating state. The characteristics of products, which lead to the permission to enter the territory or to restrictions, in this moment become part of the internal affairs of the country imposing the measure. Such a transformation does not take place in the case of NPA measures: the extraterritorial facts to which the measure is linked remain extraterritorial, even if the product crosses the border. This difference between both types of measures exists regardless of the motivation of the state imposing the measure, and irrespective of whether the measure is meant to influence foreign conduct or whether the influence is merely an unintended side-effect.[124] For that reason measures linked to

---

[121] Meng (1994), p. 76.
[122] Meng (1994), p. 82, considers the nature of such factual effects as psychological.
[123] Bartels (2002), p. 376.
[124] Howse and Regan (2000), at pp. 274–9, focus under the aspect extraterritoriality on the motivation of states adopting NPA measures. However, it seems preferable to determine

physical product characteristics fall into the category of measures with merely factual extraterritorial effects, which are *per se* permitted under international law, while NPA measures fall into the more problematic category of measures with an extraterritorial nexus.

However, this difference is not crucial for the question at issue.[125] Despite possible conflicts of interests between the concerned states as outlined above, NPA measures do not imply prescriptive regulations or binding legal consequences beyond the jurisdiction of the country adopting the measure. For this reason, it is here argued that NPA measures as measures with an extraterritorial nexus without extraterritorial regulation do not constitute impermissible extraterritorial jurisdiction.[126] While in exceptional cases there nevertheless may be a need to assess whether the consequences of such a measure in terms of factual effects on other states are excessive,[127] a *per se* violation of the principle of equal sovereignty cannot be assumed. Rather, such measures ought to be considered within the confined borders of sovereignty of the state taking such measures. In consequence of this view, the controversial legal status of this principle as a peremptory norm therefore need not be established.

---

whether or not a measure has an extraterritorial effect in an objective way. The policy objectives pursued with such measures may be relevant when it comes to justification, while they are irrelevant for the question of permissibility of measures with extraterritorial effects in the first place.

[125] The difference is however relevant for the determination whether or not NPA measures fall into the geographical scope of the general exceptions in GATT Article XX, see below at section 5.3.1.

[126] For permissibility from the perspective of extraterritorial jurisdiction: Meng, Puth, Howse and Regan; against it: Bartels. Meng (1994) considers measures linked to production methods as measures with merely factual extraterritorial effects and consequently does not consider them as legally problematic extraterritorial jurisdiction (at pp. 76, 77). Similarly, Puth (2003, at p. 147). Also Howse and Regan (2000) negate that possible extraterritorial effects of process-based measures can render such measures illegitimate under international law (at p. 274). However, measures linked to production abroad differ in a single important aspect from the other examples for measures with merely factual extraterritorial effects cited by Meng, such as the rise of the discount rate by the central bank. In the case of ecological standards, the import restriction as the relevant legal consequences is linked to a clearly extraterritorial aspect, namely, the way in which the product has been produced in a foreign country, or, as Bartels (2002), pp. 381–2, puts it, the ecological measure is *made applicable* to conduct occurring abroad. Bartels finds that activities-based measures (production) as well as product-based measures and boycott measures are relevantly extraterritorial and that legal questions of jurisdiction arise (at pp. 383–4).

[127] Meng (1994), p. 141, Bartels (2002), p. 378.

In sum, a violation of *ius cogens* is not apparent in the case of NPA measures. Therefore, permissibility of such measures depends on the legal framework established with the relevant treaties, including the GATT.

5.2.3 Result

Measures linked to NPAs are neither *per se* irreconcilable with objectives and purpose of GATT and WTO, nor do they automatically violate the chapeau of Article XX. Despite their quasi-automatic extraterritorial effects if applied to imports, this work assumes that NPA measures do not constitute extraterritorial jurisdiction. It is therefore not apparent that they fall foul of peremptory norms of public international law.

5.3 The scope of Article XX

Justification of national measures under Article XX requires that they fall into the scope of the general exceptions. If applied to NPA measures, determining the scope of Article XX is problematic in a twofold way. First, there is the question of whether or not the above-described extraterritorial reach of NPA measures exceeds the geographical scope of the exceptions. This would be the case if the exceptions would apply only to measures concerning objects or behaviour located within the country adopting the measure. Second, the particular exceptions do not cover all subject matters which states seek to regulate or influence with NPA measures. Even if a measure implements a public policy which appears legitimate under certain standards, the respective policy may not be listed in Article XX. Hence, the question arises as to whether policies that are not listed in paragraphs (a)–(j) can nevertheless be justifiable. The analysis focuses on those particular exceptions contained in Article XX that are most crucial for the justification of NPA measures, namely exceptions (b) and (g). Also, exception (a), the so-called public morals exception, is highly relevant for NPA measures. Since exception (a) provides for some particularities both with respect to geographical scope and covered subject matter, its applicability to NPA measures is analysed in a separate section.

5.3.1 The geographical scope and the problem of extraterritoriality

The particular exceptions in GATT Article XX (a)–(j) allow WTO members to deviate from GATT obligations and to restrict trade in order to implement certain public policies that have been recognized as legitimate and important. The listed categories of exceptions concern policies and respective implementing measures which serve to protect a number of specific objects, values or even the national economy as a whole. Measures seeking justification under Article XX prompt the question on the geographical scope of the particular exceptions, both with respect to the location of the objects of protection and of the targeted behaviour. The location of the objects of protection and of the targeted behaviour may well differ. For example, toxic fumes stemming from industrial production in one country may directly affect the health of the population of the neighbouring country. In cases where the neighbouring country adopted trade measures to stop imports of the products of that particular industry, the objects of protection, namely, the domestic population, would be located within the country adopting the measure, while the targeted behaviour, namely, industrial production, would be located within foreign territories. Carbon dioxide (CO_2) emissions leading to climate change may well affect life conditions of people all over the globe. The atmosphere damaged by such emissions constitutes a shared resource and belongs to the global commons. Some argue that only measures targeting objects or behaviour within the territory of the country that has adopted the measure are justifiable under Article XX. Others, in contrast, are of the view that the general exceptions do not include a geographical limitation, and thus favour a broad interpretation of the geographical scope.

Due to their special characteristics outlined above, this problem is crucial for the legal status of most NPA measures: their inherent extraterritorial reach if applied to imports renders the geographical scope of Article XX crucial for their legal status.[128] NPA measures may be intended to protect values within or without the territory of the state adopting them, but they inherently refer to circumstances or behaviour abroad if applied to imports. NPA measures will also often be part of a set of measures, with some measures targeting domestic behaviour and other measures targeting behaviour abroad.

This section discusses a possible limitation of the geographical scope with respect to NPA measures. To reiterate, international law on state sovereignty does not prohibit the use of trade measures with an extraterritorial reach. Thus, the legal status of the geographical scope depends on the relevant provisions of WTO law. This sections starts with a review of relevant GATT and WTO case law, which is here considered inconclusive.

---

[128] See above at section 5.2.2.3.

The subsequent sub-sections interpret the particular exceptions in Article XX. To reiterate, the approach to interpretation adopted by the WTO adjudicatory bodies is an integrated approach, albeit with a strong emphasis on the text.[129] Accordingly, this interpretation starts out with the language of the particular exceptions. In order to place emphasis on the differences between the particular exceptions in terms of language and negotiating history, each step in the analysis considers all relevant exceptions. Since the textual interpretation does not offer compelling evidence in one direction or the other, the objective and purpose of Article XX and negotiating history are also taken into account. The discussion then considers alternative approaches. The final sub-section reviews the findings and draws conclusions.

5.3.1.1 Insufficient GATT and WTO case law

Despite a small number of dispute settlement reports drafted under GATT and WTO that address the problem of a jurisdictional limitation of the scope of Article XX, the adjudicatory bodies have not yet settled this question. The *Tuna-Dolphin I* panel rejected an interpretation of exceptions (b) and (g) allowing for measures with an extra-jurisdictional link or purpose, invoking the original drafters' intentions and the broader consequences of such interpretation for the functioning of the multilateral framework for trade.[130] Three years later, the *Tuna-Dolphin II* panel opined that neither the text nor drafting history of Article XX provided any valid reason to conclude that measures referring to circumstances outside the territorial jurisdiction of the state imposing the measure were proscribed in an absolute manner.[131] Nevertheless, it reached the conclusion that ultimately a broad interpretation of Article XX with respect to an extraterritorial linkage would jeopardize the multilateral trading system and seriously impair the balance of rights and obligations among the contracting parties of the GATT.[132] Therefore, it found the contested measures not to be justified by Article XX. Its basic reasoning was later shared by the panel in the *Shrimp Turtle* dispute.[133]

---

[129] See above section 5.1.1.1.
[130] Panel Report, *Tuna-Dolphin I* (1991), Nos. 5.26–5.27, 5.31–5.32.
[131] Panel Report, *Tuna-Dolphin II* (1994), Nos. 5.16, 5.20, 5.31–5.33.
[132] Panel Report, *Tuna-Dolphin II* (1994), Nos. 5.26, 5.38–5.39, *Tuna-Dolphin I* (1991), above fn. 130.
[133] Panel Report, *Shrimp Turtle* (1998), Nos. 7.45, 7.61. The *Shrimp Turtle* Panel discussed this issue under the aspect of whether Article XX should be interpreted as not allowing for measures that conditioned market access to the adoption of certain policies by the

The Appellate Body in the *Shrimp Turtle* dispute gave a new impetus to the debate. The objects protected by the contested measures in this case were highly migratory sea turtles which were known to traverse waters under the jurisdiction of the defendant. In discussing justification under exception (g), conservation of exhaustible resources,[134] the Appellate Body touched upon the problem of an extraterritorial reach. However, invoking the specific facts of the case, it found that there was a 'sufficient nexus' between the sea turtle species as the protected resource at stake, on the one hand, and the country imposing the measure, on the other, because the protected species were known to occur in waters over which this country had jurisdiction. Therefore, the Appellate Body saw no need to discuss the question of an implied jurisdictional limitation in Article XX(g) in general.[135]

The Appellate Body's findings in *Shrimp Turtle* may well be interpreted to establish that, at least in the case of sufficient territorial linkage with the object of protection, measures with an extraterritorial reach may fall into the scope of the general exceptions. Some scholars invoke these findings to support the view that in cases where measures pursue policies with global effects, such as environmental measures concerning climate change or the depletion of the ozone layer, they do *per se* have a sufficient nexus with the territory of any WTO member.[136] However, since the *Shrimp Turtle* findings were explicitly limited to the specific facts of the case, they are not suitable to answer the question in general. Thus, the report does not allow for conclusions in cases where a sufficient territorial nexus is missing, or not as evident as in the case of migratory species. Since the unadopted *Tuna-Dolphin* reports also cannot serve as a basis for an established case law on the general question, existing case law does not offer much guidance on the question of whether coverage of the particular exceptions is geographically limited.

5.3.1.2 The text of the particular exceptions

The interpretation of the text considers, first, whether there are direct references to the issue of the geographical scope, and then moves on

---

exporting country. It stressed the difference with measures with an extra-jurisdictional effect on the one hand, and measures which affect other government's policies in a way that threatens the multilateral trading system (at 7.51).

[134] The United States had claimed justification under Article XX(b) only in the event that the challenged measures would not fall into the ambit of exception (g). Appellate Body Report, *Shrimp Turtle* (1998), No. 125.

[135] Appellate Body Report, *Shrimp Turtle* (1998), No. 133.

[136] van den Bossche, Schrijver and Faber (2007), p. 290.

to analyse whether the language of one or another particular exception contains aspects which allow the drawing of conclusions on this question.

5.3.1.2.1 Direct references to the geographical scope

Some of the particular exceptions contain language which refers to the location of the protected objects. For example, Article XX(f) covers measures 'imposed for the protection of national treasures of artistic, historic or archaeological value'. The adjective 'national' could indicate that only those policies can be justified which protect the described treasures within a country's borders, while measures relating to the protection of treasures located in other countries arguably would not be covered. Since exception (f) is explicitly limited to 'national' treasures, it could therefore be argued that given the absence of similar limiting adjectives in other exceptions these would not be geographically limited. However, even the term 'national' in exception (f) has been considered ambiguous: a country could, for example, restrict imports in order to help other countries protecting their 'national' treasures. In this case, a measure targeting foreign national treasures could also be covered by exception (f).[137]

Article XX(e), on the other hand, applies to measures relating to the products of prison labour. The term 'prison labour' refers to circumstances of production. Apparently, the exception was drafted in order to protect own domestic industries against 'unfair' competition by products produced with cheap labour, rather than in order to protect prisoners' rights in other countries.[138] Therefore, the prevailing view holds that this exception refers to products produced by prison labour abroad and thus covers measures with an extraterritorial nexus, namely, the circumstances of production. However, given the special subject matter of exception (e), it does not seem possible to infer from this exception the geographical scope of other exceptions. Also, the geographical scope does not need to be the same for all exceptions, which significantly differ not only regarding subject matter but also in terms of diction.[139] Nevertheless, exception (e) can indeed be invoked to underscore that it would be against the spirit and language of the exceptions to exclude *per se* measures with

---

[137] Charnovitz (1998), pp. 700–1.
[138] The EEC and the Netherlands in *Tuna-Dolphin II* interpreted Article XX(e) in this way, referring to existing state practice with respect to prison labour at the time. They argued that the prevailing systems of prison labour in GATT contracting parties were neither necessarily forced nor hard labour, and hence disbelieved in any humanitarian motivation of the drafters. Panel Report, *Tuna-Dolphin II* (1994), No. 3.35.
[139] Appellate Body Report, *US – Gasoline* (1996), pp. 17–18, after fn. 35.

an extraterritorial reach.[140] In contrast to exceptions (f) and (e), the wording of the exceptions which have so far played a crucial role in WTO dispute settlement, especially the exceptions concerning life, health and exhaustible resources, is inconclusive regarding the location of the targeted objects.

5.3.1.2.2 Indirect reference: the means–end relationship

The language of the particular exceptions contains other elements to be considered in an interpretation of the geographical scope. Textual differences with respect to the specific 'degree of connection or relationship between the measure under appraisal and the state interest or policy sought to be promoted'[141] may shed light on the question of whether a measure targeting circumstances or behaviour abroad could possibly be covered by a particular exception. While both exceptions (a) and (b) allow for justification of measures which are 'necessary' to protect certain objects and values, exception (g) applies to measures 'relating' to the conservation of exhaustible natural resources, and even other exceptions simply need to be 'imposed for' the protection of certain objects. All these requirements regard the relationship between measure and the pursued objective: the means–end relationship. The differences in language in the particular exceptions suggest that the various particular exceptions require different kinds or degrees of connection between the measure and the promoted policy.[142] Of the listed exceptions, (b) and (g) are the most relevant exceptions for NPA measures, and therefore the analysis focuses on these exceptions.[143]

5.3.1.2.2.1 'necessary'

The term 'necessary' appears in different WTO Agreements, and the meaning given to this term differs depending on its specific use.[144] Even with respect to the GATT general exceptions, the precise meaning of the term is not self-evident. Respective GATT and WTO jurisprudence has evolved over the years, and the necessity tests as applied in various disputes have placed emphasis on different aspects. The classical approach of

---

[140] Charnovitz (1994), p. 341.
[141] Appellate Body Report, *US – Gasoline* (1996), p. 17.
[142] Appellate Body Report, *US – Gasoline* (1996), p. 17.
[143] The public morals exception (a) is discussed in more detail below at section 5.3.3.
[144] E.g., in some provisions, necessity requirements are part of justification, while in others, namely, the TBT and SPS Agreements, it is part of obligations, with corresponding consequences for the allocation of the burden of proof. Neumann and Tuerk (2003), p. 226.

5.3 THE SCOPE OF ARTICLE XX

the adjudicatory bodies, which prevailed up to the 2000 Appellate Body Report in *Korea – Various Measures on Beef*,[145] can be characterized as a test of relative necessity, which compared GATT inconsistency of the adopted measures with reasonably available alternatives.[146] For example, the GATT *US – Section 337 Tariff Act* panel found that 'a contracting party is bound to use, among the measures reasonably available to it, that which entails the least degree of inconsistency with other GATT provisions'.[147] Although not stated explicitly, under the classical approach, the level of protection chosen by the country adopting the measure is the standard against which alternatives are tested.[148] The chosen level of protection was regarded as a fix value that was not put into question.[149] GATT panels and later WTO adjudicatory bodies repeatedly stressed their restraint regarding the level of protection autonomously chosen by institutions in the respective WTO member.

It is noteworthy and important that the term 'necessary' implies first of all that the measure is suitable to achieve the pursued objective. Although this fundamental requirement has not been explicitly stated in WTO jurisprudence, it certainly underlies the findings of the adjudicatory bodies. This is apparent also in the prevailing interpretation, originally adopted by the Appellate Body in *Korea – Various Measures on Beef*, which understands the term 'necessary' to comprise a whole range of degrees, with the lowest degree of necessity described as 'making a contribution' to the objective pursued, and the highest degree as 'indispensable'.[150] This interpretation shows that even the lowest degree of necessity requires a minimal positive causal relationship between measure and objective, or a 'contribution' to the achievement of the chosen objective.[151] Obviously, only measures which are suitable to achieve the objective pursued can possibly be

---

[145] For more on the classical necessity test see Neumann and Tuerk (2003).
[146] Cf., e.g., also Panel Reports, *Thailand – Cigarettes* (1990), p. 21, No. 75; *United States – Section 337* (1989), para. 5.26.
[147] Panel Report, *US – Section 337* (1989), para. 5.26.
[148] Neumann and Tuerk (2003) discuss this aspect comprehensively, but reach the same conclusion, namely, that the classical necessity test was 'never used to rule out "disproportionate" measures', at p. 209.
[149] Even the *US – Section 337* (1989) Panel apparently placed great importance on this fact. It stated: 'To avoid any misunderstanding as to the scope and implications of the above findings, the panel stresses that neither Article III:4 nor Article XX(d) puts obligations on contracting parties specifying the level of protection that they should accord to patents or the effectiveness of procedures to enforce such protection' (at para. 6.1).
[150] Appellate Body Report, *Korea – Beef* (2001), Nos. 160, 161.
[151] Appellate Body Report, *Brazil – Retreaded Tyres* (2007), Nos. 145, 146.

necessary, while measures that are *per se* unsuitable as a tool to further an objective can under no circumstances be 'necessary'. This is equally true for alternative measures to be considered under the least trade-restrictiveness test: 'the extent to which the alternative measure "contributes to the realization of the end pursued"' needs to be taken into consideration.[152]

The classical approach to interpretation of the term 'necessary' was supplemented in the 2000 *Korea – Various Measures on Beef* dispute, first with respect to exception (d) only. There, the Appellate Body stressed the need to weigh and balance alternative measures, and to consider a whole series of factors comprehensively, including the 'contribution made by the compliance measure to the enforcement of the law or regulation at issue, the importance of the common interests or values protected by that law or regulation, and the accompanying impact of the law or regulation on imports or exports'.[153] The Appellate Body later confirmed the importance of this 'weighing and balancing' process in several decisions, and extended its applicability also to exception (b).[154] In its *Brazil – Retreaded Tires* Report of 2007, the Appellate Body even stated that 'the capacity of a country to implement remedial measures that would be particularly costly, or would require advanced technologies, may be relevant to the assessment of whether such measures or practices are reasonably available alternatives to a preventive measure',[155] thus even promoting the relevance of differences between developing and developed WTO members. By introducing the weighing and balancing process, the Appellate Body established a new concept for assessing a measure's necessity, which will be discussed in more detail below.[156] For the present purpose, it is sufficient to note that the term 'necessary' is understood as requiring a minimum degree of actual causality.

5.3.1.2.2.2 'relating to' and 'imposed for'

The first panel to interpret the term 'relating to' in exception (g) was that in the *Canada – Herring* dispute. The panel asked whether 'any relationship with conservation ... is sufficient for a trade measure to fall under Article XX(g) or whether a particular relationship and conjunction are

---

[152] Appellate Body Report in *Korea – Beef* (2001), Nos. 163–6, confirmed in Appellate Body Report in *Dominican Republic – Import and Sale of Cigarettes* (2005), No. 68.
[153] Appellate Body Report, *Korea – Beef* (2001), No. 164.
[154] E.g., Appellate Body Reports, *EC – Asbestos* (2001), No. 172 and *Brazil – Retreaded Tires* (2007), No. 182.
[155] Appellate Body Report, *Brazil – Retreaded Tires* (2007), No. 171.
[156] See also below, section 5.3.3.4.3.2.

required'. Having compared the language of exception (g) with the language of the other exceptions, the panel concluded that exception (g) covered not only measures that are 'necessary' or 'essential' for the conservation of exhaustible natural resources, but a wider range of measures.[157] The panel found that given the purpose of Article XX to not hinder countries from pursuing the listed policies, in order to satisfy the 'relating to' requirement in exception (g) measures had to be 'primarily aimed at' the conservation of an exhaustible natural resource.[158] In the following years, this interpretation was followed in a number of reports,[159] although it was noted that the phrase was not treaty language and was not to be applied as a litmus test.[160] Furthermore, the Appellate Body declined that the exception required an 'empirical effects' test and alluded to practical difficulties in determining causal effects. It stated:

> in the field of conservation of exhaustible natural resources, a substantial period of time, perhaps years, may have to elapse before the effects attributable to implementation of a given measure may be observable.[161]

However, while diminishing the relevance of 'actual' effects, the Appellate Body also clarified that in the case of an apparent lack of any potential causal relationship, the requirement set up with the 'relating to' standard would not be met:

> We are not, however, suggesting that consideration of the predictable effects of a measure is never relevant. In a particular case, should it become clear that realistically, a specific measure cannot in any possible situation have any positive effect on conservation goals, it would very probably be because that measure was not designed as a conservation regulation to begin with. In other words, it would not have been 'primarily aimed at' conservation of natural resources at all.[162]

---

[157] Panel Report, *Canada – Herring* (1988), para. 4.6.
[158] Panel Report, *Canada – Herring* (1988), para. 4.6.
[159] This interpretation of the term 'relating to' was also upheld by the Appellate Body in its *US – Gasoline* (1996) Report, at p. 19. Its criticism of the appealed Panel Report regarded only the way in which the Panel had applied this interpretation, namely, to analyse whether the less favourable treatment rather than the measure at issue had been 'primarily aimed at' the conservation of clean air (p. 16). Also, Panel Report, *Tuna-Dolphin I* (1991), No. 5.32.
[160] Appellate Body Report, *US – Gasoline* (1996), p. 19.
[161] Appellate Body Report, *US – Gasoline* (1996), p. 21. The statement regards questions of causality and effectiveness, but originally regarded the additional requirement in exception (g) 'made effective in conjunction with restrictions on domestic production or consumption'.
[162] Appellate Body Report, *US – Gasoline* (1996), pp. 21–2.

The Appellate Body in the *Shrimp Turtle* dispute a few years later substantiated the interpretation of the words 'relating to' in exception (g) to require that a measure is 'primarily aimed at' the particular policy goal if there is a 'substantial relationship' between the measure and the policy of conserving an exhaustible resource.[163] With respect to the conservation measures at issue, it found the means–end relationship to be 'a close and real one' and 'every bit as substantial as that' in *US – Gasoline*.[164]

In sum, as compared with the requirement of necessity as stipulated in exception (b), the requirement that a measure be 'related to' the conservation of exhaustible natural resources is lower. According to case law hitherto, it seems that only in cases where the measure is obviously unsuited to producing any positive effect on the public good it allegedly seeks to protect, or in cases of severe inconsistencies in the design of the conservation measure, would a measure fail to meet this requirement. The term 'imposed for' which is used in exception (f) for measures to protect national treasures has not yet been interpreted by the adjudicatory bodies. However, it would seem that in this case also the standard of the causal relationship required is lower than the one established with terms such as 'necessary' or 'essential'.[165]

---

[163] Appellate Body Report, *Shrimp Turtle* (1998), paras. 136, 141.
[164] Appellate Body Report, *Shrimp Turtle* (1998), para. 141.
[165] The prevailing interpretation of the term 'necessary' has also met with criticism. Comparing the particular exceptions (a)–(j) and the requirements, there seems to be a contradiction between the required degree of connection and the hierarchy of values which may be protected through state action under GATT Article XX. At first glance, it is unintelligible why measures need to be 'necessary' to protect the highest value, namely, human life, if measures only need to be 'imposed for' the protection of objects, such as national treasures, or they only need to 'relate to' the importation of material values, such as gold and silver. Most of these contradictions, however, can be explained with the narrowly defined subject matter to which some of the exceptions relate. Due to the limited scope, e.g., products of prison labour or gold and silver, the danger of abuse of those exceptions would be relatively limited. However, this argument does not apply to the choice of language in exception (g). Under this exception, the protection of certain animal or plant species would only be reviewed based on the 'relating to' standard, while measures for the protection of life and health of human beings need to be 'necessary' – which implies a higher degree of means–end relationship (Cleveland, 2002, p. 165). Therefore, it has been argued that the 'least trade-restrictiveness' test would not be a compelling interpretation of the necessity requirement. Rather, the necessity requirement should be modified to allow for a greater accommodation of *ius cogens* and other core human rights measures, which would then include measures with an extraterritorial reach (Cleveland, 2002, p. 165). This kind of adaptation to mitigate the contradiction by abandoning the least trade-restrictiveness test, however, would imply to put at risk the consensus among WTO members that was reached with respect to the listed

5.3.1.2.2.3 Implications for the geographical scope

The question arises whether the different minimal requirements relating to a means–end relationship in exceptions (b) and (g) could possibly be fulfilled in the case of NPA trade measures. In order for a measure to have some effect on the policy objectives pursued, there must be a causal link between the measure and the policy objective. In the case of NPA measures applied to imports, this connection is the NPA to which the measure is linked. Since the NPA in question is located outside the territory of the state imposing the measure, the imposing state lacks legislative jurisdiction for the behaviour or circumstances which it seeks to influence. The potential influence of an NPA trade measure on the NPA and the protected subjects, objects or interests is very limited and depends entirely on independent circumstances, such as the private and public response of the addressee country. It could therefore be argued that NPA border measures are inherently ineffective or even unsuitable to further the policy goals they seek to achieve, since they do not have any actual effects on the circumstances or behaviour targeted. In the absence of a minimal causal means–end relationship, the justifiability of such measures would need to be rejected. This argument was actually invoked by the panel in *Tuna-Dolphin I*. The panel took into account that a country can effectively control only those production and consumption activities which are under its jurisdiction. For this reason, the panel declined an extra-jurisdictional application.[166]

This argument is even stronger with respect to those exceptions that require the highest degree of connection between measure and policy, as, for example, the health and life exception (b), which requires that measures are 'necessary'. Given the doubts regarding the mere suitability of such measures, it seems even more difficult to establish their necessity. The necessity of NPA trade measures that are hardly suited to changing circumstances or behaviour abroad could therefore easily be denied. In addition, the likelihood of alternatively available measures,

---

policies. The lower means–end relationship requirement in exception (g) can to some extent be explained by the need for accompanying internal restrictions on production or consumption. Since it would not be convincing that measures could be justified even if states could as well have taken other equally efficient measures to pursue their policies, which would be less trade restrictive, the prevailing view requiring a least trade-restrictiveness test is preferable.

[166] Panel Report, *Tuna-Dolphin I* (1991), No. 5.32. This interpretation of the term 'relating to' was upheld by the Appellate Body in its *US – Gasoline* (1996) Report, at p. 19.

that are as effective and less trade restrictive than NPA measures, would automatically usually be high.

In this sense, some are of the view that trade measures are merely third best, given that they operate at considerable distance from the cause of a problem and thus are relatively ineffective.[167] The counter-argument holds that the effectiveness of a measure has to be assessed on a case-by-case basis, since it is not impossible *per se* that NPA measures actually bring about the desired effects.[168] More than that, it could be argued that NPA measures can contribute to non-economic policy objectives with economic and political pressure just as well or even better than with legislative jurisdiction and respective enforcement mechanisms.[169] Cleveland even calls for a presumption of effectiveness for measures protecting *ius cogens* values.[170] Given that the effects or not of NPA measures on the extraterritorial facts or behaviour are difficult to prove, especially if human rights violations are concerned, a presumption of effectiveness could hardly ever be rebutted. This, however, would make an assessment of the genuineness of the measures almost impossible.

The empirical case for the effectiveness of such measures is ambiguous. While studies have shown a modestly successful record of unilateral trade sanctions for social reasons,[171] others argue that such measures have proven to be ineffective or have even worsened the position of those who were intended to benefit.[172] Even if the use of unilateral trade measures can be effective, however, their success depends on a number of factors, such as the economic power of the country imposing the measures and on the volume of trade with the addressee country.[173] Measures by big and economically powerful countries which try to influence extraterritorial behaviour in a small and weak state might be even more effective than domestic legislative or regulatory measures if adopted by a weak government or state. However, economic pressure is no guarantee of

[167] van den Bossche, Schrijver and Faber (2007), p. 210
[168] Wiers (2001), p. 108; also Diem (1996), p. 150, who does not question at all that Article XX(b) applies also to measures protecting life and health abroad.
[169] Cf., e.g., Cleveland (2002), p. 174, who states that human rights sanctions operate 'in intangible ways'.
[170] Cleveland (2002), p. 174. With this suggestion, Cleveland refers to a proportionality test under the chapeau.
[171] E.g., Schneuwly (2003), pp. 133–8; Hufbauer, Schott and Elliott (1990).
[172] See, e.g., UNICEF (1997), at p. 23, with a case study on the negative effects on children employed in the garment industry of Bangladesh through the mere threat of boycott.
[173] See Howse and Trebilcock (1996), p. 70, with further references.

compliance.[174] Also, given the principle of sovereign equality of states, economic and political powers and pressure ought not to be considered for a determination of whether or not trade measures are justifiable. If effectiveness of economic pressure were a legitimate consideration under the general exceptions, big economies could justify trade restrictive measures in circumstances under which it would be prohibited for smaller economies to adopt the same measures. This, however, would not be reconcilable with basic principles of international law and of the WTO. The decision processes and structure of the WTO are based on the principle of equality of member states, and consequently a distinction between members when it comes to the justification of trade measures is legally excluded. The economic case is therefore here considered irrelevant.

In sum, this author concludes that the stronger requirements in terms of a means–end relationship suggest that in the case of those particular exceptions that require necessity of measures, such as exception (b), there is a presumption against the suitability and necessity of the NPA measures.[175] This would imply as a corollary, that in the case of NPA measures it would be irrelevant whether the protected objects were within or without the country imposing the measure, since the requirements concerning the means–end relationship could not be met.

The recent tendency in WTO case law, manifested by the Appellate Body's repeated statements that the more vital or important are the common interests or values pursued, the easier it would be to accept as

---

[174] E.g., producers in the addressee country might choose to redirect their exports to other countries instead of complying with the NPA requirements. Furthermore, proving the suitability of measures relying on economic pressure would arguably often turn out to be difficult. See Cleveland for similar concerns with respect to human rights sanctions (2002, pp. 144–6).

[175] Puth invokes an additional contextual argument for a geographical limitation of the scope of exception (b) (2003, p. 304). This contextual argument would merely confirm the result of the textual interpretation, but is nevertheless here rejected. It is based on the fact that the SPS Agreement covers exclusively measures for the protection of certain objects 'within the territory of the Member' adopting the measure. Puth argues that this limitation of the geographical scope is transferable at least to exception (b), since the SPS Agreement can be seen as regulating the implementation of GATT Article XX, particularly exception (b). Puth, however, ignores the prevailing view, according to which the SPS Agreement is in no way contingent upon GATT Article XX, but establishes obligations in its own right (since Panel Report, *EC – Hormones* (1997), No. 8.39). Furthermore, the subject matter covered by the SPS Agreement is more specific than the scope of the general exception (b) in Article XX, since it applies to sanitary and phytosanitary measures only (Cleveland, 2002, pp. 158–9). For these reasons, there is no logical basis for an inference from the scope of the more specific SPS Agreement to the scope of the more general provision, namely, Article XX.

'necessary' measures designed to achieve these ends,[176] does not contradict this finding. First, the Appellate Body made this important point to the benefit of the country invoking Article XX in *EC – Asbestos* with respect to a measure aimed at crucial physical differences between products that were highly likely to lead to health damage within the country adopting the measure. In *Korea – Various Measures on Beef*, where not physical characteristics but origin was the aspect to which the measure was linked, the Appellate Body reached the conclusion that the measure was not necessary. More than that, it also stated:

> There are other aspects of the enforcement measure to be considered in evaluating that measure as 'necessary'. One is the extent to which the measure contributes to the realization of the end pursued ... The greater the contribution, the more easily a measure might be considered to be 'necessary'.[177]

In sum, it is not conceivable that the Appellate Body would consider the importance of the objective pursued in defence of an NPA measure. Rather, its doubtful suitability to achieve its ends might prevent an NPA measure from being justified under any of the exceptions requiring 'necessity'. Depending on the specific facts of the case, however, there is still the possibility that in certain cases NPA measures would be considered suitable, and thus possibly also necessary.[178]

In contrast to exception (b), which requires an actual causal means–end relationship, exception (g) merely requires that a justifiable measure 'relates to' the conservation of exhaustible natural resources. The 'substantial relationship' required for justification under exception (g), which according to case law hitherto would be denied only in the event that the measure could not have any positive effect on the object of protection in any possible situation, does not imply actual causality. Therefore, due to the lower threshold with respect to the means–end relationship required, exception (g) would not *per se* exclude NPA measures. However, implicit restrictions could also result from the additional requirements of exception (g) as discussed in the following section.

---

[176] Appellate Body Report, *Korea – Beef* (2001), No. 162; Appellate Body Report, *EC – Asbestos* (2001), no. 172.

[177] Appellate Body Report, *Korea – Beef* (2001), No. 163.

[178] Quick and Lau (2001), e.g., considered the EU leg-hold trap regulation necessary under Article XX(b), because the respective import prohibition was prevented by an agreement on humane trapping methods, that was concluded with the affected country.

5.3.1.2.3 Indirect reference in exception (g): domestic restrictions

Exception (g), which is of great importance for environmental NPA measures, contains an additional precondition. It stipulates that only measures that are made effective in conjunction with restrictions on domestic production or consumption fall into its scope.

5.3.1.2.3.1 History and relevant case law

For a better understanding of the reasons underlying this specific precondition, the backdrop of the relevant negotiating history will be briefly described. The GATT negotiators in the mid-1940s were preoccupied with the experience of global economic crisis and destruction resulting from the Second World War. Many countries were worried about the consequences of GATT obligations allowing for free trade because some of them already faced severe shortages of certain goods. The delegate of Czechoslovakia, for instance, invoked the example of trade in timber. He said that forests in his countries had been so depleted that it would take 10–15 years to bring them to pre-war levels even if no trees were cut at all. His concern was whether GATT obligations with respect to exports could add to the domestic shortage of timber, and he asked whether a conservation of timber reserves in terms of exports would require a corresponding conservation of domestic use.[179] The Australian delegate, in contrast, illustrated the general purpose of the requirement of associated domestic restrictions with an example, and agreed in principle that a state should not be allowed to impose export quotas or prohibitions, if at the same time domestic use of the goods concerned is freely permitted. However, he also suggested that in cases where domestic consumption is extremely conservative due to other reasons, further restrictions on domestic consumption should not be required if import restrictions were considered necessary.[180] These statements show, first, that sub-paragraph (g) was inserted to allow measures to mitigate domestic shortages rather than shortages elsewhere, and, second, that modern environmental concerns did not play a role in the discussion, since the negotiators were preoccupied with securing commodity supplies in their own countries.

---

[179] UN Economic and Social Council (ECOSOC), Preparatory Committee on the International Conference on Trade and Employment, E/PC/T/C.II/ST/PV/2, Verbatim Report, of 8 November 1946, pp. 23–5.

[180] ECOSOC, Second Session of the Preparatory Committee of the UN Conference on Trade and Employment, Verbatim Report, E/PC/T/A/PV/30, of 16 July 1947, p. 18.

The questions arise if the additional requirement implies that NPA border measures can be justifiable only if they accompany other national measures that impose restrictions on domestic consumption, and if exception (g) contains an inherent limitation to measures protecting domestic objects. GATT and WTO jurisprudence on this particular issue underwent a shift from a narrower to a wider interpretation. A GATT panel had interpreted the requirement of associated restrictions on domestic production or consumption to mean that the trade measure had to be 'primarily aimed at rendering effective' domestic production restrictions.[181] This interpretation seems to imply that the conservation policy consists primarily of internal measures, and that only trade measures accompanying the internal policy are justifiable. The panel's reasoning is understandable given the prevailing view at the time that the general exceptions were limited to measures protecting domestic as opposed to foreign objects. The Appellate Body later overturned the panel's reasoning and adopted a broader interpretation. It found the requirement of domestic restrictions to constitute a requirement of 'even-handedness'.[182] The Appellate Body's reasoning suggests that measures envisaged by exception (g) aim at the protection of an exhaustible natural resource, and that they must be part of a larger set of measures contributing to the same goal domestically. In *US – Gasoline*, the Appellate Body stated:

> we believe that the clause 'if such measures are made effective in conjunction with restrictions on domestic product[ion] or consumption' is appropriately read as a requirement that the measures concerned impose restrictions, not just in respect of imported gasoline but also with respect to domestic gasoline. The clause is a requirement of *even-handedness* in the imposition of restrictions ... upon the production or consumption of exhaustible natural resources.[183]

Also in *Shrimp Turtle*, the Appellate Body explored whether the responding member had taken measures applying to internal activities in order to pursue the same goal, and found this to be the case. The mere fact that the contested measure itself applied to imports only, therefore, was not considered an obstacle to provisional justification. Since the turtles protected by the contested measures of the United States migrated to US waters, and since the United States had similar protection measures in place that

---

[181] Panel Report, *Canada – Herring* (1988), No. 4.6.
[182] Appellate Body Report, *Shrimp Turtle* (1998), para. 143, Appellate Body Report, *US – Gasoline* (1996), pp. 20–1.
[183] Appellate Body Report, *US – Gasoline* (1996), pp. 20–1 (original emphasis).

applied to US American shrimp production and to US shrimp trawlers, the Appellate Body soon concluded that 'in principle, Section 609 is an even-handed measure'.[184] This finding implies that trade measures do not need to be subordinate compared with the corresponding domestic conservation measures. It is also important to note that with its findings in the *Shrimp Turtle* dispute, the Appellate Body confirmed that the scope of sub-paragraph (g) is wider than the class of cases that had originally been envisaged. As opposed to the examples given by the negotiators, the restricted product, for example, in the *Shrimp Turtle* dispute, shrimp, is not identical to the object of conservation, namely, sea turtles. This implies that exception (g) may in principle be invoked for a much larger range of trade measures, if they are supportive of domestic conservation policies.

5.3.1.2.3.2 Distinction between foreign and shared resources

This requirement is problematic for NPA measures, since these inherently bear on circumstances beyond the imposing state's borders. On the one hand, it could be argued that the function of the second part of exception (g) is merely to prevent protectionism disguised under the veil of a conservation measure. From this perspective, import restrictions ought to be legal provided the conservation purpose is genuine and provided that other efforts to pursue this goal are in place. For example, a state could argue that the objective of protecting foreign natural resources is not only pursued with trade measures, but also with assistance programmes or funds used for conserving the same objects. In this case, these domestic measures and programmes imposed for the protection of the foreign object might constitute conjoined measures with a restrictive effect on domestic consumption. This view, however, leads to several concerns: it is questionable if NPA trade measures and domestic protection programmes can be even-handed. An assessment of 'even-handedness' would in practice be almost impossible, given the different natures of trade measures and political programmes. It would require a determination of economic effects of extremely different types of measures, the quantification and qualification of which would be extremely difficult and complex.

At this point, it seems useful to distinguish between measures that aim exclusively at the protection of objects within the territory of other states, on the one hand, and measures that aim at the protection of the global commons or shared resources, on the other. The former case regards measures protecting exclusively foreign objects. An example would be a

---

[184] Appellate Body Report, *Shrimp Turtle* (1998), para. 144.

measure to protect tropical rain forests by means of an import prohibition on timber from such forests, for instance, if the timber has been logged illegally or without reforestation.[185] If a European state adopted such a measure, the measure would have an exclusively extraterritorial reach, because it would apply to imports from tropical countries only. Since there are no tropical rain forests in Europe and as a corollary no domestic production of tropical timber, it is questionable if such an import prohibition could possibly be part of a framework of measures pursuing the same objective by restricting domestic production. While a restriction of domestic consumption is actually embodied in the contested import restricting measure itself, this restriction can hardly be regarded as 'even-handed' in economic terms, given its apparent protective effects. An example of the latter case of measures protecting the global commons or shared resources is a measure preventing air pollution in order to protect the atmosphere. In this case, the requirement of conjoined domestic restrictions will usually not create a problem due to the nature of the objects of protection. These either exist within the territory of the state imposing the measure also, so that even-handedness may be reached by designing the measure accordingly, or responsibility is shared, in which case there is a legitimate state interest to protect.[186]

The most obvious interpretation of exception (g) suggests that the conjoined restrictions on domestic production and consumption must somehow contribute to the protection of natural resources achieved by the trade measures at issue. In the case of trade measures aimed at exclusively extraterritorial facts, the fulfilment of this requirement seems logically impossible: considering the import ban itself to be at the same time also the conjoined domestic restriction would render this requirement moot. Therefore, the view that measures aimed exclusively at foreign objects cannot be provisionally justified under exception

---

[185] This is a hypothetical example. An actual initiative of the EU to tackle the issue of illegal logging is based on partnership agreements with timber-producing countries, cf. Council Regulation (EC) 2173/2005 of 20 December 2005 (OJ L 347 of 30 December 2005), resulting from the European Action Plan for Forest Law Enforcement, Governance and Trade (FLEGT). Article 3 of the Regulation contains an import prohibition on timber products unless they are covered by a licence. The import prohibition, however, applies to shipments from partner countries only.

[186] In this direction also Puth (2003), pp. 315–16. Puth, however, does not invoke the language of Article XX(g) to reach this conclusion, but invokes the general principle of *equitable utilization*. The special status of shared resources justifies related unilateral measures also under Bartels concept of a legitimate state interest, see below at section 5.3.1.5.

(g) is preferable. This view is also consistent with the specific language of this exception. As opposed to most other sub-paragraphs, exception (g) is characterized by a low threshold for a means–end relationship indicated by the term 'relating to'. The apparent inconsistency of requirements and protected values of exceptions (g) and (b) makes sense if read together with the additional requirement included only in exception (g), namely, the requirement of conjoined domestic restrictions. If this requirement were to be ignored in cases where no domestic production of the restricted good is existent, the weak means–end relationship requirement could no longer be outbalanced. As a result, there would be a strong discrepancy between the stricter requirements for justification of health measures and the weak requirements for justification of environmental measures.

However, this restriction may not be as important as it appears, since NPA measures aimed at exclusively foreign objects will be rare. In most cases, NPA trade measures will aim at the protection of shared resources, such as the atmosphere, and often, even measures directed at exclusively foreign objects will also, or even predominantly, aim at the protection of shared resources in the long term. An example is the above NPA measure linked to illegal logging of tropical timber. While the measure directly protects an exclusively foreign resource, namely, tropical rain forests located in other countries, its ultimate objective might be the conservation of global water resources and climate protection. In this case, the above distinction would become relevant, and domestic restrictions on production or consumption contributing to the same ultimate objective could well be considered 'even-handed' domestic restrictions.

To conclude, the additional requirement of even-handed conjoined domestic restrictions indicates that exception (g) can justify NPA trade measures only if these are part of broader set of measures. Measures failing to satisfy the even-handedness requirement fall outside the scope of this exception. The additional requirement limits the geographical scope of exception (g) only for the rare case of measures aimed at the protection of exclusively foreign resources. Since most NPA measures will ultimately aim at the protection of the global commons or shared resources, the geographical scope of exception (g) does not *per se* exclude measures protecting extraterritorial values.[187]

---

[187] Against a geographical limitation also Charnovitz (2007a), p. 701.

5.3.1.3 Object and purpose

The purpose and function of Article XX within the treaty as a whole may be sought for interpretation since the text of the particular exceptions is inconclusive[188] with respect to the geographical scope of the particular exceptions. The reason to provide for these exceptions is the nature of the domestic policies listed in Article XX, which have been recognized as important and legitimate in character.[189] Thus, it is the function of the general exceptions to permit important state interests to find expression.[190]

The status of the general exceptions as compared with the obligations included in the GATT, however, is controversial. The Appellate Body in *US – Gasoline* equally stressed the purpose of Article XX not to impair the ability of WTO members to take effective measures for the protection of any of those important interests, on the one hand, and the need to do so within the limits imposed by the requirements of the WTO covered agreements, on the other.[191] The importance of finding the correct balance between the right of a WTO member to invoke an exception and the duty of that same member to respect the treaty rights of the other members was acknowledged later in *Shrimp Turtle*:

> Exercise by one Member of its right to invoke an exception, such as Article XX(g), if abused or misused, will, to that extent, erode or render naught the substantive treaty rights in, for example, Article XI:1, of other Members. Similarly, because the GATT 1994 itself makes available the exceptions of Article XX, in recognition of the legitimate nature of the policies and interests there embodied, the right to invoke one of those exceptions is not to be rendered illusory ... To permit one Member to abuse or misuse its right to invoke an exception would be effectively to allow that Member to degrade its own treaty obligations as well as to devalue the treaty rights of other Members. If the abuse or misuse is sufficiently grave or extensive, the Member, in effect, reduces its treaty obligation to a merely facultative one and dissolves its juridical character, and, in so doing, negates altogether the treaty rights of other Members. The chapeau was installed at the head of the list of 'General Exceptions' in Article XX to prevent such far-reaching consequences.[192]

Article XX can therefore be seen as the key norm for balancing the sovereign right of every contracting party to adopt and implement important

---

[188] Appellate Body Report, *Shrimp Turtle* (1998), No. 114.
[189] Appellate Body Report, *Shrimp Turtle* (1998), No. 121.
[190] Appellate Body Report, *US – Gasoline* (1996), last page (29, 30).
[191] Appellate Body Report, *US – Gasoline* (1996), last page (29, 30).
[192] Appellate Body Report, *Shrimp Turtle* (1998), No. 156.

public policies for the protection of certain objects and state interests, on the one hand, and the legitimate expectations of other contracting parties that all parties to the agreement observe their obligations, on the other. In this sense, Article XX reflects the dichotomy between a mere national prerogative to protect the sovereignty of an individual member state and the minimum standard of agreement on internationally binding obligations.[193] Consequently, interpretation of the particular exceptions requires maintaining some level of national prerogative while recognizing a set of internationally agreed standards. Under each of the particular exceptions, the degree of national prerogative as well as the degree of international agreement may vary. For instance, it has been argued that the moral exception necessarily requires some degree of deference to national decisions, while other exceptions may require a more objective interpretation.[194]

It could be argued that since the general exceptions serve to protect the sovereignty of each contracting party, only strictly national interests can possibly fall within the scope of any of the paragraphs of Article XX. In consequence, NPA measures would fall without the scope in as far as they touch matters of a foreign sovereign state, since no national interests of the state imposing the measure would be at stake. This view ignores, however, that, especially in an economically globalized world, internal and external circumstances are often connected so closely that even external circumstances may become a matter of internal concern. Furthermore, the argument is a result of circular reasoning: the question about geographical limitations of the scope of Article XX needs to be answered before it can be determined how far the particular exceptions serve to protect only national interests, or rather general interests regardless of national borders.

In sum, object and purpose of Article XX require an interpretation that takes into account a careful balancing of national interests and of the interests of all contracting parties in the rights and obligations conferred by the treaty. In this sense, object and purpose of the general exceptions do not allow for definite conclusions on the permissibility of measures with an extraterritorial reach. However, since the objective and purpose of the general exceptions is to maintain the ability of the GATT contracting parties to effectively implement the listed public policies, it is here suggested that an interpretation is required which neither hampers the

---

[193] Feddersen (2003), pp. 250–2; Feddersen (1998), p. 111.
[194] Feddersen (2003), pp. 259–68.

implementation of these policies, nor renders impossible the achievement of their objectives. In consequence of this interpretation, the relevance of the geographical location of the objects of protection would be subordinated to the effectiveness of the listed policies.

5.3.1.4 Negotiating history

Since the above interpretation of Article XX has not provided a clear answer to the question of whether NPA measures with an extraterritorial reach are covered by one or another of the particular exceptions, this section refers to the relevant negotiating history as a supplementary means of interpretation.[195] The text of the particular exceptions, in as far as is relevant for NPA measures, has remained unchanged since the adoption of the authentic text of the GATT 1947.[196]

Although there is little in terms of negotiating history on a possible jurisdictional limitation of the particular exceptions, the minutes of the preparatory committees and respective commissions provide some interesting insights. During the negotiations on the charter of the ITO, the text of the life and health exception (b) was subject to lengthy discussions.[197] The bulk of statements referred to the question of whether or not it should be required that a country restricting imports in order to protect life or health takes corresponding internal protection measures. This aspect of the travaux served as basis for the interpretation of Article XX(b) by the panel in *Tuna-Dolphin I*. The panel compared the text of the Draft Charter of the ITO, which had been proposed by the United States, with the text of the later New York Draft. The latter draft contained a proviso requiring corresponding domestic safeguards in the importing country. Although the proviso was dropped later on, the *Tuna-Dolphin I* panel interpreted the proviso to imply that 'the concerns of the drafters of Article XX(b) focused on the use of sanitary measures to safeguard life or health of humans, animals or plants within the jurisdiction of the

---

[195] Reference to the negotiating history and circumstances of the conclusion of a treaty is permitted by the VCLT if interpretation leaves the meaning obscure, or in order to confirm the result of the interpretation under the basic rule (Article 32). See also Appellate Body Report, *EC – Computer Equipment* (1998), No. 86.

[196] Apart from mere rectifications, Article XX has been changed only with respect to exception (h) concerning international commodity agreements. Article XX para. II(a) of the GATT has in part been turned into exception (j), while the remaining part of para. II was dropped completely. See GATT/CP/2 of 14 October 1948.

[197] The negotiations on the draft ITO charter are relevant for the interpretation of GATT clauses because of the close connection between the preparations for an ITO and the drafting of the GATT as a multilateral treaty (Jackson, 1997, p. 38).

importing country'.[198] This conclusion, however, is not compelling. The proviso merely required the existence of corresponding national measures without, however, referring to the location of the protected objects.[199] Furthermore, the argument must be rejected since the proviso was obviously not included in the final provision. However, other statements made in the course of the negotiations could also be invoked to support the panel's view. For example, the secretariat and the chairman of Commission A drafted an explanatory note in order to clarify this point. The text of the explanatory note slightly deviated from the text of the draft article and from the text of Article XX in its final language, by referring to measures taken by a country 'to protect *its* human, animal and plant life or health'.[200] The possessive pronoun in this text could indeed indicate that only objects under the jurisdiction of the state imposing the measure can be legitimate objects of protection. However, subsequent discussions of the explanatory note in Commission A completely ignored the use of the pronoun as well as the question of whose life or health might possibly be protected. The fact that Article XX ultimately was not drafted including the pronoun therefore can hardly be seen as a conscious decision to maintain the text of the original draft. The lack of discussion rather shows that the contracting parties did not consider deliberations on this issue necessary. Indeed, the negotiating parties and the chairman of Committee A described several situations pertinent to the additional requirement of accompanying internal measures. All of them related to the protection of internal health by restricting the importation of foreign goods.[201] The examples cited during the meetings indicate that the possibility that states could take measures in order to protect life and health outside their own territories did not even occur to the negotiators.

Charnovitz sees the 'illuminating silence' of the drafters as evidence for the significance of earlier treaties on international trade with moral exceptions, which are claimed to have served as the basis for the moral exception in Article XX(a).[202] He considers especially the negotiations on the 'International Covenant for the Abolition of Import and Export Prohibitions and Restrictions' in 1927 pertinent. From these negotiations it becomes clear that measures relating to opium, obscene photos,

---

[198] Panel Report, *Tuna-Dolphin I* (1991), No. 5.26.
[199] In this sense Puth (2003), p. 303.
[200] ECOSOC, E/PC/T/W/245 of 15 July 1947; E/PC/T/A/PV/30, of 16 July 1947, p. 8 (added emphasis).
[201] ECOSOC, E/PC/T/A/PV/30, of 16 July 1947, pp. 8–15.
[202] Charnovitz (1998), p. 705; Charnovitz (1992), pp. 203–33, before fn. 53.

lottery tickets and plumage of certain birds were within the scope of the moral exception.[203] While these measures may be primarily inwardly directed, there is no doubt that they would not address internal affairs only. Furthermore, a large amount of state practice, both in terms of unilateral measures and trade-related provisions in international treaties, regard the importation of slaves, exports of firearms into Africa, exports of opium and liquor to foreign countries, imports of pornography and goods resulting from cruelty towards animals, all of which are obviously predominantly outwardly directed subject matters.[204]

Also in *Shrimp Turtle*, in defending the challenged measures under exceptions (b) and (g), the United States referred to state practice prior to the GATT, which the contracting parties must have wanted to cover with the general exceptions. As one of several examples, the United States cited the Convention Relative to the Preservation of Fauna and Flora in their Natural State, which provided that 'the import of trophies which have been exported from any territory to which the present Convention is applicable in full, whether a territory of another Contracting Government or not, shall be prohibited'.[205] The intention of the Convention was obviously the extraterritorial protection of animals and plants. It had entered into force as early as 1936, and a number of countries which later participated in the negotiations to establish an International Trade Organization (ITO) and became original contracting parties to the GATT were parties to it.[206] Such international agreements preceding the GATT 1947 could indeed be seen as evidence that some of the most powerful original contracting parties had actually wanted the general exceptions to also cover measures aimed at extraterritorial objects, since they were obliged under specific conventions to enforce such measures. However, neither the panel nor the Appellate Body ascribed importance to the *travaux préparatoires* in this dispute.

The negotiations on exception (b) indicate that the primary intention was the protection of objects within the territory of the state imposing the measure. Similarly, the negotiations on exception (g) show that the main concern was the protection of domestic resources to prevent scarcity rather than outwardly directed modern environmental concerns. While it seems that the primary intention of the drafters was to maintain the ability of the GATT parties to protect certain objects within their

---

[203] Charnovitz (1998), p. 707.
[204] For a more detailed overview on historic state practice see Charnovitz (1998).
[205] Panel Report, *Shrimp Turtle* (1998), No. 3.192.
[206] E.g., Belgium, India, South Africa, the United Kingdom and the United States.

territory, relevant state practice at that time shows that the protection of various objects outside the territory was under certain circumstances well accepted. In sum, the negotiating history on Article XX is therefore not suitable to clarify the obscurity of the exceptions with respect to their geographical scope.[207]

5.3.1.5 Alternative approaches to extraterritoriality

To reiterate, NPA measures, despite their inherent extraterritorial links, do not violate peremptory norms of public international law.[208] Nevertheless, concerns regarding their permissibility under international law still prevail. Due to the obscurity of the particular exceptions on extraterritorial aspects,[209] some scholars have suggested alternative approaches relevant for the legal status of NPA trade measures.

Bartels, for instance, assumes with the panels and the Appellate Body in the *Tuna-Dolphin* and *Shrimp Turtle* disputes that there is indeed a valid question about the jurisdiction of the state adopting a measure with an extraterritorial reach.[210] The basic idea of his proposal is that Article XX ought to be read in the light of the rules of customary international law governing extraterritorial jurisdiction.[211] Since the 1960s, scholars have started to recognize the limits of the traditional rules on jurisdiction, namely, the territorial rule, and sought to find other concepts which would better suit the shrinking and interdependent modern world. Bartels refers here to F. A. Mann's concept of a 'meaningful connection' of a legal nature between the state and the respective subject matter, but he finds that the concept has shortcomings and a lack of precise legal meaning.[212] According to Bartels, 'rules on legislative jurisdiction are a device for balancing the sovereign interests of States in regulating matters of concern to them, regardless of where this concern is located'.[213] In his view, a state can have legislative jurisdiction even in a purely extraterritorial matter, such as human rights in another state.[214] An interest to regulate can also be derived in principle from factual or commercial effects, as opposed to strictly 'legal' interests.[215] Consequently, Bartels proposes a slightly different concept which focuses on the existence of a *legitimate state interest*, and which he sees as the minimum deciding criterion for the exercise

---

[207] In this sense also, Panel Report, *Tuna-Dolphin II* (1994), No. 5.20.
[208] See above section 5.2.2.3.   [209] See, e.g., Bartels (2002), p. 358, fn. 26.
[210] Bartels (2002), p. 386.   [211] Bartels (2002), pp. 353–403.
[212] Bartels (2002), p. 373.   [213] Bartels (2002), p. 374.
[214] Bartels (2002), p. 373.   [215] Bartels (2002), p. 372.

of legislative jurisdiction. A *legitimate state interest* may, for example, be found in cases where WTO members adopt restrictive trade measures designed to promote human rights in another member's territory – especially in cases where that other member has abdicated responsibility.[216] Thus, he does not consider extraterritoriality *per se* a threat to legality of NPA trade measures, because with his concept states can have jurisdiction even in cases of extraterritorial reach, at least as long as the measures conform to other principles relating to proportionality and other qualifying principles.[217] Permissibility of trade measures with an extraterritorial reach depends upon the circumstances or characteristics of the measures. In sum, for Bartels the crucial question under Article XX is whether the state imposing the measure is authorized by customary international law rules on legislative jurisdiction or under a treaty.[218]

Bartels' concept seems indeed to offer adequate answers in cases of measures with an extraterritorial reach. Furthermore, it is characterized by a modern approach to sovereignty, which places emphasis on an open concept of state interests and downsizes the importance of territoriality. In consequence, for example, violations of human rights could constitute valid state interests even in the absence of territorial or otherwise jurisdiction for the victims of human rights violations. Bartels considers it an important advantage that the concept ensures that Article XX neither unduly restricts nor expands the rights of a WTO member under general international law.[219] However, in addition to other concerns explained below, it is this latter aspect which appears to make it difficult to reconcile Bartels' concept with WTO law. Given that WTO members deliberately

---

[216] Bartels (2002), pp. 375, 376. It is important to note, however, that even if the *legitimate state interest* is determined, other principles need to be considered before jurisdiction can be asserted. Among such other principles is most prominently a balancing of state interests in cases of concurring jurisdiction, or the principle of non-intervention (Bartels (2002), pp. 370, 375).

[217] Bartels (2002), pp. 375, 370.

[218] Bartels (2002), pp. 366, 391–403. Bartels establishes three categories, namely: (a) measures authorized by customary international law rules on legislative jurisdiction; (b) measures under an agreement; and (c) counter-measures in response to a violation of a prior obligation. He argues that the WTO is a self-contained regime in as far as trade measures are used as counter measures, because recourse to counter measures under WTO law is allowed only in the specific cases provided for in the covered agreements (Bartels (2002), pp. 394–5). In contrast, measures in the above categories (a) and (b) are taken by way of right, and therefore ought to be permissible, subject to the proviso that they fall within the scope of the particular exceptions and that they are in line with the conditions established in the chapeau.

[219] Bartels (2002), p. 366.

5.3 THE SCOPE OF ARTICLE XX

set up specific rules establishing a multilateral trading system containing trade-related obligations as well as general exceptions, it seems impermissible to let the general rules of public international law on jurisdiction prevail over the text and specific language of Article XX. Bartels seems to assume that the silence of Article XX on the issue creates a legal vacuum that justifies resorting to public international law. However, given that Article XX contains exceptions to GATT obligations, a gap or loophole cannot be asserted, and thus a solution ought to be based on the WTO Agreements as *lex specialis*. Even if applicability of public international law could be assumed, Bartels' approach is based on a very specific concept of legislative jurisdiction. As a result of the above analysis, this work assumes that NPA trade measures do not constitute extraterritorial jurisdiction and, consequently, Bartels' approach is here rejected.

Other related approaches to interpretation of the particular exceptions are based on an additional distinction between measures protecting foreign objects and measures protecting the global commons. Many scholars argue that in cases of shared resources or a shared environment, a sufficient interest of the state taking the measure can be established[220] and an extraterritorial extension of national measures ought to be possible.[221] In the case of protection of the global commons, even the traditional jurisdictional requirement of a territorial link would be fulfilled. This means that in most cases of industrial pollution of air or water, there would be a short- or long-term effect on the global commons. In contrast, if measures are aimed at the protection of purely foreign objects, such as foreign wildlife, no such interest could be established.[222] A similar logic underlies an argument that is particularly relevant for NPA measures linked to social or human rights. Cleveland, for example, argues that over the past 50 years human rights have become matters of international concern and that respective obligations apply *erga omnes*.[223] Also, other scholars consider core human rights 'universal values equivalent to global commons and global public goods' and recommend that they ought to be treated accordingly.[224] Thus, exception (b), the human life and health exception,

---

[220] Gaines (2002), p. 431.
[221] Manzini (1999), p. 844, with respect to environmental protection measures.
[222] Gaines (2002), p. 429.
[223] Cleveland (2002), p. 160. Cleveland is of the view that there is no problem of extraterritorial jurisdiction and argues here based on the contrary assumption that there were indeed a jurisdictional problem.
[224] Cottier, Pauwelyn and Bürgi (2005a), p. 25, point to the risk of disruption and crisis in the case of violations of human rights protected under *ius cogens*.

ought to be interpreted with an evolutionary approach to cover also NPA trade measures aiming at the protection of human rights abroad.

5.3.1.6 Conclusions on the geographical scope

The above analysis shows a mixed record.[225] While there is no clear guidance on the geographical scope from the text of the most relevant exceptions, their language does contain a few indications. The term 'necessary' contained, for instance, in exception (b) establishes a requirement of a minimum causal means–end relationship, which could be interpreted to imply that only measures protecting objects and aiming at behaviour within the jurisdiction of a WTO member are justifiable. This would mean that NPA trade measures, the effectiveness of which is doubtful, such as NPA measures aimed at the protection of the health of workers abroad, would be excluded from justification under exception (b). While this interpretation seems to find confirmation in the negotiating history, it is contradicted by earlier relevant state practice. Several examples, such as the prohibition of slavery, show that measures protecting life and health abroad were accepted at the time. As regards exception (g), the negotiating history shows that the predominant concern during negotiations was the protection of domestic resources, while the record of relevant state practice at the time includes contrasting evidence, such as the acceptance of measures clearly directed at the protection of foreign objects. In this case, the weaker requirements in terms of a means–end relationship do not seem to exclude NPA trade measures with an extraterritorial reach. The additional requirement of even-handed measures restricting domestic consumption or production, however, renders those NPA measures that are exclusively aimed at the protection of extraterritorial natural resources unjustifiable. In contrast, the important group of NPA measures aimed at the protection of shared resources, even if linked to foreign objects, seems to be covered by the geographical scope of exception (g).

The general objective and purpose of Article XX is to clarify that the various trade obligations established with the GATT do not hinder the pursuit of the listed public policies.[226] The objective and purpose of the general exceptions seem to imply quite clearly that the ability of nation-states to adopt and enforce the listed policies ought to remain unaffected

---

[225] A similar result has been found by Cleveland (2002), p. 158, with a focus on measures targeting foreign human rights conduct.

[226] With respect to exception (g), this is the often quoted interpretation of the *Canada – Herring* Panel (1988), p. 12, on the purpose of the inclusion of this exception in the GATT.

by the agreements and thus prevails over possibly contrasting GATT obligations. Whether or not these public policies are limited to internal values, however, is not addressed. Therefore, it seems that the relevance of the substance of the public policies outweighs questions of geographical location.

In sum, neither the permissibility of measures with extraterritorial aspects nor a clear limitation of the geographical scope of the particular exceptions has been established. According to the basic rules on interpretation analysed above, there is no need to interpret exceptions restrictively. Given these circumstances, it would be wrong to reduce the issue of the geographical scope to a simple question of 'yes' or 'no'.

It is here suggested that the justification of measures should be assessed in an unbiased way. The above analysis shows that the focus of the assessment needs to shift from questions of geography to the crucial standards under Article XX, most importantly to the means-end relationship between measure and ultimate policy purpose. The location of objects of protection and targeted behaviour plays a subordinated role within the context of the specific requirements contained in the particular exceptions. These requirements, such as the means-end relationship in exception (b) and the requirement of even-handed domestic restrictions in exception (g), will limit the range of justifiable NPA measures considerably: in consequence of these requirements, NPA trade measures motivated by the protection of extraterritorial objects or values, such as human life and health, or shared resources, such as migratory species, will often fail to meet the specific requirements, if the effects of the measure must be expected to be limited to trade effects. Given that the burden of proof is on the WTO member invoking the exception, it will often be difficult even to provisionally justify NPA trade measures protecting objects located beyond the territory of the state imposing the measure. Nevertheless, NPA measures carefully designed and actually suitable to achieve a certain degree of protection concerning the listed policies, even if directed at behaviour abroad, are in principle justifiable – no matter where the protected objects are located.

5.3.2 *Subject coverage of the particular exceptions*

In addition to the requirements detailed above, measures are justifiable under the general exceptions only if they relate to a subject matter within the range of policies listed in Article XX. The limitation in terms of subject matter is relevant to all measures seeking justification and constitutes an additional obstacle to the justification of NPA measures. Since NPA measures are mostly adopted for reasons of public policy, the following sections focus on limitations in terms of subject matter and on policies so far not listed explicitly.

5.3.2.1 Exclusivity of listed policies

Article XX is generally viewed as a limited and conditional exception to GATT obligations,[227] and, consequently, the particular exceptions are seen as a closed list of policies recognized to override GATT obligations.[228] Subject coverage under one or another of the public policies listed in paragraphs (a)–(j) is the first hurdle for justification under the general exceptions.[229] Since the general exceptions can be seen as an important line of demarcation between policy space for WTO members and their obligations owed to other WTO members, the small number of policies and interests listed in Article XX are indeed suitable to limit the tools available to WTO members for an implementation of public policies. An important example is environmental protection, a policy field nowadays considered highly important, but that is not mentioned explicitly in Article XX. In consequence, measures adopted in order to implement environmental policies would not be justifiable under the general exceptions, unless they relate to any of the objects of protection listed in Article XX. Also, other policies which are deemed legitimate by many WTO members, such as policies in the realm of culture, animal protection, human rights, labour rights or protection of minorities, have not been included in the list of particular exceptions. In consequence, corresponding protection policies may not include measures that restrict trade in violation of the GATT.[230]

The adjudicatory bodies do not have the power to accept exceptions beyond those listed in paragraphs (a)–(j). Doing so would clearly exceed the boundaries of interpretation and competence of the DSB, and ultimately result in illicit law-making. However, the text of the particular

---

[227] Prevailing case law since Panel Report, *US – Section 337* (1989), No. 5.9; Panel Report, *Tuna-Dolphin I* (1991), No. 5.22; Appellate Body Report, *Shrimp Turtle* (1998), No. 157, cf., e.g., van Calster (2000), p. 71.

[228] Cho (2003), p. 34; Marceau (2002), p. 808.

[229] Prevailing case law since the Appellate Body in the *Shrimp Turtle* dispute confirmed the method developed in *US – Gasoline* (1996) that provisional justification under the particular exceptions is the first step in applying Article XX. Appellate Body Report, *Shrimp Turtle* (1998), Nos. 118 *et seq.*

[230] See also van den Bossche, Schrijver and Faber (2007), p. 91, fn. 277, who point out that until today there has hardly been any attempt at WTO level to amend the text of Article XX with a view to include additional public policies to the listed exceptions.

exceptions has mostly been drafted in a very concise and therefore broad way using generic rather than specific terms. Since, as detailed above, the maxim of restrictive interpretation is to be rejected and generic terms especially require an evolutionary approach to interpretation, the language of the particular exception will sometimes allow interpreting Article XX to cover public policies, although not explicitly listed in the particular exceptions.

5.3.2.2   Coverage of other policies

While some social concerns are mentioned in one or another of the particular exceptions, others are not. There are a number of policies the legitimacy of which is widely acknowledged, but that are not explicitly included in Article XX. Some of these, including the respective implementing measures, have been considered nevertheless to fall within the scope of the general exceptions. The question of where subject coverage of the particular exceptions begins and where it ends, especially with respect to policies transposed with NPA measures, is addressed in the following sections.

5.3.2.2.1   Protection of the environment

As early as 1991 Charnovitz purported that with a few exceptions Article XX includes environmental policies in general, and based this view on both a textual and a historical interpretation.[231] In the meantime, his view has gained recognition, and it has to some extent been confirmed by more recent reports of the Appellate Body. On different occasions, panels and the Appellate Body interpreted exception (g) concerning exhaustible natural resources to be sufficiently expansive to comprise measures aimed at the protection of clean air[232] and living resources, such as sea turtles, fish stock and dolphins.[233] The Appellate Body, in commenting on the interpretation of the general exceptions, stated that the term 'exhaustible natural resources' should be read in the light of 'contemporary concerns of the community of nations about the protection and conservation of *the*

---

[231] Charnovitz (1991), pp. 37–55.
[232] Panel Report, *US – Gasoline* (1996), at Nos. 6.36–6.37. The qualification of clean air as an exhaustible natural resource was not appealed explicitly (cf. the sections on preliminary questions in the Appellate Body report, *US – Gasoline* (1996), pp. 11–12), but the Appellate Body referred to this finding on various occasions and thus seems to support it (see, e.g., *US – Gasoline* (1996), pp. 14–22; *Shrimp Turtle* (1998), No. 136.
[233] Appellate Body Report, *Shrimp Turtle* (1998), at Nos. 128–131; also Panels in *Canada – Herring* (1988), No. 4.4; and *Tuna-Dolphin I* (1991), No. 5.13.

environment.[234] This statement is noteworthy. Although the text of exception (g) does not even mention the term 'environment', the Appellate Body recognizes the necessity of taking into account contemporary concerns relating to its protection and conservation. While the Appellate Body's interpretation may ultimately be in line with the intentions of some of the negotiators of the GATT 1947,[235] it made clear that interpretation is by no means limited by the original intentions, but that interpretation requires exploring the ordinary meaning of terms from a modern perspective of 'contemporary concerns'. In this sense, the Appellate Body asserted an evolutionary approach to interpretation.[236] It went as far as mentioning concerns about the 'protection' of the environment, in addition to concerns about 'conservation', a term that is much closer to the core idea of the protection of natural resources laid down in exception (g). However, it remains to be seen which aspects and applications of environmental protection could fall under this exception. Given the above-mentioned finding, that the protection of clean air is also covered by exception (g),[237] there is a real possibility that this exception will become an almost general environmental exception. NPA trade measures supplementing national policies that are based on a life-cycle analysis of products including air emissions, for instance, might well be covered by exception (g). Also, if clean air is considered an exhaustible resource, then there would be no reason to exclude clean water and soil. In this respect, the objective approach to interpretation is highly relevant: it is ultimately the existence of international treaties and other documents that give meaning to the term 'exhaustible natural resources' and thus determine the scope of exception (g). Given the above finding that interpretation of the covered

---

[234] Appellate Body Report, *Shrimp Turtle* (1998), No. 129 (emphasis added).
[235] E.g., the Legal Drafting Committee used the term 'exhaustible natural resources' in a wide sense comprising 'fisheries or wild life or other exhaustible natural resources', albeit under the Intergovernmental Commodity Arrangements chapter (United Nations Economic and Social Council, Second Session of the Preparatory Committee on the International Conference on Trade and Employment, E/PC/T/147, of 4 August 1947, pp. 29–30). The environmental connotation of exception (g) is also indicated because the negotiators rejected a proposal by New Zealand and Brazil that the term 'or other' should be included before 'resources'. The delegate had explained that the exception should not be limited to natural resources, but apparently his view did not prevail (ECOSOC, Preparatory Committee on the International Conference on Trade and Employment, E/PC/T/C.II/54/Rev.1, of 28 November 1946, p. 38, and E/PC/T/C.II/50, of 13 November 1946, p. 6). For more details on the negotiating history see Charnovitz (1991), pp. 43–47.
[236] See above at section 5.1.2.2.   [237] See above fn. 232.

agreements is by its very nature uniform, ratification of MEAs by WTO members is not relevant as such for the scope of Article XX. Therefore, MEAs can be highly relevant as evidence for the ordinary meaning of the term 'exhaustible natural resources'.[238]

In addition to subject matter, the low threshold regarding the relationship between measure and policy goal provided for in exception (g), described with a 'primarily aimed at' test and the characterization as a 'close and genuine' or 'reasonable' relationship, also facilitates provisional justification when it comes to environmental measures.[239] Hence, the importance which the Appellate Body ascribed to exception (g) with respect to the environment means that the provision is of crucial relevance for solving disputes involving trade and environmental policies in general.[240] The broad interpretation of exception (g) applied by the Appellate Body, namely, the combination of the evolutionary interpretation of the term 'exhaustible natural resources' and the low requirements for a means–end relationship, implies considerable deference to national policy-makers in choosing tools in order to implement environmental policies.

In sum, it is a truism that the drafters of exception (g) did not have modern environmental policies in mind. Nevertheless, the approach of an evolutionary and objective interpretation of the notion 'exhaustible natural resources' implies considerable potential for a wide range of environmental NPA measures to be provisionally justified under exception (g). Nevertheless, a unilateral approach might still face problems when it comes to the requirements established by the chapeau.[241] In this case, it would depend on the precise requirements of the chapeau, as discussed in more detail below,[242] whether or not justification of specific environmental measures could be successful.

5.3.2.2.2 Human rights and labour standards

The relationship between trade and human rights is highly complex.[243] The question of whether trade sanctions for the protection of human or social rights are in principle justifiable under the general exceptions is particularly controversial. None of the particular exceptions in Article

---

[238] See above section 5.1.1.4.
[239] See for a more detailed analysis McRae (2000), pp. 219–36.
[240] McRae (2000), p. 227.   [241] McRae (2000), p. 234, Ginzky (1999), p. 217.
[242] See below section 5.4.
[243] For an overview of the relationship between both fields see Cottier (2002), pp. 111–32.

XX contains an explicit reference to human or social rights beyond the protection of human life or health in exception (b). As opposed to the interpretation of exception (g) with respect to environmental measures, so far exception (b) has not been interpreted to cover policies not explicitly included in the text. Nevertheless, human rights activists regard bans on the importation of products or the suspension of trade concessions as important tools in the fight against human rights violations. Hence, there are concerns that if the GATT were understood to prohibit such measures, one of the few available tools for the protection and promotion of human rights would be lost, and human rights norms would be rendered relatively toothless.[244] Furthermore, in consequence of such an interpretation the GATT might under certain circumstances require WTO members to trade with gross human rights violators.[245] In addition to trade measures for the protection of human rights, some consider also trade measures promoting core labour rights and standards to be legitimate or even advisable.[246]

Some scholars argue that the language of some of the particular exceptions as they stand could support an interpretation that would allow the justification of other legitimate policies based on the existing exceptions. Similar to the evolutionary interpretation of exception (g) with respect to current concerns relating to the environment, so also could exceptions (a) and (b) be interpreted in the light of current concerns relating to human rights and similar social problems.[247] Indeed, since Article XX(b) explicitly mentions human health as an object of protection, it could be interpreted as embracing all measures implementing policies preventing physical harm to humans, such as those addressing genocide, summary executions, disappearances, crimes against humanity or the execution of juveniles, as well as forced labour and slave trade, because of slavery's denial of personhood.[248] Other human rights concerns and labour

---

[244] Vázquez (2003), p. 808, 809.   [245] Cleveland (2002), p. 137.
[246] There is no internationally accepted definition on the body of rights forming core labour rights. Nevertheless, in spite of its rather promotional character, the 1998 Declaration on Fundamental Principles and Rights at Work (done at the 86th Session, Geneva, 18 June 1998) adopted by the International Labour Organization is widely seen as evidence for an international consensus on the validity of certain international core labour rights. The declaration embraces rights in four areas: (1) freedom of association and collective bargaining; (2) the elimination of forced and compulsory labour; (3) the abolition of child labour; and (4) the elimination of discrimination at the workplace.
[247] Cf. Lopez-Hurtado (2002), p. 730; also Petersmann (2005a), p. 58, with respect to social rights. For more on the scope of exception (a) in this respect see below at section 5.3.3.1.
[248] Cleveland (2002), p. 162.

rights, however, might be within the scope of the moral exception, as will be detailed below, or to some extent within the security exceptions laid down in Article XXI. The latter exception is most attractive because it is suggested that national determinations of security interests are entitled to greater deference than granted under Article XX. Article XXI could be relevant for measures relating to military technology, such as the export of weapons or military technology, regardless of whether the motivation for the measure is to prevent the use of such weapons by a state, or to punish a state for other human rights violations.

With respect to core labour standards, however, the division of powers between the ILO and the WTO and other statements expressed in a number of documents seem to constitute evidence of a general reluctance to take the observance of labour standards into consideration. Especially the ILO Declaration on Fundamental Principles and Rights at Work is of importance to international trade, because its adoption needs to be seen against the backdrop of the 1996 Singapore Ministerial Declaration of the WTO. With the Ministerial Declaration, the representatives of WTO members identified the ILO as the competent body for labour standards. The represented governments affirmed that they promote these standards in general, but they also stressed that they 'reject the use of labour standards for protectionist purposes', and agreed 'that the comparative advantage of countries, particularly low-wage developing countries, must in no way be put into question'.[249] Thus, the declaration arguably implies that trade measures linked to core labour standards are not considered permissible. Also, the choice of rights constituting core labour rights under the ILO Declaration seems to be an attempt 'to lessen the accusation of protectionism and the erosion of comparative advantage', since the rights identified are process-oriented rather than outcome-oriented, and they basically aim at promoting freedom of choice and contract.[250]

Regardless of which interpretation of Article XX(b) in terms of subject coverage is adopted, the stumbling block for justification of NPA measures protecting human rights within the territories of other WTO members is ultimately the necessity requirement. According to the currently prevailing interpretation, necessity requires a certain effectiveness of the measure and a least-trade restrictiveness test. In cases where the objects of protection are located abroad, fulfilment of both requirements

---

[249] WTO Singapore Ministerial 1996: Ministerial Declaration, WT/MIN(96)/DEC, 18 December 1996, at No. 4
[250] McCrudden and Davies (2000), p. 51.

is doubtful, and justification of respective NPA measures would be very difficult. Therefore, some scholars suggest *de lege ferenda* to amend the general exceptions to cover also policies aiming at social or human rights or other social achievements requiring protection, and invoke exception (e) relating to the products of prison labour as a good example,[251] while others consider the potential of the moral exception sufficient.

5.3.2.3 Summary

Due to the objective and evolutionary approach to interpretation adopted by the adjudicatory bodies, exception (g) provides some flexibility regarding the coverage of subject matters that is relevant for NPA measures promoting environmental objectives as one of the most important type of NPA measures. Although it would be premature to consider exception (g) a general environmental exception, it is interpreted to cover measures aiming at the protection of some of the most important features of the global environment, namely, clean air. Therefore, the language of exception (g) as it stands combined with the low requirements regarding the means–end relationship have the potential to justify even NPA trade measures that aim at protecting the environment beyond the imposing state's borders. In contrast, justification of NPA measures aimed at the protection of human or social rights faces considerable difficulties arising from the limited subject coverage of the particular exceptions and from the necessity requirements stipulated in the highly relevant exception (b). Therefore, the potential for justification of human rights NPA measures aimed at protection abroad must be considered low.

5.3.3 Special consideration of the public morals exception

This section analyses the scope of the moral exception in Article XX(a), and finds it to be unlimited both in terms of geographical scope and subject matter. It may well be due to the seeming boundlessness of the moral exception, that this exception has so far hardly played any role in dispute settlement. Being aware of the risk of its abuse for protectionism, some scholars acknowledge the under-achieved potential of the moral exception for a wider range of public concerns.[252] Given the limits of the other exceptions and given that NPA measures are arguably often taken for moral reasons, the moral exception is highly relevant for the justification

---

[251] E.g., Stoll and Schorkopf (2002), pp. 257–8.
[252] Cottier and Oesch (2005), pp. 446–7

of NPA trade measures. Exception (a) offers justification for measures 'necessary to protect public morals'. Since the notion 'public morals' is vague, it is necessary to approach the determination of the exception's scope in several steps. The following sections discuss the range of subject matters to which measures under this exception can possibly relate and the perspective, or rather the standards, crucial for the determination of what is to be considered 'moral'. In other words, one needs to determine what kind of morals are to be covered and whose perspective is relevant.[253] Section 5.3.3.3 then analyses the geographical scope of exception (a).

5.3.3.1 Open subject coverage

The object of protection of exception (a) is succinctly framed as 'public morals'. According to a common definition, 'public morals' refer to 'standards of right and wrong conduct maintained by or on behalf of a community or nation'.[254] Thus, public morals are related to right and wrong conduct without, however, delimiting in any way the subject or circumstances in which the conduct at issue occurs. Due to the vague language, the value of textual interpretation for a determination of the scope of exception (a) is limited. The exception implies the existence of a violation of certain moral standards without, however, delimiting violations in terms of subject matter. This means, that measures justified by the public morals exception can potentially relate to any subject matter, whether of a social, cultural, religious, economic or other nature, as long as there are moral standards on the matter and related conduct.

This special characteristic, a distinction between a fixed object of protection, namely, public morals, on the one hand, and variable violations, which can relate to different subjects, on the other hand, distinguishes the moral exception from other particular exceptions in Article XX. Most other exceptions relate to specific objects of protection, such as life and health, gold and silver, or products made from prison labour, which at the same time determine also the nature of the violation.[255] For example, one of the objects of protection in exception (b) is animal health. Thus, measures aimed at the prevention of activities affecting animal health fall into the scope of exception (b). The distinction between a fixed object of protection, on the one hand, and variable threats, on the other, in the case of

---

[253] See also Charnovitz (1998), pp. 694, 700.
[254] Panel Report, *US – Gambling* (2004), No. 6.465.
[255] The only other exception with a broad subject coverage is exception (d), which covers measures to secure compliance with all 'laws or regulations not inconsistent with the provisions' of the GATT.

the moral exception implies an open-ended subject coverage. The objects of protection are standards of right and wrong. However, measures seeking to prevent abuse of children could as well fall into the scope of exception (a) as measures seeking to prevent blasphemy or measures aimed at the protection of minorities and their customs and traditions.

The first panel ever to be confronted with an application of the moral exception in Article XX(a), the panel in *China – Audiovisual Entertainment Products*, did not engage in an in-depth analysis of the scope of this exception, since the complainant had not contested China's assertion that an importation of the products at issue could have a negative impact on public morals in China.[256] The panel and Appellate Body in *US – Gambling*, in contrast, discussed the scope of the moral exception contained in GATS Article XIV(a) with respect to a number of measures restricting the cross-border supply of gambling and betting services. Compared with the GATT moral exception, the corresponding exception contained in the GATS also comprises measures necessary to 'maintain public order'. However, since the remainder of the GATS language is identical to the moral exception in GATT Article XX(a),[257] the elaborations are also pertinent to interpretation of the latter.[258] The *US – Gambling* panel interpreted the term 'public morals' based on the above dictionary definition relating to standards of right and wrong,[259] and stated that these can 'vary in time and space, depending upon a range of factors, including prevailing social, cultural, ethical and religious values'.[260] It is interesting to see how the panel dealt with the openness of this concept and how it applied it to the facts of the case. Having defined the concept, the panel proceeded to examine whether the concerns invoked by the defendant, namely, the prevention of underage gambling and the protection of pathological gamblers, relates to 'public morals', while the prevention of money laundering and fraud schemes could rather relate to the concept of 'public order'. Instead of considering theoretical arguments based on the definition developed by the panel, the panel was content to consider earlier and existing state practice, and found that import prohibitions on publicity and tickets for lotteries or gambling

---

[256] Panel Report, *China – Audiovisual Entertainment Products* (2009), No. 7.762. In consequence, the Panel focused on the question of whether or not the Chinese regulations and measures were necessary.

[257] GATT Article XX(a) as well as GATS Article XIV(a) refer to measures 'necessary to protect public morals'.

[258] Panel Report, *China – Audiovisual Entertainment Products* (2009), No. 7.758.

[259] Panel Report, *US – Gambling* (2004), No. 6.465.

[260] Panel Report, *US – Gambling* (2004), No. 6.465.

have been maintained for reasons of public morals by different WTO members. It backed up this evidence by referring to the historic negotiations of 1927, during which the issue of lottery tickets had also been discussed with respect to public morals.[261] In light of this evidence, the panel concluded that the measures at issue could fall within the scope of the GATS moral exception,[262] a finding later upheld by the Appellate Body.[263] The simple reference to unilateral state practice and even to deliberations during negotiations for an international agreement preceding the GATT, although appearing random as evidence, may have been justified by the need to give meaning to the sheer open-endedness of the 'public morals' exception. It can be expected that panels and the Appellate Body will proceed likewise in determining the scope of the moral exception in future cases. State practice with respect to social concerns, as well as international deliberations during negotiations of trade agreements can be expected to play a role. Also, the fact that national measures historically intended to protect both the morals of their own population, as well as the welfare of potential victims abroad,[264] might become relevant.

The panel in US – Gambling also acknowledged that the content of the public morals concept can vary in time.[265] This finding is in line with the Appellate Body in Shrimp Turtle, which stressed the need to interpret GATT provisions, especially those using generic terms, in 'light of contemporary concerns'.[266] The term 'public morals' is indeed an open concept, that requires by its very nature a constant re-determination of its meaning, which depends on views and philosophies of an ever changing society, and is therefore a prime example for the idea of evolutionary interpretation.[267] Against this backdrop, it seems adequate to argue that measures protecting particular social and human concerns other than those already reflected in the language of Article XX(b)–(j) can fall within the scope of exception (a).[268] This is certainly true for a number of human

---

[261] Panel Report, US – Gambling (2004), Nos. 6.471–6.472.
[262] Panel Report, US – Gambling (2004), No. 6.474.
[263] Appellate Body Report, US – Gambling (2005), p. 299. Interestingly, the Appellate Body was content with the finding that the measures fall 'within the scope of "public morals" and/or "public order"', thus implying that both concepts are very similar and may have a large overlap.
[264] Charnovitz (1998), p. 714.   [265] Panel Report, US – Gambling (2004), No. 6.461.
[266] Above section 5.1.2.2.
[267] In this sense also, Feddersen (2002), pp. 240–2; Howse and Trebilcock (2005), p. 290.
[268] Charnovitz concludes that the moral exception could cover the leg-hold trap regulation and trade bans on products made by indentured children, if the requirements of the chapeau were met. Charnovitz (1998), pp. 736–42.

rights concerns that do not involve physical harm and would thus fall outside the scope of exception (b). Based on the ordinary meaning of the concept, it seems today imperative to include fundamental rights in the core meaning of public morals, since public morality cannot be separated from concerns for human personhood, dignity and capacity reflected in fundamental rights.[269] In addition to human rights in general, it has also been argued that the moral exception includes labour rights[270] and, consequently, constitutes a social clause as it stands.[271] Furthermore, public morals could also be interpreted to embrace obligations *erga omnes*, such as the right to property and prohibitions against religious and gender discrimination or the overthrow of democracy.[272] Also other aspects, such as animal welfare, for example, could be covered by the variable meaning of public morals in as far as it is not covered by the health exception (b).[273]

Given the limits of a textual interpretation of exception (a), state practice has been considered important by the adjudicatory bodies in exploring subjects or circumstances relevant to this exception. On the one hand, moral justifications are relevant for prohibitions of imports of products which are considered immoral as such, or because of certain characteristics. Current examples for such measures can be derived from the US Tariff Act, which prohibits importation of obscene representations or materials, lottery tickets,[274] or cat and dog fur.[275] On the other hand, exception (a) is also highly relevant to NPA trade measures. As opposed to the large group of trade measures linked to physical characteristics, the motivation for linking trade measures to NPAs will more often than

---

[269] Howse and Trebilcock (2005), p. 290, for a consideration of at least a sub-set of human rights under exception (a); Garcia (1999), text before fn. 120. Against an attempt 'to shoehorn the international law of human rights' into the concept of public morals Vázquez (2003), p. 827.

[270] Howse and Trebilcock (2005), p. 290.   [271] Petersmann (2005a), p. 58.

[272] Cleveland (2002), p. 162.   [273] Winter (2003), p. 124.

[274] US Tariff Act of 1930, 19 USCA § 1305.

[275] US Tariff Act of 1930, 19 USCA § 1308, introduced by the Dog and Cat Protection Act, enacted on 9 November 2000. Congress expressed its multiple purposes in finding that: '(6) The methods of housing, transporting, and slaughtering dogs and cats for fur production are generally unregulated and inhumane. (7) The trade of dog and cat fur products is ethically and aesthetically abhorrent to United States citizens. Consumers in the United States have a right to know if products offered for sale contain dog or cat fur and to ensure that they are not unwitting participants in this gruesome trade. (8) Persons who engage in the sale of dog or cat fur products, including the fraudulent trade practices identified above, gain an unfair competitive advantage over persons who engage in legitimate trade in apparel, toys, and other products, and derive an unfair benefit from consumers who buy their products.' (Pub.L. 106–476, Title I, § 1442, 9 November 2000, 114 Stat. 2163).

not have a moral component. For example, in the European Union a ban prohibits importation of pelts of certain wild animal species unless they originate in countries which have been certified as prohibiting the use of so-called leghold traps, or where the methods used conform to international 'humane trapping standards'.[276] Also the prohibition by penal sanction of the importation of products produced in a foreign country by forced, convict or indentured labour, including forced or indentured child labour by the United States is based on moral reasons.[277]

In sum, the concept of public morals is in principle open-ended regarding its substantive content and subject coverage, provided there are respective standards that determine right and wrong conduct.

5.3.3.2 Standards of right and wrong

The objects of protection of exception (a), public morals, are based on ethical values, which depend upon the society or community defining and acknowledging them. Given that WTO membership includes numerous societies and communities, it is questionable which standards of right and wrong apply. Since the drafters avoided a language which would have clarified whose standards of right and wrong conduct, or whose public morals, are relevant, a subjective as well as an objective meaning of the term comes into consideration. It could be argued, on the one hand, that the content of the concept has been entirely left up to each of the states that are parties to the GATT 1947. Based on this interpretation, for instance, measures protecting 'national' moral standards, or even the moral standards of a certain community within a WTO member state, could be justified under the moral exception. On the other hand, the language of the moral exception could also be interpreted from a more objective point of view. It could be argued that in order to avoid giving too much deference to the state invoking the moral exception, the material content of the 'public morals' concept needs to be determined from the perspective of WTO membership as a whole. The danger of a random interpretation and abuse by WTO members would require a more objective or even international approach. Public morals for the purposes of Article XX would then be limited to public morals accepted at a global level or at the level of WTO membership as a whole.

---

[276] Council Regulation (EEC) No. 3254/91, Article 3:1 (OJ L 308, 9.11.1991, p. 1). An 'Agreement on international humane trapping standards' between the European Community, Canada and the Russian Federation was signed later on and has so far been ratified by Canada and the EU.
[277] US Tariff Act of 1930, 19 USCA § 1307, see also fn. 275.

In this respect, the *US – Gambling* panel considered that the meaning of the concept can vary not only in time but also in space.[278] The panel stated:

> Members should be given some scope to define and apply for themselves the concepts of 'public morals' and 'public order' in their respective territories, according to their own systems and scales of values.[279]

This statement implies that public morals may differ from one society or nation to another. However, the open-endedness of subject matter stated in the previous section, in combination with a complete deference to WTO members of the determination of standards seems to imply the danger that exception (a) could constitute an uncontrollable catch-all exception that would allow abuses by WTO members.

Feddersen[280] structures application of the moral exception by suggesting a distinction between a core meaning and a variable meaning of public morals. Under this distinction, the core material content of the term 'public morals' is universal, and it is based on an international consensus on the validity of certain values. For example, Feddersen sees a historical consensus that products with an obscene character fall within the scope of public morals.[281] The core material content can be derived from a review of international agreements with universal standing. In as far as such agreements contain consensus on particular norms and ethical values, they can be regarded as substantiation of the vague term 'public morals'. In addition to the core material content, there is also a variable meaning. The variable material content embraces those values which differ from one state or society to another. It reflects the cultural, social and political diversity of the members. The core meaning and the variable meaning are an expression of the core theme of the GATT, namely, the need for a uniform interpretation and application of GATT provisions, on the one hand, and the recognition of certain legitimate national policies which override GATT obligations, on the other. For this reason, interpretation of the moral exception can neither be interpreted entirely based on the idea of national sovereignty, nor on the need to uniformity. Rather, interpretation must consider both themes.[282]

Under Feddersen's approach, both the core and the variable moral standards can fall into the scope of the moral exception. Given that the WTO is an organization with a large membership and, consequently,

---

[278] Panel Report, *US – Gambling* (2004), No. 6.461.
[279] Panel Report, *US – Gambling* (2004), No. 6.461.
[280] Feddersen (2002), pp. 249–74. See also Feddersen (1998).
[281] Feddersen (2002), p. 260. [282] Feddersen (2002), p. 252.

incorporates great regulatory diversity, it is imperative that the variable meaning of the concept is also covered by exception (a). The distinction between both categories is nevertheless useful for the application of the moral exception, for example, as regards the evidence for the existence of certain moral standards that are disturbed. In the case of the core meaning of public morals, the existence of standards will mostly be self-evident or can be substantiated by reference to relevant international documents. Even some of the particular exceptions contained in Article XX, particularly sub-paragraphs (b) and (g), may be regarded as evidence for the existence of core moral standards comprising the protection of life and health of humans and animals. In contrast, the existence of variable standards of public morals would need to be assessed more carefully. The existence of national policies, respective provisions in the constitution or public laws or relevant regional international documents must be scrutinized in order to verify the moral standards that have been invoked.[283] Furthermore, a review of the facts of each dispute would also be required in order to delimit the member's assessment space.[284]

5.3.3.3 The geographical scope

It is unclear whether the moral exception may be invoked for measures linked to NPAs located beyond the imposing WTO member's territory. The twofold nature of exception (a), namely, the distinction between object of protection, on the one hand, and violating behaviour, on the other, requires that the analysis of the geographical scope also distinguishes between both. First, the question arises where the object of protection, namely, the threatened public morals, must be located in order for measures to be covered by exception (a). Second, the same question needs to be discussed with respect to the location of the violating behaviour.

5.3.3.3.1 Location of moral standards

To reiterate, morals are closely related to scales of values, which may change over time, and which may differ from one society or even from one person to another. From this perspective, exception (a) incorporates

---

[283] In his comment on the *US – Gambling* Panel Report, Diebold suggests that in order to identify bad faith on the part of the country invoking the exception, the WTO adjudicatory bodies ought to verify whether the number of people affected by the measure is sufficient (Diebold (2008), pp. 68, 74). However, Diebold also points out that relating to quantitative evidence alone cannot bring about adequate results, e.g., if minorities are concerned (p. 61).

[284] Feddersen (2002), p. 263.

plurality and diversity among WTO members into the multilateral trading system. Feddersen therefore concludes that moral standards are geographically limited by their very nature. In his view, only a given society is able to determine authoritatively its public morals. Due to this exclusive ability of a society to determine its own public morals, there is a need for deference to national authorities. The flip side of this ability is, however, that a society is unable to assess the variable meaning of other societies' public morals. Feddersen argues that it is inherent to the concept of variable public morals that they cannot be assessed from outside. He concludes, therefore, that only measures taken to protect internal or domestic public morals can possibly be justified under sub-paragraph (a).[285]

Given the subjective element inherent to the idea of morals, Feddersen's view is convincing. In consequence of this aspect of the nature of public morals, a distinction is necessary. In as far as the core meaning of public morals is concerned the existence of respective moral standards within the state imposing the measures does not require proof. Since the core meaning of the term 'public morals' is identical for WTO membership as a whole, a violation of core standards implies the disturbance of internal and external public morals to the same degree. The core meaning of public morals could be compared with the global commons: in as far as the global commons are threatened the interests of every state are affected. If the core meaning of public morals is disturbed, the disturbance necessarily extends to any society in the world. This means that the object of protection is global in the case of core moral standards, and that problems of extraterritoriality regarding the object of protection cannot possibly arise. In contrast, disturbances of variable public morals are limited to the society that has adopted such standards for itself. Thus, a problematic extraterritorial reach arises only if a country adopts measures in order to protect the variable public morals in other countries – a situation, however, not likely to occur.

5.3.3.3.2 Location of the threat

Exception (a) implies also the existence of a risk for or violation of public morals. Often, the violation of the moral standard will take place inside the state in which the respective moral standard exists. An example is the importation of alcohol or obscene material into a country that prohibits such products. In this case, the violating conduct, namely, distribu-

---

[285] Feddersen (2002), pp. 266, 267.

tion of such material, occurs within the state where the respective moral standards exist. Hence, no problem of interlocality arises.

It is, however, questionable if measures linked to conduct or circumstances abroad are justifiable in cases where the conduct is unacceptable according to domestic public morals. Feddersen answers this question in the affirmative, albeit with a specific explanation. He argues that in cases where a product has been produced in an offensive way in a foreign country, the production process may have rendered the product obscene.[286] Following his reasoning, the product that has been rendered obscene would itself be considered a violation of domestic moral standards. Thus, the NPA trade measure would actually protect domestic morals from a violation through domestic distribution of an obscene product. Therefore, in line with his thinking, even in the case of abhorred production methods abroad, domestic public morals would be threatened by an object within the territory of the state adopting the measures. Feddersen's argument, however, over-stretches the concept of public morals. It is ultimately not the product, but the circumstances of its production that are not acceptable from a moral point of view. If not only the condemned activity or circumstances are regarded as a violation of moral standards, but also related activities or objects, then exception (a) would indeed become a non-reviewable catch-all exception.

Justifiability of NPA trade measures linked to circumstances abroad can also be explained with the specific nature of public morals. Public morals as such are not confined to national borders. They can be affected no matter where and how the violating conduct or circumstances take place. For example, a situation in country A could well disturb the public morals existing within country B. In this respect, it is important not to confuse a violation of public morals of a society with questions of jurisdiction, which are crucial, for example, in criminal matters. If violence towards children, for example, is disapproved of in a certain society, this conduct is disapproved of no matter whether it occurs at home or in a foreign country. Enslaving adults or children in one country violates public morals of societies all over the world. While abhorrence of violence towards children forms part of core moral values that are globally valid, the nature of public morals requires that the same applies likewise in the case of variable public morals. For example, if a society considers cruelty towards animals an offence against its public morals, this society will disapprove of any such cruelty regardless of where it occurs and regardless of the nationality of

---

[286] Feddersen (2002), p. 260.

the persons involved. Therefore, due to the nature of moral standards, the location of behaviour which violates public morals is entirely irrelevant for the existence of a violation of domestic public morals.[287]

5.3.3.3.3 Preliminary conclusions

The geographical scope of exception (a) is, on the one hand, determined by the object of protection, namely, domestic public morals. Any WTO member is entitled to adopt and justify measures necessary for the protection of the moral standards of its population and society, no matter whether globally valid core public morals or variable public morals are concerned. However, it would be impermissible to adopt measures in order to protect the moral standards valid in other societies. In the case of a threat to foreign public morals, measures can be justifiable only if domestic morals are also disturbed by those extraterritorial facts.[288] On the other hand, the geographical scope is determined by the violating conduct. But due to the non-physical nature of public morals, the location of the violating conduct or circumstances is irrelevant.[289] Problems due to a possible extraterritorial reach therefore can arise only with respect to the location of the protected public morals, while the location of the violation is irrelevant.[290] Thus, concluding from the subject matter covered by exception (a), NPA measures taken for the protection of domestic public morals may indeed relate to conduct outside the adopting state's territory.

5.3.3.4 Requirements relating to the means–end relationship

As shown above with respect to the health exception in sub-paragraph (b), causal connection requirements are capable of excluding measures

---

[287] Also Feddersen (2002), who argues that there would be no problem of interlocality in case a core moral standard is violated (p. 262).
[288] In this sense Feddersen (2002), pp. 259–69.
[289] In this sense also Diebold (2008), p. 69. Also Feddersen states that even in cases where the violating conduct occurs abroad there could not possibly be a problem of 'interlocality', but he supports his view with the argument that the protected morals at issue would always be domestic. His reasoning, however, seems formalistic at this point. There is no doubt that the measure in this case would be linked to extraterritorial facts, and as shown above, an extraterritorial reach may indeed be problematic under general public international law. It is therefore preferable to recognize the extraterritorial element and to argue that the existence of the moral exception itself implies permissibility of this specific extraterritorial reach. This argument is in line with the above historical examples, which proved that moral exceptions have been invoked to also address facts outside the state adopting the measures (see above section 5.3.1.4).
[290] Even under Bartels' view on the geographical scope of Article XX, the requirement of a 'legal state interest' could be established by the disturbance of domestic public

with an extraterritorial reach from the scope of the general exceptions. While according to the previous analysis, the concept of public morals seems to permit measures with an extraterritorial reach, it will ultimately depend on the precise requirements regarding the means–end relationship whether these preliminary conclusions can be maintained. These requirements are here discussed in more detail.

In addition to proving the existence of relevant moral standards and showing that these are endangered, the member invoking exception (a) has to show that the trade measure taken was 'necessary' for the protection of these standards. The following section analyses the specific motivation and rationale for adopting genuine moral NPA measures. NPA measures adopted for moral reasons differ from other justifiable measures in their extraterritorial reach and in their lack of direct influence on the deprecated conduct or situation. Section 5.3.3.4.2 discusses the aspect of suitability, taking into account the lack of direct influence on circumstances abroad. The focus of this section is on the necessity of NPA trade measures seeking justification. Section 5.3.3.4.3 reviews different interpretations of this requirement and their related shortcomings, while section 5.3.3.4.4 suggests some modifications and draws conclusions.

5.3.3.4.1 Motivation for moral NPA trade measures

While NPA trade measures lack direct influence on the condemned conduct or situation abroad, they can ensure that the country adopting the measure does not participate or even contribute in any way to the conduct it deplores. The primary motivation for the NPA trade measure is then not an actual change of the violating situation, but the prevention of any direct or indirect participation or contribution by the country the moral standards of which are violated and its population. In many cases of NPA measures for genuine moral reasons, states adopting them arguably intend to foreclose any profits that could arise in connection with the violation. The moral character of this motivation would seem consistent with civil and criminal laws in many nations which penalize or declare impossible the legal reaping of profits from certain criminal acts, even by persons who did not participate in the primary criminal act itself.[291] In international law, the motivation could be regarded as consistent in the light of the

---

morals together with the acceptance of the importance of this aspect by GATT/WTO members.

[291] Such as the prohibition of money laundering (e.g., § 261 of the German Penal Code (Strafgesetzbuch)) or the impossibility of acquiring ownership of stolen goods (e.g., § 935 of the German Civil Code (Bürgerliches Gesetzbuch)).

accountability of a state for its own activities and for all activities, including the purchase of goods, on its territory. If according to domestic moral standards a certain conduct abroad is unacceptable, it is logically consistent that any action linked to the violation ought to be frowned upon as well. The nature of this specific motivation for moral NPA trade measures allows some conclusions for the necessity requirements. Justification is based on the idea that subsequent participations in violations of moral standards are themselves also moral violations, and that profits arising from such violations are to be frowned upon. Therefore, only measures fulfilling this purpose can be considered necessary.

5.3.3.4.2 Suitability

To reiterate, the condition that the measure be 'necessary' to protect public morals implies its suitability. The question arises which measures can be 'suitable' to protect domestic public morals, if the violation or threat happens outside a particular state's jurisdiction. Just as in the case of exception (b), the problem in this situation is the lack of jurisdiction and as a corollary a lack of influence on the violating conduct or circumstances on the part of the acting state. If, due to a lack of direct influence, a measure would be found to be unsuitable to protect public morals, then it would be unnecessary *per se*. With respect to child labour, for instance, it is often contended that unilateral trade measures have no measurable effect and therefore are not suitable to address this problem.[292] Indeed, if of all children that work in a country only 5–10 per cent are employed in export industries, then trade measures linked to child labour would probably rather lead to a shift in the employment of children from export industries to other sectors, while the number of employed children might not diminish at all.[293] Others, however, see evidence that even the threat of trade sanctions may well be sufficient to achieve a reaction in the addressee country,[294] and that a combination of trade measures, including trade incentives, accompanied by rehabilitation, educational and other supportive measures can be useful tools for helping the fight against child

---

[292] E.g., Howse and Trebilcock (2005), pp. 277–8 invoke this argument against certain voluntary instruments.

[293] In a documented case concerning Bangladesh's garment industry, the mere threat of trade measures led producers to dismiss children, who were later found to live under even worse conditions (UNICEF, The State of the World's Children, 1997, p. 23). However, there do not seem to be more comprehensive studies on the broader and long-term effects of discouraging the employment of children by economic means.

[294] Schneuwly (2003), pp. 133–8, discussing the success of the social clause in the US GSP.

labour.²⁹⁵ While the effects of trade sanctions are unclear, the possibility that in some cases there may be no measurable effects at all, or that the effects of NPA trade measures for moral reasons are very small, must be taken into consideration. A lack of suitability would lead to an exclusion of the measure from justification under the moral exception.

Due to the specific nature of moral standards as object of protection, however, trade measures may well be suitable to protect public morals, even if no measurable influence on the violation at issue is achieved. This seemingly inconsistent view is based on the special nature of public morals. Public morals have a norm-like character. Therefore, not only an ending of the violating conduct or situation is suitable to protect moral standards. Other measures that express deprecation of the conduct or that supplement political influence can also be suitable to reinforce and thus to protect the impaired moral standards. Furthermore, as explained above, the prevention of material benefits arising from the violation may render a measure suitable to protect moral standards. Therefore, in as far as the moral exception is concerned, the suitability requirement does not exclude NPA trade measures with an extraterritorial reach.²⁹⁶

5.3.3.4.3 Necessity

Given the almost open subject coverage and the existence of both core and variable public morals, a limitation of the public morals exception is indicated.²⁹⁷ While the necessity requirement for the public morals exception does not in principle differ from the same requirement in other exceptions, it has the potential to constitute a tool to achieve an adequate delimitation of the moral exception. To reiterate, in order to be necessary, a measure must be suitable to achieve the protection of a

---

[295] Humbert (2009), pp. 373–5. Humbert focuses on examples from regional trade agreements and on unilateral measures and shows that regardless of the legality of trade measures under current WTO law, an institutional cooperation between ILO and WTO would be best suited to help abandoning child labour (Humbert, 2009; Chapter 4).

[296] Similarly Howse and Trebilcock (2005), p. 292, who point to the bifurcated structure of the necessity requirement and consider necessity problematic with respect to measures aimed at inducing compliance with labour standards, but less problematic if it is seen as requiring 'a close relationship to the given objective, here protection of public morals'.

[297] Cottier warns that economic measures 'should not and cannot be applied with respect to the entire universe of international human rights guarantees' (Cottier, 2002, p. 125). Since the protection of human rights may well form part of either the core or the variable meaning of public morals, the example of human rights illustrates that an unlimited application of the public morals exception could jeopardize the functioning of the multilateral trading system.

moral standard, and from a set of equally effective measures only the least trade-restrictive measure is considered necessary. Recently, a process of 'weighing and balancing' has also gained ground. Given that the previous analysis has shown that NPA trade measures are in principle suitable for the protection of public morals, whether or not their 'necessity' can actually been asserted depends on the specific facts of the case. Especially their trade-restrictiveness and the existence of other available measures are relevant. The precise meaning of the necessity requirement is subject to an ongoing debate.

5.3.3.4.3.1 'Relative' and 'absolute' necessity

Feddersen suggests that the above distinction between core and marginal public morals is relevant also to the necessity test.[298] He suggests a 'relative necessity' test, which consists of a least trade-restrictiveness test in relation to the level of protection deemed appropriate. The satisfaction of this test would be sufficient for public morals based on the core meaning, because the importance of core public morals has implicitly been asserted by WTO membership. Variable public morals, on the other hand, lack such a consensus. For this category, Feddersen suggests an additional test of the 'absolute necessity' of the measure. Accordingly, only paramount variable public morals can override the free trade objective pursued by WTO members. Marginal moral standards, in contrast, are inferior. Hence, in this situation only less trade-restrictive measures may be permissible, even if the same level of protection for the marginal moral standard will not be achieved.

Feddersen's approach tries to produce a balance between national sovereignty, on the one hand, and the need to maintain the functioning of the multilateral trading system, on the other. He leaves the protection of moral standards, in as far as paramount values are concerned, up to the member states, with minimal reservations regarding a least trade-restrictiveness test in the case of alternative measures of equal effectiveness. In contrast, he puts marginal national moral standards under additional scrutiny: if free trade objectives are considered paramount, then nation-states have to cut back on their autonomous choice of protective measures, including the chosen level of protection. While some may be suspicious of this restriction of national sovereignty, Feddersen is basically correct in his analysis of the nature of public morals. As opposed to physical objects of

---

[298] Feddersen (2002), pp. 282–3.

protection, 'public morals' is a generic term comprising various standards, the importance of which may differ considerably. For example, while both human rights violations and cruelty towards animals may be prohibited by public morals, only the former is without doubt at the top of a hierarchy of values. Since not all moral standards are of equal importance, not all moral standards should have the potential to justify all measures protecting them.

The shortcoming of Feddersen's distinction between core and marginal public morals, however, is a lack of precision and flexibility. While Feddersen grants great variations in terms of importance of moral standards, his two-category approach prevents taking into account the specific importance of each moral standard at issue. His approach also ignores the intensity of the threat of a moral standard when determining the permissibility of a protective measure. This additional dimension is not sufficiently reflected in Feddersen's approach. While both the distinction between a core and a marginal meaning of public morals and between relative and absolute necessity is useful, a strict two-category system does not seem suitable to take the particularities of any case into account.

5.3.3.4.3.2 WTO jurisprudence on 'weighing and balancing'

WTO jurisprudence has developed a 'weighing and balancing' process as a holistic tool for assessing the necessity of a measure for achieving non-economic policy goals under some of the general exceptions.[299] This process modifies the least trade-restrictiveness test for measures, which was the previously prevailing standard in GATT/WTO jurisprudence. This test has not only been permeated with a process of weighing and balancing. In the meantime, the latter has actually come to the fore. While some see the new concept as containing relaxing elements as compared with the classical necessity test,[300] it could also be argued that the process of weighing and balancing has the potential for being more restrictive as regards the justification of national measures. This section focuses on the process of weighing and balancing with respect to the moral exception and justification of NPA trade measures.

The new approach was developed in the *Korea – Various Measures on Beef* dispute with respect to Article XX(d). The Appellate Body then

---

[299] See, e.g., Appellate Body Reports, *Brazil – Retreaded Tyres* (2007), No. 182 and *China – Audiovisual Entertainment Products* (2009), Nos. 239–42 with further references.
[300] Neumann and Tuerk (2003), p. 210.

considered the special nature of exception (d), which – just as exception (a) – is hardly delimited in terms of subject matter, and stated:

> In appraising the 'necessity' of a measure in these terms, it is useful to bear in mind the context in which 'necessary' is found in Article XX(d) … Clearly, Article XX(d) is susceptible of application in respect of a wide variety of 'laws and regulations' to be enforced. It seems to us that a treaty interpreter assessing a measure claimed to be necessary to secure compliance of a WTO consistent law or regulation may, in appropriate cases, take into account the relative importance of the common interests or values that the law or regulation to be enforced is intended to protect. The more vital or important those common interests or values are, the easier it would be to accept as 'necessary' a measure designed as an enforcement instrument.[301]

The Appellate Body therefore developed a process of weighing and balancing a series of factors,

> which prominently include the contribution made by the compliance measure to the enforcement of the law or regulation at issue, the importance of the common interests or values protected by that law or regulation, and the accompanying impact of the law or regulation on imports or exports.[302]

However, the Appellate Body in *Korea – Various Measures on Beef* not only found the weighing and balancing of factors especially useful given the specific nature of exception (d), it also limited the weighing and balancing process to cases where measures were found not to be 'indispensable'.[303] Since the *Korea – Various Measures on Beef* dispute, the

---

[301] Appellate Body Report, *Korea – Beef* (2001), No. 162.
[302] Appellate Body Report, *Korea – Beef* (2001), No. 164.
[303] Appellate Body Report, *Korea – Beef* (2001), No. 164. Also the *EC – Asbestos* Report does not constitute proof of a general extension of the process of weighing and balancing to all instances of the necessity requirement in the general exceptions. There, the Appellate Body considered weighing and balancing of factors with respect to the health exception contained in Article XX(b) (*EC – Asbestos* (2001), No. 172), and so seems to have extended the scope of application of the weighing and balancing process. This would come as a surprise, however, given the comparatively clear delimitation of the health exception in terms of subject matter. In contrast to exceptions (a) and (d), the adoption of the health exception itself is proof of a consensus on the paramount importance of the non-economic policy objective health protection. In applying the weighing and balancing test, however, the Appellate Body follows the previously prevailing procedure for determining least trade-restrictiveness: after having established that an alternative measure would not achieve the same level of protection, the Appellate Body concludes that the measure is necessary for the protection of a value of vital importance. It does not actually proceed to weigh and balance (*EC – Asbestos* (2001), Nos. 172–5).

process of weighing and balancing of factors in order to determine necessity has been applied in a few other disputes.[304]

More recently, and with respect to the moral exception, the adjudicatory bodies in *US – Gambling* and later in *China – Audiovisual Entertainment Products* carried out a comprehensive process of weighing and balancing of relevant factors. In analysing the moral exception in the GATS, the *US – Gambling* panel discussed: (a) the importance of the interests or values that the measures were intended to protect; (b) the extent to which these measures contributed to the realization of the ends pursued; and (c) the respective trade impact of the measures. It identified as protected interests or values the protection of society against the threat of money laundering, organized crime, risks to children and health. The panel found a key element of the 'necessity' test to be whether the respondent had 'explored and exhausted reasonably available WTO-consistent alternatives to the ... prohibition on the remote supply of gambling and betting services that would ensure the same level of protection',[305] and so treated the classical necessity test as merely one aspect to be considered in the assessment of necessity. The panel derived from the specific market access commitment an obligation to consult with the complainant before and while imposing its prohibition on the cross-border supply of gambling services,[306] and was not convinced by the view of the respondent that its specific concerns could not have been met through consultations. The panel found that, although the respondent had considered the measures indispensable, it would have been obliged to explore other less WTO-inconsistent options before imposing an import prohibition, and therefore concluded that the necessity requirement at issue had not been fulfilled.[307]

However, the panel's main lines of reasoning were overruled by the Appellate Body. The Appellate Body seized the occasion for some general explanations on the assessment and function of the necessity requirement. It began its elaborations with the very important finding that necessity must be assessed 'independently and objectively' based on the evidence in

---

[304] E.g., the *Dominican Republic – Import and Sale of Cigarettes* (2004) Panel undertook a comprehensive process of the weighing and balancing in order to determine necessity under exception (d) (confirmed by the Appellate Body, *Dominican Republic – Import and Sale of Cigarettes* (2005), Nos. 71–4). In a similar way to *Korea – Beef* (2000) the process of weighing and balancing was applied by the Panel in *Canada – Wheat Exports and Grain Imports* (2004), also with respect to Article XX(d), paras. 6.302 *et seq.*
[305] Panel Report, *US – Gambling* (2004), para. 6.528.
[306] Panel Report, *US – Gambling* (2004), para. 6.531.
[307] Panel Report, *US – Gambling* (2004), paras. 6.533–6.534.

the record before a panel.[308] The Appellate Body then turned to the core question. It stated that a measure is necessary in a situation where there is no WTO-consistent alternative 'reasonably available'.[309] Interestingly, it did not even mention the relevance of a 'less WTO-inconsistent' alternative,[310] but continued to outline how the process of 'weighing and balancing' is to be carried out:

> The process begins with an assessment of the 'relative importance' of the interests or values furthered by the challenged measure. Having ascertained the importance of the particular interests at stake, a Panel should then turn to the other factors that are to be 'weighed and balanced'. The Appellate Body has pointed to two factors that, in most cases, will be relevant to a Panel's determination of the 'necessity' of a measure, although not necessarily exhaustive of factors that might be considered. One factor is the contribution of the measure to the realization of the ends pursued by it; the other factor is the restrictive impact of the measure on international commerce.
>
> 307. A comparison between the challenged measure and possible alternatives should then be undertaken, and the results of such comparison should be considered in the light of the importance of the interests at issue. It is on the basis of this 'weighing and balancing' and comparison of measures, taking into account the interests or values at stake, that a panel determines whether a measure is 'necessary' or, alternatively, whether another, WTO-consistent measure is 'reasonably available'.[311]

Without here analysing related questions pertaining to the burden of proof, the Appellate Body stated that alternative measures may be found not to be 'reasonably available' if they are 'merely theoretical in nature, for instance, where the responding Member is not capable of taking it, or where the measure imposes an undue burden on that Member, such as prohibitive costs or substantial technical difficulties'.[312] Perhaps most important is the Appellate Body's finding that the alternative measure would need to preserve for the responding member 'its right to achieve its desired level of protection with respect to the objective pursued'.[313]

In applying these general rules to the panel's findings, the Appellate Body did not consider consultations as such as an alternative measure to achieve the objectives regarding the protection of public morals or the

---

[308] Appellate Body Report, *US – Gambling* (2005), No. 304.
[309] Appellate Body Report, *US – Gambling* (2005), No. 308.
[310] Appellate Body Report, *US – Gambling* (2005), Nos. 304–11.
[311] Appellate Body Report, *US – Gambling* (2005), Nos. 306–7.
[312] Appellate Body Report, *US – Gambling* (2005), No. 308.
[313] Appellate Body Report, *US – Gambling* (2005).

maintenance of public order, and therefore reversed the panel's findings.[314] It then went on to complete the analysis, which it based on the *prima facie* case for the necessity of the measure established by the respondent ('but for' the lack of negotiations with the complainant). Without exploring further alternative measures reasonably available, the Appellate Body took note of the complainant's failure to suggest such measures, and therefore concluded that in the absence of other reasonably available alternative measures, the import prohibition adopted by the respondent was indeed 'necessary'.[315] The Appellate Body confirmed this sequential process for a comprehensive analysis of necessity more recently in its *China – Audiovisual Entertainment Products* Report.[316]

On the one hand, by rejecting a general obligation to consult and negotiate with trading partners before adopting a measure under the general exceptions, the Appellate Body in *US – Gambling* seems to turn the balance slightly towards the autonomy of competent national institutions. On the other hand, the Appellate Body moves the process of an overall 'weighing and balancing' open to any factor considered relevant to the fore. The existence of less trade-restrictive measures making an equivalent contribution to the relevant objective is but one of the factors to be included in that process.[317] This new approach could be interpreted as an introduction of certain 'relaxing elements' into the least trade-restrictiveness necessity test.[318] However, this approach seems equally suited to undermining the autonomy of national authorities. An analysis of the process of weighing and balancing shows that all factors, including possibly available alternatives and the relative importance of values and interests, are weighed and balanced comprehensively.[319] More than reviewing national decision-making processes from the angle of WTO law, the adjudicatory bodies themselves undertake a comprehensive weighing and balancing of interests, values and alternatives if presented by the complainant – a

---

[314] Appellate Body Report, *US – Gambling* (2005), Nos. 317, 321.
[315] Appellate Body Report, *US – Gambling* (2005), No. 327.
[316] Appellate Body Report, *China – Audiovisual Entertainment Products* (2009), No. 242.
[317] Appellate Body Report, *China – Audiovisual Entertainment Products* (2009), No. 242.
[318] Neumann and Tuerk (2003), p. 210.
[319] The Appellate Body in *US – Gambling* (above fn. 311), clarified that the negative effects on commerce are relevant factors in the weighing and balancing process. Therefore, the process of weighing and balancing can indeed be characterized as a proportionality test. This is rejected by Desmedt (2001), at pp. 470, 476, who bases his view on the Appellate Body report *Korea – Beef* (2001) and *Shrimp Turtle* (1998). For a discussion on the existence of a proportionality test see also Hilf and Puth (2002) and Neumann and Tuerk (2003).

task usually reserved for national legislators. Panels, indeed, have not refrained from delving into assessing the importance of certain interests for certain states. For instance, in the *Dominican Republic – Import and Sale of Cigarettes* dispute, the adjudicatory bodies recognized that 'the collection of tax revenue (and, conversely, the prevention of tax evasion) is a most important interest for any country and particularly for a developing country such as the Dominican Republic'.[320] More than reviewing the genuineness the Dominican Republic's interest in the collection of tax revenue, the adjudicatory bodies actually commented on the importance of the policy of collecting respective tax revenues in general, and for the Dominican Republic in particular. It is questionable whether a review of the importance and usefulness of certain economic policy tools is mandated by the task of reviewing coverage of the particular exceptions.

Furthermore, the Appellate Body report is ambiguous regarding the crucial questions: although it implied in a number of reports that the chosen level of protection is an absolute benchmark that the adjudicatory bodies need to take for granted,[321] the factors explicitly mentioned by the Appellate Body to be weighed and balanced for the necessity assessment are comprehensive and include the importance of the interests concerned, the effectiveness of the measure or its contribution and the trade restrictiveness.[322] It is on this basis that the existence of 'reasonably available' alternatives is determined. The Appellate Body now equalizes the existence of reasonably available alternatives with the definition of necessity.

The concept as applied by the Appellate Body mixes aspects of suitability, necessity and, ultimately, proportionality.[323] Among the factors that need to be considered in the process is the contribution of the measure to the achievement of the objective, which is an aspect of suitability. While the existence of other equally suitable, but less trade-restrictive, measures is a question of necessity, the consideration of the importance of the protected interests and values is an indication of a proportionality test.

---

[320] Panel Report, *Dominican Republic – Import and Sale of Cigarettes* (2004), para. 7.215, confirmed by the Appellate Body, *Dominican Republic – Import and Sale of Cigarettes* (2005), No. 71.

[321] Appellate Body Report, *US – Gambling* (2005), Nos. 308, 311, Panel Report, *US – Gambling* (2004), Nos. 6.528 and 6.461, there referring to Appellate Body Reports, *Korea – Beef* (2001), para. 176, and *EC – Asbestos* (2001), para. 168.

[322] Also Desmedt (2001) finds the Appellate Body's approach to the level of protection not entirely consistent. As an example, Desmedt mentions the Appellate Body's lack of hesitance in rejecting the truthfulness of Korea's stated 'level of enforcement' with WTO consistent laws and regulations, at p. 465.

[323] In this direction Tietje (1998), pp. 320 *et seq.*, Epiney (2000), p. 84.

Since the level of protection is certainly to be considered in determining the importance of a protected value, it is unclear how the Appellate Body wants to ensure that the determination of the level of protection is excluded from the process of weighing and balancing. For instance, if the protected interest is the protection of children from hard labour, different degrees of protection are imaginable. The minimum age for working, for example, might be put at five years of age, or at fifteen. Likewise, the minimum working hours defining illegal 'hard labour' with respect to children may be put at two hours work per day, or at eight. In assessing the importance of the protected value, namely, the freedom of children from labour, the level of protection is crucial for the importance of the protected interest. Certainly, it should be considered more important to protect smaller children from work than older children, and it should equally be considered more important to prevent children from working eight hours per day than from two hours or less. Since the process of weighing and balancing includes all relevant aspects, this process would ultimately repeat and replace all considerations that should be taken into account by a 'good' legislator. In weighing and balancing comprehensively the importance of the protected value or interest and intensity of threats, the Appellate Body seems to review tasks that have traditionally been assigned to national law-makers. It would then hardly be possible to reconcile this approach with the objectivity of a measure's necessity proclaimed by the Appellate Body at the outset of its elaborations. The more aspects that are taken into account in the process of weighing and balancing, the less checkable and reviewable is the decision.

An integration of the least trade-restrictiveness test, which tests the effectiveness of the measure to achieve the specifically chosen level of protection, and the consideration of an open list of aspects in the weighing and balancing process, is neither relaxing the least trade-restrictiveness test nor is it tightening this test. Indeed, the process of weighing and balancing may be applied so as to find more measures justifiable, but it is as suitable to reject justifiability of measures, and is therefore neutral in terms of outcome. However, as a process, a comprehensive weighing and balancing of aspects and measures is more intrusive vis-à-vis the autonomy of national legislators in choosing and designing non-economic policies. There seems to be an almost complete overlap of aspects considered by legislators and the aspects to be weighed and balanced in the review of a WTO adjudicatory body. The more comprehensive the process of 'weighing and balancing' is, and the fewer standards for executing this process exist, the less transparent is any outcome of the process.

The process implies options for the broad consideration of non-economic aspects, but at the same time defies any critique and control.

A separation of the different aspects that are relevant, and a structure which contains different steps to be followed in the process, seems therefore indispensable. It is suggested that a comprehensive necessity test as outlined below, which is based on the least trade-restrictiveness test and which adds a separate and limited proportionality test, would provide for reviewability while still allowing for flexibility through consideration of relevant aspects.

5.3.3.4.3.3   Other approaches

Some reject all of the above approaches to necessity. According to Puth, for instance, provisional justification under one or another of the exceptions requires only verification of the legitimacy of the policy objective in relation to any of the listed exceptions, and the suitability of the measure to achieve the stated objective. He rejects the least trade-restrictiveness test as well as the process of weighing and balancing, since these consider relevant the measure's trade effects and in his opinion turn upside down the interpretation of Article XX. His argument is that the 'necessity' requirement in several of the particular exceptions characterizes the relationship of the measure at issue and the policy objective, namely, protection of one of the listed objects. In consequence, Puth rejects the relevance of effects on international trade for provisional justification under one or another of the particular exceptions.[324] His view is based on an extremely broad interpretation of the term 'necessary'. Indeed, some scholars favour an interpretation based on the language of the other exceptions which ranks the term necessary in between the least direct connection, indicated by the term 'relating to' in exception (g), and 'essential', as in exception (j). This interpretation favours the meaning 'suitable', which means a connection that is closer than 'relating to', but less direct than 'essential'.[325] Puth suggests that trade effects ought to be considered instead under the chapeau of Article XX, namely, under the aspect of 'unjustifiable discrimination'.[326]

The panel in *Argentina – Hides and Leather* also took an approach to interpretation of necessity which seems to be in line with this reasoning. With respect to provisional justification under Article XX(d), the panel detected a difference in the approaches to interpretation of the term 'necessity' on the sides of complainant and respondent. At this stage,

---

[324] Puth (2003), p. 310.   [325] Puth (2003), p. 311.   [326] Puth (2003), pp. 341 *et seq.*

the panel did not engage in a comprehensive analysis, but found rather quickly that the respondent had adduced 'argument and evidence sufficient to raise a presumption that the contested measures, in their general design and structure', were 'necessary'.[327] Only when examining as a requirement under the chapeau whether the measure did not unjustifiably discriminate, however, did the panel take note of the specific details and consequences of the measure. It implied that justifiability of a measure is closely related to the question of whether the measure, considering alternative courses of action, is unavoidable. It found that certain of the measure's consequences for importers were not 'unavoidable' for achieving the purpose of the measure and held that the requirements of the chapeau had not been met.[328]

The view that necessity or unavoidability of a measure is a question to be considered under the chapeau is not convincing. Puth's approach ignores prevailing case law since the *US – Gasoline* case on the chapeau of Article XX, according to which the chapeau relates to the way in which a measure is applied, in particular, with respect to possible discriminatory application.[329] Even more importantly, it seems that an interpretation which equalizes 'necessary' and 'suitable' for provisional interpretation ignores the ordinary meaning of both terms. If only the existence of a minimal degree of connection is tested for provisional justification, and necessity is an aspect to be considered under the chapeau, the different requirements indicated by the different terms in the particular exceptions (a)–(j) would be blurred.[330]

As synonyms describing the meaning of the term 'necessary' the words 'compulsory', 'required' or 'indispensable' are often mentioned. Something is considered necessary only if there are no alternative ways to achieve a certain goal. From a set of alternative measures, only the one that has the least negative effects needs to be considered necessary. For all these reasons, a comparison with alternative measures is logically inherent to the term 'necessary', just as suitability of a measure is inherent as a minimum requirement pertaining to the degree of connection.

5.3.3.4.4 Conclusions for an adequate 'necessity' test

The above interpretations of the necessity requirement aim at satisfying two opposing needs, namely, the need to give structure and allow for

---

[327] Panel Report, *Argentina – Hides and Leather* (2000), paras. 11.305–11.307.
[328] Panel Report, *Argentina – Hides and Leather* (2000), paras. 11.324–11.331.
[329] Appellate Body Report, *US – Gasoline* (1996), p. 22.
[330] In this direction also Neumann and Tuerk (2003), p. 228.

reviewability of the assessment of trade measures, on the one hand, and the need to provide for sufficient flexibility and allow for the consideration of all relevant aspects, on the other. While it is here suggested that a strict separation between core and variable, paramount and marginal values does not provide the flexibility needed, the most fundamental difference between the current 'weighing and balancing' approach and the proposal outlined below is a clear separation of steps that lead to an assessment of necessity.

Drawing on the approaches discussed above, this section suggests an approach to specifically assess the necessity of measures for the protection of public morals. It is based on the assumption that the importance of moral standards varies gradually and that differences in the intensity of the threat ought also to be taken into account. The first step regards the general suitability of the measure to achieve its objective, namely, the protection of a certain domestic moral standard. The second step regards the relative necessity, which is asserted if there is no other equally suitable measure as regards the specific objective that is at the same time less trade-restrictive. The third step is an absolute necessity test that assesses if the measure is proportional with regard to its positive achievements and negative consequences on trade.[331]

5.3.3.4.4.1 Step 1

Not all NPA trade measures are actually suitable for protecting public morals. In order to prevent abuses, suitability ought to require a link between the product to which the measure applies, on the one hand, and the violating conduct or circumstances, on the other. Only in the case of a link can the objective of achieving a protection of certain moral standards be realized. Indirect links should not be sufficient. For instance, if a measure is linked to the origin of a product that has been produced under a political regime frowned upon by the imposing state, it could hardly prevent a participation in the violation. The violator, in this case, would not be the producer, but the government of the country of production. The link between the particular violation and the NPA to which the measure is linked (origination in a certain regime) would not be sufficiently tight. Therefore, general economic sanctions affecting all products originating in a certain country in which, for example, grave human rights violations

---

[331] These steps correspond to the principle of proportionality (*Verhältnismäßigkeitsgrundsatz*) in German law, with special consideration of the characteristics of NPA trade measures and of the nature of public morals.

occur, would in most cases not be considered suitable to achieve protection of specific domestic moral standards. Since all of the approaches to necessity outlined above require as a basic condition the suitability of a measure regarding its objective, measures linked to NPAs that constitute broad economic sanctions or similar bans would not be justifiable under sub-paragraph (a). Justification of economic sanctions under Article XXI would naturally remain unaffected by this qualification.[332] Therefore, fears about opening the door to 'a war between public orders' arising from what is perceived as a broad interpretation of the public morals exception would therefore not be justified.[333] Only in cases of a direct link between the ban and the violation could suitability be asserted. In this sense, for example, import prohibitions against carpets produced by small children or export prohibitions pertaining to technical equipment used in connection with human rights violations, could well be suitable to protect public morals because of a direct link between the banned product, on the one hand, and the violation of the moral standard, on the other.

5.3.3.4.4.2 Step 2

The least trade-restrictiveness test requires an exploration of alternative measures that are equally suited to achieving the specific objective, namely, the protection of a domestic moral standard. As has been detailed above, the protection of the moral standard is reached by preventing subsequent participation in the violation and the gain of profits or advantages from it. In most cases, NPA import prohibitions will relate to products that have been produced under a violation of the moral standard. Since only an import prohibition is able to prevent economic gains linked to the violation completely, relative necessity will usually be found in cases of import bans linked to NPAs for moral reasons. This aspect is most important, since alternatives, such as diplomatic means or labelling of products, will then not be considered equally effective tools. Only an import ban would be capable of completely preventing involuntary economic participation in the violation. However, trade measures alone will usually not be

---

[332] Howse and Trebilcock cite as an example for an acceptable sanction the United States Burmese Freedom and Democracy Act (Howse and Trebilcock, 2005, p. 282). However, an authorization by the ILO would hardly be permissible under GATT Article XXI.

[333] See, e.g., Bagwell, Mavroidis and Staiger (2002), p. 75. The measure given by the authors as an example, namely, an EU ban against all imports from the United States as long as the United States continues to apply the death penalty, would therefore neither be suitable nor justifiable under this approach to interpretation of the necessity requirement of the moral exception.

sufficient to effectively remedy a violation of human rights.[334] Therefore, the existence of accompanying policies or programmes pursuing the same objective would not render an import ban unnecessary.

5.3.3.4.4.3 Step 3

The final and crucial step suggested here ought to verify the absolute necessity of a measure. A measure ought to be considered absolutely necessary if it is adequate. The test suggested here basically consists of a test of proportionality, and its purpose is to ensure that the positive and the negative effects of the measure are not entirely out of balance.[335] Among the aspects to be considered for the assessment of absolute necessity is the importance of the protected value. Since, regardless of the category, this value forms part of domestic public morals, its importance needs to be assessed with a view to the domestic sphere. Here, there is an inherent privilege for public morals belonging to the core meaning. Thus, values reflected in public international law, in particular values and norms reflected in *ius cogens* or obligations *erga omnes*, ought to be given great importance. Paramount moral standards belonging to the variable meaning of the term ought to be considered equally important. However, existence and importance of variable values would need to be assessed carefully. The claim of paramount importance could be substantiated with the national constitution, relevant national laws and regulations as well as national documents or any other relevant evidence. Also the existence of non-trade policies and programmes pursuing the same objectives could be considered evidence for measure's genuineness and for the rank of the moral value.

Another aspect to be taken into account is the intensity of the violation together with the chosen level of protection. For instance, if a country internally prohibits children below the age of fifteen years from working, then production of goods by children aged fourteen years would be a violation of the standard, but the violation would be less intense than in the case of production by children below six years of age. The consideration of the chosen level of protection, however, does not imply any judgement regarding whether or not that level is adequate. This aspect would be entirely in the

---

[334] Cottier, Pauwelyn and Bürgi (2005a), p. 25.
[335] Also this aspect distinguishes the test suggested here from the process of weighing and balancing as applied by the Appellate Body. As a result of weighing and balancing, adjudicatory bodies may even consider alternative measures that are not equally effective to achieve the desired level of protection, if they do not consider that the objective is of paramount importance.

internal sphere of the WTO member taking the measure, in as far as it would not be subject to international law.

The prior aspects then need to be balanced with the impairment in terms of trade to other WTO members affected by the measure. The importance of this interest is verified by the WTO Agreements. However, also here, the intensity of impairment must be taken into consideration. While the adjudicatory bodies implement the proportionality test, the test ought to lead to a negative result only in cases of an apparent imbalance between the effects of the measure with respect to the goal pursued, on the one hand, and the trade effects, on the other. Only then, should a measure be considered unproportional.

This step allows for flexibility, as does the process of weighing and balancing. Compared with the weighing and balancing test applied by the WTO adjudicatory bodies, however, it is more restricted. For instance, a reconsideration of aspects that have been considered before, namely, suitability and relative necessity, are excluded. This is relevant especially for the 'universe' of reasonably available alternative measures. Therefore, the three-step approach suggested here is more structured and accordingly more transparent and reviewable than the process of weighing and balancing. In contrast to the test suggested by Feddersen, on the other hand, the basic lines of the test apply equally to core and variable public morals. This does not mean that the approach suggested here ignores the differences between these categories. Rather, it is suggested that the differences concerning importance of the moral standards at issue are inherently reflected in the test, since the importance of the protected value is to be taken into account in assessing proportionality. An inherent consideration is preferable to a categorical difference between core and variable public morals, because the importance of the value should not alone be decisive in the assessment. Rather, the importance of the value needs to be considered together with the intensity of the threat and the impairment caused by the measure.

5.3.4 Summary

Depending on the public policy objective they pursue, NPA trade measures can indeed fall into the scope of the general exceptions. Nevertheless, there are considerable constraints. These arise mainly from two aspects: first, subject coverage of Article XX is limited to the policies listed in sub-paragraphs (a)–(j) and, second, given the lack of direct influence on circumstances abroad, there are doubts about the suitability and necessity of NPA measures relating to objects outside the imposing state's borders.

As regards the first limitation, it is noteworthy that subject matters such as general environmental policies, human rights, core labour rights, cultural policies and protection of minorities are not listed explicitly. For environmental NPA measures, the approach of interpreting in particular generic terms in an evolutionary way together with the comparably low requirements relating to the means–end relationship is of paramount importance. Recent developments indicate that exception (g) on the protection of natural resources has the potential to cover policies addressing at least the most pressing environmental concerns, in as far as they are of global relevance. This means that NPA measures targeting the protection of air, soil or water are justifiable, even if they relate to circumstances and conduct abroad. In contrast, exception (b) will rarely prove suitable to justify NPA trade measures aimed at the violation of human rights abroad. Even if a broad interpretation of human life and health covering human rights were adopted, the stricter requirements regarding the means–end relationship, namely, the necessity requirement, would prevent justification. As regards most other public policies that would come into consideration, such as cultural protection or protection of minorities, they are not directly reflected in any of the sub-paragraphs of Article XX.

However, under certain circumstances, the public morals exception (a) covers NPA trade measures also if linked to other policies. Due to the vagueness of the notion of public morals, the exception has the twofold potential to serve as a catch-all provision for legitimate NPA measures excluded from the scope of the other particular exceptions. First, the scope of the public morals exception in terms of subject matter is ultimately open-ended; therefore, measures taken to protect human rights or cultural, religious, environmental or other values and interests could be justified under this exception, provided that the protection qualifies as a moral standard. Second, given the non-physical nature of public morals, the location of the violation of the moral standard is not relevant, as long as it violates domestic moral standards. The necessity requirement, including suitability, in this case does not exclude NPA measures. Depending on the facts of the case, NPA measures can be suitable to protect and enforce domestic public morals by expressing deprecation of a condemned conduct and by preventing economic participation in immoral conduct or circumstances.

The object of protection of exception (a), domestic public morals, consists of a whole range of moral standards that can be sub-divided into core public morals and variable public morals. These categories, however, are merely crutches in structuring application of this exception. Paramount and marginal public morals are not closed categories, rather, the importance of moral standards differs gradually on a scale from lowest marginal to highest paramount moral standards. If, however, the threatened morals belong to the core meaning of public morals, international acceptance or consensus among WTO members will facilitate proof of the existence of such standards and of the moral standards' importance.

Since there is no presumption of a 'broad' or 'narrow' interpretation of any of the exceptions, including the case of the moral exception, the terms need to be given meaning by applying the ordinary means of interpretation. At the same time, there is a need to protect legitimate expectations and preserve the functionality of the multilateral trading system. Therefore, no moral concern ought to be sufficient to justify trade restrictions.[336] Due to the vagueness and open-endedness of the term 'public morals', it is imperative that precise conditions for invoking the exception are developed. The necessity requirement seems suitable to give structure to the application of the exception and to limit the applicability of the exception to a reasonable degree. Therefore, it is here suggested that the necessity of a measure is assessed in three steps as detailed above. This approach would only slightly modify the comprehensive weighing and balancing test applied by the adjudicatory bodies, but it would increase the reviewability of the assessment considerably.

5.4 The chapeau and other requirements regarding the application of measures

While the general design of a measure seeking justification is assessed under sub-paragraphs (a)–(j), its application needs to conform to other standards. In addition to general due process requirements, the chapeau of Article XX requires that measures falling under one or another of the exceptions contained in sub-paragraphs (a)–(j):

> are not applied in a manner which would constitute a means of arbitrary or unjustifiable discrimination between countries where the same conditions prevail, or a disguised restriction on international trade.

---

[336] Cottier (2002), p. 125, stressing the extremely broad range of human rights guarantees which would render unacceptable a broad permission of trade measures based on human rights.

For its interpretation of the chapeau, the Appellate Body has placed far greater importance on the object and purpose of the chapeau than on the ordinary meaning of terms.[337] This approach seems justified, since the text of the chapeau is characterized by the use of generic terms and concepts rather than by establishing precisely defined requirements. It is widely recognized that the general purpose and function of the chapeau is to prevent measures justified by the general exceptions being abused.[338] The Appellate Body in *US – Gasoline* stated that the exceptions:

> should not be so applied as to frustrate or defeat the legal obligations of the holder of the right under the substantive rules of the *General Agreement*. If those exceptions are not to be abused or misused, in other words, the measures falling within the particular exceptions must be applied reasonably, with due regard both to the legal duties of the party claiming the exception and the legal rights of the other parties concerned.[339]

Beyond the purpose of preventing abuse, the chapeau is regarded as an expression of the principle of good faith. Therefore, the Appellate Body highlighted the need to apply the general exceptions '*bona fide*, that is to say, reasonably'.[340] More precisely, the requirement of reasonable application means, that the exercise of the right:

> should at the same time be *fair and equitable as between the parties* and not one which is calculated to procure for one of them an unfair advantage in the light of the obligation assumed. A reasonable exercise of the right is regarded as compatible with the obligation. But the exercise of the right in such a manner as to prejudice the interests of the other contracting party arising out of the treaty is unreasonable and is considered as inconsistent with the bona fide execution of the treaty obligation, and a breach of the treaty.[341]

Thus, the requirement of reasonable application concerns the legal duties of the state invoking the exception as well as the legal rights of other WTO members.[342] Naturally, the chapeau applies to both NPA measures and measures linked to product characteristics. Given the extraterritorial

---

[337] McRae (2000), p. 235.
[338] McRae (2000), p. 229. This interpretation corresponds to the core function attributed to the chapeau by the negotiators on the Havana Charter. GATT *Analytical Index*, Vol. I, at pp. 563, 564.
[339] Appellate Body Report, *US – Gasoline* (1996), p. 22.
[340] Appellate Body Report, *Shrimp Turtle* (1998), No. 158.
[341] Appellate Body Report, *Shrimp Turtle* (1998), fn. 156, quoting B. Cheng, *General Principles of Law as Applied by International Courts and Tribunals* (Stevens & Sons, 1953), chapter 4, in particular, p. 125 (emphasis added by the Appellate Body).
[342] Appellate Body Report, *US – Gasoline* (1996), p. 22.

5.4 THE CHAPEAU AND OTHER REQUIREMENTS

reach inherent only to NPA measures, however, the requirements for justification arising from the chapeau might differ between both types of measures.

This chapter will not give a comprehensive overview of the chapeau and the other requirements on application of measures, but focuses instead on possible particularities of the requirements with respect to measures linked to NPAs. This section starts with a discussion on the general need of a balancing process under the chapeau. Section 5.4.2 analyses the general and the particular requirements resulting from the chapeau with special consideration of NPA measures.

5.4.1 A 'balancing process' under the chapeau?

The recognition that the rights of both the member invoking the exception and the members affected by a measure need to be taken into account has triggered the question of whether the chapeau establishes a separate 'balancing' requirement.[343] Some scholars argue that a balancing of contrasting interests by applying proportionality concepts is indicated, since it would be in line with the function of the chapeau and with the rule of law itself.[344] In the absence of such a balancing process, a measure might be found to be justified even if its application in a specific case would be entirely out of proportion. Another argument relates to the assessment of the genuineness of the measure under the chapeau. It is claimed, that 'some balancing between the purported benefits of a measure and their costs' would be inevitable.[345]

This view is ultimately a consequence of the idea of a strict separation between a measure's design and its application, which as a corollary would need to be assessed separately under the particular exceptions and the chapeau, respectively. To reiterate, the chapeau is widely regarded as concerning the application of a measure, while its design and structure are subject to a review under the particular sub-paragraphs.[346] A distinction between design and application could indeed give structure to

---

[343] McRae (2000), pp. 230, 231, recognizes that the meaning ascribed to the term discrimination by the Appellate Body does indeed justify a 'balancing' of interests.
[344] Puth (2003), pp. 324–5; Hilf and Puth (2002) p. 216. Puth ascribes paramount importance to the principle of proportionality by stating that the principle guides the application of the chapeau (Puth, 2003, p. 342).
[345] McRae (2000), p. 235.
[346] Prevailing case law since Appellate Body Report, *US – Gasoline* (1996), section IV, p. 22; for a more recent confirmation see Appellate Body Report, *US – Gambling* (2005), No. 390 (albeit with respect to GATS Article XIV).

the assessment of measures under Article XX. A review of the design of the measure under the standards of the particular exceptions can help to identify unjustifiable measures before delving into the factually more difficult realm of application of a measure in specific cases. Only if the measure has been found to meet all requirements concerning its basic design is a review of the measure in its entirety, including its specific application, required. Finally, the distinction seems to correspond to the explicit language of the chapeau, which requires that measures 'are not applied' in a certain manner.

The understanding of Article XX as establishing such a distinction, however, has also met criticism.[347] The question arises if a distinction between design and application of a measure would not be artificial. It might often be difficult to assess whether certain guidelines or decisions constitute measures themselves, or whether they merely constitute application of other measures. Also, a strict separation would imply that the application of a measure does not need to meet necessity requirements, since these would apply only to the design of the measure, and this only in some cases, such as the health and public morals exceptions.[348] In consequence, even measures applied in a most inappropriate way could still be justified under Article XX.

It seems that the Appellate Body did not intend to establish a strict separation in the first place. It did not limit the chapeau requirements to pertain only to the application of the measure,[349] as has been maintained by some critics. Instead, the Appellate Body has recognized that, given the general purpose and function of the chapeau with respect to a final review of measures, its requirements apply to substantial as well as to procedural discrimination.[350] Furthermore, the chapeau obviously contains horizontal requirements that apply to all measures seeking justification, no matter to which policy they relate. Therefore, the chapeau could also be interpreted to establish at least in part additional general requirements, the limitation of which to the stage of application would not seem justified.

---

[347] Puth, e.g., argues that the requirement of unjustifiable discrimination, including a necessity test, concerns the substance of the measure, while only the requirement of arbitrary discrimination concerns the application of the measure. Puth (2003), pp. 323–8.

[348] Desmedt (2001), p. 475.

[349] The Appellate Body stated that the chapeau concerned '*not so much* the questioned measure or its specific contents as such, but *rather* the manner in which that measure is applied' (Appellate Body report, *US – Gasoline* (1996), p. 22).

[350] Appellate Body Report, *Shrimp Turtle* (1998), No. 160.

5.4 THE CHAPEAU AND OTHER REQUIREMENTS

Indeed, the debate on a balancing process as a distinct requirement of the chapeau can be solved if the term 'measure' under Article XX is interpreted more broadly. The distinction between measures and their application under Article XX is based on the idea that the legislative act itself constitutes the measure, while administrative decisions and activities constitute application. However, there is nothing in the agreements that would suggest such an understanding of the term 'measure'. In contrast, the provisions of the agreements are in general interpreted most comprehensively to include all kinds of acts issued by the central state or other bodies or institutions. Therefore, administrative acts could also be regarded as measures, so that the requirements contained in any one of the sub-paragraphs (a)–(j) together with the requirements contained in the chapeau would apply to all measures, whether legislative or other acts.

It is here suggested to use the distinction between measure and application merely as a tool to give structure to Article XX, and to make all official acts seeking justification subject to all requirements laid out in this article. In consequence, a process of balancing or rather of weighing and balancing to assess the absolute necessity of measures is indicated only for measures that need to meet necessity requirements, and under the relevant particular exception. Furthermore, as will be shown below, the non-discrimination requirement of the chapeau allows for the consideration of relative necessity, even if a process of balancing or a distinct absolute necessity test is rejected here. This is of great importance for measures relating to the protection of exhaustible resources, since sub-paragraph (g) does not establish a 'necessity' requirement in the first place.

In sum, a distinct process of balancing of rights and interests or an assessment of proportionality under the chapeau does not seem indicated,[351] since the non-discrimination requirement allows for an adequate consideration of different interests and circumstances.

5.4.2 *The requirements*

There are three aspects in the chapeau of Article XX, namely 'arbitrary discrimination between countries where the same conditions prevail', 'unjustifiable discrimination between countries where the same conditions prevail' and 'disguised restriction on international trade'. Since there is little GATT and WTO jurisprudence on the application of the

---

[351] Neumann and Tuerk (2003), p. 231; Desmedt (2001), p. 474.

chapeau, none of these different aspects have been explored comprehensively yet.

5.4.2.1 Introductory remarks

The vague language of the chapeau poses considerable problems.[352] The Appellate Body has so far not defined the different aspects mentioned in the chapeau in a meaningful way, but nevertheless has offered some guidance. It approached the non-discrimination requirements by identifying and categorizing different flaws in the application of the contested measures.

From this assessment, it is apparent that there is considerable overlap in terms of coverage of both non-discrimination requirements[353] and, in consequence, the assessment of measures remains uncertain.[354] It seems indeed natural that both requirements are closely interrelated. In the case of arbitrary discrimination, such discrimination would in most cases also be unjustifiable. The meaning of the third aspect of a 'disguised restriction' has not yet been addressed in detail. It has been suggested that there might be cases of measures with certain 'hidden features', such as concealed privileges to domestic producers, that might fall into this category.[355] However, such measures would usually also amount to unjustifiable discrimination. The overlap stated for both non-discrimination standards therefore seems to extend even to the requirement that the measure does not constitute a disguised restriction on international trade – measures that are applied in a certain unreasonable manner may at the same time infringe all requirements set out in the chapeau.[356] Interpretation of the

---

[352] E.g., it seems that earlier panels had interpreted the first two of these aspects as a single requirement of non-discrimination (see, e.g., *Tuna-Dolphin II* (1994), Nos. 5.15, 5.31). In *Shrimp Turtle*, however, the Appellate Body established that there are three different standards contained in the chapeau (Appellate Body Report, *Shrimp Turtle* (1998), No. 150. The Appellate Body Report on *US – Gasoline* (1996) is ambiguous on a distinction between 'arbitrary' and 'unjustifiable' discrimination (cf., e.g., at pp. 23 and 25, where a distinction is made, but the review of the measure with result on discrimination at pp. 25–9)). Thus, preference was given to an interpretation of the chapeau that gives a distinct meaning to both non-discrimination requirements.

[353] Cf., e.g., the elaborations on 'arbitrary discrimination' with respect to the rigidity and inflexibility in the administration of certification processes, which had before been found to constitute 'unjustifiable' discrimination, Appellate Body Report, *Shrimp Turtle* (1998), No. 177.

[354] Feddersen (2002), p. 288; Panel Report, *US – Gambling* (2004), No. 6.580.

[355] Quick (2000), p. 255.

[356] Cf. Panel Report, *US – Gambling* (2004), No. 6.580, stating overlap between all three aspects contained in the chapeau (here regarding GATS Article XIV).

5.4 THE CHAPEAU AND OTHER REQUIREMENTS

three standards is further complicated by the Appellate Body's statement that their meaning depends on the category of measure under the different sub-paragraphs of Article XX. As an example, the Appellate Body invoked measures that purport to be necessary to protect public morals, and stated that, for example, the standard of 'arbitrary discrimination' may be different for such measures than for measures relating to the products of prison labour.[357]

The Appellate Body overcame problems relating to the overlap between the different aspects of the chapeau and their different meanings by stating that:

> The fundamental theme is to be found in the purpose and object of avoiding abuse or illegitimate use of the exceptions to substantive rules available in Article XX.[358]

This approach is reasonable. While the language of the chapeau is very broad and differences between the different aspects unclear, there is consensus on its object and purpose. For this reason, the Appellate Body has identified a number of due process requirements which must be met in order not to violate the chapeau.[359] Also, given the overlap between 'unjustifiable' and 'arbitrary' discrimination, it seems more important to identify categories of flaws in the application of discriminatory measures which quasi-automatically render discrimination unjustifiable and/or arbitrary. Other problems relate to the burden of proof: it is not entirely clear whether the complainant or the respondent needs to prove the existence or absence of an arbitrary or unjustifiable discrimination.[360]

Therefore, section 5.4.2.2 below analyses the more general requirements arising from the chapeau, namely, from the specific non-discrimination standard and from due process requirements. Given the little relevance of the third aspect, disguised restriction on international trade, in hitherto jurisprudence and given that no special relevance for NPA measures is conceivable, the third aspect is not considered separately. Section 5.4.2.3

---

[357] Appellate Body Report, *Shrimp Turtle* (1998), No. 120.
[358] Appellate Body Report, *US – Gasoline* (1996), p. 25.
[359] For more details on these general requirements, see below section 5.4.2.2.4.
[360] See, e.g., Appellate Body Report, *US – Gambling* (2005). Here, the respondent was refused the moral exception, because it had not demonstrated that these measures had been applied consistently with the requirements of the chapeau (para. 369). The respondent's attempts to demonstrate consistent application in the subsequent compliance Panel were unsuccessful, mainly because the Panel refused to accept further evidence on consistency in the absence of measures taken to comply (Panel Report, *US – Gambling (Article 21.5)* (2007), para. 6.93).

discusses two specific problem fields, namely unilaterality and a possible obligation to negotiate, and section 5.4.2.4 addresses the specific applications of the general requirements that are of particular importance to NPA trade measures.

5.4.2.2 General requirements and principles

Discrimination under the chapeau must not be equated with the non-discrimination requirements contained in primary GATT obligations.[361] If a case of 'discrimination' has been found in the course of the review, for example, between a domestic and a foreign like product, the crucial question under the chapeau is whether the discrimination is unjustifiable and/or arbitrary. Related questions have been approached by the adjudicatory bodies in different ways. In some reports, some specific flaws in the administration or application of a measure were determined as unjustifiable and/or arbitrary. The following sections analyse the general meaning of the non-discrimination standard and due process requirements relating to the application and administration of measures. While these requirements apply to all measures under Article XX, some are of special importance for NPA measures.

5.4.2.2.1 An 'unavoidable' standard of justifiability?

The panel in *Argentina – Hides and Leather* approached the issue of discrimination in a more general way with respect to a measure falling into the scope of sub-paragraph (d). It focused on the question of justifiability and explored whether the specific discrimination had been 'unavoidable' in terms of nature and extent. The panel found that the measure in principle had been necessary to achieve the stated objective. However, it also found that the specific discrimination, namely, additional interest lost or paid, had not been 'unavoidable', because alternative measures had been available to the respondent.[362] In the end, although the measure had provisionally been justified under Article XX(d), the measure, or more specifically, the amount of discrimination in which it resulted, was found not to be justified. Ultimately, the panel's view amounted to an equalization of the meaning of 'justifiable' and 'unavoidable'. This interpretation, however, seems too narrow. While the term 'justifiable' suggests that it is not required that a measure is 'unavoidable', one needs to agree with the panel that vice versa an unavoidable discrimination ought to be justifiable.

---

[361] Appellate Body Report, *US – Gasoline* (1996), p. 23.
[362] Panel Report, *Argentina – Hides and Leather* (2000), Nos. 11.324–11.331.

5.4 THE CHAPEAU AND OTHER REQUIREMENTS

Any other interpretation would render the general exceptions moot. This report was, however, not appealed and hence the Appellate Body has not yet confirmed this interpretation.

If confirmed, however, this approach could turn out to be especially relevant to NPA measures. Since these are linked to facts occurring abroad, enforcement of such measures at the border requires considerable administrative efforts in order to verify the existence or not of the relevant NPA. Therefore, the administration might often place some part of this burden on the importers, while domestically, the state might put into place national structures to verify the NPAs. It would then be subject to the specific facts of the case to assess whether or not the amount of discrimination is unjustifiable. The panel's view is here rejected. It seems that discriminations would nearly always be avoidable, however, at potentially excessive costs. In consequence, any disadvantage of importers would lead the measure to fail justification – a result that could hardly be brought in line with the function of Article XX to strike a balance between WTO members' rights and obligations. For this reason, and given the wording of the chapeau, only arbitrary and unjustifiable discrimination ought to lead to a violation of the chapeau.

5.4.2.2.2 Relevance of different conditions in countries

The second part of the discrimination standard in the chapeau clarifies that the discrimination must relate to 'countries where the same conditions prevail'. Similar to the prohibition of discrimination between 'like products', the chapeau prohibits discrimination between 'like' countries, namely, between those where the same conditions prevail. The term 'countries' comprises the importing country as well as exporting countries.[363] Hence, a comparison between the domestic situation and the situation in the exporting country is relevant, as well as a comparison between several exporting countries. Given its purpose, the phrase obviously comprises discrimination between products originating in different countries where the same conditions prevail.[364]

This precondition is of particular importance to NPA measures. To reiterate, in the case of measures linked to product characteristics, the product bears on the country of importation via its physical properties. It seems therefore that physical characteristics are of equal importance,

---

[363] Appellate Body Report, *US Shrimp* (1998), para. 150; Appellate Body Report, *US – Gasoline* (1996), at pp. 23–4.
[364] Panel Report, *Argentina – Hides and Leather* (2000), No. 11.314.

no matter which conditions prevail in the country of origin. In contrast, NPA measures inherently relate to conditions in other countries also, while mostly they do not have any direct effect on the country of importation. Therefore, conditions in other countries are of paramount importance for design as well as application of NPA measures. It is therefore plausible that other conditions in the producing countries apart from the specific NPA may also be relevant for an assessment of discrimination.

The question arises whether beyond the situation of 'same conditions', discrimination also needs to be justified if countries where different conditions prevail are treated alike.[365] To reiterate, the function of the non-discrimination requirements contained in the chapeau is to prevent an abuse of the general exceptions. In the light of this objective, the phrase 'in countries where the same conditions prevail' cannot be regarded as a *proviso* which qualifies the relevance of discrimination under the chapeau. It is here suggested that, in contrast, the phrase instead amounts to a specific application of the general principle of equality. Equality before the law is a fundamental principle of law, enshrined in the UN Charter and applicable also in international trade law.[366] The essence of the principle is that 'like should be treated like, and unlike treated unlike in and before the law'.[367] Hence, if different conditions prevail in countries, and if these conditions are relevant, then such conditions are aspects capable of justifying a differentiation. Likewise, a differentiation based on relevant conditions in different countries cannot be considered arbitrary. There are the first signs indicating recognition of the relevance of the general principle of equality in WTO jurisprudence. The Appellate Body in *Shrimp Turtle* found that lack of flexibility could also result in discrimination if the application of the measure does not allow for an inquiry into the appropriateness of a regulatory programme for the respective exporting country.[368] In *Shrimp Turtle (Article 21.5)* it repeated that in its view, 'a measure should be designed in such a manner that there is sufficient flexibility to take into account the specific conditions prevailing in *any* exporting Member'.[369] With this requirement, the Appellate Body implicitly extended the prohibition to discriminate between countries where

---

[365] In this sense also Quick (2000), pp. 253–4.
[366] Cottier (2006), at p. 795.
[367] Cottier (2006), at p. 796.
[368] Appellate Body Report, *Shrimp Turtle* (1998), para. 165.
[369] Appellate Body Report, *Shrimp Turtle (Article 21.5)* (2001), para. 149.

5.4 THE CHAPEAU AND OTHER REQUIREMENTS

the same conditions prevail to a prohibition of treating equally those countries where different conditions prevail.[370]

It is a specific characteristic of NPA measures that they take into account the existence of certain conditions or circumstances in the exporting country. This certainly does not mean that all NPA measures are consistent with the requirements of the chapeau.[371] The crucial question is which conditions are relevant and need to be taken into account, and whether there is sufficient flexibility to accommodate them in the application of the measure. This could be particularly relevant if the protection of moral standards with NPA measures is concerned. It would then be required that the application of the measure leaves sufficient flexibility to accommodate differences in countries which would cast a positive or negative light on the threatening situation.

The consideration of conditions prevailing in different countries, including the country of importation, is relevant also with a view to consistency regarding the protected value. Also, this aspect is of great importance to NPA measures. The NPA to which the measure is linked needs to be considered equally important with regard to domestic as well as to foreign conduct or circumstances.[372] Otherwise, a measure protecting domestic morals that is linked to circumstances abroad must be considered an unjustifiable and arbitrary discrimination.

---

[370] Also the Panel in *EC – Tariff Preferences* (2003) seems to apply standards amounting to a general principle of equality. The Panel criticized the fact that the EC could not provide evidence of similar conditions with respect to drug problems prevailing in a number of beneficiary countries, or evidence of not sufficiently similar conditions in other drug-affected developing countries to which the preferential schemes did not apply (para. 7.234).

[371] Gaines (2002), p. 430, argues that the fact that producers in one country use a PPM and producers in another country do not creates a presumption that the same conditions prevail, and that the discrimination is therefore neither arbitrary nor unjustifiable under Article XX. His view does not imply that other conditions are irrelevant, but merely leads to a shift of the burden of proof to the country challenging the measure. While the issue of the burden of proof is not addressed in this work, it seems clear that in light of the nature of the reference to conditions in Article XX as an application of the general principle of equality, all relevant aspects need to be taken into account for the assessment whether in a specific case particular PPMs create a legitimate basis for a distinction.

[372] The aspect of 'consistency' in the enforcement or application of a moral standard was also considered in *US – Gambling*, albeit as part of a review of the measure under the chapeau. There, the panel found that the respondent had failed to show that it treated domestic and foreign suppliers of horse-betting services equally, because apparently in certain situations the provision of remote gambling and betting services was permitted to domestic but not to foreign services suppliers. Panel Report, *US – Gambling* (2004), paras. 6.599–6.600, Appellate Body Report, *US – Gambling* (2005), Nos. 348–51.

5.4.2.2.3 Special and differential treatment

The objective of sustainable development features prominently as one of the objectives of the WTO.[373]

The chapeau does not explicitly provide for special treatment of developing countries. Nevertheless, there are good arguments that the chapeau requirements differ depending on the economic situation of the affected country. The requirement to differentiate according to the level of economic development could arise directly from the principle of special and differential treatment of developing countries (SDT).

5.4.2.2.3.1 The principle of SDT

WTO members have repeatedly committed themselves to improving the situation of developing countries, especially of the least developed among them. This is reflected, for example, in the first recital of the preamble of the Marrakesh Agreement and in several Ministerial Declarations.[374] Since the 1960s, provisions providing for special treatment of developing countries have been introduced into the agreements.[375] Today, about 150

---

[373] Pascal Lamy, Director-General of the WTO, Speech 'Towards Shared Responsibility and Greater Coherence: Human Rights, Trade and Macroeconomic Policy', Colloquium on Human Rights in the Global Economy, Geneva, 13 January 2010.

[374] See, e.g., Doha Ministerial Declaration, fn. 295, p. 74, paras 42–4; also Hong Kong WTO Ministerial Declaration, 2005, WT/MIN(05)/DEC, adopted on 18 December 2005, paras. 35–8.

[375] The most general rule of SDT is contained in Part IV of the GATT, titled trade and development, which has been introduced after the Kennedy Round in 1964–5. According to Article XXXVI:8, developed contracting parties do not expect reciprocity for commitments made by them. The respective Note (GATT 1947, Annex I, Notes and Supplementary Provisions, Ad Article XXXVI, paragraph 8) explains this provision by stating that developing countries should in the course of trade negotiations not be expected to make contributions inconsistent with their individual development, financial and trade needs. This applies to both reduction and elimination of tariffs, and aims at providing developing countries with preferential market access. In consequence, developing countries retain the right to keep tariffs and other trade barriers, while they can profit from concessions of developed members (Kipel, 1996, p. 640). Article XXXVI:8 constitutes an exception to the general WTO principle of reciprocity. In addition, as a GATT waiver to the principle of non-discrimination, developed countries were allowed to maintain their GSP. Another exception to reciprocity is included in the so-called 'Enabling Clause' (Decision of 28 November 1979 (WTO:L/4903) on 'Differential and more favorable treatment, reciprocity and fuller participation of developing countries'), which grants developing country members the right to preferential access to the markets of developed countries, regardless of comparable conditions concerning access to their own markets. The right of developing countries to notify preferential trade agreements among themselves constitutes an exception to the principle of MFN treatment.

different rules providing special and differential treatment are contained in the WTO Agreements,[376] and for the least developed countries among them there are even more. In addition, SDT is acknowledged in the preambles of the WTO Agreements and in repeated declarations that developing countries are accorded special treatment in the WTO Agreement. Taken together, the insular provisions render SDT of developing countries a principle that permeates the WTO covered agreements and that is fully incorporated into the trade regime.[377]

Originally, SDT was intended to give time to developing countries to catch up in industrialization, so that they could better integrate themselves into the multilateral trading system afterwards.[378] Given that many of these time-lines have expired, the primary rationale for SDT is now based on the assumption that further adjustment through market opening causes unavoidable costs to national economies, and that those economies need special treatment to keep these costs at a lower level.[379] Such provisions, which are also contained for example, in the Agreement on Agriculture, the TBT Agreement and the Agreement on Trade-Related Investment Measures, are supposed to address the special needs of those member states which are still in a stage of economic development. Some SDT provisions aim at enhancing trading opportunities,

---

A mechanism for treating developing countries more favourably is offered in Articles XXIV and XXV with respect to free trade agreements and customs unions, even if they do not explicitly refer to developing countries. Article XVIII GATT provides protection to domestic industries of developing countries. This provision had nevertheless been applied to both developed and developing countries until 1955 (Pangestu, 2000, p. 1286), and has been reaffirmed to constitute a SDT provision (Decision of 14 November 2001, WT/MIN(01)/DEC/17, Implementation-related issues and concerns. Developing countries under certain circumstances are entitled to take protective measures, such as modifying or withdrawing from concessions for promoting an industry (Article XVIII:2, 3 and section A) and restrictions in the case of balance of payments problems (paras. 2, 3 and section B). Paragraph 4 and sections C and D even allow under certain preconditions the use of measures inconsistent with other GATT provisions. This permission of section C does not include the right to deviation from the principle of MFN, which is constituted by Article I, and from the non-discrimination provision of Article XIII. In reverse, as Article XVIII:20 refers explicitly only to section C, this also means, that the permission of the other sections includes also the right to deviate even from these articles.

[376] The WTO Secretariat identified 155 such provisions (Implementation of Special and Differential Treatment Provisions in WTO Agreements and Decisions, Note by the Secretariat, WT/COMTD/W/77 Rev.1 of 21 September 2001, at p. 14).
[377] See, e.g., Leebron (2002), p. 19. Cottier and Oesch (2005) consider SDT a 'constitutional principle' and an important mainstay of WTO law (chapter XII; p. 552).
[378] Pangestu (2000), p. 1286.   [379] Fukasaku (2000), p. 15.

others require developed countries to safeguard the interests of developing countries, still others give developing countries some flexibility by granting them more favourable thresholds, mandate support measures, provide for some safeguard-type measures or grant limited time derogation from the application of rules.[380] In some of these cases, SDT even over-rules the principle of MFN and the non-discrimination provision Article XIII.

Despite the variety of SDT provisions, it has been argued that traditional avenues of SDT have largely failed, and that a redesign of the concept is urgently needed. In consequence of these difficulties, Mitchell argues that the 'principle of non-discrimination would almost undoubtedly rise above the principle of S&D'. Postulating a certain hierarchy of principles, however, seems contrary to the general function of principles as higher norms informing all norms of a legal system. More importantly, however, this suggested hierarchy would be contrary to the intentions of WTO signatories, who chose to stress the importance of SDT by framing concrete objectives in the preamble of the WTO Agreement.

Today, there is no doubt that the concept of SDT is accepted and well anchored in WTO law.[381] Given the general relevance of SDT in the agreements, and given the great importance ascribed to it, SDT must be considered one of the fundamental principles of the WTO. Only the equal ranking of SDT with other fundamental principles of the WTO explains why developing countries may derogate from principles such as non-discrimination or reciprocity.[382] Reassuring the importance of SDT, Pascal Lamy points out that trade liberalization may entail social costs and stresses the responsibility of the international community to help countries negatively affected by the opening of markets:

> This is what I have called the 'Geneva consensus', under which the opening of markets is necessary to our collective well-being, but does not suffice in itself. It does not suffice unless strong safety nets help correct the imbalances between winners and losers at the national level. It does not suffice unless the countries which do not enjoy sufficient human, technical, and financial resources to build the necessary infrastructure or to put in place such safety nets domestically are assisted by the international community.[383]

---

[380] Youssef (1999), III.2, pp. 17–18.
[381] Cottier (2006), at p. 787. For on overview of the evolution of special and differential treatment see pp. 783–7.
[382] Mitchell (2008), p. 245. [383] See above fn. 373.

5.4.2.2.3.2 Relevance of SDT for the chapeau

Turning now to the chapeau, even without direct reference to the principle of SDT its language reflects the idea that factual conditions in different countries need to be taken into account if the application of a measure ought to meet the standards of the chapeau. More precisely, discrimination between 'countries, where the same conditions prevail' requires justification and must not be arbitrary. Given that, as detailed above, this phrase is an application of the general principle of equality, equal treatment provided to countries where different conditions prevail would also constitute discrimination.[384] The chapeau itself, however, does not give any guidance as to which conditions are relevant. According to the principle of SDT for developing countries it is imperative that the economic situation and the level of development of the affected member is among those conditions that need to be taken into account. Since the principle of SDT permeates the covered agreements, it must be considered relevant for the interpretation of the chapeau also. Thus, the application of measures seeking justification under Article XX must accommodate interests of developing countries whenever this is indicated and feasible. Given that NPA measures inherently relate to aspects subject to domestic regulation, it seems obvious that the principle of SDT is particularly relevant. The specific consequences and requirements arising from the principle of SDT under the chapeau are outlined in the sections on specific requirements below.

5.4.2.2.4 Due process and general principles

According to the prevailing view, the general requirements arising from the chapeau include observance of due process. The principle of due process, or procedural fairness, respectively, is reflected in various provisions in the WTO Agreements,[385] and it is relevant also for the application of measures seeking justification. The Appellate Body in *Shrimp Turtle* derived their applicability from an interpretation of the chapeau, more precisely of the notion 'arbitrary discrimination', together with Article X:3, which contains a number of due process requirements such

---

[384] See above at section 5.4.2.2.2.
[385] E.g., Article X contains a number of different due process objectives with respect to the legal instrument at issue and with respect to the manner in which it is administrated by the WTO member adopting the instrument. Similarly, DSU Article 6.2 contains requirements that apply to dispute settlement proceedings.

as transparency[386] and basic fairness. The Appellate Body reasoned that these requirements, which usually apply to measures consistent with WTO obligations, must *a fortiori* apply to measures falling under the general exceptions. It stated that:

> rigorous compliance with the fundamental requirements of due process should be required in the application and administration of a measure which purports to be an exception to the treaty obligations of the Member imposing the measure and which effectively results in a suspension *pro hac vice* of the treaty rights of other Members.[387]

In addition to transparency and fairness in the administration of trade regulations as applications of the principle of due process, the Appellate Body in *Shrimp Turtle* mentioned explicitly the right to be heard, the requirement to provide formal notice of decisions, the need to provide reasons for the decision and the existence of formal legal procedures for review.[388] Furthermore, the principle of good faith is also applicable in WTO law[389] and thus informs the chapeau. This principle can be described as general faithfulness to obligations and is recognized to find expression, for example, in the doctrine of the abuse of rights, protection of legitimate expectations and equity.[390]

In general, the above requirements apply equally to all measures. However, due process requirements could prove to be especially important to NPA measures. The verification of the non-physical aspects that determine the legal consequences for the respective products is characterized by practical difficulties. Often, instead of an actual verification of the facts at the border, the legal consequences will depend on the existence of valid documents certifying the respective NPAs. Thus, NPA measures will often

---

[386] The applicability of general transparency requirements is widely acknowledged. Some derive these from the rules applying to publication of regulations of general application, others from the requirement of 'reasonableness' contained in Article X:3 (the latter view is purported by Puth (2003), p. 353).

[387] Appellate Body Report, *Shrimp Turtle* (1998), para. 182.

[388] Appellate Body Report, *Shrimp Turtle* (1998), para. 183.

[389] Appellate Body Report, *US – Offset Act ('Byrd Amendment')* (2003), paras. 295–7. The Appellate Body recognized explicitly that there is a basis for the adjudicatory bodies to determine whether a WTO member has not acted in good faith (at para. 297). Thus, it is clear that the importance of this principle is not limited to treaty interpretation, but that it permeates the agreements and is relevant also for assessing compliance with WTO obligations.

[390] Cottier and Nadakavukaren Schefer (2000), pp. 48–55. The Appellate Body Report, *US – Offset Act ('Byrd Amendment')* (2003), marks the recent developments in WTO law on the principle of good faith (above fn. 389).

require greater administrative support and international cooperation than other measures. Hence, the principle of due process requires that NPA measures are applied in a highly transparent way and that producers are given a real chance to meet the conditions specified in the law or regulation.

5.4.2.3 Specific problem fields

The Appellate Body approached the non-discrimination requirement by exploring specific flaws in the application of measures which amount to unjustifiable or arbitrary discrimination. This section discusses problem fields relevant to all measures. Both aspects discussed below are often perceived as sources of flaws.

5.4.2.3.1 No prohibition of unilateral measures

The unilateral character of a measure alone does not preclude justification under Article XX. This is indicated by the strong language of Article XX, which states that 'nothing in this agreement shall be construed to prevent the adoption or enforcement by any contracting party' of measures meeting the requirements set out in Article XX. In this respect, the Appellate Body in *Shrimp Turtle* stated, albeit in a very careful language, that:

> conditioning access to a Member's domestic market on whether exporting Members comply with, or adopt, a policy or policies unilaterally prescribed by the importing Member may, to some degree, be a common aspect of measures falling within the scope of one or another of the exceptions (a) to (j) of Article XX.[391]

Hence, the general exceptions are neither reserved to measures adopted by groups of WTO members nor to measures based on international agreements.[392] To reiterate, under certain conditions, international agreements may determine legal relations among WTO members, and international recognition may be crucial for an interpretation of the particular exceptions. Nevertheless, a unilateral measure is not *a priori* excluded from the scope of Article XX.[393]

---

[391] Appellate Body Report, *Shrimp Turtle* (1998), para. 121.
[392] As Charnovitz points out, the distinction between unilateral and multilateral measures is not suitable to depict the far more complex reality. He suggests taking into account the 'degree of multilateral approval' in evaluating the appropriateness of a measure. 'Multilateral approval' of a NPA would render a measure less likely to be protectionist or arbitrary (Charnovitz, 2002, pp. 105–6).
[393] E.g., Quick (2000), pp. 255–6; Gaines (2001), p. 808; Howse (2002), pp. 502–3; Charnovitz (2002); Chang (2005), pp. 44–5; also in WTO jurisprudence, e.g., Panel Report, *Shrimp Turtle (Article 21.5)* (2001), No. 5.65.

Closely related to the issue of unilaterality is the question of an obligation to reach international agreement before adopting a measure.[394] The chapeau of Article XX clearly does not contain an obligation to conclude an international agreement before adopting measures under the general exceptions.[395] As the Appellate Body stated in *Shrimp Turtle (Article 21.5)*, such an obligation would in effect provide any WTO member with a veto over whether another country could fulfil its obligations under the WTO Agreements.[396] This result would indeed ultimately render naught the right of WTO members to invoke the general exceptions. Consequently, the Appellate Body also rejected an obligation to conclude international agreements as a pre-requirement of the chapeau.[397]

5.4.2.3.2 Are serious negotiations obligatory?

The question remains whether the non-discrimination principle set out in the chapeau implies other cooperation requirements, such as a pre-requirement to conduct serious international negotiations on the subject matter, whether or not these result in an agreement.

The WTO adjudicatory bodies have repeatedly stressed the importance of 'serious good faith efforts' in negotiations with all affected trading partners prior to the adoption of the contested measures.[398] The Appellate Body in *Shrimp Turtle (Article 21.5)* stated that a multilateral approach, as far as possible, was indeed strongly preferred,[399] and cited an international agreement, namely, the Inter-American Convention for the Protection and Conservation of Sea Turtles 'as evidence that an alternative course of action based on cooperation and consensus was reasonably open to the United States'.[400] This approach, however, has also met with criticism. The reports in the *Shrimp Turtle* dispute especially have been criticized for interpreting the chapeau in a way that would reduce Article XX to an

---

[394] This argument was put forward by Malaysia in the *Shrimp Turtle (Article 21.5)* (2001) dispute (Panel Report, No. 3.104).
[395] Howse (2002), p. 509, also invokes in this respect the difference between Article XX and Article XXI(c).
[396] Appellate Body Report, *Shrimp Turtle (Article 21.5)* (2001), para. 123.
[397] Appellate Body Report, *Shrimp Turtle (Article 21.5)* (2001), para. 124.
[398] Cf. Panel Report, *Shrimp Turtle (Article 21.5)* (2001), para. 5.67, similarly, Appellate Body Report, *Shrimp Turtle* (1998), Nos. 166–72.
[399] Appellate Body Report, *Shrimp Turtle (Article 21.5)* (2001), No. 124.
[400] Appellate Body Report, *Shrimp Turtle (Article 21.5)* (2001), No. 128. The statement shows the twofold importance of negotiations. On the one hand, negotiations may constitute reasonably available alternative courses of action, and may therefore be relevant for the necessity requirement and for the weighing and balancing process, and as proof of the absence of unjustifiable discrimination on the other.

5.4 THE CHAPEAU AND OTHER REQUIREMENTS

emergency measure 'that can be applied only in direct connection with ceaseless efforts to reach a multilateral agreement'.[401] It has been argued that whether or not a measure is a result of negotiations or a unilateral act cannot be decisive for the finding of discrimination. Otherwise, Article XX would be supplanted with a rule based on negotiated exceptions.[402]

Indeed, there is some evidence that the findings on negotiations in the *Shrimp Turtle* dispute cannot be generalized, since they were based on the specific facts of the case. Among these facts was a provision in the respective legislative act which directed the respondent's authorities to initiate negotiations for the development of bilateral or multilateral agreements for the protection of sea turtles.[403] Given that the respondent had indeed entered into negotiations with some states but not with others, and so discriminated against those other states, it was consistent that the adjudicatory bodies explored reasons that could justify the lack of comparable negotiations. Since no reasons were found, the finding that the lack of comparable negotiations with all affected trading partners amounted to unjustifiable discrimination is convincing for this particular dispute. However, there is some evidence that the Appellate Body considered serious negotiations crucial not only because of the specific facts of the case but also in general, since it stated:

> Given the specific mandate contained in Section 609, and given the decided preference for multilateral approaches voiced by WTO Members and others in the international community in various international agreements for the protection and conservation of endangered sea turtles that were cited in our previous Report, the United States, in our view, would be expected to make good faith efforts to reach international agreements that are comparable from one forum of negotiation to the other.[404]

With this statement, the Appellate Body showed that the requirement to make good faith efforts to reach international agreement is a result not only of the relevant law at issue, but also of the 'decided preference for multilateral approaches voiced by WTO Members and others'.

A requirement to negotiate prior to the adoption of trade restrictive measures was also addressed in the *US – Gambling* dispute, albeit not under the chapeau. The panel discussed the lack of negotiations with respect to necessity of the measures when assessing provisional justification under

---

[401] Gaines (2001), p. 814.   [402] McRae (2000), p. 234.
[403] Appellate Body Report, *Shrimp Turtle* (1998), No. 166. An excerpt of section 609 is reprinted in Panel Report, *Shrimp Turtle* (1998), Annex I, p. 296.
[404] Appellate Body Report, *Shrimp Turtle (Article 21.5)* (2001), No. 122.

the moral exception of the GATS. In the weighing and balancing process, the panel relied on the Appellate Body's statements in *Shrimp Turtle* and considered the lack of negotiations as decisive for declining the necessity of the contested measures.[405] This finding, however, was over-ruled by the Appellate Body. It stated:

> consultations are by definition a process, the results of which are uncertain and therefore not capable of comparison with the measures at issue in this case.[406]

Consequently, the Appellate Body found that the panel had been wrong to consider negotiations as a reasonably available alternative to achieve the stated objective. Although the Appellate Body also reviewed the panel's assessment of the requirements contained in the chapeau, it did not explore whether the lack of negotiations could be relevant in this respect. Since the specific facts underlying the *US – Gambling* dispute suggested that negotiations would not be fruitful, however, the Appellate Body's silence on the relevance of the lack of negotiations in this respect cannot be interpreted to indicate a general irrelevance of negotiations under the chapeau.

In sum, so far, there is no well-established WTO jurisprudence on the relevance of negotiations under the chapeau. If, however, negotiations were conducted with some of the affected trading partners, then the non-discrimination principle under the chapeau indeed requires comparable efforts with all other affected countries, provided there is a chance that these will be fruitful. While a general obligation to seriously negotiate cannot be derived directly from the language of Article XX, it might arise from general due process requirements, such as the principles of good faith and basic fairness. To date, however, a respective obligation has been strongly contested.[407] An outright refusal of a serious offer to negotiate, however, would usually violate the principles of good faith and basic fairness and thus amount to a disguised restriction in violation of the chapeau.

5.4.2.4 Specific requirements for NPA measures

While the above section explored the general relevance of negotiations, the following sections explore whether the specific characteristics of NPA measures lead to any particular requirements.

---

[405] Panel Report, *US – Gambling* (2004), paras. 6.531–6.535.
[406] Appellate Body Report, *US – Gambling* (2005), No. 317.
[407] E.g., Chang (2005), pp. 44–50.

5.4.2.4.1 Relevant characteristics of NPA measures

The crucial difference between NPA measures and measures linked to product characteristics is the existence of an extraterritorial reach, and this difference does indeed seem relevant for non-discrimination requirements. In the case of measures linked to physical product characteristics, objects in the country imposing the measure may be affected. This is usually not the case if NPA measures are concerned. Products restricted because of NPAs cannot transfer the deprecated aspects into the country imposing the measure. Thus, the country of importation is not physically affected. Also, in contrast to other measures, among the objectives of NPA measures is an influence on situations or conduct within the jurisdiction of another WTO member. It seems that the lack of jurisdiction on the side of the country imposing the measure is also a relevant factor to be considered for the interpretation of the chapeau. Due to the lack of jurisdiction, there is no direct influence on the respective NPAs. In sum, the relevant specific characteristics of NPA measures comprise: (1) a lack of physical impact on the country of importation, which imposes the measure; (2) a lack of jurisdiction of the country of importation for the respective NPA; and (3) factual differences between different countries of production in which the respective NPAs are present.

The general principle of non-discrimination under the chapeau requires that any discrimination between the country imposing the measure, or products produced in it, and other countries or products originating within these must be justifiable and not be arbitrary. This discrimination standard has been interpreted as including a requirement of basic fairness. Therefore, one could argue that since the country imposing the measure lacks jurisdiction for the situation or conduct aimed at, discriminations between products are justifiable only if the authorities competent for regulating the situation or conduct have been involved in the process. Given their lack of direct effect on the NPAs in question, NPA trade measures will often be less urgent than measures that seek to prevent physical effects on objects within the territory of the country imposing the measure. It is important to note, however, that the previous elaborations do not apply equally to all NPA measures. If a measure targets NPAs affecting the country of importation, for example, in cases of environmental damage arising from production in a neighbouring country, then the remaining differences would need to be assessed for a determination of the specific requirements under the chapeau.

The following specific requirements are in part more procedural in nature, namely, those regarding negotiations and implementation periods, and in part more substantial in nature, when it comes to accompanying activities, such as transfer of technologies or funds.

5.4.2.4.2 Consultations and negotiations

NPA measures are characterized by their extraterritorial effects and by the fact that their objectives relate to conduct or circumstances within the jurisdiction of other countries. In addition, due to their non-physicality NPAs usually do not endanger objects in the country of importation and, in consequence, they will usually be less urgent than product measures linked to physical aspects, if these are harmful or bear risks. It could therefore be argued that the above due process applications lead to different requirements for NPA measures.

For example, if an NPA measure is not considered urgent, then due process could require the imposing state to take into account the interests of affected states at an earlier stage. The right to be heard, if applicable in the drafting stage of measures, would then imply that affected countries have the opportunity in consultations to voice their concerns and interests even before the measure is imposed. Consultations are the most basic form of international cooperation, and at the same time a pre-requirement for any other form of cooperation. The same argument, however, could also be invoked to require active negotiations beyond consultations in order to find a solution.

Another argument for a requirement to enter into consultations with respect to NPA measures is the language of the chapeau, which states that it is crucial to take into account the different conditions prevailing in the affected countries. Given that this language is an expression of the general principle of equality, this requirement should not be limited to the application of measures, but also apply to the drafting stage. Therefore, relevant differences in the affected WTO members should be taken into account in the law-making process. This is especially relevant in the case of NPA measures necessary to protect domestic public morals. The particular situation in the country will usually be decisive for the question of whether or not trade measures are necessary for protecting domestic public morals. A uniform application of the measure with respect to all countries, ignorant of the particular conditions prevailing there, will often have to be considered arbitrary. There will usually be time and opportunity to find solutions that suit the conditions prevailing in each affected country.

Finally, the requirement to consult with affected trading partners could also be derived from application of the general principle *pacta sunt servanda* together with the obligation to apply treaties in good faith.[408] According to Article 18 of the Vienna Convention, states are obliged to refrain from acts which would defeat the object and purpose of a treaty.[409] This obligation could be interpreted to imply that states ought to resort to trade-restrictive measures only if truly necessary.

In sum, depending on the object of protection and on the specific facts of the case, consultations with affected countries will usually be indicated and, given the lesser time constraints, they will often be feasible. Therefore, if alternatives to NPA measures have not even been explored in consultations with affected trading partners, then the resulting discrimination usually ought to be considered unjustifiable under the chapeau. In contrast to consultations, negotiations aim at avoiding restrictions on trade altogether. They allow different stakeholders to truly participate and will often result in modifications of original decisions or otherwise influence outcomes. In addition to the elaborations on cooperation requirements for all measures outlined above,[410] it seems that given the lesser urgency of NPA measures the principles of good faith and basic fairness can indeed require efforts that go beyond mere consultations.[411] However, these negotiation requirements must not be interpreted in a way that would render NPA measures impossible in cases where such negotiations fail.

5.4.2.4.3 Implementation periods

The Appellate Body considered the granting of reasonable time-lines for affected countries crucial for the determination of unjustifiable discrimination. Such time-lines would allow countries to decide and possibly to adapt to the respective requirements and to implement necessary regulatory programmes. The Appellate Body also stressed the relationship between time periods and the onerousness of compliance:

> The length of the 'phase-in' period is not inconsequential for exporting countries desiring certification. That period relates directly to the onerousness of the burdens of complying with the requisites of certification

---

[408] Cf. Appellate Body Report, *US – Offset Act ('Byrd Amendment')* (2003), para. 296.

[409] This same argumentation led the Panel in *Shrimp Turtle* to refer to the preamble for determining objective and purpose of the WTO Agreement. While the reference to objective and purpose of the WTO Agreements was strongly criticized by the Appellate Body, the reference to the principles *pacta sunt servanda* and good faith was not (No. 116). The Appellate Body's statements in *US – Offset Act ('Byrd Amendment')* (2003), paras. 295–7, confirmed the validity of the latter principles.

[410] Above at section 5.4.2.3.2.

[411] In this direction also the recommendations *de lege ferenda* by Cottier, Pauwelyn and Bürgi (2005a), at p. 25.

and the practical feasibility of locating and developing alternative export markets for shrimp. The shorter that period, the heavier the burdens of compliance, particularly where an applicant has a large number of trawler vessels, and the greater the difficulties of reorienting the harvesting country's shrimp exports. The shorter that period, in net effect, the heavier the influence of the import ban.[412]

Although the Appellate Body did not explicitly give the legal reasons for considering such practical difficulties, it seems that underlying this reasoning is a consideration of basic fairness. In this respect, practical problems of WTO members facing restrictive measures affecting their exporting industries also need to be taken into account. Since the requirement of reasonable time periods arises from general principles of basic fairness, it applies to all measures under Article XX. Also, different timelines must conform to the different factual conditions prevailing in these countries. Due to the general principle of equality, uniform phase-in periods will often tend to constitute unjustifiable discrimination. In consequence of the principle of SDT, the economic situation in affected developing countries is a crucial factor to be considered in determining the length of the phase-in period.

In the *Shrimp Turtle* Report, which prompted the Appellate Body to expressly mention regulatory difficulties of the affected WTO member and adequate time-lines, the contested measure was actually an NPA measure. While in cases of measures linked to physical properties producers also need to adapt production in order to meet the particular requirements, it seems that reasonable implementation periods are even more appropriate in the case of NPA measures. First, the general absence of serious time constraints, given the lack of direct effect on the NPA at issue, is the crucial difference relevant for the justification of NPA measures and also bears on the need to offer reasonable implementation periods. Second, the administration of NPA measures will often require considerable administrative efforts, and putting in place functioning structures to verify and document NPAs may take time. To reiterate, due to their non-physical character, NPAs cannot be checked on importation, and the importing country will often rely on documents and certification instead. This aspect is reflected in the *Shrimp Turtle* Report, where the Appellate Body ascribed great importance to:

> the administrative and financial costs and the difficulties of governments in putting together and enacting the necessary regulatory programs and

---

[412] Appellate Body Report, *Shrimp Turtle* (1998), No. 174.

'credible enforcement effort', and in implementing the compulsory use of TEDs on hundreds, if not thousands, of shrimp trawl vessels.[413]

Thus, a lack of serious time constraints and administrative difficulties that typically accompany NPA measures account for the importance of reasonable phase-in periods in the case of NPA measures.

At this point, the principle of SDT is also highly relevant: given the efforts necessary to allow developing country producers to comply with the NPA requirements at issue, the level of development and the specific circumstances in developing WTO members need to be taken into account for determining the length of adequate phase-in periods.

5.4.2.4.4 Transfer of technologies, administrative and financial support

A possible requirement of a transfer of technologies and general support was discussed in the *Shrimp Turtle* dispute, and thus in a dispute concerning a NPA measure. Assessing the existence of unjustifiable discrimination, the Appellate Body pointed out that requirements of certification usually assume a successful previous transfer of a specific technology, in this case, for example, so-called turtle excluder devices (TEDs) for shrimp trawlers. It stated:

> Differing treatment of different countries desiring certification is also observable in the differences in the levels of effort made by the United States in transferring the required TED technology to specific countries. Far greater efforts to transfer that technology successfully were made to certain exporting countries – basically the fourteen wider Caribbean/western Atlantic countries cited earlier – than to other exporting countries, including the appellees. The level of these efforts is probably related to the length of the 'phase-in' periods granted – the longer the 'phase-in' period, the higher the possible level of efforts at technology transfer. Because compliance with the requirements of certification realistically assumes successful TED technology transfer, low or merely nominal efforts at achieving that transfer will, in all probability, result in fewer countries being able to satisfy the certification requirements under Section 609, within the very limited 'phase-in' periods allowed them.[414]

Since the respondent had failed to make equal efforts to transfer technologies to various affected countries, unjustifiable discrimination was

---

[413] Appellate Body Report, *Shrimp Turtle* (1998), No. 174.
[414] Appellate Body Report, *Shrimp Turtle* (1998), No. 175.

asserted, albeit 'in their cumulative effect' with discrimination relating to different phase-in periods and other treatment.[415]

Therefore, the question of whether a transfer of technologies is a general requirement for justification of NPA measures or whether it was merely a consequence of the facts underlying the *Shrimp Turtle* dispute, namely, that the respondent had actually provided technical assistance to some countries but not to others, as yet remains unanswered. While the differences in treatment of countries were obviously crucial in that dispute, the last sentence of the above quote stresses the importance of technology transfers for the satisfaction of certification requirements in rather general language. Against such a requirement it could be invoked that neither Article XX nor any other provision in the GATT mentions technology transfer explicitly, and that in consequence technology transfer could play a role only in combination with discriminatory treatment.

Several of the WTO covered agreements drafted in the 1990s, however, stress the general importance of technology transfers.[416] The preamble of the TBT Agreement, for example, shows that WTO members considered 'the transfer of technology from developed to developing countries' as desirable and as an objective of that agreement.[417] The concept of transfers of technologies from developed to developing countries is well established in international law. This is apparent, for example, from the 1982 UN Convention on the Law of the Sea (UNCLOS), which promotes the transfer of relevant technologies and scientific knowledge, both in general and particularly with respect to developing states.[418]

However, it seems that a general requirement of a transfer of technologies would considerably limit the right to invoke Article XX. Transfers of technologies imply costs for providing expertise, equipment, technical assistance and training. Depending on the measure at issue, these costs may be immense. Given that neither the language of Article XX nor of other relevant GATT provisions requires such transfers, it is here argued that the chapeau cannot be interpreted as establishing a general requirement of technology transfer to affected countries. Nevertheless, in rare cases, a refusal to provide technical assistance despite the existence of an

---

[415] Appellate Body Report, *Shrimp Turtle* (1998), No. 176.
[416] Cf., e.g., TRIPS Agreement Article 7, Objectives: 'should contribute to the promotion of technological innovation and to the transfer and dissemination of technology'.
[417] Also the GATS Annex on Telecommunications encourages a transfer of technology from foreign providers to enable developing countries to support the development of telecommunications infrastructure (at No. 6(d)).
[418] Cf., e.g., UNCLOS Article 144 and Part IV.

5.4 THE CHAPEAU AND OTHER REQUIREMENTS

offer that would imply no or little costs to be borne by the country imposing the measure, might violate the obligation to good faith and basic fairness. Therefore, although there is no general requirement, such a refusal could under certain circumstances amount to a disguised restriction in the sense of the chapeau.

At this point, the principle of SDT assumes a crucial role for the justification of NPA measures. A main concern about the justification of NPA measures is that they shift considerable costs to the country of production for complying with rules that have been put in place by other countries. Therefore, developing countries especially fear that often they will simply not be able to comply with NPA measures and as a corollary will be hampered in their economic development. This problem has been recognized in scholarship. For example, Charnovitz stresses the necessity for policymakers adopting NPA measures to be sensitive to the financial burden that is being shifted to developing countries, and regrets that there are currently no mechanisms to 'provide for fair burden sharing'.[419] Cottier, Pauwelyn and Bürgi stress the need for affirmative action and postulate that 'PPMs alone should not be recognized without a component of transfer of resources', including investment and technology transfer.[420]

It is here suggested that the principle of SDT, if taken seriously, provides a suitable tool for sharing the burden of compliance commensurate with the level of economic development of the countries concerned. The chapeau of Article XX, informed by the principle of SDT, requires that NPA measures are designed taking into account the level of economic development of affected countries. Together with the commitment to sustainable development, the chapeau requires a WTO member imposing an NPA measure to provide technical assistance to enable affected developing country members to meet the requirements imposed by it. The same reasoning that applies to the provision of technologies must likewise apply to costs related to a change in the regulation of the developing WTO member affected by the measure. In *Shrimp Turtle*, the Appellate Body stressed the high 'administrative and financial costs' and other difficulties of governments in enacting the necessary regulatory programmes.[421]

---

[419] Charnovitz (2002), pp. 74–5.
[420] Cottier, Pauwelyn and Bürgi make this point with respect to human rights and beyond the realm of special and differential treatment (Cottier, Pauwelyn and Bürgi, 2005a, p. 25). However, it seems that only the principle of SDT and the economic inequality between WTO members provides a basis for transfers. Measures affecting developed countries, if otherwise justified under Article XX, should not be subjected to any transfers.
[421] Appellate Body Report, *Shrimp Turtle* (1998), No. 174.

Although the transfer of technologies is an important point, it may not necessarily be the only one crucial for many developing countries. The requirement to provide assistance to developing countries, where indicated, extends therefore from technical, to administrative and, consequently, even financial assistance in order to allow developing country producers and administrations to satisfy the requirements imposed by the importing country.

5.5 Conclusions

The above analysis of applicability and scope of the particular exceptions to NPA measures proves ample opportunity to justify a range of NPA measures under existing WTO law. While a number of public policies which might be relevant for NPA measures, such as culture or minority protection, are excluded from the scope of the exceptions, many policies that are highly relevant for NPA measures are included or otherwise reflected in sub-paragraphs (a)–(j). For example, the important group of environmental NPA measures falls into the scope of exception (g), provided the measures aim at the protection of domestic or shared resources. Also NPA trade measures aimed at the prevention of serious human rights violations abroad are generally justifiable under the public morals exception. This flexibility of Article XX towards NPA measures is due to the vague language of the particular exceptions, the predominant use of generic terms, together with an objective and evolutionary approach to interpretation. The more established a value or the urgency of a need for action is at international level, the greater is the likelihood that this recognition can at some point translate into the incorporation of the body of core or variable public morals. Nevertheless, the public morals exception cannot be invoked as a catch-all exception. The necessity requirement in sub-paragraph (a), together with the requirements of the chapeau as developed in WTO case law, provide useful handholds to prevent abuse. The principle of special and differential treatment for developing countries in particular is of utmost importance to the justification of NPA trade measures. This principle together with the rule that different conditions prevailing in affected WTO members need to be taken into account has the potential to render illegal any NPA measure that is not designed in a way which allows developing countries, and in particular developing country producers, to actually comply with the measure. Given that NPA measures need to be justified based on legitimate public policies, it seems consistent that only genuine NPA measures which ultimately aim at an actual change of specific circumstances or conduct can possibly be justifiable. The flipside of the flexibility of Article XX, which ultimately stems from vague language, is considerable legal uncertainty. Much is left for decision by the adjudicatory bodies, namely, the difficult task of striking a balance between policy space for WTO member states as bodies competent for public policies, on the one hand, and the need to preserve the functioning of the multilateral trading system, on the other.

In sum, while the language of the particular exceptions and of the chapeau allows for a reasonable assessment and justification of NPA trade measures, there are also shortcomings. To reiterate, certain policies that clearly ought to be considered legitimate are excluded from the scope of Article XX. This applies to all policies that are not reflected in subcparagraphs (b)-(j) and that do not have a strictly moral dimension. The *per se* exclusion of related NPA measures seems to limit the policy space of WTO members unnecessarily. Also, the legal uncertainty itself amounts to a problem. Legal uncertainty, if related to fundamental questions, has the potential to create mistrust and disrupt the smooth functioning of the trading system. Therefore, while Article XX provides a suitable basis to determine the status of NPA measures as it stands, further development in WTO jurisprudence, authoritative interpretations and carefully drafted amendments are necessary to seize its potential and to provide for the necessary legal certainty.

6

The status of PPM measures under the TBT Agreement and the SPS Agreement

6.1 Introduction

In contrast to the GATT, both the TBT and the SPS Agreement explicitly mention 'processes and production methods'. This chapter therefore explores whether PPM measures have a special legal status under both agreements. Despite the explicit reference, however, it is unclear whether both agreements cover all types of PPM measures, or whether coverage is limited to incorporated PPMs. The question arises if the GATT remains of any actual relevance, since a large part of NPA measures could fall within the scope of the TBT and the SPS Agreements as *lex specialis*. While this issue is very complex and contentious for the TBT Agreement, section 6.3 explains that the SPS Agreement covers only incorporated PPMs and is therefore of little importance to this work. The TBT Agreement, on the other hand, relates to a specific subject matter, namely, technical barriers to trade, and therefore cannot cover all PPM, let alone NPA, measures. In addition, the relationship between the TBT Agreement and the GATT in the case of conflicting provisions is not entirely clear. The following section argues that the TBT Agreement is applicable to an important group of technical norms, namely, labelling regulation, even if these concern unincorporated PPMs. Its focus is on the consideration of consumer information as a legitimate objective highly relevant to labelling requirements concerning unincorporated PPMs.

6.2 The TBT Agreement and PPMs

Given the lack of international harmonization, technical standards and regulation have the potential to create substantial non-tariff barriers to international trade. The importance of such barriers has increased vis-à-vis other trade restrictions, in particular tariffs, which have been lowered to a

6.2 THE TBT AGREEMENT AND PPMS

fraction of their pre-GATT level.[1] In response to the trade-restrictive effects of such barriers, the GATT parties in the Tokyo Round adopted the so-called Standards Code. The Code was later substituted by the TBT Agreement and has been adopted by WTO members in the Uruguay Round. Whatever their trade effects, technical standards are necessary to ensure that safety and quality requirements are met. The basic intention of the TBT Agreement is therefore not to abolish technical standards, but to mitigate possible trade-restrictive effects. The TBT Agreement establishes certain transparency procedures and requires notification of relevant regulation. In respect of substantive requirements, it obliges WTO members to draft and apply only standards pursuing legitimate objectives, and only in a way that is not more trade-restrictive than necessary.[2] The increasing importance of technical barriers to trade is reflected in the increasing number of notifications which reached an all-time high of 1,410 new notifications in 2009.[3]

The TBT Agreement is most relevant to the debate on PPM measures as it explicitly refers to 'processes and production methods'. However, the agreement does not define the notion in more detail. Hence, coverage of the agreement with respect to PPMs, especially unincorporated PPMs, is contested.[4] PPM-based measures falling into the scope of the TBT Agreement might be national technical regulations and standards, packaging and labelling requirements relating to production processes or methods of production.

6.2.1 Applicability of the TBT Agreement

The TBT Agreement contains provisions relating to technical regulations, standards and to procedures assessing conformity with both types

---

[1] E.g., average tariffs on industrial goods in developed countries have been lowered from around 40 per cent the 1940s to an average of 3.8 per cent in the Uruguay Round (Stewart and Venables, Note on Globalisation prepared for the Select Committee on Economic Affairs (22 November 2002), available at www.parliament.the-stationery-office.co.uk/pa/ld200203/ldselect/ldeconaf/5/514.htm, accessed 9 August 2010). The number of imports whose tariff rates are bound have increased to 99 per cent of product lines in developed countries (WTO, 2007a, p. 25).
[2] Cf. TBT Agreement, Article 2:2.
[3] Fifteenth Annual Review of the Implementation and Operation of the TBT Agreement, Note by the Secretariat, G/TBT/28 of 5 February 2010, at p. 39.
[4] The debate has been going on for several decades. It began under the Tokyo Round Agreement on Technical Barriers to Trade of 12 April 1979, see, e.g., Committee on Technical Barriers to Trade, Decisions and Recommendations Adopted by the Committee

of norms. The scope of application therefore depends on the determination of whether a norm constitutes a technical regulation or a standard. Technical regulations are defined in Annex 1 to the agreement as documents which lay down 'product characteristics or their related processes and production methods'.[5] Standards, compliance with which is not mandatory unlike technical regulations, are documents which provide 'rules, guidelines or characteristics for products or related processes and production methods'.[6] The agreement points out that both technical regulations and standards can also consist in requirements relating to terminology, symbols or, most prominently, labelling requirements 'as they apply to a product, process or production method'. The limitation of the TBT Agreement's scope on norms of a technical character implies that the broader group of NPAs measures is in principle excluded. Accordingly, social NPAs, such as observance of labour rights, fall outside the scope of the TBT Agreement.[7] PPMs are the notable exception from this rule. Due to the explicit language of the definition in this respect, PPMs seem to be covered by the provisions of the TBT Agreement. However, even with respect to PPM measures, doubts concerning its applicability remain.

6.2.1.1 Categorization of relevant norms linked to unincorporated PPMs

There is consensus that technical norms relating to incorporated PPMs, namely, production methods bearing on physical characteristics, fall into the scope of the TBT Agreement. In contrast, the question of whether or not this agreement covers, or whether it should cover, technical regulations and standards requiring use of certain unincorporated PPMs is subject to an ongoing scholarly debate. For the analysis below it is important to distinguish between two types of measures relating to unincorporated PPMs.

The first type, addressed in the following section, are laws or regulations directly prescribing specific technical requirements that must be met in order for products to be placed on the domestic market. Such laws and regulations can impose requirements with respect to production that must be met in order for the respective products to be allowed to be placed on the market. An example is the notification by Belgium of a prohibition

---

since 1 January 1980, TBT/16/Rev.2 of 11 October 1984. To date, WTO members have not yet reached an explicit agreement on this question.

[5] TBT Agreement, Annex 1, No. 1.   [6] TBT Agreement, Annex 1, No. 2.

[7] For direct technical norms, this finding is in line with the view that unincorporated PPMs are not covered. For labelling requirements, see below at section 6.2.1.3.2.2.

on production and marketing of skins of seal pups if the seals have been not hunted by the Inuit people in a traditional way.[8] Other examples of unincorporated PPMs to which technical regulations can be linked are procedural or formal requirements, for example, relating to product safety. For instance, in order to prevent the use of dangerous substances in toys, national regulations may oblige producers to adhere to certain formal administrative procedures, for example, relating to registration and authorization of use and presence of certain chemicals in products. Producers failing to meet these formal requirements may thus face a prohibition on placing a product on the market, even if the product itself would be in conformity with the substantive requirements.

The second type of regulation relevant for PPM measures, addressed in section 6.2.1.3, is the group of labelling requirements. These seek to increase consumer information and usually require or encourage that information on specific aspects is disclosed and labelled on the product. The most prominent case is labelling of ingredients on food products, and similar requirements may relate to PPMs if the required information pertains to aspects of production. An example is a requirement to label products with information on the use of environmentally or animal friendly production methods, such as consumer information on farming methods used in the production of eggs.[9]

6.2.1.2 Technical regulations and standards

In the practical implementation of the TBT Agreement there is considerable legal uncertainty on the scope of the agreement with respect to the first type of measures, technical norms, in as far as they prescribe the use or not of unincorporated PPMs. While the prevailing view seems to hold that these norms do not fall within the scope of the TBT Agreement, some countries have actually notified such technical regulations to the TBT Committee.[10]

The starting point for the analysis of the scope of the TBT Agreement is the text of the agreement. The definitions of both technical regulations and standards in Annex 1 of the TBT Agreement refer to 'processes and production methods' in addition to products; for example, a technical regulation is a 'document which lays down product characteristics or

---

[8] Notification of Belgium, G/TBT/N/BEL39 of 8 March 2006.
[9] E.g., Notification of South Africa, G/TBT/ZAF/57 of 28 July 2006, notifying a regulation requiring an indication of 'free range' or 'barn' on fresh eggs.
[10] A recent example is the Belgian notification with respect to methods of obtaining seal pup skins (above fn. 8).

their *related* processes and production methods'. Likewise, a standard is a document that provides for non-mandatory 'rules, guidelines or characteristics for products or *related* processes and production methods'.[11] The word 'relate' has been interpreted to mean 'having a physical impact on the end product'.[12] This view holds that only PPMs altering the physical characteristics of a product, so-called incorporated PPMs, are covered by the TBT Agreement. The small difference between the wording of the definition of technical regulations ('their related processes and production methods') and the definition of standards which omits the possessive pronoun ('related processes and production methods') does not seem to imply a different meaning. Thus, the prevailing view understands the language of the TBT Agreement to indicate that only requirements on PPMs incorporated in the product can possibly constitute technical regulations or standards, and therefore can be subject to the provisions of the TBT Agreement.[13] Accordingly, requirements with respect to unincorporated PPMs would be excluded from the scope of the TBT Agreement. This view finds support in the negotiating history of the TBT Agreement.

The question of whether or not requirements with respect to unincorporated PPMs should be covered by the TBT Agreement has been subject to repeated discussions in the course of negotiations. A proposal by the United States in 1988 to extend all major disciplines in the agreement to technical requirements relating to all PPMs was motivated by the recognition that such requirements constitute a growing body of measures with a high potential for creating unnecessary trade barriers. While the proposal found a good deal of support, it was met with scepticism by others.[14] In the final phase of negotiations in the Uruguay Round, Mexico, however, proposed that the coverage of PPM-based measures in the definitions should be clarified, and negotiators agreed that the word 'related' should be inserted. Mexico had made clear that the intent was to exclude PPMs

---

[11] Emphasis added.
[12] According to the UNCTAD (Dispute Settlement, 3.10, Technical Barriers to Trade (2003) at p. 10) this is the view generally held on this question. Although this interpretation has not always been acknowledged explicitly, it is a necessary precondition for the arguably prevailing opinion. The discussion obviously draws from the 'likeness' debate discussed in more detail below.
[13] E.g., Tietje (2003), p. 286; Joshi (2004), pp. 69–92, at 75; Schoenbaum (1997), pp. 268–313, at 288; Puth (2003), pp. 216–17.
[14] WTO, Negotiating History of the Coverage of the Agreement on Technical Barriers to Trade, Note by the Secretariat, WT/CTE/W/10, G/TBT/W/11 of 29 August 1995, CXX–CXXIII.

that are unrelated to the characteristics of a product.[15] At a later stage, Mexico proposed in addition to insert the word 'their' before the word 'related' in the definition of a technical regulation in order to ensure that the Agreement would address only a narrow selection of PPMs.[16] This wording was finally carried into the text of the TBT Agreement. In sum, it seems that the intention of the majority of the negotiators was to exclude technical regulations and standards relating to unincorporated PPMs from the TBT Agreement.

Less clear, however, is what kind of legal status the negotiators had actually wanted for such measures. The negotiating history gives evidence of a general scepticism with regard to the legitimacy of linking trade measures to unincorporated PPMs. It seems that the exclusion of PPMs from the scope of the TBT Agreement was misunderstood as implying a general rejection of such measures. Scepticism about unincorporated PPMs was indeed expressed by a number of participants. New Zealand, for instance, viewed PPM-based requirements as generally more trade-restrictive than requirements relating to product characteristics. Therefore, it was of the view that in order to prevent a circumvention of the disciplines of the TBT Agreement, PPM-based requirements should be included.[17] Scepticism with respect to the legitimacy of PPM-based norms is also apparent in the draft text for the TBT Agreement circulated in July 1990, which expressed a hierarchy under which technical regulations should, whenever appropriate, be drafted in terms of performance rather than in terms of PPMs.[18] The confusion with respect to the legal consequences of inclusion or exclusion of measures relating to unincorporated PPMs also becomes apparent in a note by the Secretariat summarizing the negotiating history: it observed in a rather complicated way that many participants were of the view that standards based on unincorporated PPMs 'should not be considered eligible for being treated as being in conformity with the TBT Agreement'.[19] Based on the objective and purpose of the TBT Agreement, some do indeed argue for the inclusion of all PPM-based norms into the agreement: pointing out the legal consequences of the exclusion of such measures from the scope of the agreement, they stress that excluded

---

[15] Note by the Secretariat, WT/CTE/W/10, G/TBT/W/11 of 29 August 1995, at CXLVI.
[16] Note by the Secretariat, WT/CTE/W/10, G/TBT/W/11 of 29 August 1995, at CXLVII.
[17] Proposal by New Zealand, MTN.GNG/NG8/W/58 of 22 November 1989.
[18] WTO, Note by the Secretariat, WT/CTE/W/10, G/TBT/W/11 of 29 August 1995, at CXLII, Article 2.5.
[19] WTO, Note by the Secretariat, WT/CTE/W/10, G/TBT/W/11 of 29 August 1995, at III(c).

measures would automatically be subject to the arguably less stringent provisions of the GATT. They warned that it would be curious if 'non-PPM technical regulations were subject to the more stringent requirements of the TBT Agreement, while the less transparent PPM type technical regulations, possibly justified by Article XX of GATT, were not'.[20] Others, in contrast, wondered why the TBT Agreement should not render all kinds of PPM norms subject to the principle of proportionality.[21]

The stated perplexity is arguably based on two doubtful presumptions: first, it is not clear why technical requirements relating to PPMs should be less transparent than those relating to product characteristics. There is no obvious reason why production requirements should not be as transparent, or as obscure, as technical requirements relating to physical product characteristics. Difficulties may indeed arise in assessing whether or not the requirements have been met, but many smaller physical differences in products, for example, the absence of certain chemical substances, are also difficult to detect and require sophisticated testing methods. The second doubtful premise relates to the argument that the exclusion of unincorporated PPMs would be curious because GATT disciplines were less stringent than those of the TBT Agreement. Indeed, the Appellate Body has found that the TBT Agreement establishes requirements that are *different* from, and *additional* to, the obligations imposed on members under the GATT 1994.[22] The most crucial difference in this respect is arguably the requirement in TBT Agreement Article 2.2 that technical regulations are not more trade-restrictive than necessary. This applies also to non-discriminatory regulations and therefore exceeds considerably the non-discrimination requirements contained in the GATT. However, as shown above, technical regulations creating barriers to international trade and distinguishing between products because of PPMs will usually be considered in violation of GATT obligations under Article XI and/or Article III, provided that less favourable treatment has been accorded to imported products. The legality of such regulations would then depend on justification under the general exceptions in Article XX. Therefore, although disciplines under the TBT Agreement and under the GATT differ to some extend, referring PPM-based technical norms to the GATT would not undermine disciplines for technical norms. Given that the substantive provisions of the TBT Agreement might also offer

---

[20] Marceau and Trachtman (2002), pp. 811–81, at 861.
[21] Cottier and Oesch (2005), p. 762.
[22] Appellate Body Report, *EC – Asbestos* (2001), para. 80.

an adequate regime for measures linked to unincorporated PPMs, one may find that the different legal treatment of technical norms depending on whether or not they relate to incorporated or unincorporated PPMs may not be entirely convincing. Therefore, in order to achieve greater legal certainty and predictability, it would appear reasonable to refer all PPM regulation to the more specific standards of the TBT Agreement and so achieve greater uniformity of the law. However, the finding of an unacceptable contradiction seems to overstate the differences in the substantial provisions of the GATT and the TBT Agreement. Even if objective and purpose of excluding unincorporated PPMs from the scope of the TBT Agreement are neither self-evident nor convincing, there is also no paramount reason for an interpretation contrary to the wording of the TBT Agreement as it stands in order to include technical norms for unincorporated PPMs into its scope.

To reiterate, the text of a provision is of primary importance for its interpretation. Given that the principle of effective treaty interpretation[23] requires giving meaning to all terms of an agreement, it must be concluded that the word 'related' in the definition of technical regulations and standards implies that only technical requirements relating to incorporated PPMs are covered by the TBT Agreement. Therefore, the view which rejects coverage of technical norms linked to unincorporated PPMs is here preferred.[24] While the incidences of WTO members notifying norms linked to unincorporated PPMs mentioned above are irrelevant for the law as it stands, they could indicate a changing attitude among WTO members and negotiators, which could lead to an authoritative interpretation or to a future amendment of the TBT Agreement.

6.2.1.3 Labelling requirements

A crucial difference between the legal status of labelling regulations and other technical regulations relating to unincorporated PPMs is often overlooked. In addition to direct technical regulation, the question of coverage of the TBT Agreement also arises with respect to labelling requirements relating to PPMs. Labelling, as understood here, refers to all

---

[23] See above, Chapter 1, fn. 157, with relevant WTO adjudication.
[24] Also Appleton (2002), pp. 239–40. Vranes (2009a), pp. 337–42, in contrast, finds that also regulations prescribing PPMs that do not leave physical traces in products fall within the scope of the TBT Agreement, provided that such prescriptions are sufficiently related to the end-product. Outside the scope of the TBT Agreement would therefore be general prescriptions such as general labour standards or family allowances programmes (at p. 342).

specific information that is provided by producers and usually attached to the product in the form of a label. For this analysis, it is irrelevant whether the information is presented in an explicit way with descriptive language or through a specific symbol or mark which presents certain precisely defined information.

The use of labelling regarding unincorporated PPMs has increased over recent years, both in the form of mandatory labelling as a policy tool and in the form of voluntary labelling that is often used by producers for marketing purposes. Technological progress has not only enabled producers to seize economic advantages of different conditions of production in different countries, it has also increased demand for, and supply of, information on products and on the way they are produced or generated. Labelling, particularly in the field of environmental and health policy, has become a valued regulatory technique offering more flexibility and reduced costs to producers.[25] Paralleling this development, freedom of information and the protection of consumers have been achieving status as well-established and recognized values in many countries and international organizations.[26] Kysar argues that regardless of the various pros and cons of consumer behaviour as a regulatory tool, consumer information is a basic requirement for the evaluative function assigned to consumers, particularly by proponents of the liberal market vision. He finds the distinction between legitimate information on products as opposed to illegitimate information on processes too thin and formalistic a conceptual device to address broader social and environmental questions.[27]

However, the legitimacy of information relating to production is still often being questioned. Some fear that consumers can be influenced too easily and that their concerns would be exploited and abused for

---

[25] Cheyne (2009), p. 931.

[26] Various consumer protection laws promoting information are in force in developed as well as in developing countries. Also the UN expanded Guidelines for Consumer Protection (Decision 54/449) declare as legitimate needs which the guidelines are intended to meet: '(c) Access of consumers to adequate information to enable them to make informed choices according to individual wishes and needs ... (g) The promotion of sustainable consumption patterns". Also, both values are for instance reflected in the Charter of Fundamental Rights of the European Union, namely in Article 11 on freedom of expression and information, and Article 38 on consumer protection' (OJ, C364/1–22 of 18 December 2000). The European Court of Justice has consistently held that consumer protection is a 'mandatory requirement' that may justify unilateral measures (see, e.g., the Judgment of the Court of 12 March 1987, *Commission of the European Communities* v. *Federal Republic of Germany*, Case 178/84 regarding purity requirements for beer).

[27] Kysar (2004), pp. 533–5.

protectionism. Developing countries especially are suspicious of product labelling concerning unincorporated PPMs, mostly for economic reasons.[28] Compliance with labelling regulations or standards relating to PPMs can imply considerable costs. The economic advantages enjoyed by producers in developing countries could so be considerably diminished, even if they complied with the substantial requirements. Otherwise, labelling norms could even result in *de facto* denial of market access, since developing country producers often may not be able to afford the increased costs of compliance. Furthermore, there is concern about the lack of representation of stakeholders from developing countries in the non-governmental standard-setting bodies. Since these bodies may often represent alliances of economic and non-economic interests prevailing in developed countries, it is feared that standards relating to PPMs are often designed as disguised restrictions on international trade to the detriment of developing countries.[29] Ultimately, there are concerns on the fair and equitable application of labelling regulations.

The following section addresses legal problems concerning labelling requirements relating to unincorporated PPMs against the backdrop of an exemplary EU regulation serving to illustrate the problem.

6.2.1.3.1 The EU regulatory framework on egg labelling

The amended EU legal framework on marketing standards for eggs, which entered into force on 1 July 2007, shall serve as an example for NPA labelling requirements. The intention of the regulation is to enable consumers to distinguish between eggs of different quality and weight grade and to identify the farming method used. It applies to eggs produced in the EC, even if they are intended for export, as well as to eggs imported into the EC from third countries.[30] According to the regulation, eggs shall be marked with a distinguishing number containing codes that indicate among other elements the country of production and the farming method used, namely, 'free range', 'barn' or 'cage'.[31] Member states within the EC are required to establish a system that attributes a unique number to each production site or establishment, and they may add additional numbers

---

[28] For more on developing countries' concerns see Appleton (2002), pp. 240–5.
[29] Ghandi (2005), pp. 856–7.
[30] Council Regulation (EC) No. 1028/2006, OJ, L 186/1 of 7 July 2006, Article 1:1.
[31] Council Regulation (EC) No. 1028/2006, OJ, L 186/1 of 7 July 2006, Articles 4 and 2:9, together with point 2 of the Annex to Directive 2002/4/EC, OJ, L 30/44 of 31 January 2002).

to identify different flocks kept in separated buildings of the registered establishment.[32]

As regards imports, the regulation requests the Commission to evaluate marketing standards for eggs, including rules on labelling, farming methods and controls, in exporting countries. If the evaluation finds that for a specific country the respective rules are equivalent to EC rules, then eggs shall be marked with a number equivalent to the EC producer code.[33] The Commission is requested to conduct negotiations with third countries aimed at finding ways of offering guarantees as to equivalence with Community legislation where necessary.[34] The regulation stipulates:

> If sufficient guarantees as to equivalence of rules are not provided, imported eggs from the third country concerned shall bear a code permitting the identification of the country of origin and the indication that the farming method is 'unspecified'.[35]

The relevant EU laws distinguish between products based on welfare conditions accorded to laying hens,[36] and enable consumers to choose between eggs of different quality and to identify the farming method used.[37] Since imports failing to meet the Community standards of production are not banned from the internal market, the EU legal framework would not amount to a quantitative restriction. However, label of 'unspecified' farming methods will place respective imported eggs at a considerable disadvantage, since many European consumers ascribe considerable importance to this aspect. Since the respective provisions relate to the process of egg 'production' in complete ignorance of the physical impact of the regulated methods on the end-products, they constitute an example of labelling requirements regarding unincorporated PPMs. Whether these are subject to the provisions of the TBT Agreement is explored in the next section.[38]

---

[32] Directive 2002/4/EC, Article 1 together with point 2.3 of the Annex.
[33] Council Regulation (EC) No. 1028/2006, OJ, L 186/1 of 7 July 2006, Article 6:1.
[34] Council Regulation (EC) No. 1028/2006, OJ, L 186/1 of 7 July 2006, Article 6:2.
[35] Council Regulation (EC) No. 1028/2006, OJ, L 186/1 of 7 July 2006, Article 6:3.
[36] See. e.g., reference to Council Directive 1999/74/EC, OJ L 203 of 3 August 1999, pp. 53–7, which lays down minimum standards for the protection of laying hens.
[37] Council Regulation (EC) No. 1028/2006, OJ, L 186/1 of 7 July 2006, Preamble, No. 5.
[38] The TBT Agreement applies to all products, including agricultural products (TBT Agreement Article 1:3). Also, the labelling provisions pertaining to farming methods at issue do not constitute sanitary measures that would fall under the SPS Agreement as *lex specialis* (TBT Agreement Article 1:5).

6.2.1.3.2 Coverage with respect to labelling of PPMs and NPAs

The importance of the TBT Agreement for labelling regulation has been discussed in detail in recent years, albeit mostly with respect to voluntary labelling standards. The large number of labels reflects an increased demand for information on infinite aspects, such as quality, safety and ingredients, but also information on various NPAs. Consumers have become increasingly concerned about environmental or ethical problems and demand relevant information as a basis for their purchase decisions. A qualitative study on consumers' attitudes towards labelling published in 2005 stated:

> But, whereas [concerns of an environmental and ethical nature] only appeared very infrequently in the studies carried out a few years ago, they have now gone beyond this marginal stage to become a factor impregnating people's attitudes – at least in a substantial minority of consumers: questions concerning methods of cultivation or breeding (organic farming, GMO, hormone treatment, anti-natural manipulations revealed by recent health crises), interest in fair-trade products that are beginning to become quite widely known in the case of coffee, and sometimes also chocolate.[39]

The flood of different labels containing information on different aspects accredited by various non-governmental organizations, including producer associations and companies,[40] however, has often led to confusion. Recent developments show that legislators have become aware of the need to channel the numerous labels in order to provide reliable information to consumers. As a consequence, compulsory labelling requirements have become more important.

6.2.1.3.2.1 Labelling of unincorporated PPMs

Both, voluntary programmes and compulsory labelling requirements often relate to both incorporated and unincorporated PPMs. While the

---

[39] OPTEM, The European Consumers' Attitudes Regarding Product Labelling, Qualitative Study in 28 European Countries, Study at the request of the European Commission, Directorate General Health and Consumer Protection, May 2005, at p. 8 (available at http://ec.europa.eu/consumers/topics/labelling_report_en.pdf, accessed 9 August 2010).

[40] The Verbraucher Initiative e.V., a German association concerned with consumer protection and sponsored by the German Federal Ministry for the Environment, Nature Conservation and Nuclear Safety, estimates that about 1,000 labels accredited by various organizations and producers are used on the German market (press release of 11 February 2004, available at http://www.verbraucher.org/verbraucher.php/cat/53/aid/709/title/ www.label-online.de).

difference between technical regulations and standards relating to PPMs is relevant in terms of the substantive disciplines of the TBT Agreement, the difference is irrelevant for the question of the general applicability of the agreement. The text of Annex 1 explicitly extends the definitions of both technical regulations and standards to labelling requirements. The second sentence of each definition reads:

> It may also include or deal exclusively with terminology, symbols, packaging, marking or labelling requirements as they apply to a product, process or production method.[41]

This sentence was copied from the definition of a 'technical specification' contained in the earlier Tokyo Round agreement, the so-called Standards Code.[42] Compared with the second sentence of the Standards Code definition, two important changes were made during the Uruguay Round. First, the word 'also' was included, supposedly in order to clarify that the second sentence was additional to the first one,[43] and that the listed instances of technical norms were not exclusive. The second modification regards the inclusion of the term 'process or production method' as a supplement to the list. Although there is little negotiating history on the inclusion, it seems that it resulted from the understanding that the effectiveness of the agreement should not be weakened by an exclusion of PPMs. For this reason, the draft presented by the United States in 1988 to amend the definition of 'technical specifications' included a general reference to 'processes, conditions of growth and production methods'. Interestingly, while the discussions on the question of whether only those PPMs that affect product characteristics should be covered by the TBT Agreement led negotiators to insert the word 'related' before 'processes and production methods' in the first sentence of the definition,[44] the negotiators did not insert the word 'related' into the second sentence. Given the absence of the word 'related' in the second sentence, which is crucial for labelling requirements, the conclusion that all labelling requirements relating to PPMs fall into the scope of the TBT Agreement seems compelling.[45]

---

[41] TBT Agreement, Annex 1, second sentence of Nos. 1 and 2.
[42] Tokyo Round Agreement on Technical Barriers to Trade, Annex 1.
[43] WTO, Note by the Secretariat, WTO, Note by the Secretariat, WT/CTE/W/10, G/TBT/W/11 of 29 August 1995, at XXI.
[44] For a comparison with technical regulations and standards, see above section 6.2.1.2.
[45] For coverage, see also Marceau and Trachtman (2002), at p. 861. This view finds also support by the decision of the TBT Committee agreeing that notification requirements with respect to standards apply to voluntary labelling, no matter what information is concerned (Triennial Review, below fn. 55), also Wiers (2001), p. 110.

6.2 THE TBT AGREEMENT AND PPMS

The arguably prevailing view holds, in contrast, that the text of the Annex contains single definitions for both technical regulations and standards, and that therefore sentence 1 and 2 of each definition should be read together. Based on the negotiating history, particularly on the debates regarding insertion of the term 'their related' processes and production methods, it is argued that the exclusion of unincorporated PPMs in the first sentences of both definitions extends also to the second sentences.[46] Consequently, labelling requirements relating to unincorporated PPMs would not fall into the scope of the TBT Agreement.[47]

The same instances of negotiating history, however, could also be invoked as evidence for the contrary opinion: given that inclusion of the term 'related' into the first sentence was subject to repeated debates, it cannot be regarded as mere negligence by the negotiators that they did not add the term 'related' in the second sentence as well. Furthermore, it seems problematic to ascribe greater importance to the negotiating history than to the text of the agreement. Following the principle of effective treaty interpretation, the fact that the second sentence omits the word 'related' must be given meaning. Only inconsistent legal consequences because of the then applicable substantive provisions of the agreement could be invoked against this approach. In this respect, it is important to note that the nature of a labelling requirement differs fundamentally from other technical norms bearing on unincorporated PPMs directly. Labelling laws merely require disclosure of specific information, while other technical norms require that certain technical standards are actually observed in the production of a good. In light of this fundamental difference, the conclusion that coverage with respect to labelling requirements and coverage with respect to technical norms must be identical is neither compelling nor manifest. To the contrary, the text-based interpretative

---

[46] E.g., Gehring and Jessen (2005), pp. 353–5; Puth (2003), pp. 212–17; Schoenbaum (1997), p. 288; Rege (1994), p. 110, also Tietje (1995). Tietje recognizes the remaining uncertainty with respect to coverage and argues that eco-labelling programmes, even if considered to fall into the scope of the TBT Agreement, do not fulfil legitimate objectives under the TBT Agreement and thus are unnecessary obstacles to trade, at pp. 134–6.

[47] Chang (1997), p. 146, bases his view that labelling requirements referring to unincorporated PPMs are excluded from the scope of the TBT Agreement mostly on the drafters' intentions, which clearly were 'to exclude non-product-related PPMs from the coverage of the TBT Agreement in general, rather than from the scope of the first sentence only, otherwise, the insertion of the words "or related" into the first sentence would become meaningless'. His argument fails, however, because, as explained in the text, a single legal framework applicable to all labelling requirements seems more rational than an artificial divide between labelling of incorporated and labelling of unincorporated PPMs.

approach here leads to a reasonable legal result: a single legal framework for all labelling requirements, no matter what kind of information is concerned.[48] Only this interpretation seems to give proper weight to the fact that the definition explicitly includes labelling requirements.

6.2.1.3.2.2 Other NPAs

According to the definition of technical regulations and standards in the Annex, labelling requirements are covered by the TBT Agreement if 'they apply to a product, process or production method'. While PPMs constitute a sub-set of the larger group of NPAs, the specific description of covered technical norms in the TBT Agreement refers explicitly to PPMs only. Therefore, the TBT Agreement could be interpreted to apply to technical requirements only and to ignore general conditions relating to labour and human rights in the country of production. Social and environmental aspects that are not strictly related to the production of a specific good, even if highly relevant to consumers, would then be considered to fall outside the scope of the TBT Agreement.

The term 'process or production method' could, however, also be understood as to merely indicate the object of 'terminology, symbols, packaging', etc. The Annex stipulates that technical regulations may deal exclusively with 'labelling requirements as they apply to a product'. In the literal sense of the term, 'as they apply to a product' must be understood to indicate all requirements concerning labels that need to be physically attached to products – no matter what information the label provides. Against this understanding it cannot be invoked that the alternative term 'labelling requirements as they apply to a … process or production method' would be bare of meaning. The second sentence of the definition of technical regulations contains several itemizations and alternatives, and a textual interpretation does not require that all combinations of all terms and all alternatives make sense. Since there are certainly documents which deal exclusively with terminology or symbols applying to processes and production methods, there is more than one combination of items with the alternative 'process and production method' describing a specific form of a technical regulation. Hence, the definition does not require that labelling requirements would apply to processes and production methods.

---

[48] The suggestion that labelling regulations relating to both physical and non-physical product characteristics be assessed under both GATT and the TBT Agreement for the respective part of the regulation is not workable from a practical viewpoint (Appleton, 2002, p. 257).

Considering that there would be no convincing reason to assess labelling requirements concerning PPMs differently from labelling requirements concerning physical properties or NPAs, it is here argued that labelling requirements concerning NPAs not strictly related to production also fall into the scope of the TBT Agreement.[49]

6.2.2 Substantive provisions

While technical norms stipulating requirements concerning unincorporated PPMs have been found to fall outside the scope of the TBT Agreement, corresponding labelling requirements are covered. Thus, the substantive provisions of the TBT Agreement are applicable. Some hold, however, that labelling requirements concerning unincorporated PPMs are *per se* in violation of its basic principles and substantive provisions. The next section rebuts this view. The following sections then review the relevance of the substantive provisions for PPM labelling requirements, and consider in this respect the importance of consumer information as a legitimate objective of national regulations.

6.2.2.1 No *per se* illegality

Against coverage of the TBT Agreement for labelling requirements relating to unincorporated PPMs or other NPAs it has been argued that the substantive provisions of the TBT Agreement imply an exclusion of such measures from its scope.[50] Since the scope of the agreement is determined by the definitions contained in the Annex, the legal consequence of the alleged inconsistency of substantive provisions would not be the exclusion of such measures from the scope, but rather their *per se* impermissibility. The argument that labelling requirements relating to unincorporated PPMs inherently violate the TBT Agreement is based on several references to the WTO core principle of non-discrimination by

---

[49] For coverage of labelling relating to the broader social conditions of production by the TBT Agreement see Lopez-Hurtado (2002). A Belgian notification also shows that some WTO members interpret coverage of the TBT Agreement in this way: Belgium notified a draft law which it described as creating 'a label which companies can affix to their products if the latter meet criteria and standards recognized in particular by the International Labour Organization. These criteria are monitored by accredited bodies and a committee for socially responsible production has been set up to monitor the allocation of labels and procedures for assisting developing countries that wish to have the label.' (WTO, Committee on Technical Barriers to Trade, Notification, G/TBT/N/BEL/2, 16 January 2001).

[50] Joshi (2004), at p. 78.

use of the term 'like products' in the TBT Agreement.[51] For instance, TBT Agreement Article 2:1 requires members to ensure that, with respect to technical regulations, foreign products are to be accorded treatment no less favourable than national 'like products' or 'like products' originating in other WTO members. With respect to standards, Annex 3 opens a 'Code of Good Practice for the Preparation, Adoption and Application of Standards' to acceptance by the standardizing bodies in the territory of WTO member states. The first substantive provision of this Code then repeats the requirement to provide non-discriminatory treatment to 'like products' originating in the territory of any other WTO member.[52] Since the prevailing view asserts likeness of products regardless of the methods applied in production, labelling requirements distinguishing between products based on unincorporated PPMs would *per se* violate the TBT Agreement.

Underlying the view of the *per se* illegality of labelling requirements relating to PPMs is the assumption that the term 'like products' in the TBT Agreement has the same meaning as the term 'like products' in GATT Article III. In this case, likeness of products would be determined based on the traditional criteria, while aspects not incorporated in the physical characteristics of a product would be irrelevant. There are, however, several arguments against this interpretation of the term 'like products' in the TBT Agreement. It is conventional knowledge that the meaning of the term 'like products' does not need to be interpreted in a uniform way in the different provisions of the GATT.[53] *A fortiori*, the meaning of the term 'likeness' may vary between different WTO Agreements. Also in the TBT Agreement, the meaning of the term likeness 'must be determined by the particular provision in which [it] is encountered as well as by the context and the circumstances that prevail in any given case to which that provision may apply'.[54]

Since the context is relevant, the definitions contained in the Annex play a role in an interpretation of the term 'likeness'. Since the analysis in the previous chapter has shown that labelling requirements concerning unincorporated PPMs are also covered by the TBT Agreement, it would be inconsistent to interpret the vague notion 'like products' as used in

---

[51] This argument has actually played an important role in the discussion at the WTO, cf., e.g., the summary of concerns under the TBT Agreement by Motaal (2002), pp. 272–4.
[52] TBT Agreement, Annex 3, D.
[53] Appellate Body Report, *Japan – Alcoholic Beverages* (1996), p. 21; see also above section 4.2.2.1.1.3.
[54] Appellate Body Report, *Japan – Alcoholic Beverages* (1996), p. 21.

this agreement in a way that would lead to *per se* impermissibility of this group of measures. Furthermore, it cannot be ignored that the second sentence in both definitions omits the term 'related' with respect to PPMs. The language indicates, first, that labelling requirements relating to unincorporated PPMs do fall within the scope of the TBT Agreement. This has at least implicitly been confirmed with respect to the Code of Good Practice relating to standards, which establishes certain transparency requirements in paragraph L. In 1997, the TBT Committee clarified that the requirement to publish a notice specifying the start of the minimum period of time allowing for comments applies to voluntary labelling, no matter which information is concerned. The Committee agreed:

> (e) without prejudice to the views of Members concerning the coverage and application of the Agreement, the obligation to publish notices of draft standards containing voluntary labelling requirements under paragraph L of the Code is not dependent upon the kind of information provided on the label.[55]

Second, the difference in language must be seen against the backdrop of the premises underlying the TBT Agreement. As opposed to the GATT, the basic idea of which is to abolish all unjustified trade barriers other than tariffs, the TBT Agreement starts from the premise that technical regulation is *prima facie* legitimate. It therefore does not aim at abolishing technical norms, but at ensuring that technical regulations are not more trade-restrictive than necessary to fulfil a legitimate objective. In this sense, the second sentence of Article 2:5 explicitly establishes a rebuttable presumption of legitimacy of a technical regulation based on international standards. Also, the first sentence of that paragraph, which requires an explanation and justification in terms of the specific requirements of the TBT Agreement of a technical regulation only in case of a request of another WTO member, seems to presume the legitimacy of technical norms. The lack of a general rejection of technical norms is also reflected in the relationship of rule and exception: the TBT Agreement does not rely on general exceptions comparable with GATT Article XX, but rather establishes specific rules which need to be observed in the process of drafting and adopting such norms. Because of this crucial difference between GATT and TBT Agreement, a simple transfer of the meaning of the concept of 'like products' from GATT Article III to

---

[55] WTO, Committee on Technical Barriers to Trade, First Triennial Review of the Operation and Implementation of the Agreement on Technical Barriers to Trade, G/TBT/5, 19 November 1997, para. XII.

provisions of the TBT Agreement is neither appropriate nor justifiable. Considering the specific rule–exception relationship in the GATT, with an exclusive list of exceptions, it seems that the term 'like products' in Article 2:1 of the TBT Agreement must be construed more narrowly.[56] PPMs therefore need to be taken into account when determining whether or not products are like. Consequently, the use of different PPMs leads to the finding that the respective end-products are not 'like' in the sense of the TBT Agreement, and that regulation that distinguishes between products based on these PPMs is not *per se* discriminatory.[57]

This conclusion is supported by the definition of technical regulations and standards. Since the TBT Agreement explicitly includes labelling requirements with respect to processes and production methods in its scope, one needs to give meaning to the fact that the substantive norms do not declare this type of technical norms illegal. To the contrary, the substantive provisions of the TBT Agreement, if referring to PPMs, also omits the word 'related' – an indication, that PPMs, no matter whether incorporated or unincorporated, are subject to the requirements laid down in the substantive provisions. For example, Article 2:12 requires reasonable periods of time for producers in other countries to adapt 'their products or method of production' to the requirements of the importing country. Giving meaning to the lack of the word 'related' in this provision as compared with the first sentence of the definitions contained in the Annex requires interpreting this provision to apply to all kinds of PPMs. A distinction between 'related' PPMs and PPMs in general in one provision of the agreement, that is, the definitions in the Annex, indicates that the provisions which do not make use of the distinguishing adjective refer to the entire set of PPMs, namely, incorporated as well as unincorporated PPMs.

---

[56] Marceau and Trachtman (2002), p. 822.
[57] Lell (2004), arrives at the same conclusion, albeit with a different argument, which is particularly relevant for food production using GMOs, if no traces of GMOs remain in the end-product. According to Lell, the use of GMOs as a production method is relevant for the traditional criterion 'consumers' tastes and preferences', so that even the traditional criteria would lead to the finding that the products are not 'like' (at p. 110). This argument may indeed be most relevant with respect to labelling. Labelling requirements arguably will be adopted only if there is evidence that consumers are sufficiently interested in the labelled information. Therefore, in most cases of labelling laws as opposed to direct regulation it can be expected that also the traditional criteria for likeness would allow regulators to distinguish between products based on unincorporated PPMs, in as far as labelling laws are concerned.

Other general arguments against labelling of unincorporated PPMs are of a more political nature. It has been argued that such labelling would undermine the territorial sovereignty of WTO members.[58] Given that labelling requirements, as opposed to other NPA trade measures, merely provide information and allow consumers to distinguish between products, this argument is weak. To the contrary, declaring such national labelling requirements impermissible seems to considerably limit the autonomy of importing WTO members. For the same reason, the argument that labelling of unincorporated PPMs also imposes inappropriate standards from outside is inconclusive: information requirements, whether in the form of labels or otherwise, cannot 'impose' standards on other countries.[59] The developmental concerns underlying this argument, however, are justified but need to be addressed in a different way, which is discussed in more detail below.

In sum, the substantive provisions of the TBT Agreement which cover all types of labelling requirements cannot be invoked against requirements to label unincorporated PPMs. It is here argued that 'like products' in the TBT Agreement need to be interpreted in a broader way, taking into account different PPMs. The substantive norms contained in the TBT Agreement therefore apply also to labelling requirements relating to unincorporated PPMs and other NPAs.

6.2.2.2 Substantive requirements on technical regulations and standards

Depending on the form of the technical norm, the provisions of the TBT Agreement pertaining to either technical regulations or standards are applicable.

6.2.2.2.1 Overview of substantive requirements

Compulsory labelling requirements, such as the EU legal framework for marketing of eggs discussed above, need to conform to the requirements for technical regulations established in Articles 2 and 3. For example, according to Article 2.4 members are required to base their labelling laws on international standards whenever possible, and Article 2.6 obliges members to play a full part in international standardizing bodies in the preparation of international standards within the limits of their resources. Article 2 also states specific transparency requirements in paragraphs

---

[58] Motaal (2002), p. 275.   [59] Motaal (2002), p. 275.

9–11, while Article 3 concerns technical regulations by local government bodies or non-governmental bodies. Most important, however, are the principle of non-discrimination laid down in Article 2.1 encompassing both national treatment and MFN, and each member's obligation to ensure that technical regulations are not prepared, adopted or applied in a way that creates unnecessary obstacles to international trade.

The latter obligation is detailed in Article 2.2 and reflects the central idea of the TBT Agreement, namely, the presumption that technical regulations are in principle permissible. It is, however, crucial that the regulation pursues a legitimate objective and is not more trade-restrictive than necessary, 'taking account of the risks non-fulfilment would create'.[60] Like other technical norms, labelling requirements with respect to unincorporated PPMs also need to jump this hurdle. In contrast to GATT Article XX, legitimate objectives for technical norms are not listed exhaustively in the agreement. The agreement names as legitimate objectives *inter alia* national security requirements, the prevention of deceptive practices and protection of human health or safety, animal or plant life or health or of the environment. In assessing whether the technical norms fulfil a legitimate objective, the non-exclusive list of the TBT Agreement provides more flexibility than GATT Article XX. This aspect is discussed in more detail in section 6.2.3 below.

Voluntary labelling requirements, on the other hand, are standards for the purposes of the TBT Agreement. Article 4 requires members to ensure that standardizing bodies comply with the Code of Good Practice for the Preparation, Adoption and Application of Standards in Annex 3. Of particular relevance are again the principle of non-discrimination and the requirement that standards should not be more trade-restrictive than necessary.[61] There is nothing with respect to the necessity requirement comparable with the phrase in Article 2.2 relating to technical standards, which requires that 'the risks non-fulfilment would create' for the determination of necessity should be taken into account.

Other substantive provisions relate to the assessment of conformity with technical regulations and standards. Article 5 obliges members to ensure compliance with certain procedural and substantive rules when positive assurance of conformity with technical norms is required. Those rules again include the principle of non-discrimination in the preparation, adoption and application of conformity assessment procedures, and the requirement

[60] TBT Agreement, Article 2.1.   [61] TBT Agreement, Annex 3, D and E.

that there is no effect or intention to create unnecessary obstacles to international trade. Article 6 prescribes, under certain conditions, recognition of the results of such procedures in other members, and Articles 7 and 8 extend the rules contained in Articles 5 and 6 on conformity assessment by local government bodies and by non-governmental bodies.

Rules prescribing transparency and supply of information on technical regulations, standards and assessment procedures are contained in Article 10. Articles 11 and 12 are applications of the principle of SDT and provide for technical assistance and for differential and more favourable treatment for developing country members. Also, the relevance of SDT for labelling requirements concerning unincorporated PPMs is addressed in the discussion below in more detail.

6.2.2.2.2 The distinction between regulations and standards

The distinction between technical regulations and standards in the TBT Agreement has important consequences in terms of the applicable substantive requirements. The crucial difference between these categories of technical norms is the degree to which they are compulsory. According to Annex 1, technical regulations are mandatory, while standards have a voluntary character.[62] As the above overview shows, standards are privileged in many respects. For example, the requirement of a legitimate objective applies in the case of 'mandatory' technical regulations, but not in the case of 'voluntary' standards. The substantive privileges for standards arise from the idea that they are non-mandatory and that they merely serve to overcome practical obstacles for private commercial activity in a highly diversified economy. They are believed to be well suited to facilitating international trade if they are harmonized on an international basis. Furthermore, standardizing bodies usually consist of private entities and state control of their activities is limited. Thus, their legitimacy does not need to be established in a way similar to Article 2.2. The Code of Good Practice in Annex 3 merely requires that standards should not create unnecessary obstacles to trade (Annex 3, E).

The distinction between both types of technical norms, however, has been criticized as artificial. Related concerns pertain to the status of NGO technical regulations and standards, which may be privileged in that they are not subject to the requirements established with the TBT Agreement. Compared with the treatment of technical regulations and standards by governmental bodies, this privilege seems inconsistent. It has been

---

[62] TBT Agreement, Annex 1, No. 2.

argued that even non-mandatory labelling for example, labelling schemes developed by NGOs, can have economic effects on enterprises giving a *de facto* mandatory character to the scheme. NGO standards may indeed create economic disadvantages for producers, which are presumed to be highly relevant for developing country producers. Against the backdrop of the objectives of the TBT Agreement, standards designed by NGOs do not seem to deserve any privileges, since they do not address merely technical problems but are designed to achieve social goals. Some argue that under the TBT Agreement, a broad interpretation of the term 'non-governmental standardizing body' should be adopted so that NGOs could also be potential designers of technical regulations and standards. At least the substantive requirements for standards in Article 4 should also apply to so-called voluntary labelling schemes developed by NGOs.[63]

NGOs, however, are private organizations, characterized by their purposeful independence from state institutions. Clearly, they are not covered by the definition of 'non-governmental bodies' in Annex 1,[64] since they do not have the legal power to enforce technical regulations.[65] For this reason, NGOs without such legal power do not constitute recognized standardizing bodies under the TBT Agreement. Thus, neither provisions on technical regulations nor provisions on standards by non-governmental bodies as contained in Articles 3 and 4 of the TBT Agreement are applicable. NGO standards, often relating to unincorporated PPMs or other NPAs, therefore do not fall into the scope of the TBT Agreement or any other of the WTO covered agreements.

6.2.2.3 Legitimacy of the objective pursued: special consideration of consumer information

Article 2.2 of the TBT Agreement which applies to all technical regulations[66] requires that such norms may be imposed only to fulfil a

---

[63] Gandhi (2005), p. 875.   [64] TBT Agreement, Annex 1, No. 8.

[65] National labelling laws might be a remedy to prevent such effects. Also, labels accredited by NGOs must conform to the national legal framework of the country where the labelled products are offered for sale. Should NGO labels be designed to pursue protectionist purposes, then national consumer protection laws, such as laws against unfair trade practices, might be applicable. However, the lack of action by a government to address such deceptive business practices cannot constitute a measure subject to scrutiny under the TBT Agreement. The WTO Agreements create obligations on WTO members only, and it is questionable whether they could be interpreted to establish obligations to take action against private standardizing bodies or entities.

[66] Article 2.2 applies to technical regulations adopted by government bodies, and read together with Article 3.1 also with respect to technical regulations adopted by local government bodies and non-governmental bodies.

'legitimate objective'. To reiterate, the list of legitimate objectives in Article 2.2 is not exhaustive. This openness of the TBT Agreement could be decisive for the permissibility of labelling requirements relating to unincorporated PPMs.

The relevance of this consideration is apparent from the example mentioned above, the European marking requirements relating to farming methods for laying hens. It should be noted that animal health is among the legitimate objectives explicitly mentioned both in GATT Article XX and in TBT Agreement Article 2.2, and as detailed above, the protection of laying hens is indeed among the objectives of the framework. Thus, the legitimacy of the objective would be determined in a similar way under both agreements. The TBT Agreement clearly establishes a balancing test,[67] by requiring that the risks of non-fulfilment need to be taken into account in the determination of the least trade-restrictiveness. To reiterate, the necessity requirement under GATT Article XX(b) also includes a process of weighing and balancing. Whether or not the labelling requirements would be suitable, or even necessary, for the protection of animal health would therefore depend on an assessment of the framework together with the specific market situation and economic effects. In the case of a labelling requirement, a positive impact on animal health could arguably arise only in the long term, if at all. Producers might decide to change from conventional to animal friendly farming methods in response to economic pressure resulting from greater demand for products produced with such methods. Whether or not producers would actually be prompted to implement the desired changes, however, would be uncertain. In the case of labelling requirements, a possible impact on the behaviour of producers would depend on the reaction of consumers in the domestic market. Consumers could find the labelled information irrelevant, or they might for other reasons decide to make their purchasing decisions regardless of the labelled information. Correspondingly, it could be argued that the risks created by the mere non-fulfilment of labelling requirements might be insignificant. This argument has been made with respect to eco-labelling requirements which usually promote protection of the environment with a broader perspective,[68] and it could likewise apply to labelling requirements with respect to the protection of animal welfare. In sum, although there may be specific cases where suitability of labelling requirements to reach certain social objectives cannot be denied, the nature of labelling requirements prevents the finding of a general suitability to promote certain social objectives.

---

[67] Marceau and Trachtman (2002), at p. 831.   [68] Tietje (1995), p. 135.

These questions, however, would be irrelevant for the legal status of labelling requirements if their legitimacy arises from an entirely different consideration. There are good reasons to argue that consumer information is in itself a legitimate objective covered by the TBT Agreement.[69] If this were the case, then labelling requirements serving this objective would be legitimate *per se*, provided that they are consistent with other requirements established by the agreement. There are two strong arguments supporting the claim that consumer information is a legitimate objective under the TBT Agreement. The first argument stems from the field of fundamental rights, while the second argument relates to the economic foundations of the WTO Agreements.

6.2.2.3.1 Consumer information as an internationally recognized value

Consumer protection, at the core of which is the consumer's right to information, is an internationally recognized value.[70] In the light of concerns about disguised protectionism detailed above, it is often argued that consumers have a right to information only in as far as the information at issue is important to them. Some argue that this is the case only if certain dangers are inherent to the product. This applies, for example, in the case of food labelling where many ingredients or substances may pose health risks. On the other hand, one could argue that consumers have the right to decide for themselves which information is important to them and which is not. From this point of view, labelling requirements would serve legitimate objectives, no matter which aspects are concerned, and no matter if there are any physical risks for consumers.

In different countries and contexts, different views on the importance of consumer protection and of consumer information prevail and, accordingly, the way and intensity of protection also differs. In the United States, for example, the right to consumer protection gained importance on the political agenda with a message from President Kennedy to Congress in 1962. Kennedy declared:

> Additional legislative and administrative action is required, however, if the Federal Government is to meet its responsibility to consumers in

---

[69] Lell (2004), at p. 110.
[70] Cottier and Khorana (2005), p. 246, consider freedom of active and passive information, together with other freedoms relating to the freedom of expression, as being at the core of classical human rights. See their fn. 2 for a list of international agreements recognizing the importance of those rights.

the exercise of their rights. These rights include: ... (2) The right to be informed – to be protected against fraudulent, deceitful, or grossly misleading information, advertising, labeling, or other practices, and to be given the facts he needs to make an informed choice. (3) The right to choose – to be assured, wherever possible, access to a variety of products and services at competitive prices; and in those industries in which competition is not workable and Government regulation is substituted, an assurance of satisfactory quality and service at fair prices.[71]

From a regulatory point of view, consumer information in the United States is often discussed with respect to the commercial speech doctrine, which in a broader sense encompasses both the right of producers to supply information for commercial purposes, such as advertisement, and the consumer's right to receive information. The commercial speech doctrine, based on the ruling of the United States Supreme Court in *Valentine v. Chrestensen*,[72] concerns certain limits to the constitutionally protected right to free speech as reflected in the First Amendment. It limits the freedom of speech for commercial purposes, and is mostly relevant for private companies engaging in advertising. The US Supreme Court reversed this longstanding jurisprudence in 1976 when it stated:

> Moreover, there is another consideration that suggests that no line between publicly 'interesting' or 'important' commercial advertising and the opposite kind could ever be drawn. Advertising, however tasteless and excessive it sometimes may seem, is nonetheless dissemination of information as to who is producing and selling what product, for what reason, and at what price. So long as we preserve a predominantly free enterprise economy, the allocation of our resources in large measure will be made through numerous private economic decisions. It is a matter of public interest that those decisions, in the aggregate, be intelligent and well informed. To this end, the free flow of commercial information is indispensable.[73]

---

[71] John F. Kennedy, Special Message to the Congress on Protecting the Consumer Interest of 15 March 1962. Kennedy focused on information relating to product characteristics and protection of consumers from fraud. Because of this speech, 15 March was picked as the date for the annual World Consumer Day, which was introduced in 1983 by Consumer International.

[72] In the 1942 *Valentine v. Chrestensen* case, the US Supreme Court recognized that so-called commercial speech is afforded less protection under the First Amendment than non-commercial or political speech. The case concerned a regulation banning the distribution of advertising handbills in New York City on city-owned streets. The Supreme Court said that the Constitution imposes 'no such restraint on government as respects purely commercial advertising' (*Valentine v. Chrestensen*, 316 US 52, at 54).

[73] *Virginia State Board of Pharmacy v. Virginia Citizens Consumer Council, Inc.*, 425 US 748, at 765 (1976).

Other cases, however, have been concerned with laws that actually require the disclosure of information by companies through product labels or otherwise with respect to production processes.[74] The US Supreme Court has confirmed the right of consumers to receive information in a number of decisions. For instance, in 1977 it declared consumers' interests in receiving factual information about prices as valuable, and it held that price competition and access to information about it were in the public interest.[75] However, more recent litigation in the United States relating to food produced with bovine growth hormones[76] suggests the establishment of a new distinction between the right to information relating to product characteristics and information relating to processes – a distinction which is of particular importance in the context of PPM labelling.[77] A group of consumers challenged not only the respective approvals by the US Food and Drug Administration (FDA), but also the FDA's failure to oblige producers and retailers to include appropriate labelling. The district court rejected the claims, and based its findings on, among other things, the absence of detectable differences in the end-product. More important for the purposes of this analysis are challenges to labelling laws adopted at state level which required producers to place a blue dot on milk and milk products produced from cows treated with growth hormones. Also in this case, *International Dairy Foods Association* v. *Amestoy*,[78] the Second Circuit based its ruling on the impossibility of distinguishing between milk from hormone-treated cows and milk from other cows, and dismissed the state interest in adopting the law as mere consumer concern. The court was of the view that curiosity alone was insufficient to support a law that required producers to disclose facts, even if accurate, against their will.[79] The court decision implies that there needs to be a manifest interest for a state to adopt a law that requires private companies to disclose

---

[74] Another important case with respect to commercial information on PPMs is the *Nike* v. *Kasky* case (123 SCt 2554 (2003); 45 p.3d 243 (Cal. 2002)), which is relevant for voluntary disclosure of process information, whether accurate or not, rather than for questions of labelling. The case has been interpreted to illustrate the instability of the First Amendment divide between commercial and non-commercial speech (Kysar, 2004, at p. 578).
[75] *Bates* v. *State Bar of Arizona*, 433 US 350 (1977), at 386, 389, 404. Justices Burger, Powell, Stewart and Rehnquist dissented.
[76] Several law suits in the US relate to growth hormones developed by Monsanto, Inc. in the 1990s. For an overview, see Kysar (2004), pp. 569–74.
[77] For more details on the related litigation see Kysar (2004), pp. 569–70.
[78] *International Dairy Foods Association* v. *Amestoy*, 92 F.3d 67, 69–70 (2nd Cir. 1996).
[79] *International Dairy Foods Association* v. *Amestoy*, 92 F.3d 67, 74. For more details on the case see Kysar (2004), pp. 569–74.

6.2 THE TBT AGREEMENT AND PPMS

factual information. Consumer concerns relating to production methods were dismissed as irrelevant – even if the production methods cause, an allegedly insignificant, physical difference in the end-product.

Also in Europe, potentially harmful effects of the right to free speech on commercial activities have in a few instances been subject to discussion and court decisions.[80] In contrast, as regards information requirements on producers, laws on the labelling of production methods and other NPAs are gaining ground. So far, there has been little protest from producers. This difference might be due to the different regulatory traditions.[81] These may have led to the recognition among European producers and consumers that private business may operate freely only within the limits set by national regulation, while in the United States producers may challenge respective regulatory measures based on the premise that mere consumer concern about production methods does not create sufficiently manifest interests. For the question of the existence of an internationally accepted value of consumer protection, it is more important to recognize the similarities of both systems. Both systems in principle permit states to require producers to disclose facts, provided a legitimate interest for such information can be asserted. Likewise, both systems recognize limitations to claims for consumer information, for example, if they violate legitimate interests of the producer or if otherwise illegitimate effects are intended. The general relevance of rights pertaining to information has been acknowledged also with respect to the international trading system. It has been claimed that respect for some categories of human rights, such as free expression, are essential for a well-functioning economy and as a corollary for a well-functioning trade regime.[82] Hence, both the right to free expression and the right to information are relevant for the international trading system.[83]

---

[80] In the Swiss *Hertel* case, e.g., a private person and non-competitor published controversial information on alleged health risks relating to microwave ovens. On a complaint, he was prohibited by pain of penalties from repeating the contested statements. The case was later referred to the European Court of Human Rights. For a detailed legal analysis of this case see Cottier and Khorana (2005), pp. 245–72. Since this case relates to the freedom of speech rather than to national requirements that producers provide information to consumers, this case is not strictly relevant to the legal question at issue. However, in the course of their analysis, Cottier and Khorana state a curious imbalance between the obligation of private persons to express their views in a balanced manner, while there is no corresponding obligation on producers to inform comprehensively about advantages and disadvantages of their products (at p. 254).

[81] See above section 2.1.2.   [82] Vázquez (2003), p. 839.

[83] Cottier and Khorana (2005) even suggest that freedom of expression and information, if they are not anyway applicable in relations between the parties of a dispute, could to some

These considerations lead back to the question of under which conditions the requirement to supply information in form of product labelling can constitute a legitimate objective in the sense of the TBT Agreement. One view, represented, for example, by the court in the *International Dairy* case detailed above, regards consumer concerns on production methods as irrelevant. This view is perhaps not so much based on the assumption that consumer concerns are scientifically naive,[84] but rather on the assumption that consumer concerns are legitimate only if health or other values of the consumer are at risk. The opposite view holds that state requirements relating to accurate information on conditions of production are generally legitimate.

The term 'legitimate objective' as used in the TBT Agreement constitutes a generic term[85] and encompasses objectives other than those explicitly listed in Article 2:2. The term 'legitimate' refers to general ethical concepts and requires a normative assessment. Neither a consensus of the parties to the agreement nor support of the objective in the domestic laws of all parties is necessary for the determination of which objectives are legitimate. Guidance as to the meaning of legitimacy may be found in internationally accepted documents.[86] Given that ethical concepts change over time, more recent official documents in particular may be considered pertinent. With respect to consumer information, the UN Guidelines on Consumer Protection ('the Guidelines') need to be taken into account as evidence for the legitimacy of consumer information on production methods. If the Guidelines show that consumer information on production methods is supported by the United Nations, this would constitute strong evidence for consumer information being a legitimate objective of public policies and respective measures in the sense of Article 2.2.

The Guidelines do indeed recognize the great importance of consumer information and go as far as assigning governments the task of promoting it. The Guidelines describe the role of governments with respect to consumer information as follows:

> Governments should develop or encourage the development of general consumer education and information programmes, including

---

extent be recognized as fundamental principles of law under Article 38 of the Statute of the ICJ, or could perhaps be taken into account as a matter of customary law (pp. 267–8).

[84] This, however, is assumed by Kysar (2004), pp. 595–7.

[85] Indicated by the term '*inter alia*' before the list of examples for such legitimate objectives.

[86] See Chapter 5, section 5.1.1.1, for the relevance of international law and international documents for interpretation of the WTO Agreements.

information on the environmental impacts of consumer choices and behaviour and the possible implications, including benefits and costs, of changes in consumption, bearing in mind the cultural traditions of the people concerned. The aim of such programmes should be to enable people to act as discriminating consumers, capable of making an informed choice of goods and services, and conscious of their rights and responsibilities.[87]

This statement refers to the possible implications of consumer choices and behaviour in an extremely open way. It suggests that NPAs, such as production methods, should also be addressed, and supports sustainable consumption in order to meet the needs of present and future generations for goods and services in ways that are economically, socially and environmentally sustainable.[88] The Guidelines assign the responsibility for sustainable consumption to all members and organizations of society with informed consumers, government, business, labour organizations and others. They also state:

> Informed consumers have an essential role in promoting consumption that is environmentally, economically and socially sustainable, *including through the effects of their choices on producers*. Governments should promote the development and implementation of policies for sustainable consumption and the integration of those policies with other public policies.[89]

The Guidelines are, first, evidence for the internationally recognized legitimacy of consumer information as objective of state action. More than that they are unambiguous in their support for the influence consumers should have on producers, if the objective of such influence is of an environmental, economic or social nature.

While the Guidelines merely constitute evidence of the international recognition of comprehensive consumer information as legitimate, there are also a number of material arguments for the legitimacy of consumer information relating to processes. Kysar, for example, argues that the presumption that information on processes is illegitimate means ignoring the instrumental account for process preferences – consumer preferences for processes can well reflect normatively consistent demand for changes in production. He invokes the long tradition of process-oriented consumer

---

[87] UN Guidelines for Consumer Protection (as expanded in 1999), adopted by the General Assembly at its 87th Plenary Meeting (22 December 1999, 54/449), at 35.
[88] UN Guidelines for Consumer Protection, at 42.
[89] UN Guidelines for Consumer Protection, at 43 (added emphasis).

activism, which enjoys a long pedigree in the United States, and he points out that this activism has received constitutional recognition under the First Amendment from the US Supreme Court.[90] Furthermore, Kysar argues that the legitimacy of consumer preferences for processes, and as a corollary the legitimacy of information on such processes, resonates 'well with a variety of forces that have combined to place the consumer and the market at the center of twenty-first century culture and governance'. In his view, process preferences might help to overcome the democratic deficit that the forces of globalization have created.[91] He claims that this era increasingly regards the consumer and his or her pursuit of individual welfare 'as a central orienting concept of law, politics, and culture', and he concludes that process preferences as outlets for public-regarding consumer expression should not be dismissed.[92]

Indeed, comprehensive information is crucial in our so-called information age. Evidence for this can be found in the strong demand for information on all kinds of subjects, including production processes, working conditions and environmental and other social impacts of production. It would be incoherent not to recognize the legitimacy of labelling laws requiring disclosure of production-related information, if a number of international organizations and institutions such as the United Nations appeal to the responsibility of consumers who have reached an unprecedented level of education and knowledge.

However, there is no doubt that labelling laws can also be illegitimate, for example, if they violate the legitimate interests of the producer, such as keeping sensitive business information secret, or if information would impair other protected interests, such as human rights. Furthermore, labelling requirements should not be imposed arbitrarily, and it has been suggested, that in order to prevent disguised protectionism, labelling requirements should be justified by certain important and legitimate consumer interests.[93] In as far as consumer information is in line with the UN Guidelines, however, it must be considered legitimate. This means, that information on environmentally and socially relevant production methods constitutes a 'legitimate objective' in the sense of the TBT Agreement.

---

[90] Kysar (2004), at p. 586. Kysar shows that campaigns and boycotts relating to aspects other than the product itself were at the heart of the civil rights campaign in the United States, e.g., when a widening of options for African American labourers was sought with the slogan 'Don't Buy Where You Can't Work'. See also fn. 261 in Kysar's article.
[91] Kysar (2004), at p. 580.   [92] Kysar (2004), pp. 639–40.
[93] Lell (2004), p. 111.

6.2.2.3.2 Consumer information as precondition for the functioning of markets

Consumer information is highly relevant for the legal status of labelling requirements concerning unincorporated PPMs under the TBT Agreement. The demand for consumer protection and information is predominantly characterized as a social movement to further corrective action against the misuse of both market and political powers held by the suppliers of goods.[94] While protection of consumers as the weakest group of market participants certainly has a strong social component, this perspective is too narrow and tends to neglect another crucial dimension of consumer protection, and most importantly, consumer information. Consumer information is not a function, but a precondition for achieving a maximum of welfare from international trade. Thus, more than a right of the individual consumer, consumer information is a necessary requirement for competition and for the functioning of markets. This dimension is often overlooked, and consumer information or labelling is consequently often discussed under the false premise that labelling requires justification due to seemingly trade-restrictive effects.

It is a basic insight of micro-economic theory that the welfare of the individual consumer is inextricably linked with the welfare of society as a whole.[95] It is assumed that under certain conditions there is no need for government intervention because by pursuing their own interests, individuals lead the economy to produce what is needed and in the cheapest possible way. As detailed above, the theory is, however, based on certain assumptions, such as the existence of perfect competition, which rarely exist in the real world.[96] A crucial aspect of perfect competition is full information of all market participants.[97] It is therefore essential for the

---

[94] MacGowan (1978), p. 8. See also Guest (2002), who describes contemporary activities and concerns of the consumer movement in the United States.

[95] This idea is the basic argument for free markets as made by Adam Smith, when he referred to the 'invisible hand' (see also Chapter 2, section 2.1.3.1). Indeed, during Smith's time, consumers were confronted with a smaller number of options due to mobility constraints and smaller markets with rather simple products, and often common knowledge may have been sufficient for consumers to make rational choices (Maynes, 2003, p. 199). Given the information asymmetries and the meagre performance of micro-economic models existing in the modern real world, Stiglitz refers to Smith's 'invisible hand' as 'palsied', or even a non-existent hand (e.g., Stiglitz (2003), p. 6).

[96] See above Chapter 2, section 2.1.3.2.1.

[97] See, e.g., Sen (1999), pp. 159, 160, Cottier and Khorana (2005), p. 246. For the economic implications of information asymmetries see the analysis in Cottier and Khorana (2005), pp. 254–60.

model and for Smith's idea of an invisible hand that market participants are guided by their true preferences. Only if consumers have a full understanding based on full information of the options available to them are they able to act according to what they truly want.[98] The reason for the need for full information is obvious: positive private and social goals can be achieved by the tool of choice, that is, the market, only if the individual choices are exercised freely and intelligently. Hence, in order to allow markets to function, consumers must have access to information.[99] Only informed consumers can look after their own interests, and so make the market work. Indeed, assuming perfect information, a large part of other consumer protection laws would be redundant or have less significance.[100] Swagler, for example, suggests that in the whole range of consumer issues, consumer information may be considered the most important element. He states:

> Everyone makes mistakes, but with better information, such mistakes should be minimized. This marks the consumers as the first line of defense against abuses in the market. If individual choice is to have any meaning, individuals must have the information to make these choices. Given that information, consumers can emerge as a powerful force within the marketplace. Without it, they are no better than sheep, and the best they can hope for is that some benevolent shepherd will look after them.[101]

In the absence of relevant information on the part of consumers, the situation of an information asymmetry arises. In this situation, consumers will base their decisions on the incomplete information at hand, and will arrive at adverse choices that do not adequately reflect the facts. For example, if the buyer is unable to assess the quality of a specific product, he or she might base his or her choice on information on the average quality of the respective type of products. Since choices of this kind will not reward exceptional quality or punish poor quality of the product at issue, there is no incentive for producers to produce products of high quality. Hence, producers cannot compete on quality. In consequence, the market fails and leads to an inefficient allocation of resources.[102]

Whether in a national or an international market, the importance of consumer information for competition and the functioning of markets

---

[98] Maynes (2003), p. 196.   [99] Stern (1971), p. 96.
[100] Swagler (1979), p. 88.   [101] Swagler (1979), p. 88.
[102] For more details on market failure due to information asymmetries Vahrenkamp (1991), pp. 39–42.

6.2 THE TBT AGREEMENT AND PPMS

is beyond doubt.[103] Some might argue that information is just one good among others, and that the market for information will efficiently regulate the supply of all information for which there is a corresponding demand. Since information is a precondition for making a purchasing decision, it could be regarded as a mere transaction cost and as such a mere factor relevant for decision-making. This view, however, ignores some structural problems inherent to the market for information that prevent an optimal solution. The group most likely to possess all information relating to the product is the producers. However, since the supply of such information has an impact on the sales of the respective product, there is no incentive for producers to provide comprehensive information, since part of that information could render the product less attractive. The position of producers with respect to information relating to a specific product is a monopolist one which cannot be efficiently regulated by the market. In addition, not even producers might have at hand all information relating to a product that might be of interest to consumers. Producers intend to maximize their profits and will therefore possess all cost-relevant information. But they will usually not invest resources in order to gain information on cost-neutral aspects, such as information relating to waste management or environmental impacts of production. Hence, consumers would have to invest huge resources in achieving full information, which would normally by far exceed the value of the good they intend to purchase. It is therefore reasonable to assume that markets are not usually capable of providing all information of interest to consumers, and that there are great information asymmetries. This means that one of the most basic assumptions of micro-economic models, namely, perfect information of all market actors, does not exist in real life. For this reason, in as far as labelling serves to diminish information asymmetries and enables consumers to meet their preferences, labelling is welfare enhancing.[104]

Having sufficiently described the importance of full information from an economic perspective, and so ascertained the legitimacy of policies addressing this problem, the question of which information is needed is as yet unanswered. One view holds that only information on product

---

[103] In 2001, Professors Akerlof, Spence and Stiglitz won the Nobel Prize in Economic Science precisely for their work in information economics and the consequences of information asymmetries on markets, which challenged the way economists had traditionally thought about markets. See, e.g., Stiglitz (1975) on the consequences of imperfect information on product markets, and more recently for the general importance of markets Stiglitz (2003 and 2004).
[104] van den Bossche, Schrijver and Faber (2007), p. 230

price and quality are necessary for consumers to arrive at rational decisions. This view is based on the assumption that aspects which do not have a direct impact on the consumer or his or her belongings are irrelevant. Others argue that in addition to information on price, quality and health effects, 'product-related' basic knowledge, including information on the side-effects of products and on external effects such as pollution, is also relevant.[105] As numerous studies show, there is demand for information on aspects which do not affect consumers' lives or belongings, and despite an obvious free-riding problem, labels seem to influence choices of an increasing number of consumers, especially in developed countries.[106]

From an economic perspective, the question of which information is relevant depends on the results the market is intended to achieve. In as far as markets are regarded as tools to ensure that goods are supplied in a way that ensures a certain ratio of good quality and low prices, information on externalities might indeed be considered irrelevant to consumers. If, however, the market is used as a tool to achieve likewise a positive effect on certain social or economic externalities, consumers need all information relating to such externalities in order to make informed choices that foster economic, social and environmental welfare. Labelling then helps to remove information asymmetries and can contribute to internalize externalities, such as environmental or social damage through production.

In the case of the WTO, the goals to be achieved are determined by the agreements. As discussed in more detail above,[107] the WTO Agreements are designed to contribute to a large number of different welfare objectives, such as raising living standards, 'while allowing for the optimal use of the world's resources in accordance with the objective of sustainable development, seeking both to protect and preserve the environment'.[108] The TBT Agreement, which is particularly designed to reduce other, that is, technical, barriers to trade, has been drafted with the desire 'to further the objectives of GATT 1994' and is aimed at 'improving efficiency of production and facilitating the conduct of international trade'.[109] Hence, under the WTO Agreements, international markets are used as a tool for

---

[105] Vahrenkamp (1991), p. 25.
[106] From the vast number of empirical studies showing an increase in the relevance of eco-labelling for purchasing decisions, see, e.g., Imkamp (2000) on a raised interest in information on ecological aspects of the products, and Loureiro and Lotade (2004), for the receptiveness of consumers towards fair-traded coffee.
[107] See above Chapter 2, section 2.2.1.1.
[108] WTO Agreement, Preamble, 1st recital, reflecting the language of the preamble of GATT 1947, 2nd recital. The GATT 1947 forms part of the GATT 1994 (GATT 1994 1(a)).
[109] TBT Agreement, Preamble, 1st recital.

promoting objectives beyond product quality and lower prices. The WTO Agreements thus imply that information on environmental and social aspects of production also constitutes information relevant to consumers. The reference to 'sustainable development' in particular shows that economic and social welfare also form part of the objectives. Therefore, consumer information on these aspects must necessarily constitute a 'legitimate objective' in the sense of the TBT Agreement. Any other interpretation would render the achievement of the explicitly framed goals of the WTO agreements impossible.

Finally, it is noteworthy that economic theory acknowledges problems relating to perfect information. Obviously, in the real world the precondition of perfect information does not exist. Informational deficits and asymmetries can possibly also arise from an excess of information. It is likewise obvious that even the most comprehensive information requirements could not lead to the full realization of the preconditions for the micro-economic model in the real world. For example, an excess of information can arise if information is too specific and therefore understandable only to experts, or if processing of information would incur high costs to consumers. Also, information may be presented in a confusing way. It has even been argued that there is a psychological threshold relating to information, often referred to as an information overload.[110] Information overload may impede the processing of information, with the consequence that consumers base their choices on incomplete information despite the availability of full information. An excess of information may cause individuals to ignore some information and to take less optimal purchasing decisions.[111] This argument has been invoked to support standardized information, which is easier for consumers to extract and which lowers respective transaction costs.[112]

From an economic point of view, it is therefore preferable that the optimal level of information is provided. In determining the optimal level of information for a society or individual, it is necessary to consider all relevant circumstances. For example, information overload is a ubiquitous problem in a period sometimes referred to as the 'information age'. Due to various technical developments, most importantly the Internet, information is available and more accessible than at any former time. However, the need to channel information and to filter necessary and

---

[110] Vahrenkamp (1991), p. 38.
[111] See Teisl and Roe (1998), p. 148 with further references.
[112] Teisl and Roe (1998), pp. 142–3.

relevant information from the abundant information available has even led to the creation of new branches of economic activity. In addition, non-commercial associations and interest groups today look upon the provision of comprehensible information to their members as being among their most important tasks. Last, but not least, the average human ability to deal with information in many societies has to a great extent paralleled technical developments. Thus, given that sophisticated methods to deal with information exist, the optimal level of information will usually equal the highest possible level of information. While regardless of technological developments full information as an ideal condition will remain impossible to achieve, there is ample scope to raise the level of information on products, including information on NPAs.

6.2.2.3.3 Preliminary conclusions

The legal account and the economic account for consumer information lead to nearly congruent results. From a legal perspective, consumer information is a legitimate objective, because it constitutes an internationally recognized right of consumers. From an economic perspective, consumer information is a necessary precondition for the functioning of markets. More than conferring a right to individual consumers to be protected, adequate consumer information protects the market itself and as a corollary also the benefits of international trade. While traditionally only information relating to prices or quality has been considered relevant to fulfil this function, the stated objectives of the WTO Agreements imply that information on a whole range of other social and environmental aspects is equally important. In the light of the objectives of the WTO, the precondition of perfect information for markets to function extends to consumer information on incorporated as well as unincorporated PPMs if these are economically, environmentally or socially relevant.

Given the legitimacy of accurate information from both a legal and economic point of view, consumer information must be considered a legitimate objective in the sense of Article 2:2 of the TBT Agreement.[113] This view conforms to an increased demand for information on various NPAs, which can be observed at the market.[114] Since it is information itself which

---

[113] Appleton (2002), at p. 259, considers similar arguments with respect to the requirement in Article 2:2 that the measure be least trade-restrictive.

[114] Examples are the strong demand for bio-food, which consumers expect to conform to certain health as well as to ecological standards, including environmental protection, animal welfare and protection of species (cf., e.g., 'Drei Viertel aller Konsumenten bereit zu Bio-Aufpreis', *Wirtschaftswoche*, 24 October 2007), as well as the demand for

must be considered legitimate, it is irrelevant for the legal assessment whether obligatory information requirements or whether voluntary provision of information is concerned.[115] Consumer information and labelling serving this objective are desirable in principle.[116]

Nevertheless, the *prima facie* case for legitimacy should be subject to rebuttal, since the case for consumer information is not absolute. Given the importance of information as a prerequisite for the functioning of markets, it is self-evident that only true information can be legitimate. Thus, laws against unfair competition constitute an important pillar in a legal framework on information requirements, in order to ensure that only true information is offered in a way that is not misleading to consumers. Furthermore, information requirements may be illegitimate in cases where they are designed in a deceptive or abusive way, for example, in cases of sensitive information, or if they result in an unjustifiable excess. Certainly, labelling or information abused in order to lead consumers to discriminate based on race, colour, sex and other aspects listed in Article 2 of the Universal Declaration of Human Rights would not constitute a legitimate objective.

Laws prescribing the disclosure of information, whether in the form of labelling, publication in the Internet or otherwise, have to be assessed in the light of the above considerations. The burden of proof, which is currently placed on those applying labelling and information schemes, thus needs to be reversed. Suspicious attitudes towards consumer information and labelling overlook the point that legitimate information improves rather than jeopardizes the functioning of markets. Suggestions

---

ecologically produced textiles (cf., e.g., 'Moral kommt in Mode', *Wirtschaftswoche*, 17 April 2008).

[115] van den Bossche, Schrijver and Faber (2007), p. 231 warn that voluntary labelling in exceptional cases may lead to inefficient outcomes. Costs on the provision of information are part of production costs, thus the decision on voluntary labelling is a decision on costs. If returns on accurate voluntary information are promising, producers would seize this opportunity to reap additional benefits. Nevertheless, these benefits would reflect consumer choices based on a higher level of information and thus be entirely consistent with the idea of competitive markets. Therefore, this argument against voluntary labelling must be rejected. However, given that information by voluntary labelling is welfare enhancing and thus profitable to society as a whole, international or national funds to support the provision of information by small or by developing-country producers also ought to be considered in line with the objectives of the WTO agreements.

[116] See also Charnovitz (2002), p. 109, who considers truthful labels a market-friendly response; Esty (2000), p. 250; Esty and Geradin (1998), p. 38, where Esty suggests that mechanisms should be developed to ensure a greater degree of convergence among the schemes and non-discriminatory application.

to subject mandatory PPM labelling to narrow conditions[117] or to a proportionality approach[118] do not reflect the general legitimacy and even necessity of consumer information. They ignore the fact that uninformed consumer choices, that is, consumer decisions made despite a lack of relevant information, are in contradiction to the basic economic rationales of the multilateral trading system. Given the legal and the economic case for information and corresponding requirements, it is the lack of information that requires justification.

6.2.2.4 Necessity

In addition to the requirement of a legitimate objective, Article 2.2 requires that technical regulation shall not be more trade-restrictive than necessary to fulfil a legitimate objective, taking account of the risks non-fulfilment would create. It seems clear that information requirements are by their very nature less trade-restrictive than direct regulation. Since consumer information is not only a legitimate objective, but actually promotes the functioning of markets, it is questionable what exactly constitutes the trade-restrictive effects that need to be considered: while labels obviously influence consumers, a consumer's free and informed choice not to buy a product cannot be considered trade-restrictive.[119] In contrast, the choice not to buy one product is as desirable from a market perspective as the choice to buy another one instead.

However, it cannot be denied that labelling requirements or other requirements to publish information place a burden on producers. This burden may indeed be considered trade-restrictive. From this point of view, certain labelling laws could be more trade-restrictive than necessary

---

[117] Swinbank (2006) purports to defend mandatory labelling, but establishes a number of extremely restrictive conditions for rendering mandatory labelling 'an acceptable international practice' (at p. 707). His reasoning and conclusions are therefore inconsistent. On the one hand, he acknowledges a 'right' of consumers to receive information on the way products have been produced, while he restricts legitimacy of mandatory labelling to exceptional circumstances, on the other.

[118] Cheyne (2009), at pp. 942–51, suggests a proportionality test for deciding on the legitimacy of labelling schemes. The test is based on various spectra of consumers' decision-making in order to 'avoid undue harm to those most affected by that consumer choice'. While the analysis of different consumer motivations for decision-making is instructive, Cheyne misses the legitimate nature of information in the first place. She sees the possibility of 'undue harm' due to labelling, but ignores that consumer choices have impacts *per se*. In the absence of labelling or other information, uninformed consumer choices likewise have impacts which currently remain unquestioned, although they do cause inadequate harm.

[119] Similarly Appleton (2002), at p. 259.

6.2 THE TBT AGREEMENT AND PPMS

to fulfil a legitimate objective if equally suited alternatives are at hand. The risks created by non-fulfilment consist in the lack of information that would otherwise have been available to individual consumers, and the corresponding negative effects on the functioning of competitive markets.[120]

One could argue that voluntary labelling is a less trade-restrictive alternative as compared with compulsory labelling or information requirements. Since the costs of labelling can be substantial, some producers might decide to stay out of a certain national market due to labelling requirements. In the case of voluntary labelling, however, the producer might stay in the market, save the costs of labelling and try to outbalance marketing disadvantages by a cost advantage due to the saved labelling costs.

However, necessity is to be assessed with a view to the objective pursued. As detailed above, labelling requirements always pursue the improvement of consumer information. It is questionable, however, whether voluntary labelling is equally suited to achieve this goal. One could argue that voluntary labelling results in some producers labelling their products, while others decide not to. The additional information in the case of voluntary labelling therefore is not available for all products, as would be the case in compulsory labelling, but only for some of the products concerned. Furthermore, there are other objections against information by means of voluntary labelling. Since there is no ubiquitous application of voluntary labels, they might not be able to achieve the same degree of popularity among consumers. Unknown labels, often consisting in symbols or icons, even if implying useful information are in this case not capable of contributing to a general improvement of information among consumers. Only a few consumers with expert knowledge would profit from such labels. The level of information that may be achieved by voluntary labelling provisions is therefore usually lower than the level resulting from mandatory labelling.[121]

Only in a few cases might the use of voluntary labels constitute a real alternative. For example, voluntary labelling of food products free of certain allergens might be sufficient, because the product is especially directed at a limited group of consumers looking for this particular

---

[120] In as far as the information relates to physical aspects and is therefore relevant for consumption, the lack of information may lead to other risks, such as risks for consumer health.

[121] Lell (2004) explores this argument with respect to labelling of products produced by GMOs.

feature. Producers would therefore usually voluntarily add the information 'gluten free' on food products, since this information will make the product more attractive to certain customers. In contrast, it would be insufficient to provide information with a negative marketing effect, such as the existence of allergens in certain food (e.g., 'contains milk'), on a voluntary basis.

The idea of labelling relating to unincorporated PPMs is to provide consumers with information which allows them to come to an informed decision. Both voluntary and compulsory labelling come into consideration. However, the necessity of compulsory information will usually depend on the desired level of information. Since usually a high level of reliable information will be intended, voluntary labelling cannot constitute an equally suited alternative to compulsory labelling.

6.2.3 *The relationship of the TBT Agreement and the GATT*

Product labelling with information on environmentally or socially relevant production methods is here considered consistent with the TBT Agreement, provided that the general requirements for technical norms have been met. However, the question arises as to whether GATT provisions can nevertheless apply to labelling requirements. The GATT/WTO adjudicatory bodies so far have not considered the TBT Agreement *lex specialis* relative to the GATT. It would therefore be conceivable that in the light of the more limited list of exceptions contained in GATT Article XX, which lists animal health but not consumer information, a labelling requirement that is consistent with TBT provisions could fall foul of the GATT.[122] This question may well become relevant for the *Tuna-Dolphin III* panel, since Mexico holds that the labelling regulations of the United States are illegitimate under GATT rules as well as under the TBT.[123]

This situation could fall under the conflict rule contained in the General Interpretative Note to Annex 1A. Under this rule, in the event of a conflict between the GATT and a provision of another agreement in Annex 1A, 'the provision of the other agreement shall prevail to the extent of the conflict'. Since this rule applies only in the case of a conflict, the meaning of the term 'conflict' needs to be reviewed. In scholarship and jurisprudence, a narrow interpretation, similar to the prevailing interpretation of

---

[122] See above Chapter 4. Also Appleton (2002), pp. 250–1, finds that labelling of unincorporated PPMs would violate the national treatment standard under the GATT.

[123] *Tuna-Dolphin III*, Request for Consultations by Mexico, 28 October 2008, WT/DS381/1. See also above Chapter 4, section 4.2.2.1.2.1(iii).

the term in public international law, and a wider interpretation have been suggested. According to the narrow interpretation, a conflict requires a situation, where adherence to the one provision leads to a violation of another provision.[124] Here, however, there would be no situation of contradictory obligations, since the TBT Agreement would only allow, but not require, labelling laws relating to unincorporated PPMs that could violate GATT obligations. Supporters of this view have argued that provisions of the GATT and the TBT Agreement apply cumulatively,[125] with the strictest provision prevailing. In the case at hand, consistency with the TBT Agreement would therefore *per se* be irrelevant for GATT-inconsistent labelling provisions.

A different view interprets the term conflict in a broader way. For example, earlier case law in the *EC – Bananas* case also regarded as conflicts situations where one agreement allowed what another agreement prohibited.[126] Also, Pauwelyn argues that the strict definition of conflict hardly ever allows for an application of this rule. He finds that due to the rule-exception structure of the GATT, the definition would mean overemphasizing the obligations contained in the WTO Agreements vis-à-vis the exceptions, which ultimately constitute the WTO members' rights.[127] In the light of these arguments, a broader interpretation of the term 'conflict' seems clearly preferable. As a result, a finding of consistency of labelling requirement laws with the TBT Agreement would prevail over any possible contrary finding under the GATT.

6.2.4 Special and differential treatment

Developing countries' concerns about labelling requirements pertaining to PPMs have been explained above, and SDT for developing countries is a principle particularly relevant to the TBT Agreement. The importance ascribed to SDT in the TBT Agreement is reflected in the high number of provisions relating to the special needs and concerns of developing countries, and especially of the least developed among them. Also, the preamble of the TBT Agreement stresses its special importance for developing countries by pointing out that international technology can make

---

[124] Marceau and Trachtman (2002), pp. 868–78; Tietje (1995), pp. 136–7. The narrow interpretation was applied by the Appellate Body, e.g., in *Guatemala – Cement I* (1998), para. 65, and in *US – Hot Rolled Steel* (2001), para. 55.
[125] Marceau and Trachtman (2002), pp. 873–5.
[126] Panel Report, *EC – Bananas (Mexico)* (1997), para. 7.159.
[127] Pauwelyn (2002), p. 80.

an important contribution to the transfer of technologies from developed to developing countries, and that WTO members are desirous of assisting developing countries in their endeavours relating to the use of technical regulations, standards and conformity assessment. Against this backdrop, the need to explore to what extent SDT exists in the TBT Agreement and how it affects the legal status of labelling laws relating to unincorporated PPMs when applied to products originating in developing countries is indicated.

Interestingly, PPMs are frequently mentioned with respect to developing country members in the TBT Agreement. Articles 2.12 and 5.9, for example, require members to allow reasonable time for producers in exporting member states, in particular in developing countries, 'to adapt their products or methods of production to the requirements of the importing Member' with respect to technical regulations and conformity assessment. More than merely granting additional time, Article 11 urges WTO members to grant technical assistance and to advise other members, especially developing country members, regarding the preparation of technical regulations, the establishment of national standardizing bodies and participation in respective international bodies, the establishment of national regulatory bodies, or bodies for the assessment of conformity with technical regulations, and the methods by which their technical regulations can best be met.[128] Even more importantly, members shall on request likewise grant assistance regarding 'the steps that should be taken by [the requesting member's] producers if they wish to have access to systems for conformity assessment operated by governmental or nongovernmental bodies within the territory of the Member receiving the request'.[129] In addition, Article 12 establishes general principles of SDT which require members to provide differential and more favourable treatment, including through the relevant provisions of other articles of the TBT Agreement. Article 12 requires members to take into account the special development, financial and trade needs in the implementation of the TBT Agreement, 'with a view to ensuring that such technical regulations, standards and conformity assessment procedures do not create unnecessary obstacles to exports from developing country Members'.[130]

While Article 12 and other provisions providing for SDT stipulate more favourable treatment in terms of additional adaptation periods and technical assistance, they leave the substantive provisions of the TBT

[128] TBT Agreement Articles 11.1, 11.2, 11.3.1 and 11.3.2.
[129] TBT Agreement, Article 11.5.   [130] TBT Agreement, Article 12.3.

Agreement untouched. As a consequence, developing country members cannot challenge labelling regulations and standards if these conform to the requirements laid down in the agreement. The only provision allowing for deviations from the substantive provisions, Article 12.8, relates to exceptions for obligations to developing country members under the agreement. This provision is important with respect to technical regulations and standards adopted by developing countries, but it is not designed to tackle developing countries' main concerns with respect to technical norms, namely, their ability to meet requirements or standards adopted by developed countries. Given that technical norms need to be designed to pursue legitimate objectives, however, it seems consistent that developing countries are not offered exceptions relating to conformity requirements with technical norms.

The TBT Agreement's approach, namely, to provide assistance and thus enable developing countries to comply with legitimate technical norms, is therefore preferable. However, it is questionable whether the SDT provisions are actually capable of achieving this goal, which is based on the development and improvement of technical abilities of developing countries requesting assistance. Extended adaptation periods may be useful if a country is on its way to achieving these abilities, but they are of no use if no development takes place. Also, technical assistance with respect to producers' access to conformity assessment systems may not be sufficient if the financial means to comply are not at hand.

Ultimately, even if the provisions are able to make a contribution to the ability of developing country members to have access to highly regulated product markets, the provisions lack the legal quality which would render them enforceable rights. The language used, such as members 'shall' advise or take measures, and the failure to state in detail the nature of technical assistance or the reasonable measures that are required, indicates that the SDT provisions in the TBT Agreement mostly contain soft law.

Nevertheless, the provisions might have some effect. So far, no developing country member has challenged the lack of technical assistance offered by a WTO member that has imposed a relevant technical norm. The example above, the EU laws on marking of eggs, may be a promising candidate for evaluating this option. Article 6 of the EU Regulation 1028/2006 regulates the import of eggs from third countries and the labelling options available to such eggs. The marking of the eggs depends on an evaluation of marketing standards in third countries. If these are found to be equivalent to the EU standards, then such eggs shall be marked with a distinguishing number equivalent to the producer code. If there are no guarantees for equivalence, then such eggs shall bear a code permitting identification of the country of origin and 'the indication that the farming method is "unspecified"'.[131] Although the Commission is required to implement negotiations with third countries aimed at finding appropriate ways for offering guarantees, there is no provision stating rules on special assistance to developing countries. Whether or not the EC will offer meaningful technical assistance remains to be seen – if not, the discriminatory impact of such regulation on products from developing countries seems inevitable. While often producers in developing countries actually do apply sustainable farming methods as detailed in the EC legal framework, the marketing standards in these countries will most likely not conform to EC standards. Hence, eggs imported from developing countries will usually be marked with the indication that the farming method is unspecified, and sales of imported eggs will suffer from the negative implications of this mark, even if sustainable farming methods have actually been used. In this case, the application of the information requirements would actually have been counter-productive since they would have failed to supply accurate information.

Developing country concerns about eco-labels are often limited to concerns about their capability to assess conformity in a way that would allow them to profit from the label. Arguably, production in developing countries would often meet the substantial requirements of eco-labels, even if merely due to a lack of availability of expensive pesticides in agricultural production for example. Therefore, developed countries claiming to adopt genuine technical norms such as eco-labelling requirements ought to take the principle of SDT seriously and provide developing country producers with real opportunities to comply. While under the GATT the chapeau of Article XX together with the principle of SDT establishes such requirements, it could be argued that the same requirements result from the preamble of the TBT Agreement, which repeats the requirements of the chapeau.[132] It could also be questionable if in this case the member adopting the technical norm truly complies with the requirement in Article 2:2 to ensure that the regulation is not applied 'with the effect of creating unnecessary obstacles to international trade'.

---

[131] Regulation (EC) 1028/2006, OJ, L 186/1 of 7 July 2006, Article 6:3.
[132] 6th recital: 'Recognizing that no country should be prevented from taking measures ... subject to the requirement that they are not applied in a manner which would constitute a means of arbitrary or unjustifiable discrimination between countries where the same conditions prevail or a disguised restriction on international trade.'

6.3 The SPS Agreement

The SPS Agreement deals with sanitary and phytosanitary (SPS) measures affecting trade. Its scope of application is limited to SPS measures which are precisely defined in Annex A. SPS measures are defined by their objectives rather than by their design or the shape they take. The four constitutive objectives enlisted in the Annex refer to the protection of human, animal or plant life or health or to the prevention of other damage, and all are limited to the protection of values 'within the territory of the Member'.

Measures under the SPS Agreement seek to protect the values listed above from a limited number of ills, among them pests, diseases or harmful substances. As regarding the design and type of measures, all kinds of laws, requirements or regulations are appropriate if they include certain enlisted aspects, such as product criteria, testing procedures, etc. Also packaging and labelling requirements 'directly related to food safety' are included in the definition. The SPS Agreement explicitly mentions 'processes and production methods' as a potential aspect included in a sanitary or phytosanitary measure. Like the TBT Agreement, the SPS Agreement does not contain a definition of the notion 'processes and production methods'.

The SPS Agreement stipulates the requirements which legitimate sanitary and phytosanitary measures have to fulfil, thus approaching the legal status of these measures from a different angle than the GATT. While the GATT prohibits certain measures unless they are not justified, for example, under GATT Article XX, the SPS agreement does not focus on prohibited measures, but rather assumes legality of these measures provided they are in line with the requirements set forth in its provisions.[133] The SPS Agreement rather elaborates rules for the application of GATT provisions, in particular those of Article XX(b) including the chapeau.[134] For this reason, explicit obligations to non-discrimination appear only to a small extent regarding control, inspection and approval procedures,[135] while the measures in general have to live up to the standards set by Articles 2 and 3, which include a provision reflecting the chapeau of GATT Article XX.

Although the agreement states explicitly that SPS measures can refer to processes and production methods as well as to product characteristics,

---

[133] Matsushita, Schoenbaum and Mavroidis (2004), p. 486.
[134] SPS Agreement, preamble and fn. 1.
[135] SPS Agreement, Annex C 1(a) and (f).

measures relating to unincorporated PPMs are not covered by the SPS Agreement. For the contrary opinion, one could invoke the position that the principle of effective treaty interpretation requires that any term has meaning and effect of its own in a legal text.[136] If only incorporated PPMs were subject to the SPS Agreement, then the explicit mention of processes and production methods in Annex A would be superfluous, because SPS measures referring to PPMs would then implicitly also relate to product characteristics. Furthermore, as opposed to the TBT Agreement, the adjective 'related' is omitted in the phrase mentioning processes and production methods in the SPS Agreement.

However, stronger textual arguments support the prevailing view that unincorporated PPMs as well as all NPA measures are *per se* excluded from the scope of the SPS Agreement. The main argument for this view is the nature of SPS measures, which according to the definition in Annex A may exclusively serve to protect values within the borders of the state imposing the measure. In the case of imported products, dangers or risks can arise only if the physical characteristics of these products carry the respective risks across the border. It has also been argued that the SPS Agreement does not apply to unincorporated PPM measures, because Annex A 1.lit (b) requires explicitly that risks arise from certain substances, and also the alternatives in lit (a), (c) and (d) apply only in relation to imports of animals or plants or products thereof.[137] Therefore, trade measures referring to PPMs can be subject to SPS provisions only in cases where they are connected to any of the risks listed in Annex 1 of the agreement, such as the spread of pests and diseases. The SPS Agreement applies only to a small sub-set of measures addressing certain risks affecting objects and values within the territory of the importing state.

There is broad agreement that incorporated PPMs are relevant under the SPS Agreement. A recent example is the *EC – Biotech* dispute, in which the panel reviewed almost all challenged measures relating to genetically modified products under the SPS Agreement. However, considering that the main intention of the SPS Agreement is to encompass all measures with the objective of preventing certain risks in advance and not only the actual damage,[138] SPS measures might in exceptional cases be linked also to aspects other than product characteristics. This could be the case if factual reasons prevent the detection of the actual physical characteristics which might carry diseases or harmful substances to territories of other

---

[136] Appellate Body Report in: *US – Gasoline* (1996), p. 21(IV).
[137] Puth (2003), at pp. 208, 209.   [138] Gehring and Jessen (2005), p. 366.

member states, and if regulators found a reasonable connector, possibly even an NPA. An example could be a ban on meat derived from animals carrying certain diseases. Regulators could decide that, in the face of the non-existence of reliable tests to detect a particular disease, the ban ought to be linked to facts that are typically related to a particular disease, such as the use of particular feed in meat production combined with origin. Even in this case, however, the relevant PPMs would actually be incorporated in the end-product. Although this fact would not be apparent, the measure would serve to avert dangers to the country adopting it.

The prevailing view is thus preferable. According to the definition, SPS measures are limited to measures protecting certain values 'within the territory of the Member', and hence only measures addressing products which are capable of physically carrying risks into the member imposing the measure can constitute SPS measures. Since unincorporated PPMs or other NPAs by definition do not cause physical differences in the end-product, whether dangerous or not, measures addressing unincorporated PPMs do not fall within the scope of the SPS Agreement. The same must be true also for packaging and labelling requirements 'directly related to food safety'. PPMs may bear on food safety only if they cause physical differences; hence, labelling requirements for food products relating to unincorporated PPMs would not fall within the scope of the SPS Agreement. As labelling requirements, they would instead be subject to the provisions of the TBT Agreement. This finding is consistent with the precise and detailed definition of SPS measures and the corresponding delimitation of the scope of the agreement. The preciseness of the definition indicates that the agreement is highly specialized, and that its substantive provisions are designed to address only a small specific sub-set of measures which would otherwise be subject to the GATT, especially Article XX. In sum, measures relating to unincorporated PPMs causing risks in third countries will therefore be subject to the provisions of the GATT, while SPS measures relating to incorporated PPMs do not provide for any specialities as compared with other SPS measures.

6.4 Result

For the analysis of the TBT and the SPS Agreements, it is necessary to distinguish between PPMs and other NPAs, since neither of the agreements covers the latter category of measures directly. In contrast, both agreements deal with PPMs and related measures in a special way. Therefore, a further distinction between incorporated and unincorporated PPMs proves useful. The analysis of the SPS Agreement shows that measures linked to unincorporated PPMs are excluded from its scope. The SPS Agreement has been designed to cover measures protecting values such as health within the territory of the member taking the measure. Since unincorporated PPMs by definition cannot cause additional risks, coverage of the SPS Agreement is limited to measures linked to incorporated PPMs.

An interpretation of the ambiguous language of the TBT Agreement, together with the unambiguous reluctance of the drafters to include such measures, shows that general technical norms referring to unincorporated PPMs are not covered by the TBT Agreement. However, this conclusion does not affect the coverage of labelling requirements concerning unincorporated PPMs. Since labelling requirements are covered by the TBT Agreement in general, it is irrelevant whether they relate to information on incorporated or unincorporated PPMs or even other NPAs. Applying the substantive provisions of the agreement to labelling relating to unincorporated PPMs shows that such labelling is not *per se* discriminatory or otherwise impermissible. Instead, permissibility depends on the requirement in Article 2.2 that technical norms should pursue a legitimate objective. Since consumer information as a policy objective must generally be considered legitimate, both on a legal and an economic account, both voluntary and compulsory information requirements, including labelling, must be presumed to be legitimate. The presumption of legitimacy is subject to rebuttal, however, for example, if the information to be disclosed violates the rights of others. Compulsory labelling will also usually not be considered more trade-restrictive than necessary, since it is less trade-restrictive compared with direct regulation. Although it may affect producers more than voluntary labelling, the latter will usually not be equally suited to reach the objective of a general improvement of the level of consumer information. Finally, it is here suggested that the provisions of the TBT Agreement prevail over the GATT for measures falling into its scope. Hence, permissibility of labelling laws relating to unincorporated PPMs need to be assessed exclusively on basis of the TBT Agreement.

In sum, only labelling provisions relating to unincorporated PPMs are referred to scrutiny under the TBT Agreement, while the GATT remains the applicable agreement for all other technical regulations and standards relating to NPAs.

PART III

Outlook: new perspectives on the legal status of NPA measures

The legal analysis *de lege lata* has shown that perhaps contrary to the conventional view, the WTO Agreements offer considerable flexibility concerning NPA measures. Since states will often find it sufficient to publish information on PPMs on products or to adopt other information requirements that producers must adhere to, the TBT Agreement is of great importance. Although this has not yet been confirmed in dispute settlement, the TBT Agreement has enormous potential to render a large number of NPA measures, namely, labelling requirements concerning unincorporated PPMs, legal under WTO law. Also, even though most NPA measures would fall foul of GATT obligations, the general exceptions offer scope for finding many genuine NPA measures legal. The adjudicatory bodies will most probably proceed in interpreting the general exceptions with an evolutionary approach. Since several provisions in Article XX contain generic terms, as is most obvious in the case of the moral exception, many NPA measures that are used to implement internationally recognized public policies can be justified. Of equal importance are the findings on the principle of special and differential treatment for developing countries. This principle, if taken seriously, establishes that NPA measures take into account adequately the concerns of affected developing countries. Only if the conditions emerging from this principle are fulfilled, may NPA measures be covered by one or another of the particular exceptions. This means, that in order to be consistent with WTO law, NPA measures must be both genuine in terms of the public policies they pursue and provide for remedies to prevent disadvantageous economic effects on developing countries. In this sense, assessing NPA measures under Article XX may lead to balanced solutions as regards the opposing interests involved.

Despite this potential in the existing agreements, however, the legal situation is not entirely satisfactory. First, despite an evolutionary approach to interpretation, not all legitimate interests are reflected in the general exceptions. Furthermore, the use of generic terms, while allowing for flexibility, also implies legal uncertainty. This is most obvious in the case of the moral exception: views among members might differ considerably when it comes to determining the precise content of public morals.

In this situation, it is indicated to move ahead. The following two chapters provide an outlook on the subject. Chapter 7 reviews existing reform proposals and discusses their relevance for NPA measures. Chapter 8, drawing on the foundations outlined in Part I, then develops a specific perspective on the legal status of NPA measures under WTO law which may offer guidance as to the legal status of NPA measures *de lege lata* as well as *de lege ferenda*.

7

The interface of international trade and public policies: an overview over existing proposals for reform

National NPA measures will often be justified as pursuing important public policies. Therefore, the legal status of NPA measures under WTO law is an important part of the broader 'trade and ...' or 'linkage' debate, which discusses the general interface of trade and non-economic public policies. Many suggestions *de lege ferenda* have been made from the perspective of a certain policy, such as environmental or social and human rights policies, and some of these are highly relevant to the legal status of NPAs in general. Therefore, this chapter reviews and comments on existing suggestions and their usefulness for a new general perspective on NPAs.[1]

7.1 Review

The proposals presented below concern diverse issues such as institutional, procedural and substantive matters and questions of competence. Most scholars favour mixed approaches which relate to changes in several categories. This chapter summarizes these approaches into three categories. The first category, denial of WTO competence, comprises views that completely deny linkage or the desirability of developing such linkage. It is important to note, however, that the motivation for the denial differs considerably. The two remaining categories describe various suggestions made by the 'supporters' of linkage. Most proposals suggest more complex changes in substance and procedure. Section 7.1.3, on institutional change and governance, presents some more general approaches to reform international

---

[1] For an overview over the main positions and the complexity of arguments in the debate see the Symposium 'Boundaries of the WTO', in *American Journal of International Law* 96(1) (2002), with contributions by Alvarez; Leebron; Charnovitz; Bagwell, Mavroidis and Staiger; Trachtman; Howse; Jackson; Bhagwati; and Steger. Since the literature on this topic is enormous and since most suggestions are very complex, this review cannot be comprehensive. Its purpose is rather to provide an overview as a starting point for the proposal presented in Chapter 8.

economic law, often aimed at better embedding international economic law into the broader field of public international law.

7.1.1 Denial of competence?

The most basic question relates to the competence of the WTO vis-à-vis other international organizations for non-economic policies. This basic issue is often equalized with the 'linkage' or 'trade and …' debate. Except for the United Nations and various organizations for regional integration, international organizations focus on a specific subject matter. For example, while the WTO deals with the policy domain of international trade, the ILO's focus is on employment and conditions of work, and UNEP coordinates environmental activities. Naturally, however, globalization and deeper economic integration, accompanied by a huge volume of international trade, cannot be dealt with in isolation. Economic activity, by its very nature, brings along environmental damage and social change in many different respects. For this reason, the terms 'linkage' or 'trade and…' debate are misleading: what is discussed is not whether there is actually some kind of link between international trade and various social issues. Given the strong impact that international trade has on economic activities and the manifold impacts of such activities on society and the environment, the existence of many and diverse factual links cannot be denied. Also, links between trade and social policies are pervasive in the WTO Agreements already, as reflected, for example, in the particular exceptions listed in GATT Article XX. What is hotly debated, however, is whether these links should be extended, amended or limited – and if so, how they should best be incorporated into the WTO and into the covered agreements. This debate can be seen as part of a process from the legacy of fragmentation towards greater coherence in international law.[2] It has been argued that the WTO cannot deal with international trade while officially ignoring its manifold social implications. As will be shown below, the group of those supporting the need to link trade and other non-economic concerns sees different ways to realize such links. Prominent suggestions are, for instance, the inclusion of so-called social clauses into the WTO Agreements and/or increased institutional cooperation between the WTO and other international organizations.

Others, however, reject the need or desirability of linkage. They are of the view that the WTO is competent only with respect to its core task and

[2] Cottier, Pauwelyn and Bürgi (2005b), p. 3.

should therefore leave other matters to arguably more specialized organizations. The view of the latter group is what is here categorized as a denial of competence of the WTO for dealing with non-economic issues. The most radical view against a link between the WTO as an organization fostering free trade and social or environmental issues would be based on a neo-liberal economic theory. Particularly with respect to environmental protection, it could be argued that different environmental standards are part of the factor endowment decisive for a country's comparative advantages. Differences between countries, the exploitation of which is the very idea of comparative advantage, are often reflected in countries' regulations. In this view, linking trade measures to environmental protection would be against the very spirit of the WTO agreements.[3] It could also be argued that economic growth resulting from free trade will ultimately lead to higher demand for environmental protection. Trade restrictions, however, impede economic growth, especially for poor countries, which would therefore not be able to improve their environmental standards. In consequence of this view, free trade is the ultimate cure and must therefore be placed beyond environmental protection. Therefore, linking the WTO in some way to non-economic issues would be counter-productive. Taking this argument to its end, the view might even decline the need to address environmental concerns at all, because the economic welfare created by free trade would automatically lead to an optimal level of environmental protection.[4]

Bhagwati also rejects the need for linkage, albeit with a different rationale. He argues that the underlying principle of the GATT and the WTO is Adam Smith's proposition that non-coercive trade between countries is a mutually beneficial phenomenon. The WTO Agreements must therefore be designed to benefit all WTO members, including developing countries. Bhagwati argues that from this point of view, the TRIPS does not belong to the WTO, since it basically results in the payment of royalties by poor countries, which consume intellectual property, to rich countries, which produce it. According to him, other issues supported by northern

---

[3] E.g., Roessler (1998), p. 224.
[4] For an explanation of environmental and social effects of international trade see Anderson (1998). Anderson gives a mixed account. He concludes that 'it should be acknowledged by liberal traders that it is not possible to claim with certainty that trade liberalization will improve the environment and welfare for different groups of countries in the presence of significant environmental externalities without appropriately offsetting environmental policies in place. But equally it should be acknowledged by environmental groups that in many situations trade liberalization may actually help not only the economy but also the environment' (p. 240).

lobbies, such as labour and the environment, would also not meet the mutual benefit test and should therefore be rejected. Bhagwati compares the TRIPS with a third leg of the WTO which does not belong and which prompts the growth of other legs, so that the WTO turns from a tripod 'into a centipede, slowing down the freeing of trade as the poor countries object and protest and walk away from negotiations'.[5] Bhagwati invokes a second argument against linkage, namely, the dominance of trade associations at the WTO. He argues that these associations represent the most important commercial interests which are located in the developed world. According to Bhagwati, this explains why the social agendas discussed at the WTO usually relate to subject matters where developing countries will most likely be defendants. Other social issues, on the other hand, such as sweatshops and treatment of migrant labour, which would hurt industries located within developed countries, are ignored. According to Bhagwati, the choice of social or moral issues on the WTO agenda is therefore evidence of the hidden interests of competing industries.[6] It seems that Bhagwati's rejection of linkage is to a large extent based on the WTO's lack of competence for subject matters and values other than trade, together with the organization's shortcomings as a real-world institution influenced by various competing interests.

Other scholars are also of the view that social policies and other non-economic issues must be dealt with outside the WTO.[7] Anderson, for example, suggests that for strategic reasons some engagement by the WTO may be wise, even if limited to reminding the world of some of the non-trade measures and actions otherwise available.[8] Instead, he supports engagement of the trade community in drafting multilateral environmental agreements outside the WTO, if these are likely to include trade provisions, and to ensure that these meet certain requirements which render them acceptable.[9] Nevertheless, he interprets the existing exceptions, such as those in GATT Article XX, narrowly when it comes to environmental or other social trade measures, and rejects any amendments to the WTO Agreements. Jones' main concern, in contrast, is that the WTO would be weakened as an institution if non-trade rules were to be integrated into the WTO system. Such rules would exceed the limits set by the core agreements, which reflect the common goal among its members,

---

[5] Bhagwati (2002), pp. 127, 128. Bhagwati strongly opposes linkage, with the notable exception of competition policies.
[6] Bhagwati (2000), p. 494.
[7] E.g., Grossmann, Busse, Fuch and Koopmann (2002), Anderson (1998), Jones (2002).
[8] Anderson (1998), p. 246.   [9] Anderson (1998), p. 249.

namely, the achievement of free trade.[10] According to Jones, there are beneficial effects of trade on environmental and social goals as part of a long-term process. He therefore suggests:

> Yet governments should avoid any systematic retreat from trade liberalization, even as part of a strategic effort to enforce global social and environmental standards. Such efforts will harm all countries and erode the economic foundations for progress.[11]

Jones argues that the difficulties in achieving 'non-trade goals'" do not lie in the WTO or in a democratic deficit, but in a global institutions deficit.[12] He therefore suggests that achieving non-economic goals, instead of linking them to international trade as fostered by the WTO, may require a 'variable geometry' of institutional arrangements from organizations of regional economic integration to specific treaties and multilateral organizations.[13]

Similar arguments have been invoked against the incorporation of a social clause dealing with labour standards into the WTO. Stern, for example, argues that the developmental history of Western countries like the United States and other industrialized countries shows that improvement in labour standards requires an active role for government together with broad public support, rather than strict enforcement of ILO labour standards. He therefore suggests that what is needed is technical and financial assistance to low income countries to promote welfare-enhancing economic progress, and that the role of the ILO is to provide a multilateral forum that enhances its authority in improving labour standards internationally.[14] Also, Addo rejects the inclusion of a social clause into Article XX, allowing for trade sanctions, and instead favours an approach based on cooperation between countries.[15] He also suggests creating a direct connection between labour and trade issues within the ILO process.[16]

Although many view trade as an improper tool with which to pursue non-economic public policies, it is rare that the need to link international trade and social issues is rejected outright. Maskus, for example, argues that the question of whether or not regulatory standards should be put on the WTO agenda depends on the substance matter. He sees a

---

[10] Jones (2002), p. 260.   [11] Jones (2002), p. 265.
[12] Jones' finding has been confirmed by the Report by the Consultative Board to the Director-General Supachai Panitchpakdi, Report on the Future of the WTO (2004), which states that globalization has created a governance deficit (p. 39, No. 171).
[13] Jones (2002), p. 272.   [14] Stern (2000), pp. 431-7.
[15] Addo (2002), pp. 295-9.   [16] Addo (2002), pp. 301-3.

strong case for linking trade and competition policy, and a weaker one for environmental or even labour concerns.[17] Others argue that changes are necessary to achieve a balance that reflects the concerns of contemporary societies,[18] or stress the need to better integrate existing international bodies and organizations in a multi-level system of governance,[19] or see a more general need for continual attention and work.[20] The question of linkage therefore is one of how and how much, rather than a question of yes or no. As Leebron put it:

> Carefully tailoring the modality of linkage to the substantive ... claims advanced for linkage will enable us to see that these are not all-or-nothing claims but, rather, steps in the evolution of a complex multilateral regulatory framework across a variety of issue areas. Linkage so pursued should not obstruct agreement; on the contrary, it should further enhance the coherence of that multilateral world and the legitimacy of its institutions.[21]

7.1.2 Changes at WTO level

Most scholars seem to agree on the point that social and environmental issues as a general matter should be dealt with primarily outside the WTO. Nevertheless, the arguably prevailing view acknowledges existing links between trade and non-trade policies. Many find that the WTO as it stands already recognizes the precedence of certain public policy objectives over the freer trade goals, and argue that this balance requires some modifications.

The decreasing importance of tariffs, which triggered the need to discipline other trade-related policies in order to successfully dismantle trade barriers, has been seen as the main reason for the emergence of links. As a consequence of this development, the WTO has to deal with measures that are considered to pursue legitimate policies but that are not entirely consistent with obligations of WTO members. Cottier argues that the need to balance different interests has effectively rendered the system multifunctional.[22] The strongest constituency in this respect are environmentalists, who urge the need to 'green' existing international institutions and the GATT. Boyce, for example, argues that there is no intrinsic reason why institutions should not consider environmental goals, or why

---

[17] Maskus (2002), pp. 135–52. [18] Steger (2002), pp. 143–5.
[19] See, e.g., Trachtman (2002), who describes this problem as one of horizontal, vertical and functional allocation of jurisdiction.
[20] Schoenbaum (1997), p. 313. [21] Leebron (2002), p. 27. [22] Cottier (1998), p. 58.

'trade agreements must rule out consideration of environmental impacts arising from production and process methods'.[23] Charnovitz posits the WTO is already – among other functions – an environmental agency. In his view, thinking in terms of 'linkage' is outdated, since the WTO is a multifunctional organization with multiple objectives, among them biodiversity and public health.[24]

Scholars have discussed different approaches to shape 'linkage' or even multifunctionality and to anchor it within the legal framework of the WTO. The very diverse suggestions differ not only in substance, but also in procedure. In principle, different ways come into consideration in order to realize the substantive suggestions, such as an amendment to Article XX, broader interpretation of the existing provisions through an authoritative interpretation, or via development of specific case law. This chapter first reviews proposals on substantive changes and turns then to the procedures that have been suggested to implement them.

7.1.2.1 Substance

The most obvious suggestions for change relate to the prevailing interpretation of the term 'like products' and to the scope of the general exceptions. Regarding the term 'like products', there are different suggestions which would lead to the finding that products are not 'like' if they differ in certain aspects, even if these are not incorporated in the product.[25] This would allow WTO members to pursue public policies by means of a distinction between products based on all relevant aspects. Likewise, it has been suggested that the Article XX exceptions should be read more broadly,[26] by changing the current interpretation of the allegedly too strict necessity test in several particular exceptions,[27] and interpreting the chapeau more rigorously. In consequence, environmental measures could actually be justified, even if their preparation or implementation suffers from flaws of minor importance,[28] such as a lack of consistency in import restrictions with respect to all goods produced in an objectionable

---

[23] E.g., taking an economic approach to environmental degradation, Boyce (2004), p. 122.
[24] Charnovitz (2007b), chapter IV, text accompanying fn. 146.
[25] For more details on the arguments dominating the discussion see above Chapter 4.
[26] E.g., Petersmann (2005a) argues that future WTO jurisprudence may well hold that with the moral exception in GATT Article XX(a), the GATT already includes a social as well as a human rights clause, at p. 58, fn. 83.
[27] Schoenbaum (1997), p. 313, who limits this suggestion to trade measures protecting domestic values and rejects measures relating to extraterritorial objects.
[28] Gaines (2001), pp. 849–60.

manner.[29] These suggestions regard interpretation of the existing texts or, alternatively, an explicit change of the underlying rules.

Another group of suggestions implies amendments to the texts. Cottier asks whether there is a 'minimal standard catalogue of truly universal civil, political, social, economic, and cultural rights', integration of which could prove essential for promoting coherence between trade rules and human rights.[30] Most suggestions focus on the general exceptions in GATT Article XX: the list of policy objectives that override free trade goals could be adapted to the contemporary concerns of humankind. These proposals mostly relate to the protection of the environment and labour rights. Against this approach, however, has been argued that in recent disputes concerning environmental measures the measures failed the requirements of the chapeau after they had been regarded as provisionally justified. Therefore, adding new exceptions to the list in Article XX cannot provide for more flexibility, since the chapeau would still prevent justification of respective measures.[31] Brack, for example, suggests a new WTO side agreement on MEAs instead, which would create a clear set of rules applying only to MEAs. Topics covered in this agreement could be the definition of MEAs and of the different categories of trade measures to which it applies, non-trade measures which would need to accompany trade measures to off-set negative developmental effects, and clarification of competence regarding the institution charged with the resolution of disputes. Due to the specificity of such an agreement, Brack expects that negotiation of such an agreement would be easier.[32]

Given existing case law and given that the terms of the general exceptions potentially cover environmental protection measures, even more suggestions concern labour rights as value not explicitly listed in Article XX. For example, it has been suggested that all widely accepted international conventions on human rights and labour rights should be reviewed, and that the most fundamental values be identified, which could then be included explicitly in the list of particular exceptions in Article XX.[33] This so-called social clause would introduce core labour standards into Article XX, possibly in a similar fashion to existing social clauses in the GSP of some developed countries. Which labour rights should be included in this clause, however, is subject to debate. Various labour

---

[29] Howse and Trebilcock (2005) argue that 'as a matter of international trade law there should be a negative duty not to discriminate for protectionist reasons, but there should not be a positive duty to take affirmative action', p. 279.
[30] Cottier (2002), p. 131. [31] Brack (2002), p. 347.
[32] Brack (2002), pp. 347–9 [33] Steger (2002), p. 144.

rights have been classified as human rights or otherwise acknowledged in a number of international documents, such as in the UN Universal Declaration of Human Rights[34] or the ILO Declaration of Fundamental Principles and Rights at Work, and it could be argued that a link between trade and labour standards should be limited to those appropriately characterized as human rights. Trebilcock and Howse argue that core labour standards promote human freedom of choice and are in this sense entirely consistent with a liberal trading regime seeking to ensure other human freedoms, namely, the right to engage in market transactions.[35]

Schneuwly, in contrast, refers to empirical evidence on the effectiveness of sanctions and distinguishes between norms which can be implemented without negative side-effects and which therefore do not depend on the addressee country's level of development, and other norms which are better promoted with incentive regimes. He suggests incorporating only the former group into the WTO, and limiting the role of the WTO in supervising the sanctions, while relying on expertise provided by other organizations such as the ILO.[36]

A suggestion which would bring about changes of a more fundamental nature is harmonization of rules.[37] Harmonization could help to mitigate concerns about unfair competition, and would limit the scope for conflict between different regulatory regimes. The need for trade measures to discourage the use of certain PPMs would consequently disappear. The reference to international standards in the TBT and the SPS Agreements are steps in this direction.[38] However, there is a great deal of scepticism towards substantive harmonization.[39] Harmonization implies positive integration – a concept that is hotly debated. Integration is often perceived as being inconsistent with the WTO's commitment to regulatory diversity, and beyond that as undesirable.[40] As Esty has pointed out, however, substantive harmonization can take different shapes, which are in part reconcilable with diverse national regulation. He lists as a number of

---

[34] In particular Articles 4, 20 and 23.
[35] Howse and Trebilcock (2005), pp. 272–3.
[36] Schneuwly (2003), pp. 140–1.   [37] E.g., Cottier (1998), p. 57.
[38] Although both agreements contain more elements of procedural than substantive harmonization, see also Cho (2005), p. 665, who characterizes respective harmonization in TBT and SPS Agreement as 'quasi-harmonization'.
[39] See the discussion at the 6th Annual WTO Conference, 2006, London, as summarized by van Damme (2006), pp. 761–2.
[40] Cho (2005), on the other hand, is of the view that the WTO's telos is ultimately 'integrationist', and thus requires strengthening the free trade/social regulation linkage, pp. 628, 646–7.

different harmonization strategies including uniform, minimum, maximum and differentiated standards, multi-tier and goal harmonization and standardization of options. Esty states:

> When properly applied, harmonization may allow the advantages of diversity, preserving the freedom of each nation to exploit its natural comparative advantages, and at the same time permit policy co-ordination to prevent market allocative inefficiencies resulting from externalization of costs or other market failures.[41]

While uniform harmonization will often not be optimal, other strategies are promising, depending on circumstances and objectives. For instance, a multi-tier approach to harmonization implies the adoption of standards for groups of countries, tailored to local conditions without losing advantages as a consequence of uniform requirements. Environmental standards, for example, could be developed for the group of countries which are economically most advanced, while imposing more modest standards for other groups of countries according to their respective level of development.[42] Since most harmonization approaches leave sufficient policy scope to national regulators, harmonization would not *per se* exclude the benefits of regulatory competition.[43]

Great emphasis has also been placed on the need to clarify the relationship of MEAs and the WTO Agreements. In 2001, WTO members agreed to negotiate 'the relationship between existing WTO rules and specific trade obligations set out in multilateral environmental agreements',[44] and reaffirmed the mandate at the Hong Kong Ministerial Conference in 2005.[45] To date, the negotiations have failed to reach agreement on crucial questions. Nevertheless, many WTO members are signatories to a number of international environmental agreements and have approved certain objectives and even agreed to a set of measures or activities therein. As detailed above, however, the application of MEAs as sources of law in WTO agreements is currently problematic. Due to the requirements established in the VCLT, and given nearly universal membership of the WTO, even MEAs with a large membership arguably cannot be taken into account for the legal relations among all WTO members at present.[46] Therefore, some have suggested that trade measures in pursuance of MEAs should be 'relevant to the aims set out in subparagraphs (b) or (g) and the

---

[41] Esty and Geradin (1998), p. 39.   [42] Esty and Geradin (1998), p. 42.
[43] For more arguments against harmonization see Cho (2005).
[44] Doha Declaration, para. 31(i).   [45] Hong Kong Ministerial Declaration, para. 30.
[46] See above Chapter 3, section 3.2.

headnote of GATT Article XX',[47] that they should be considered 'necessary' in the sense of the relevant particular exception or that they even be exempted entirely from scrutiny of Article XX, so that the member would not need to show that a measure is covered by the particular exceptions.[48] Other scholars have developed more sophisticated frameworks which would allow reference to MEAs within the GATT legal framework, for example, via the introduction of a particular exception for MEAs,[49] or following the blueprint set in NAFTA's Article 104. The latter suggestion would imply that those MEAs to which WTO membership could agree would be named explicitly in the text of Article XX, while future MEAs could follow a specific procedure to be included.[50] Many scholars and practitioners seem to agree that the assessment of any trade measure under Article XX must take into account whether it is based on an international agreement, or at least whether the number of countries pursuing similar policies is low or high. A majority considers international acceptance highly important when it comes to justification under Article XX.

It is essential for any suggestion addressing frictions between trade and non-economic policies, especially those relating to NPAs, to take into account developing countries' special concerns and the WTO principle of SDT. Different authors have addressed this issue. Charnovitz, focusing on environmental PPMs, argues that measures relating to PPMs create costs, and that it would be useful to explore ideas on a cooperation effort between the parties. These should include hearings held by the WTO to investigate the costs and explore possible alternatives for achieving the policy objective in question. He then draws on SDT provisions relating to technical assistance, as well as to provisions in the TBT Agreement and the TRIPS Agreement, which require developed countries to take into account the 'special development, financial and trade needs' of developing countries. Acknowledging that these provisions are too vague to contain legal rights, Charnovitz is of the view that these may nevertheless serve as the basis for a query about their implementation.[51]

Bhagwati clearly opposes trade measures linked to unincorporated PPMs. His arguments, however, shed light on the implications of the special status of developing countries. He suggests that many PPM trade measures might be superfluous, since their policy goals could as well or

---

[47] WTO, Submission by the European Communities, TN/TE/W/1, 21 March 2002, paras. 6–8.
[48] WTO, Submission by Switzerland, TN/TE/W/4, 6 June 2002, para. 8.
[49] Hudec (1996).   [50] Neumayer (2002), pp. 155–6.
[51] Charnovitz (2002), p. 109.

better be achieved by providing simple technical or financial assistance to developing countries.[52] Bhagwati postulates that if certain issues are promoted by developed countries, then these should enable developing country producers, even by monetary means, to adhere to the respective standards.[53] Anderson also supports the idea of compensation for developing countries in this respect, especially if environmental measures are concerned.[54]

7.1.2.2 Procedure

There are three main approaches to an implementation of the suggested changes.[55] Changes could be realized (1) by amending the texts of the WTO Agreements, (2) by adopting authoritative interpretations and (3) through case law by the WTO adjudicatory bodies. Many scholars argue that the interrelations between international trade and non-economic policies are of great importance and therefore require political negotiations and a solution supported by all WTO members.[56] Indeed, the WTO is designed as a member-driven organization,[57] and negotiations would be the best option. The obvious problems, however, lie in the difficult procedures for amending the WTO Agreements[58] and in the necessity of ratification in most WTO members. In the light of the apparent impossibility of agreeing a suggestion on the politically sensitive issues relating to linkage in general and to NPA measures in particular, alternative solutions need to be contemplated. A second-best option could be the adoption of authoritative interpretations by the Ministerial Conference and by the General Council according to Article IX:2 of the Marrakesh Agreement.[59] The advantage of this procedure is that authoritative interpretations do not require national ratification in order to take effect. Furthermore, as opposed to amendments, a three-fourths majority of WTO members

---

[52] Bhagwati (2000), pp. 494–5.
[53] Bhagwati (2000), p. 134.   [54] Anderson (1998), p. 250.
[55] Procedural issues are not the main concern of this work and are therefore summarized only briefly.
[56] E.g., Charnovitz (2002), p. 108; Steger (2002), 143–5. Quick and Lau (2003) 'urge WTO Membership not to continue to be politically inactive and ignore important issues such as environment, animal welfare or even labour standards. If the law maker is unable to adapt the law to new developments, the judge will be tempted to step in and "regulate"' (p. 458).
[57] See, e.g., Report on the Future of the WTO (2004), p. 69, No. 313.
[58] Marrakesh Agreement, Article X.
[59] For more details on this tool, which so far has never been used, see Ehlermann and Ehring (2005), pp. 803–24.

would be sufficient. However, the use of authoritative interpretations is obviously rather limited. They may not be used in order to circumvent the procedures for amending the agreements, but are strictly limited to interpretations.[60] These restrictions, however, could also turn into an advantage: since interpretation relates to specific term or provisions, the subject matter concerned would naturally be limited, and thus the probability of agreement would be higher. Authoritative interpretations have the advantage that they are adopted by the competent policy-making authorities of the WTO and may therefore lead to nuanced interpretations of enduring value.[61]

The third option is that the Appellate Body would revise its approach to interpretation, especially of Article XX. The disadvantage of this alternative is obviously the unpredictability of future judgments and reliance on the Appellate Body. Furthermore, it has been questioned whether the WTO adjudicatory bodies are competent to develop case law in a way similar to national judicial bodies, given the lack of a functioning system of checks and balances. This option is nevertheless considered promising by scholars, who feel that the required changes can indeed be achieved on the basis of the existing agreements.[62] It has been argued that such case law could allow rules to be looked at 'from a constitutional angle, taking into account the overall responsibility of the system'.[63] Other suggestions relating to the third option include proposals for institutional changes, such as outsourcing competences on social issues to competent international organizations, or the creation of respective expertise within the WTO. Since the large WTO membership and the higher likelihood of political impasse often prevent negotiated solutions, the development of case law is gaining in importance. However, despite a number of promising developments in recent disputes, and despite a *de facto* rule of precedent, panels and the Appellate Body cannot develop comprehensive solutions, but merely decide as far as necessary in order to settle particular disputes.[64] Cottier, Tuerk and Panizzon therefore postulate a need to develop appropriate structures for negotiations in order to overcome

---

[60] For the problems relating to the fine line between interpretation and amendment see above Chapter 5, section 5.1.1.4.
[61] E.g., Gaines (2001), p. 860.
[62] E.g., Bagwell, Mavroidis and Staiger (2002), p. 76, with respect to pecuniary externalities; Cho (2005), pp. 651–9, who favours the jurisprudence approach together with a 'multifaceted list' of other options.
[63] Cottier (1998), p. 60.
[64] Cottier, Tuerk and Panizzon (2003), p. 163.

political impasse and question the traditional functional approach to trade policy.[65] Nevertheless, even case law not meeting the approval of WTO membership could ultimately contribute to a solution by creating a motivation for WTO members to actively address matters in negotiations and to reach agreement.

7.1.3 Institutional changes and governance-related suggestions

Many ideas involve more or less modest institutional changes at the WTO and/or other international organizations, and some focus on the broader institutional framework of contemporary multi-level governance and develop fundamentally new approaches. While different authors suggest different institutional responses to linkage, the review of suggestions shows that there is agreement on the nature of the problem, and even on the broad lines of possible institutional changes. In consequence of these suggestions, NPA trade measures might become redundant, because underlying regulatory differences or conflicts could be solved at a different stage. The public policies that NPA measures help to implement might then be managed in institutional settings altogether different from the existing ones.

7.1.3.1 Institutional changes

Many scholars feel that a mere change of the WTO Agreements would not do justice to the nature of the trade and social policies interface. Since issues for which expertise is available at other international organizations are involved, it is suggested that cooperation procedures or other institutional linkages to ensure that issues are decided by the most competent body by taking into account its expertise are established. In this way, the advantages of an 'institutional division of labour' could be ensured.[66]

The most far-reaching suggestion is perhaps Guzman's proposal for turning the WTO into a more powerful World Economic Organization (WEO). His point is that a narrow focus on trade will not be sustainable, because it is inconsistent with the needs of an increasingly global economy.[67] His conclusion, an expansion of the WTO to include non-trade issues, would require fundamental institutional changes. Guzman sketches the organizational structure of a new WEO, which would try to retain the WTO's advantages as a stable and effective international

---

[65] Cottier, Tuerk and Panizzon (2003), p. 166.
[66] Howse and Trebilcock (2005), p. 284.   [67] Guzman (2004), p. 305.

7.1 REVIEW 441

organization, as including different departments with responsibilities for different subject areas. The departments would, for example, include a department for trade in goods, one for trade in services and an environmental department to name but a few. Each department would hold negotiating rounds.[68] Guzman stresses that these departments would not constitute regulatory agencies with decision-making powers, but rather have the nature of a form of 'collective governance'.[69] With his proposal, Guzman addresses one of the main shortcomings of the contemporary system of specialized international institutions: the absence of a forum for negotiations across issue areas, and the absence of effective agreements addressing trade-offs between trade and social policies.[70] Other scholars, even if pleading for a new WEO, also suggest the creation of new international bodies rather than merely intensifying ties between existing organizations. Many scholars criticize, for example, the lack of a central international organization with broad competences relating to environmental policies.[71]

Others are in favour of creating more or less close institutional ties between the WTO and other international institutions. For instance, it has been suggested that international agreements providing for trade measures to sanction labour rights violations should be implemented and lead-managed by the ILO. Respective settlement of disputes should be operated by an independent body, consisting of representatives of different international organizations, among them the WTO. It has been argued that in this way, consistency of trade sanctions with the WTO legal framework could be ensured, while the body with the greatest expertise for the violation at issue would retain the main competences.[72] Another idea, which also aims at improving expertise for a special subject matter, albeit in the realm of the WTO itself, is the establishment of a new arm within the WTO responsible for trade measures aimed at human rights violations. Member states intending to adopt such trade measures would notify these to the human rights body at the WTO, which would have the power to assess facts, consider alternative types of measures and, finally, to authorize the trade measure before it is actually imposed.[73] Also, the idea of requiring that a certain number of panellists should have explicit expertise in specific matters relevant to the

---

[68] Guzman (2004), p. 307.   [69] Guzman (2004), p. 341.   [70] Guzman (2004), p. 351.
[71] E.g., Schlagenhof (1995), p. 154; or more recently Boyce (2004), pp. 121, 122.
[72] Grossmann et al. (2002), pp. 81–2.   [73] Vázquez (2003), p. 836.

case aims at improving expertise on non-trade subjects within WTO dispute settlement.[74]

Also Howse and Trebilcock reject a sharp and exclusive division of powers among international institutions, for example, by assigning the competence to sanction violations exclusively to the international body competent for the respective subject matter. Instead, they suggest horizontal coordination by dividing specific tasks. This would require assigning the competent international organization the task of determining the violation of human rights or labour standards, while the WTO would oversee the implementation of sanctions and ensure that these were not abused by protectionism or that they do not constitute unjustifiable discriminations. An important feature of this suggestion is that the competence to determine 'necessity' of measures to achieve the desired protection would be outsourced from the WTO to other international agencies.[75]

Cho concludes that institutional cooperation, according to the cooperation agreements with a few other international organizations such as the IMF, has met many problems and not produced any impressive result. He favours an approach of 'co-optation' instead, which he describes as 'a process of incorporating new elements into the policy-making structure of an organization in order to overcome challenges of stability'.[76] This approach could also be relevant to WTO dispute settlement. Indeed, a first step in this direction was taken by the GATT panel in the *Thailand – Cigarettes* case. In this dispute, the panel turned to the WHO for a regulatory opinion on the question of whether the ban on Western cigarettes could be justified for health reasons.[77] Cho has argued that although the opinion was ultimately dismissed by the panel, the procedure could be a promising precedent for 'judicial co-optation' in dispute settlement.[78] Cho's suggestion for co-optation is arguably covered by the adjudicatory bodies' right to seek information, and is in this respect consistent with the suggestions of Director-General Panitchpakdi's Consultative Board. The Consultative Board opposes the idea of cooperation procedures involving other international organizations within the dispute settlement system of the WTO, except on a case-by-case basis within the existing right to seek information. It invokes the special

---

[74] Neumayer discusses, but rejects this idea as unnecessary given the existing right to seek information (2002), p. 152.
[75] Howse and Trebilcock (2005), pp. 284–5; Schneuwly (2003), pp. 140–1.
[76] Cho (2005), p. 673.
[77] Panel Report, *Thailand – Cigarettes* (1990), Submission by the WHO, at paras. 50–7.
[78] Cho (2005), pp. 673–74.

characteristics and nature of the dispute settlement system, which it sees as self-contained in its jurisdictional responsibilities and recommends maintaining this policy.[79]

7.1.3.2 Governance in a multi-level system

In recent years, several scholars have been discussing regulatory problems in a global system of multi-level governance.[80] Some of the concepts with a stronger focus on WTO law are outlined briefly. The starting point for most concepts is the observation that technological progress and globalization have brought about challenges that reach far beyond the boundaries of the traditional nation-state.[81] While the approaches are primarily aimed at general problems of multi-level governance, they are highly relevant for the linkage of trade and non-trade policies and, hence, for NPA measures.

After the breakdown of the ministerial meeting in Seattle in 1999, Cottier observed that there were hardly any answers to fundamental questions on the interface of trade and non-trade policies. He explained:

> I would argue that trade liberalization, at some point, inherently starts to require, rely upon and develop positive integration, i.e., it depends on common and shared standards and perceptions, or at least, upon mutual recognition of national or regional standards. Moreover, trade liberalization, at some point, inherently leads to the adoption of flanking policies which are in a position to balance detrimental effects of trade liberalization.[82]

In this sense, a 'functional paradigm' of a multilateral trading system predominantly aimed at trade liberalization would not be capable of dealing with complex contemporary challenges.[83] In consequence, several scholars agree that the WTO cannot simply be viewed in narrow

---

[79] The Future of the WTO (2004), p. 39, No. 167. In this direction also Neumayer (2002), p. 152.
[80] For an overview over different constitutional approaches see Petersmann (2006), pp. 35–6, further references also in Cottier and Hertig (2003), pp. 270–5. Approaches by Jackson (2006) and Trachtman (2002) are discussed in more detail below. See also the collections of articles by Joerges, Sand and Teubner (2004); Joerges and Petersmann (2006), and Griller (2003).
[81] E.g., Cottier (1996), observes the emergence of international rules and a corresponding intrusion into formerly national domains and calls for adequate modes of multilateral governance that are able to cope with increasingly complex issues, such as genetic engineering and information technologies. See also Jackson (2002), p. 122, who stresses the importance of technological innovation for international cooperation.
[82] Cottier (2000a), p. 221.   [83] Cf. Cottier (2000b).

economic terms[84] and call for a 'constitutionalization' of the multilateral trading system,[85] while others vehemently reject this idea.[86] While in the debate neither the concept nor the term 'constitutionalization' is used in a uniform manner,[87] most suggestions seem to be based on a certain core idea of constitutionalism. In a modest sense, constitutionalization has been defined as 'an attitude and a framework capable of reasonably balancing and weighing different, equally legitimate and democratically defined basic values and policy goals of a polity dedicated to promote liberty and welfare in a broad sense'.[88]

Cottier and Hertig start their search for an adequate structure for the interaction of different layers of governance from the premise that over the last century, constitutionalism and international law have gradually been converging. They observe:

> The goals of liberty, justice and dignity, of equity but also efficiency and security all remain unimpaired. But ways and means to secure them in coming decades and perhaps centuries need to be developed in the context of an increasingly globalized society … interaction of states and societies has considerably increased, leading from traditional coexistence to cooperation and even to integration by means of international law and organizations. It is obvious that Constitutionalism of the 21st century needs to address these complexities and to reach beyond the boundaries of the Nation State.[89]

Ultimately, Cottier and Hertig take an intermediary view on constitutionalism. They reject the idea of a state-centred concept of constitutionalism, or of a 'Constitution with a capital C',[90] and instead view constitutionalism as a process to 'discipline the power of emerging non-state polities by law' and to 'eliminate inconsistencies stemming from the traditional separation of domestic and international law'.[91] Cottier and Hertig detect about five levels in the multi-layered system of governance, with the state having the position as *'pouvoir intermédiare'* in between rather than a position of

---

[84] Petersmann (2006), p. 36
[85] E.g., Petersmann (2006), Hilf (2003), Cottier (2002). For an overview over different positions in the discussion see Cottier and Hertig (2003), pp. 270–5.
[86] E.g., Howse and Nicolaidis (2003), p. 331, argue that acquiring legitimacy from the constitutional route 'would require something like a world democratic state, and this in turn require the end of politics as we know it'.
[87] Cf., e.g., the more recent approach labelled a 'divided democratic constitutionalism' by Herwig and Hüller (2008), who focus on fairness considerations and legitimacy in decision-making procedures.
[88] Cottier (2000b), p. 221.   [89] Cottier and Hertig (2003), p. 262–3.
[90] Cottier and Hertig (2003), p. 298.   [91] Cottier and Hertig (2003), pp. 297–8.

supreme authority.[92] Constitutionalism then serves to allow for a fruitful interaction among the different layers. Cottier and Hertig identify several key principles to guide the interaction: shared sovereignty; the principle of supremacy of higher levels, albeit with exceptions; a set of normative safeguards, such as international human rights instruments; a set of substantive and procedural remedies regarding the allocation of powers; and a set of standards of review that would allow the judiciary to overcome the dichotomy between domestic and international review.[93]

John H. Jackson also explores the allocation of decision-making power in a system of multi-level governance. In several publications[94] he postulates that traditional ideas of sovereignty, based on the traditional Westphalian notion of the nation-state, are not only outdated, but misleading.[95] He cites, for example, the principle of non-interference that is based on traditional ideas of sovereignty but no longer reflects the contemporary world, where action by one state usually influences and possibly constrains the domestic affairs of other states. Jackson does not suggest rejecting the concept of 'sovereignty' completely, but rather to disaggregate the notion and to focus on the more complex problems that should be taken up and that involve real policy issues.[96] In this way, 'slices' of sovereignty should be maintained as a *prima facie* norm for which exceptions can be devised – a concept Jackson terms 'sovereignty-modern'.[97] Jackson hypothesizes that underlying current policy debates involving sovereignty is actually the question about the allocation of power, normally 'government decision-making power'.[98] Although Jackson does not touch upon the issue of NPA trade measures with an extraterritorial effect, it seems obvious that the question he identifies is crucial in the debate on these measures. Jackson's point of departure is the recognition that due to the increasing globalization of the economy and due to increasing factor mobility, more and more often states can no longer regulate matters effectively. In these situations, the question about the locus of decision-making arises. Jackson sees three dimensions of allocation of power: first, a vertical dimension, from international organizations to sub-federal units or vice versa; second, a horizontal dimension, which concerns the different government segments at the respective governance level; and a third dimension, relevant even

---

[92] Cottier and Hertig (2003), p. 303.
[93] Cottier and Hertig (2003), pp. 304–26.
[94] Jackson (2001), p. 72; Jackson (2002), pp. 122–5 with a focus on competition policy to illustrate his points, Jackson (2003), Jackson (2006).
[95] Jackson (2003), pp. 788, 789.   [96] Jackson (2006), p. 69.
[97] Jackson (2006), p. 217.   [98] Jackson (2003), p. 790.

within both other dimensions, regarding the appropriate type of institution, namely, government or private, profit or non-profit.[99] He then creates a 'policy analysis matrix' containing a number of questions which arise in each of these dimensions, and which must be considered for determining the allocation of power for a particular subject matter. Starting points for the analysis are the identification of the goals or objectives being undertaken and the assessment of whether there is a need for government action. Other questions relate to legitimacy, determination of level and choice of government unit, competence of the institution, effectiveness of national regulation and the existence and characteristics of adequate international institutions.[100] Consequently, Jackson denies that there could be a one-size-fits-all answer to the question of allocation and rejects a presumption in favour of international organizations, nation-states, or any other institution as the appropriate locus of 'power'.[101] Among the 'application situations' discussed by Jackson to illustrate his points are, for example, the protection of the environment, health and human rights[102] – all subject matters prominent in the linkage debate and highly relevant to NPA measures. Jackson seems to assume the necessity to address large parts of these matters on a global scale in order to reach effective regulation, but purposefully refrains from answering the complex questions which according to him need to be answered in deciding where to allocate which 'slice' of sovereignty.[103] For example, with respect to health Jackson touches upon numerous questions relating to competences of existing or not yet existing international bodies, subsidiarity, non-government relations and so forth. Jackson's focus are changing fundamentals in international law, namely, with respect to sovereignty, and he sees an increasing importance of international institutions and a development in the international law system towards 'constitutional law'.

Trachtman approaches the issue from an entirely different perspective. In addressing linkages between trade and non-trade matters, Trachtman develops a concept to administer jurisdictional conflicts. Similar to Jackson's unveiling of sovereignty, Trachtman also sees linkage mainly as a problem of allocation of jurisdiction, which he defines as a state's legal authority to prescribe. The distinctive feature of Trachtman's approach

---

[99] Jackson (2006), pp. 72, 218. [100] Jackson (2006), pp. 70–6, 218–19.
[101] Jackson (2006), pp. 212, 213.
[102] See for an application of this type of policy analysis on competition policy Jackson (2002), pp. 123–5.
[103] Jackson (2006), ch. 7.

is his starting point, namely, an economic theory based on private property rights, which he applies to questions of jurisdiction. To illustrate his point, Trachtman cites the 'Grand Bargain', in which developed countries made concessions in agriculture and textiles for concessions in intellectual property rights and services.[104] In his view, the states party to this bargain ultimately made a deal involving the transfer of jurisdiction on different subject matters. Trachtman does not address problems relating to jurisdiction predominantly from a perspective of international law, but primarily applies concepts of law and economics and new institutional economics. One of his basic premises is that prescriptive jurisdiction of a state, or international organization, is analogous to property in a private context.[105] Just as property rights can be transferred, incurring a certain amount of transaction costs, prescriptive jurisdiction can also be transferred among and between states and international organizations. Trachtman uses the term 'transfer of jurisdiction' to denote the acceptance of constraints on jurisdiction, namely, by preventing states from regulating a specific subject matter or by requiring a state to regulate in a specific way. He presumes, not surprisingly, that states act to maximize achievement of their preferences, and therefore sees allocation of jurisdiction as a function depending on certain variables, namely, the extent of achievement of preferences through transfer on the positive side, and transaction costs on the negative side. He distinguishes between initial and subsequent transactions, with initial transactions creating property rights of jurisdiction, which can then be transferred among states or states and international organizations. Trachtman argues that the linkage problem is not about different values such as trade or labour, but rather 'about societies and their respective interests, and how authority is allocated among them so as to maximize the achievement of those interests'.[106] In Trachtman's view, linkage problems are created by the incompleteness of rules allocating jurisdiction. Neither is territorial sovereignty necessarily precise, nor are the rules on jurisdiction based on nationality or effects.[107] He does not take a position on specific linkage claims, but attempts to give structure to the relevant data and their analysis,[108] and also arrives at a few more specific conclusions. For instance, especially in cases where the transaction costs, in terms of negotiations, for initial allocation and reallocation of jurisdiction would be high, there would be a strong case for the

---

[104] Trachtman (2002), pp. 78–79. [105] Trachtman (2002), p. 80.
[106] Trachtman (2002), p. 80. [107] Trachtman (2002), p. 82.
[108] Trachtman (2002), p. 78.

establishment of an organization to 'hold' and reallocate jurisdiction.[109] Furthermore, he concludes that as regards the allocation of jurisdiction among international organizations, a hegemon or central government is needed to reduce inter-jurisdictional externalities. He contemplates that this function could be fulfilled by the United Nations or the ICJ, but that a currently inconceivable 'constitutional moment' would be required to induce states to confer this power.[110]

Trachtman's theory provides useful insights into quasi-bargaining processes among states and international organizations. However, his theory has been criticized for declaring irrelevant the underlying normative issues relating to real-life situations.[111] Instead, Trachtman focuses on an approach to allocate the solution of problems to the 'appropriate' body at the 'appropriate' level of governance, that is, a body that regulates the problem in a way that constitutes the optimal ratio of achievement of preferences at minimal transaction costs. It is Trachtman's starting point, namely, a comparison of a state's jurisdiction with property rights in a private context, which is questionable indeed. Comparing jurisdiction, that is, the legal power to regulate, to private property seems to limit the role of the state or its government to maximize power rather than the welfare of its citizens. Trachtman's theory is useful in explaining bargaining processes and transfers of jurisdiction among and between states and other bodies, but does not solve the substantive problems underlying the linkage debate.

In a sense, all 'constitutional' approaches[112] develop basic rules for the allocation of jurisdiction and power beyond the nation-state, and thus have the potential to solve, or avoid, conflicts of linkage in general and conflicts about NPA measures with extraterritorial effects in particular.

7.2 Comment

The 'linkage' or the 'trade and ...' debate is characterized by vagueness. NPA measures as the most prominent application of the debate, in contrast, trigger very specific problems of WTO law. Both debates, the

---

[109] Trachtman (2002), p. 84.   [110] Trachtman (2002), p. 92.
[111] Steger (2002), p. 137.
[112] Cottier and Hertig (2003); Jackson (2006), albeit pointing out the different meanings of the term, characterizes his approach in this way (e.g., at p. 268); Trachtman (2002) states the need for a 'constitutional moment' for an implementation of his concept (at p. 92). For a comprehensive discussion of the meaning of the term see Cotter and Hertig (2003), pp. 275–98.

governance debate and the legal debate on the status of NPA measures, therefore need to be viewed together.

Despite the wide range of views on the interface of trade and non-economic public policies and broader questions on the multi-level system of governance in the contemporary world, however, the majority of approaches presented above show that there is also important common ground. First, there seems to be almost agreement on the existence of factual effects of international trade on a number of matters falling into the realm of social policies. Second, it is important to note that the different views rarely disagree on values: all seem to recognize the need to improve social policies, to address contemporary environmental challenges and to fight poverty and other social problems. Interestingly, there is even considerable agreement when it comes to the way in which these objectives should be pursued: Most scholars seem to believe that substantive questions relevant for social policies should in general be dealt with outside the WTO, and that to this end strong international institutions would be necessary. Indeed, there is no doubt that the first best solution for conflicts at the trade and social policies interface, including those arising from NPA measures, would be a comprehensive network of effective international organizations and other forums allowing for maximum international cooperation.

In the meantime, however, legal conflicts need to be solved by the most competent institutions in the existing system with the tools currently available, including WTO law; despite the shortcomings and legal uncertainty described in Part II. Given the existence of factual links and trade-offs between different policies, and given that some of the arguably most important social policy objectives are included in the existing WTO Agreements already, it is of utmost importance to the system that in case of conflicts WTO law allows the legitimate interests involved to be appropriately balanced:

> The problems encountered ... point to the need of a new framework. Whether or not this is called a constitutional model or a further development of embedded liberalism is not of importance. The model must be able to reconcile different and diverging values, and ... this requires balancing market access and equally legitimate non-economic goals within WTO law.[113]

In reflecting on the diversity of opinions expressed by different scholars on the adequate scope of the WTO, Jackson suggested that 'the issue seems

---

[113] Cottier, Pauwelyn and Bürgi (2005b), p. 21.

not to be one of logical imperatives, but rather one of pragmatic considerations'.[114] Many of the approaches presented above discuss the problem of linkage from a governance perspective, focusing on procedural and institutional changes in order to provide for greatest competence and coherence, to enhance participation and deliberation in decision-making. Indeed, it seems urgently necessary to improve the institutional structure available to address important contemporary challenges together with the coherence of different fields of international law.

This book focuses on specific legal problems that may become relevant in disputes today. The following chapter develops a perspective, or a set of 'pragmatic considerations', with a double intention: the perspective might serve to structure future negotiations on changes to the WTO system, while in the meantime and within the yet imperfect institutional structure existing today, its basic insights might be considered for the interpretation of the WTO Agreements and thus for solving disputes on the permissibility of NPA measures.

---

[114] Jackson (2006), p. 133, referring to articles printed in the 'Symposium: The Boundaries of the WTO', *American Journal of International Law* 96 (2002), pp. 1–158.

8

A regulation-based perspective on NPA trade measures

> But more importantly, trade is a means to an end; and the end is raising the standards and conditions of living of all.[1]

Most suggestions relating to linkage of trade and social policies discussed in Chapter 6 above focus on a particular issue area, such as environmental protection or labour rights. It seems, however, that a number of important legal questions or considerations relating to NPA measures are equally relevant for such measures, no matter which public policy objectives they pursue. This chapter develops a more general approach, or rather a perspective, on substantive questions concerning NPA measures.

The starting point is the well-established premise that rather than being an objective in itself, freer international trade is merely the means chosen by WTO members to achieve a number of broader economic and social objectives. Underlying the choice of this tool are the convincing rationales of free markets developed in economic theory. In cases where markets fail totally or in part, however, economic as well as non-economic objectives of the system cannot be reached by the tool of choice, namely, international trade. At this point, alternatives need to come into play in order to allow the system to adhere to its objectives. At the domestic level, a common alternative means by which to achieve economic and non-economic goals is state intervention by regulation, including regulation by means of NPA measures.

The basic idea developed in this chapter is to bring the key rationales of domestic regulation in line with the economic rationales and various objectives of the multilateral trading system. It is assumed that there is an enormous overlap between the different national systems within WTO member states and the multilateral trading system in terms of key rationales and objectives. This chapter tries to explore this overlap and to draw

---

[1] Pascal Lamy, Director-General of the WTO, speech 'Towards Shared Responsibility and Greater Coherence: Human Rights, Trade and Macroeconomic Policy', Geneva, 13 January 2010.

conclusions on basic considerations relevant for the permissibility of NPA measures under WTO law as it stands and *de lege ferenda*. In other words, the perspective developed below seeks to give answers to the question of when and under which conditions national regulation by means of NPA measures ought to be permissible. It is here suggested that the respective answer ought to be based on a comparison of the extent to which the national NPA measure at issue is consistent with either WTO economic key rationales, WTO objectives, or both.

This approach can therefore be characterized as a regulation-based perspective on the legal status of NPA measures under WTO law: consistency of national regulation with WTO key rationales and objectives or the lack of such consistency indicate the way in which WTO law ought to determine whether or not such measures are permissible. This perspective could serve as a basis for negotiations in future agreements on NPA measures. Some ideas, however, may also be relevant to an interpretation of the existing agreements. It is hoped that the approach could help to bridge opposing views on the legitimacy of NPA measures by putting international trade into the perspective of the higher-ranking objectives to which all WTO members have subscribed.[2]

This first section of this chapter considers possible implications of freer international trade on domestic regulation. It reviews these implications from the perspective of WTO law and considers also the present international institutional structures. Section 8.2 concludes on a framework for assessing NPA measures by actually comparing certain categories of national NPA measures with WTO economic key rationales and objectives.

8.1 Regulatory problems linked to international trade

The possibly crucial consideration in the development of a regulation-based perspective is the gap between the globalization of markets and the stand-still in the competencies of regulators. The motivation is to find a way to bridge this gap, at least in as far as WTO law is concerned, in order to maintain essential problem-solving capacities in the existing multi-level system of governance. The following sections describe problems of market failures caused or exacerbated by international trade and a related dilemma faced by national regulators. As will be shown, NPA measures have potential to play a crucial role in this dilemma.

[2] See reprint of WTO objectives, above p. v.

8.1.1 Side-effects of international trade

Besides the desirable economic effects described above in Chapter 2 which make the economic case for trade liberalization, moving from national to international trade has numerous other effects on the trading nations. These side-effects are in part positive and in part negative. Among the positive non-economic side-effects is an increase in trans-national contacts, which brings a mutually beneficial exchange of ideas and cooperation, better cultural understanding, personal ties and an overall improvement in foreign relations with other trading nations. There are, however, also a whole range of other side-effects. It is self-evident that international trade results in an increase in production which is inextricably linked to externalities. For example, an increase in goods production will usually be accompanied by an absolute increase in pollution.[3] International trade leads to an increase in transportation of goods, likewise leading to pollution. In sum, the globalization of markets is accompanied by a globalization of market failure, most visible in the case of pollution.[4]

International trade also leads to distributional problems. Deterioration in the personal situation of individuals employed in sectors which cannot withstand the fierce international competition is unavoidable,[5] and in countries where bad governance prevails, the economic situation of the population may deteriorate overall. Predatory governments carry the idea of comparative advantage to absurdity, since they will use gains resulting from exports for the importation of goods serving the interests of individuals or clans instead of goods serving the public interest. An example is the use of export profits for the purchase of weapons or the consumption of luxury goods, while the essential needs of the majority of the population remain unsatisfied.

---

[3] Interestingly, international trade may also lead to less pollution, e.g., in a situation where production of a 'dirty' product is moved to a country which is able to produce the product in a cleaner way. The likelihood that production is moved to the country with an environmental comparative advantage would be high if prices reflected environmental costs, which is currently not the case. Instead, the existence of external costs in the form of pollution will usually lead to market failure. For more on pollution due to international trade see Ahmad and Wyckoff (2003).

[4] See Boyce (2002), for the examples of increasing worldwide pollution and a loss of crop diversity due to international trade. Boyce argues against the conventional view that since the Industrial Revolution the main direction of environmental dumping has been from North to South, and pleads for policies to translate the comparative environmental advantage of many developing countries into a comparative economic advantage (at p. 99).

[5] See Samuelson and Nordhaus (2005), p. 302.

The focus of this chapter, however, is on how to address the negative side-effects of freer international trade that arise even if the participating nations subscribe to the ideal of good governance. These negative side-effects arise if markets fail and if alternative means, such as regulatory policies to prevent and mitigate such effects, are not deployed, or where existing policies are not effective. Two problems need to be distinguished. First, some problems need collective action, because due to their limited jurisdiction and means nation-states are incapable of solving certain problems autonomously. An example is global warming, a problem that can be addressed effectively only by concerted action, since national action alone will usually be insufficient. The second problem is an impairment of the effectiveness of national regulation due to the multilateral trading system. Both problems are interlinked. The focus here is on the impairment of effective national regulation due to international trade and WTO law. Based on the analysis of legal problems relating to NPA measures, the next section illustrates how WTO law can impair effectiveness of national regulations.

8.1.2 The regulatory dilemma

With freer international trade formerly national markets, regulated by national governments and regulators, turn into international markets. As described above in Chapter 2, markets may fail whether they are national or international, and market failure is usually prevented or mitigated by national regulation. WTO law bears upon national regulation, and it is here suggested that in some instances it impairs national regulation in terms of the choice of measures and arguably also in terms of regulatory effectiveness. This section discusses the effectiveness of national regulation in regulating markets in times of freer international trade, first without constraints and then with constraints due to WTO law. It is argued that WTO law puts national regulators in a dilemma, since, as will be shown below, there are theoretical arguments which suggest a trade-off between effective regulation and economic sustainability or increased polarization.

8.1.2.1 Effectiveness of unimpaired national regulation

Before discussing how WTO law impairs the effectiveness of national regulation concerning NPAs, it will briefly be described how unconstrained national regulators can achieve their regulatory goals if they are allowed to accompany internal regulation with border measures. The internal regulation discussed here is regulation of NPAs, for example, by enforcing certain standards or by prohibiting certain deprecated methods of production. Given international competition due to foreign producers who produce unimpaired by internal regulation, however, regulators might find it necessary to impose border measures to accompany national regulation.[6] Border measures that accompany regulatory measures range from import prohibitions for products produced with the deprecated production method, to tariffs offsetting competitive disadvantages of domestic producers over product labelling to other measures.

An import prohibition on products produced with certain deprecated methods would leave the entire domestic market to the domestic industry in the short term, but in the long term foreign competitors could decide to adapt production to the requirements of the importing country and to re-enter the market. In as far as the regulatory objectives concern dangers or damages within the territory of the country imposing the measure, the regulatory goals would be fulfilled: domestic industry would produce under the conditions imposed by internal regulators and yet remain competitive. The economic costs for national regulation would in part be borne by national consumers who would pay higher prices reflecting the higher costs of production. However, in the absence of most foreign competition, and depending on the structure of the national market, the domestic industry might raise prices beyond even the actual costs of complying with national regulation. Depending on the size of the national market, foreign producers might decide to adapt to the regulatory regime of the importing country. In this case, regulators would have extended their regulatory achievements, whether purposeful or not, to objects located in foreign territories, quasi as a side-effect. However, diminished foreign competition, or even the complete lack thereof, would not only exclude foreign competitors from the domestic market, but also exclude the importing country from the various advantages of international trade and higher competition.

An alternative tool would be a tariff offsetting the competitive disadvantages of the domestic industry vis-à-vis foreign competitors due to the costs of complying with the NPA regulation. Also, this measure would allow regulators to achieve their regulatory goals. The costs of internalization would again be borne by domestic consumers, since they would not be able to profit from the lower prices of foreign competitors due to higher

---

[6] The need for accompanying border measures is explained in the next section, which describes the effects of national regulation without accompanying measures.

environmental pollution in the country of production. Nevertheless, the advantage of such countervailing duties is that the importing country would still be able to profit from increased competition, since even the foreign producers producing with the condemned production method would remain present at the domestic market, albeit at higher costs due to the tariff. The regulatory success would therefore be limited to the territory of the regulating state.

Duties offsetting the cost advantages due to lower national standards in other countries could be designed precisely to 'level the playing field', in the sense that they would merely offset the actual costs of national producers of complying with national regulation.[7] This means that foreign producers would not be put at a disadvantage: rather, they would be prevented from reaping the profits linked to higher pollution in the country of production. In the case of duties based on NPAs, foreign products produced in compliance with the required standards would not be burdened. The costs of higher national standards, as reflected in higher prices of end-products, would thus be borne by consumers in the regulating state, while the measure would be cost-neutral to foreign competitors. A tariff would therefore be less trade-restrictive compared with an import prohibition, it would be more efficient from an economic perspective, and at the same time it would also preserve effectiveness of national regulation.

8.1.2.2 Effectiveness of impaired national regulation

In some situations, WTO law allows its members to deviate from their obligations in order to pursue their own regulatory policies. For example, totally free international trade could result in the importation of dangerous products, even if the production of such products were prohibited within the territory of a state. In this situation, WTO law allows the importing state to deviate from its obligations and to restrict importation of the respective product. This became evident, for example, in the famous *EC – Asbestos* dispute where national health policies were at stake.

As described in the previous chapters, the situation is different if production hazards are concerned. Naturally, under WTO law regulators may choose to prohibit a dangerous production method internally, so that domestic producers will have to develop other, perhaps more costly, production methods. In this way, avoiding negative externalities in production places producers at a competitive disadvantage vis-à-vis producers

---

[7] The strongly contested argument of 'levelling the playing field' will be addressed in more detail below.

in states that do not prohibit a cheaper but more dangerous production method. In order to maintain the competitiveness of domestic industries, regulators could consider, as described above, accompanying the internal prohibition or regulatory standard with a prohibition on the importation of foreign products produced with the deprecated method or with charges on importation in order to offset the additional costs incurred in domestic production. In this situation, WTO law is most suspicious about the accompanying border measure. Since end-products would be 'like', such border measures would, according to the prevailing view, violate WTO obligations of the importing country.[8] Furthermore, the accompanying border measures might not be considered to fall under any of the exceptions listed in Article XX.[9] In order to allow for a comparison and to illustrate the regulatory dilemma, it is here assumed that the NPA trade measure accompanying a certain national NPA regulation would be in violation of WTO law.

In this situation, WTO law would prevent national regulators from taking accompanying border measures. Regulators would therefore face a dilemma. They would be left with two options: either to maintain the comparably higher internal requirements for production, or to lower the requirements to the level prevailing in other countries. Lowering the requirements beyond what they would find appropriate for the given situation in their country, however, is not a choice consistent with the task and function of regulators.

The other choice, however, would imply strong disadvantages. In cases where regulators decide to uphold the higher internal requirements, in theory, they will in the short term be able to achieve their regulatory goal to avoid the dangers of production or pollution caused by the condemned method of production. In the long run, however, the competitive advantage of foreign competitors would place a heavy burden on domestic producers. Depending on the nature of this burden, domestic industries

---

[8] See above Chapter 4.
[9] As described in Chapter 5 in more detail, views on interpretation of the general exceptions diverge and there is a considerable lack of legal certainty in this respect. For this reason, the presumption that NPA border measures violate WTO law is not merely hypothetical. The prevailing view seems not to accept measures linked to NPAs abroad, unless the object of protection is considered a global common. The interpretation of the moral exception suggested in this work would allow the linking of measures to NPAs, even if the direct objects of protection are located beyond the borders of the regulating state. However, the scope of the moral exception is limited to severe violations of public morals, and it is questionable whether this could be the case if ordinary environmental damage were concerned.

might lose market share or in the worst case even be forced from the market. In a globalized world with a relatively high mobility of production, this situation might prompt producers to opt out and to switch production to countries or areas with lower requirements in order to be able to (re-)import their products. For regulatory success this would mean that the use of the dangerous production methods would not be avoided, but rather be moved to production sites elsewhere. From a broader regulatory perspective, intending to avoid the respective dangers completely no matter where they arise, the regulatory measure would have failed. However, assuming that national regulators aim at achieving regulatory goals only within their jurisdiction and thus to avoid dangers only for objects or individuals within their territory, regulation could ultimately be considered successful. This regulatory success, however, would come at a high cost: not only would the dangerous or polluting aspects of production have been avoided or shifted to other countries, but possibly even production in general. Therefore, this regulatory choice would most probably not be sustainable because the costs, namely, the loss of industries and related jobs, may well be unaffordable to the society concerned in the long run.

Interestingly, from a merely economic point of view also this regulatory measure must be considered a failure. International trade is based on the idea of competitive markets. Competitive markets function – in the sense of achieving an efficient reallocation of resources – only if the most efficient competitors are rewarded. In the present example, however, foreign competitors are not rewarded for higher efficiency: they would actually be rewarded for the more *laissez-faire* style of regulation chosen by the regulators in their countries. The foreign producers' competitive advantage would not be their greater efficiency in production, but a lack of internalization of external costs, for example, in terms of environmental damage through lower standards.[10] In this way, producers profit – or have disadvantages – from differences in the regulatory regimes of different countries. The cost advantage inherent to regulatory differences may even out-balance inefficiencies in production. Depending on the costs incurred by the regulation, foreign competitors may be able to push domestic producers out of the markets, even if the domestic producers are more efficient in terms of production.

This implies that regulators have to choose between a healthier national environment, combined with the risk of a partial or total loss of a particular domestic industry, or a dirty environment at no economic cost at all.

---

[10] See Daly (1993).

Of course, reality is not black and white and regulators will evaluate other options. It is conceivable that regulators will negotiate with the regulatees, the domestic industry, and offer them compensation in terms of other advantages; often, however, this option will be affordable only to wealthy societies. Nevertheless, it is beyond doubt that constraints imposed by WTO law affect regulators' decisions.

Before concluding that national regulation could actually be impaired by WTO law, however, the above argument needs to be put into perspective. The theoretical argument illustrated above is a reminder of the general discussion on regulatory competition. A well-known claim is that international trade brings about 'a race to the bottom' between competing states with different regulatory regimes, for example, with respect to environmental standards. According to this argument, competitive pressures lead regulators to lower standards in order to attract investment and industries. With respect to production, the argument is based on the producer's option of moving production to countries with the lowest production or process standards. Therefore, national regulators would be prompted to lower national production standards below those of competing states and so forth. This situation, which has been referred to as 'competition-in-laxity',[11] has been claimed to lead to a 'regulatory chill'. This line of thinking is not commonplace even amongst the environmentalist lobby. Others have also granted that 'there is no doubt that a race-to-the-bottom is a theoretical possibility, and that trade and investment liberalization could exacerbate such tendencies'.[12]

However, the theory is far from being proven correct. Other analyses of the effects of globalization on national regulation even suggest the contrary. Some scholars argue that there is actually a trend to convergence at the top. They argue that growing environmental concerns lead to ecological modernization, with spill-over effects to countries with lower environmental standards.[13] Others make the simple point that only countries with higher incomes can afford environmental protection. Since international trade would lead to higher incomes, freer trade would ultimately foster environmental protection. Even others describe a mixed scenario. Boyce, for example, argues that neither an upwards nor downwards trend is correct, but describes the possibility that globalization could promote polarization.[14] He posits that globalization increases possibilities

---

[11] E.g., Murphy (2005), p. 897.   [12] Nordström and Vaughan (1999), p. 43.
[13] For a summary of the different theories see Boyce (2004), pp. 107–13.
[14] Boyce (2004), p. 113.

for environmental cost-shifting by widening the spatial distance between those who profit from pollution and those who bear the external costs. Boyce then argues that globalization, because of income inequalities and power disparities, combined with a lack of sympathy due to the spatial distance between polluters and pollutees, could lead to 'environmental polarization between North and South and to an increase in the total magnitude of environmental degradation worldwide'.[15] Murphy illustrates that there are three basic 'trajectories' for any given issue: whether the outcome of regulatory competition leads to the lowest or highest common denominator or rather to heterogeneity depends on a number of factors: that is, the locus of regulatory activity; the structure of the market; and its asset specificity. Murphy's analysis suggests that in contrast to product regulation, regulation of manufacturing processes may indeed spawn competition-in-laxity, leading to regulatory havens.[16] Also, based on public choice rationales, Esty has concluded that 'a presumption that regulatory competition will operate as theorized to maximize welfare cannot be supported'.[17] So far, however, empirical studies have neither confirmed nor refuted either theory.[18] In sum, there are diverse theories and a lack of empirical evidence on the effects of economic globalization on national regulation, creating uncertainty about an actual 'race to the bottom', 'ecological modernization' or rather a 'polarization of environmental degradation'. Empirical evidence, however, will remain hard to achieve because of the difficulty of quantifying political forces that lead to specific regulations and regulatory outcomes.

The dilemma presented above is not based on any one of the above theories. However, it seems important to bear in mind that none of the theories, including a downwards trend in regulation of production, can be ruled out. From a legal perspective, there is no doubt that the WTO Agreements limit the ability of WTO members to supplement national non-economic policies with border measures. Limitations actually arise in a twofold way: although the precise extent of the limitations is very much under debate, it is clear that nearly all trade-restrictive border measures other than tariffs, no matter which motivation underlies them, are *prima facie* inconsistent with the WTO Agreements. This is the very core of the multilateral trading system. This is also true for internal NPA

---

[15] Boyce (2004), p. 118.
[16] Murphy (2005), pp. 897–907, 916. In his analysis, Murphy focuses on offshore banking centres.
[17] Esty and Geradin (1998), p. 23.
[18] Boyce (2004), p. 110; Nordström and Vaughan (1999), p. 45.

measures if these also apply to imports. Given a *prima facie* violation of GATT obligations, existing possibilities for justification under the agreements are limited. In this sense, WTO law imposes direct disciplines on national regulation. Perhaps even more importantly, the effectiveness of permissible internal regulation can possibly be undermined by WTO obligations in the way illustrated above. Even if the existence of a global downwards trend in regulatory standards or of polarization is uncertain, it is apparent that national regulators take the above scenario into consideration, and consequently there will be instances where, as a consequence of WTO law, the above considerations will determine their decisions.

Limitations which affect the effectiveness of national social regulation, however, must be taken seriously. Also, international markets, created by international trade, fail when it comes to environmental and other social damage. The above analysis shows that national regulators assigned with the task of reducing or remedying the effects of market failure are impaired in their free choice of tools due to WTO law, and that effectiveness of national regulation and problem-solving capacities can in consequence be impeded. The following section considers the consequences of international market failure and restraints on national regulation from the perspective of objectives and key rationales of the WTO Agreements.

8.1.3 Market failure and the lack of international institutions

While market failures within national economies are addressed by national institutions and policies, comparable institutions at the international level are almost inexistent. Often, international cooperation in areas other than trade takes the form of soft law rather than legally binding treaties. This is particularly true for those areas that would be considered constitutional in the domestic sphere.[19] To the extent that effective international regulatory structures are missing, globalization of markets takes place in a regulatory vacuum. This regulatory deficit leads to a number of negative side-effects for various social policies and even impedes the proper functioning of the global markets themselves. This situation has led to concerns, expressed, for example, Jackson:

> As outlined by very eminent economists in recent decades ... markets will not work unless there are effective human institutions to provide the framework that protects the market function. Therefore, the core problem is the globalization-caused need to develop appropriate international

[19] Pauwelyn (2006), p. 201

institutions. If a thorough analysis led to the conclusion that the WTO is a good place in which to concentrate some of these cooperation activities, one could see the WTO becoming essentially an international economic regulatory level of government. This prospect, of course, is scary to many people.[20]

Whether or not strong international institutions or formalized cooperation among nation-states and with international organizations would be the best way to solve related global problems or to provide a framework for national regulatory policies is beyond the focus of this work. For the concept suggested below, however, it is important to note that international institutions sufficient to bridge the regulatory gap do not yet exist. Although some 'regulatory' institutions do exist, which in part contribute to harmonization and to further certain regulatory goals, such as the Codex Alimentarius Commission in the field of food safety,[21] with respect to most subject matters an effective regulatory system of governance does not exist beyond nation-state level. Regardless of whether regulation by nation-states remains the first- or second-best solution to social problems caused or exacerbated by international trade, for the time being in most areas they are the only bodies capable of dealing with social problems in an effective way.

As detailed in Chapter 2 above, the objectives of the WTO Agreements include sustainable development and protection and preservation of the environment. It would be inconsistent should the WTO Agreements by freeing international trade ultimately impede the achievement of their very objectives. It is therefore necessary to consider the complex interactions between WTO law, international trade, including its economic and social side-effects, and the effective implementation of non-economic policies, which in turn are strongly related to the objectives of the multilateral trading system as reflected in the preambles. Markets fail for a number of established reasons, and given that national regulators are impaired in the choice of their regulatory tools due to WTO law, the focus of attention must be on the problem-solving capacities of the

---

[20] Jackson (2003), p. 799.
[21] For an assessment of the Codex Alimentarius Commission (CAC) as an international regulatory institution see Hüller and Meier (2006). They find that the CAC has created a large body of international food safety regulations, including hundreds of standards (at pp. 267–8). Nevertheless, Hüller and Meier come to mixed conclusions on the quality of the CAC as a regulatory body. E.g., they detect considerable inequalities in state participation and find that the institutional design favours unequal opportunities (at pp. 296–9).

multi-level system of governance. Since markets cannot achieve it all, institutions ensuring the proper functioning of the market to achieve the desired outcome, and to correct it if it fails, are indispensable. Due to the absence of international institutions providing a framework for regulation to achieve objectives in the case of market failure, nation-states remain the only bodies competent to intervene in the market and to implement social policies. Therefore, it is here suggested that an understanding of WTO law which would impair the ability of nation-states to regulate effectively, without equally effective alternatives at other levels in the multi-layered system of governance in place, is inconsistent with the very objectives of the organization.

8.1.4 Regulatory failure is not in line with objectives and key rationales of the WTO

While the prevailing view among economists is that environmental and social damage linked to production are the result of market failure, the views on the relevance of this type of market failure for the multilateral trading system differ greatly. This section presents the more prevalent arguments made with respect to environmental policies, but the same arguments apply *mutatis mutandis* to other social damage.

Some consider low environmental standards illegitimate and argue that their effects are similar to those of subsidies. They argue that just as any other illegitimate subsidy it would be necessary that low environmental standards may also be legally countervailed with corresponding trade measures by importing states in order to 'level the playing field'. Others, however, claim that the environment is simply part of the natural endowment of each country, and that it may be 'used' for production just as any other natural resource, subject to the conditions imposed by the government. From this perspective, environmental damage may be regrettable, but does not constitute a case of market failure, since the damage is actually internalized and voluntarily borne by the country of production. Hence, views advocating a 'level playing field' are sometimes branded as 'totally invalid', and often with arguments referring to the normality of a ruthless competitive process, justified by the well-being of domestic consumers who would otherwise be denied 'the right to choose the widest possible selection of goods in the marketplace'.[22]

---

[22] Husted and Melvin (2006), p. 198.

The arguments challenging the need to 'level the playing field' are problematic both from a normative and an economic point of view. First, it is often based on the wrong factual assumption that the effects of environmental damage can be confined to the territory of a single state. Important cases of environmental damage, such as pollution of the air, soil and ground water, will generally have short- or long-term effects beyond the borders of a single state. In such cases, low standards cannot be considered in determining comparative advantages, since they instead constitute the result of a simple strategic cost-shifting behaviour.[23] Likewise, the understanding that social unrest, for example, due to inhumane working conditions, is limited to national borders seems outdated.[24] Second, the argument often seems to be based on the idea that the value of the environment is quantifiable like the value of other goods and that it differs from one country to another. Some conclude that differences in the environment and related standards 'may be desirable in order to reflect differences in income and ability to pay for environmental quality. After all, the opportunity cost of environmental polices in terms of forgone income may differ considerably among poorer and richer countries, and neither would be served well by setting the standards at the average.'[25] This view, however, misses the human dimension of environmental damage. Severe environmental damage will often cause disease and hardship for present and for future generations. Therefore, reducing the value of a healthy environment to income forgone, that is lower in poor than in wealthy countries, ignores fundamental human rights and challenges the equality of all human beings.[26] Although a distribution-blind understanding of optimality may be common in neo-classical economics, the obliviousness of this argument to even the most basic of normative standards disqualifies it as a basis for policy.[27] Boyce therefore suggests that 'a rights-based allocation of access to a clean and safe environment ... is an attractive alternative to the wealth-based allocation principle founded on willingness to pay'.[28] Last, the argument is problematic because it does not adequately take into account the fact that environmental and social damage

---

[23] Esty and Geradin (1998), p. 22.
[24] Cottier (2002), p. 118, observes that the treatment of individuals, such as protection of minorities, became an international concern as a consequence of the internationalization of human rights after the Second World War.
[25] Nordström and Vaughan (1999), p. 45.
[26] As, e.g., stated in Article 1 of the Universal Declaration of Human Rights by the General Assembly of the UN, of 10 December 1948.
[27] In this sense Boyce (2004), p. 107. [28] Boyce (2004), p. 107.

constitute costs. Whether or not the damage is consistent with the laws and regulations in force within the country of production is entirely irrelevant. The question is, then, whether or not competitive advantages of producers polluting the environment without having to bear these costs can be considered legitimate. The advantage does not arise from competition, but from the ability to shift costs, in many cases to human beings who are neither involved in the process of production and sale of products, nor have the power to prevent these costs or at least claim adequate damages from the producer or from consumers benefiting from lower product prices. Environmental pollution is a negative externality and not in line with a properly functioning market according to the classical micro-economic model. Therefore, invoking the legitimacy of the competitive advantage of producers who pollute for free means promoting the results achieved by failing markets to the desired efficient allocation of resources. Not only from a normative, but also from an economic point of view, this position is untenable.

The objectives of the WTO provide guidance as to the relevance of environmental damage for its system. They suggest a more normative evaluation of the idea of competitive markets which considers environmental damage a negative externality. If economic efficiency were the only objective of the WTO, opposing arguments could be considered defensible. Since the WTO, however, has subscribed to the objective of sustainable development, including the protection and preservation of the environment, environmental damage cannot be ignored, and environmental pollution must not be allowed to lead to competitive or comparative advantages for producers or countries. Therefore, arguments for 'levelling the playing field' should not be dismissed as illegitimate attempts to disguise protectionism.[29]

Regulations to level the playing field do indeed serve to shield domestic industries, albeit not from more efficient foreign producers, but from competitive advantages that need to be considered illegitimate if the objectives of the WTO are taken seriously. Only if regulation 'to level the playing field' over-reaches in that it places a burden on imports that is higher than necessary in order to offset the illegitimate advantages would it be protectionist. Genuine regulations 'to level the playing field' rather aim at upholding national regulatory competence and efficiency in order

---

[29] E.g., Charnovitz (2002), who argues that 'economic motivations' underlying measures linked to PPMs in order 'to level the playing field' should not be shielded by the WTO. Charnovitz, however, seems to miss the regulatory dimension of the problem, which is inextricably linked to the 'economic motivation' (at p. 106).

to address market failure – ultimately for the sake of a proper functioning of the market itself.

It is here suggested that policies, including NPA border measures to 'level the playing field', are legitimate to the extent necessary to maintain effectiveness of national regulations in order to achieve objectives in line with the objectives of the WTO. This does not mean, however, that any measure ought to be considered legal under WTO law: genuine measures to level the playing field will be difficult to administer. Levelling the playing field would imply that border measures should take into account the different regulatory and other conditions in each exporting state. Some exporting states may even have higher standards, which would lead to a right to compensation in the 'level playing field' logic. Despite these problems, however, it is noteworthy for the regulatory-based perspective presented below that the logic of such measures is not illegitimate, given the unambiguous objectives and key rationales of the WTO.

8.1.5 Conclusions

Domestic regulation, as described above, serves to maintain functioning markets and to avoid negative externalities of production, for example, by internalizing external costs. While environmental damage is mainly invoked as an example of negative externalities, other damage, such as damage to public health, for example, due to polluting production or to unsafe conditions at the work place, can also be considered a negative externality. Freer international trade impairs the ability of nation-states to internalize externalities and to correct the allocation of resources achieved by a failing market. Additional reasons for market failure in this sense are regulatory differences between nation-states, which internalize negative externalities to a higher or lower degree. This market failure could be remedied with international harmonization, with a higher level of enforcement of regulations within different nation-states or by international institutions providing for framework regulations.

However, in the absence of such remedies, an impairment of effective national regulation is problematic. In a situation where effectiveness of national regulation is diminished, without alternative mechanisms that can take over certain tasks in place, the achievement of WTO objectives is put at risk. Maintaining effective problem-solving capacities in a way that is consistent with WTO objectives and key rationales must be the crucial measure for any proposal addressing the regulatory deficit in the multi-level system.

8.2 Applying the regulation-based perspective

The regulation-based perspective suggested in this chapter approaches the issue of NPA measures from the perspective of global regulatory deficits. To reiterate, international trade leads to a globalization of market failure. The basic conditions for markets to achieve economic optimality, namely, the characteristics of a perfectly competitive market, cannot be generated by the market but need to be supplied from outside. In addition, other recognized instances of market failure need to be remedied. Since the results achieved by the market will not match ideas of fairness, active redistribution is required. All these 'services' must be provided by institutions outside the market.

Within nation-states, this function is taken over by governments and national regulators. The globalization of market failure, however, has not sufficiently been accompanied by a globalization of governance and regulatory institutions. Thus, there is a regulatory deficit or a case of governance failure. The lack of properly functioning international cooperation and the absence of effective international institutions with regard to most subject matters will be due to a lack of political will. In contrast to the different approaches presented in the previous chapter, this approach seeks to offer a way to deal with the current situation characterized by political deadlock and in a situation of a regulatory deficit in the multi-layered system of governance. Since in many policy fields, national regulators are the only institutions with authority and competence to regulate effectively, it is of utmost importance to maintain these capacities. International agreements must be designed and interpreted in a way that does not impair the effectiveness of legitimate national regulation as long as there are no institutions able to take over the regulatory tasks. Otherwise, essential problem-solving capacities would be lost, and the 'proper' functioning of international markets, in terms of achieving the objectives of the WTO, would be at risk.

8.2.1 Deduction of the regulation-based approach

The motivation of the regulation-based approach is to allow society to maintain its problem-solving capacities despite globalization of market failure in a situation of a regulatory deficit. Boyce, focusing on environmental aspects of governance problems caused by globalization, concludes:

> In principle, the globalization of governance can counter adverse environmental impacts arising from the globalization of market failure that

accompanies the integration of world markets. But there is nothing automatic about this 'double movement' – it rests on human agency, and on balances of power between those who stand to gain and lose from environmental governance.[30]

Apparently, positive efforts are needed to surmount the challenges faced by society today and in the future.

The perspective adopted in this chapter builds on a fact illustrated in Chapter 2: despite great differences in national regulations among WTO members, ultimately all governments in the world, no matter how conservative or how liberal, regulate their economies.[31] Nevertheless, differences relating to regulatory tools, objectives and substance are considerable, and hence the difficulties of reaching agreement on the legitimacy of different regulatory policies. At this point, the objectives and key rationales of the WTO come into play, since they are here considered the common ground to which WTO members have formally subscribed. Thus, these rationales and objectives allow one to draw conclusions on a structure that could help to assess national regulations allegedly falling foul of WTO law.

Other approaches have also been based on the consideration of consistency of non-trade policies with the key rationales of the WTO, albeit to a different end. For example, Maskus analysed the degree of consistency of intellectual property rights protection, competition policy and environmental and core labour standards with basic rationales of the WTO with the intention of assessing whether or not the particular regulatory policies should be conducted at the national or the international level, for example, at the WTO.[32] The regulatory approach here, in contrast, takes existing regulatory deficits for granted and focuses on the powers of existing competent regulators at the national level. The idea is that the greater the consistency of a regulation with objectives as well as key rationales of the WTO, the stronger the case for its permissibility, and, since WTO members have subscribed to the WTO objectives, the higher the probability for approval among WTO members. Therefore, it is here suggested that in as far as effective national regulation contributes to the objectives of the multilateral trading system, and in as far as it is in line with the economic key rationales, such regulation should be presumed *prima facie* consistent with WTO law.[33]

---

[30] Boyce (2004), p. 123.   [31] See also Samuelson and Nordhaus (2005), p. 34.
[32] Maskus (2002).
[33] This presumption does not extend to national regulation that is independent from objectives of the multilateral trading system and does not build on the key rationales. However,

8.2.2 Categorization of national regulation

The approach distinguishes between three groups of national regulation by reflecting their regulatory rationales. The idea underlying the categorization is that the more the national regulation at issue matches with the economic key rationales of the WTO, namely, competitive markets and comparative advantage, and the economic and non-economic objectives of the multilateral trading system, the stronger is the case for considering the respective national regulations *prima facie* consistent with WTO law. It is here argued that there should be a presumption in favour of legitimacy of regulations with high consistency values as described below. The finding of a lower consistency value, however, must not be understood vice versa as indicating a finding of illegality. For example, a finding of consistency with WTO objectives coinciding with a finding of neutrality with regard to the economic key rationales is still a slight presumption in favour of consistency, albeit a weak one. If neither consistency with economic key rationales nor objectives of the WTO can be established, this does not imply that the national regulations are *prima facie* inconsistent with WTO law. Rather, the national regulation is then simply not linked to the rationales and objectives of the WTO. For this latter category, it will arguably be difficult to reach agreement in future negotiations.

The categories of national regulation established here correspond to the categories of regulations identified in Chapter 2. Naturally, there is a whole range of policies with various degrees of linkage or remoteness to WTO objectives and rationales. The following three categories merely serve as a tool to illustrate the basic idea of the framework – an assessment of consistency in a specific case would need to explore the objectives of the measure at issue, as well as consistency with WTO rationales and objectives on a case-by-case basis.

8.2.2.1 Category 1: Regulation reducing market imperfections

The first category comprises all national regulation serving to reduce market imperfections or to supply the necessary preconditions for the market to work. Both key economic rationales underlying the multilateral trading system build on the proper functioning of competitive markets. The efficiency of markets, in turn, depends on certain prerequisites, which can

these policies, of course, should not be presumed to violate WTO law. Instead, their consistency *de lege lata* should be assessed according to WTO law as expounded in Part II of this book.

be summarized as 'perfect competition'. As detailed in Chapter 2, perfect markets are characterized by price-taking, product homogeneity, mobility of resources and perfect information. Since all WTO members approve of the key economic rationales underlying the WTO, there should be consensus on the legitimacy, or even necessity, of WTO members adopting regulation with a view to reduce market imperfections, and to improve in this way the proper functioning of markets. Given that WTO members chose the economic key rationales as a means of achieving other ultimate objectives, such as raising the standards of living, coherence of measures promoting perfect competition with the objectives of the WTO Agreements must be presumed. Therefore, national regulation to reduce market imperfections is characterized by great consistency with the key economic rationales of the WTO, together with consistency as regards the economic objectives of the WTO, namely, the objective 'to increase the pie'. Among national regulatory policies in this category are competition and antitrust policies[34] serving to prevent accumulation of market power, arguably certain consumer protection policies, including regulations to ensure a minimum level of product safety which help to maintain general consumer confidence in products, reduction of tariffs and non-tariff barriers to trade, and consumer information policies.

This work considers the example of information policies and respective regulation, since these seem to be of greatest relevance for the legal status of NPA measures. In Chapter 6 above, I have argued why consumer information constitutes a legitimate objective of technical regulations in the sense of Article 2.2 of the TBT Agreement. The same considerations apply also to all other information policies and regulations, whether or not they fall into the scope of the TBT Agreement. For example, states might consider obliging companies to disclose certain NPA data in form other than labelling. Since product labelling allows only the provision of certain key data, states could oblige companies to provide more comprehensive information with different means. Information technologies offer ample opportunity for the provision and distribution of information, even of complex data. Information requirements in general contribute to the proper functioning of markets and must therefore be considered legitimate, provided they are not abusive.

The latter qualification leads to the question of whether information on NPAs is relevant, or if information requirements with respect to

---

[34] For the consistency of competition policies with the multilateral trading system see, e.g., Bhagwati (2002), p. 129, 130; Maskus (2002).

8.2 APPLYING THE REGULATION-BASED PERSPECTIVE 471

NPAs should be considered abusive *per se*. Here, it should be noted that information serves two objectives of economic regulation. First, perfect information is a prerequisite for the functioning of markets. Thus, the provision of accurate and relevant information is a legitimate end in itself. Second, information can help to remedy market failure in the case of negative externalities. Thus, the provision of information can also constitute a means of achieving other legitimate objectives. In the case of information on NPAs in the multilateral trading system, both functions will often be closely interrelated. This section, however, focuses on the former function, while the second function of information will be discussed in the next section dealing with measures addressing market failure.

In the light of the nature of information as an end in itself, there should be a general presumption of legitimacy of information requirements. However, the presumption ought to be rebuttable. The determination of legitimacy of specific information requires a consideration of the WTO objectives.[35] These are the determinants for a proper functioning of markets in the multilateral trading system. To reiterate, the multilateral trading system created by the WTO intends to use the tool of freer international markets to promote economic efficiency as well as a number of other economic and non-economic objectives. Thus, in as far as the NPAs on which information is required are in some way linked to market activities, such as production, transportation of goods, marketing or consumption, measures requiring the supply of truthful information should be legitimate.

It must not be ignored, however, that even requirements relating to truthful information can be illegitimate. Legitimate information requirements should not constitute disguised protection or be otherwise abusive. It seems that the chapeau of Article XX, supplemented with a proportionality test, could be a suitable basis for assessing the legitimacy of information requirements. For example, misleading information requirements, such as a requirement for information on negligible environmental damage to be placed on the product in a way that suggests that the damage is overly severe relative to information on other, possibly favourable, information, should not be considered proportional and is thus abusive. In addition, irrelevant and abusive information requirements pertaining to aspects such as religious or political convictions of producers are

---

[35] See on the importance of information for the functioning of markets and for the question which information is relevant above Chapter 6.

likewise illegitimate.[36] As a mere presumption of consistency of information requirements, including those relating to NPAs, *per se* legitimacy of information does not imply that such requirements could not be found to be inconsistent with WTO law.[37] However, the possibility that a legitimate policy objective can also be abused for illegitimate purposes is not a particularity of information policies but a general feature of all public policies. Given that handholds in WTO law to exclude such abusive policies exist already, for example, the requirements of the chapeau of Article XX, there is no reason to believe that the identification of abusive information policies would be more difficult than with respect to any other public policy. Hence, while concerns pertaining to the possibility of abusive information requirements may not be unfounded, they cannot amount to a general objection against the legitimacy of information in principle.

Understanding availability of truthful information as an end in itself leads to a number of important conclusions. First, just as information requirements ought to be presumed consistent with WTO law, unjustified national restrictions on the provision of information ought to be presumed illegal. This consequence results from the fact that in contrast to other legitimate non-economic public policies, the availability of information serves as a direct precondition for the functioning of markets. Second, since information is legitimate *per se*, regulatory measures concerning information and other measures aimed towards the same end must not be considered alternatives.[38] Information requirements are in principle legitimate irrespective of whether or not other regulatory measures are in place. While in some cases, information requirements might render additional regulatory measures unnecessary, the reverse conclusion would be wrong. Even the most effective regulatory measures could not prejudice in any way the *per se* legitimacy of information on the same matter. Third, the legitimacy or relevance of information does not dependent

---

[36] For exceptions to the *prima facie* case of legitimacy see also above Chapter 6, section 6.2.2.3.

[37] As will be shown in the next section, there is an important difference between information linked to the broad set of NPAs and information linked to the sub-set of PPMs. Since production often leads to negative externalities, information on PPMs should generally be presumed consistent with WTO law.

[38] van den Bossche, Schrijver and Faber (2007), p. 211, discuss the effectiveness and efficiency of labelling compared with other measures and conclude that in cases where externalities are excepted by consumers, more interventionist measures are required. If information is understood to be legitimate *per se*, however, there is no need to explore the effectiveness or efficiency of information, since as a prerequisite for the functioning of markets legitimate information is beyond these standards.

8.2 APPLYING THE REGULATION-BASED PERSPECTIVE

on consumer preferences that exist at a given point of time. Consumer preferences change over time, and often this is a result of the availability of information. While society's expectations and assumptions with respect to certain products or NPAs can make the need for information even more urgent, the lack of related expectations cannot render information abundant. Related suggestions for further preconditions for the consistency of information requirements with WTO law must therefore be rejected.[39] Ultimately, the phenomenon of a change in consumers' purchasing decisions or general preferences triggered by information should not be distrusted. It is actually an indication that the market is functioning properly.

8.2.2.2 Category 2: Regulation addressing market failure

In a situation of a failing market the resource allocation is sub-optimal and thus inefficient. In these situations, government action is required in order to increase efficiency. Nevertheless, the WTO Agreements determine freer international trade as the tool of choice to achieve a number of objectives. This means, that in cases of market failure, the tool chosen by WTO members is unsuitable for achieving the objectives agreed upon – arguably, this is an important shortcoming of the WTO Agreements. Considering that the chosen means must be of secondary importance as compared with the objectives agreed upon, regulation to either prevent or remedy the well-established situations of market failure in principle ought to be consistent with WTO law.[40] As detailed in Chapter 2, among those well-established situations of market failure are public goods and externalities.

This section focuses on negative externalities, since NPA measures are often designed to address these cases. Negative externalities occur

---

[39] E.g., the strict conditions for the legitimacy of labelling requirements as suggested by Swinbank (2006) show a presumption against the permissibility of such requirements. This view does not reflect the paramount importance of information for markets.

[40] A neo-liberalist view would hold that markets bring about optimal results, and that negative externalities, such as environmental pollution, merely reflect differences in the value ascribed to certain objects or circumstances in different countries of the world. However, there are several indications that the WTO Agreements are not based on neo-liberalism. First, the WTO Agreements are not even strictly free trade agreements, but rather agreements to foster 'freer' trade, while accepting a large number of exceptions to the rule. Also, the WTO Agreements subscribe to the principle of sustainable development, which implies that a special consideration of social and environmental objectives is necessary. In this respect, the WTO Agreements even recognize the need for 'positive efforts' to improve the situation of developing countries, a statement irreconcilable with neo-liberalist views.

if production of goods implies damage to other values, without creating corresponding costs reflected in product prices. The most prominent case of negative externalities is pollution and damage to the environment. A polluted environment may diminish considerably the quality of life and even life expectation of affected people. Such damages constitute costs which are not usually, or not totally, borne by the producer. In consequence, prices of end-products will not reflect these costs adequately. Hence, markets cannot lead to optimal results either in terms of the economic or the non-economic goals of the multilateral trading system. Just like environmental damage, other social damage also constitutes a negative externality. In addition, dangerous or otherwise inadequate conditions at the workplace can result in damage to life and health. Depending on contracts, collective labour agreements and/or the relevant laws in the country of production these costs may be borne by the producer, but are often shifted to those directly affected or to society as a whole.

Regulation addressing negative externalities, by internalizing external costs, should also be considered consistent with WTO law. One way to remedy externalities is to supply full information on the real costs of production, thus utilizing the second function of information mentioned above. Although information cannot actually internalize costs, consumers might take externalities into account when making purchase decisions. Since purchase decisions are to a greater or lesser extent based on all information concerning a product, such as price, quality, outer appearance of a product, environmental impact of the product through consumption or waste disposal, information on NPAs, if available, will usually also be considered.[41] Therefore, measures relating to the provision of information on all environmental or social aspects of a product's life cycle should be presumed to be in line with WTO law. Whether or not consumers are willing to pay a higher price for products produced with less negative externalities, however, depends on their personal preferences. Hence, consumer information will be suitable, even though not necessarily sufficient, to remedy negative externalities.

---

[41] Critiques of information on NPAs invoke two contradictory arguments. First, it is argued that such information is objectively irrelevant and that it would illegitimately influence consumer behaviour. This argument has been discussed and rejected in Chapter 6. Second, it is claimed that due to collective action problems consumers would not consider it rational to pay higher prices for products without a 'moral taint' (Howse and Trebilcock, 1996, p. 72, with respect to the second argument). Today, however, there is overwhelming empirical evidence that consumers actually do respond to information relating to NPAs.

8.2 APPLYING THE REGULATION-BASED PERSPECTIVE 475

Consumer information is certainly not the only tool available to regulators in order to internalize externalities. A prominent example for a different attempt to internalize air pollution is the EU scheme for 'greenhouse gas emission allowance trading'.[42] The scheme provides incentives for producers to reduce emissions by penalizing higher levels of emissions with the need for producers to buy pollution allowances from their competitors. In addition to emission trading, there is a whole variety of other market-based measures to address negative externalities, among them environmental tax reforms, subsidies and charges.[43] Although there is a broad range of measures to reduce emissions that are not specifically trade-related,[44] states may find merely internal measures insufficient to achieve their desired level of protection.

In sum, national regulation remedying different cases of market failure in principle can be considered in line with the key economic rationales, and in many cases also with the objectives, underlying the multilateral trading system. Nevertheless, the assessment of such measures is more difficult than the assessment of measures supplying the basic conditions for the functioning of markets discussed in the previous section. These measures are covered by the consensus of WTO members that have chosen free markets as means of achieving certain objectives. Hence, the consensus must logically cover all measures that support the proper functioning of markets. In contrast, in cases of market failure the market is simply not suitable as a tool for achieving optimality, even according to classical economic models. The WTO Agreements, as reflected in the various exceptions to the rule, recognize the existence of market failure and the need for affirmative action. However, neither economic theory nor the WTO Agreements offer precise answers as to how and to what extent market failure should be remedied. Given the importance of WTO objectives relative to the economic means of achieving them agreed upon by WTO members, the fact of a situation of market failure in the assessment of a measure in violation of WTO law cannot be ignored. Certainly, merely assuming

---

[42] See the EC Directive 2003/87EC, OJ L 275/32 of 25 October 2003.
[43] See for an overview on suggestions for market-based instruments, Commission of the European Communities, Green Paper on market-based instruments for environment and related policy purposes, COM (2007) 140 final, of 28 March 2007.
[44] See, e.g., Goh (2004), who points out that neither the UN Framework Convention nor the Kyoto Protocol requires governments to implement policies that are trade-related. The measures listed in Article 2.1(a) of the Kyoto Protocol, e.g., would be applicable consistent with WTO rights and obligations (at p. 415).

the legitimacy of all national measures to remedy market failure would exceed the boundaries of presumed consensus among WTO members. These are reflected, however, in the objectives of the WTO Agreements. Thus, measures to remedy a situation of market failure ought to be consistent with WTO law, at least in those situations where the measure serves as an alternative tool in pursuit of the core objectives of the WTO Agreements. Assessing measures to remedy market failure is therefore more complex than assessing measures in the first category. As a first step, a situation of market failure must be established. In a second step, the assessment must focus on consistency or not of a particular measure with WTO objectives. Only if both assessments provide a positive answer should the measure be considered to be in line with WTO law.

Questions relating to design and intensity of measures addressing market failure also need to be answered. The guiding idea for the assessment of such measures must be to ensure the effectiveness of existing mechanisms that serve to improve the inefficient allocation produced by the failing market. Therefore, location of the externality and of its negative impacts ought to be crucial aspects in deciding about the competent political body in the multi-level system of governance, and as a corollary about the political process to which the determination of the measure to remedy market failure should be deferred.

If location and effects are within the territory of a single WTO member state, then this state must be considered competent to address the market failure with adequate means. Internal measures to remedy negative externalities are in many cases consistent with WTO law as it stands. Thus, the problem-solving capacities are in this case not impaired in any way by WTO law. Similar measures that affect international trade, on the other hand, ought to be considered consistent with WTO law if either the effectiveness of the corresponding internal measures would otherwise be impaired, or if internal measures are unsuitable to achieve the regulatory objective. The latter argument would apply to cases where the location of the market failure is in a country other than the state imposing the measure, while the negative externalities and damage are located within the country imposing the measure. Since this situation, as discussed above, implies a cost-shifting from the polluting to the polluted state, trade measures should be allowed in line with the polluter pays principle applicable in international environmental law.

If, in contrast, location or effects of market failure are international or global, then the question about the competent political body in the multi-level system arises. This will often be the case if negative externalities

8.2 APPLYING THE REGULATION-BASED PERSPECTIVE 477

relate to the global environment, such as the atmosphere or the climate. Here, the first crucial question is whether or not international institutions able to effectively address the problem exist.[45] At this point in time, this will often not (yet) be the case. Then, competence should fall back to the nation-states as alternative political bodies in a position to regulate effectively. Measures addressing negative externalities which affect the global commons should be presumed legitimate, as long as the multi-level system of governance does not address the externality effectively at a higher level. The national regulation chosen to address international market failure should then be assessed like other national measures. Also here, maintaining problem-solving capacities must be the guiding idea. This means that in order to address international or global problems caused or exacerbated by international trade, nation-state internal regulation to address market failure should be presumed effective and thus consistent with WTO law. Just as in the case of national market failure, product measures linked to NPAs applicable to imports should also be considered consistent to the extent necessary to ensure effectiveness of the internal regulation. However, especially if product measures linked to NPAs are at stake, the existence of international agreements should play a role.

It is therefore suggested that regulation based on certain international standards or rules should be presumed effective to remedy market failure and thus consistent with WTO rationales and objectives. Which agreements are considered relevant would be subject to negotiation. For example, WTO members could agree on a general rule for the relevance of international agreements if these have been signed by a certain *quorum* of WTO members. The proviso relating to *de minimis* impacts of internal regulation on costs of domestic production, which would normally lead to inconsistency of the measure, should be irrelevant if the NPA measure would be in line with relevant international rules.

In sum, since the provision of truthful information, including information on external costs, is considered to enforce market mechanisms, respective measures should always be considered to be consistent with WTO law, no matter which function of information is actually prevailing. This presumption, however, is not applicable in general to regulatory measures remedying market failure. The assessment of consistency with the international trading system is more complex: while regulation

---

[45] This assessment corresponds to the four questions asked by Jackson in the similar context of determining whether a particular policy ought to be 'brought under the GATT/WTO umbrella'. Jackson (2002), pp. 123–5.

addressing established cases of market failure is in line with the key economic rationales of the WTO, consistency with its objectives will need to be positively established. While such measures will often be consistent with one or another of the objectives, the WTO Agreements are silent on the question of how to address such situations. In the assessment, the existence of competent and effective regulatory bodies in the multilayered system of governance also needs to be considered. In cases where only nation-states offer this quality, suitable and adequate national measures consistent with WTO objectives and designed to remedy market failure ought to be permissible. International agreements could be used to facilitate the assessment of whether measures are adequate to achieve regulatory goals or not.

8.2.2.3   Category 3: Distributive regulation

Even if a Pareto-optimal result is achieved by a market, this does not establish anything about distributional issues or fairness. Hence, according to their normative preferences, governments will find it necessary to correct the outcome achieved by the market. This type of regulation constitutes the third category. Most economic schools of thought deliberately ignore distributional issues, since these are considered political questions to be decided at the ballot box.[46] Consistency with economic rationales of the multilateral trading system is therefore not applicable in the case of purely distributive regulation. Nevertheless, national social regulation may often be perfectly in line with one or another economic or non-economic WTO objective. In the absence of positive consistency with economic key rationales, however, congruence is least in the third category of regulation (cf. Table 8.1).

As demonstrated in Chapter 2, redistributive policies which consist in a direct transfer of resources to consumers, for example, to the poor or unemployed, will not usually create barriers to international trade in goods if they do not specifically discriminate against foreign products. Examples are the supply of, or subsidies to, basic services of general interest, such as basic transportation systems and infrastructure, education or health, which must be considered WTO-consistent.[47] Often, distributive measures, whether in the form of subsidies or otherwise, will be linked to NPAs. Subsidies in whatever form, however, are particularly

---

[46] E.g., Samuelson and Nordhaus (2005), p. 39.
[47] In this respect, however, problems can arise under the GATS. These problems relating to trade in services are beyond this work, which focuses on trade in goods.

Table 8.1 *Regulation-based approach to WTO conformity of NPA measures*

Type of regulation Rationales and objectives	Category 1: Regulation reducing market imperfections	Category 2: Regulation addressing market failure	Category 3: Distributive regulation
Key economic rationales (means)			
Theory of competitive markets	Yes	Yes (in established situations of market failure, such as externalities)	./.
Theory of comparative advantage	Yes		./.
Ultimate objectives of the WTO (ends)			
Raising standards of living	pbWTO	tba	tba
Full employment	pbWTO	tba	tba
Growing volume of real income and effective demand	pbWTO	tba	tba
Expanding production	pbWTO	tba	tba
Seeking protection and preservation of the environment	pbWTO	tba	tba
Manner consistent with needs and concerns of WTO members at different levels of development	pbWTO	tba	tba

pbWTO = presumed by WTO Agreements.
tba = to be assessed.

problematic when they benefit domestic producers, possibly via subsidizing their products, such as farmers or agricultural products, since they may protect domestic farmers from their foreign competitors. In such cases, even consistency with WTO objectives will be difficult to establish. For example, in as far as full employment or an increase in production in a certain sector of a particular WTO member is cited as the objective of a distributive measure, the effects of the measure on other countries need to be taken into account. It is difficult to perceive of purely distributive measures, whether or not linked to NPAs, being in violation of WTO law situations in which the regulation-based approach might lead to a finding of consistency. Hence, the regulation-based approach does not imply a presumption of consistency of such measures with WTO law. This does not mean, however, that such measures ought to be presumed *prima facie* inconsistent with WTO law. The silence of the WTO on most distributive measures merely reflects the position that WTO law and distributive policies are not assumed to be strictly interlinked. Arguably, all countries in the world implement some distributive policies, and hence the need and legitimacy of correction of market outcomes seems sufficiently established. Nevertheless, the diversity in the specific objectives as well as the specific tools and availability of resources to achieve these objectives is great.

In this respect, it is important to note that there is overlap between the second and the third category: the prevention of situations that lead markets to fail, such as policies to internalize external costs, has here been considered in the second category, although it also has a distributional dimension. Distributive measures in order to offset advantages or damages incurred in situations of market failure may well be considered under the second category and thus be found consistent with the agreements. Often, however, the question of whether or not there is a situation of market failure will be difficult to answer. Certain external costs of production are not reflected explicitly within the objectives listed in the Marrakesh Agreement. Examples are human rights violations linked to the production of goods, social costs arising from poor conditions at the workplace, cultural costs arising from increased imports of cultural products that may force products relevant to the domestic culture out of the market, or regulation offering incentives for animal friendly farming methods. In many cases, WTO objectives do encompass certain benefits to individuals and therefore are amenable to the legitimacy of distributive policies, for example, by stressing the need to raise 'standards of living' or by subscribing to the objective of sustainable development. In these cases, whether or not a situation of market failure and consistency with WTO objectives can be established under the second category needs careful assessment on a case-by-case basis.

In sum, distributive regulation may be found to be consistent with the multilateral trading system if linked to situations of market failure. In contrast, whether or not purely distributional policies are reflected in the WTO objectives needs to be positively established, based on an assessment of the characteristics of the regulatory measure at issue. Although consensus on a general need for distributive policies can be assumed, the WTO objectives offer little common ground for presuming acceptance by WTO members of distributive policies violating obligations in WTO law. In consequence, even in cases of an overlap with WTO objectives, the relationship of such policies with WTO law should be determined in negotiations by WTO members.

8.2.3 General conditions of consistency

The regulation-based perspective serves to assess the consistency of trade-related national policies with WTO law. From this perspective, consistency depends on the category to which the regulation at issue belongs. For some regulations, it has been argued that consistency ought to be presumed *prima facie*. Beyond the three categories outlined above, however, there are some requirements that national regulations ought to meet.

8.2.3.1 General requirements

National regulations under the above Category 1, regulation to reduce market imperfections, and regulations under Category 2, regulation addressing market failure, profit to a greater or lesser extent from a presumption of consistency with WTO law. Nevertheless, it must be recognized that all national regulation, no matter how high the goals allegedly pursued, can be abused. There is no doubt that competition policy, albeit in principle perfectly legitimate as a policy, can be abused to protect domestic firms. The same is true, for example, for regulations concerning consumer information. Therefore, despite the legitimacy in principle of such policies, laws and regulations that are drafted or applied abusively must be excluded from this scheme. Therefore, the chapeau of Article XX should be applied, both to design and application of measures, to identify illegitimate measures. Hence, laws and regulations of all categories that discriminate arbitrarily or unjustifiably would be found to be in violation of WTO law.

8.2.3.2 National regulation and SDT

Furthermore, there ought to be a general requirement that even justified measures must conform to the principle of SDT. This does not seem indicated for the first category of measures that contribute to the proper functioning of markets. The reason is that properly functioning international markets according to the key rationale of comparative advantages benefit all countries, including developing countries. Although the second category also contains measures that are in principle consistent with key rationales of the WTO, it is here suggested that such measures ought to conform to the principle of SDT. Since the WTO merely recognizes market failure, without, however, giving guidance on how to address it, there should be the requirement that measures under the second category must adhere to the principle of SDT. Measures addressing market failure should provide for mechanisms that prevent or mitigate negative economic effects on developing countries. For example, if national measures addressing pollution, according to the requirements detailed above, are applied to imports in order to 'level the playing field' and to maintain regulatory effectiveness, developing countries' concerns must be taken into account. Often, technical assistance, including transfer of know-how and funds, possibly together with sufficient implementation periods to enable developing country producers to comply with the requirements requested by other countries will be sufficient. Requiring countries to 'pay' for measures that are otherwise justified to address market failure effectively seems inconsistent at first glance only. This requirement is necessary given the WTO objective of sustainable economic development in developing countries and given the recognition of the need for positive efforts. Due to the trade measures restricting imports of products that have been produced by incurring external costs, developing country producers lose an, albeit illegitimate, competitive advantage vis-à-vis producers in countries with a higher degree of internalization. Technical assistance, including transfer of know-how and related costs, should prevent the loss of export opportunities and at the same time would enable developing country producers to compete on a level playing field. Last, the obligation to supplement trade measures addressing market failure with technical assistance for developing countries is also justified by basic ideas of fairness. This is especially clear when it comes to pollution. Since the beginning of industrialization, the economic development of industrialized countries has been the cause of large external costs. These externalities have been, and are still being, borne by developed and developing countries and their populations. For example, it is thought that climate change has predominantly been caused by CO_2 emissions from industrialized nations. Therefore, it is believed that developing countries will suffer disproportionately from the externalities of industrial production. Hence, it would be inequitable not to provide assistance in order to avoid additional external costs, no matter where they incur. Since the principle of SDT ought to apply even if measures under the second category are concerned, the case for applying the principle to distributive measures is even stronger.

8.2.4 Conclusions

The approach described in this chapter is not intended to offer black and white answers to the question of consistency of NPA measures with WTO law. It utilizes the core idea of the WTO Agreements, namely, economic key rationales and general objectives, in order to develop a new perspective on the legal status of national regulatory measures with WTO law.

The perspective has led to a strong argument for consistency of all national measures suitable for ensuring the functioning of markets by reducing imperfections and supplying the necessary preconditions. Most relevant to NPA trade measures is the finding that measures improving consumer information ought to be *prima facie* WTO-consistent. For WTO law as it stands, however, this argument could be used to support the consideration that labelling or other information requirements are least trade-restrictive when it comes to an assessment under Article XX. More importantly, it supports the case for consumer information as a legitimate objective under Article 2.2 of the TBT Agreement.

The second category of national measures, namely, measures to prevent or address market failure as reflected in the WTO Agreements, shows a mixed record. Nevertheless, there should be a presumption in favour of consistency with WTO law, since such measures address situations where the means chosen in the WTO Agreements fails to bring about the desired optimality result. It is here suggested, that the principle of SDT requires countries to supplement their regulatory measures with assistance to developing country producers in order to help them to compete on a 'level playing field' as desired by the country of importation.

The third category of measures, namely, measures implementing distributional policies, is characterized by weaker links to the WTO Agreements. Hence, in as far as there are interactions between such policies and international trade, their legal status under WTO law should be subject to negotiations. The approach should not be to negotiate on a package of measures or policies. Chances for consensus will be higher if negotiations focus on specific policies, or even specific questions arising under specific policies. *De lege ferenda*, it would seem reasonable to move those distributional policies, which are not yet explicitly reflected in the WTO Agreements but nevertheless widely recognized on the international stage, to the second category. This should encompass all policies and measures that reflect compulsory international law (*ius cogens*). This would apply, for example, with respect to measures fighting child labour or other human rights violations. Since the principle of SDT requires assistance to developing countries, which should in principle be designed to avoid the costs of compliance, agreement on questions relating to child labour and labour rights might be more probable than sometimes expected.

The regulation-based approach can be relevant *de lege lata* to interpretation of the agreements by placing greater weight on foundations and telos of the multilateral trading system. Given the limited legal relevance ascribed to economic key rationales and objectives as stipulated in the preamble to an agreement, the perspective adopted here could in addition be used *de lege ferenda* to bridge opposing views on consistency of certain national measures. Adopting a regulation-based perspective might facilitate negotiations in which members could come to agreement on the consistency of particular national policies and specific regulatory measures. The basic ideas of the agreements, as reflected in the underlying economic rationales as well as in the objectives laid down in the Marrakesh Agreement offer plenty of common ground, if taken seriously by the 153 WTO members who have subscribed to them.

Summary and concluding remarks

The question of whether NPA and PPM measures are permissible under WTO law is often understood as unveiling certain general views or beliefs held by 'supporters' and 'opponents' of these measures. This work shows that the question, if taken for what it is, is completely unsuited to splitting the WTO community into two opposing groups. NPA measures are neither *per se* good nor bad. A simple 'yes' or 'no' as a response to the PPM or NPA question in WTO law is flawed, since it misses the complexity of the problem.

Part I Foundations

A preliminary legal analysis, a review and cursory analysis of the relevant political and economic background constitute the starting point of the analysis and the development of a new regulatory perspective on the issue. The legal foundations consist in the main in a preliminary analysis of relevant case law and of the relevant provisions of the WTO Agreements in order to identify the legal key issues. It confirmed the utmost importance of the concept of 'like products', as used in several provisions in different WTO Agreements. It is the uncertainty on the relevant factors for the determination of 'like products', in particular, the relevance of non-physical aspects, which makes measures linked to such aspects an object of extensive legal research. In addition, the cursory analysis showed that a certain 'extraterritorial reach' inherent to NPA measures, as well as the unilaterality or multilaterality characterizing design and application, are considered crucial for justifiability under the general exceptions. Furthermore, the explicit use of the term 'processes and production methods' in the TBT and SPS Agreements implies that production methods do have a specific legal relevance under both agreements, while no evidence for a comparable status of PPMs under the GATT could be identified. Based on these preliminary findings, this work distinguishes between measures linked to non-physical aspects, or NPA measures, on the one hand, and measures linked to processes and production methods, or PPM measures, on the other. Due to the use of the 'like products' concept the TBT and SPS Agreements also, this work distinguishes as well between unincorporated PPMs and incorporated PPMs. Since this work focuses on NPA measures, only the former set of PPMs is relevant to the comprehensive legal analysis in Part II.

The political and economic background described in Chapter 2 sheds light on the relevance of NPA measures as a tool of national regulation. While differences in meaning as well as in nature of regulation prevail in different countries, this work adopts a broad notion of regulation that corresponds to the applicability of WTO law on all national measures, whether laws, regulations or other official acts. From an economic perspective, national regulation equals government intervention in free markets. Three regulatory rationales are widely accepted among economists, namely, regulation to safeguard competitive markets, regulation to address market failure and regulation in pursuit of distributional goals. All these categories are relevant to NPA measures, and the approach developed in Part III builds to a considerable extent on this concept. Chapter 2 then moves to the international dimension of the subject: It addresses the relevance of NPA measures in a situation of international trade within the multilateral trading system as fostered by the GATT and the WTO Agreements. From an economic perspective, it is apparent that the multilateral trading system is based on the idea of free markets as a tool to provide for an optimal allocation of resources according to neo-classical economic theory. The gates for a consideration of national regulation and national public policies in the WTO Agreements are mostly located in the general exceptions, that is, GATT Article XX, which accepts the predominant importance of a number of listed public policies. Furthermore, a brief analysis of WTO key rationales and objectives shows that the multilateral trading system as designed by the WTO Agreements pursues co-equal non-economic as well as economic objectives. The political background briefly reviews a number of general concerns about NPA measures. All aspects considered in this background section, as well as the national regulatory rationales and the objectives and key rationales of the multilateral trading system, are relevant and taken up in the legal analysis in Part II and for considerations on a new perspective in Part III.

Part II   Legal analysis

The legal analysis shows that the legal status of NPA measures is determined by different aspects. The permissibility of a certain NPA measure depends on the specific subject matter to which the measure relates, on the existence of relevant international law outside the WTO, as well as on design and application of the measure.

The first junction is the law applicable in the relations between the parties. The WTO is not a self-contained regime. Given the speedily growing body of international law, it is more and more likely that specific provisions in specific agreements may override WTO obligations under certain circumstances. For example, provisions prohibiting trade in certain species contained in specific bilateral or international agreements, even if defined under reference to NPAs, may as *lex specialis* prevail over GATT obligations to accord national or MFN treatment. If the WTO covered agreements are applicable, on the other hand, it is necessary to determine which agreement is relevant. For this determination it is necessary to distinguish between measures linked to PPMs, which are accorded a special legal status under the TBT Agreement, and those linked to other NPAs. This work argues that the TBT Agreement provides the legal regime applicable to all labelling requirements. Thus, labelling regulations and norms concerning incorporated as well as unincorporated PPMs or concerning any other aspect, including NPAs, are assessed under the standards of the TBT Agreement. As to the material content of these standards, the analysis suggests that consumer protection and consumer information are legitimate objectives in the sense of the TBT Agreement. Therefore, this work has concluded that labelling requirements providing accurate information are *prima facie* legal under the TBT Agreement, no matter to which specific subject matter they relate. Only discriminatory or otherwise abusive requirements must be considered inconsistent with WTO law. Furthermore, it is here argued that the TBT Agreement, to the extent that it allows certain measures, prevails over provisions of the GATT.

NPA measures other than labelling requirements fall within the scope of the GATT, with the consequence that the concept of 'like products' is crucial. Some approaches to the concept, namely, the theory on aims and effects or market-based approaches, would in some instances permit NPA measures, depending on the genuineness of underlying regulatory intentions or depending on the view of market agents. This analysis, however, mainly agrees with the arguably prevailing view on the concept of 'likeness' and favours an 'objective' determination of the concept. Normative considerations are therefore relevant at a later stage in the legal assessment. In consequence of this view, NPA measures will usually violate GATT obligations, such as the prohibition to quantitative restrictions or obligations arising from the principle of non-discrimination. Consequently, the legitimacy of the NPA measures depends largely on their justifiability under the general exceptions.

This work argues that Article XX does not exclude any NPA measure *per se*. Even NPA measures aimed at the protection of objects abroad are in principle justifiable, although they meet specific problems. Also with respect to justifiability, NPA measures must be assessed on a case-by-case basis. NPA measures are provisionally justifiable if they fall into one or another of the particular exceptions (a)–(j). Since these exceptions are drafted in a succinct and very general language, interpretation of key terms can be crucial for NPA measures relating to contemporary concerns. It is here argued that interpretation is an objective exercise, and that for this reason relevant international instruments may constitute evidence for the ordinary meaning of terms. Although their importance as evidence may depend on the level of their acceptance, interpretation by its very nature requires that reference to such documents is not subjected to congruence in terms of membership or signatories. This approach is in line with an evolutionary interpretation of generic terms, as applied by the WTO adjudicatory bodies. International instruments, even if not directly applicable, may therefore indeed be highly relevant to the justifiability of certain NPA measures. For example, environmental NPA measures are provisionally justifiable under Article XX(g) if they relate to the protection of shared exhaustible resources, provided they meet the further requirements of this exception. Much of the global commons, including atmosphere and ozone layer, water and soil, may be considered exhaustible resources and thus allow related NPA measures to be justified.

As regards other particular exceptions, the means–end relationship required, for example, by the term 'necessity' will often prevent justification of NPA measures, since their influence on foreign objects of protection is inherently limited. Since the direct effects of such NPA measures are limited to trade effects, and since it will often be difficult or even impossible to verify any impact on protected objects through a change of circumstances or behaviour in the addressee country, NPA measures would thus need to be assumed unsuitable to further their ultimate objectives. Therefore, this work assumes that it would often be difficult to justify NPA measures linked to child labour or unacceptable working conditions under the life and health exception in Article XX(b). The same reasoning would apply to measures aiming at the protection of exhaustible natural resources located exclusively within a third country, unless the state imposing the NPA measure could prove the existence of even-handed domestic measures sufficiently flanking the contested NPA measures.

Against this backdrop, the public morals exception in Article XX(a) becomes highly relevant to NPA measures: neither limitation in terms of subject matter nor in terms of a certain means–end relationship is relevant for justification under this exception. Due to the nature of public morals, the territorial incongruence of the object of protection, namely, domestic public morals, and targeted situation or conduct abroad, is irrelevant. NPA measures may be well suited to protect domestic public morals, in as far as they prevent any participation in certain immoral situations or activities, no matter where, merely by dissociating the importing country imposing the measures. Thus, in as far as NPA measures do have a moral dimension they are justifiable under the moral exception, no matter to which aspects in terms of subject matter or geographical location they relate. The idea underlying the public morals exception provides sufficient handholds in order to prevent its abuse. However, the review of an NPA measure justified by the public morals exception would require a careful and unbiased examination by the WTO adjudicatory bodies. While I see strong arguments for this interpretation of Article XX, relevant case law is limited, and thus a high degree of legal uncertainty on the scope of Article XX in general and of the public morals exception in particular prevails.

Also the chapeau of Article XX contains aspects that are especially relevant to NPA measures. I argue that the principle of special and differential treatment is a principle of WTO law that also informs the chapeau. Given that the chapeau reflects the need to take into account different conditions prevailing in different countries, measures seeking justification under Article XX need to take into account the level of economic development of the countries concerned in order to meet the requirements of the chapeau. This is highly relevant for NPA measures, given that these are often opposed by developing countries fearing that they lack the resources necessary to comply with certain environmental or other social standards adopted by industrialized countries. Other characteristics of NPA measures, in particular, their lack of direct influence on factual matters in other countries, lead to a number of requirements that are especially relevant to NPA measures. First, despite doubts about a general obligation to negotiate, a lack of serious consultations and negotiations with all countries affected by an NPA measure may lead to unjustifiable discrimination under WTO law. Second, the principle of special and differential treatment, together with the obligation to basic fairness and good faith requires WTO members taking NPA measures to allow for adequate implementation periods, and to transfer resources and assistance needed to the developing countries concerned in order to enable developing country producers to comply with NPA requirements.

Part III Outlook

The analysis of the legal status of NPA measures under WTO law showed considerable potential for justifiability of NPA measures. However, given the small number of relevant reports by the adjudicatory bodies on Article XX in general and with respect to NPA measures in particular, and the lack of a consistent view on the crucial legal questions in scholarship, the legal situation is characterized by enormous legal uncertainty. Beyond the legal uncertainty, numerous NPA measures that would also arguably be considered justifiable by most WTO members are barred from justification under the general exceptions. This is relevant for NPA measures implementing public policies outside the scope of Article XX, such as information policies, protection of minorities, protection of consumers or protection of cultural heritage.

The public policies to which NPA measures can relate show that their legal status forms an important application of the broader debate on the interface of non-economic public policies and WTO law, the 'trade and …' or 'linkage' debate. A cursory review of this broader debate shows a large variety of opinions on desirability and the need to reform the WTO and/ or the current system of multi-layered governance in general. The review proves the existence of some common ground: most scholars seem to agree that international trade and therefore also the WTO Agreements affect social matters within nation-states and on a global scale. Also, the prevailing view holds that the proper location for social policies in general ought to be outside the WTO, and that the strong institutions which would be urgently needed to address contemporary challenges are not yet in place or not yet functioning effectively.

This work does not offer any suggestions as regards the future of the multi-layered system of governance. However, it develops a perspective which could contribute to the determination of whether NPA measures ought to be permissible under WTO law in the meantime. The perspective is based on a comparison of the rationales of national regulation with the various objectives and economic key rationales of the multilateral trading system. The idea is that the greater the consistency of rationales and objectives, the stronger the case for permissibility of such NPA measures in WTO law. The strongest case for consistency with WTO law of NPA measures occurs where national measures safeguarding the functioning of markets are concerned. It is argued, that given that the multilateral trading system is based on neo-classical theory on markets, such regulation should not be considered trade restrictive. An application of this perspective shows that NPA measures requiring the disclosure of relevant information or antitrust and competition laws ought to be consistent with WTO law, since they improve the proper functioning of markets. The case of regulation, including NPA measures, addressing market failure, however, is more complicated. The WTO Agreements recognize market failure, but do not give any guidance as to how to address these situations. The guiding idea to approach this situation ought to be the recognition that society's problem-solving capacities must not be impaired. This means that if with respect to a particular subject matter nation-states are at a given point in time the only bodies competent to address severe cases of market failure in an effective way, then non-discriminatory or abusive NPA measures ought to be permissible. This could play a role, for example, in the event of damage to common resources or serious violations of human rights. Information, however, can contribute to mitigate market failure, since it can be suitable for internalizing externalities. Therefore, there are several reasons for consistency of information-related regulation with WTO law. Regulation for distributional reasons will often be unrelated to WTO rationales and objectives, if not, distribution of resources to developing countries is implied. In other cases of distributive regulation its permissibility ought to be addressed on a case-by-case basis and, as first-best solution, in negotiations.

Concluding remarks

Exploring the potential of the WTO Agreements for the legal status of NPA measures has shown that, despite considerable legal uncertainty, there is ample scope for finding balanced and coherent answers on the permissibility of NPA measures even *de lege lata*. Seizing this scope, however, implies that difficult and sensitive legal questions need to be addressed and answered in one way or another. The uncertainty existing today is in part a consequence of the simple fact that the adjudicatory bodies as well as the WTO member states as parties to disputes have refrained from touching upon questions, such as the public morals exception in Article XX(a), answers to which could easily have wider implications not desired by all stakeholders and constituencies.

However, doing justice to the legal texts underlying the multilateral trading system requires giving meaning to what has been stipulated and agreed upon by the WTO members.

Also, the approach developed with this analysis as a new perspective on national regulatory measures cannot serve as a simple roster to distinguish in a black and white style between permissible and impermissible NPA measures. However, the essential common ground identified, most importantly the basic reasoning of national regulation and of rationales and objectives of the WTO and the covered agreements may help to bridge opposing views on NPA measures by putting the debate into perspective: trade is a means, and neither a value of its own nor an end in itself. As a means, the WTO Agreements implicitly subordinate free international trade to the objectives they pursue and which are explicitly stated in the legal texts. Therefore, it is here argued that the WTO Agreements, if taken seriously, must be interpreted to allow for alternatives in the event that the chosen means, namely, freer international trade, fails to foster the very objectives of the system.

Given that the prevailing political impasse may well prevent the first-best solution, namely, agreements providing clear rules on specific groups of NPA measures, for some more time, one must hope that the adjudicatory bodies will not refrain from making full use of the potential of the agreements, in particular when it comes to interpretation of the general exceptions and to relevant implications of the principle of special and differential treatment.

This work has explored but a small fraction of a larger problem. Uncertainty on the legal relevance of NPAs arises not only with respect to trade in goods, but may lead to specific and even more complex problems for trade in services or government procurement. Furthermore, NPA measures are but one application of the tensions at the interface of WTO law and national social regulation. While these complex problems appear rather static, in particular, from a legal perspective, they are certainly not. They occur against the backdrop of the current decline of the power of the nation-state in a world where globalization of governance lags far behind the global activities of private actors and globalization of environmental and other social problems. Much genuine political will, of all stakeholders within and without the international trading system, is needed to develop equitable, sustainable and coherent structures of governance that will enable the global community to meet the most pressing challenges of humankind ahead. Legitimacy of the WTO within these structures cannot be derived from formal adherence to its objectives which are laid down in the agreements and reprinted on page v of this book. Rather, the WTO will have to measure up to expectations that the multilateral trading system actually fosters these objectives in an active way, and refrains from any measures with the potential to impair their achievement.

BIBLIOGRAPHY

Aaker, David A. and Day, George S. 1971. *Consumerism. Search for the Consumer Interest* (New York, 1971).
Abbott, Frederick M. 2005. 'Toward a New Era of Objective Assessment in the Field of TRIPS *And* Variable Geometry for the Preservation of Multilateralism', *Journal of International Economic Law* 8: 77–100.
Addo, Kofi 2002. 'The Correlation Between Labour Standards and International Trade', *Journal of World Trade* 36(2): 285–303.
Ahmad, N. and Wyckoff, A. 2003. 'Carbon Dioxide Emissions Embodied in International Trade of Goods', *OECD Science, Technology and Industry Working Papers*, 2003/15, OECD Publishing.
Anderson, Kym 1998. 'Environmental and Labor Standards: What Role for the WTO?', in Krueger (ed.), *The WTO as an International Organization*.
Appleton, Arthur E. 1999. 'Shrimp/Turtle: Untangling the Nets', *Journal of International Economic Law* 2(3): 477–96.
  2002. 'Environmental Labelling Schemes Revisited: WTO Law and Developing Country Implications', in Sampson and Chambers (eds.), *Trade, Environment, and the Millennium*, pp. 235–66.
Bacchus, James 2005. 'Appellators: The Quest for the Meaning of *And/Or*', essay based on remarks made at the Advisory Centre on WTO Law, Switzerland, June, available at www.acwl.ch/e/about/cooperation_e.aspx, accessed 18 October 2007.
Bagwell, Kyle, Mavroidis, Petros C. and Staiger, Robert W. 2002. 'It's a Question of Market Access', *American Journal of International Law* 96(1): 56–76.
Baldwin, Robert and Cave, Martin 1999. *Understanding Regulation* (Oxford).
Bartels, Lorand 2002. 'Article XX of GATT and the Problem of Extraterritorial Jurisdiction – The Case of Trade Measures for the Protection of Human Rights', *Journal of World Trade* 36(2): 353–403.
Berger, Joseph R. 1999. 'Unilateral Trade Measures to Conserve the World's Living Resources: An Environmental Breakthrough for the GATT in the WTO Sea Turtle Case', *Columbia Journal of Environmental Law* 23: 355–411.
Berrisch, Georg 2003. 'Das allgemeine Zoll- und Handelsabkommen (GATT 1994)', in Prieß and Berrisch, *WTO-Handbuch*, pp. 71–168.

Bhagwati, Jagdish 2000. 'On Thinking Clearly about the Linkage between Trade and the Environment', *Environment and Development Economics* 5: 485–96.
  2002. 'Afterword: The Question of Linkage', *American Journal of International Law* 96(1): 126–34.
Bhagwati, Jagdish and Hudec, Robert E. (eds.) 1996. *Fair Trade and Harmonization* (Cambridge).
Bhala, Raj and Kennedy, Kevin 1998. *World Trade Law* (Charlottesville).
Bishop, Matthew, Kay, John and Mayer, Colin (eds.) 1995. *The Regulatory Challenge* (Oxford).
Bodansky, Daniel 2000. 'What's So Bad about Unilateral Action to Protect the Environment?', *European Journal of International Law* 11(2): 339–47.
Bogdandy, Armin von, Mavroidis, Petros C. and Mény, Yves (eds.) 2002. *European Integration and International Co-ordination* (The Hague).
Bogdandy, Armin von and Wolfrum, Rüdiger (eds.) 2003. *Max Planck Yearbook of United Nations Law: Vol. 7* (Leiden).
Boss, Alfred, Laaser, Claus-Friedrich, Schatz, Klaus-Werner et al. 1996. *Deregulierung in Deutschland*, Kieler Studien 275 (Tübingen).
Boyce, James K. 2002. *The Political Economy of the Environment* (Cheltenham).
  'Green and Brown? Globalization and the Environment' 2004. *Oxford Review of Economic Policy* 20(1): 105–29.
Boyer, Robert and Saillard, Yves (eds.) 2002. 'A Summary of *Régulation* Theory', *Régulation Theory. The State of the Art* (London), pp. 36–44.
Brack, Duncan 2002. 'Environmental Treaties and Trade: Multilateral Environmental Agreements and the Multilateral Trading System', in Sampson and Chambers (eds.), *Trade, Environment, and the Millennium*, pp. 321–52.
Breyer, Stephen 1979. 'Analyzing Regulatory Failure: Mismatches, Less Restrictive Alternatives, and Reform', *Harvard Law Review* 92: 549–609.
  1984. 'Analyzing regulatory failure: Mismatches, Less Restrictive Alternatives, and Reform', in Ogus and Veljanovski (eds.), *Readings in the Economics of Law and Regulation*, p. 238.
  1990. 'Regulation and Deregulation in the United States: Airlines, Telecommunications and Antitrust', in Majone (ed.), *Deregulation or Re-Regulation?*, pp. 7–58.
Bronckers, Marco and McNelis, Natalie 2002. 'Rethinking the "Like Product" Definition in GATT 1994: Anti-Dumping and Environmental Protection', in Cottier and Mavroidis (eds.), *Regulatory Barriers and the Principle of Non-Discrimination*, pp. 345–85.
Bronckers, Marco and Quick, Reinhard (eds.) 2000. *New Directions in International Economic Law* (London).
Bürgi Bonanomi, Lisa 2007. 'Agricultural Trade: Taking Integration Seriously', 21 May 2007, available at http://papers.ssrn.com/sol3/papers.cfm?abstract_id=980208.

Bydlinski, Franz 1991. *Juristische Methodenlehre und Rechtsbegriff*, 2nd edn. (Wien).
Cameron, James, Demaret, Paul and Geradin, Damien 1994. *Trade and the Environment: The Search for Balance* (London).
Cassese, Antonio 1995. *Self-Determination of Peoples* (Cambridge).
Chang, Howard F. 2000. 'Toward a Greener GATT: Environmental Trade Measures and the Shrimp-Turtle Case', *Southern California Law Review* 74: 31-47.
  2005. 'Environmental Trade Measures, the Shrimp-turtle Rulings, and the Ordinary Meaning of the Text of the GATT', *Chapman Law Review* 8: 25-51.
Chang, Seung Wha 1997. 'GATTing a Green Trade Barrier. Eco-Labelling and the WTO Agreement on Technical Barriers to Trade', *Journal of World Trade* 31(1): 137-59.
Charnovitz, Steve 1991. 'Exploring the Environmental Exceptions in GATT Article XX', *Journal of World Trade* 25: 37-55.
  1992. 'GATT and the Environment. Examining the Issues', *International Environmental Affairs* 4(3): 203-33.
  1994. 'Green Roots, Bad Pruning: GATT Rules and their Application to Environmental Trade Measures', *Tulane Environmental Law Journal* 7(2): 299-352.
  1997. 'WTO's Alcoholic Beverages Decision', *RECIEL* 6(2): 198-203.
  1998. 'The Moral Exception in Trade Policy', *Virginia Journal of International Law* 38: 689-745.
  2001a. 'Solving the PPMs Puzzle', *PSIO Occasional Paper* (Geneva).
  2001b. 'Rethinking WTO Trade Sanctions', *American Journal of International Law* 95(4): 792-832.
  2002. 'The Law of Environmental "PPMs" in the WTO: Debunking the Myth of Illegality', *Yale Journal of International Law* 27: 59-110.
  2005. 'Belgian Family Allowances and the Challenge of Origin-based Discrimination', *World Trade Review* 4(1): 7-26.
  2007a. 'The WTO's Environmental Progress', *Journal of International Economic Law* 10: 685-706.
  2007b. 'A New WTO Paradigm for Trade and Environment', *Singapore Year Book of International Law*, e-publication.
Cheyne, Ilona 2009. 'Proportionality, Proximity and Environmental Labelling', *Journal of International Economic Law* 12: 927-52.
Cho, Sungjoon 2003. *Free Markets and Social Regulation: A Reform Agenda of the Global Trading System* (London).
  2005. 'Linkage of Free Trade and Social Regulation: Moving Beyond the Entropic Dilemma', *Chicago Journal of International Law* 5(2): 625-74.
Choi, Won-Mog 2003. *Like Products in International Trade Law. Towards a Consistent GATT/WTO Jurisprudence* (New York).
Christian, Ernest and Hufbauer, Gary Clyde 2004. 'End this Damaging Tax and Trade Charade', *Financial Times*, 8 March.

Cleveland, Sarah H. 2002. 'Human Rights Sanctions and International Trade: A Theory of Compatibility', *Journal of International Economic Law* 5(1): 133–89.
Cordonier Segger, Marie-Claire 2009. 'The Role of International Forums in the Advancement of Sustainable Development', *Sustainable Development Law and Policy* 10(4).
Cottier, Thomas 1996. 'The Impact of New Technologies on Multilateral Trade Regulation and Governance', *Chicago-Kent Law Review* 415–35.
  1998. 'The WTO and Environmental Law: Three Points for Discussion', in Fijalkowski, Agata and Cameron, James (eds.), *Trade and the Environment: Bridging the Gap* (London), pp. 56–64.
  2000a. 'From Progressive Liberalization to Progressive Regulation in WTO Law', *Journal of International Economic Law* 9: 779–821.
  2000b. 'Limits to International Trade: the Constitutional Challenge', *ASIL Proceedings* 220–2.
  2002. 'Trade and Human Rights: A Relationship to Discover', *Journal of International Economic Law* 5(1): 111–32.
Cottier, Thomas and Hertig, Maya 2003. 'The Prospects of 21st Century Constitutionalism', in Bogdandy and Wolfrum (eds.), *Max Planck Yearbook of United Nations Law*, pp. 261–328.
Cottier, Thomas and Khorana, Sangeeta 2005. 'Linkages between Freedom of Expression and Unfair Competition Rules in International Trade: The *Hertel* Case and Beyond', in Cottier, Pauwelyn and Bürgi (eds.), *Human Rights and International Trade*, pp. 245–72.
Cottier, Thomas and Nadakavukaren Schefer, Krista 2000. 'Conflict Resolution in the World Trade Organization. Assessing the story so far: hope on the horizon?', in Ward and Brack (eds.), *Trade, Investment and the Environment*, pp. 187–202.
Cottier, Thomas and Mavroidis, Petros C. 2002a. *Regulatory Barriers and the Principle of Non-Discrimination in World Trade Law* (Ann Arbor).
  2002b. 'Conclusions', in Cottier and Mavroidis (eds.), *Regulatory Barriers and the Principle of Non-Discrimination*, pp. 389–94.
  2003. *The Role of the Judge in International Trade Regulation. Experience and Lessons for the WTO* (Ann Arbor).
Cottier, Thomas and Oesch, Matthias 2005. *International Trade Regulation. Law and Policy in the WTO, the European Union and Switzerland* (London).
Cottier, Thomas, Pauwelyn, Joost and Bürgi, Elisabeth 2005a. *Human Rights and International Trade* (New York).
  2005b. 'Linking Trade Regulation and Human Rights in International Law: An Overview', in Cottier, Pauwelyn and Bürgi (eds.), *Human Rights and International Trade*, pp. 1–26.
Cottier, Thomas, Tuerk, Elisabeth and Panizzon, Marion 2003. 'Handel und Umwelt im Recht der WTO: Auf dem Weg zur praktischen Konkordanz', *ZUR* Sonderheft 155–66.

Dahm, Georg, Delbrück, Jost and Wolfrum, Rüdiger 2002. *Völkerrecht. Bd. 1.3, Die Formen völkerrechtlichen Handelns*, 2nd edn. (Berlin).

Daly, Herman 1991. 'The Perils of Free Trade', *Scientific American* 269(5): 50–7.

Davey, William J. and Pauwelyn, Joost 2002. 'MFN Unconditionality: A Legal Analysis of the Concept in View of its Evolution in the GATT/WTO Jurisprudence with Particular Reference to the Issue of "Like Product"', in Cottier and Mavroidis (eds.), *Regulatory Barriers and the Principle of Non-Discrimination*, pp. 13–50.

Deardorff, Alan V. 2000. 'The Economics of Government Market Intervention, and its International Dimension', in Bronckers and Quick (eds.), *New Directions in International Economic Law*, pp. 71–84.

Demaret, Paul and Stewardson, Raoul 1994. 'Border Tax Adjustments under the GATT and EC Law and General Implications for Environmental Taxes', *Journal of World Trade* 28(4): 5–65.

Desmedt, Axel 2001. 'Proportionality in WTO Law', *Journal of International Economic Law* 4(3): 441–80.

Diebold, Nicolas F. 2008. 'The Morals and Order Exceptions in WTO Law: Balancing the Toothless Tiger and the Undermining Mole', *Journal of International Economic Law* 11(1): 43–74.

Diem, Andreas 1996. *Freihandel und Umweltschutz in GATT und WTO* (Baden Baden).

Ehlermann, Claus-Dieter and Ehring, Lothar 2005. 'Are WTO Decision-making Procedures Adequate for Making, Revising, and Implementing Worldwide and "Plurilateral" Rules?', in Petersmann (ed.), *Developing Countries in the Doha Round*, pp. 91–118.

Ehring, Lothar 2002. '*De Facto* Discrimination in WTO Law: National and Most-Favored-Nation Treatment – or Equal Treatment?', *Journal of World Trade* 36(5): 921–77.

Epiney, Astrid 2000. 'Welthandel und Umwelt – Ein Beitrag zur Dogmatik der Art. III, IX, XX GATT', *Deutsches Verwaltungsblatt* 2: 77–86.

Esty, Daniel C. 2000. 'Environment and the Trading System: Picking up the Post-Seattle Pieces', in Schott (ed.), *The WTO after Seattle*, pp. 243–52.

Esty, Daniel C. and Geradin, Damien 1998. 'Environmental Protection and International Competitiveness. A Conceptual Framework', *Journal of World Trade* 32(2): 5–46.

Fauchald, Ole Kristian 2003. 'Flexibility and Predictability under the World Trade Organization's Non-Discrimination Clauses', *Journal of World Trade* 37(3): 443–82.

Feddersen, Christoph T. 1998. 'Focusing on Substantive Law in International Economic Relations: The Public Morals of GATT's Article XX(a) and "Conventional" Rules of Interpretation', *Minnesota Journal of Global Trade* 75–122.

2002. *Der ordre public in the WTO. Auslegung und Bedeutung des Art. XX lit a) GATT im Rahmen der WTO-Streitbeilegung* (Berlin).
Ferrell, Jessica K. 2005. 'Controlling Flags of Convenience: One Measure to Stop Overfishing of Collapsing Fish Stocks', *Environmental Law* 35: 323–90.
Frank, Robert H. 2005. *Microeconomics and Behavior* (New York).
French, Duncan 2005 'Treaty Interpretation and the Incorporation of Extraneous Legal Rules', *International and Comparative Law Quarterly*, 55(2): 281–314.
Frowein, Jochen A. 1994. 'Reactions By Not Directly Affected States to Breaches of Public International Law', *Recueil des Cours* (Collected Courses) 248(4): 345–437.
Fukasako, Kiichiro 2000. 'Special and Differential Treatment for Developing Countries: Does it Help to Help Themselves?', UN-WIDER, Working Papers No. 197.
Gaines, Sanford E. 2001. 'The WTO's Reading of the GATT Article XX Chapeau: A Disguised Restriction on Environmental Measures', *University of Pennsylvania Journal of International Economic Law* 22(4): 739–860.
2002. 'Processes and Production Methods: How to Produce Sound Policy for Environmental PPM-Based Trade Measures?', *Columbia Journal of Environmental Law* 27: 383–432.
Gallagher, Kevin P. and Werksman, Jacob 2002. *International Trade & Sustainable Development* (London).
Gandhi, Samir R. 2005. 'Regulating the Use of Voluntary Environmental Standards Within the World Trade Organization Legal Regime: Making a Case for Developing Countries', *Journal of World Trade* 39(5): 855–80.
Garcia, Frank 1999. 'The Global Market and Human Rights: Trading Away the Human Rights Principle', *Brooklyn Journal of International Law* 25: 51–97
Gehring, Markus W. and Jessen, Henning 2005 'Gesundheitspolizeiliche und pflanzenschutzrechtliche Massnahmen (SPS)', in Hilf and Oeter (eds.), *WTO-Recht. Rechtsordnung des Welthandels*, p. 366.
Geradin, Damien 2000. 'Overview: A Lawyer's View', in Ward and Brack (eds.), *Trade, Investment and the Environment*, pp. 91–101.
Germann, O. A. 1967. *Probleme und Methoden der Rechtsfindung* (Bern).
Ginzky, Harald 1999. 'Garnelen und Schildkröten – Zu den umweltpolitischen Handlungsspielräumen der WTO-Mitgliedstaaten', *ZUR* 4: 216–22.
Goettsche, Götz 2005. 'WTO als Rechtsordnung', in Hilf and Oeter (eds.), *Trade, Investment and the Environment*, § 7.
Goh, Gavin 2004. 'The World Trade Organization, Kyoto and Energy Tax Adjustments at the Border', *Journal of World Trade* 38(3): 395–423.
Goodwin, Neva, Nelson, Julie and Ackerman, Frank 2004. *Microeconomics in Context* (Boston, MA).

Graber, Christoph Beat 2006. 'The New UNESCO Convention on Cultural Diversity: A Counterbalance to the WTO?', *Journal of International Economic Law* 9: 553–74.

Griffin, Keith 2000. 'Delinking Trade, Environmental Protection, and Labor Standards', *Environment and Development Economics* 5: 504–10.

Griller, Stefan 2003. *International Economic Governance and Non-Economic Concerns* (Wien).

Grossmann, Harald, Busse, Matthias, Fuchs, Deike and Koopmann, Georg 2002. *Sozialstandards in der Welthandelsordnung* (Baden Baden).

Guest, Jim 2002. 'Consumers and Consumerism in America Today', *The Journal of Consumer Affairs* 36(2): 139–49.

Guzman, Andrew T. 2004. 'Global Governance and the WTO', *Harvard International Law Journal* 45: 303–51.

Hawkins, Keith 1989. 'Rule and Discretion in Comparative Perspective: The Case of Social Regulation', *Ohio State Law Journal* 50: 663–79.

Heintschel von Heinegg, Wolf 2004 'Die völkerrechtlichen Verträge als Hauptrechtsquelle des Völkerrechts', in Ipsen (ed.), *Völkerrecht*, pp. 112–209.

Herwig, Alexia and Hüller, Torsten 2008. 'Zur normativen Legitimität der Welthandelsordnung, in Meinhard Hilf (ed.), *Perspektiven des Internationalen Wirtschaftsrechts*.

Hahn, Michael J. 1996. *Die einseitige Aussetzung von GATT-Verpflichtungen als Repressalie* (Berlin 1996).

Hilf, Meinhard 2000. 'Freiheit des Welthandels contra Umweltschutz?', *Neue Zeitschrift für Verwaltungsrecht* 481–90.

  2001. 'Power, Rules and Principles – Which Orientation for WTO/GATT Law?', *Journal of International Economic Law* 4(1): 111–30.

  2003. 'Die Konstitutionalisierung der Welthandelsordnung. Struktur, Institutionen und Verfahren', *Berichte der Deutschen Gesellschaft für Völkerrecht* 40: 257.

Hilf, Meinhard and Oeter, Stefan 2005. *WTO-Recht. Rechtsordnung des Welthandels* (Baden Baden).

Hilf, Meinhard and Puth, Sebastian 2002. 'The Principle of Proportionality on its Way into WTO/GATT Law', in Bogdandy, Mavroidis and Mény (eds.), *European Integration and International Co-ordination*, pp. 199–218.

Horlick, Gary N. and Clarke, Peggy A. 1994. 'The 1994 WTO Subsidies Agreement', *World Competition* 17(4): 41.

Howse, Robert 2002. 'The Appellate Body Rulings in the Shrimp/Turtle Case: A New Legal Baseline for the Trade and Environment Debate', *Columbia Journal of Environmental Law* 27: 491.

Howse, Robert and Nicolaidis, Kalypso 2003. 'Legitimacy through "Higher Law"? Why Constitutionalizing the WTO is a Step Too Far', in Cottier and Mavroidis (eds.), *Regulatory Barriers and the Principle of Non-Discrimination*, pp. 307–48.

Howse, Robert and Regan, Donald 2000. 'The Product/Process Distinction: An Illusory Basis for Disciplining "Unilateralism" in Trade Policy', *European Journal of International Law* 11(2): 249–89.

Howse, Robert and Trebilcock, Michael J. 1996. 'The Fair Trade-Free Trade Debate: Trade, Labour, and the Environment', *International Review of Law and Economics* 16: 61–79.

  2005. 'Trade Policy and Labor Standards', *Minnesota Journal of Global Trade* 14(2): 261–300.

Howse, Robert and Tuerk, Elisabeth 2006. 'The WTO Impact on Internal Regulations', in G. Bermann and P. Mavroidis (eds.), *Trade and Human Health and Safety*, p. 91.

Hudec, Robert E. 1990. *The GATT Legal System and World Trade Diplomacy*, 2nd edn. (Salem).

  1996. 'GATT Legal Restraints on the Use of Trade Measures against Foreign Environmental Practices', in Bhagwati and Hudec (eds.), *Fair Trade and Harmonization*, pp. 95–174.

  1998. 'GATT/WTO Constraints on National Regulation: Requiem for an "Aims and Effects" Test', *The International Lawyer* 32: 619–49, and in *Essays on the Nature of International Trade Law* (London, 1999).

  2000. 'The Product–Process Doctrine in GATT/WTO Jurisprudence', in Bronckers and Quick (eds.), *New Directions*, pp. 187–217.

  2002. '"Like Product": The Differences in Meaning in GATT Articles I and III', in Cottier and Mavroidis (eds.), *Regulatory Barriers*, pp. 101–23.

Hufbauer, Gary Clyde, Schott, Jeffrey J. and Elliot, Kimberly Ann 1990. *Economic Sanctions Reconsidered: History and Current Policy*, 2nd edn. (Washington, DC).

Humbert, Franziska 2009. *The Challenge of Child Labour in International Law* (Cambridge).

Hunter, David, Salzman, James and Zaelke, Durwood 2002. *International Environmental Law and Policy*, 2nd edn. (New York).

Husted, Steven and Melvin, Michael 2006. *International Economics*, 7th edn. (Boston, MA).

Hüller, Thorsten and Meier, Matthias Leonhard 2006. 'Fixing the Codex? Global Food Safety Governance under Review', in Christian Joerges and Ernst-Ulrich Petersmann (eds.), *Constitutionalism, Multilevel Trade Governance and Social Regulation* (Oregon), pp. 267–99.

Imkamp, Heiner 2000. 'The Interest of Consumers in Ecological Product Information is Growing – Evidence from Two German Surveys', *Journal of Consumer Policy* 23(2): 193–202.

Ipsen, Knut 2004. *Völkerrecht*, 5th edn. (Munich).

Isaac, Grant E. and Kerr, William A. 2003. 'Genetically Modified Organisms and Trade Rules: Identifying Important Challenges for the WTO', *The World Economy* 26: 29–42.

Iwasawa, Yuji 2002. 'WTO Dispute Settlement as Judicial Supervision', *Journal of International Economic Law* 5(2): 287–305.

Jackson, John H. 1969. *World Trade and the Law of GATT: A Legal Analysis of the General Agreement on Tariffs and Trade* (Charlottesville).

   1989. 'National Treatment Obligations and Non-Tariff Barriers', *Michigan Journal of International Law* 10: 207–24.

   1992. 'World Trade Rules and Environmental Policies: Congruence or Conflict?', *Washington and Lee Law Review* 49: 1227–78.

   1994. 'Greening the GATT: Trade Rules and Environmental Policy', in Cameron, Demaret and Geradin (eds.), *Trade and the Environment*, pp. 39–51.

   1997. *The World Trading System*, 2nd edn. (Cambridge).

   2000a. *The Jurisprudence of GATT and the WTO – Insights on Treaty Law and Economic Relations* (Cambridge).

   2000b. 'Comments on Shrimp/Turtle and the Product/Process Distinction', *European Journal of International Law* 11(2): 303–07.

   2000c. 'The Perils of Globalization and the World Trading System', *Fordham International Law Journal* 24: 371–82.

   2001. 'The WTO "Constitution" and Proposed Reforms: Seven "Mantras" Revisited', *Journal of International Economic Law* 67(4).

   2002. 'Afterword: The Linkage Problem-Comments on Five Texts', *American Journal of International Law* 96(1): 118–25.

   2003. 'Sovereignty-Modern: A New Approach to an Outdated Concept', *The American Journal of International Law* 97(4): 782–802.

   2005. 'The Role of International Law in Trade', *Georgetown Journal of International Law* 36(3): 663–67.

   2006. *Sovereignty, the WTO and Changing Fundamentals of International Law* (Cambridge).

James, Allan 1986. *Sovereign Statehood: The Basis of International Society* (London).

Jenny, Frédéric 2003. 'WTO Core Principles and Trade', *International Antitrust Law and Policy: Annual Proceedings of the Fordham Corporate Law Institute* 30: 703–61.

Joerges, Christian 2006. 'Constitutionalism in Postnational Constellations: Contrasting Social Regulation in the EU and in the WTO', in Joerges and Petersmann (eds.), *Constitutionalism, Mulitlevel Trade Governance and Social Regulation*, pp. 491–527.

Joerges, Christian and Petersmann, Ernst-Ulrich (eds.), *Constitutionalism, Multilevel Trade Governance and Social Regulation* (Oregon), pp. 5–58.

Joerges, Christian, Sand, Inger-Johanne and Teubner, Gunther 2004. *Transnational Governance and Constitutionalism* (Oxford).

Jones, Kent 2002. 'The WTO Core Agreement, Non-Trade Issues and Institutional Integrity', *World Trade Review* 1(3): 257-76.
Joshi, Manoj 2004. 'Are Eco-Labels Consistent with World Trade Organization Agreements?', *Journal of World Trade* 38(1): 69-92.
Kay, John and Vickers, John 1990. 'Regulatory Reform: An Appraisal', in Majone (ed.), *Deregulation or Re-Regulation?*, pp. 223-51.
Kelly, J. Patrick 2005. 'The Seduction of the Appellate Body: Shrimp/Sea Turtle I and II and the Proper Role of States in WTO Governance', *Cornell International Law Journal* 38: 459-91.
Kipel, Alice Alexandra 1996. 'Special and Differential Treatment for Developing Countries', in Stewart (ed.), *The World Trade Organization*, p. 617.
Koskenniemi, Martti and Leino, Päivi 2002. 'Fragmentation of International Law? Postmodern Anxieties', *Leiden Journal of International Law* 15: 553-79.
Koskenniemi, Martti and Mosley, Christopher 2004. 'The Work of the International Law Commission at its Fifty-Fifth Session', *Nordic Journal of International Law* 73(1): 99-134.
Krueger, Anne O. 1998. *The WTO as an International Organization* (Chicago).
Kube, Hanno 2001. *National Tax Law and the Transnational Control of State Aids*, EUI Working Paper LAW No. 2001/9.
Kuijper, Pieter Jan 1994. 'The Law of GATT as Special Field of International Law. Ignorance: Further Refinement or Self-contained System of International Law?', *Netherlands Yearbook of International Law* XXV: 227-57.
Kysar, Douglas A. 2004. 'Preferences for Processes: The Process/Product Distinction and the Regulation of Consumer Choice', *Harvard Law Review* 118: 525-642.
Lauterpacht, Hersch 1970. *International Law. Collected Papers: Vol. I* (Cambridge).
Lammenett, Klaus 1964. *Die Behandlung von Wohlstandseffekten in der reinen Theorie des internationalen Handels* (Mainz).
Leebron, David W. 2002. 'Linkages', *American Journal of International Law* 96(1): 5-27.
Lell, Ottmar 2004. 'Die neue Kennzeichnungspflicht für gentechnisch hergestellt Lebensmittel - ein Verstoß gegen das Welthandelsrecht?', *EuZW* 108-12
Lennard, Michael 2002. 'Navigating by the Stars: Interpreting the WTO Agreements', *Journal of International Economic Law* 5: 17-87.
Lopez-Hurtado, Carlos 2002. 'Social Labelling and the WTO', *Journal of International Economic* 5(3): 719-46.
Lopez-Mata, Rosendo 2001. 'Income Taxation, International Competitiveness and the World Trade Organization's Rules on Subsidies: Lessons to the US and to the World from the FSC Dispute', *Tax Lawyer* 54(3): 577-616.
Loureiro, Maria L. and Lotade, Justus 2004. 'Do Fair Trade and Eco-labels in Coffee Wake Up the Consumer Conscience?', *Ecological Economics* 53(1): 129-38.
Lowenfeld, Andreas 2002. *International Economic Law* (New York).

Lowi, Theodore 1986. *The Welfare State, the New Regulation, and the Rule of Law* (Siegen).

MacGowan, Daniel A. 1978. *Consumer Economics* (Chicago).

Macklem, Patrick 2002. 'Labour Law Beyond Borders', *Journal of International Economic Law* 5(3): 605–45.

Majone, Giandomenico (ed.) 1990a. *Deregulation or Re-Regulation? Regulatory Reform in Europe and the United States* (New York).

1990b. 'Introduction', in Majone (ed.), *Deregulation or Re-Regulation*.

1996a. *Regulating Europe* (London).

1996b. 'Regulation and its Modes', in Majone (ed.), *Deregulation or Re-Regulation*, pp. 9–27.

1996c. 'Theories of Regulation', in Majone (ed.), *Deregulation or Re-Regulation*, pp. 28–46.

1996d. 'The Rise of Statutory Regulation in Europe', in Majone (ed.), *Deregulation or Re-Regulation*, pp. 47–60.

1997. 'The New European Agencies: Regulation by Information', *Journal of European Public Policy* 4(2): 262–75.

Malanczuk, Peter 1997. *Akehurst's Modern Introduction to International Law*, 7th edn. (London).

Mankiw, Nicholas Gregory 2006. *Principles of Microeconomics*, 4th edn. (London).

Mann, Howard and Porter, Stephan 2003. *The State of Trade and Environment Law 2003. Implications for Doha and Beyond* (Winnipeg).

Manzini, Pietro 1999. 'Environmental Exceptions of Art. XX GATT 1994 Revisited in the Light of the Rules of Interpretation of General International Law', in Mengozzi (ed.), *International Trade Law on the 50th Anniversary of the Multilateral Trade System*, pp. 811–48.

Marceau, Gabrielle 1999. 'A Call for Coherence in International Law: Praises for the Prohibition Against "Clinical Isolation" in WTO Dispute Settlement', *Journal of World Trade* 33(5): 87–152.

2001. 'Conflicts of Norms and Conflicts of Jurisdictions. The Relationship between the WTO Agreement and MEAs and other Treaties', *Journal of World Trade* 35(6): 1081–131.

2002. 'WTO Dispute Settlement and Human Rights', *European Journal of International Law* 13(4): 753–813.

Marceau, Gabrielle and Trachtman, Joel P. 2002. 'The Technical Barriers to Trade Agreement, the Sanitary and Phytosanitary Measures Agreement, and the General Agreement on Tariffs and Trade. A Map of the World Trade Organization Law of Domestic Regulation of Goods', *Journal of World Trade* 36(5): 811–81.

Maskus, Keith 2002. Regulatory Standards in the WTO: Comparing Intellectual Property Rights with Competition Policy, Environmental Protection, and Core Labor Standards', *World Trade Review* 1(2): 135–52.

Matsushita, Mitsuo, Schoenbaum, Thomas J. and Mavroidis, Petros C. 2004. *The World Trade Organization: Law, Practice, and Policy* (Oxford).
Mattoo, Aaditya and Subramanian, Arvind 1998. 'Regulatory Autonomy and Multilateral Disciplines: the Dilemma and a Possible Resolution', *Journal of International Economic Law* 1(2): 303–22.
Mattoo, Aaditya and Sauvé, Pierre (eds.) 2003. *Domestic Regulation and Service Trade Liberalization*, The World Bank.
Mavroidis, Petros C. 2000a. 'Trade and Environment after the Shrimps-Turtles Litigation', *Journal of World Trade* 34(1): 73–88.
  2000b. 'Remedies in the WTO Legal System: Between a Rock and a Hard Place', *European Journal of International Law* 11(4): 763–813.
  2005. *The General Agreement on Tariffs and Trade. A Commentary* (New York).
  2007. *Trade in Goods. The GATT and the Other Agreements Regulating Trade in Goods* (New York).
Maynes, Scott E. 2003. 'Marketing – One Consumer Disaster', *The Journal of Consumer Affairs* 37(2): 196–207.
McCrudden, Christopher 1999. 'International and Economic Law and the Pursuit of Human Rights: A Framework for Discussion of the Legality of "Selective Purchasing" Laws under the WTO Government Procurement Agreement', *Journal of International Economic Law* 2: 3–48.
McCrudden, Christopher and Davies, Anne 2000. 'A Perspective on Trade and Labour Rights', *Journal of International Economic Law* 3: 43–62.
McEldowney, John 1995. 'Law and Regulation: Current Issues and Future Directions', in Bishop, Kay and Mayer (eds.), *The Regulatory Challenge*, pp. 408–23.
McLachlan, Campbell 2005. 'The Principle of Systemic Integration and Article 31(3)(c) of the Vienna Convention', *International and Comparative Law Quarterly* 54: 279–319.
McNair, Arnold Duncan 1986. *The Law of Treaties* (New York).
McRae, Donald 2000. 'GATT Article XX and the WTO Appellate Body', in Bronckers and Quick (eds.), *New Directions in International Economic Law*, pp. 219–36.
McRae, Peter 2002. 'The Search for Meaning: Continuing Problems with the Interpretation of Treaties', *Victoria University of Wellington Law Review* 33(2): 8.
Meng, Werner 1994. *Extraterritoriale Jurisdiktion im öffentlichen Wirtschaftsrecht* (Berlin).
Mengozzi, Paolo (ed.) 1999. *International Trade Law on the 50th Anniversary of the Multilateral Trade System* (Milan).
Mitchell, Andrew D. 2008. *Legal Principles in WTO Disputes* (Cambridge).
Mitnick, Barry 1980. *The Political Economy of Regulation* (New York).
Mosler, Herrmann 1980. *The International Society as a Legal Community* (Alphen aan den Rijn).

Motaal, Doaa Abdel 2002. 'The Agreement on Technical Barriers to Trade, the Committee on Trade and Environment, and Eco-labelling', in Sampson and Chambers (eds.), *Trade, Environment, and the Millennium*, pp. 267-85.

Murase, Shinya 1995. 'Perspectives from International Economic Law on Transnational Environmental Issues', *Recueil des Cours* (Collected Courses) 253: 283-431.

Murphy, Dale D. 2005. 'Interjurisdictional Competition and Regulatory Advantage', *Journal of International Economic Law* 8(4): 891-920.

Nadakavukaren Schefer, Krista 2010. *Social Regulation in the WTO. Trade Policy and International Legal Development* (Cheltenham).

Neumann, Jan and Türk, Elisabeth 2003. 'Necessity Revisited: Proportionality in World Trade Organization Law after Korea-Beef, EC-Asbestos and EC-Sardines', *Journal of World Trade* 37(1): 199-233.

Neumayer, Eric 2002. 'WTO Rules and Multilateral Environmental Agreements', in Gallagher and Werksman (eds.), *International Trade & Sustainable Development*, pp. 137-65.

Nielsen, Laura, *The WTO, Animals and PPMs* (Leiden).

Nivola, Pietro S. (ed.) 1997. *Comparative Disadvantages? Social Regulations and the Global Economy* (Washington).

Nordström, Hakan and Vaughan, Scott 1999. 'Special Studies: Trade and the Environment', WTO.

Nowotny, Ewald 1999. *Der öffentliche Sektor*, 4th edn. (Berlin).

Oesch, Matthias 2003a. 'Commentary on *EC - Asbestos*', *International Trade Law Reports* VI: 441-60.

2003b. *Standards of Review in WTO Dispute Resolution* (Oxford).

Ogus, Anthony 1992. 'Regulatory Law: Some Lessons from the Past', *Legal Studies* 12(1): 1-19.

Ogus, Anthony and Veljanovski, Cento (eds.) 1984. *Readings in the Economics of Law and Regulation* (Oxford).

Ohlhoff, Stefan 2003 'Streitbeilegung in der WTO', in Prieß and Berrisch (eds.), *WTO-Handbuch*, p. 677.

Olson, Mancur 1965. *The Logic of Collective Action: Public Goods and the Theory of Groups* (Cambridge, MA).

Ortino, Federico 2006. 'Treaty Interpretation and the WTO Appellate Body Report in *US-Gambling*: A Critique', *Journal of International Economic Law* 9: 117-48.

Oxley, Allan 2002. 'Environmental Trade Sanctions: What is at Stake?', *Policy* 18(4): 17-22.

Palmeter, David and Mavroidis, Petros C. 1998. 'The WTO Legal System: Sources of Law', *American Journal of International Law* 92: 398.

Pangestu, Mari 2000. 'Special and Differential Treatment in the Millennium: Special for Whom and How Different?', *The World Economy* 23(9): 1285-302.

Pauwelyn, Joost 2002. 'Cross-agreement Complaints before the Appellate Body: A Case Study of the EC – Asbestos Dispute', *World Trade Review* 1(1): 63–87.
  2003. *Conflict of Norms in Public International Law* (Cambridge, MA).
  2004. 'Diversity or Cacophony?: New Sources of Norms in International Law Symposium, Reply to Joshua Meltzer', *Michigan Journal of International Law* 25: 924–7.
  2006. 'Non-Traditional Patterns of Global Regulation: Is the WTO Missing the Boat?', in Joerges and Petersmann (eds.), *Constitutionalism, Multilevel Trade Governance and Social Regulation* (Oregon), pp. 199–227.
Petersmann, Ernst-Ulrich 1994. 'Trade and Environmental Protection: The Practice of GATT and the European Community Compared', in Cameron, Demaret and Geradin (eds.), *Trade and the Environment*, pp. 147–81.
  2000. 'Prevention and Settlement of International Trade Disputes between the European Union and the United States', *Tulane Journal of International and Comparative Law* 8: 233–60.
  2005a. 'Human Rights and International Trade Law: Defining and Connecting the Two Fields', in Cottier, Pauwelyn and Bürgi (eds.), *Human Rights and International Trade*, pp. 29–94.
  2005b. *Developing Countries in the Doha Round* (Florence).
  2006. 'Multilevel Trade Governance in the WTO Regime Requires Multilevel Constitutionalism', in Joerges and Petersmann (eds.), *Constitutionalism, Multilevel Trade Governance and Social Regulation*, pp. 5–58.
  2008. 'State Sovereignty, Popular Sovereignty and Individual Sovereignty, in Wenhua Shan, Penelope Simons and Dalvinder Singh (eds.), *Redefining Sovereignty in International Economic Law* (Oxford), pp. 27–60.
Pindyck, Robert and Rubinfeld, Daniel 2004, *Microeconomics* (New Jersey).
Porges, Amelia and Trachtman, Joel P. 2003. 'Robert Hudec and Domestic Regulation: The Resurrection of Aims and Effects', *Journal of World Trade* 37(4): 783–99.
Prieß, Hans-Joachim and Berrisch, Georg M. 2003. *WTO-Handbuch* (Munich).
Puth, Sebastian 2003. *WTO und Umwelt: Die Produkt-Prozess-Doktrin* (Berlin).
  2005. 'WTO und Umwelt', in Hilf and Oeter (eds.), *WTO-Recht*, § 30, pp. 577–600.
Quick, Reinhard 2000. 'The Community's Regulation on Leg-Hold Traps: Creative Unilateralism Made Compatible with WTO Law through Bilateral Negotiations?', in Bronckers and Quick (eds.), *New Directions in International Economic Law*, pp. 239–57.
Quick, Reinhard and Lau, Christian 2001. 'Kreativer Unilateralismus und die WTO – Die Tellereisen-Verordnung der EG im Lichte der "Shrimp/Turtle"-Entscheidung', *ZEuS* 4(1): 97–126.
  2003. 'Environmentally Motivated Tax Distinctions and WTO Law', *Journal of International Economic Law* 6(2): 419–58.

Raustiala, Kal 2000. 'Sovereignty and Multilateralism', *Chicago Journal of International Law* 1: 401.

Regan, Donald 2002. 'Regulatory Purpose and "Like Products" in Article III:4 of the GATT (With Additional Remarks on Article III:2)', *Journal of World Trade* 36(3): 443–78.

Rege, Vinod 1994. 'GATT Law and Environment-Related Issues Affecting the Trade of Developing Countries', *Journal of World Trade* 6: 95–169.

Reiterer, Michael 1994. 'The International Legal Aspects of Process and Production Methods', *World Competition Law and Economics Review* 17: 111–28.

Roessler, Frieder 1996. 'Diverging Domestic Policies and Multilateral Trade Integration', in Bhagwati and Hudec (eds.), *Fair Trade and Harmonization*, pp. 21–56.

1998. 'Domestic Policy Objectives and the Multilateral Trade Order: Lessons from the Past', in Krueger (ed.), *The WTO as an International Organization*, pp. 213–29.

Ruge, Nicole 2002. *Die Zulässigkeit staatlicher Umweltschutzsubventionen nach dem EG-Vertrag und dem GATT 1994/WTO Regelwerk* (Osnabrück).

Sampson, Gary P. and Chambers, W. Bradnee (eds.) 2002, *Trade, Environment, and the Millennium*, 2nd edn. (Tokyo).

Samuelson, Paul A. and Nordhaus, William D. 2005. *Economics*, 18th edn. (New York).

Sands, Philippe 2000. '"Unilateralism", Values, and International Law', *European Journal of International Law* 11(2): 291–302.

Schlagenhof, Markus 1995. 'Trade Measures Based on Environmental Processes and Production Methods', *Journal of World Trade* 29(6): 123–55.

Schlesinger, Arthur 1958. *The Age of Roosevelt. The Coming of the New Deal* (Boston, MA).

Schneider, Egon and Schapp, Friedrich E. 2006. *Logik für Juristen* (Munich).

Schneuwly, Philippe 2003. 'Sind Handelssanktionen ein geeignetes Mittel zur Durchsetzung von Arbeitsnormen? Eine Untersuchung der Wirksamkeit der Sozialklausel im US GSP', *Aussenwirtschaft* 58(1): 121–44.

Schoenbaum, Thomas 1992. 'Free International Trade and Protection of the Environment: Irreconcilable Conflict?', *American Journal of International Law* 86: 700–27.

1997. 'International Trade and Protection of the Environment: The Continuing Search for Reconciliation', *American Journal of International Law* 91(2): 268–313.

Schott, Jeffrey J. (ed.) 2000. *The WTO after Seattle* (Washington DC).

Selznick, Philip 1985. 'Focusing Organizational Research on Regulation', in Roger G. Noll (ed.), *Regulatory Policy and the Social Sciences* (Berkeley, CA), pp. 363–7.

Sen, Anindya 1999. *Microeconomics* (New Delhi).

Shaw, Malcolm 1997. *International Law*, 4th edn. (Cambridge).

Showalter, Stephanie 2005. 'The United States and Rising Shrimp Imports From Asia and Central America: An Economic or Environmental Issue?', *Vermont Law Review* 29: 847–75.

Sinclair, Ian 1984. *The Vienna Convention on the Law of Treaties*, 2nd edn. (Manchester).

Smith, Adam 1776. *An Inquiry into the Nature and Causes of the Wealth of Nations* (Edinburgh).

Steger, Debra P. 2002. 'Afterword: The "Trade and ..." Conundrum – A Commentary', *American Journal of International Law* 96(1): 135–45.

Stern, Louis L. 1971. 'Consumer Protection Via Increased Information', in David A. Aaker and George S. Day (eds.), *Consumerism* (New York), pp. 94–103.

Stern, Robert M. 2000. 'Labor Standards and Trade', in Bronckers and Quick (eds.), *New Directions in International Economic Law*, pp. 425–38.

Stewart, Terence P. (ed.) 1996. *The World Trade Organization* (Washington, DC).

Stigler, George J. 1975a. *The Citizen and the State* (Chicago).

1975b. 'The Process of Economic Regulation', in Stigler (ed.), *The Citizen and the State* (reprint from the *Antitrust Bulletin* 17(1), Spring 1972).

Stiglitz, Joseph E. 1975. 'Equilibrium in Product Markets with Imperfect Information', *American Economic Review* 339–45.

2003. 'Information and the Change in the Paradigm in Economics, Part 1', *The American Economist* 47(2): 6–26.

2004. 'Information and the Change in the Paradigm in Economics, Part 2', *The American Economist* 48(1): 17–49.

Stoll, Peter-Tobias and Schorkopf, Frank 2002. *WTO – Welthandelsordnung und Welthandelsrecht* (Cologne).

Swagler, Roger M. 1979. *Consumers and the Market* (Lexington).

Swinbank, Alan 2006. 'Like Products, Animal Welfare and the World Trade Organization', *Journal of World Trade* 40(4): 687–711.

Sykes, Alan O. 2003. The Economics of WTO Rules on Subsidies and Countervailing Measures, John M. Olin Law and Economics. Working Paper No. 186, Chicago Working Paper Series, May.

Teisl, Mario F. and Roe, Brian 1998. 'The Economics of Labeling: An Overview of Issues for Health and Environmental Disclosure', *Agricultural and Resource Economics Review* 140–50.

Thaggert, Henry L. 1994. 'A Closer Look at the Tuna-Dolphin Case: "Like Products" and "Extrajurisdictionality" in the Trade and Environment Context', in Cameron, Demaret and Geradin (eds.), *Trade and the Environment*, pp. 69–95.

Tietje, Christian 1995. 'Voluntary Eco-Labelling Programmes and Questions of State Responsibility in the WTO/GATT Legal System', *Journal of World Trade* 29(5): 123–58.

1998. *Normative Grundstrukturen der Behandlung nichttarifärer Handelshemmnisse in der WTO/GATT-Rechtsordnung* (Berlin).

2003. Das Übereinkommen über Technische Handelshemmnisse', in Prieß and Berrisch (eds.), *WTO-Handbuch*, pp. 273–326.

2006. 'Questionnaire International Economic Law', in Zimmermann and Hofmann (eds.), *Unity and Diversity in International Law* (Berlin).

Trachtman, Joel P. 2002. 'Institutional Linkage: Transcending "Trade and ..."', *American Journal of International Law* 96: 77–93.

2003. 'Lessons for the GATS from Existing WTO Rules on Domestic Regulation', in Mattoo and Sauvé (eds.), *Domestic Regulation and Service Trade Liberalization*, pp. 57–81.

2004. Book review: *Conflict of Norms in Public International Law*. By Joost Pauwelyn. *American Journal of International Law* 98: 855–61.

Vahrenkamp, Kai 1991. *Verbraucherschutz bei asymmetrischer Information. Informationsökonomische Analysen verbraucherpolitischer Maßnahmen* (Munich).

van Calster, Geert, *International and EU Trade Law: The Environmental Challenge* (London).

van Damme, Isabelle 2006. 'Sixth Annual WTO Conference: An Overview', *Journal of International Economic Law* 9(3): 749.

2009. *Treaty Interpretation by the WTO Appellate Body* (New York).

van den Bossche, Peter, Schrijver, Nico and Faber, Gerrit 2007. *Unilateral Measures addressing Non-Trade Concerns*, The Ministry of Foreign Affairs of the Netherlands, The Hague

van Scherpenberg, Jens and Thiel, Elke (eds.) 1998. *Towards Rival Regionalism? US and EU Regional Regulatory Regime Building* (Baden Baden).

Vázquez, Carlos Manuel 2003. 'Trade Sanctions and Human Rights – Past, Present, and Future', *Journal of International Economic Law* 6(4): 797–839.

Verdross, Alfred and Simma, Bruno 1984. *Universelles Völkerrecht: Theorie und Praxis*, 3rd edn. (Berlin).

Verhoosel, Gaetan 2002. *National Treatment and WTO Dispute Settlement* (Oxford).

Villiger, Mark E. 1985. *Customary International Law and Treaties* (Leiden).

Vogel, David 1997. 'Trouble for Us and Trouble for Them. Social Regulations as Trade Barriers', in Nivola (ed.), *Comparative Disadvantages?*, pp. 98–145.

Vranes, Erich 2009a. *Trade and the Environment. Fundamental Issues in International Law, WTO Law, and Legal Theory* (Oxford).

2009b. 'The WTO and Regulatory Freedom: WTO Disciplines on Market Access, Non-Discrimination and Domestic Regulation Relating to Trade in Goods and Services', *Journal of International Economic Law* 12(4): 953–87.

Wallace, Rebecca M. M. 2002. *International Law*, 4th edn. (London).

Ward, Halina and Brack, Duncan (eds.) 2000. *Trade, Investment and the Environment* (London).

Westen, Peter 1983. 'The Meaning of Equality in Law, Science, Math, and Morals: A Reply', *Michigan Law Review* 81: 604–63.
Wiers, Jochen 2001. 'WTO Rules and Environmental Production and Processing Methods (PPMs)', *ERA Forum, scripta iuris europaei* 4: 101–11.
Wilcox, William K. 1998. 'GATT-based Protectionism and the Definition of a Subsidy', *Boston University International Law Journal* 16: 129–63.
Winerman, Marc 2003. 'The Origins of the FTC: Concentration, Cooperation, Control, and Competition', *Antitrust Law Journal* 71(1): 1–97.
Winter, Gerd 2003. 'The GATT and Environmental Protection: Problems of Construction', *Journal of Environmental Law* 1592: 113–40.
Wirth, David A. 1995. 'The Rio Declaration on Environment and Development: Two Steps Forward, and One Back, or Vice Versa?', *Georgia Law Review* 29: 599–652.
Woolcock, Stephen 1998. 'European and North American Approaches to Regulation: Continued Divergence?', in van Scherpenberg and Thiel (eds.), *Towards Rival Regionalism?*, pp. 257–76.
Youssef, Hesham 1999. 'Special and Differential Treatment for Developing Countries in the WTO', T.R.A.D.E. Working Papers No. 2, Southcentre, June.
Zeitler, Helge Elisabeth 2000. *Einseitige Handelsbeschränkungen zum Schutz extraterritorialer Rechtsgüter* (Baden Baden).
Zrecny, Alan Isaac 1994. 'The Process/Product Distinction and the Tuna/Dolphin Controversy: Greening the GATT through International Agreement', *Buffalo Journal of International Law* 1: 79–133.

Official documents

GATT 1995. *Guide to GATT Law and Practice: Analytical Index: Vol. I*, 6th edn, Geneva (GATT Analytical Index).
GATT Secretariat 1971. Note 'Industrial Pollution Control and International Trade', L/3538, 9 June.
GATT Secretariat 1992. *Trade and the Environment*, Study GATT/1529, 12 February.
OECD 1994. *Trade and Environment: Processes and Production Methods, 1994* (OECD).
OECD 1997. *Processes and Production Methods, 1997* (OECD).
World Commission on Environment and Development, Report 1987. *Our Common Future*, in General Assembly Resolution A/RES 42/187, 96th Plenary Meeting, 11 December (Brundtland Report).
UNICEF 1997. *The State of the World's Children 1997*, Carol Bellamy (UNICEF).
WTO 2007. *Analytical Index, Guide to WTO Law and Practice*, 2nd edn., available at www.wto.org/english/res_e/booksp_e/analytic_index_e/analytic_index_e.htm (WTO Analytical Index).

WTO 2007b. *Matrix on Trade Measures Pursuant to Selected Multilateral Environmental Agreements*, Note by the Secretariat, WT/CTE/W/160/Rev.4, TN/TE/S/5/Rev.2, 14 March (WTO).

WTO 2010. *Understanding the WTO*, 4th edn. (WTO).

WTO Secretariat 2004. *Trade and Environment: Background Document*, April (WTO).

INDEX

AAA. *See* Agricultural Adjustment Administration
abus de droit, 125
actionable subsidies, 50
AD Agreement. *See* Anti-Dumping Agreement
administrative support requirements for NPA measures, 369–72
Agenda 21, 129, 252
Agricultural Adjustment Administration (AAA), US, 76
aims and effects theory, 206–22
    concept of, 206–7
    conclusions regarding, 245
    controversial nature of, 206n.289
    criteria for, 208–9
    critique of, 220–2
    diverse forms of, 211
    indirect taxation and NPAs, 42, 43
    NPA measures, significance for, 211–12
    objective or traditional approach, perceived problems with, 207
    protective effects of measure, 208
    as public policy approach, 220, 237
    rationale for, 207, 237
    regulatory aims, relevance of, 221–2
    regulatory purpose, identification of, 208
    scope and relevance of, 41n.133, 209–10
    in WTO adjudication, 212–20
        Canada – Periodicals (1997), 218
        Dominican Republic – Import and Sale of Cigarettes (2005), 219
        EC – Asbestos (2001), 219
        EC – Bananas (1997), 215–18
        EC – Biotech (2006), 220
        Japan – Alcoholic Beverages (1996), 214–15
        Japan – Film (1998), 218
        Tuna-Dolphin disputes, 212
        US – Malt Beverages (1992), 213–14
        US – Taxes on Automobiles (1994), 214–15
amendment of WTO Agreement texts, reform proposals regarding, 438
Anderson, Kym, 429n.4, 430, 438
Anti-Dumping (AD) Agreement, 46–8, 238n.380
anti-dumping duties, 46–8
applicability of WTO and other international law to NPA measures, 119–46
    conclusions regarding, 487
    conflicts of law. *See* conflicts between WTO and other international law instruments
    general applicability of international law versus applicability of specific treaties; 124–8, inherent relationship of NPA measure to matter other than trade or tradable good; 119, international treaty obligations, likelihood of relationship of NPA measure to; 119, 129, interpretive tool, international law as; 122, jurisdictional issues121
    lack of clarity in WTO law regarding applicable sources, 125

applicability of WTO and other
international law to NPA
measures (*cont.*)
no preclusion of applicability of
one international regime by
applicability of another, 121
relevance of conventional
international law in WTO
disputes, 121–2, 124–8
requirements for WTO law to be
applicable, 120–1
self-contained regime, WTO not
regarded as, 122–4, 141, 487
state responsibility, customary
international law on, 140–5
TBT Agreement, applicability of.
See *under* TBT Agreement
Article XX chapeau. See chapeau,
Article XX
Article XX general exceptions.
See justification of NPA
measures under general
exceptions asymmetric impact
test for detrimental treatment
241–4, 246
asymmetrical conflicts between WTO
and other international law
instruments, 133–4
Austrian school of economic thought,
84n.64
average cross-price supply
substitutability rate of the
concerned industry (IASR
standard), 225n.339

Bacchus, James, 261n.54
balancing requirements
chapeau, Article XX, balancing
of rights and interests
requirement attributed to,
347–9
of TBT Agreement, 397
weighing and balancing approach to
public morals exception, 331–8,
332n.303, 343, 397
Bartels, Lorand, 123n.10, 141,
280n.126, 304, 306n.218
Bates v. State Bar of Arizona (USC,
1977), 400n.75

Bhagwati, Jagdish, 429, 437
Bodansky, Daniel, 109
border tax adjustments, 43–6
exports, 45–6
general exceptions, interpretation
of, 457n.9
imports, 44–5
'like products' concept and, 45,
172–3, 207
national regulation, combined with,
455, 457
Border Tax Adjustments, Report of
Working Party on
'like products' determinations and,
172–3, 204, 207
national treatment obligations, 158
bovine spongiform encephalopathy
(BSE), 72–4
Boyce, James K., 432, 453n.4, 459,
464, 467
Brack, Duncan, 434
Britain, rail transportation in, 81
British Independent Television
Agency, 79
British Monopolies and Merger
Commission, 79
Brundtland report, 94, 94n.92
Bundeskartellamt, German, 79
Bürgi, Elisabeth, 371

CAC. See Codex Alimentarius
Commission
Chang, Seung Wha, 387n.47
chapeau, Article XX, 54–5,
345–72
balancing of rights and interests
requirement attributed to,
347–9
conclusions regarding, 489
disguised restriction on
international trade, prohibition
on, 349, 350, 351
due process requirements, 359–61,
366
environmental measures failing
requirements of, 434
good faith principle (reasonable
application requirement)
in, 346

negotiations, good faith efforts at, 362–4, 366–7
non-discrimination requirements under, 54–5, 349–61
   arbitrary and unjustifiable discrimination, prohibition on, 349–51
   different conditions in different countries affecting, 353–5, 367, 372
   distinguished from non-discrimination principle of primary GATT obligations, 352
   NPA measures, relevant characteristics of, 365
   SDT principle, 354, 356n.375, 369, 371
   'unavoidable' standard of justifiability, 352
NPA measures, specific requirements for, 365–72
   consultations and negotiations, 366–7
   implementation periods, 367–9
   relevant characteristics of NPA measures, 364–6
   technology transfers and administrative and financial support, 369–72
objectives and purpose stressed more than ordinary meaning of terms, 346
per se violations of, 274
public morals exception necessity requirement viewed as determinable under, 338–9
regulation-based perspective, consistency between national regulation and WTO measures under, 481
SPS Agreement and, 419
on unilateralism, 361–2
Charnovitz, Steve, xviii, 106, 284–99, 303, 371, 433, 437, 465n.29
Charter of Economic Rights and Duties of States (1974), 276
Charter of Fundamental Rights of the European Union (2007), 381n.24

Cheyne, Ilona, 412n.118
Chicago school of economic thought, 84n.64
Cho, Sungjoon, 442
Choi, Won-Mog, 224–5, 225n.337
classical free market theory, 84–5
Cleveland, Sarah H., 292, 307
climate change, collective action required to address, 454
Codex Alimentarius Commission (CAC), 462, 462n.21
collective action, international trade side-effects requiring, 454
commercial freedom of speech, 398–404
Commission technique des ententes et des positions dominantes, France, 79
comparative advantage, theory of, 99, 429, 453, 458, 464
competitive markets
   international trade, NPA measures affecting, 110–12
   'like products' concept and. *See* 'market-based or economic approaches' under 'like products' concept
   national regulatory dilemma and, 458–61
   regulations safeguarding, 86
   WTO agreements on efficiency of, 99
compulsory labelling, 393–4, 412n.117, 413, 414
conflicts between WTO and other international law instruments, 128–40
   asymmetrical conflicts, 133–4
   CITES example, 135–6, 137
   conflict rule in General Interpretive Note to Annex IA, 414–15
   defining existence of conflict, 128–32
   prevailing conflict rules, 132–3
   symmetrical conflicts, 134–8
   TBT Agreement and GATT, relationship between, 414–15

congruence of WTO membership and state signatories within disputes, 255–7
consistency of national regulation and WTO measures. *See under* regulation-based perspective on NPA measures
consistency of NPA measures with GATT obligations, 147–246
  conclusions regarding, 244–6
  detrimental treatment, determining, 240–4, 246
  justification arguments tending to supersede, 147–8
  'like products', 149, 168–9. *See also* 'like products' concept
  national treatment obligations, 148, 149–62. *See also* national treatment obligations
  non-discrimination principle, 149, 162–8. *See also* non-discrimination principle
consistency of standards and use of public morals exception, 351n.360, 355, 355n.372
'constitutionalization', reform proposals regarding, 444–5, 446, 448
consultation and negotiation
  good faith effort requirement under chapeau, 362–4, 366–7
  NPA measures, specific requirements for, 366–7
consumer information, 396–412
  conclusions regarding, 410
  as disguised restriction on international trade, 398–404, 481
  free market, as precondition for functioning of, 405–10
  as internationally recognized value, 398–404
  legitimacy of objectives and, 397–412
  national regulations on, 382n.26
  no more trade restrictive than necessary requirement regarding, 412–14

  regulation-based perspective on market failures, addressing, 474–5
  market imperfections, addressing, 470–2, 483
  UN Guidelines on Consumer Protection, 381n.24, 402–4
consumer preference in determination of 'like products', 172, 173, 236
consumption, regulation of, 72
Contingent Valuation Analysis on Proportional Cross-Price-Demand Substitutability (CVA-PCPDS), 225, 225n.337, 225n.339
Convention on Biological Diversity (1993), 252
Convention on International Trade in Endangered Species of Wild Flora and Fauna (CITES, 1963), conflicts with WTO law, 135–6, 137
Convention Relative to the Preservation of Fauna and Flora in their Natural State (1936), 304
Corporate Average Fuel Economy law (CAFE), US, 186–7
Cottier, Thomas, 329n.297, 371, 432, 434, 443, 444–5
counter-measures under customary international law, NPA measures as, 140–5
cross-price elasticity, 225n.337, 227, 229, 233
cultural differences and similarities on consumer information, 398–404
regulatory cultures. *See under* national regulation and NPAs
customs tariffs, 32–6
  international rules other than GATT relating to, 33–5
  MFN obligations, 35
  NPAs, as basis for tariffs under Article II, 32–3

de lege ferenda suggestions regarding NPA measures linked to PPMs in WTO law. *See* reform proposals
de lege lata review of NPA measures linked to PPMs in WTO law, 57
Deardorff, Alan V., 87n.72
decision-making, reform proposals for allocation of, 445–6
Declaration on Fundamental Principles and Rights at Work (ILO, 1998), 314n.246, 315, 435
demand substitutability, 225n.337, 234
denial of competence, different arguments for, 428–32
deregulation
  in European Union/Western Europe, 80–1
  in United States, 77, 82
Desmedt, Axel, 336n.322
detrimental treatment and NPA measures, 240–4, 246
developing countries, special and differential treatment of. *See* SDT principle
diagonal test for detrimental treatment, 240
different conditions in different countries principle under chapeau, Article XX, 353–5, 367, 372
discrimination. *See* entries at non-discrimination
  chapeau prohibition on, 349, 350, 351
  consumer information requirements as, 398–404, 481
distributional issues
  congruence/consistency of distributive regulation with WTO objectives, 478–81, 483
  international trade, distributive side-effects of, 453
  national regulation to obtain distributional objectives, 90–1

Dog and Cat Protection Act (2009), US, 320n.275
Doha Ministerial Declaration of 2001, 95, 101n.113
domestic regulation. *See* national regulation and NPAs
DSU (Understanding on Rules and Procedures Governing Settlement of Disputes)
  applicability of international law norms specifically mentioned in, 125–7
  countermeasures authorized by, 142, 143
  institutionalized links to international law in, 123
  jurisdictional issues, 121
due process requirements of chapeau, Article XX, 359–61, 366

eco-dumping, 46
eco-labels, 40n.127, 387n.46, 397, 418
economic theory. *See also* competitive markets; free market economy; market failures
  comparative advantage, 99, 429, 453, 458, 464
  of consumer information, 405–10
  denial of WTO competence according to, 429
  'invisible hand', 405n.95, 406
  'like products' and. *See under* 'like products' concept
  multilateral trading system, rationales for, 98–100
  of national regulation. *See under* national regulation and NPAs
  'race to the bottom' arguments and counter-arguments, 459–60
editorial content and 'like content' determinations, 197–200
egg labelling, EU regulatory framework on, 374–84, 393, 397, 417–18
Ehring, Lothar, 241, 243–4
end-use in determination of 'like products', 172, 236

environmental protection
  ability of international trade rules to account for environmental production costs, 1
  chapeau, Article XX, failing requirements of, 434
  concept of social regulation aimed at, 68–70
  denial of competence, economic argument for, 429
  eco-labels, 40n.127, 387n.46, 397, 418
  'exhaustible natural resources', particular exception for, 312n.235, 313, 372
  global warming, collective action required to address, 454
  greenhouse gas emission allowance trading scheme, EU, 475
  international trade and national regulation, nexus between, 103
  'like product' determinations
    based on environmental impacts, 200–1
    based on genetic modifications, 203–4
    based on toxicity/risk differences, 201–3
  location of protected objects, jurisdiction over, 104–6
  national regulation
    distributive regulations, 478–81
    market failure, addressing, 469–81
    in pursuit of distributional or social objectives, 91
  NPA measures involving. See NPA measures linked to PPMs in WTO law
  objectives and purposes of WTO, environmental damage not in line with, 462
  under particular exceptions, 311–13
  public morals exception and ordinary environmental damage, 457n.9
  reform proposals regarding, 432, 434

  sanitary and phytosanitary measures. See SPS Agreement
  side-effect of international free trade, pollution as, 453
  sustainable development, as WTO objective, 94, 94n.91
UNEP, 428
Environmental Protection Agency (EPA), US, 77, 186
equality before the law, chapeau viewed as enshrining, 354
equilibrium result of free market as Pareto-efficiency, 83, 83n.61, 87, 478
erga omnes obligations, priority of, 132
Esty, Daniel C., 435, 460
Euphorbia trigona, 139–40
European Action Plan for Forest Law Enforcement, Governance and Trade (FLEGT), 298n.185
European Court of Justice, 82
European Union/Western Europe. *See also* specific countries
  anti-cartel laws, 80
  Charter of Fundamental Rights of the European Union, 381n.24
  consumer information and commercial free speech in, 381n.24, 401
  egg labelling, regulatory framework on, 374–84, 393, 397, 417–18
  greenhouse gas emission allowance trading scheme, 475
  Oilseeds Agreement, 256
  public morals exception, state practice regarding, 321
  regulatory culture in, 66, 67, 78–83
  services, trade in, 102
  Treaty of Paris establishing European Coal and Steel Community, 80
  Treaty of Rome establishing European Economic Community, 80
exceptiones sunt strictissimae interpretationis, 251
exceptions. *See* justification of NPA measures under general

exceptions; particular
        exceptions
'exhaustible natural resources',
        particular exception for,
        312n.235, 313, 372
exports, border tax adjustments for,
        45–6
expressio unius est exclusio alterius,
        262
extraterritoriality
    alternative approaches
        to, 305–8
    conclusions regarding, 485
    customary international law
        governing, 277–81, 305
    geographical scope of Article XX as
        issue of. *See* geographical scope
        of Article XX
    international trade and NPA
        measures, 106–8
    legitimate state interest as
        determinant of, 306
    NPA measures, relevant
        characteristics of, 365
    particular exceptions and, 53–4
    sovereignty and extraterritorial
        jurisdiction, 277–81

Faber, Gerrit, 411n.115, 472n.38
FDA. *See* Food and Drug
        Administration
Feddersen, Christoph T., 285, 324, 325,
        326n.289, 330–1
Federal Trade Commission (FTC),
        US, 75
fees and taxes. *See* taxes and fees
financial support requirements for
        NPA measures, 369–72
First Amendment protection of
        commercial free speech, 399,
        404
Food and Drug Administration (FDA),
        US, 400
Foreign Trade Act (1992),
        India, 166
France, Commission technique des
        ententes et des positions
        dominantes, 79

free market economy
    consumer information as
        precondition for functioning
        of, 405–10
    liberalization of trade as WTO
        means rather than objective
        in, 451
    nature of, 83
    neo-classical/neo-liberal theory of,
        84–5, 429, 473n.40
    WTO Agreements on efficiency of, 99
free speech, commercial, 398–404
free trade
    social regulation in terms of, 70
    as WTO means rather than
        objective, 451
Frowein, Jochen A., 144
FTC. *See* Federal Trade Commission

General Agreement on Tariffs and
        Trade (GATT), NPA measures
        linked to PPMs under. *See* NPA
        measures linked to PPMs in
        WTO law
General Agreement on Trade in
        Services (GATS), 57–9, 101–2,
        478n.47
general exceptions. *See* justification of
        NPA measures under general
        exceptions
genetically modified organisms
        (GMOs) and 'like content'
        determinations, 203–4, 392n.57
geographical scope of Article XX, 281
    alternative approaches to, 305–8
    conclusions regarding, 308–9
    GATT and WTO case law on,
        insufficiency of, 283–4
    legitimate state interest as
        determinant of, 306
    negotiating history as means of
        clarifying, 302–5
    object and purpose of Article XX
        shedding light on, 300–2
    in particular exceptions, 283
        direct references, 283–4
        foreign versus shared resources,
            295–7

geographical scope of Article XX (cont.)
  means–end relationship, indirect references involving, 286–94
  national restrictions, measures required to be in conjunction with, 295–9
  'necessary', use of, 286–8
  'relating to' or 'imposed for', use of, 288–90, 299
  public morals exception, 323–6
  sovereignty principle not violated by, 282
  SPS Agreement and, 293n.175
Germany
  anti-cartel laws, 80
  Bundeskartellamt, 79
  rail transportation in, 81
  trade and services deregulation in, 81
global warming, collective action required to address, 454
globalized market failure, regulation-based proposal to counter. *See* regulation-based perspective on NPA measures
globalized market, NPA measures in. *See* NPA measures linked to PPMs in WTO law
GMOs. *See* genetically modified organisms
good faith principle (reasonable application requirement) in chapeau, Article XX, 346
goods, focus on trade in, 57–60
governance, multi-level, reform proposals regarding, 440, 443–8
government (public) procurement, NPAs in, 59–60
GPA Agreement, 59
Great Britain. *See* entries at Britain and British
greenhouse gas emission allowance trading scheme, EU, 475
Guzman, Andrew T., 440

harmonization of rules, WTO reform proposals regarding, 435–6
Harmonized System (HS), 33–5, 36, 172, 257
health. *See* human life and health
Hertig, Maya, 444–5
Hong Kong Ministerial Conference (2005), 436
horizontal test for detrimental treatment, 240
Howse, Robert, 108, 280n.126, 329n.296, 435, 442
HS. *See* Harmonized System
Hudec, Robert E., 25, 26, 29, 61, 209
human life and health
  'like content' determinations, health risk levels as basis for, 201–3
  particular exception for, 302, 314, 332n.303
  sanitary and phytosanitary measures. *See* SPS Agreement
human rights
  institutional reform proposals regarding, 441, 442
  particular exception for, 313, 372

IASR standard (average cross-price supply substitutability rate of the concerned industry), 225n.339
ICJ. *See* International Court of Justice
ILO. *See* International Labour Organization
IMF. *See* International Monetary Fund
implementation periods for NPA measures, 367–9
imports
  anti-dumping duties, 46–8
  border tax adjustments, 44–5
  national regulations and international trade, nexus between, 103–4
  prohibitions and restrictions on, 36–8
  'imposed for', indirect references to geographical scope in use of, 288–90
  incongruence of WTO membership and state signatories within disputes, 257

information polices and regulations.
    See consumer information
institutional issues
    denial of competence, institutional
        arguments for, 431
    market failures
        competent political body to
            address, determining, 476
        lack of international institutions
            for dealing with, 461–3
        reform proposals for institutional
            changes, 440–3
intellectual property rights, TRIPS
    Agreement on, 96, 429, 437
Inter-American Convention for the
    Protection and Conservation
    of Sea Turtles (2001), 362.
    See also Shrimp Turtle
internal regulation. *See* national
    regulation
international collective action
    international trade side-effects
        requiring, 454
International Convention on the
    Harmonized Commodity
    Description and Coding System
    of the WCO (1983), 33–5
International Court of Justice (ICJ),
    126, 448
International Covenant for the
    Abolition of Import and Export
    Prohibitions and Restrictions
    (1927), 303
International Dairy Foods Association
    v. *Amestoy* (US 2nd Circuit,
    1996), 390n.51, 402
International Labour Organization
    (ILO), 314n.246, 315, 428, 431,
    435, 441
international law
    applicability to NPA measures.
        See applicability of WTO and
        other international law to NPA
        measures
    conflicts with WTO Agreements.
        See conflicts between WTO
        and other international law
        instruments

interpretation of Article XX
    regarding general exceptions,
    relevance for, 249
treaty obligations, likelihood of
    relationship of NPA measure
    to, 119
International Monetary Fund (IMF),
    442
international trade and NPA measures,
    92
    design parameters of multilateral
        trading system, 100
    economic rationales for,
        98–100
    identifying objectives of WTO
        agreements, 92–5
    relevance of objectives of WTO
        agreements, 96
    multilateral agreements, NPA
        measures in, 106
    national regulation and, 100–4
        GATT provisions regarding,
            100
        imports, NPA measures applied
            to, 103–4
        WTO awareness of issues related
            to, 100–3
    political aspects of, 104–12
        competitiveness, 110–12
        location of protected objects,
            jurisdiction over, 104–6
        sovereignty and
            extraterritoriality, 106–8
        unilateralism, 107, 108–10
international trade, disguised
    restriction on
    chapeau prohibition on, 349, 350,
        351
    consumer information requirements
        as, 398–404, 481
international trade liberalization
    social regulation in terms of, 70
    as WTO means rather than
        objective, 451
International Trade Organization
    (ITO), 302, 304
international trade, side-effects of,
    453–4

interpretation of Article XX regarding general exceptions, 249
border tax adjustments and, 457n.9
chapeau, objectives and purpose stressed more than ordinary meaning of terms in, 346
in GATT and WTO case law, 251, 252–4
restrictive interpretation, rejection of, 266–7
signatories-based approach, 254–8
static versus evolutionary interpretation, 267
VCLT, use of, 252–4
inter se understandings, 264–5
international law guidelines for, 249
objective approach, 258
advantages of, 263
nature of interpretation versus rule-making and, 258–9
ordinary meaning of terms, use of international instruments in determining, 260–3
reform proposals regarding, 433, 436–7
restrictive interpretation principle, rejection of, 265–7
signatories-based approach, 254–8
advantages of objective approach over, 263
congruence within disputes, 255–7
incongruence within disputes, 257
static versus evolutionary approach to, 267–8
textualism, predominance of, 251, 266–7
VCLT, use of, 250
in GATT and WTO case law, 252–4
ordinary meaning of terms, use of international instruments in determining, 262, 263
signatories-based approach, 255
static versus evolutionary interpretation, 267

Interstate Commerce Commission, US, 75
'invisible hand', 405n.95, 406
Iran v. *United States* (*Oil Platforms* case; ICJ, 2003), 262n.60
Island of Palmas case (Permanent Court of Arbitration, 1928), 275n.105
ITO. *See* International Trade Organization
ius cogens
means–end relationships and geographic scope of Article XX, 292
NPA measures justified as, 145, 146
priority in conflicts of laws, 132
sovereignty principle, objections to justification of NPA measures under general exceptions based on, 275–81
state responsibility rules not regarded as, 142, 143

Jackson, John H., 94, 445–6, 449–50, 461
Jones, Kent, 431
jurisdiction
extraterritorial, 277–81
legitimate state interest as determinant of, 306
NPA measures, relevant characteristics of, 365
over WTO disputes, 121
reform proposals for transfer of, 426
sovereignty, as central feature of, 277
justification of NPA measures under general exceptions, 52–5, 247–373
chapeau requirements. *See* chapeau, Article XX
conclusions regarding, 372, 488
consistency of measures with GATT obligations primary to, 147–8
geographical scope of Article XX and. *See* geographical scope of Article XX
interpretation of Article XX regarding. *See* interpretation of

Article XX regarding general exceptions
'like products' concept linked to, 246
objections to, 269–72
   chapeau, *per se* violations of, 274
   conclusions regarding, 278
   irreconcilability with WTO objectives and purposes, 272–3
   on sovereignty grounds, 270–1, 275–81
   vagueness of, 271
under public morals exception. *See* public morals exception
public policy focus of, 247
reform proposals regarding, 433–4
sovereignty, general exceptions as means of protecting, 247, 301
subject matter coverage under particular exceptions, 309–10. *See also* particular exceptions
public morals exceptions, openness of, 317–21

Kennedy, John F., 398
Kiel Canal (*SS Wimbledon*) case (PCIJ, 1923), 122n.6, 124
Kyoto Protocol, 475n.44
Kysar, Douglas A., 382, 403

labelling requirements
   applicability of TBT Agreement to, 377, 381–9
   coverage with respect to labelling of PPMs and NPAs, 385
   EU regulatory framework on egg labelling, 374–84
   NPAs other than PPMs, 388–9
   unincorporated PPMs, 382–3, 385–8
   compulsory, 393–4, 413, 414
   consumer information issues. *See* consumer information
   defined, 381
   eco-labels, 40n.127, 387n.46, 397, 418
   legitimacy of objectives regarding, 397–412

'like products', references to, 390–3, 392n.57
national regulations, 396n.65
per se illegality of labelling requirements relating to unincorporated PPMs, rejection of, 389–93
PPM debate, increasing importance of, 25
proportionality test, 412n.118
SDT principle, 415–18
SPS Agreement coverage of packaging and labelling requirements directly related to food safety, 419, 421
technical regulations and standards distinguished, 381
voluntary, 394, 411n.115, 413–14
labour standards
   denial of competence, arguments for, 431
   particular exception for, 313, 314n.246
   reform proposals regarding, 434–5, 441, 442
laissez-faire economics, 84
Lamy, Pascal, 358
Lauterpacht, Sir Hersch, 127
least trade-restrictiveness test
   public morals exception, 330–1, 341
   TBT Agreement
      balancing legitimate objective with trade-restrictiveness under, 397
      necessity, 412–14
      technical regulations and standards, 394
Leebron, David W., 432
legitimate state interest, 306
Lell, Ottmar, 392n.57
Lennard, Michael, 255
'level the playing field' arguments, 462
lex posterior derogat legi priori, 132, 135–7, 145

lex specialis
  conflicts of law and, 133, 137–8, 145–6
  counter-measures in WTO law as, 141, 145
  NPA measures falling under scope of TBT and SPS Agreements as, 374
  self-contained regimes as subcategory of principle of, 122
  WTO Agreements viewed as, 307
liberalization of trade
  social regulation in terms of, 70
  as WTO means rather than objective, 451
life and health. *See* human life and health
'like countries' rule, non-discrimination requirements under chapeau, Article XX, 353–5, 367, 372
'like products' concept, 149, 168–9
  aims and effects theory of. *See* aims and effects theory
  anti-dumping duties and, 46
  border tax adjustments and, 45, 172–3, 207
  comparison of different approaches to, 236–9
  conclusions regarding, 236–9, 244–6, 485, 487
  conflict of laws and, 138–9, 140
  consumer preference in determination of likeness, 172, 173, 236
  crucial nature of, 56, 61, 237
  defining, 38, 179n.127
  end-use in determination of likeness, 172, 236
  environmental protection and. *See under* environmental protection
  general exceptions, linked to interpretation of, 246
  indirect taxation and, 42
  labelling requirements and, 390–3, 392n.57
  market-based or economic approaches to, 222–36
    advantages of, 226
    conclusions regarding, 245–6
    critique of, 232–6
    cross-price elasticity, 225n.337, 227, 229, 233
    CVA-PCPDS, 225, 225n.337, 225n.339
    NPA measures, significance for, 226–7
    rationale for, 223–5, 237, 238
    traditional or objective approach compared, 232
    in WTO adjudication, 228–32
  MFN and national treatment, importance to, 148
  non-discrimination principle applicable only to 'like products', 164–5
  NPAs used to determine applicability of, 167–8
  objective determination approach of DSB. *See* objective determination of 'like products'
  physical characteristics as criterion. *See* physical characteristics in determination of 'like products'
  reform proposals regarding, 433
  SCM Agreement on, 229n.359
  subsidies and, 51
  substitutability, 42, 199–200, 223–5, 225n.337, 227, 229n.359, 230, 232, 234, 238, 239
  tariff classification as criterion, 175–6, 236, 237
  TBT Agreement and, 55, 390–3, 392n.57
  traditional criteria for. *See* objective determination of 'like products'
  in *Tuna-Dolphin* II, 15
Lomé Convention (1975), 131
Lowi, Theodore, 77

mad cow disease (bovine spongiform encephalopathy or BSE), 72–4
Majone, Giandomenico, 67, 78, 82
mandatory labelling, 393–4, 412n.117, 413, 414
Mann, F. A., 305
Marceau, Gabrielle, 127n.37, 255

INDEX

Marine Mammal Protection Act (MMPA, 1972), US, *Tuna-Dolphin* disputes and. *See Tuna-Dolphin* disputes
market-based approaches to 'like products'. *See under* 'like products' concept
market economy. *See* free market economy
market failures
  distributive regulations addressing, 480
  economic case for national regulation of, 84–5, 88–90
  international trade, linked to, 452–66
  lack of international institutions for dealing with, 461–3
  objectives and purposes of WTO, not in line with, 462
  regulation-based perspective as means of addressing. *See under* regulation-based perspective on NPA measures
Marrakesh Agreement (1994)
  authoritative interpretations, adoption of, 438
  conflicts between WTO and other international law instruments, 129, 131
  external production costs not explicitly addressed by, 480
  international trade and NPA measures, 93, 94, 95, 96
  on interpretation, 256
  regulation-based perspective on, 484
  scope of legal analysis and, 60
  SDT principle, 356
Maskus, Keith, 431, 468
means–end relationship
  indirect references to geographical scope involving, 286–94
  public morals exception and, 326–43
MEAs. *See* Multilateral Environmental Agreements
Meng, Werner, 278, 280n.126
Mexico
  on TBT Agreement, 378

Tuna-Dolphin disputes. *See Tuna-Dolphin* disputes
MFN. *See* most-favoured-nation treatment
MMPA. *See* Marine Mammal Protection Act, 1972
moral exception. *See* public morals exception
most-favoured-nation (MFN) treatment
  detrimental treatment, determining, 240–4, 246
  as key legal issue, 35
  'like products' concept and, 149. *See also* 'like products' concept
  national treatment obligations and, 148, 163. *See also* national treatment obligations
  non-discrimination principle central to, 163
  scope of analysis and, 59
  technical regulations and standards, 394
multi-level governance, reform proposals regarding, 440, 443–8
multilateral agreements, NPA measures in, 106
Multilateral Environmental Agreements (MEAs)
  clarification of relationship between WTO Agreements and, 436–7
  as modification of WTO Agreements, 136–7
  ordinary meaning of 'exhaustible resources', as evidence for, 313
  peaceable coexistence with WTO agreements, 129, 130, 131, 255n.37
  WTO side agreement regarding, proposal for, 434
multilateral trade. *See* entries at international trade
Murphy, Dale D., 460

NAFTA. *See* North American Free Trade Agreement, 1994
Namibia Advisory Opinion (ICJ, 1971), 268n.79

National Industrial Recovery Act
    (NIRA, 1933), US, 75
National Institute for Occupational
    Safety and Health (NIOSH),
    US, 76
National Recovery Administration
    (NRA), US, 75
national regulation and NPAs, 65–92
  aim and effects theory
    regulatory aims, relevance of,
      221–2
    regulatory purpose, identification
      of, 208
  conclusions regarding, 486
  consumer information laws, 382n.26
  consumption, regulation of, 72
  differences and similarities in
      regulatory cultures, 66, 74–5
    assessment of, 81–3
    deregulation. *See* deregulation
    European Union/Western
      Europe, 66, 67, 78–83
    services, trade in, 102
    United States, 67, 75–8
  direct versus indirect regulation,
    70–4
  economic case for state regulation
    competitive markets,
      safeguarding, 86
    distributional or social objectives,
      obtaining, 90–1
    effectiveness dilemma, 458–61
    market economy, nature of, 83
    market failures, dealing with,
      84–5, 88–90
    neoclassical free market theory,
      84–5
  environmental protection and.
    See under environmental
    protection
  geographical scope of Article XX
    and, 295–9
  history and concept of regulation
    generally, 66–8
  international trade and.
    See under international trade
    and NPA measures
  labelling requirements, 396n.65

'like products', objective
    determination of, 192–6
  Belgium – Family Allowances
    (1952), 192–5, 196
  Tuna-Dolphin I (1991) and *Tuna-
    Dolphin II* (1994), 195–6
non-tax, 38–9
product regulation and production
    regulation, overlap between,
    70–4
public ownership as means of
    regulation, 79
public policy, justified as pursuing,
    427
reform proposal aimed
    at consistency with
    international trade laws.
    See under regulation-based
    perspective on NPA measures
services, trade in, 101–2
social regulation, concept of,
    68–70
taxes and fees, 39–43
    direct taxation, 43
    indirect taxation, 40–3
national treasures, particular
    exception for, 284
national treatment obligations, 148,
    149–62
  applicability to NPA measures,
    149–50, 155–6, 161–2
  Border Tax Adjustments, Report of
    Working Party on, 158
  comparison of GATT Article III:2
    and III:4 regarding, 156–8
  detrimental treatment, determining,
    240–4, 246
  measures 'of the same nature', Note
    Ad Article III on, 158–61
  non-discrimination principle
    central to, 163. *See also* non-
    discrimination principle
  technical regulations and standards,
    394
  terminological issues, 150–6
    'affecting', broad interpretation
      based on use of, 152–5
    conclusions regarding, 155–6

'products', narrow interpretation based on use of, 151–2
in *Tuna-Dolphin* disputes. See under *Tuna-Dolphin* disputes
necessity
  geographical scope of Article XX indirectly referenced by, 286–8
  prevailing interpretation, criticism of, 290n.165
  public morals exception and. See under public morals exception
  reform proposals regarding, 433
  TBT Agreement, no more trade restrictive than necessary requirement under, 412–14
negotiation and consultation
  good faith effort requirement under chapeau, 362–4, 366–7
  NPA measures, specific requirements for, 366–7
neo-classical/neo-liberal free market theory, 84–5, 429, 473n.40
NGO. See non-governmental organization
Nike v. *Kasky* (USC, 2003), 400n.74
NIOSH. See National Institute for Occupational Safety and Health
NIRA. See National Industrial Recovery Act, 1933
Nixon, Richard, 77
non-discrimination principle, 149, 162–8
  chapeau non-discrimination requirement distinguished from, 352
  concept of, 163–5
  detrimental treatment, determining, 240–4, 246
  'like products'
    applicable only to, 164–5
    NPAs as means of determining, 167–8
  MFN treatment, importance to, 163
  national treatment, importance to, 163
  origin-based discrimination, clear prohibition of, 165–7
  SPS Agreement, 419
  technical regulations and standards, 394
non-discrimination requirements of chapeau. See under chapeau, Article XX
non-governmental organization (NGO) technical regulations and standards, 395–6
non-intervention principle, 276
non-physical aspect (NPA) measures. See entries at NPA
non-product-related PPMs, concept of, 28–9, 62
Nordhaus, William D., 83
North American Free Trade Agreement (NAFTA, 1994), 132, 137, 137n.85, 437
North Sea Continental Shelf case (ICJ, 1969), 265n.68
NPA (non-physical aspect) measures
  defined, 12
  linked to measures other than PPMs, 12
  linked to PPMs. See NPA measures linked to PPMs in WTO law
NPA measures linked to PPMs in WTO law, 1–6, 11
  applicable law. See applicability of WTO and other international law to NPA measures
  broader outlook on, 5–6
  chapeau requirements. See under chapeau, Article XX
  conclusions regarding, 485–93
  consistency with GATT obligations. See consistency of NPA measures with GATT obligations
  de lege ferenda proposals regarding. See reform proposals
  de lege lata, 57
  definition of issue, 1–3
  extraterritoriality, 53–4

NPA measures linked to PPMs in WTO law (cont.)
  foundational legal, political, and economic dimensions of, 3–4, 485–6
  GATT, focus on, 60–1
  general exceptions under Article XX, justification under. See justification of NPA measures under general exceptions
  goods, focus on trade in, 57–60
  inherent relationship of NPA measure to matter other than trade or tradable good, 119
  international trade and. See international trade and NPAs
  international treaty obligations, likelihood of relationship to, 119
  legal analysis of, 4–5, 486–90
  legality of, 13
    Shrimp Turtle (1998). See Shrimp Turtle
    Tuna-Dolphin I and II. See Tuna-Dolphin disputes
  national regulation and. See national regulation and NPAs
  NPAs, as term or concept, 61
  NPAs, defined, 12
  particular exceptions for. See particular exceptions
  PPM debate, overview of. See PPM debate
  PPMs, as term or concept, 62
  PPMs, defined, 12, 27–8
  product regulation, defined, 11
  public policy arguments for. See public policy
  regulation-based perspective on. See regulation-based perspective on NPA measures
  scope of legal analysis, 57
  social and environmental costs, ability of international trade law to account for, 1
  socio-economic context, 64–5
  SPS Agreement and. See SPS Agreement
  TBT Agreement and. See TBT Agreement
  theoretical legal issues, synoptical analysis of, 31, 56
NRA. See National Recovery Administration

objective approach to interpretation. See under interpretation of Article XX regarding general exceptions
objective determination of 'like products', 169–206
  aims and effects theory as corrective for, 207
  Border Tax Adjustments, Report of Working Party on, 172–3, 204, 207
  on case-by-case basis, 170, 177
  characteristics or qualities, assessment of, 171, 172–4
  conclusions regarding, 204–6, 237, 244, 246
  consumer preference, 172, 173, 236
  degree of similarity, assessment of, 171, 177–9
  dictionary definitions of likeness, 170
  as DSB approach, 169
  end-uses, 172, 236
  market-based or economic approaches compared, 232
  national regulation and NPAs, 192–6
    Belgium – Family Allowances (1952), 192–5, 196
    Tuna-Dolphin I (1991) and Tuna-Dolphin II (1994), 195–6
  output and producer characteristics, cases dealing with NPAs linked to, 183–9
    EC – Seal Products (2009), 188–9
    US – Gasoline (1996), 187–8, 189
    US – Malt Beverages (1992), 184–6, 189

US – Section 337 (1989), 183–4, 189
US – Taxes on Automobiles (1994), 186–7, 189
physical characteristics.
  See physical characteristics in determination of 'like products'
PPMs in narrow sense, cases dealing with NPAs linked to, 179–83
  Shrimp Turtle (1998), 182, 196, 196n.209
  Tuna-Dolphin I (1991), 179–81
  Tuna-Dolphin II (1994), 181
  Tuna-Dolphin III (2009), 181
price, cases dealing with NPAs linked to, 189–92
relevance of different perspectives, variance in, 170, 171, 174–7
tariff classification as criterion, 175–6, 236, 237
Occupational Safety and Health Act (OSHA, 1970), US, 76
Occupational Safety and Health Administration, US, 76
OECD. See Organization for Economic Cooperation and Development
Oesch, Matthias, 256
Ogus, Anthony, 79
Oil Platforms case (Iran v. United States; ICJ, 2003), 262n.60
Oilseeds Agreement, 256
Organization for Economic Cooperation and Development (OECD), on PPM concept, 27–8
origin-based discrimination, clear prohibition of, 165–7
OSHA. See Occupational Safety and Health Act, 1970
output characteristics, 'like product' determinations involving. See under objective determination of 'like products'
Oxley, Alan, 270

packaging and labelling requirements directly related to food safety, SPS Agreement coverage of, 419, 421

pacta sunt servanda, 96, 126, 366
pacta tertiis rule, 133, 145, 261
Panitchpakdi, Supachai, 442
Pareto-efficiency, equilibrium result of free market as, 83, 83n.61, 87, 478
Paris, Treaty of (1951), 80
particular exceptions, 53–4
  conclusions regarding, 488
  environmental protection, 311–13
  exclusive and limited nature of, 310–11
  geographic scope, references to. See under geographical scope of Article XX
  labour standards, reform proposal to include, 434
  policies acknowledged as legitimate but not specifically mentioned in, 311–16
  public morals. See public morals exception
  subject matter requirements of, 309–10
Pauwelyn, Joost, 125–7, 136n.81, 142, 256, 371, 415
physical characteristics in determination of 'like products'
  characteristics or qualities, assessment of, 172, 236, 237
  minor physical differences, relevance of, 176–7, 196–204
    editorial content, 197–200
    environmental impacts, 200–1
    genetic modifications, 203–4
    toxicity/risk levels, 201–3
  varying relevance of, 175–7
phytosanitary measures. See SPS Agreement
PPM debate, 20
  concept of PPMs, 27–8
  continuing legal uncertainties in, 29–30
  emergence of, 21–2
  labelling, increasing importance of, 25
  product–process distinction, 25

PPM debate (*cont.*)
  product-related and non-product-related PPMs distinguished, 28–9
  Shrimp Turtle dispute affecting, 16, 24, 30
  Tuna-Dolphin disputes affecting, 22–4, 30
PPMs (process or production methods) debate regarding. *See* PPM debate
  defined, 12
  'like product' determinations involving PPMs in narrow sense. *See under* objective determination of 'like products'
  NPA measures linked to. *See* NPA measures linked to PPMs in WTO law
  in TBT Agreement, 25, 63
price substitutions equivalence (PSE) standard, 225n.337, 225n.339
'primarily aimed at' text, 313
prison labour, particular exception for, 60
process or production methods. *See* entries at PPM
producer characteristics, 'like product' determinations involving. *See under* objective determination of 'like products'
product labelling. *See* labelling requirements
product–process doctrine, 25
product regulation and production regulation, overlap between, 70–4
product regulation, defined, 11
proportionality test for labelling schemes, 412n.118
PSE. *See* price-substitutions equivalence standard
public choice theory, 66, 86, 460
public morals exception, 316–45
  boundlessness of, 316, 372
  conclusions regarding, 344–5, 489
  consistency of standards, 351n.360, 355, 355n.372
  core versus variable or marginal morals, 285, 330–1
  in GATT and WTO case law, 316, 318–19, 322
  geographical scope of, 323–6
  human rights and labour standard within scope of, 313, 314n.246, 372
  least trade-restrictiveness test, 330–1, 341
  location of moral standards, 323–4
  location of threat to moral standards, 324–6
  means–end relationship and, 326–43
  motivation for adopting measure, 327–8
  necessity requirement, 329–43
    absolute necessity, 330–1, 342–3
    chapeau, as matter to be determined under, 338–9
    comparison with alternative measures logically inherent to, 339
    relative necessity, 330–1, 341–2
    steps required for adequate necessity test, 339–43
    suitability and, 331, 340–1
    weighing and balancing approach to, 331–8, 332n.303, 343, 397
  ordinary environmental damage and, 457n.9
  sovereignty and, 330
  standards of right and wrong conduct, defined as, 317, 321–3
  state practice, importance of, 320
  subject matter coverage, openness of, 317–21
  suitability of measure for protecting public morals, 328–9, 331, 340–1
public ownership as means of regulation in Europe, 79
public policy
  aims and effects theory as public policy approach, 220, 237
  conclusions regarding, 490
  denial of competence arguments based on, 428–32
  general exceptions focused on, 247
  interface of international trade and, 427

national NPA regulation justified as
    pursuing, 427
public procurement, NPAs in, 59–60
Puth, Sebastian, 129, 280n.126,
    293n.175, 338, 339

quantitative restrictions, 36–8
'race to the bottom' arguments and
    counter-arguments, 459–60

rail transportation in United States
    versus Europe, 80
ratione materiae conflicts, 129–31
ratione personae conflicts, 131
reasonable application requirement
    (good faith principle) in
    chapeau, Article XX, 346
redistributive policies.
    See distributional issues
reform proposals, 427–50
    conclusions regarding, 448–50, 490
    'constitutionalization' proposals,
        444–5, 446, 448
    denial of competence, different
        arguments for, 428–32
    governance, multi-level, 440, 443–8
    for institutional changes, 440
    regulation-based perspective.
        See regulation-based
        perspective on NPA measures
    for WTO-level changes, 432–40
        procedural suggestions, 438–40
        substantive suggestions, 433–8
Regan, Donald, 108, 221, 280n.126
regulation-based perspective on NPA
    measures, 451–84
    conclusions regarding, 483–4, 490–1
    consistency between national
        regulation and WTO measures,
        481–3
    chapeau, Article XX, general
        agreement with, 481
    distributive regulations, 478, 483
    market failure, national
        regulations addressing, 473,
        477–8, 483
    market imperfections, national
        regulations aimed at reducing,
        470, 483

SDT principle, conformity with,
    482–3
consumer information policies and
    regulations
    market failures, addressing,
        474–5
    market imperfections, addressing,
        470–2, 483
market failures
    competent political body to
        address, determining, 476
    distributive regulations
        addressing, 480
    lack of international institutions
        for dealing with, 461–3
    linked to international trade,
        452–66
    national regulation addressing,
        473–8, 483
    objectives and purposes of WTO,
        not in line with, 462
    regulation-based perspective as
        means of addressing, 467
national regulation, 454–61
    categorization of, 469–81
    distributive regulations, 478–81,
        483
    effectiveness when impaired by
        WTO laws, 456–61
    effectiveness when unimpeded,
        454–6
    market failure, addressing, 473–8,
        483
    market imperfections, aimed at
        reducing, 469–72, 483
    multilateral trading system, need
        for consistency with, 451–2
    side-effects of international trade
        impairing effectiveness
        of, 454
outline of problem, 467
    rationale for, 467–8
side-effects of international trade,
    453–4
regulation generally, history and
    concept of, 66–8
'relating to', indirect references to
    geographical scope in use of,
    288–90, 299

Resolution on Assistance to
    Developing Countries (2006),
    252
Ricardo, David, 99
right and wrong conduct, public
    morals defined as standards of,
    317, 321-3
Rio Declaration on Environment and
    Development (1992), 108, 129,
    130
risk levels as basis for 'like content'
    determinations, 201-3
Rome, Treaty (1957), 80
Roosevelt, Franklin D., 75

Samuelson, Paul A., 83
sanitary and phytosanitary measures.
    See SPS Agreement
Schneuwly, Philippe, 435
Schrijver, Nico, 411n.115, 472n.38
SCM Agreement (Agreement on
    Subsidies and Countervailing
    Measures)
  Article XX and subsidies, 52n.160
  border tax adjustment for exports, 45
  illegitimate subsidization, low
      standards constituting, 51-2
  on 'like products', 229n.359
  NPAs, subsidies legitimately linked
      to, 48-51
SDT principle (special and differential
    treatment of developing
    countries)
  chapeau, Article XX, non-
      discrimination requirements
      under, 354, 356n.375, 369, 371
  reform proposals regarding, 437-8
  regulation-based perspective on,
      482-3
  TBT Agreement and, 395, 415-18,
      437
Seattle Ministerial Conference (1999),
    443
SEC. See Securities and Exchange
    Commission
Securities Act (1933), US, 76
Securities and Exchange Commission
    (SEC), US, 76

self-contained regime, WTO law not
    regarded as, 122-4, 141, 487
Selznick, Philip, 67, 78
services, NPAs in trade in, 57-9, 101-2,
    478n.47
Shrimp Turtle (1998), 16-20
  Appellate Body report on, 18-20,
      97-8
  justification of NPA measures under
      general exceptions in, 248
  chapeau, non-discrimination
      requirements in, 354
  due process requirements, 359-60
  geographical scope of Article XX
      and, 284, 290, 296, 300, 304,
      305
  implementation period, 368
  interpretation of Article XX
      regarding, 252, 254, 258, 260,
      267
  negotiations, good faith efforts at,
      362-3
  objections to, 270, 271, 272, 274
  public morals exception, 319
  technology transfers and
      administrative and financial
      support, 369-70, 371
  unilateralism, 362
  'like product' determinations, 182,
      196, 196n.209
  Malaysian compliance case, 20
  Panel Report on, 17-18
  PPM debate affected by, 16, 24, 30
  public morals exception, 319
  on relevance of objectives of WTO
      Agreements, 97-8
  unilateralism, 55
side-effects of international trade,
    453-4
signatories-based approach to
    interpretation of Article XX.
    See under interpretation of
    Article XX regarding general
    exceptions
Singapore Ministerial Declaration of
    the WTO (1996), 315
Smith, Adam, 84, 405n.95, 406, 429
social dumping, 46

social regulation
  ability of international trade rules to account for social and environmental costs, 1
  concept of, 68–70
  consumer information, 398–404. *See also* consumer information
  denial of competence arguments for purposes of, 428–32
  national regulation in pursuit of distributional or social objectives, 90–1
  NPA measures involving. *See* NPA measures linked to PPMs in WTO law
  objectives and purposes of WTO, social damage not in line with, 462
socio-economic context of NPA measures linked to PPMs in WTO law, 64–5
sovereignty
  extraterritoriality and, 106–8
  geographical scope of Article XX not violating, 282
  jurisdiction as central feature of, 277
  justification of NPA measures under general exceptions, objections to, 270–1, 275–81
  means-end relationships and geographic scope of Article XX, 292
  non-intervention principle, importance of, 276
  public morals exception and, 330
  public policy nature of general exceptions and, 247, 301
  reform proposals regarding, 445–6
  traditional understanding of, 275
special and differential treatment of developing countries. *See* SDT principle
specificity of subsidies linked to NPAs, 49–50
SPS Agreement (Agreement on the Application of Sanitary and Phytosanitary Measures), 56, 374, 419–21
  chapeau, Article XX and, 419
  conclusions regarding, 421–2, 485
  GATT compared, 419
  geographical scope of Article XX and, 293n.175
  harmonization of rules, WTO reform proposals regarding, 435
  lex specialis, NPA measures falling under scope of agreement as, 374
  national regulations, trade-restrictive effects of, 102
  non-discrimination principle and, 419
  packaging and labelling requirements directly related to food safety, 419, 421
  PPMs explicitly mentioned in, 63, 419
  unincorporated PPMs, 420–2
  WTO and GATT case law on, 420
standards of right and wrong conduct, public morals defined as, 317, 321–3
stare decisis in WTO law, technical absence of, 169
state practice and public morals exception, 320
state regulation. *See* national regulation and NPAs
state responsibility, customary international law on, 140–5
state sovereignty. *See* sovereignty
Stern, Louis L., 431
Stigler, George J., 77
subsidies, 48–52. *See also* SCM Agreement
  actionable, 50
  Article XX, justification under, 52n.160
  as distributive regulations, 478
  illegitimate subsidization, low standards constituting, 51–2
  legitimately linked to NPAs, 48–51
  specificity requirements, 49–50

substitutability and 'like products' concept, 42, 199–200, 223–5, 225n.337, 227, 229n.359, 230, 232, 234, 238, 239
support requirements for NPA measures, 369–72
sustainable development, as WTO objective, 94, 94n.91, 409
Swagler, Roger M., 406
Swinbank, Alan, 412n.117
Swiss Hertel case (ECHR, 2010), 401n.80
Switzerland, on relationship between MEAs and WTO Agreements, 255n.37
symmetrical conflicts between WTO and other international law instruments, 134–8

Tariff Act of 1930, US, 183–4, 320, 320n.275
tariffs. *See also* customs tariffs
  competitive disadvantage of domestic industry, off-setting, 455
  decreasing importance of, 432
  'like products', tariff classification as criterion for, 175–6, 236, 237
taxes and fees
  border taxes. *See* border tax adjustments
  national regulation of internal taxes and NPAs, 39–43
  direct taxation, 43
  indirect taxation, 40–3
TBT Agreement (Agreement on Technical Barriers to Trade), 55, 374
  applicability of, 375–89
    classification of relevant norms linked to unincorporated PPMs, 376–7
    to labelling requirements. *See under* labelling requirements
    to technical regulations and standards, 377–81
  balancing test, 397
  conclusions regarding, 421–2, 485, 487
  consumer information issues. *See* consumer information
  GATT, relationship to, 414–15
  harmonization of rules, WTO reform proposals regarding, 435
  labelling requirements. *See* labelling requirements
  least trade-restrictiveness requirement. *See under* least trade-restrictiveness test
  lex specialis, NPA measures falling under scope of agreement as, 374
  'like products' concept and, 55, 390–3, 392n.57
  national regulations, trade-restrictive effects of, 102
  per se illegality of labelling requirements relating to unincorporated PPMs, rejection of, 389–93
  PPMs under, 25, 63
  SDT principle, 395, 415–18, 437
  substantive provisions of, 389
  technical regulations and standards. *See* technical regulations and standards
  unincorporated PPMs, 376–7, 382–3, 385–8, 421–2
technical regulations and standards
  applicability of TBT Agreement to, 377–81
  assessment of conformity with, 394
  distinction between regulations and standards, 395–6
  labelling requirements distinguished, 381
  least trade-restrictiveness test, 394
  mandatory versus voluntary, 395
  of NGOs, 395–6
  non-discrimination principle, 394
  SDT principle, application of, 395
  substantive provisions regarding, 393–6

transparency and supply of
 information, 395
technology transfer requirements for
 NPA measures, 369–72, 482
TEDs. *See* turtle excluder devices
Tehran Hostages case (ICJ, 1980), 122
theoretical legal issues, synoptical
 analysis of, 31
Tokyo Round, 375, 375n.4, 386
toxicity levels as basis for 'like content'
 determinations, 201–3
Trachtman, Joel P., 127, 446–8
trade associations, WTO dominance
 of, 430
trade liberalization
 social regulation in terms of, 70
 as WTO means rather than
  objective, 451
transfer of jurisdiction, reform
 proposals for, 426
transfer of technology requirements
 for NPA measures, 369–72,
 482
Treaties, Vienna Convention on Law
 of. *See* VCLT
Treaty of Paris (1951), 80
Treaty of Rome (1957), 80
Trebilcock, Michael J., 329n.296, 435,
 442
TRIMS Agreement (Agreement on
 Trade-Related Investment
 Measures), 167n.74
TRIPS Agreement (Agreement on
 Trade-Related Aspects of
 Intellectual Property Rights),
 96, 429, 437
Tuna-Dolphin disputes
 aims and effects theory and, 212
 consistency of NPA measures with
  GATT, *Tuna-Dolphin II*'s
  attitude toward, 147
 interpretation of Article XX
  regarding general exceptions in
  Tuna-Dolphin I, 252
 justification of NPA measures under
  general exceptions in
  geographical scope of Article XX
  and, 282, 283, 284, 291, 305

 interpretation of Article XX
  regarding, 252
 objections to, 271
 particular exceptions, 285n.138
 'like product' determinations
  national regulation, 195–6
  output and producer
   characteristics cases compared,
   184
  price as criterion in *Tuna-Dolphin
   I*, 191
  Tuna-Dolphin I, 179–81, 195–6
  Tuna-Dolphin II, 181, 195–6
  Tuna-Dolphin III, 181
 national treatment obligations,
  interpretation of applicability
  of
  comparison of GATT Article III:2
   and III:4, 156–8
  measures 'of the same nature'
   in Note Ad Article III, *Tuna-
   Dolphin I* on, 159, 161
  terminological considerations,
   151–2, 153, 155–6
 PPM debate affected by, 22–4, 30
 on quantitative restrictions
  prohibition, 37
 TBT Agreement and GATT,
  relationship between, 414
 Tuna-Dolphin I (1991), summary of,
  13–14
 Tuna-Dolphin II (1994), summary
  of, 15
 Tuna-Dolphin III (2009), summary
  of, 181
turtle excluder devices (TEDs) for
 shrimp trawlers, 369

UNCLOS. *See* United Nations
 Convention on the Law of the
 Sea
Understanding on Rules and
 Procedures Governing
 Settlement of Disputes.
 See DSU
UNEP. *See* United Nations
 Environment Programme
unilateralism, 55, 107, 108–10, 361–2

unincorporated PPMs
  SPS Agreement, 420–2
  TBT Agreement, 376–7, 382–3, 385–8, 421–2
United Kingdom. *See* entries at Britain and British
United Nations Charter
  equal sovereignty of states in, 276
  equality before the law in, 354
United Nations Convention on the Law of the Sea (UNCLOS, 1982), 252, 370
United Nations Environment Programme (UNEP), 428
United Nations Framework Convention, 475n.44
United Nations Guidelines on Consumer Protection, 381n.24, 402–4
United Nations, reform proposal involving allocation of jurisdiction by, 448
United Nations Universal Declaration of Human Rights (1948), 435
United States
  consumer information and commercial free speech in, 398–401, 403
  deregulation in, 77, 82
  multilateral agreements, NPA measures in, 106
  public morals exception, state practice regarding, 321
  rail transportation in, 80
  regulatory culture in, 67, 75–8, 81–3
  services, trade in, 102
  Shrimp Turtle (1998). *See Shrimp Turtle*
  on TBT Agreement, 378, 386
  Tuna-Dolphin disputes. *See Tuna-Dolphin* disputes
Universal Declaration of Human Rights (1948), 435
Uruguay Round, 23n.51, 23n.52, 24, 33, 102, 257, 375, 375n.1, 378, 386

Valentine v. *Chrestensen* (USC, 1942), 389n.49

van den Bossche, Peter, 411n.115, 472n.38
Vienna Convention on the Law of Treaties, 1980 (VCLT)
  applicability in WTO disputes, 125, 126
  asymmetrical conflicts, 133
  on conflicts in international law instruments, 130, 132, 133, 134, 136–7
  consultation and negotiation requirements for NPA measures and, 367
  general exceptions, interpretation of Article XX regarding. *See under* interpretation of Article XX regarding general exceptions
  MEAs, clarification of relationship between WTO Agreements and, 436
  object and purpose statements, importance ascribed to, 96
  on peremptory norms, 275n.103
  symmetrical conflicts, 134, 136–7
Virginia State Board of Pharmacy v. *Virginia Citizens Consumer Council, Inc.* (USC, 1976), 399n.73
voluntary labelling, 394, 411n.115, 413–14
Vranes, Erich, 223, 381n.24

WCO. *See* World Customs Organization
Wealth of Nations (Adam Smith), 84
weighing and balancing approach to public morals exception, 331–8, 332n.303, 343, 397
WEO. *See* World Economic Organization
Western Europe. *See* European Union/Western Europe
WHO. *See* World Health Organization

World Customs Organization (WCO), 33–5
World Economic Organization (WEO), proposal for, 440
World Health Organization (WHO), 442

World Trade Organization (WTO), NPA measures linked to PPMs in. *See* NPA measures linked to PPMs in WTO law

Zeno (Roman emperor), 66

Made in the USA
Lexington, KY
04 October 2014